Special Edition

USING
POWERBUILDER™5

ALI FAROKHI

Special Edition

USING
POWERBUILDER™ 5

Written by Charles A. Wood

Chuck Boudreau • Blake Coe • Bill Heys • Raghuram Bala
David J. O'Hearn • Scott L. Warner • Mike Seals • Greg McAteer
Peter MacIntyre • Blaine Bickar • Dave Fish • Ron L. Cox
Victor Rasputnis • Anatole Tartakovsky

ALI FAROKHI

Special Edition Using PowerBuilder 5

Credits

PRESIDENT
Roland Elgey

PUBLISHER
Joseph B. Wikert

PUBLISHING MANAGER
Fred Slone

TITLE MANAGER
Bryan Gambrel

EDITORIAL SERVICES DIRECTOR
Elizabeth Keaffaber

MANAGING EDITOR
Sandy Doell

DIRECTOR OF MARKETING
Lynn E. Zingraf

ACQUISITIONS EDITOR
Al Valvano

ACQUISITIONS COORDINATORS
Angela C. Kozlowski
Bethany Echlin

PRODUCT DIRECTOR
Nancy D. Price

PRODUCTION EDITORS
Mark Enochs
Elizabeth A. Bruns

PRODUCT MARKETING MANAGER
Kim Margolius

ASSISTANT PRODUCT MARKETING MANAGER
Christy M. Miller

TECHNICAL EDITOR
Scott L. Warner

TECHNICAL SPECIALIST
Nadeem Muhammad

OPERATIONS COORDINATOR
Patty Brooks

EDITORIAL ASSISTANT
Andrea Duvall

BOOK DESIGNER
Kim Scott

COVER DESIGNERS
Dan Armstrong
Nathan Clement

PRODUCTION TEAM
Steve Adams
Jason Carr
Chad Dressler
Joan Evan
DiMonique Ford
Jessica Ford
Amy Gornik
Jason Hand
Daniel Harris
Clint Lahnen
Bob LaRoche
Michelle Lee
Casey Price
Laura Robbins
Bobbi Satterfield
Kelly Warner
Jeff Yesh

INDEXERS
Tim Griffin
Brad Herriman

Composed in *Century Old Style* and *MCPdigital* by Que Corporation.

About the Authors

Charles Wood is a Systems Engineer at Analytical Technologies. He graduated with bachelor's degrees in computer science and finance from Ball State University in 1986, and is a Certified PowerBuilder Developer (CPD). Along with developing software in PowerBuilder, C++, COBOL, and QuickBasic, Charles has instructed in C and C++ at Indiana Vocational Technical College. He is currently pursuing his MBA at Butler University (when he can find the time). He lives in Indianapolis with his wife, Lyn, and his two daughters, Kelly and Kailyn.

Chuck Boudreau (CPD, CPI) is a Director at PowerCerv Corporation. His humorous presentation style, industry knowledge, and ability to connect with developers and project managers keep Chuck in high demand as an instructor and conference speaker around the world. His fortes include goal-oriented design, graphical user interface design, object-oriented techniques, team development, and best practices for enterprise developers. He writes for several magazines including *PowerBuilder Advisor, PowerBuilder Developers Journal*, and *Pure Power*.

Blake Coe is a Senior Analyst and Project Manager and has been designing and developing database applications for eight years. He is currently developing applications for the Federal Communications Commission using PowerBuilder and Sybase. He currently resides in the northern Virginia area with his wife, Holly and his son, Joshua.

Bill Heys is a Technology Partner with Waterfield Technology Group, Inc., a Powersoft Premier Channel Partner located in Lexington, MA. Bill is a Professional Certified PowerBuilder Developer and Certified Powersoft Instructor. He has been using PowerBuilder since version one. Bill has been a regular columnist for *PowerBuilder Advisor* magazine since its premier issue. In addition to PowerBuilder, he has taught C, C++, GUI Design, DB2, and a variety of mainframe technologies. Bill resides in Franklin, MA and can be reached at 74720,3364@compuserve.com (preferred), bheys@tiac.com, (800) 381-7811 (voice), or (617) 863-8408 (fax).

Raghuram Bala is a Senior Software Engineer at Pencom Software, with seven years experience in software development and consulting. He holds an M.S. degree in computer science from Rensselaer Polytechnic Institute, and bachelor's degrees in computer science and mathematics from SUNY-Buffalo. He also served as an Adjunct Faculty member at Columbia University. Raghu's technical interests lie in Internet application architectures and distributed computing and object technologies. He is a Certified PowerBuilder Developer, and a contributor to several magazines and trade journals. He can be reached at rbala@1-2000.com.

David O'Hearn graduated from Harding University in 1986 with a bachelor's degree in computer science. O'Hearn has worked as a computer programmer and systems analyst in the insurance industry for the past six years. He is currently working as a consultant for Computer Horizons Corporation. O'Hearn resides in Plainfield, IN, with his wife Amy.

Scott L. Warner is a programmer/analyst for Service Graphics, Inc. in Indianapolis. He received his degree from Purdue University's Computer Technology Department. In addition to Delphi, Scott also develops applications in PowerBuilder and Visual Basic. He can be reached on the Internet at swarner@iquest.net.

Mike Seals is a Senior Consultant at Source Consulting's Indianapolis office. He has extensive experience in client/server and telecommunications technologies. He holds a degree in entrepreneurship from Ball State University, is a Certified Netware Engineer, and a Certified PowerBuilder Developer Professional. He works with Visual Basic, Access, PowerBuilder, and other development tools. He can be reached on the Internet as mseals@iquest.net, and on CompuServe at 73753,274.

Blaine Bickar is an independent consultant, operating as Grey Matter Systems. He is a Certified PowerBuilder Developer and a Certified PowerBuilder Instructor. Bickar has extensive experience with PowerBuilder, having built several systems ranging in size from individual applications utilizing local database-management systems to enterprise-wide client/server applications utilizing mainframe and mid-range database management systems. He has mentored many people in PowerBuilder, graphical design, regression testing, and general client/server architecture issues. Bickar graduated from Carnegie-Mellon University with a B.S. in industrial management.

Dave Fish is a Certified PowerBuilder Developer who has been designing and developing database applications for nine years. He has worked with DBMSs on mainframes, VAX, UNIX, and PC networks. He has been developing client/server Windows and Motif applications for two years, and has written several PowerBuilder applications using Oracle, Sybase, and MS SQL Server. His most recent application was a document-tracking system for a U.S. government agency, which supports over 100 concurrent users. Dave resides in Washington, D.C., and can be reached on CompuServe at 73503,3151 or on the Internet at 73503,3151@compuserve.com.

Ron L. Cox is a Project Manager with Computer People Unlimited in Milwaukee, WI. He focuses on client/server consulting, and is a Certified PowerBuilder Developer. Cox lives with his wife, Jean, in Waukesha, WI. He can be reached on CompuServe at 71621,1551.

Victor Rasputnis has a Ph.D. in computer science from the Moscow Institute of Robotics. He is the cofounder of CTI, a software development and consulting company in New York, which specializes in client/server, multimedia, and other emerging technologies. Rasputnis is a Certified PowerBuilder Developer and has over 12 years of software development and consulting experience with financial and manufacturing companies. He leads development of CTI PowerBase Class Library for PowerBuilder, and can be contacted on CompuServe at 74643,1755.

Anatole Tartakovsky graduated from Kharkov University in 1986, with an M.S. degree in math, and has a Ph.D. in computer science from the Moscow Institute of Robotics. He is the cofounder of CTI, a software development and consulting company in New York, specializing in client/server, multimedia, and other emerging technologies. Tartakovsky is a Certified PowerBuilder Developer and has over 10 years of software development and consulting experience with financial and manufacturing companies. He leads a number of projects, including the development of imaging add-ons, custom controls, and application framework libraries for PowerBuilder. Tartakovsky can be contacted on CompuServe at 74250,1550.

Acknowledgments

I would like to thank the contributing authors Chuck Boudreau, Blake Coe, Bill Heys, Raghuram Bala, Scott Warner, David O'Hearn, Greg McAteer, Mike Seals, Peter MacIntyre, Blaine Bickar, Dave Fish, Ron L. Cox, Victor Rasputnis, and Anatole Tartakovsky for all their difficult, mind-numbing work.

I would also like to thank Nancy Price, Al Valvano, Elizabeth Bruns, Mark Enochs, and the rest of the staff at Que for their exhaustive effort to get this book out. A special thanks goes to Cecile Roux and the Powersoft staff for their tireless help and hours of phone calls during the development process.

Most of all, I would like to thank my wife, Lyn, for her infinite patience and understanding while this book was being written. I couldn't have done it without you.

—CW

Dedication

We'd Like to Hear from You!

As part of our continuing effort to produce books of the highest possible quality, Que would like to hear your comments. To stay competitive, we *really* want you, as a computer book reader and user, to let us know what you like or dislike most about this book or other Que products.

You can mail comments, ideas, or suggestions for improving future editions to the address below, or send us a fax at (317) 581-4663. Our staff and authors are available for questions and comments through our Internet site, at **http://www.mcp.com/que**, and Macmillan Computer Publishing also has a forum on CompuServe (type **GO QUEBOOKS** at any prompt).

In addition to exploring our forum, please feel free to contact me personally to discuss your opinions of this book: I'm **avalvano@que.mcp.com** on the Internet, and **74671,3710** on CompuServe.

Thanks in advance—your comments will help us to continue publishing the best books available on new computer technologies in today's market.

Al Valvano
Acquisitions Editor
Que Corporation
201 W. 103rd Street
Indianapolis, Indiana 46290
USA

Contents at a Glance

VII | **References**

| **Appendixes**

Table of Contents

II   Using PowerScript

III   Using DataWindows

IV Delivering the Final Product

21 DataWindows Tips and Tricks   573

22 Exploiting the Power of Inheritance   589

VII   References

Appendixes

Introduction

Windows development is usually considered to be difficult and tedious. With all of the aspects of a graphical user interface to consider, Windows developers were usually forced to develop in hard-to-learn text-based languages. PowerBuilder has changed all of that.

PowerBuilder is quickly becoming the premier Windows development tool. The capabilities of PowerBuilder have upped the ante on all Windows development, and programmers are starting to develop PowerBuilder applications *in droves!* Companies realize that PowerBuilder is an excellent way to develop in Windows, while consulting firms can't hire enough PowerBuilder programmers. (All the more reason to buy this book, right?)

Special Edition Using PowerBuilder 5 fulfills two functions. First, it steps the beginning PowerBuilder programmer through an entire application. Second, it is a one-stop resource for intermediate and advanced PowerBuilder developers. ◼

The Emerging Client-Server Environment

In recent years, people have discovered the need to share information with each other through the PC. Instead of passing disks around with needed information, companies have turned to the *client-server environment*. A client-server environment is where several PCs (called *clients*) can access one centralized database (or databases) on one centralized PC (called a *server*).

FIG. I.1

An example of a simple client-server setup.

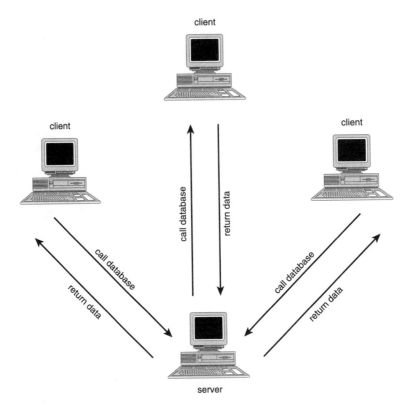

In figure I.1, you see a client-server setup. Here, three client PCs are accessing a database on the server PC. Since they all can access and update the same data, there is more control over the database. The database is in one location, there needs to be only one backup procedure for the database, and all clients can access up-to-date information entered by other clients.

Part of PowerBuilder's popularity is due to the demand for client-server applications. Typical databases will support client-server technology. Because of its extensive database support, PB developers have easy access to client-server technology. Simply put, since databases address problems like distributed access, security, and multiple user access, and since PowerBuilder interfaces *easily* with these databases, the PB developer is able to concentrate on functionality!

Trends in Application Development

Software developers are now expected to make their applications graphical (usually much to their dismay!). As the DOS market shrinks and the Windows market grows, demand for graphical programs increases. Add to this the *incredible need* for faster development. Many programming shops are *years* behind in development. Clearly, older methods of development will have to be replaced.

What this means to you, the typical developer, is that your newly developed programs are supposed to be better than before, and you're supposed to develop them in less time! It's fortunate that PowerBuilder came along.

What to Expect from Using PowerBuilder 5

Using PowerBuilder 5, developers can expect several benefits: rapid development, less training time, and professional Windows programs.

Rapid Development

The time it takes to develop an application will *decrease dramatically*. Typical client-server Windows applications that took years can now take months or even weeks! You can now design a program as you write it. Maintenance will also be much easier due to the object-based nature of PowerBuilder 5. You will be able to concentrate on program analysis and design without worrying about hours and hours of tedious coding.

Less Training Time

Remember when you first learned to program? Unless you were a prodigy, it usually took you months to learn the language and years to get up-to-speed. (If you don't believe me, try dusting off some of those first programs and take a look!) With PowerBuilder, you can begin quality client-server Windows development immediately. Your typical "up-to-speed" training time is around three months of normal working days.

Professional Windows Programs

Even with such quick development and less training time, you can develop really great Windows single-user or client-server applications. You will be astounded at the high quality of code that such little effort produced.

New Features

PowerBuilder 5 includes several new features:

- PowerBuilder 5 can now compile into machine code executables. Earlier versions of PowerBuilder actually delivered interpreted applications. Machine code applications can run 10 to 100 times faster than interpreted applications.

■ PowerBuilder 5 now supports tab controls. Tab controls allow the developer to group controls together and show one group of controls at a time. Tab controls also allow you to navigate around your windows without messy bitmap coding or forcing a C++ interface.

■ PowerBuilder 5 now has Rich Text Edit (RTE) controls and DataWindows. Now, slow, resource-expensive operations (like OLE links to Microsoft Word, WordPerfect, etc.) may no longer be needed because of the addition of RTE controls. You can even use RTE DataWindows for form letters that look as professional as those developed in a high-end word processor.

■ PowerBuilder 5 now allows n-tier client-server development. You can code user obects designed to run on a server rather than a client machine. This allows the server to do work it should be allowed to do and lightens the burden on the client machine as well as the network traffic.

■ And much, much more!

Who Should Use This Book?

There is something in this book for every PowerBuilder developer:

■ Beginners will find this book especially useful because it written to show how to develop an application from database modeling through window, DataWindow, and menu development to delivering an executable.

■ Intermediate and advanced audiences will find topics not covered in any other PowerBuilder book, including the C++ interface, using Sybase SQL Anywhere, getting certified in PowerBuilder with a CPD designation, and object-oriented design and development, just to name a few.

■ All users will love the reference sections found in this book. No other PowerBuilder book covers as much reference material.

What to Expect with *Special Edition Using PowerBuilder 5*

If you know Windows, this book will help you become a PowerBuilder developer:

■ Throughout this book, I will take you step-by-step through the development of an Inventory Tracking system. (You'll find it on the CD included with this book.)

■ This book is full of detailed syntax, troubleshooting tips, cautions, and notes that help guide you through the intricacies of PowerBuilder development.

■ Suggested standards, like naming conventions, are given. This will make your programming easier and more maintainable.

■ The appendixes of this book contain lists of PowerBuilder training partners, PowerBuilder consultants, and third-party products that can interface with PowerBuilder to make your development a little easier.

If you already develop in PowerBuilder, this book is still a must for you:

■ This book delves into all the new features of PowerBuilder 5, including Tab Controls, Rich Text Edit controls, n-tier development, and compiling your application into machine code, just to name a few.

■ We all know that knowing a language inside and out does not necessarily make you a great developer. Advanced database design and object-oriented design is covered in depth *as they relate to PowerBuilder.*

■ Interfacing with other languages using OCXes or C++ is defined in this book.

■ "Techniques from the Pros" is a section in this book that details how PowerBuilder is used in the field.

■ This book is an invaluable reference. Part VII of this book contains several chapters that list and describe all PowerBuilder functions, events, attributes, enumerated data types, and messages. The CD contains a PBAPI, a program that searches for the proper Windows API function based on a keyword search and even returns the PowerBuilder function prototype for the function. No longer will you have to sift through numerous help screens or manuals to find that needed reference. This book and the CD will be the best way to find an obscure function or attribute.

Simply put, if you're a PowerBuilder developer, then this book should be in your collection. There is no finer reference, tutorial, or guide to advanced PowerBuilder features.

Special Notes About the CD

The Inventory Tracking system included on the CD was developed using a late-breaking beta version of PowerBuilder 5. This shows Que's and the authors' commitment to delivering an up-to-date edition of a *Special Edition Using PowerBuilder* when version 5 came out, just when you needed it most.

Because a beta was used to write the Inventory Tracking system, you will need to migrate the Inventory Tracking system to the production version of PowerBuilder 5. To migrate the Inventory Tracking system to the production version of PowerBuilder 5, you'll need to perform the following steps:

1. Copy the inventory tracking files from your CD to your hard drive.
2. Try to open the ap_inventory_tracking application. When you do, you should receive a message asking you which libraries to migrate, as seen in figure I.2.

FIG. I.2

PowerBuilder will tell you
if you need to migrate
your application to the
production version of
PowerBuilder 5.

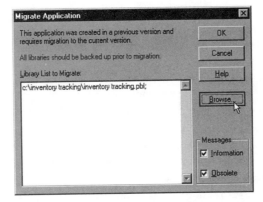

3. Next, be sure to select the Ancestor.pbl to add to your application library list, as seen in figure I.3.

FIG. I.3

You can choose which
PBLs to migrate.

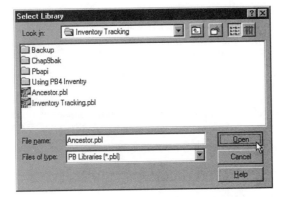

4. Finally, your Migrate Application dialog box should show both Ancestor.pbl and Inventory Tracking.pbl. Click OK, and your system should be migrated.

FIG. I.4

The Migrate Application
dialog box shows both
Ancestor.pbl and
Inventory Tracking.pbl.

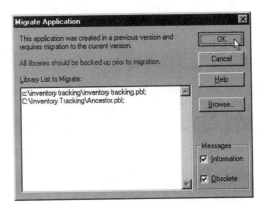

How to Use This Book

This book contains many conventions that you'll find extremely useful. Names of dialog boxes are capitalized. Messages that appear on the screen are written in a special font: `Could not connect to database`. New terms are introduced in *italic* type. Text that you have to type is in **boldface**. Any programming uses a special script:

```
//This is a comment in PowerBuilder
```

You'll also notice the following icons:

 This icon indicates features not available in previous versions of PowerBuilder but available in PowerBuilder 5.0.

 This icon indicates applications found on the CD.

You will also find Notes, Tips, Cautions, and Troubleshooting sidebars.

 T I P

Tips suggest easier or alternative methods for executing a procedure.

N O T E Notes indicate additional information that may help you avoid problems or that should be considered during development. ■

CAUTION

Cautions warn you of pitfalls when you develop your PowerBuilder application.

 TROUBLESHOOTING

How do I troubleshoot my PowerBuilder application? Troubleshooting is a question-answer format that provides guidance on how to find solutions to common problems. Specific problems you may encounter are shown in bold. Possible solutions to your problem appear immediately after the problem.

▶ **See** "Using PowerBuilder as an Object-Based Environment," **p. 13**

Cross-references show you related text that you may want to view or review while reading about a topic.

Special Edition Using PowerBuilder 5 is a must for every PowerBuilder developer. You simply can't find a better, more complete reference.

Introducing PowerBuilder

Introducing PowerBuilder

by Charles A. Wood

5.0

This chapter is designed to give an introduction to using the various aspects of PowerBuilder 5 with the new Windows 95 operating system and to establish a foundation of knowledge for the rest of the book to build from. If you're an intermediate or advanced user, much of this chapter will be a review. If you're new to PowerBuilder, however, this chapter is probably the most important chapter in the entire book.

Throughout this book, you'll be developing an Inventory Tracking system, which tracks the purchase and disbursement of inventory while explaining how to develop in PowerBuilder. By developing a small application, you can see what it takes to bring an application from requirements to implementation.

This chapter discusses the major components of PowerBuilder and introduces you to libraries, applications, windows, and menus. At the end of the chapter, you'll finish your first (albeit small) PowerBuilder application! ■

Identify the major components of PowerBuilder.

PowerBuilder gets its "power" from several different types of objects. These objects include menus, windows, and DataWindows.

Define visual and iterative design.

No longer do you need to worry about next year's phase during this year's development. PowerBuilder makes iterative design easy. Your applications will never be quicker to develop, and will never look better.

Know how to create Power-Builder libraries, applications, windows, and menus.

The key to PowerBuilder development is in its objects. PowerBuilder libraries contain these objects. PowerBuilder application objects hold information relevant to the entire application. Menus and windows are part of the visual effect you strive for when developing an application.

Build a small application to run the application inside the PowerBuilder environment.

You'll be able to see just how easy it is to create PowerBuilder applications.

Describing the Main PowerBuilder Components

PowerBuilder's environment consists of five components that are linked together. They are listed next and covered in detail in later chapters.

■ **PowerBuilder Painters**—PowerBuilder painters are sub-environments in PowerBuilder that allow the developer to implement Windows constructs (such as windows and menus). These painters can be accessed through the PowerBuilder library painter or through the PowerBuilder toolbars. The majority of this book describes how to use these painters to build a Windows application.

■ **PowerBuilder Libraries**—PowerBuilder Libraries (known as PBLs, or *pibbles*) contain object-based constructs (such as windows and menus) used in PowerBuilder.

■ **PowerBuilder Database**—The PowerBuilder database painter cannot be accessed through the library; it must be accessed through the Database icon on the PowerBar. This allows the developer to act as a Database Administrator (DBA) and administer the database.

■ **Toolbars**—Toolbars (as shown in figs. 1.1 and 1.2) are the picture buttons found on every painter. They include the PowerBar (used throughout the PowerBuilder environment), the PainterBar (which is unique for every painter), and the StyleBar. More about PowerBuilder toolbars will be discussed later in this chapter.

FIG. 1.1

PowerBuilder's default shows the toolbar with no text. This gives room for a lot of toolbar items.

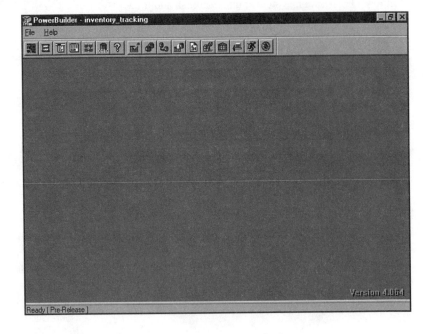

FIG. 1.2
You can alter the appearance of your toolbar to show text and to be positioned on any side of the window, or to float as shown in the figure.

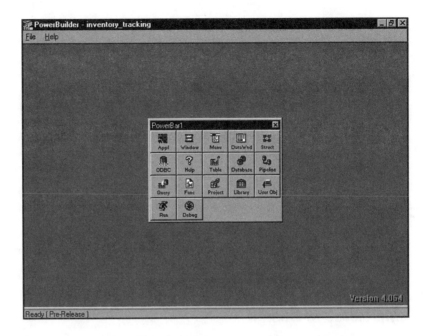

- **Online Help**—PowerBuilder's context sensitive online help is very extensive. Most of PowerBuilder's online documentation is contained in the online help. More about help is mentioned later in this chapter.

N O T E Even though some developers don't need the PowerBuilder manuals, which are available for an additional cost from Powersoft, this book is instrumental in leading you through a development process that is not focused on in the manuals. Add to that the references, Sybase SQL Anywhere help, and "Techniques from the Pros," and you have a very good buy. The CD includes fully working shareware, scaled down programs, and demos so that you can add to your system easily. ■

Using PowerBuilder as an Object-Based Environment

A lot could be said about object-oriented programming (OOP). To put it simply, object-oriented languages consist of three primary ways of doing things. First, every function and group of related functions (called classes) should not be allowed to affect the data values in other functions—this is called *encapsulation*. Second, the language should allow you to reuse much of your code in similar functions instead of the old-style way of copying your old code and making changes; this is called *inheritance*. Third, functions that inherit from each other should be allowed to customize themselves if necessary; this is called *polymorphism*.

The object-oriented *paradigm* (or way of doing things) is difficult for some to adjust to. Once implemented, OOP greatly facilitates iterative design. Iterative design, described in detail in this section, is a design that can be added to later with little work.

PowerBuilder is an object-oriented environment, which means it implements all of the features found in object-oriented environments. Some of these features include inheritance (discussed later in this chapter) and iterative design.

5.0 **N O T E** In earlier versions of PowerBuilder, it was often said that PowerBuilder is object-based rather than object-oriented, because PowerBuilder had yet to fully implement some object-oriented features. However, PowerBuilder contains features such as function overloading (polymorphism) as well as variable access that includes private, protected, and read-only (encapsulation), as well as the inherited objects not found in many other visual development tools. Few can now argue that PowerBuilder is fully object-oriented. ■

Using Visual Design

As you will see, PowerBuilder is visual in a way that other "visual" development environments can't match. You don't program your application—you paint it. If any programming is needed, it's implemented behind the painted objects. This may seem a little odd right now, but soon you will be using painters to develop your application.

Using Iterative Design

Iterative design is designing a little bit of your application at a time. Iterative design (also called *phased design*) is a by-product of object-oriented development. Iterative design enables you to develop your application in "chunks" from start to finish. While one chunk is being evaluated and tested, you can add to previous work easily.

Iterative design is different from old school design in that, using non-object languages, modifying existing code is difficult and perilous! Previously, analysis, design, and development each were separated into sections, and each had to be completed before another began, as if each were separated by a brick wall (see fig. 1.3).

FIG. 1.3
Moving between phases of development was very difficult—it was as if a wall existed between phases.

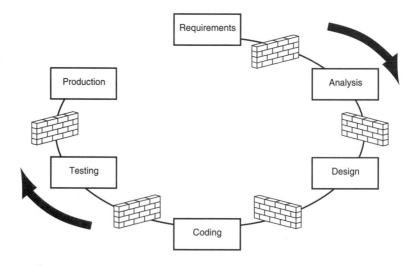

It was expensive and difficult to go back to a previous phase, and often the application suffered for it. Maintenance was a nightmare, and a program could not keep up with its environment. Eventually, systems became so out-of-date that a whole new system needed to be written from scratch! Data processing departments fell years behind in development (literally) as a result. (Indeed, some are still years behind.)

Clearly, something had to be done. PowerBuilder and iterative design are answers to this dilemma. Not only can you return to the analysis phase, but you can easily modify your application to evolve with your work environment. In this chapter, you see iterative design (of sorts) by developing a working application and adding to it throughout the book until you develop a more fully featured Inventory Tracking application. You'll find that iterative design allows the developer to move freely between design phases, as represented in figure 1.4.

FIG. 1.4
Using iterative design, movement between phases is easily done.

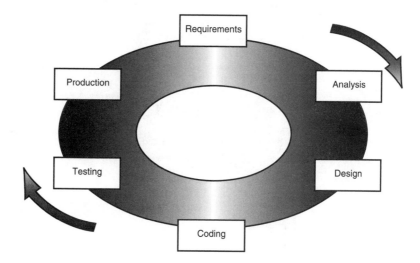

Installing PowerBuilder

PowerBuilder's installation is simple and straightforward. Follow these steps:

1. Insert the PowerBuilder CD. (Obviously, you will need a CD drive.) Go to your Windows 95 taskbar, click on Start, and then choose Run. (If you're in Windows 3.x, click on File, Run in the Program Manager.)

2. Enter D: SETUP and click OK.

3. Answer the questions that follow. (If you need any help, see the Getting Started manual provided with your PowerBuilder documentation.)

4. Double-click on the PowerBuilder icon in your Windows environment to start the application.

Using PowerBuilder Libraries

▶ **See** "Using the Library Painter," **p. 414**

PowerBuilder puts all of its objects (such as windows and menus) into a library. This library always has a .PBL extension. Powersoft put libraries into PowerBuilder to help you organize your work. Every library is a single file ending in .PBL. (Hence, every PowerBuilder library is called a "pibble.") Every library has members that you can access through PowerBuilder. These members are PowerBuilder objects that you develop while making your application.

To enter the library painter, click on the Library icon on the PowerBar. This icon might not have text depending on how you set your preferences, but the picture still appears.

N O T E You don't always have to use the icons provided by PowerBuilder in the PowerBar. Usually, there is some menu equivalent. For instance, you could start to create a new PBL by clicking on Library, Create as seen in figure 1.5. ■

FIG. 1.5
You can start to create a library by clicking Library, Create, or by clicking the Create Library icon.

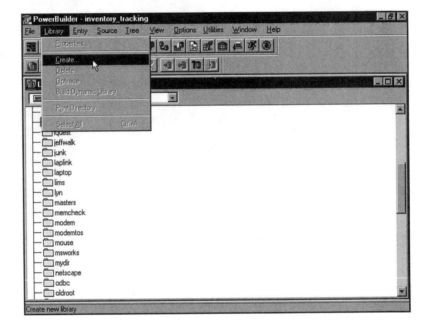

Creating a Library

To create a library, click on the Create Library icon on the PainterBar. The Create Library dialog box appears (as shown in fig. 1.6). In the Create Library dialog box, you enter the file name of your library and the directory where you want it stored. When you finish, click Save or press the Enter key.

N O T E Your default directory will be \PowerBuilder 5.0 (or your default PowerBuilder directory). To avoid cluttering your PowerBuilder directory, you probably want to change your default to another directory for each system. First, create a directory through Windows Explorer (or File Manager). Then click on the proper directory in the library painter before creating your PBL. ■

N O T E Several of you will be going to Windows 95 soon, if you haven't already. Here are some thoughts about using Windows 95 that you may consider:

- Windows 95 allows you to create filenames (and library names) up to 256 characters in length. (Long file names are used in the Inventory Tracking system.) However, if your PBLs are accessed on a network by people using DOS and Windows 3.x systems, you may consider limiting your library names for now to 8 characters. Otherwise, your coworkers will need to access somewhat cryptic library names. (For instance, "Inventory Tracking.PBL" would look like "INVENT~1.PBL" to Windows 3.x users.)

- Windows 95 uses Windows Explorer for file manipulation. (See your Windows Documentation or *Special Edition Using Windows 95* from Que for more information.) However, File Manager is still included with Windows 95. To add File Manager to your desktop, right-click on a blank area on your Windows 95 desktop, click on New, Shortcut, and type C:\WINDOWS\WINFILE.EXE.

File Manager allows you to do several things that Explorer does not. You can open several directories within one window, or group rename files, just to name two. However, File Manager still is limited to 8 character file names, so Windows 95 file names are encrypted to six characters followed by a tilde (~) and a number. Still, if you can get used to it, you'll have the convenience of File Manager with the power of Windows 95. ■

FIG. 1.6

The Create Library dialog box appears every time you create a library.

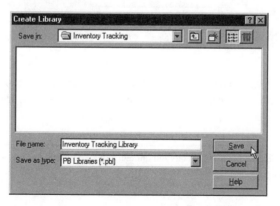

Now the Property Sheet for the library appears, as seen in figure 1.7. The property sheet for libraries allows you to enter comments for a PBL.

FIG. 1.7
The library Property
Sheet lets you add
comments to a library.

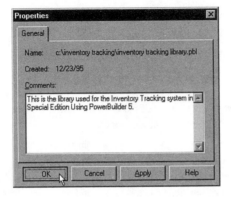

> **T I P** Comments should be entered every time PowerBuilder asks for them!

FIG. 1.8
For the Inventory
Tracking system, the
Ancestor PBL also
needs to be created.

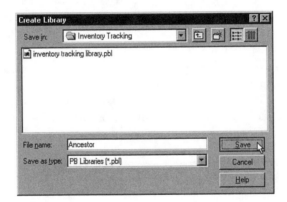

> **N O T E** In the Inventory Tracking system, two PBLs are to be used. The *Inventory Tracking Library*
> PBL is created in figures 1.6 and 1.7. The *Ancestor* PBL is created in figures 1.8
> and 1.9. ▪

> **T I P** You cannot move a PBL from one subdirectory to another using PowerBuilder. Instead, use Windows
> Explorer or File Manager.

▶ **See** "PowerBuilder Libraries," **p. 413**

> **N O T E** Using the Comments area, enter a description of what you are creating every time you
> create an object. Comments not only help those who are lucky enough to work on your
> system later, but they'll also help you when you look at old code a year from now! ▪

FIG. 1.9
Don't forget to enter the comments for the Ancestor PBL in the library Property Sheet.

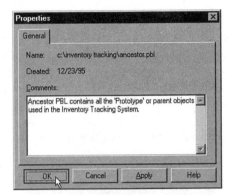

Using Libraries

Libraries cannot be used to create new objects. (To do this, you need to use the PowerBar.) However, they can be used to navigate around existing objects in the PowerBuilder environment. The more you use PowerBuilder, the more you'll probably tend to use libraries to work with existing objects.

To work on another object in the PowerBuilder Library, simply double-click on that member. This causes the proper painter to come up with that member ready to be worked on.

Using PowerBuilder Application Painter and Applications

To get into the application painter, either access the application through the library painter or click on the Application icon in the PowerBar. The application painter is unique among PowerBuilder objects in several ways:

▶ **See** "What Is Contained in an Application Object," **p. 106**

- You always start a new project by defining an application.
- You can only work with one application at a time, whereas with most painters, you can access several different objects of the same object type (several windows, menus, etc.) at a time.
- You are always attached to an application.
- The application is always executed when the program runs.

More information on applications will be covered in chapter 3, "Understanding Applications."

Selecting Your Application

When you first enter PowerBuilder, you are in the Sample Application. You need to change your application to the application you are working on. This is done by selecting the Open icon pictured at the start of this section. Clicking on the Open icon opens the Select Application Library dialog box, shown in figure 1.10. Using this dialog box, you choose the PBL where the application does (or will) reside.

> **TIP** You must create a PBL for an application in the library painter before creating a new application.

FIG. 1.10
Select the application's PBL in the Select Application Library dialog box.

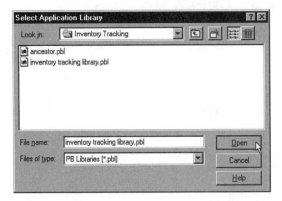

This allows you to choose a different application or create a new one using the Select Application dialog box shown in figure 1.11.

FIG. 1.11
The Select Application dialog box allows you to switch from one application to another or to create a new application.

To create a new application, simply click on the New button in the dialog box pictured in figure 1.11, which opens the Select New Application Library dialog box, shown in figure 1.12. Here, you select the PBL where the new application will reside. For the Inventory Tracking system, we chose the Inventory Tracking Library.PBL that we created earlier in this chapter. When you're finished selecting the PBL for the new application, click on Save.

 5.0 **N O T E** If you want to go straight to the Select New Application Library dialog box to create a new application without reviewing existing applications, click on the New Painterbar icon. ▪

FIG. 1.12
Choose the PBL of the new application in the Select New Application Library dialog box.

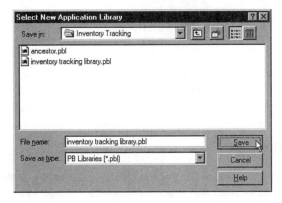

Now the Save Application dialog box opens, pictured in figure 1.13. Within this dialog box, you can create new applications and store them in the appropriate PBL.

N O T E Notice that the application is saved with the name ap_inventory_tracking. This is the name used throughout the book for this application. ▪

FIG. 1.13
The Save Application dialog box appears when you choose New in the Select Application dialog box.

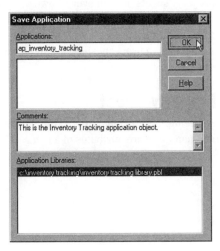

After saving your application, PowerBuilder displays a message box, shown in figure 1.14, asking if you would like PowerBuilder to generate an Application template. If you click Yes, PowerBuilder will build a minor application framework for you to work with, consisting of an MDI window and menu, a main window, and an About window. You can use this handy short-cut later in your own applications. However, in order to learn how to use PowerBuilder in a development environment, for now choose No.

FIG. 1.14
PowerBuilder always asks if you want to generate a template when developing a new application.

While this might suit your needs, often you will find the need to develop your own framework customized to your own system, as you do with the Inventory Tracking system. However, there's nothing wrong with letting PowerBuilder do the work for you if you can.

TROUBLESHOOTING

I know I created a PBL, but can't seem to find it in the library painter. Why is this? If you can't find the PBL with your application in it, you are probably viewing the wrong directory. This window allows you to change your drive and directory and search other areas on your hard drive.

Understanding Property Sheets

PowerBuilder 5 introduced property sheets. (Property Sheets were seen earlier for use in the library painter.) You will find property sheets used in every PowerBuilder 5 object. Property sheets are a new and more understandable way to specify attributes of the PowerBuilder object you are currently working on. The library property sheet (see figures 1.7 and 1.9) shows the attributes available to a library. To pull up a property sheet for an object, click on the properties icon found on most PainterBars.

Viewing the Application Property Sheet

The application property sheet (see fig. 1.15) is much more complicated, since there are many more attributes of an application than there are attributes of a PBL.

FIG. 1.15

There are many attributes that you can specify in the application property sheet.

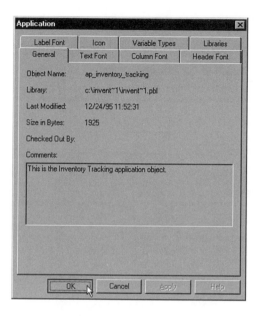

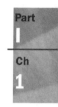

The application property sheet and other object property sheets will be covered in this chapter and in other chapters.

▶ **See** "The Application Property Sheet," **p. 106**

Specifying a Library Path

Every PowerBuilder application searches its own PBL for any references to windows or other PowerBuilder objects. Sometimes, however, you may want to split your work up into multiple PBLs. For this reason, PowerBuilder lets you specify a library path. A library path is a list of PBLs that your application accesses when looking for objects, variable references, and other PowerBuilder constructs created during application development.

A library path is specified using the application property sheet. When the property sheet is pulled up, click on the Libraries tab. This will display the Libraries sheet seen in figure 1.16.

To add another PBL to your search path, you can either type it directly in the Library Search Path multi-line edit box or click the Browse button. If you click the Browse button, you will see the Select Library dialog box, as seen in figure 1.17. Here, you will choose PBLs that you can add to your search path.

FIG. 1.16
The Select Libraries dialog box lets you choose which libraries are searched (which library search path is used) in order to run the program.

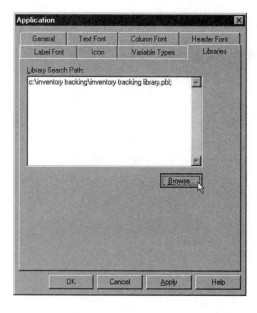

FIG. 1.17
When you're finished, clicking Open will return the name of the PBL you've chosen to be in your library search path, as seen in figure 1.18.

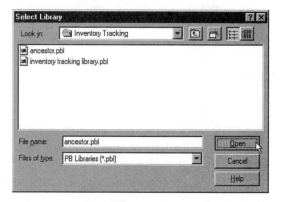

N O T E   Be sure that both Inventory Tracking Library.PBL and Ancestor.PBL are in the search path for the application. Since our application object (inventory_tracking) is already in Inventory Tracking Library.PBL, you will find that Inventory Tracking Library.PBL is already in the search path. You should also add Ancestor.PBL to your search path. ■

FIG. 1.18

Any additions chose while browsing for PBLs will be reflected in the library search path.

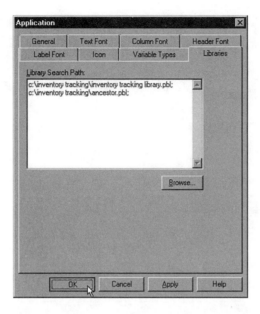

Using Menu Options in PowerBuilder Painters

Each PowerBuilder painter has its own menu. Some menu items you will find consistent in most of the PowerBuilder painters. The following sections discuss those menu items that you'll use most often.

Saving Your Work

After you complete your work, you'll need to save it. To do this, you need to open the File menu and choose Save (see fig. 1.19). This saves your PowerBuilder object (in this case, your PowerBuilder application) with the new settings.

Closing the Painters

You'll want to close your painter after working with it. This not only frees up more memory, but also allows for easier movement between the painters you use. To close the painter you are currently working on, open the File menu and choose Close. This closes your current painter. If you have made changes but have not saved them, PowerBuilder asks if you want to save your changes before completely closing the painter.

FIG. 1.19

To save work in a PowerBuilder painter, choose File, Save.

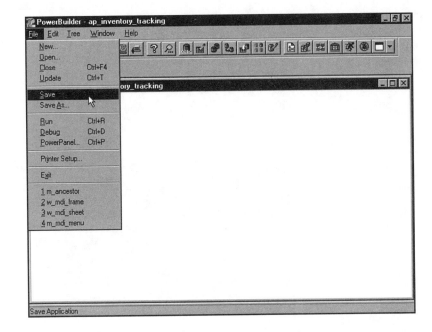

Exiting PowerBuilder

To exit PowerBuilder completely, click File, Exit. Before exiting, PowerBuilder closes all open painters and asks if you want to save any unsaved changes, as seen in figure 1.20. Here, answer Yes to save changes and exit, No to exit without saving changes, and Cancel to not exit at all.

FIG. 1.20

To exit PowerBuilder, choose File, Exit. PowerBuilder will ask if you want to save any unsaved changes.

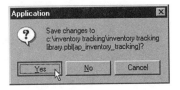

Using Control Menu Boxes

There is a difference between the *Sheet* (or *Painter*) control menu box and the *Frame* (or *Application*) control menu box. The frame control menu box is the little square on the upper left corner of your screen when PowerBuilder is running. The square looks like the icon of the application. (In Windows 3.x, it has a big minus sign in the middle of it.) The frame control menu box is the smaller box down from the frame control menu box. The square looks like an icon of the painter. (In Windows 3.x, it also has a little minus sign in the middle of it.)

You can double-click either the sheet control menu box or the frame control menu box rather than go through the menu. By double-clicking the sheet control menu box, you close that painter. If you have made changes in the painter, PowerBuilder will ask if you want to save your changes.

 T I P To free up memory, navigate more easily, and to run more efficiently, you should periodically close all your painters so that just the PowerBar is showing.

By double-clicking the frame control menu box, you close the entire PowerBuilder application. Any open painters automatically close (and ask if you wish to save any unsaved changes). PowerBuilder asks if you really want to exit. If you answer OK, PowerBuilder ends. You can double-click either the sheet control menu box or the frame control menu box, rather than go through the menu.

N O T E Rather than double-clicking the control box on a frame or sheet window, you can also close an application in Windows 95 by clicking the close button. The close button is the button with an 'x' on the upper right of the title bar on every Windows 95 window. The close button will close your window identically to double-clicking on the control box. ▨

FIG. 1.21
Windows 95
PowerBuilder
developers take the
easy way out of a
painter by clicking
on the close button.

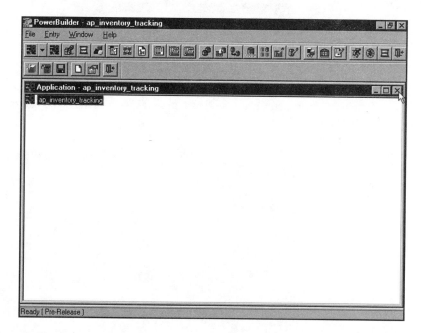

Try using the toolbars, close buttons, and control menu boxes instead of the menus for saving and exiting. You will find that this way is easier and quicker. However, you should use the menu to save your work without exiting. This is a good idea if you have a large task before you inside a painter.

Using Menus

▶ **See** "Developing Your Menu Using the Menu Painter," **p. 167**

Menus, which appear at the top of applications, are important for navigating between windows and for performing certain tasks. To get to the menu painter, click the Menu icon. This displays the Select Menu window, shown in figure 1.22.

FIG. 1.22
The Select Menu window allows you to either view/update an existing menu or create a new menu.

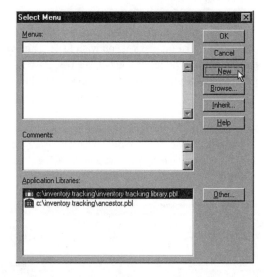

To create a new menu, click the New button. This opens the menu painter shown in figure 1.23.

FIG. 1.23
In the menu painter, enter your menu bar choices and menu options.

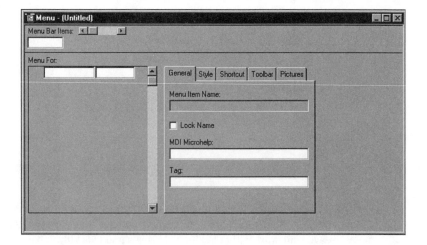

N O T E Notice the tab controls on the right side of the menu painter. The menu painter does not contain a Properties icon, but rather places the properties sheet right on the painter. ■

Making Your Menu

Now you decide what to put on your menu. On the top menu bar, you should include menu items similar to the following:

- ■ File for file and exit options
- ■ Edit for undoing, cutting, and pasting
- ■ Inventory for inventory-related functions
- ■ Window for any window-related functions
- ■ Help to pull up online help

These items are called *menu bar items*. For now, limit your options under File to Save, Close, and Exit. You can add other options later.

For each menu item underneath the main options, PowerBuilder allows you to enter MDI MicroHelp. The MicroHelp is displayed every time the cursor passes over the menu item or the menu's toolbar item (while the left mouse button is held down). This is a very handy way to make your programs more user-friendly without a lot of work.

 To create the file, type File in the first Menu For text box. Then type &Save, &Close, and E&xit in the following text boxes to create Save, Close, and Exit. Use the Insert icon each time to insert a new row. (The Insert icon is the icon on the far left on the PainterBar.) Notice how inserting a row option adds the row above the current option. If you want to rearrange your menu items, use the Move icon (the icon that looks like a hand) to position your options how you want them.

N O T E An ampersand (&) in front of a menu item does several things:

- An underline appears under the following letter when focus leaves that menu item and when the application is running.

- On menu items, (i.e., Save, Close, and Exit), the & establishes an accelerator key. An accelerator key allows the user to press the underlined letter when the menu list is displayed. This will allow the user to immediately jump to a menu item (i.e., Exit) when the menu list is displayed and the accelerator key (i.e., 'x') is pressed.

- On the menu bar (in this case, File, Edit, Inventory, Window, and Help), the & establishes a shortcut key of ALT+letter to mimic if you clicked the menu item with the mouse pointer. For instance, &File shows File and allows you to use ALT+F to pull down menu items under File. Shortcut keys are discussed in more depth in chapter 5.

Every menu bar item should have a shortcut, and every menu item should have an accelerator. ■

▶ **See** "Using Shortcut Keys," **p. 169**

To add another column, left-click the scroll bar that the mouse pointer is sitting on in figure 1.24, or click on the right arrow, or press the Tab key. This blanks out your screen and allows you to type both the next menu bar item and your options for the next menu bar item (see fig. 1.25). Don't worry if what you just typed disappears. It reappears once you click the left side of the scroll bar or the left arrow or press BACKTAB, or Shift+Tab (see fig. 1.26). Add additional menu bar items Edit, Inventory, Window, and Help. (Make sure that these items are added to the menu bar, not as options on a single menu bar item.) You'll add more menu bar items and options to menus later in the book.

FIG. 1.24

Notice how Save, Close, and Exit are typed underneath File. For each menu option, you also should assign an accelerator, and MDI MicroHelp.

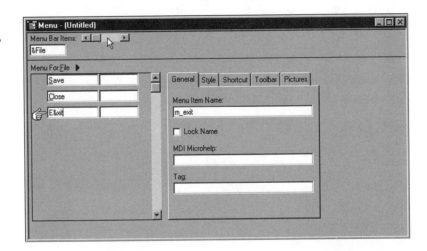

FIG. 1.25

Notice how adding a new menu bar item appears to clear out the previous menu bar item. Click on the left side of the scroll bar next to Menu Bar Items to make previous entries reappear.

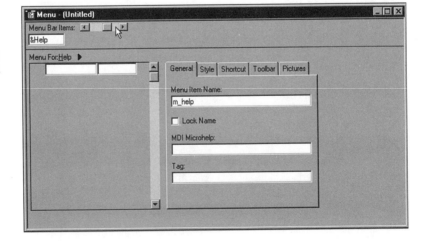

FIG. 1.26

See? The other menu items are still there. You can see these again by clicking on the left side of the scroll bar or the left arrow where the pointer is now.

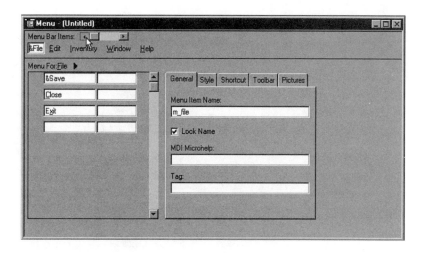

N O T E A *Tag* is allowed to be entered for many objects, and many controls on those objects. A tag is not used by PowerBuilder internally, but can be used by the developer as a means of identifying the object or control.

Tags should be used cautiously. Many third-party packages use tags, and can change the ones you've previously entered. Often, there are other ways to uniquely identify an object, such as object name. ■

Saving Your Menu

When you want to save your menu, choose File, Save. This opens the Save Menu dialog box, pictured in figure 1.27. Now you can save your menu.

N O T E In the Inventory Tracking system, you will create one menu and call it m_ancestor. It will go into Ancestor.PBL and become a menu ancestor. *Menu ancestors* are prototypes for other menus. (Windows can also have ancestors.) You'll learn more about ancestors and what else you can do with menus in the menu chapter later in this book. ■

▶ **See** "Implementing Window Inheritance," **p. 157**
▶ **See** "Implementing Menu Inheritance and Toolbars," **p. 173**
▶ **See** "Inheritance," **p. 470**

FIG. 1.27
You save your menu
using the Save Menu
dialog box. As always,
don't forget the
comments.

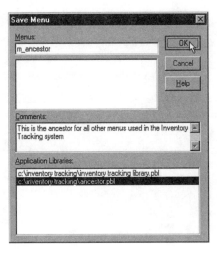

Using Windows

A *window* is a rectangular box that appears on your screen when you run a Windows program.
You may already know what a window is, but you may not know that there are several types of
windows and lots of different ways to program for them.

To define a window, click the Window icon. This opens the Select Window dialog box, shown
in figure 1.28.

FIG. 1.28
The Select Window
dialog box allows you to
either view or update an
existing window or create
a new window.

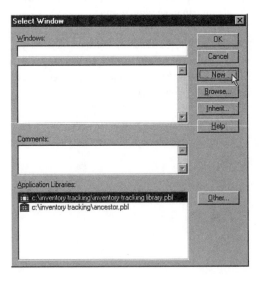

To create a new window, click New. This opens the window painter, shown in figure 1.29.

FIG. 1.29

In the window painter, the rectangular box in the upper left corner represents the window that will appear.

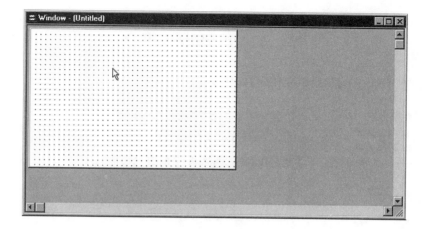

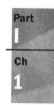

▶ **See** "Using the Windows Property Sheet," **p. 116**

By double-clicking the window you are creating or by clicking the properties icon, you will see the window property sheet, as seen in figure 1.30. As you can see, the title of the new window, *Using PowerBuilder 5*, has been typed in. Also, the window color and the MDI Client color have been changed to Silver. Finally, MDI Frame with Microhelp was the choice for the window type.

▶ **See** "General Window Properties," **p. 116**

FIG. 1.30

The window property sheet allows you to change the attributes of a window.

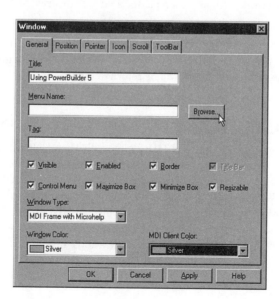

> **N O T E** I changed the Window Color to match the MDI Client Color. This is personal preference only. You can change your window color to anthing you prefer. ■

Joining Your Menu to Your Window

FIG. 1.31

The Select Menu dialog box allows you to associate a menu with a window.

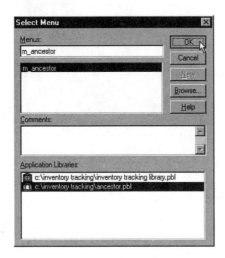

▶ **See** "Associating a Menu with a Window," **p. 180**

Now you need to attach a menu to the MDI frame. (In Version 5, MDI frame windows are no longer allowed to be saved without a menu associated with the frame.)

You can enter the name of a menu into the Menu Name text box. Also, by clicking the Browse command button in the window property sheet as seen in figure 1.30, the Select Menu dialog box appears, as seen in figure 1.31. Here, you choose which menu gets displayed when your window opens. The menu you choose will be returned to the property sheet, as seen in figure 1.32.

Comparing SDI vs. MDI Frame

Notice you can choose MDI Frame and MDI Frame with MicroHelp as the window type in the Window Style dialog box (see fig. 1.30). MDI stands for *Multiple Document Interface*. (As you probably guessed, SDI stands for *Single Document Interface*.) Most Windows applications are MDI applications. With an MDI application, all windows (called *sheet windows*) are opened "inside" a master window. This master window is called an MDI Frame. All sheet windows opened can reference each other easily, and movement between sheet windows is clean. SDI is typically used for single-window applications. The sample Inventory Tracking system is

MDI; therefore, an MDI Frame must be created to hold the other windows in the Inventory Tracking system.

▶ **See** "Defining Window Types," **p. 118**

FIG. 1.32
The Select Menu dialog box will fill the Menu Name text box with the appropriate menu.

Using MicroHelp

MicroHelp messages are short help messages that can appear at the bottom of an MDI frame. These messages are a good way to communicate an idea to the user (such as Save was successful or Enter a numeric field) without having to stop the program with a response window (often called a dialog box). Since MicroHelp is only available with MDI programs, most of your programs will be developed using MDI Frame with MicroHelp, instead of only an MDI Frame (without MicroHelp).

N O T E   Figure 1.33 shows an MDI frame window with a sheet window inside of it. This set of windows is not part of the Inventory Tracking system, but was made to explain frame windows, sheet windows, menus, toolbars, and MicroHelp. ■

▶ **See** "Using MDI Frames and MDI Frames with MicroHelp," **p. 119**
▶ **See** "Opening a Window Sheet," **p. 161**

FIG. 1.33
Inside the MDI frame, you can place other windows. The MicroHelp message is located at the bottom of the window.

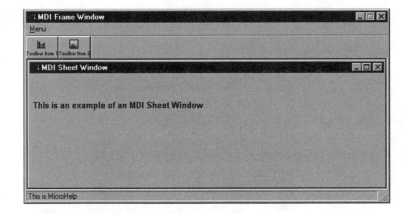

Saving Your Window

When you want to save your window within the application painter, choose File, Save. This opens the Save Window dialog box, pictured in figure 1.34; from there you can save your window. In the Windows text box, enter the name of your window (w_inventory_frame). Provide the appropriate comments, click the appropriate PBL (inventry.pbl), and click OK.

 TIP When you saved the window, the name you saved it under started with a w_. This is not required by PowerBuilder, but naming conventions in PowerBuilder make your code easier to use and debug. Appendix A shows a list of suggested naming conventions.

▶ **See** "Using Naming Conventions," **p. 759**

FIG. 1.34
After creating your window, you need to save it. This is similar to other save windows you've seen so far. Don't forget the comments!

Pulling It Together with PowerScript and Events

PowerScript is the language of PowerBuilder; it is how you control the flow of your application and how you code for certain events.

Exploring PowerBuilder Events

Event programming is the main area in which Windows programs differentiate from old-style MS-DOS and mainframe applications. In older operating systems, sequential programming (in which steps needed to follow a set of procedures) was necessary. This caused programs and procedures to be set in action sequentially. When these programs were finished running, they would typically set other programs or procedures in motion. This continued until processing was done.

Soon it became apparent that most businesses did not do their business functions sequentially, but rather in response to events that take place. Programs that attempted to mirror businesses were hard to develop, hard to maintain, and often cumbersome to run.

Event programming allows the programmer to program for a specified event. Examples of typical events are mouse clicks, starting or ending the application, opening or closing a window, pressing the Enter key, or choosing a menu item. Windows programmers program for these and other events.

▶ **See** "Understanding Events," **p. 188**

▶ **See** "Programming in PowerScript," **p. 223**

Programming in PowerScript

In PowerBuilder, events control the flow of an application. Specific PowerScript is executed every time a corresponding event occurs. In this section, you can code three events in PowerScript.

 Application Events   Using the library painter, you can pull up your existing PowerBuilder objects. Pull up the library by clicking on the Library icon. The library painter will automatically display the members (also known as entries) of the current application's PBL, although you can open other directories and PBLs by double-clicking them as they appear in the painter.

By double-clicking an entry (like the application, as seen in fig. 1.35), you automatically open that entry in its proper painter (much like the Windows Explorer or File Manager starts the associated program with a file on the disk drive).

FIG. 1.35

By double-clicking an entry in the library painter, you automatically open that entry in its proper painter.

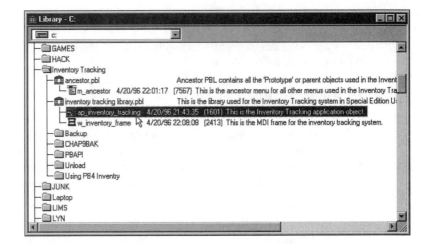

Using the Library or the Application icon, run the application painter for the Inventory Tracking application. Now, click the Script icon to enter the script painter. Your screen should now look like the one in figure 1.36.

FIG. 1.36

When you click the Script icon, the script painter opens.

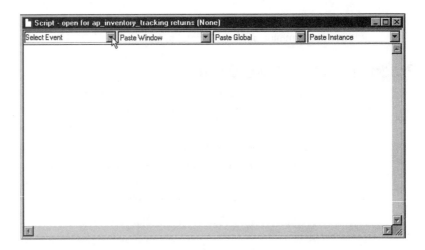

Notice how the script painter for your application automatically opens with the application open event. PowerBuilder does a reasonably good job of determining which event you want to code first. If you want to code for another event, PowerBuilder gives you several events in each PowerBuilder object in which you can place PowerScript, as seen in figure 1.37. These events will be discussed in later chapters. You can select an event by clicking the Select Event box and clicking the event you want to code for.

FIG. 1.37
When you click the Select Event box, all the available events for the PowerBuilder object you're coding for are displayed.

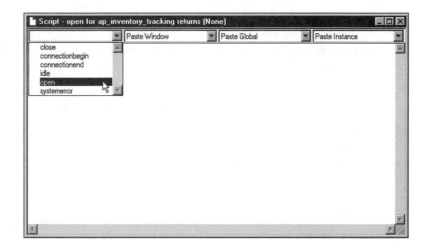

Be sure the open event is selected. Without coding for the open event in the application, your application cannot run! In the application painter, the open event is executed when the application opens. Right now, just code an open statement for your window. Do this by simply typing **open(w_inventory_frame)** in the PowerScript editor (see fig. 1.38).

FIG. 1.38
With the PowerScript painter, simply enter your commands. Here, you want to open your MDI frame window as soon as the application opens.

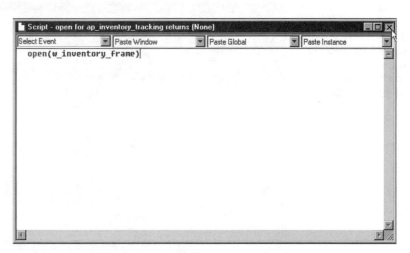

To close, use the menu or double-click the Script Control menu box (where the arrow is pointing in figure 1.36). PowerBuilder asks if you want to keep your changes. Click on Yes. Now close the application painter. Also, clicking the Return icon returns to the application painter and automatically saves any changes. The Return icon looks the same as the object the script is for. A window script uses a window for the return icon, a menu script uses a menu for the Return icon, and an application object uses an application icon for the Return icon.

▶ **See** "Using Child Windows," **p. 119**

▶ **See** "Using Pop-Up Windows," **p. 119**

Menu Events   One of the first actions pre-Windows developers learned was to always code the exit first. (That way, you can always get out of your program!) With Windows, that is no longer such a great concern (because you can always terminate a task), but old habits die hard, so code the Close and Exit events in the menu.

When you built your menu (m_ancestor), you told PowerBuilder what you wanted the choices to be, but not what to do when the choices were selected. This is done through PowerScript.

Click the Menu icon to run the menu painter and select m_ancestor. Within the menu painter (not on the menu bar), click on &File, and then on E&xit in the Menu For: File area. Now click the Script icon (see fig. 1.39).

> **N O T E**   When you click on &File and E&xit, be sure you are doing this in the menu painter, not on PowerBuilder's menu bar. Clicking File and Exit on the menu bar makes you exit out of PowerBuilder. ■

This brings you into the script painter for the Exit event. Type **Halt Close** in the script painter, as seen in figure 1.40. Halt immediately terminates your application; Halt Close executes the close event of the application and then terminates the application.

FIG. 1.39

Choose which event you want to code for, and then click the Script icon (where the pointer is) to enter PowerScript for that event.

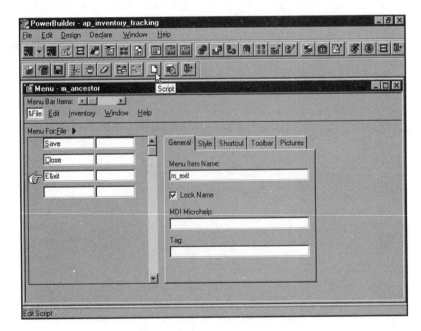

FIG. 1.40

This code immediately executes the application close event and then exits the application.

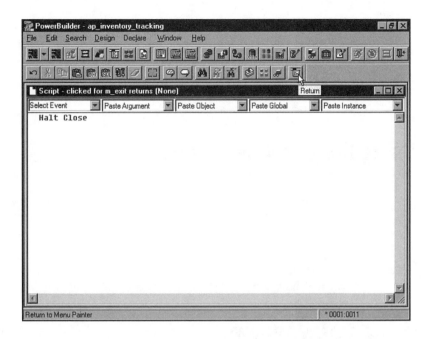

After coding PowerScript for your Exit event, leave the script painter and repeat the process for Close. Here, instead of entering Halt Close, type **close (ParentWindow)**, as shown in figure 1.41. This closes whatever window the menu is attached to, but usually does not close the application. However, if there are no more windows open in the application, the application closes. Now exit out of the script painter and out of the menu painter.

FIG. 1.41

Here is the code to close the window that the menu is attached to.

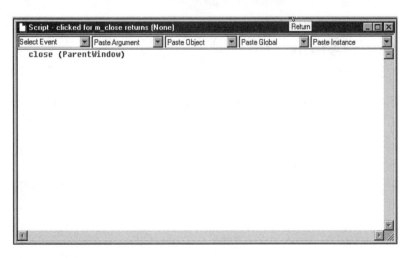

Other Events You have just scratched the surface of available events. Every PowerBuilder object can use PowerScript to enhance it.

N O T E   PowerBuilder is not case-sensitive. Therefore, Halt Close, halt close, HALT CLOSE, and hAlT ClOsE all do the same thing. Perhaps capitalizing functions may make them more readable, but it's really a matter of preference. ▪

▶ **See** "Understanding Analysis, Design, and Databases," **p. 49**
▶ **See** "Programming in PowerScript," **p. 223**

Using the Database Interface

▶ **See** "Designing a System with the PowerBuilder Database Painter," **p. 71**

One of PowerBuilder's strong points is its capability to interface with many databases. These database interfaces are transparent to the end user and (for the most part) also transparent to the developer.

You'll find that the database cannot be accessed through the library. It can only be accessed through the Database icons on the PowerBar. The database interface is coded through the open event of the application. (The next chapter explains this process.)

Using DataWindows

▶ **See** "Using the DataWindow Painter," **p. 268**

After defining the database, DataWindows are used as data-entry screens and reports connected to these databases. They are an integral part of PowerBuilder and are covered in detail in the DataWindow chapters (chapters 9 through 12). You won't create any DataWindows until after you go through the database.

Using Online Help

PowerBuilder's online help is extraordinary! All functions, attributes, and ways to do things can be found in the online help. You'll find yourself using PowerBuilder's help quite often. To access help, click the Help menu bar item. (In the next section, "Customizing Your PowerBuilder Toolbars," you'll see how to get an icon for searching help added to your PowerBar.)

N O T E   To get help on a specific command in the PowerScript painter, type that command, position your cursor in the middle of that command, and press Shift+F1. To open the help table of contents, press F1. ▪

N O T E   If you're stuck on a problem, try searching through online help. In most cases, you can save a lot of time with an online search, as opposed to a manual one.

I find it much easier to pull up the online help and immediately perform a search (by clicking on the Search button) for the desired topic, rather than reading through the table of contents. ▪

Customizing Your PowerBuilder Toolbars

Depending on what you are in, you can have up to three toolbars:

- The PowerBar runs all of the time in PowerBuilder. It allows you to navigate between most of the painters, and it contains some tools (such as the Run Current Application icon, which runs your program).

- The PainterBars are different for each painter. They contain tools that you'll want to use when inside that painter.

- The StyleBar is for text manipulation. With the StyleBar, you can change any text's size, font, or style.

Before you go any further, open your w_inventory_frame window in the window painter. The window painter gives you access to all the toolbars.

Using the Toolbars Dialog Box

To get to the Toolbars dialog box, click Window and choose Toolbars, as seen in figure 1.42. The Toolbars dialog box controls the toolbars (see fig. 1.43). From here, you can hide or show toolbars, move the toolbars to a desired location, control the text display within the toolbar, or customize the toolbar by adding or deleting icons from it.

FIG. 1.42

You can manipulate your toolbars by clicking Window, Toolbars.

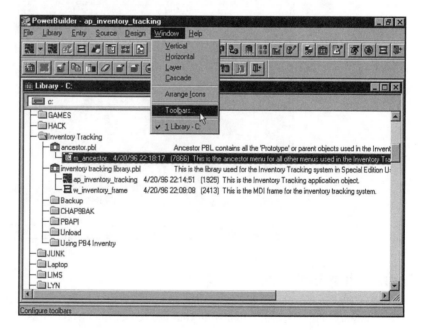

FIG. 1.43
The Toolbars dialog box allows you to manipulate your toolbars.

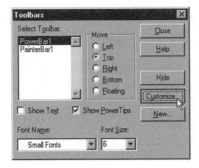

N O T E There are many ways to manipulate toolbars. If you don't want to go through the menu, try right-clicking a toolbar. This opens a pop-up menu that is functionally equivalent to the Toolbars dialog box (see fig. 1.44). From here, you can do anything that could be done through the Toolbars dialog box. Try it and see which one you like better. ▪

FIG. 1.44
You can get to this toolbar pop-up menu by right-clicking any toolbar.

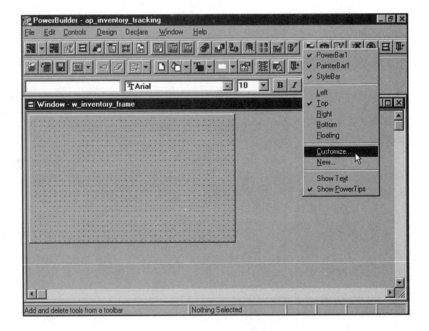

Positioning Toolbars

By clicking on the appropriate toolbar and then choosing how you want that toolbar displayed, PowerBuilder moves the toolbar to your desired location. You can also hide a toolbar completely if you wish.

N O T E PowerBuilder lets you drag the PowerBar and PainterBar to the position of your choice. Simply click an empty area on the toolbar, hold down the left mouse button, and drag the toolbar to where you want them to go. ▪

Showing Text

When you first start using PowerBuilder, you may want to display text underneath your toolbar icons. Although this makes PowerBuilder easier to use, it makes the icons on the toolbar take up a lot more space. Most experienced developers eventually turn off the text on the toolbars, especially with PowerTips turned on. (See next section, "Showing PowerTips.")

To toggle the toolbar text on and off, click the Show Text check box in the Toolbars dialog box, as seen in figure 1.43.

Showing PowerTips

PowerTips are used both in the PowerBuilder environment and in any application you develop. When Show Text for a menu is turned off, PowerTips appear if your mouse cursor sits on a toolbar item for about two seconds.

FIG. 1.45
PowerTips are displayed when Show Text is off and the mouse cursor is stationary on an icon for about two seconds.

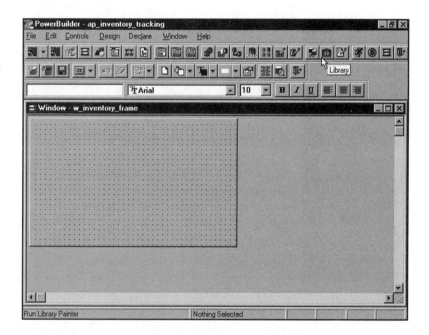

In figure 1.45, the mouse is stationary on the Library icon. After a few seconds, the PowerTip appears, describing what that icon is used for.

PowerTips make the PowerBuilder environment and any applications you develop more friendly, especially for beginning users.

Adding, Deleting, and Rearranging Icons

By clicking the Customize button in the Toolbars dialog box, you arrive at the Customize dialog box, which lets you place icons on a toolbar, take them off a toolbar, or rearrange icons on a toolbar. Simply find the icon you want and drag it where you want it, as shown in figure 1.46.

FIG. 1.46
The Customize dialog box shows the Run Window icon being dragged from the selected palette to the current toolbar.

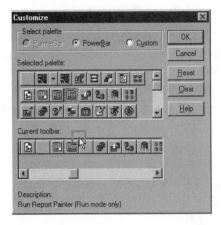

N O T E Are you confused about what all those icons do? If you don't know what an icon's function is, look at the bottom of the window at PowerBuilder's MicroHelp. Every time you click on an icon, its MicroHelp is displayed. ▓

N O T E Although I leave most PainterBars alone, there are several icons I like to add to the PowerBar:

● Search (the magnifying glass) runs the help search. I put this icon right next to the Help icon (the question mark).

● Run Report Painter and Run Report Painter (Run mode Only) help with reports. These icons resemble the DataWindow icon, except that they resemble reports a little more closely. I put these icons right next to the DataWindow icon.

● The Database Administration icon allows you to enter SQL commands directly to your database from anywhere in your application.

● The Arrange Window icon is actually a drop down icon containing several icons within itself. The icons contained in the drop down Arrange Window icon allow you to arrange

(Tile, Cascade, Layer, etc.) any open painters in your PowerBuilder environment.

Again, it's personal preference. If you find yourself frequently using a function that PowerBuilder has provided an icon for, then put that icon on one of the toolbars. It'll save you loads of mouse wear and tear! ▓

Running Your PowerBuilder Application

To run your application, click the Run icon, which opens your window and first application. Your first application can be seen in figure 1.47. Of course, right now you can't do much with it except open the File menu and choose either Exit or Close, both of which do the same thing.

Still, it's an important start. Chapter 2, "Understanding Analysis, Design, and Databases," discusses what you want the application to do and tells you why these initial building blocks are important.

FIG. 1.47

Here you see the Windows 95 application we have created so far using PowerBuilder 5.

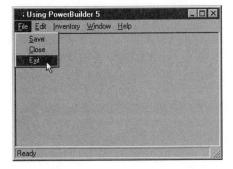

From Here...

By now, you should know how to build a small application in PowerBuilder. You've also gone over the concepts of visual and iterative design and most of the PowerBuilder components including PowerBuilder Libraries (PBLs), windows, and menus.

One of the many great things about PowerBuilder is its capability to build on existing work. Use what you started in this chapter; in the following chapters, you'll examine the components in more detail as you come closer to finishing the Inventory Tracking system.

This chapter serves as an introduction to the rest of the book, and all other chapters reference and build on this chapter. Some especially useful chapters include:

- Chapter 2, "Understanding Analysis, Design, and Databases," shows you how to analyze your user's requests into a coherent database design. (A good data model is a must for any development!)

- Chapter 3, "Using the Application Painter," shows you how to define your application in more detail.

- Chapter 4, "Exploring Windows," shows you the ins and outs of window design and development inside PowerBuilder. Window controls are also discussed here.

- Chapter 5, "Designing Menus," shows you how to build on your menu that you started in this chapter.

CHAPTER 2

Understanding Analysis, Design, and Databases

by Charles A. Wood

Although database and program analysis and design chapters are usually discussed last in most books, they are probably the most important parts of any project. Because you're designing a system as you learn PowerBuilder, it is wise to define what you are developing. Here is your crash course in requirements, resource allocation, analysis, and design.

This chapter has something for every level of experience. It is one of the most complex chapters in *Special Edition Using PowerBuilder 5*, yet it covers concepts so vital to an application that every developer should be aware of the techniques discussed herein. ■

Analyze what is needed in an application using Entity/Relationship Modeling.

Modeling a system before actually developing can be crucial to the development process.

Learn how to normalize your entity relationship model into a database design.

Database normalization is extremely important to any application. More systems that fail do so because of poor database design and normalization than any other reason. This chapter shows you how to normalize your database, and the pitfalls to avoid during database design.

Implement your database design using the PowerBuilder database painter.

The database painter is an extremely powerful and visual tool. This chapter shows you how to use your database painter.

Create, maintain, and administer the database.

Using the database painter, you can create, update, and administer your database.

Access and update data in your database tables using the database painter.

PowerBuilder's database painter also allows you to add or update data on your database.

Understanding the Systems Development Cycle

The systems development cycle provides the usual steps developers go through to implement a system. Traditionally, the seven phases of the systems development cycle are:

1. Requirements	The requirements phase is where the end-user specifies what he or she requires your system to do.
2. Resource Allocation	After your requirements have been set up, you should allocate resources to your project. This would include people (programmers and developers, testers, etc.), hardware (new computers, new devices, new printers, etc.), software (case tools), and time needed. Resource allocation also includes setting the scope and needed quality of your system.
3. Analysis	Analysis consists of determining the major components of your system and how they relate together.
4. Design	Design consists of converting your analysis to a relational format that can be handled *effectively* by a relational database.
5. Development	Development consists of the actual implementation of your requirements using the analysis and design. The production stage is where all the PowerBuilder development takes place.
6. Testing/ Implementation	Testing consists of debugging your application and implementing it on the end-user's platform.
7. Feedback	Feedback consists of monitoring how well your system is received by the end-user. Feedback is converted into requirements for the next version of your system.

Although all seven of these phases are covered (at least somewhat) in this book, it primarily concentrates on Development. However, this chapter primarily deals with Analysis and Design.

N O T E   I've seen cycles that had anywhere from three to nine phases. The cycles with a different number of phases have combined other phases together (i.e., Analysis/Design) or split them apart (i.e., Unit Testing, System Testing, and Implementation). ▪

Completing Requirements

Requirements are perhaps the most important phase of the systems development cycle. All your work in analysis, design, and production should be targeted toward completing your requirements. Before beginning design, you must first get requirements of your system. Although this may seem intuitive, developers are often forced to start coding *before* requirements arrive. Occasionally, the end-user will tell the developer to develop a system and *only then* will the end-user offer any substantial comments on what he/she wants!

Requirements should only contain system outputs, or what outputs are desired from the proposed system. System outputs should consist of statements of what the system should do (i.e., "I want a system to be able to track and report items from ordering to selling point...") or an actual example of output forms, such as invoices or order sheets.

> **CAUTION**
>
> Requirements *should not* contain screen layouts, system flow, or *any interim steps* in reaching your final required system outputs. There are companies that submit 100+ page requirements documents for systems with one report as the desired output! Not only does this take a long time to develop, but the requirements are then too hard to follow and then are usually rewritten as detailed analysis occurs.
>
> Think of requirements as a goal for your system rather than a step-by-step development plan. After your requirements are set, everything you do in development should be devoted to meeting those requirements.
>
> Some users will want a more active hand in screen design and system flow. Nonetheless, requirements should *only* consist of system outputs desired by the end-user. If the end-user still wants a more active role, then have the end-user lend a hand during the design phase, where screen layouts and system flow are determined.

N O T E   We only have two requirements for the Inventory Tracking system we are developing in this book.

1. We want to be able to track items from ordering (from the supplier) to selling point (to the customer). Each item category can only be stored in one warehouse at a time and purchased from one supplier. (In other words, you cannot have 1/4" bolts residing at several warehouses and you only buy 1/4" bolts from one supplier.)

2. We want the selling point to be invoice driven. The invoice should look like figure 2.1

FIG. 2.1
This is the required invoice.

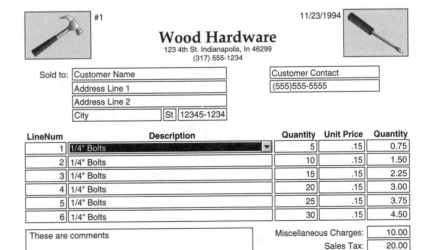

continues

continued

Now *everything* we analyze, design, and develop should help achieve the requirements. Although most requirements will contain more forms, you can see that the medium-sized system requirments should probably not exceed 10 pages. Large-sized system requirements should probably not exceed 30 pages. ▪

Understanding Resource Allocation

After you get the requirements for your system, you then need to allocate resources to develop your system. There are four components of resources available to developers: scope, material resources, time, and quality (see fig. 2.2).

Scope	Scope is the size of the system. Scope includes the number of data entry windows, the number of reports, and the complexity of a system.
Material Resources	Resources (usually) are the machines and tools purchased and the developers added *at the beginning of a project*. (Any tool or developer added during the project actually *takes away* from resources.)
Time	Time is the amount of time you get to complete the project.
Quality	Quality is the number of bugs *eliminated* and level of sophistication present in the system when delivered.

FIG. 2.2
There is always contention between the four components of resource allocation.

If you ask your end-user which of these four components is most important, the probable response will be all of them. However, it's good to prioritize components in order of importance. The cardinal rule of resource allocation is that you can't *increase* one of the components of development without *decreasing* another.

> **CAUTION**
>
> If you add features to a project without adding resources, you either have to increase the time it takes to develop the system or expect the overall quality of the delivered system to be reduced. This seems pretty intuitive, but many end-users do not understand this! Here are some examples of resource contention that often aren't addressed by the end-user or management:
>
> - Often you will have an end-user adding to the scope of a project, but refusing to push back the date or add costs. System quality will suffer.
>
> - Management may transfer a valuable developer to another section (or a valuable developer may quit). Then they replace the seasoned developer with a new developer that needs to be trained. All this will occur without pushing back the date. Again, system quality will suffer.
>
> - Management doubles the scope of a system, and then requires programmers to work double shifts. Productivity drops due to fatigue. The time and quality suffer.
>
> There are many, many more examples of how one component of resource allocation is increased without adjusting the other components. Usually this leads to a buggy, late, and expensive system.

Part

I

Ch

2

Exploring Analysis

N O T E Experienced developers know that there are many different analysis methodologies. In addition, each methodology is implemented slightly different from developer to developer. The methodology I use is a hybrid of several different methodologies, and is well-suited for system analysis by hand into PowerBuilder if no CASE (Computer Aided Software Engineering) tool is available.

The analysis methodology mentioned in this chapter is designed to give developers without an analysis tool a methodology which they can evolve (or mutate) to meet their specific needs.

Keep in mind that your analysis methodology should be flexible enough to support iterative design, and should organize your system in such a way so that you can deliver a quality system with a minimum amount of time.

If possible, use a CASE tool; it helps with analysis and system documentation. ▓

In this phase of a project, the language you're using (PowerBuilder), the operating system (Windows), and the computer you're using (a PC) are not considered. Analysis deals only with description of the current business activities and the software that needs to be developed. Therefore, the analysis discussion in this chapter does not deal with PowerBuilder in detail. (Don't worry, though—in the following parts of the chapter, you'll see how to implement design using PowerBuilder and you'll get into the database painter.)

Entity Relationship Modeling

In analysis, an entity is a real-world object whose attributes can and should be recorded on a database. (For example, an Item would be an entity in the inventory tracking system since you would be recording the item's order price, selling price, and location.) In the past several years, object-oriented development has caused a push to make your programs mimic real-world processing as much as possible. This is effectively done with an Entity Relationship Model (ERM). Developing an ERM requires four steps:

1. Identifying all the entities (tables) that are required for your deliverables
2. Identifying all the relevant attributes and states (columns) of those entities
3. Eliminating unused entities
4. Determining relationships between your entities

Identifying All the Entities (Tables) That Are Required for Your Deliverables   Once more, look at the requirements of your system. With Inventory Tracking, we must track an item, and be able to issue invoices. We must first identify those entities required by the deliverables. By reviewing the requirements, you can determine what entities are needed:

■ Requirement 1 states that we need to track items. Therefore, you know that an Item entity is needed as well as Warehouse and Supplier entity.

■ Requirement 2 says that we need to produce an invoice, so an Invoice entity is needed, and we'll also add a Salesperson entity.

Figure 2.3 lists the entities needed (so far) in the Inventory Tracking system.

FIG. 2.3
Here you see every entity in a box.

| Supplier | | Invoice |

| Item |

| Warehouse | | Salesperson |

N O T E   Some of you may have noticed that some needed entities have been left out. This is purposefully done to show you how normalization can find and correct errors in your analysis. ■

N O T E   Remember that entities are always nouns! If you write down an entity that is not a person, place, or thing, what you have written down is not an entity. (However, it could be an entity relationship. See the next section for details.) ■

CAUTION

You could name about 80 percent of the entities in any system in a few minutes. The last 20 percent, however, require some in-depth research. Be prepared for a long and laborious process of interviews, research, and analysis to name all of the entities.

Eventually, each entity you find turns into a database table. Using analysis, you need to define which tables you'll need on your database.

Identifying All the Relevant Attributes and States (Columns) of Those Entities   Now we take the entities we've defined along with the requirements specified and assign attributes to each entity based on the requirements:

1. To track items as mentioned in requirement 1, you need a warehouse ID listed in the Item entity. The Warehouse entity will need a warehouse ID, warehouse name, contact, address, and phone.

2. Since your end-user provided a form layout for you, you then assign each field on the form to an attribute.

All the attributes will eventually become columns on your database tables. Attributes have been added to your ERM in figure 2.4.

Part

I

Ch

2

FIG. 2.4

Attributes have been added to all the entities based on the requirements.

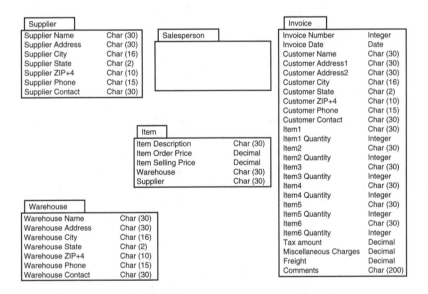

Also be sure to add the data types (Integer, Character, Decimal, etc.) to the attributes, as was done in figure 2.4.

> **N O T E**   Selecting all the attributes and assigning data types is tedious, but not as tedious as I've made it above. As mentioned earlier, there are some severe analysis flaws in the above ERM that will be addressed during normalization discussed later in this chapter. ■

Eliminating Unused Entities   Notice in figure 2.4 that the Salesperson entity that we chose as one of our initial entities was never used by any attribute in our requirements. If an entity has no attributes, then it does not belong in your system. Figure 2.5 shows the ERM with Salesperson deleted.

FIG. 2.5

Since it was not used, Salesperson has been deleted from the ERM.

Supplier	
Supplier Name	Char (30)
Supplier Address	Char (30)
Supplier City	Char (16)
Supplier State	Char (2)
Supplier ZIP+4	Char (10)
Supplier Phone	Char (15)
Supplier Contact	Char (30)

Item	
Item Description	Char (30)
Item Order Price	Decimal
Item Selling Price	Decimal
Warehouse	Char (30)
Supplier	Char (30)

Warehouse	
Warehouse Name	Char (30)
Warehouse Address	Char (30)
Warehouse City	Char (16)
Warehouse State	Char (2)
Warehouse ZIP+4	Char (10)
Warehouse Phone	Char (15)
Warehouse Contact	Char (30)

Invoice	
Invoice Number	Integer
Invoice Date	Date
Customer Name	Char (30)
Customer Address1	Char (30)
Customer Address2	Char (30)
Customer City	Char (16)
Customer State	Char (2)
Customer ZIP+4	Char (10)
Customer Phone	Char (15)
Customer Contact	Char (30)
Item1	Char (30)
Item1 Quantity	Integer
Item2	Char (30)
Item2 Quantity	Integer
Item3	Char (30)
Item3 Quantity	Integer
Item4	Char (30)
Item4 Quantity	Integer
Item5	Char (30)
Item5 Quantity	Integer
Item6	Char (30)
Item6 Quantity	Integer
Tax amount	Decimal
Miscellaneous Charges	Decimal
Freight	Decimal
Comments	Char (200)

TROUBLESHOOTING

I think that Salesperson is a pretty important entity. Surely it would contain valuable information about who made sales to what customers, etc. Shouldn't the Salesperson entity still be in the Inventory Tracking system? Everyone would agree that sales information is pretty important. Indeed, placing Salesperson on the ERM in the first place was due to the usual importance of tracking the salesperson. However, salesperson information was not on the requirements. By adding an additional entity, you create work for yourself for a system feature that was not requested. Developing for entities that were not requested could cause your scope to increase as well as increase the complexity of your easy-to-use small system.

Perhaps salesperson information is desired. If you really think it's an oversight of the requirements, then return to your end-user and ask if he or she would find salesperson information useful. You may find that you'll have to add it anyway, or you may find that your inventory personnel don't care about your sales personnel.

TROUBLESHOOTING

Aren't I making my system inflexible if I only put in entities that are on the requirements? This question is often asked by developers who have been using traditional mainframe development tools (COBOL, RPGII, etc.). With older tools, maintenance was so difficult that developers often were forced to second-guess what future enhancements may occcur to a system.

Thanks to the iterative design capabilities of PowerBuilder discussed in chapter 1, PowerBuilder allows you to add to existing systems fairly easily. Adding new features later requires little more work than adding them during development. By keeping your system as small as possible and using a good, normalized database design, you can implement features needed today by the end-user as quickly and easily as possible.

Determining Relationships Between Your Entities After determining the entities, you must find out how the entities relate to each other. This is done with functions. In other words, entities relate to each other by doing some action. Draw arrows with words on them between the entities to show the relationship, as seen in figure 2.6.

Part

I

Ch

2

FIG. 2.6
When displaying relationships, connect the two entities with a line and describe the relationship.

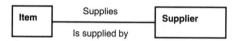

 T I P Two entities can have more than one relationship between them. Don't be afraid to draw more than one relationship, and don't feel forced to choose between two valid relationships.

N O T E Remember that functions are always verbs! If you write down a relationship between two entities that is not an action, rethink your entities. ■

The reason we show relationships is to once more ensure that all the entities belong to our system:

- If we cannot find a relationship between one entity and any other entity, then that entity probably does not belong on this system.

- If you see a set of entities that are not related to another set of entities, then you are probably trying to design two (or more) different systems.

In a traditional language such as C, COBOL, or BASIC, each relationship translates into a function, subroutine, or paragraph. Using PowerBuilder, you can also code relationships as functions, as command buttons on a window, or as menu bar items.

Notice that the relationship, or function, of the left (or top) entity is listed above (or on the left side of) the line connecting the entities. The relationship of the right (or bottom) entity is listed below (or on the right side of) the line connecting the entities. Therefore, you can read the relationship between supplier and item in figure 2.6 as "The Supplier supplies the Item" and "The Item is supplied by the Supplier."

Figure 2.7 shows all the relationships between entities in the Inventory Tracking system.

FIG. 2.7

Now you see the relationships between the entities.

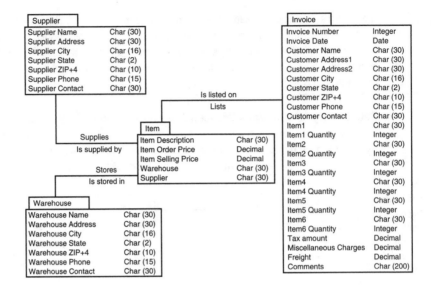

Showing Ordinality After you define the entities and relationships, you need to define ordinality, which describes the number of entities that can exist with another entity. For example, how many Warehouses can exist for each Item? (The answer is one—and only one—Warehouse can exist for each Item.) How many Items can exist for each Warehouse? (The answer is zero to many Items can exist for each Warehouse. Thus, Items and Warehouses have a one-to-many relationship, or a one-to-many ordinality.)

N O T E I have heard many people use *cardinality* as opposed to *ordinality* in design when referring to relationships, but ordinality fits the definition better. If you look up *ordinal number* vs. *cardinal number* in the *Random House College Dictionary* like I did, you'll see that:

- A cardinal number is defined as any of the numbers that express an amount, such as one, two, three, and so on.

- An ordinal number is defined as any of the numbers that express degree, quality, or position in a series, such as first, second, third, and so on.

You could argue that relationships like "one-to-one" are cardinal in nature, while relationships like "many-to-many" are ordinal in nature. However, I think "ordinality" fits a little better than "cardinality" since ordinal numbers seem more relational-, degree-, and series-oriented than cardinal numbers, which are isolated and stand alone. ■

Graphically Showing Ordinality Figure 2.8 indicates that each instance of Entity One can have no (zero) corresponding instances of Entity Two, or can have one corresponding instance of Entity Two. (This is referred to as a none-or-one relationship.) Often, entities that have large text fields that are optional (for example, comments) separate those comments out into separate tables and establish a none-or-one relationship between an entity and its comments.

FIG. 2.8

Entity One has a none-
or-one relationship with
Entity Two.

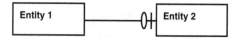

The symbol shown in figure 2.9 indicates that each instance of Entity One can have one and only one corresponding instance of Entity Two. This is referred to as a one-and-only-one relationship. In this Inventory Tracking system, an Item entity must be supplied by only one Supplier entity. Therefore, each Item has a one-and-only-one relationship with a Supplier.

FIG. 2.9

Entity One has a
one-and-only-one
relationship with
Entity Two.

Figure 2.10 indicates that each instance of Entity One can have no (zero) corresponding instances of Entity Two or can have many corresponding instances of Entity Two. This is referred to as a zero-through-many relationship. In this Inventory Tracking system, a supplier could sell us no items (and therefore not have any corresponding Item entities) or a supplier could have sold us lots of different items (and therefore have several corresponding Item entities). Supplier, therefore, has a zero-through-many relationship with Item.

FIG. 2.10

Entity One has a
zero-through-many
relationship with
Entity Two.

Figure 2.11 indicates that each instance of Entity One must have at least one corresponding instance of Entity Two, but can have many corresponding instances of Entity Two. This is referred to as a one-through-many relationship. In this Inventory Tracking system, each invoice must list at least one item. However, an invoice might list several items. Therefore, Invoice has a one-through-many relationship with Item.

FIG. 2.11

Entity One has a
one-through-many
relationship with
Entity Two.

Adding Ordinality to Your ERM In an ERM, you need to apply ordinality to each entity in a relationship. Study figure 2.12.

FIG. 2.12

Ordinality has been applied to both Item and Supplier.

Viewing figure 2.12, you could say that Item has a one-and-only-one relationship with Supplier, and Supplier has a zero-through-many relationship with Item. Often this is shortened to indicate maximum values only to say that Supplier and Item have a one-to-many relationship.

In figure 2.13, ordinality is added to our ERM:

- Supplier and Item have a many-to-one relationship. (Each supplier can supply many items, but each item must be supplied by only one supplier.)

- Invoice and Item have a many-to-many relationship. (Each invoice can contain many items, and each item may be contained on many invoices.)

- Warehouse and Item have a one-to-many relationship. (Each warehouse can store many items, but each item can be stored in only one warehouse, per the requirements.)

FIG. 2.13

Now you add all of the ordinalities.

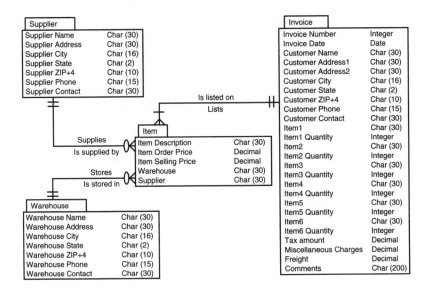

Normalization

Your ERM is starting to look a lot like a database layout. Indeed, most developers by this stage start calling your ERM a data model. However, as was pointed out earlier in the chapter, there are some serious analysis problems that were introduced while the ERM was created. These problems will be resolved while we discuss normalization.

Here are some data model terms that we will need to use during the rest of analysis and design:

Table	All entities are now called tables. (for example, The Item entity is now the Item table.) A table contains information about an entity. This information is stored in rows (also called instances or records) and columns (also called attributes or fields).
Database	A database is a collection of tables.
Data Model	A data model is a layout of a database. Although not quite yet in database format, a data model is to a database what a blueprint is to a building.
Column	All attributes on the ERM are now columns. A column (also called a field) is a bit of information about each occurrence (or instance) of an entity. For example, a column on the Item table would be order price.
Row	A row is an instance or occurrence of an entity. For example, if you had five different suppliers that you ordered from, then you would have five rows on your Supplier table.

Before we begin to design your database into PowerBuilder's database painter, your data model should be *normalized*. Normalization is the process of making a data model as "normal" as possible. In database terms, a "normal" database is a database that is efficient as well as easy to use and understand.

The normalization process takes us through several *normal forms*. A normal form is a set of rules that your database should follow. We cover six normal form rules.

N O T E   There are many "normal forms." Periodically, a database designer (usually a Ph. D. from the academic community) publishes yet another normal form.

Since a normal form is a set of rules that your database should follow, there is a near infinite number of database design rules that *could* be called normal forms. However, most normal forms (including 4th and 5th normal forms covered in this chapter), while usually valid, cover situations in database design that don't occur too often. ▪

TROUBLESHOOTING

I've heard that you should never normalize past 3rd normal form and that you can over-normalize. How true is this? Such statements are common among some database developers, but not really valid. Basically what you're saying is that there may be valid rules that you should be following, but you choose to ignore because the rule has been called a normal form higher than number 3.

However, sometimes normalization will result in a database design that is hard to work with and non-intuituitive. When this occurs, the database developer can and should denormalize to make the database easier to work with. An example of when denormalization should occur is covered later in this chapter.

First Normal Form (1NF) First normal form (1NF) is simply assigning a primary key to each table. A primary key is a column (or several columns) that *uniquely* identify a table. Figure 2.14 shows the data model developed so far with primary keys on all tables and foreign key designations when necessary.

FIG. 2.14

Now your data model has all primary keys and foreign keys identified.

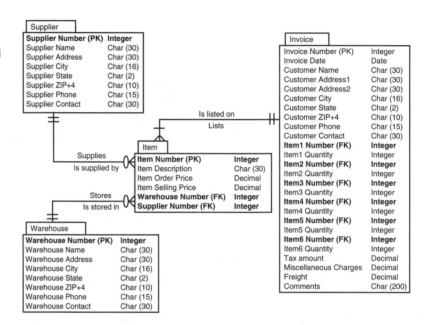

 TIP All changes made to your data model are in bold.

Now your data model has at least one unique identifier. Notice that if a unique identifier wasn't present, one was created. Primary keys are identified with a (PK) at the end of the column name. Foreign keys are identified with an (FK) at the end of the column name. (Foreign Key is defined below.) The foreign keys' names and data types have been changed to reflect any changes in the corresponding primary key's name and data type. (For example, in the item table, 'supplier char(30)' has changed to 'supplier number integer' to reflect on the item table the changes made to the supplier table.)

Primary Key   A primary key is a column (or set of columns) that makes this row unique from other rows. For instance, item_number is unique to each item row.

Foreign Key   A foreign key is a column (or set of columns) indicating that rows have either a zero or one, or a one-and-only-one correspondence to a row in another table. For instance, because each Item is stored in one and only one Warehouse, you need to include warehouse_number in every Item row.

TROUBLESHOOTING

What's a foreign key, and why are they important to me? Foreign keys play a vital role in relational database development. Databases can restrict users and developers from deleting a row from a table if that row's primary key is being accessed as a foreign key on another table.

Without foreign keys, relational databases would lose their relational information. A foreign key allows you to specify a relationship between two tables. Databases use this relational information for performance and data integrity.

1NF should be very intuitive for most developers. There are, however, some mistakes and misconceptions that occur which cause two problems that mutate into headaches for every developer:

- You must pick a primary key that *uniquely* identifies a row on your database table. If your primary key can be duplicated across rows, then it will not function as a primary key.

- You should not pick more columns than are necessary to identify a row on a table. Developers do this often because they feel a column is "important" enough to be a primary key, or they mistakenly believe that every column in a primary key has an index attached to it. (Sometimes, even the entire primary key will not have a true index associated with it!) This practice results in overly-complicated table queries.

Now that you've identified a primary key for each table, you are now able to address some of the analysis problems that have cropped up using second normal form (2NF) and third normal form (3NF).

Second Normal Form (2NF)   If you look at your invoice table, you'll notice an undesirable situation. On the invoice table, we limit the number of items per invoice to 6. Also, we always allocate storage for 6 items, even if less are used.

A series of foreign keys (item number 1, item number 2, etc.) is called a *repeating dependency*. Repeating dependencies occur with many-to-many relationships. (Obviously, relational databases can't handle many-to-many relationships very well.) Second normal form (2NF) tells us to remove any repeating dependency from our tables. In other words, 2NF tells us to eliminate all many-to-many relationships.

To eliminate many-to-many relationships, you introduce an *associative table*. Figure 2.15 shows this.

FIG. 2.15

The invoice line table has been added to eliminate many-to-many relationships.

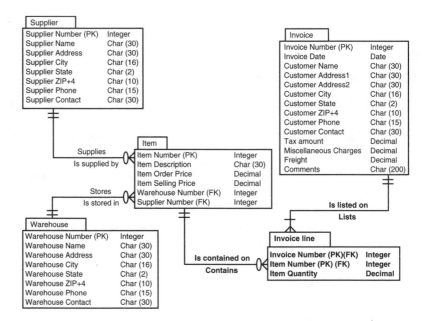

The new invoice line table has a one-to-many relationship with the item table and the invoice table. Now, as you can see, all many-to-many relationships have been resolved.

You should notice several things about this new data model:

- The data model looks less complicated now. This is because a series of repeating fields in the invoice table has been reduced to three columns in the invoice line table.

- Also notice how we placed the invoice line table in 1NF. Every time you add a table or normalize to a new normal form, you must determine ordinality and also re-normalize your new table.

- The invoice line table has two columns for a primary key. Multi-column primary keys often occur with associative tables.

- Associative tables have foreign keys to multiple tables. (The invoice line table has foreign keys to the item table and the invoice table.) By their very nature, associative tables relate to at least two other tables, and therefore need at least two foreign keys.

- You'll find that associative tables usually have the columns of their primary key also serve as foreign keys.

Third Normal Form (3NF)   While our database in 2NF is now easier to work with, there still is a problem with the data model. Notice the customer information in the Invoice table in figure 2.15. If a customer orders more than one item using an invoice, that customer's name, address, phone, etc., will be duplicated for each invoice. Also, if that customer changes address, name, etc., then our information will be out of date and hard to modify.

The problem with placing customer information inside an Invoice table is that a customer is not dependent upon an invoice. A customer could still be a customer, if you deleted an invoice with the customer's information on it.

Third normal form (3NF) states that you should remove all *non-dependencies* from all tables. In other words, any information on a table that is not dependent on the table's entity should be removed and, if desired, a new table should be created to contain the non-dependent information (see fig. 2.16).

FIG. 2.16

The Customer and Customer Address tables were created to hold customer information previously found on the Invoice table.

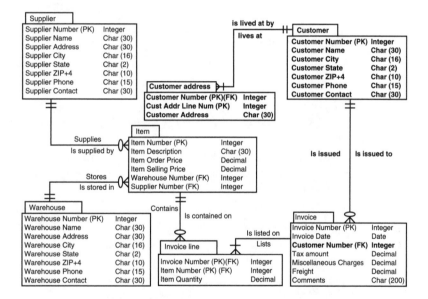

Denormalization   Notice that a new table was created called Customer Address. The customer address lines repeated on the invoice, and so they were removed to place the table in 2NF. However, removing two lines of address would create a lot of additional work and overhead, not to mention make the database harder to use. Since normalization is supposed to make the database easier to use, forcing 2NF in this situation would seem a little inflexible.

Sometimes, a developer is forced to *denormalize* a data model when normalization makes a database less understandable and harder to use, but adds nothing in the way of data integrity or data management (see fig. 2.17).

FIG. 2.17

The Customer Address table was merged back into the Customer table. Even though this violates 2NF, most would agree that such denormalization makes the database easier to use and easier to understand.

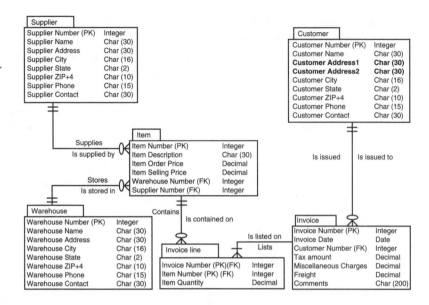

CAUTION

Denormalization can cause severe problems if done too freely. Here are some guidelines you can use for denormalization:

- Never denormalize without diagramming or at least understanding how the normalized form of the datamodel would look and act. Be sure that your denormalization is not an excuse to avoid the sometimes hard work of normalization.

- Always keep a table in 1NF. In other words, always find a unique identifier for a table, and make sure you don't have extra columns in the identifier that aren't needed to uniquely identify rows in a table.

- 2NF denormalizations are often used when the repeating dependency only repeats for a limited number. For instance, there are only two address lines in customer.

- 3NF denormalizations are often used with one-to-one relationships, or on tables where the non-dependent entity information would make an entire key.

3 1/2 (Boyce-Codd) Normal Form (BCNF)   Assume you were developing a system with the following system requirements:

1. All salespeople work for one or more counties.

2. All salespeople/county relationships are serviced by a branch office.

You *could* develop the model shown in figure 2.18. Indeed, the model is in 3NF since all repeating dependencies have been resolved.

FIG. 2.18

This model is in 3NF since all repeating dependencies and non-dependencies have been resolved. However, there are still problems with the design.

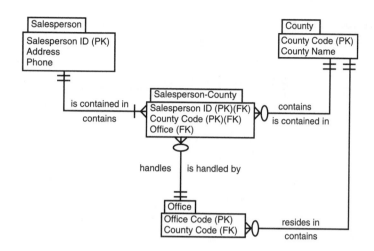

However, the above model has some problems. An office resides in a county. Each salesperson/county relationship is handled by an office. However, that data model *does not insure* that the branch office handling the salesperson/county relationship resides in the same county.

This deficiency in 3NF was noticed by Dr. E. Codd and Dr. R. Boyce. These two professors enhanced 3NF to eliminate some of these deficiencies. This new 3NF is called Boyce-Codd Normal Form, or BCNF. (I like to call it 3 1/2 normal form since it is an extension of 3NF.)

With a BCNF violation, there is usually a circular relationship once all foreign keys have been mapped out on the entity relationship model. Usually, this can be resolved by reorganizing the foreign keys in the tables.

In figure 2.19, we change the Salesperson-County table to the Salesperson-Office table. We then force any inquiries about county to first go through the Office table. Now all branches servicing a salesperson are *guaranteed to be* a valid branch for that county.

FIG. 2.19

BCNF resolves all conflicting determinants.

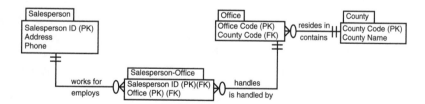

Other Normal Forms   In most cases, a developer does not need to normalize past BCNF. However, there are some very rare situations where other normal forms would also apply. For instance, 4th and 5th normal form occur only with a three (or more) column primary key. Also, usually 4th and 5th normal form result from some bugs that can be introduced during the normalization process.

Fourth Normal Form   Consider the many-to-many-to-many relationship with Office, Salesperson, and Item in figure 2.20.

FIG. 2.20

This many-to-many relationship violates 2NF and must be resolved.

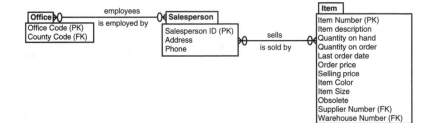

You *could* resolve the relationship with a three-way associative table that relates to all three tables, as seen in figure 2.21.

FIG. 2.21

The Sales/Office Information table resolves the many-to-many relationships seen in figure 2.20, but creates other problems.

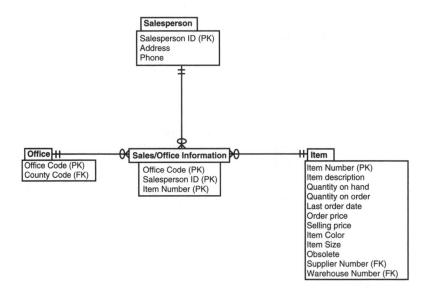

The design in figure 2.21 meets BCNF. However, as you can see in figure 2.21, the design has some flaws:

- There is no way to assign a salesperson to an office before he or she sells anything.

- The salesperson will have to list every item-office combination. This could create a very large and cumbersome table.

4NF states that you should not resolve more than one many-to-many relationship in one table. This is shown in figure 2.22, where two associative tables were added to the design in figure 2.22 to achieve 2NF.

FIG. 2.22

Adding two associative tables resolves the many-to-many relationships found in figure 2.21.

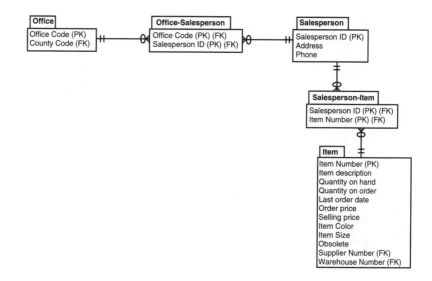

You should analyze a table for 4NF violations, if both the following conditions apply:

- The table has three or more columns in the primary key.
- The table has relationships with at least three other tables.

Fifth Normal Form The fifth normal form (5NF) is more rule-based than entity-based. 5NF deals with when you should stop normalizing. If you had the requirement that investment brokers have to be certified to trade a type of securities on an exchange, table 2.1 could describe a table to meet this requirement.

Table 2.1 Investment Table

Investment Broker	Exchange	Security Type
Jones	Nikkei	Bonds
Jones	Nikkei	Stocks
Jones	NYSE	Stocks
Jones	NYSE	T-Bills
Smith	Nikkei	Bonds
Smith	NYSE	Stocks

You may see some duplicate data on the exchange and security type and try to normalize the data by splitting the above table into three tables (seen in tables 2.2, 2.3, and 2.4).

Table 2.2   Broker-Exchange Table

Investment Broker	Exchange
Jones	NYSE
Jones	Nikkei
Smith	NYSE
Smith	Nikkei

Table 2.3   Broker-Security Type Table

Investment Broker	Security Type
Jones	Bonds
Jones	Stocks
Jones	T-Bills
Smith	Bonds
Smith	Stocks

Table 2.4   Exchange-Security Type Table

Exchange	Security Type
NYSE	Stocks
NYSE	T-Bills
Nikkei	Stocks
Nikkei	Bonds

However, if you separated these tables out like this, you could (through the entity relation-ships) reason that:

1. Smith can sell on the Nikkei exchange (table 2.2).
2. Smith can sell stocks (table 2.3).
3. Stocks are sold on the Nikkei exchange (table 2.4)
4. Ergo, Smith can sell stocks on the Nikkei exchange.

The conclusion that Smith can sell stocks on the Nikkei exchange based on the information in tables 2.2, 2.3, and 2.4 violates the information found in table 2.1, where Smith *cannot* sell stocks on the Nikkei exchange.

Fifth normal form (5NF) specifies that you should not normalize *join dependencies* out of tables. A join dependency is when every column of a key in a table is dependent on every other key column. In this case, investment broker, exchange, and security type all are dependent on each other and therefore should not be normalized into separate tables without losing some information.

There is no easy method for determining if there are 5NF violations. The analyst must make sure that the requirements given to him or her are reflected in the table design.

Designing a System with the PowerBuilder Database Painter

 "So," you ask, "all this analysis stuff is really great, but how do I put it into PowerBuilder?" After you decide what your entities are and how they relate, implement your analysis inside the database painter by clicking the Database icon. This allows you to "draw" your entities into your PowerBuilder system. PowerBuilder's database painter lets you identify instances of entities (with primary keys) and assign relationships to other entities (with foreign keys).

Creating a Database

As soon as you click the Database icon for the first time, you see the *Powersoft Demo DB (V5)* appear (as shown in fig. 2.23). This is the database that PowerBuilder uses for its sample application. (Of course, it's not the database you need for the Inventory Tracking system—you must create a new database.)

FIG. 2.23
The first database that opens when you click on the Database icon is not the database you need, so you need to create a new database.

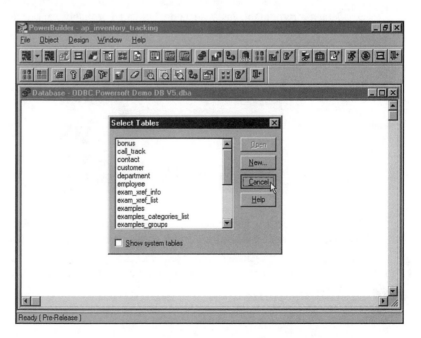

To create a new database, click the Cancel button (see fig. 2.23). Then choose File, Create Database, as shown in figure 2.24.

FIG. 2.24

In the database painter, open File to find Create Database.

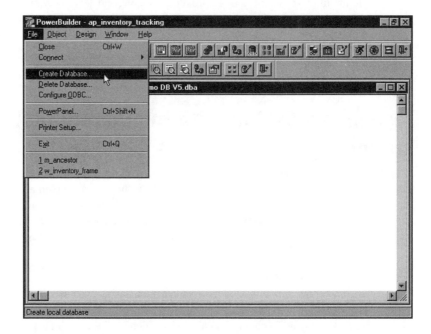

The Create Local Database dialog box appears (see fig. 2.25). You can enter the name of your new database right in the database name, but you'd probably want to click the Browse command button (as seen in figure 2.25) to select the proper directory. Otherwise, your database will be created in the current working directory.

FIG. 2.25

Use the Create Local Database dialog box to create your database.

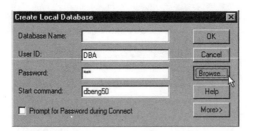

If you click the Browse command button, another Create Local Database dialog box will appear (as seen in figure 2.26) which will let you choose the directory and file name of your database.

In Windows 3.x your new database must not exceed 8 characters. In Windows 95, the limit is 256 characters.

FIG. 2.26
This dialog box allows you to specify the file name and path of your new database.

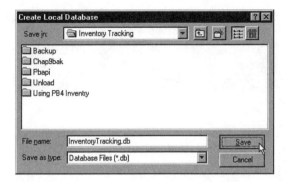

PowerBuilder hides some of the details from you when creating a database. Sybase SQL Any-where included with PowerBuilder 5 contains options that can be used when the database is created to improve on the speed of the database and/or customize your database for your work environment and security needs. (For instance, the page size has been increased to 4096 from 1024 to allow large databases to process more data at one time, thereby adding to perfor-mance.)

To get to these options, click More, as seen in figure 2.27. The Create Local Database dialog box will then be expanded to include some other options for creating your database.

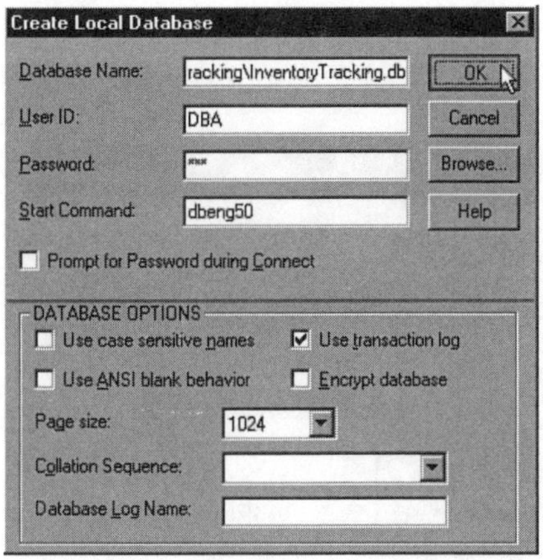

FIG. 2.27
Clicking More in the Create Local Database dialog box can allow you to further customize your local database options.

Connecting and Customizing Your Database

As you can see from the database painter window title in figure 2.28, my database was created with the name InventoryTracking.DB. This may or may not suit your needs. If you want to call the database something more personally suitable or use a more descriptive name, you would use the profile setup.

FIG. 2.28

The name of the current database is displayed in the database painter.

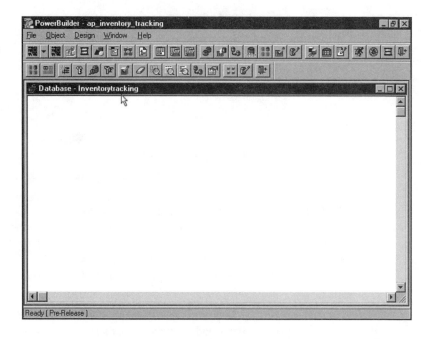

By choosing File, Connect, PowerBuilder allows you to connect to various databases that have already been created and defined. By then choosing Setup, as seen in figure 2.29, you allow PowerBuilder to edit your database profiles or to create new profiles from existing databases.

FIG. 2.29

You can help configure your database by choosing File, Connect and then Setup.

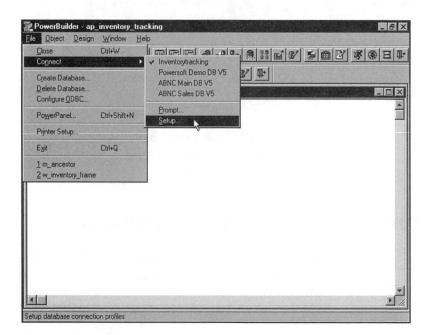

PowerBuilder now displays all valid database profiles for you to choose from in the Database Profiles dialog box, as shown in figure 2.30. Pick Inventorytracking and click Edit.

FIG. 2.30

The Database Profiles dialog box allows you to choose which profile you want to edit, or to create or delete database profiles.

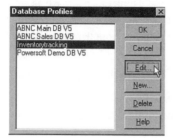

The Database Profile Setup dialog box appears (see fig. 2.31). In the Profile Name field, you can change the name to Inventory Tracking. Type the name, the user ID, and the password, and click OK.

FIG. 2.31

You can change the name in the Database Profile Setup dialog box.

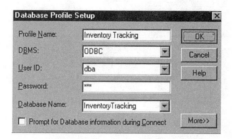

N O T E PowerBuilder allows you to type in a user ID and a password into the Database Profile Setup dialog box. This defaults in PowerBuilder to a user ID of dba and a password of `sql`. If you assign the user ID and password when you connect to your database, your users will not be forced to enter a user ID and password every time they use your system. ■

After you click OK, the Database Profiles dialog box appears once more (see fig. 2.32). Notice that Inventory Tracking appears. By clicking OK here, Inventory Tracking will be brought up in the database painter.

FIG. 2.32

Inventory Tracking now shows in the Profiles field.

Creating Tables

Right now, you have an empty database. That is, you have a database that contains no tables, which are groups of data inside a database. Think of a database as a file cabinet; each table represents a file within that file cabinet. In any system, the entities developed in analysis track directly to each table. Therefore, you will have a Supplier table, an Item table, a Customer table, and so on.

 To create a table, either click the Open icon and click the New button, or click the New Table icon.

 This opens the table painter, as seen in figure 2.33. The column names can be entered in lower-case letters only.

FIG. 2.33
The table painter is where you create tables for the database.

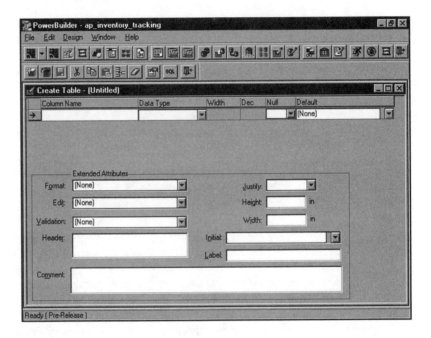

 TIP Some of the data has scrolled off in figure 2.34. Be sure you enter all the item columns.

FIG. 2.34
Now enter all the columns needed for the item table. Notice how the columns scroll down as you enter them.

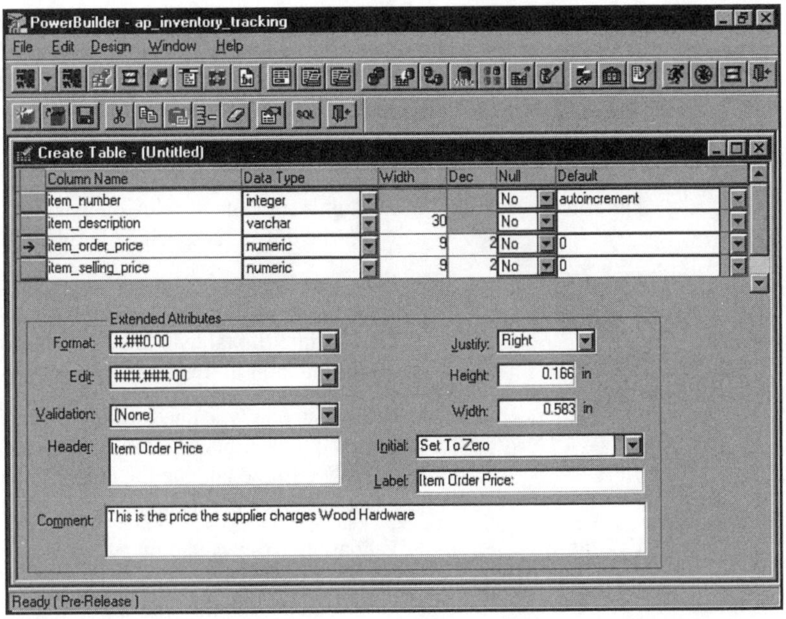

Many options you can enter using the table painter will affect how a column is *initially* placed on your DataWindow. The following are options you can enter when you are defining your table:

Column Name

Column Name is the name of your column on the database table. Column name is how PowerBuilder and other development languages will access your database column.

Data Type

Data type is the category of data (for example, string, integer, boolean, etc.) of each column.

Width (Column)

Column width (if applicable) is the maximum length of your column. Some data types, such as integer, don't allow column width. (Not to be confused with display width below.)

Dec

Dec (if applicable) is the number of decimals in a field. Using the Sybase SQL Anywhere that comes with PowerBuilder 5, only Decimal data types allow you to specify the number of decimals. (However, Float and Double both allow decimals internally.)

Null

Null is a checkbox that determines whether or not NULLs are allowed to be stored in this column when a new row is added to the database.

N O T E *NULLs* are not zeros; they are empty columns in a row on your database. (An empty column contains nothing—no zeros, no spaces, no anything!) Most columns require some entry, so most databases allow you to define a column as Not NULL when you create it. By declaring a column Not NULL, you force the database to not allow an update when the column in question is NULL. ■

Default	Default is the default value on a database. Default is only used when the default is specified in the SQL.
Format	Format is the display format when this column is placed on a DataWindow. Formats also can control how data is entered directly into the table in the database painter. Formats are discussed later in this book.
Edit	Edit is the edit type used when this field is placed on a DataWindow. Edits also can control how data is entered directly into the table in the database painter. Edit types are discussed later in this book.
Validation	Validation is the validation rule used during data entry when this column is placed on a DataWindow. Validation rules are discussed later in this book.
Header	Header is the text placed at the top of a grid or tabular style DataWindow.
Label	Label is the text placed to the left of the column in a freeform DataWindow (for example, *Label:* _____).
Justify	Justify is how the data is justified initially when viewing the data on a table or when placing a column on a DataWindow.
Height	Height is how "tall" the data entry field for this column will be when the DataWindow is created.
Width (Display)	Display width is how long the data entry field for this column will be when the DataWindow is created.
Initial	Initial is the initial value of this column's data entry field on a DataWindow when the DataWindow is created.
Comments	Comments allow you to enter any column-specific information.

CAUTION

In the database painter, the database data types are the same as the ones used in the database. They are not the same data types as in PowerBuilder. Furthermore, little checking is performed to make sure numbers are still within the range for a data type.

For instance, in Sybase SQL Anywhere, *integer* is defined as any value from -2,147,483,648 through 2,147,483,647. In PowerBuilder, integer is defined as any value from -32,768 through 32,767. If you were to read an integer from SQL Anywhere into an integer in PowerBuilder, a wrap-around might occur, and you would end up with a random number some of the time. This is a hard bug to catch. (By the way, if you define an integer in SQL Anywhere, make sure that any values do not exceed the PowerBuilder limit or use a long data type in PowerBuilder. A long data type in PowerBuilder has the same range as an integer data type in SQL Anywhere.)

 Using Table Property Sheets By clicking the properties icon on the table painter bar, you open a table's property sheet, as seen in figure 2.35.

FIG. 2.35
The table property
sheet allows you to
specify attributes of a
table.

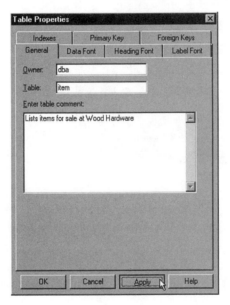

When you first open a table property sheet, you are allowed to enter the table owner, the table name, and any comments you have about the table.

 You will be prompted for a table name when you exit the table painter if you don't enter one on the general table property sheet.

Picking Primary Keys After entering all of your fields into your table, you need to tell your database what sets every row in a table apart from each other. For this you need a primary key, a unique indicator that allows you to address individual table entries. Every table should have a primary key defined.

Adding a primary key is much easier in PowerBuilder 5 than in previous versions. To add a primary key, simply click the Primary Key tab in the table property sheet. Then click the columns you want to add to your primary key, as shown in figure 2.36.

FIG. 2.36

Choose item_number as your primary key.

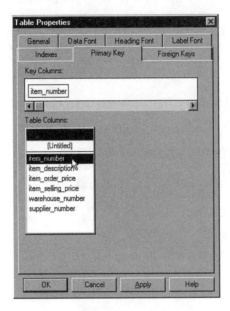

Using Indexes   Sometimes, you'll want to look up data using criteria other than the primary key. For instance, even though you have declared customer_number for your primary key, you are more likely to look up people by name. Hence, you should probably have names indexed.

Indexing speeds up data retrieval immensely! If you often use a field to look up data, an index on that field speeds things up. To index a field, click the Index tab on the table property sheet. This will display the Indexes tab, as shown in figure 2.37. Click New to add a new index to your table.

After clicking New, the Create Index dialog box appears. Here, you click the columns you want to use for your index, as seen in figure 2.38.

FIG. 2.37

Clicking the Indexes tab on the table property sheet will allow you to create or edit indexes.

FIG. 2.38

The Create Index dialog box allows you to create a new index.

N O T E   You can avoid the table painter when creating indexes, if you wish. On a created table, perform the following steps:

1. Open a table by clicking the open icon and selecting a table.

2. Click the Index icon on the database painterbar.

3. The Create Index dialog box will then appear for that table. This is the same dialog box shown in figure 2.38. Fill in the proper name and columns, and you're finished creating an index without using the table painter. ▪

N O T E   Indexes decrease querying time in a database, so you can retrieve records faster using an index. However, indexes increase the time needed to update or add to your tables, so use them only when you need them.

Also, the longer the key, the longer both queries and updates are, so try to keep your keys reasonable in length. For instance, if you only need customer_name and customer_contact as keys, don't also include customer_phone.

Because graphical applications tend to run slower than old-style text-based applications, you should do what you can to speed things up! ▪

CAUTION

Believe it or not, there are situations in which you'll want to index your primary key. Although a primary key serves as an index itself, often it is paired with all the foreign key combinations. Therefore, if you have one primary key with several thousand foreign keys, an index on the primary key may significantly speed up your searches.

However, for most tables, there is no need to index a primary key. Indexes increase the time it takes to add or update your data. Use them, but only when you need to.

Choosing Fonts   By clicking the Data Font tab on the table property sheet, you are allowed to choose the data font of the table. The data font is the font used when the table rows are displayed. (Similarly, you can specify the heading font and the label font for the table.) You can choose the font (i.e., Times New Roman), the font style (i.e., Regular, Bold, Italic, or Bold Italic), and the point size of the font, as seen in figure 2.39.

FIG. 2.39

The Table Properties sheet allows you to specify display fonts.

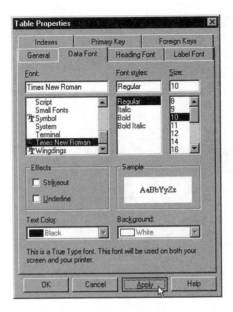

Creating the Inventory Tracking System

You've created the Item table in your database. Now repeat the process of creating tables for the rest of the Inventory Tracking system:

1. Create all the tables in the database painter found on your data model.

2. Add all the columns to each table while it is being created.

3. Choose a primary key and any indexes that you want to use on the tables.

If you'd like to see a list of the tables and columns, you can view a table listing in the next section in figure 2.42.

N O T E   A table sometimes will have more than one primary key (known as a *composite key*). In the invoice_line table, the primary key invoice_number tells you which invoice this invoice_line is a part of, while item_number describes the item being sold (as seen in fig. 2.40). ■

Part

I

Ch

2

FIG. 2.40
The invoice line table
has a two column
primary key.

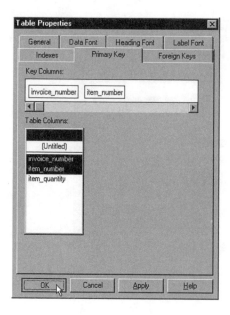

Viewing Tables in the Database Painter

When you enter the database painter, PowerBuilder will connect to the database you previously were connected to. The database painter will automatically display a list of tables, as seen in figure 2.41.

FIG. 2.41
A database's table list
can be seen when you
enter the database
painter.

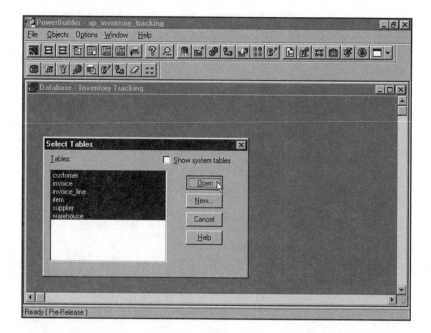

TIP A table listing can be viewed from within the database painter by clicking on the Open icon.

To view any table or tables in your database, click on the table name. In figure 2.41, all the table names have been chosen. When you're finished choosing which table names you want to view, click OK. All selected tables will now open.

Each table in the database painter is resizable. The tables in figure 2.42 have been resized and rearranged so that you can see all the tables and their columns in one screenshot.

FIG. 2.42
This is a graphical representation of all the tables in the inventory tracking system.

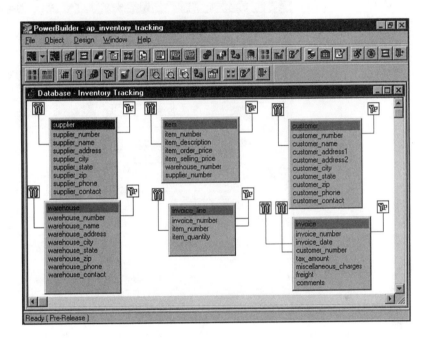

Modifying Tables

Now you have created tables.

Say you take your design to your end-user. (You should do this to make sure your design is on the right track.) The end-user reviews your design, and makes some additional requirements:

1. Item, Supplier, Warehouse, and Customer must all contain a comments field to place free form text. (A comments field in major tables is often a good idea in a design anyway to allow the end-user some flexibility, if the design is missing a column or columns.)

2. Item is missing quantity_on_order, quantity_on_hand, and last_order_date columns. (This would have been a major oversight. Having an end-user review a design often catches these major oversights.)

3. It's easier to track an item in the warehouse if color and size are included on the item table. (Again, the end-user would know this, but the developer might not.)

As development goes on, you'll often need to modify your tables. A general rule is that you can't make a table smaller, but you can increase it. You can increase the size of variables or add new variables, but you can't decrease the size of variables, or change variable data types. You can, however, delete existing columns and then re-add them with the same name but different (or smaller) data types.

To modify an existing table, double-click that table. This will open the table painter and allow you to alter your table, as seen in figure 2.43.

FIG. 2.43

You can alter a database table using the table painter.

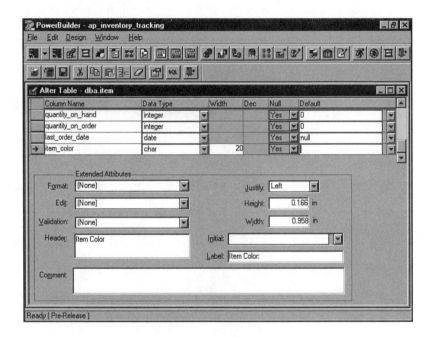

> **N O T E** Like most PowerBuilder menu bar functions, there are several ways to open the table painter. You can double-click the customer table shown in the database painter. You can also right-click the table name and choose Definition. This may be preferable to some, though probably less intuitive. Finally, you can click Objects, Extended Definition from your menu to open the table painter. ▓

For the database painter to show your changes, you must close the table and reopen it or close the database painter and then re-enter the database painter. As you can see in figure 2.44, the database painter now reflects the changes made in the Alter Table dialog box.

FIG. 2.44
All changes from new requirements are now reflected in the database painter.

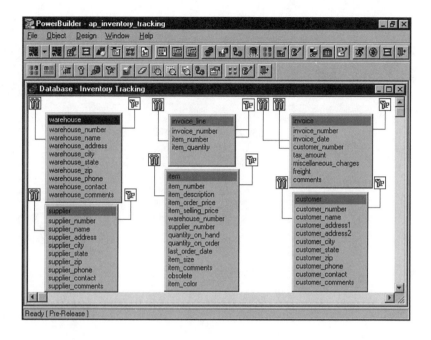

Part
I

Ch
2

Right-Clicking in the Database Painter

Using the right mouse button to click on items is a quick and easy way to manuver in your database painter. Right-clicking different areas in your database painter will produce different pop-up menus.

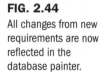

Right-Clicking on Empty Space in the Painter Right-clicking an empty space in the database painter lets you set options for the database painter, as seen in figure 2.45. The following options are valid:

Select Tables	Select Tables pulls up the Select Table dialog box. It has the same effect as clicking the Open icon.
Arrange Tables	Arrange Tables arranges any open tables in an orderly fashion.
Show Comments	Show Comments toggles the comments display on and off. If you want to save room, turning the comments off may make tables and relationships in your database painter more readable.
Show Index Keys	Show Index Keys toggles the index key display on and off. Index key lines can often intersect with primary and foreign key lines, making your database painter a little confusing.
Show Referential Integrity	Show Referential Integrity toggles the primary and foreign key displays on and off.

FIG. 2.45

Right-clicking the gray area on the database painter allows you to choose your preferences for your database painter.

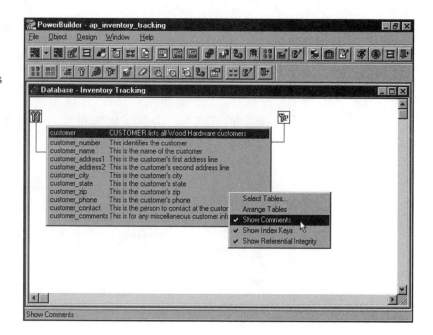

Right-Clicking on a Table Title Right-clicking the table title will give you to execute table operations and set some table display options, as seen in figure 2.46.

The following options are available:

Close Closes the database table. This will allow you to no longer display the table on your database painter.

> **T I P** Often you will need to close and reopen a table for some database changes to be reflected in the database painter.

Definition Definition will open the table painter.

Properties Properties will open a scaled-down table property sheet, as seen in figure 2.47. All the properties you can set are also available in the table painter.

New New creates a new table.

Drop Table Drop Table deletes the table from the database. It is equivalent to clicking the Drop icon on the database PainterBar.

Data Manipulation Data Manipulation puts you in the data manipulation painter (discusssed later in this chapter). It is equivalent to clicking the Preview icon.

Data Pipeline Data Pipeline formats the columns of this table into a data pipeline. This option is equivalent to clicking the Pipeline icon. Data Pipelines are covered later in the book.

Print   Print produces a detailed report of all the columns, data types, and the column attributes (edit, validation, etc.).

FIG. 2.46

Right-clicking a table title in the database painter allows you to run table operations and set table display options.

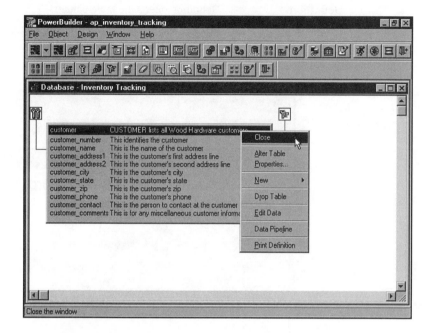

FIG. 2.47

A scaled-down property sheet is available when you right-click a table name or primary key and choose Properties.

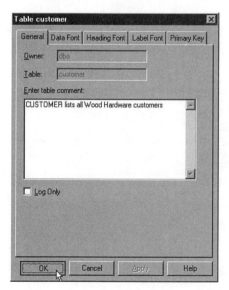

Right-Clicking on a Column Right-clicking a database column, as seen in figure 2.48, lets you do some database column operations:

Definition	Definition opens the table painter.
Properties	Properties opens up a property sheet for the column. In this property sheet (see fig. 2.49), you can specify comments and extended attributes.

FIG. 2.48
Right-clicking a database column allows you to perform some database column operations.

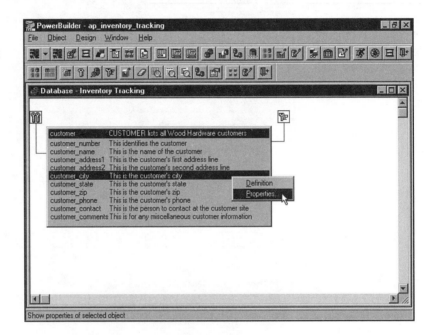

FIG. 2.49
The column property sheet allows you to set some database column attributes.

Right-Clicking on a Primary Key   To easily manipulate the primary key of a table, right-click that primary key, as shown in figure 2.50. This will open a pop-up menu that will allow you to enter the primary key property sheet, open dependent tables, or drop a primary key.

FIG. 2.50

Right-clicking the primary key opens a pop-up menu that allows you to perform operations on the primary key of a table.

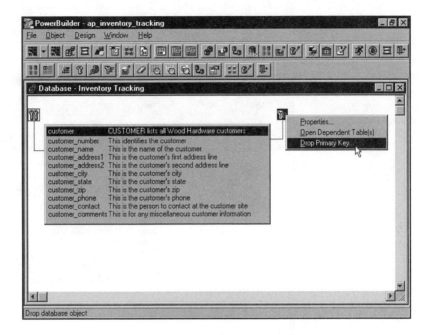

Part

I

Ch

2

Properties	Properties opens up the same table property sheet as found in figure 2.47.
Open Dependent Tables	Open Dependent Tables opens up tables that have a foreign key relating to your primary key. Foreign keys are discussed later in this chapter.
Drop Primary Key	Drop Primary Key allows you to drop the primary key from your table.

CAUTION

Dropping a primary key from a table usually is not a good idea. Relational databases rely on primary keys to establish relationships with other databases. You may be limiting database integrity, execution speed, and table maintenance by deleting a primary key from a database table.

Right-Clicking on an Index   Right-clicking an index key on the database painter, as shown in figure 2.51, allows you two options:

Browse	Browse allows you to display information about the index, as seen in figure 2.52.
Drop Index	Drop Index allows you to delete the index from the database table.

FIG. 2.51

You can Browse or Drop Index by right-clicking an index key in the database painter.

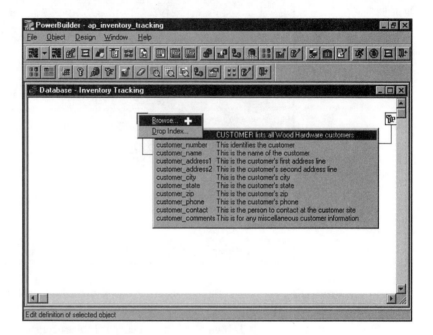

FIG. 2.52

You can review an index's name, type, order, and columns by right-clicking the index key and choosing Browse.

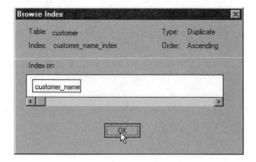

Using the Table Painter Icon

You can enter the database anytime in your application without entering the database painter. Clicking the table icon pulls up the select table dialog box as seen in figure 2.53. Here, choose the table you want to alter (or click New to create a new table), and the table painter will appear for that table.

FIG. 2.53
The table painter is a way to add or alter a table from anywhere in PowerBuilder.

Adding Foreign Keys

Now that you defined all of the primary keys, you can start working on your foreign keys. As mentioned previously, a foreign key is a field (or set of fields) indicating that table entries have either a zero or one, or a one-and-only-one correspondence to a table entry in another table. Foreign keys are defined by taking the corresponding table's primary key and duplicating it in the related table. Often, foreign keys stop you from making a grievous error and help you track down bugs caused by database irregularities.

T I P If TABLE1 has a foreign key to TABLE2, TABLE1 is said to be *dependent* on TABLE2.

For example, because every entry in the Item table has one and only one corresponding Warehouse entry, and because every entry in the Item table has one and only one corresponding Supplier entry, Item will have foreign keys to Warehouse and Supplier.

To add a foreign key to your database table, double-click one of the open tables in your database painter. This will open the table painter. Then click the Properties icon and the Foreign Keys tab, as seen in figure 2.54. Click New to create a new foreign key.

T I P You can also open the Foreign Key Definition dialog box by right-clicking on a table and choosing New, Foreign Key from the pop-up menu.

FIG. 2.54

The Foreign Keys tab
allows you to edit or
define a foreign key.

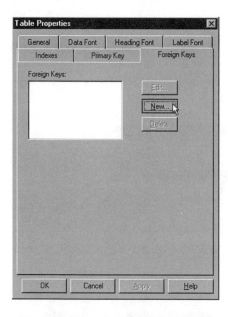

FIG. 2.54

The Foreign Keys tab
allows you to edit or
define a foreign key.

FIG. 2.55

Warehouse_fk is chosen
as one of the foreign
keys for the item table.

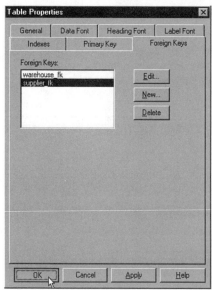

To define a foreign key, perform the following steps:

1. Enter a foreign key name as seen in figure 2.55. (This will probably be a name ending in _key or _fk.)

2. Choose the columns you want to relate by clicking a column in the Select Columns list box.

3. Choose the table you want to relate in the Primary Key Table drop-down list box. (The primary key of the Primary Key Table is shown automatically.)

4. Choose the type of referential integrity you want to enforce in the On Delete of Primary Table Row group box. Your choices are as follows:

   ■ You cannot allow a primary key table row to be deleted if a foreign key table row (dependent row) exists. This is called Restrict referential integrity.

   ■ You can delete dependent rows, if a primary key table row is deleted. This is called Cascade referential integrity.

   ■ You can set the foreign keys to NULL, if the foreign keys reference a deleted row. This is called Set NULL referential integrity.

CAUTION

If you use Set NULL referential integrity, make sure you did NOT define your column as NOT NULL when you created it. Otherwise, you'll receive an error when you try to save your definition.

5. Click OK to return to the table painter.

N O T E   We have several foreign keys defined in the Inventory Tracking system:

   ● Item has a foreign key to warehouse, as seen in figure 2.55.

   ● Item has a foreign key to supplier, as seen in figure 2.56.

   ● Invoice_line has a foreign key to Item.

   ● Invoice_line has a foreign key to Invoice.

   ● Invoice has a foreign key to Customer.

You will need to alter your database using the table painter to include these foreign keys. ■

FIG. 2.56
The Inventory Tracking system also needs a foreign key from item to supplier.

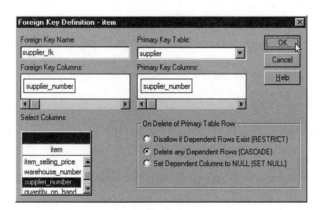

When you are finished defining your foreign keys, notice how they are then displayed in the Foreign Keys tab in the table property sheet, as seen in figure 2.57.

FIG. 2.57

All your foreign keys are listed in the property sheet Foreign Keys tab.

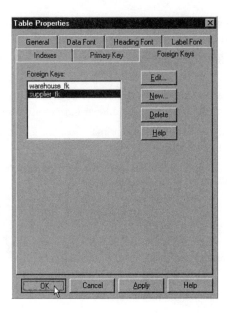

Establishing a foreign key in PowerBuilder enforces a somewhat complicated universal database concept called referential integrity. Referential integrity implies that if you have a foreign key in table 1 referencing a primary key in table 2, that primary key will definitely be in table 2, or you will not be allowed to add your table entry in table 1. Furthermore, you will not be able to delete your entry in table 2 until all corresponding foreign keys in table 1 have been either deleted or changed to another entry in table 2.

For example, suppose that you have several entries in your supplier table. If you try to add an Item entry in the Item table, SQL Anywhere (or other databases) automatically makes sure that the supplier_number you entered in the Item table corresponds to an existing entry in the Supplier table. Otherwise, SQL Anywhere (or other databases) will not allow the item to be added, and will return an error to PowerBuilder giving some cryptic message that referential integrity has been violated.

If you try to delete an entry in your Supplier table and that entry has a corresponding supplier_number in the item table, SQL Anywhere (or other databases) will not allow you to delete the Supplier and return another referential integrity error to PowerBuilder.

In any case, using foreign keys is a good way to catch your errors during development and ensures that future developers do not make mistakes that can mess up your database. Foreign keys also maintain the integrity of your database for your users and any third-party database packages that can alter the contents of your database.

Now you're finished defining foreign keys. When you exit the database painter and then return, foreign keys will be noted, as seen in figure 2.58.

FIG. 2.58
Foreign key relation-ships are added to the graphics in the database painter.

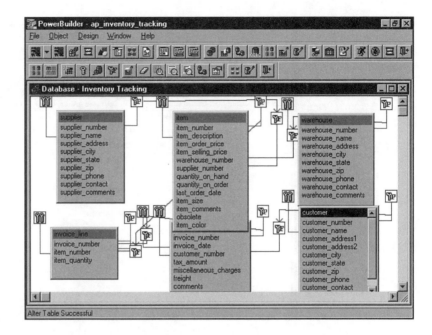

N O T E Although the screen in figure 2.58 looks complicated, it is even more so when you first open it. After opening all of the tables, the foreign key lines looked like spaghetti! It took a lot of time to resize the table windows and move the table windows and key boxes around so that the window was more readable. You should not pull up more than three tables at a time, if you want to check out foreign key relationships. ■

Manipulating Data in a Table

Now that you've created the table, you need to know how to get data inside it. Normally, this is done through the application in either a DataWindow or through PowerScript. However, PowerBuilder gives you two ways to access and alter data in your PowerBuilder environment: through the Data Manipulation window, and through the database administrator painter and SQL.

  Using the Data Manipulation Dialog Box You get to the Data Manipulation window (as shown in fig. 2.59) through the database painter. Click the Grid, Tabular, or Free Form icon, which opens the Data Manipulation window for the table you selected.

T I P You can also use the table's right-click pop-up menu to get to the Data Manipulation window show in figure 2.59.

FIG. 2.59

In the Data Manipulation window for your table, you can add, change, or delete table entries.

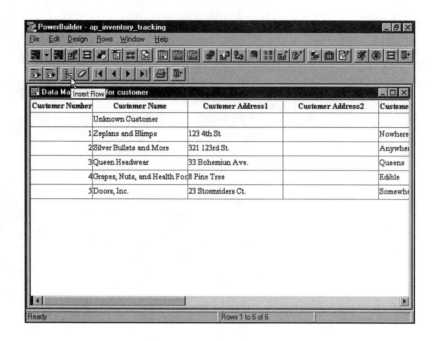

This window contains the following utilities for quick updates to your table:

■ Retrieve lets you re-retrieve your data in your table. It's handy if you want to start over on your manipulations.

■ Update Database lets you write any changes you've made to your table.

■ Insert Row lets you add a new row to your database.

■ Delete Row lets you delete the current row from your database.

■ Scroll to First Page allows you to go to the beginning of your table.

■ Scroll to Last Page brings you to the end of your table.

■ Scroll to Previous Page pages up for you.

■ Scroll to Next Page pages down for you.

In addition to the PainterBar commands, you will find the menu bar commands very helpful. Within File, you will find many commands that help you print your table. Within Rows, you have two commands that are particularly helpful—Filter and Sort.

Clicking Rows, Filter on the menu opens up the Specify Filter dialog box, as shown in figure 2.60. The Specify Filter dialog box screens out certain rows so that you're only working with the rows you want.

FIG. 2.60

By opening Filter and choosing Rows, you can specify which rows on your table you want to work with. Here you choose to display those rows that don't have NULL in the comments field.

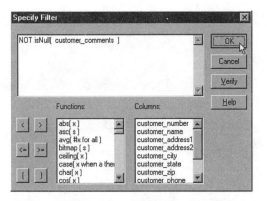

Clicking Rows, Sort on the menu opens the Specify Sort Columns dialog box, as shown in figure 2.61. Using your mouse, drag each field from the Source Data area to the Columns area. The Specify Sort Columns dialog box displays the rows in any order you want.

FIG. 2.61

In the Specify Sort Columns dialog box, you can specify the row order in which you want to display your table.

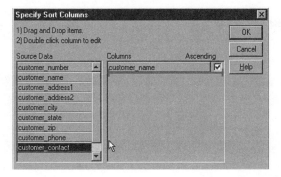

TROUBLESHOOTING

I'm trying to change or delete a row on a table, but my database and PowerBuilder won't let me. I keep getting this cryptic `primary keys` message. How do I drop a row I don't want? Sometimes you will try to delete or alter a primary key on a table that has foreign keys attached to it. This can be maddening because you can have several tables with corresponding foreign keys to your table's primary key. All foreign keys must be tracked down before you make any alterations to a primary key.

To do this quickly in the database painter, maximize the table you are working on (so that the fields and keys are all displayed). Then right-click the primary key box. A pop-up menu appears with an Open Dependent Tables selection, as shown in figure 2.62. If you click this choice, all tables that have foreign keys that relate to this primary key are displayed.

You can also open any referenced tables by right-clicking the foreign key box, as shown in figure 2.63.

You need to reassign or delete all foreign keys that reference the primary key of the row you are trying to delete before you can delete that row.

FIG. 2.62
Open Dependent Tables opens any table with a foreign key that relates to a table.

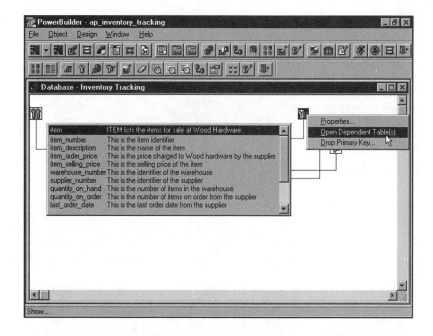

FIG. 2.63
Right-clicking the foreign key box will allow you to open any referenced tables.

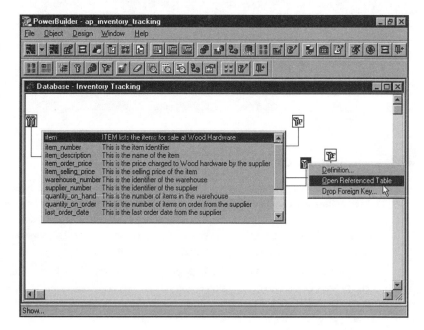

Using the Database Administration Painter and SQL If you know SQL pretty well, you will spend a lot of your development time in the database administration painter, which allows you to issue SQL commands to your database. To enter the database administration painter pictured in figure 2.64, click the DB Admin icon.

When you've entered your SQL, click the Execute icon on the database administration PainterBar. This will execute any SQL commands you use. You'll learn about SQL commands in chapter 8, "Using SQL in PowerBuilder."

FIG. 2.64

From the Database Administration window, you can alter any table in the database you are connected to. For example, you can delete all records from the customer table.

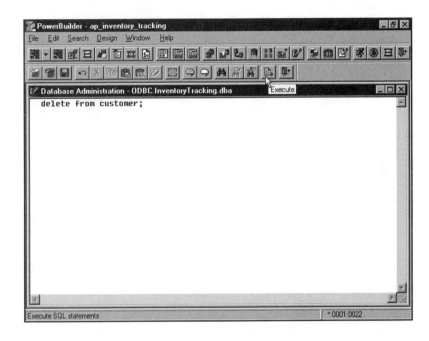

> **TIP**
>
> The database administration painter is good for massive operations on huge tables that would be impractical using the Data Manipulation window.

> **TIP**
>
> Use the data manipulation painter to do minor data manipulation, and use SQL to do major data manipulation.

Implementing Database Changes with a Spreadsheet It may be easier to implement changes into a database by going outside of PowerBuilder, especially in a spreadsheet. This is done using the following steps:

1. Back up your database! This is probably the most important step. That way, if all your manipulation destroys needed data, you'll have a backup to return to.

2. Drop all foreign keys. This can be done several ways, but the easiest is to pull up your table; open dependent tables, as shown in figure 2.62; and then drop the foreign keys.

Part

I

Ch

2

3. Go into the data manipulation painter and choose File, Save Rows As from the menu. This allows you to save your database rows in several popular formats (see fig. 2.65) and to include or exclude headers.

FIG. 2.65
In the Save Rows As dialog box, you can save your table in several formats, such as text format.

4. Go to the database administration painter and type a delete command to delete all rows off the table, as shown in figure 2.64.

5. Work on your data in the spreadsheet. After you complete your changes, save the data in tab-delimited text format. (You can also use dBASE II or dBASE III format. These are the only formats that PowerBuilder imports.)

6. Go to the Data Manipulation window. Choose Rows, Import from the menu. The Select Import File dialog box appears, in which you can enter the name of your new file, as shown in figure 2.66. Save from the spreadsheet into tab-separated format.

FIG. 2.66
You import the data in this dialog box.

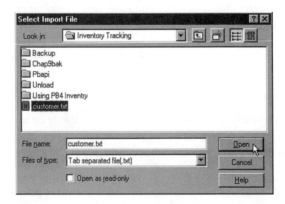

7. Finally, go back to table painter, as shown in figures 2.54 and 2.55, and reassign all your foreign keys.

If you mess up during this process, restore immediately! This seven-step process will help out if you are proficient with a spreadsheet, and your data manipulation will go faster in a spreadsheet than in the database painter.

Dropping a Table

 Of course, there will be times when a table is no longer needed. Click on a table to select it, and then click on the Drop icon to drop a table from your database.

> **CAUTION**
>
> When you drop a table with data in it, you lose all that date. Furthermore, any foreign key relationships between the dropped table and other tables are dissolved.

Exploring PowerBuilder Database Independence

One of the nice things about PowerBuilder is its database independence. Using the fields you defined, you can use any database you want to implement or (usually with little effort) switch between them. If you are using Oracle at work with the PowerBuilder Enterprise Edition, you could work at home on the same application using SQL Anywhere with the PowerBuilder Desktop Edition. Similarly, if you are using DB2 but want to change your database to Oracle, such a change is accomplished relatively easily by editing your database profile.

> **CAUTION**
>
> Although switching between databases is, in theory, transparent, not all databases support the same data types. Before you switch databases, be sure that you are using datatypes that exist in both databases.
>
> Also, some databases implement a "nonstandard" form of SQL. Sometimes, minor syntax changes can be a problem. For instance, Sybase (Version X and XI) has to have strings in double quotes; Sybase SQL Anywhere has them in single quotes.

From Here...

This chapter is the most complex chapter in this book. However, once you understand the techniques discussed, the rest of development will become much easier.

Analysis and design normally should take roughly twice as long as the actual development; but done properly, analysis and design will mean the difference between a mediocre application and a great application. If you've mastered analysis and design, you'll be worth your weight in gold to your company.

For more information about analysis, design, and the database painter, see the following chapters:

- Chapter 1, "Introducing PowerBuilder," mentions iterative design, which speeds up PowerBuilder development considerably.

- Chapter 8, "Using SQL in PowerBuilder," shows how to incorporate SQL into your application.

- Appendix B, "Using SQL Anywhere Database and SQL Anywhere," shows how you can use SQL Anywhere to implement your application. Also covered in this chapter are Sybase SQL Anywhere functions and SQL commands not allowed inside the PowerBuilder environment.

CHAPTER 3

Using the Application Painter

by Charles A. Wood

Application objects are often confused with applications or executables when talking about PowerBuilder development. In a nutshell, an application is the finished product of the developer. Applications are also called executables, EXEs, or computer programs.

An application object, on the other hand, is specific to PowerBuilder. An application object contains attributes and controls events that occur on a system-wide scale. ■

What is contained in an application object.

The application controls several aspects of your application, from global variables to database connections.

What properties you can set in the application object's property sheet.

The application object can affect how the rest of your application looks and functions. This chapter shows how and why you set certain application properties from the application property sheet.

What Is Contained in an Application Object

▶ **See** "Using PowerBuilder Application Painter and Applications," **p. 19**

You have seen some of the application painter and application objects in chapter 1. An application object is unique among all other PowerBuilder objects in that:

- There can be only one application object per PowerBuilder application. On a similar note, you can run only one application at a time in the PowerBuilder environment, and can be attached to only one application at a time.

- The PowerBuilder library search path is contained in the application. You are not allowed to save changes to library members that are not in your application's library search path.

  ▶ **See** "Variable Scope," **p. 195**

- All global variables that are defined are stored in the application object.

  ▶ **See** "Making Your Menu," **p. 29**

  ▶ **See** "Making a Toolbar," **p. 175**

- Many PowerBuilder features, such as Toolbars or the MDI display messages, are set in the application object.

  ▶ **See** "Using Project Objects," **p. 458**

- The application object is the first entry point to your PowerBuilder application. Futhermore, you are not allowed to compile or run an application without coding for the Application Open Event.

- Many times, database connections occur in the application object.

All these features make your application object one of the integral parts of your PowerBuilder program.

The Application Property Sheet

 PowerBuilder allows you to declare settings that affect the application during run time and/or affect the development of the application. These settings are set in the application property sheet. You've already seen the application property sheet in chapter 1 when the library search path was set. There are other attributes you can set using the application property sheet by clicking the property sheet icon from within the application painter, as seen in figure 3.1.

FIG. 3.1
You can change settings on your application object by clicking the property sheet icon from within the application painter.

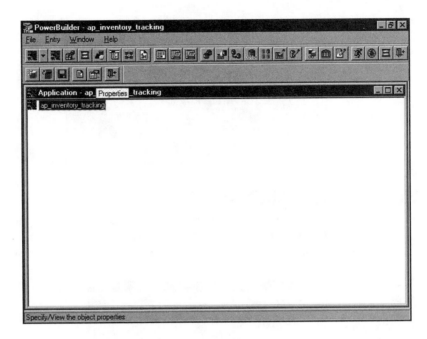

Libraries

▶ **See** "Specifying a Library Path," **p. 23**

Application Libary paths were discussed in chapter 1. Using the application painter, you can tell PowerBuilder to search through several application libraries when running an application.

TROUBLESHOOTING

I'm trying to run an application (like the Inventory Tracking system), but when I do, I get an error message similar to the error message seen in figure 3.2. Why is that? The error message in figure 3.2 says that you are accessing an object that cannot be found. More often than not, this is because you have not placed all the libraries in the appropriate library path in your application object. For instance, the error in figure 3.2 occurs when you try to run the inventory tracking system on the CD without including ancestor.pbl in your library path.

FIG. 3.2

An error can occur if you reference an object that is not defined within your library path.

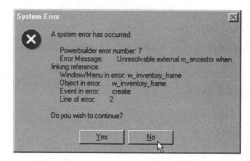

Viewing General Attributes

General Settings allows you to view the application name, library, last modified date, application object size (in bytes), who the application is checked out by (if anyone), and the application comments. Figure 3.3 shows how the application general attributes are displayed.

FIG. 3.3

You can view some settings in your application by opening the property sheet. This displays the general properties for an application.

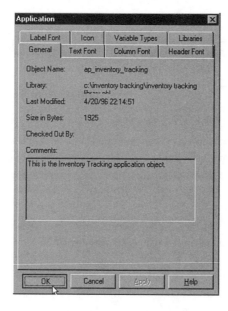

Using Default Fonts

To standardize your application, you should choose a default font that you are comfortable with. The default for all text, data, headings, and labels is Arial 10 point. However, you can adjust this to suit your own needs. By clicking on one of the font tabs in the application painter (fig. 3.4), you can choose the way your fonts look throughout your application. You can also differentiate between how text, data, headings, and labels look in your application.

FIG. 3.4

The font tabs in the application painter are used for setting the default fonts in the major objects in PowerBuilder.

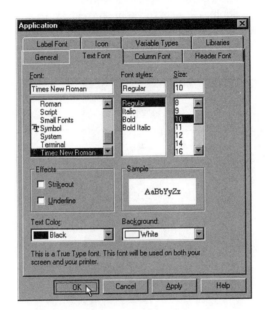

Part

I

Ch

3

 TIP Set defaults that consistently apply throughout the application. That way, all your windows will look consistent since they all have the same font style and font size.

> **CAUTION**
>
> Nearly every end-user will be using VGA monitors with Windows applications. Although you may be tempted to use color throughout your application, be careful that your target audience does not use black-and-white screens, such as those that come with many laptops. Colors may not look as clear on gray scale monitors. At the very least, test your color choices with gray scale monitors to make sure they are usable!
>
> For those who have color monitors, some color combinations clash and may have a detrimental effect on your application. Color choice is important and should be considered during development and testing.

N O T E   In the Inventory Tracking system, you will use the default font of Times New Roman 10 point for all of your windows. Of course, this is personal preference. You can set the font to any setting you wish. ■

Setting the Application Icon

You can set the application icon using the application property sheet. The application icon is the icon that the end-user double-clicks to run your application. To set an icon for your application, click on the Icon tab on your application property sheet. This will display the tab shown in figure 3.5

FIG. 3.5

The Icon tab in the application property sheet allows you to choose an icon for your application.

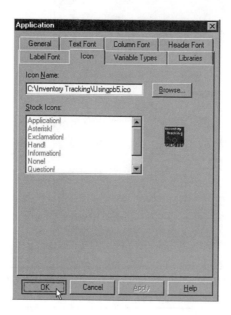

The application sheet allows you to enter the path of the icon you want to use for your application. If you don't know the name of the icon, click on Browse. This will pull up the Select Drag Icon dialog box, as seen in figure 3.6.

From the Select Drag Icon dialog box, you can select an icon directly from your hard drive.

N O T E   In Windows 95, you get to actually see the icon you are choosing from the list view provided in the Select Drag Icon dialog box. Unfortunately, this feature is not implemented in Windows 3.1. ■

N O T E   You can't build an icon from within PowerBuilder. However, there are several resource managers, including those available on the PowerBuilder CD and also available from many online sources, like CompuServe and the Internet. Using these tools, you can build your icons fairly simply for use with your application. ■

FIG. 3.6
The Select Drag Icon dialog box allows you to select an icon for your application.

After you choose your icon by double-clicking on it in the Select Drag Icon dialog box, click on Open. This will assign the icon to your application, as seen in figure 3.7. Notice in figure 3.7 that not only is the icon name displayed, but a picture of the icon is also shown.

FIG. 3.7
The Icon tab shows the pathname and the picture of the icon you've chosen.

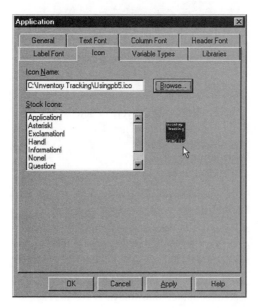

Setting Variable Types

FIG. 3.8

The default global data types can be changed inside the Variables tab of the application property sheet.

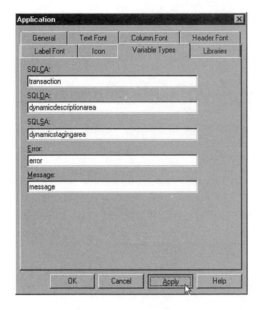

By clicking the Variables tab in the application property sheet (as seen in figure 3.8), you can see five global variables that are defined by PowerBuilder. These five global variables are present in every PowerBuilder application, and are described as follows:

Variable	Description
SQLCA	SQLCA is a Transaction object. Every time you access a database, you need a transaction object to contain your database's connection information.
SQLDA	SQLDA is a DynamicDescriptionArea data type. SQLDA is used to store information about the input and output parameters used in dynamic SQL
SQLSA	SQLSA is a copy of the dynamic staging area for your database, and is used in conjunction with dynamic SQL. SQLSA stores the SQL statement used in your PREPARE statement, the number of parameters, and the transaction object (usually SQLCA) for use during your dynamic SQL statements.
ERROR	ERROR contains information about system errors that can occur. Often, system errors in a PowerBuilder application lead to immediate termination of that PowerBuilder application. Often, developers will code an intercept routine in the application SYSTEMERROR event to describe the error to the end-user and allow processing to continue.
MESSAGE	The MESSAGE object captures all parameters when an object is opened "WITHPARM".

These five structures can be redefined based on your personal needs as well as your particular database. However, most developers leave them alone.

From Here...

In this chapter, you learned about the application painter. Here are some other chapters and sources you may find interesting and informative:

- Chapter 1, "Introducing PowerBuilder," covers how to create an application and how to set up a library list in an application.

- Chapter 6, "Using Events, Functions, and the PowerScript Language," describes variable access (that is, Global variables) as well as event programming for applications.

- To find out more about dynamic SQL and the Watcom SQL database, ask for QUE's book *Special Edition Using Watcom SQL* by Charles A. Wood (ISBN: 0-7897-0103-0). It is the *only* book that covers Watcom SQL. (Note that Sybase SQL Anywhere is a Watcom SQL database.)

CHAPTER 4

Exploring Windows

by Charles A. Wood

The biggest push in application development today is the need for a *graphical user interface*, or *GUI*. The main thrust of GUI development centers around the window.

This chapter describes much of what you can do with a window in the Windows environment. You've already touched on windows in the first chapter, so this chapter will add to what you've already learned. ■

Describe and differentiate between different window types.

There are many different types of windows that will perform different uses during your application development.

Set window properties through the window property sheet.

The windows property sheet can help you control and track your window's properties.

Add and implement window controls.

There are many controls, like tab controls or command buttons, that you can add to a window. PowerBuilder 5 has added even more controls than before to help you develop a professional application with remarkable ease.

Implement window inheritance.

Inheritance is an extremely powerful tool. This chapter introduces you to window inheritance and will show you how inheritance can make your programming task a lot easier.

Using the Windows Property Sheet

You've seen a little bit of window properties in the Windows Property Sheet when w_inventory_frame was defined. The following sections discuss the other window properties that can be set inside the Windows Property Sheet and why you should use them.

There are four ways to pull up a window property sheet inside the window painter:

- Double-click the window (as shown in chapter 1).

- Click the Properties icon while in the PowerBuilder window painter.
- Click Edit, Properties as shown in figure 4.1.

FIG. 4.1
You can open the Windows Property Sheet by using the PowerBuilder menu.

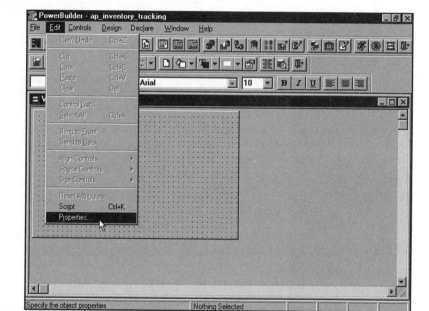

- Right-click the window and choose Properties (as shown in fig. 4.2).

General Window Properties

When you open the window property sheet, the General tab page is displayed. The General tab page allows you to set window general properties, which are defined as follows:

- **Title Bar.** The title bar is the bar at the top of a window with the title in it. The title bar also contains the Control menu icon (called Control menu in PowerBuilder's window painter), Maximize box, and Minimize box. If any of these are active, the title bar is also active.

FIG. 4.2
You can also right-click
the window to pull up a
property sheet.

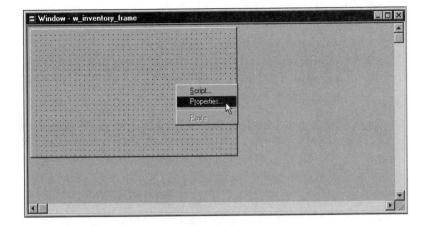

N O T E   The title of the MDI Frame (or the main window in an SDI application) is also the name of
the application. The title will be displayed when you pull up your Windows 95 taskbar and
when you press Ctrl+Tab to switch between applications. ■

- **Menu Name.** The Menu Name option tells PowerBuilder which menu to attach to the window. Because you have created only one menu, m_ancestor, that's the one you'll have to use for now.
- **Visible.** The Visible indicator tells whether you want this window shown when it's pulled up. This indicator may seem a little odd—you may ask, why create a window and then make it invisible? Sometimes it's more expedient to hide a window by making it invisible and only show it when it's needed.
- **Enabled.** Sometimes you will want to display a window but not allow entry into it. Clicking this off disables a window.

N O T E   All windows in the Inventory Tracking system will be visible and enabled. The visible and
enabled properties are most often handled using PowerScript. If you want to make a
window or window control invisible, use the windowname.Hide() command. If you want to make a
window or window control visible, use the windowname.Show() command.

It should also be noted that instead of using Hide and Show commands, it's faster to directly assign
the window attribute:

```
windowname.visible = TRUE
windowname.enabled = FALSE
```

Using the enabled attribute is the only way to choose whether or not a window is enabled or disabled.
Note that all these properties can be affected by setting the proper attribute. Chapter 27, "Property
Quick Reference," lists all of the properties for all of the objects and controls in PowerBuilder. ■

Part

I

Ch

4

■ **Border.** Border controls whether a border surrounds the window. Main and MDI windows must have borders. Getting rid of a border on a window creates the illusion of one window, when in fact there are two.

■ **Control Menu.** The Control menu icon is the picture in the upper left-hand corner of your window containing your application (or window) icon. This controls whether you have a Control menu box on your window.

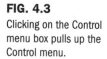 **N O T E** It's easy to get confused when discussing the Control menu with other Windows users. The Control menu box is also called the Control box. The Control menu appears when you click once on the Control box. PowerBuilder groups the Control menu box and the Control menu into one and calls it the Control menu (see fig. 4.3). ■

■ **Maximize Box.** The Maximize box is the box in the upper right-hand corner of your window. It acts as a toggle between full-screen and its normal area.

■ **Minimize Box.** The Minimize box is the box in the upper right-hand corner of your window. It reduces your window to an entry on the task bar (or an icon in Windows 3.x).

■ **Resizable.** Clicking on Resizable resizes the window.

FIG. 4.3

Clicking on the Control menu box pulls up the Control menu.

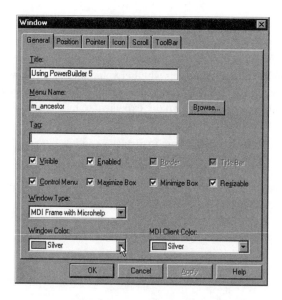

Defining Window Types In chapter 1, MDI and SDI windows were discussed. PowerBuilder lets you choose between several other window types. These window types and how they are used are described in this section.

▶ **See** "Using Windows," **p. 32**

Using Main Windows You will probably use main windows more than any other type. Main windows are stand-alone windows (unless inside an MDI frame). If you aren't using an MDI frame, the first window opened will be a main window.

N O T E Even in a simple Windows application, you may find yourself wanting to use MDI frame with MicroHelp as a "shell" for all your main windows. MicroHelp is great for displaying short messages to the user, and MDI frames look more professional than stand-alone main windows.

Inside your MDI frame, all your major sheet windows will probably end up being main windows. ■

Using Pop-Up Windows   Pop-up windows are usually opened from within another window (they have a parent window). Although the pop-up window can't be overlaid by its parent window, it can extend beyond the boundaries of its parent window. When the parent window is closed or minimized, the pop-up window is also closed or minimized.

Pop-up windows are commonly used as support windows. For example, if you were asked to enter a customer number, a pop-up window would display all customer numbers with names for you.

N O T E Pop-up windows are a good way to tie one window to another window, but be careful not to overuse them. An application with tons of pop-up windows is usually a sign that an MDI frame should have been used, especially if the windows don't seem to relate to each other. ■

Using Child Windows   Child windows are also opened from within another window and also have a parent window. There are some strong differences, however:

- ■ Child windows can never exist outside of the parent window.
- ■ Child windows are never considered active.
- ■ When a child window is maximized, it only fills the space of the parent window.
- ■ Child windows can't have menus.

   ▶ **See** "Programming for Window Event," **p. 240**

Although child windows aren't used that often, they can be a type of pop-up window if you want to avoid activating and deactivating your parent window because of some PowerScript you have written.

Using Response Windows   Response windows are a type of pop-up window. They differ from pop-up windows in that they are application modal (no other window in the application can be accessed until the response window is closed).

Response windows are often called dialog boxes. You'll use response windows often. For example, they are useful if you don't want the user to continue with your application until some questions have been answered. If your changes have not been saved, a response window appears and asks if the changes should be saved. The user won't be able to continue until the question has been answered.

Using MDI Frames and MDI Frames with MicroHelp   An MDI frame is a window (called a frame) which contains other windows (called sheets). You only have one frame per application but can have many sheets within your frame.

▶ **See** "Comparing SDI vs. MDI Frame," **p. 34**

Part

I

Ch

4

In any complex (and usually any simple) Windows application, you should use an MDI frame. The MicroHelp works well as an easy way to convey a message to the user (Save was successful!, Performing Calculations., Please wait., and so on) without stopping your application.

 T I P If you use an MDI frame, you should use it with MicroHelp. (MicroHelp is easy to use; it won't noticeably impact your application's performance.)

N O T E Most books start you with an SDI application, claiming that MDI is too advanced. This is simply not so! PowerBuilder has done a fine job implementing MDI, and using MDI allows you more freedom in development. Also, your final project will be more professional.

You should be careful about suggesting an SDI application. You may wish you hadn't. MDI offers MicroHelp and easy interaction between windows for the user that SDI applications can't match. All this is done with very little extra effort from the developer. ■

N O T E If you already defined your window as a certain type and then later change your mind and want it to be a different type, go into the Window Style dialog box and simply choose a new type. This may cause some difficulty if you're changing from an SDI application to an MDI application, but otherwise there should be little problem. ■

Color You can also change the background color of your window in the Window Style dialog box. In the Window Color drop-down listbox, you can choose the color you want for your main window. If your window is an MDI frame, the MDI Client Color drop-down listbox can control the background color of all your sheet windows.

Position

By clicking on the Position tab on the windows property sheet, as seen in figure 4.4, you can define the position of your window. Not only does PowerBuilder allow you to enter the height, width, and (X,Y) coordinates of your window, but you also get a graphical representation of how your window looks in relationship to your monitor screen.

N O T E When you ran your application after chapter 1, the MDI frame took up a small section of the screen. You probably want to change it so the MDI frame takes up the whole screen. To do this, open Design and choose Window Position. ■

The Position tab also allows you to define the initial state of your window. (The initial state can be Maximize, Minimize, or Normal.)

 T I P MDIs look best when they're full-screen. Adjust the size of the frame window so there is no "bleeding" application on either side of it. Your user won't be distracted while running your application.

FIG. 4.4

In the Position tab page of the window property sheet, you can choose Window Position to change the size and opening position of your window.

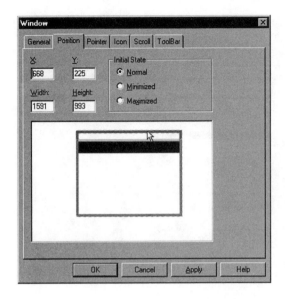

Pointer

Usually, you want to keep the default pointer icon when the mouse pointer moves over your window. However, if you want to change the way your mouse pointer appears while crossing your window, you use the pointer tab to choose a new pointer for your window, as seen in figure 4.5.

N O T E PowerBuilder comes with many icons and several pointers, but you can't create new icons or pointers within PowerBuilder. These are created by using third-party Windows development toolkits.

Watcom Image Editor comes with the PowerBuilder Enterprise Edition, and is available as a stand-alone product. ■

Icon

The window icon appears in the upper left corner of your application. (In Windows 3.1, this is not true, but if your window is minimized, the window icon representing your window will appear.) This icon defaults to the Application! icon. If you want to change your icon to another, click the Icon tab page in the window property sheet, as shown in figure 4.6.

If you want to use a different icon for your minimized window, this is the place to do so. PowerBuilder lets you choose one of its stock icons or browse for the icon file you want to use.

Part
I

Ch
4

FIG. 4.5

Use the Pointer tab page to see a different pointer when the pointer is over your window.

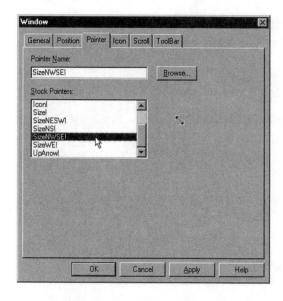

FIG. 4.6

Select an icon to represent your window if your window is minimized. The default is the Application! icon.

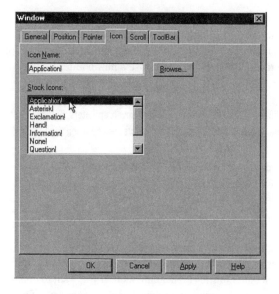

Scroll

The scroll tab on the windows property sheet, as seen in figure 4.7 allows you to specify scroll characteristics. The following scroll characteristics can be specified:

FIG. 4.7

The Scroll tab page on the window painter property sheet allows you to specify scrolling characteristics of your window.

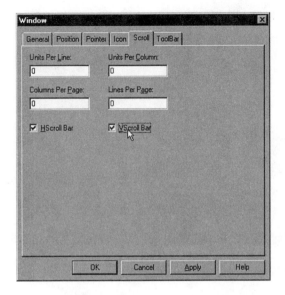

- **Units Per Line.** Units per line allows you to specify how much you want to scroll when the user clicks the vertical scroll tab. The default (0) indicates that one unit per line will be allowed for each click on the scroll bar arrow.

- **Units Per Column.** Units per column allows you to specify how much you want to scroll when the user clicks the horizontal scroll tab. The default (0) indicates that one unit per column will be allowed for each click on the scroll bar arrow.

- **Columns Per Page.** Columns per page indicates how many columns will be scrolled over when the user clicks the scroll bar to page over.

- **Lines Per Page.** Lines per page indicates how many lines will be scrolled down (or up) when the user clicks the scroll bar to page down (or up).

- **HScroll Bar.** A horizontal scroll bar places a scroll bar at the bottom of your window. This lets you "shift" the window over, in case your information is wider than your window.

- **VScroll Bar.** A vertical scroll bar places a scroll bar on the right side of your window. This lets you "shift" the window down, in case your information is longer than your window.

Toolbar

The toolbar tab page, as seen in figure 4.8, allows you to set the following toolbar properties of a window:

- **Alignment.** Alignment controls the placement of the window toolbar. You can choose top, bottom, left, right, or float.

- **X and Y.** X and Y control the position (in units) of your toolbar on the window.

Part

I

Ch

4

FIG. 4.8
The toolbar tab page allows you to set the toolbar properties of a window.

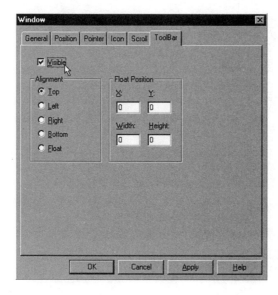

■ **Width and Height.** Width and height control the appearance of your toolbar while your application is running.

■ **Visible.** Visible indicates whether or not your toolbar is visible when your application is running.

Adding Window Controls

A window control is anything you put in a window. The window PainterBar mostly contains different controls you can place on your window. Controls are necessary for every window; without controls, a window is simply a box with no functionality displayed on your screen.

 To place a control on a window, you can use the drop-down icon list. This displays all the control icons that you can choose, as seen in figure 4.9.

 You can easily add controls to your window by clicking on an icon, and then on the window where you want the control placed.

New Controls in PowerBuilder 5

PowerScript has added several new controls, some of which can greatly enhance PowerBuilder applications.

 Tab Controls   Probably the most awaited control has been the tab control. Tab controls are an easy and efficient way to place multiple controls on a system. For instance, say you had two related DataWindows: DataWindow 1 and DataWindow 2. Also assume that you wanted a tab folder used to separate and select between the two DataWindows.

FIG. 4.9

A drop-down list can be used to place controls on a window.

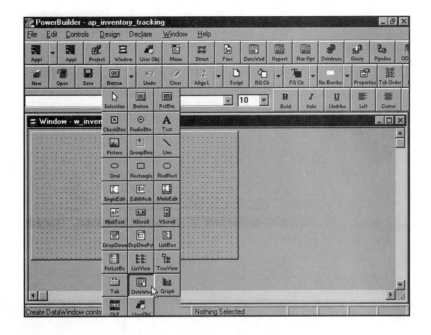

N O T E DataWindows are covered in detail in "Part III: Using DataWindows" later in this book. In the interest of expediency, the DataWindows (DataWindow 1 and DataWindow 2) have been created for you. ■

First, you must create a tab folder control. This is done by clicking the tab icon and then clicking anywhere in your window area. When you are finished, you should have a very rough looking tab, as seen in figure 4.10.

Now right-click anywhere on the tab *except the tab name*. A menu should pop up from which you can select the property sheet for the entire tab control, as seen in figure 4.11.

You can now change the properties of the tab control, as seen in figure 4.12. Typically the name and colors are changed on a tab control.

The following properties are available to tab controls:

Picture On Right	Specifies whether a picture that is part of the tab label is to the right (clicked on) or left (clicked off) of the text.
PowerTips	Specifies whether PowerTipText for a tab page is displayed as a PowerTip (a pop-up label for the tab) when the mouse pointer pauses over the tab.
Fixed Width	Specifies whether tabs have a fixed width, meaning they do not shrink to the length of their text labels.
Focus On Button Down	Specifies whether each tab gets focus when the user clicks on it.

FIG. 4.10
A tab control with one tab labeled "none" is placed on your window.

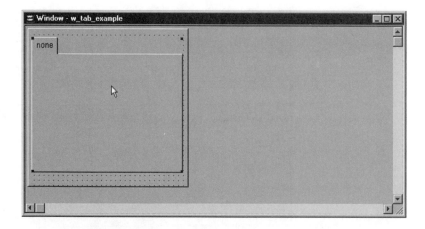

FIG. 4.11
The tab control pop-up menu can be seen by right-clicking on the tab control.

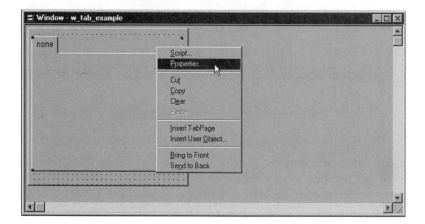

Show Text	Specifies whether the text specified for each tab label is displayed.
Show Picture	Specifies whether the picture selected for each tab is displayed.
Perpendicular Text	Specifies whether the tab labels are drawn perpendicular to the tab page.
MultiLine	Specifies whether the tabs can appear in more than one row. If there is not room for all the tabs in a single row, a dual arrow control will display to allow the user to scroll to tabs that don't fit.

Ragged Right	Specifies whether tabs are stretched so that they fill space along the edge of the control.
Bold Selected Text	Specifies whether the text for the selected tab is bold (clicked) or the text on the selected tab has the same setting as the other tabs.

FIG. 4.12

The tab control dialog box.

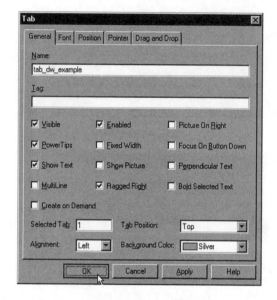

Next you should set the properties on each tab page. Right-click the tab page name ("none") as shown in figure 4.13. This will pull up the tab page property sheet, as seen in figure 4.14.

On the tab page properties sheet, you can set the colors of each tab page or the PowerTip that will appear as your mouse cursor rests on the tab page.

After you've set the properties for your tab page, you'll probably want to add another. The second (third, forth, etc.) tab page will have the same properties as those of the last tab page that you've changed. To add another tab page, right-click the tab control and click Insert Tab Page, as seen in figure 4.15.

As you can see in figure 4.16, a new tab page has been added to the old tab page. Although this tab page also needs to be customized, much of the customization done to tab page 1 is carried over into tab page 2.

Now we can place a DataWindow control onto the tab page, as seen in figure 4.17. This tab page now contains the DataWindow. When the tab page is no longer in view, the DataWindow is also taken from view.

Part

I

Ch

4

FIG. 4.13

Each tab page has its own properties.

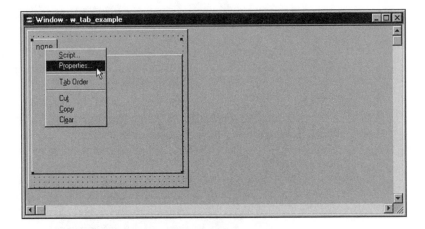

FIG. 4.14

The tab page properties are different than the tab control properties.

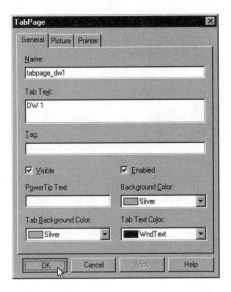

Then, in the development environment, we click on the second tab page. Notice in figure 4.18 that both the first tab page and any controls on that first tab page disappear except for the folder tab.

FIG. 4.15
Right-click the tab control to insert more tab pages.

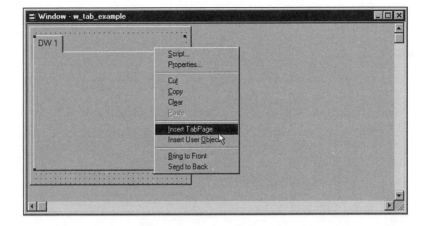

FIG. 4.16
Any additional tab pages have much of the same properties found in the previous tab pages.

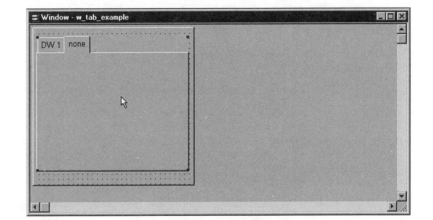

Part
I

Ch
4

FIG. 4.17
Tab pages can hold any window controls.

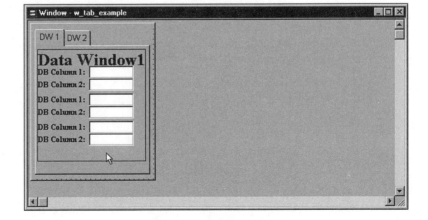

FIG. 4.18
Other tab pages of a tab control are pulled up by clicking on the folder tab.

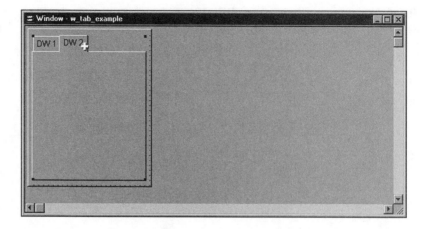

Now we can add other controls to the second folder. In this case, we add a different DataWindow than the one added before, as you can see in figure 4.19.

FIG. 4.19
Different tab pages can contain many different controls.

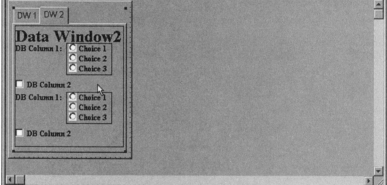

Now when you run your application, a window appears containing a tab control (see fig. 4.20). DataWindow1 is on the first tab page.

However, when you click on another folder tab, the first tab page and all of its controls become hidden. You then see the second tab page with all its controls, as seen in figure 4.21.

FIG. 4.20
Controls that are placed on a tab folder appear one tab page at a time.

FIG. 4.21
Clicking on the tab folder brings up a new tab page with new controls.

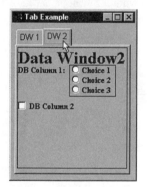

Part

I

Ch

4

Rich Text Edits   Rich Text Edits are controls that give your application word-processing capabilities, including the ability to change the font and appearance of your text. As you can see by the Rich Text Edit control way back in figure 4.9, a Rich Text Edit control contains many of the same features as Microsoft Word or WordPerfect.

Placing a rich text edit on your window is easy. Simply click the Rich Text Edit icon and then on the area of your window where you want it to be placed.

Due to the word-processing nature of the rich text edit, properties, as seen in figure 4.22, have been separated into general properties (which are similiar to properties of other controls) and document properties (which are unique to rich text edits). The document properties of a rich text edit are as follows:

Document Name	The name that will display in the print queue when the user prints the contents of the control.
Tabs Visible	Specifies whether tabs are visible.
Header-Footer	Determines whether or not the RichTextEdit control has a header/footer section.

Popup Menu	Indicates whether or not the user has access to pop-up menu by clicking the right mouse button on the rich text edit.
Returns Visible	Specifies whether carriage returns are visible.
Spaces Visible	Specifies whether spaces are visible.
Field Names Visible	Indicates whether input field names are displayed in input fields, rather than the input field values.
Fields Visible	Specifies whether input fields are visible.
Ruler Bar	Indicates whether or not a ruler bar is visible above the editing area.
Tab Bar	Indicates whether or not a bar for setting tabs is visible above the editing area.
Word Wrap	Indicates whether or not text wraps automatically to the next line when the line reaches the margin.
Pictures As Frame	Indicates whether or not the rich text edit will display pictures (bitmaps) as frames.
Tool Bar	Indicates whether or not a tool bar for formatting text is visible above the editing area.
Background Field Color	Default background color for input fields.
Undo Depth	Sets the maximum number of activities that Undo will undo.
Left Margin	The width of the left margin on the printed page.
Top Margin	The width of the top margin on the printed page.
Right Margin	The width of the right margin on the printed page.
Bottom Margin	The width of the bottom margin on the printed page.

FIG. 4.22

The document tab of a Rich Text Edit control property sheet contains those properties which are unique to a rich text edit.

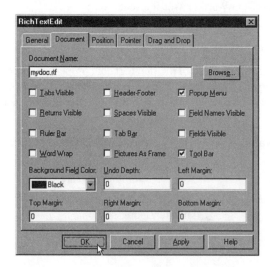

NOTE There is a rich text edit type of DataWindow which allows such things as form letters to be written. These will be covered in the DataWindow section. ■

Picture Listboxes and Drop-Down Picture Listboxes   Picture listboxes are identical to standard listboxes except that each word has a picture associated with it. The properties for picture listboxes are also identical except for the Pictures and Item property sheet.

The Pictures tab on the Picture ListBox property sheet, as seen in figure 4.23, allows you to choose pictures to be associated with your listbox.

FIG. 4.23
You can associate pictures with your listbox by using the Pictures tab on the Picture ListBox property sheet.

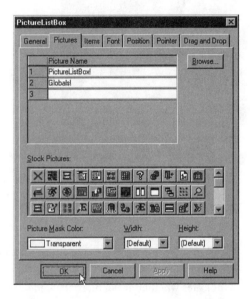

You can then associate the picture with a particular item or items in the Items tab of the Picture ListBox property sheet, as seen in figure 4.24. After typing in the text for your choice, as you did with standard listboxes, choose the picture number (picture index) of the picture you want associated with this item.

Listviews   Listviews are a lot like picture listboxes, except that you have much more control over how your items in your listview are displayed. You can display listviews as one of the four following presentation styles:

- **Large icon view**—This is equivalent to a group view inside windows. (An example of this is in figure 4.9.)
- **Listview**—This shows small icons with the text next to the icon.
- **Small icon view**—This is similar to listview except that the icons can be rearranged.
- **Report View**—This displays the name and detail information for each list item. Report views are set using PowerScript.

Part

I

Ch

4

FIG. 4.24

You associate a particular picture with a particular item in the Items tab of the Picture ListBox property sheet.

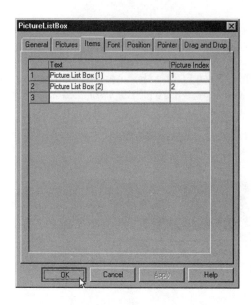

The general properties of a listview can be seen in figure 4.25. They are as follows:

Fixed Locations — Indicates whether or not icons are in fixed locations (clicked) or the user can drag icons to a new location (not clicked).

Edit Labels — Indicates whether or not the editing of labels is permitted in a listview.

Auto Arrange — Indicates if icons are automatically arranged in a large or small icon view.

Extended Select — Indicates whether or not more than one item can be selected at one time.

Button Header — Report view header appears as pushable buttons instead of labels.

Deleted Items — Indicates whether or not the end user can delete items from the listview with the delete key.

Label Wrap — Indicates that labels of items should be wrapped instead of being forced onto one line.

Scrolling — Indicates whether or not scrolling is permitted in the listview.

Show Header — Indicates whether or not headers should be shown in a report view.

View — Changes the view to Large Icon, Small Icon, List, or Report.

As you can see in figure 4.26, you can associate pictures with your listview control. You can set different pictures for large, small, and state views of your listview.

FIG. 4.25
Listview properties can
be seen in the general
tab of the ListView
property sheet.

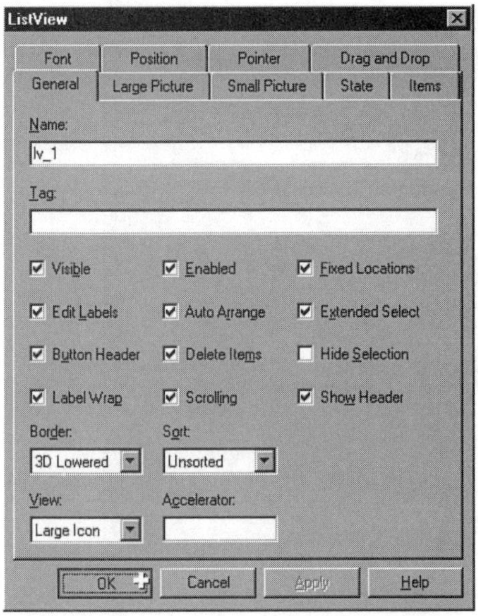

FIG. 4.26
Listviews allow you to
associate pictures with
your listview.

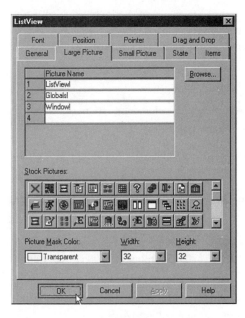

Finally, just as with picture listboxes, you add items to your listview and associate the picture
index to them, as seen in figure 4.27. Depending on which view you're using and the state of
your items in your listview, different pictures may be used for the same item.

FIG. 4.27

You can associate a state, large, and small picture with your listview item in the Items tab of your listview.

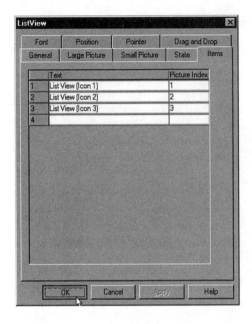

Treeviews   Treeviews allow you to use PowerScript to establish a tree structure control on your window. This tree structure is similar to the tree structure you see using Windows Explorer or File Manager. Features of treeview controls include:

- Text and graphical (bitmap) representation for each node.
- Easy drag-and-drop manipulation.
- Easy manipulation of tree nodes using copy, cut, paste, delete, and insert of tree nodes.
- Easy expanding and collapsing of tree nodes.

Treeviews, as you can see in figure 4.28, have some unique properties:

Show Buttons	Displays + and - buttons next to each parent root.
Disable Drag and Drop	Indicates that items may not be dragged.
Show Lines	Indicates that lines connect the items on the treeview.
Lines at Root	Indicates that there are lines connecting all root items.
Indentation	The number of PowerBuilder units that are used for indentation between levels in a treeview.

You then can associate the picture with your treeview to be used with PowerScript. This will then associate with your tree, as seen in figure 4.29.

▶ **See** "Programming for Treeviews," **p. 245**

N O T E   Actually implementing treeviews requires some understanding of how they work and of PowerScript. For more on developing treeviews, see chapter 7, "Programming in PowerScript." ■

FIG. 4.28
The General tab of the TreeView property sheet is used to set properties for a treeview.

FIG. 4.29
You can associate pictures with your treeview using the Pictures tab in the TreeView property sheet.

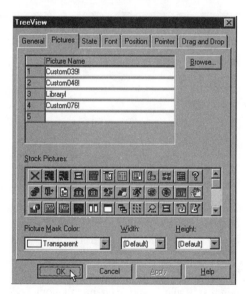

Other Types of Window Controls

There are several different types of controls you can choose from. Most of the controls are shown in figure 4.30. The icon for each control precedes each control description in the following sections.

FIG. 4.30
Many different window
controls are displayed
here, but usually you
have only one or two
types of window controls
at a time.

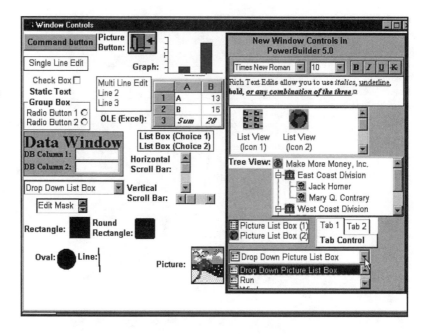

Although all controls are somewhat different from each other, the property sheets are almost identical in that most controls save for the General properties tab. You can get to your property sheet for a control by:

■ Double-clicking the control.

■ Right-clicking the control and choosing Properties.

■ Selecting the control by clicking it and clicking the Properties icon on your window painter bar.

The following property sheets can be found on most controls:

General	The General property sheet tends to differ (at least slightly) for most controls. The General property sheet lets you define control-specific properties. (Pictures of General property sheets can be viewed for the specific control later in this chapter.)
Font	The Font tab, as seen in figure 4.31, is available in controls that contain text. It allows you to change the font, style, color, size, and font effect. It is identical to the Font property sheets reviewed in chapter 3.

FIG. 4.31
The Font tab allows
you to set your typed
character properties on
a window control.

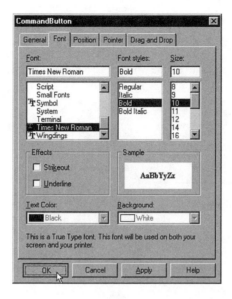

Position   The Position tab, as seen in figure 4.32, allows you to specify the size of the control and the position of the control in relation to the upper left corner of the parent window.

Pointer   The Pointer property sheet is identical to the Window Pointer property sheet seen in figure 4.5. The Pointer property sheet allows you to define which pointer appears when the mouse cursor passes over your control.

FIG. 4.32
The Position tab allows
you to define the size
and placement of a
control on a window.

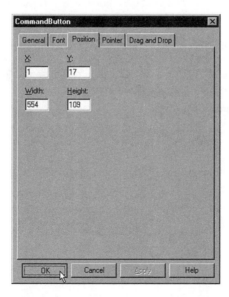

Part
I

Ch
4

Drag and Drop   Several controls can be dragged onto other controls or even into other programs. The Drag and Drop tab (see fig. 4.33) allows you to define the icon that appears when you start to drag your control. It also allows you to define whether or not drag will be automatically allowed.

FIG. 4.33
You can choose and view the drag icon in the Drag and Drop tab.

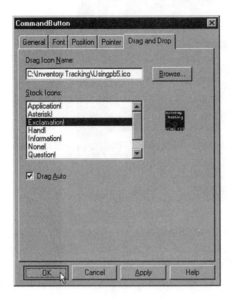

Command Buttons   Command buttons look like buttons on your window. When clicked, command buttons give a pushed-in look while the mouse button is depressed. To put a command button on your window, click on the Command Button icon and then click on the window where you want the command button to go in the window you are defining.

When command buttons are "pushed" (clicked on), PowerScript defined in command button events is executed. Command buttons are often not used on a window where a menu toolbar is available. However, command buttons are often used on response windows since the menu is inoperable when a response window is active.

▶ **See** "Adding an About Window," **p. 428**

The general tab on the command button property sheet, as seen in figure 4.34, allows you to change the following:

Name   PowerBuilder lets you change the name of your controls. Name is common to all general property sheets for every control.

FIG. 4.34

The Command Button General property sheet allows you to define properties for your command button.

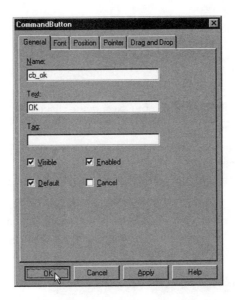

N O T E Controls are named by PowerBuilder. For instance, this command button was called cb_1 at first. When you start accessing these controls, cb_1 is hard to work with because it's not intuitive and not very maintainable.

To pull up the property sheet of any control, double-click that control. In figure 4.34, the command button's name is changed. (You can also change what is displayed on the button and certain properties regarding that button.) You should rename all your controls to better fit their descriptions. By renaming this command button to cb_ok, you and your coworkers now know that you are dealing with the OK command button. ∎

Text	The text that is displayed on your command button (or other window controls).
Tag	The tag is an identifier that you can assign a control for identification later in the PowerBuilder program.
Visible	The visible checkbox tells if the command button (or any control) defaults to visible or invisible when the parent window opens.

N O T E Invisible controls take as long as visible controls to create and bring up. If possible, minimize the controls on your window. You'll be surprised at how slow a window with a lot of controls compares to a window with little controls. ∎

Enabled	Enabled tells if the command button (or any control) can be accessed or not when the parent window opens.

T I P Invisible controls are always disabled.

Default Default tells PowerBuilder to execute the clicked event of the command button if the user hits the Enter key.

Cancel Cancel tells PowerBuilder to execute the clicked event of the command button if the user hits the Escape key.

Picture Buttons Picture buttons are just like command buttons except they have pictures on them. Pictures can make the words on the picture button hard to read, but there are times when a picture button can enhance the presentation quality of an otherwise nondistinct window.

To put a picture button control on your window, click the Picture Button icon and then click where you want the picture button to go in the window you are defining. When you double-click on a picture button, the Picture Button property sheet appears (see fig. 4.35).

FIG. 4.35
You can change properties of a picture button control using the Picture Button property sheet.

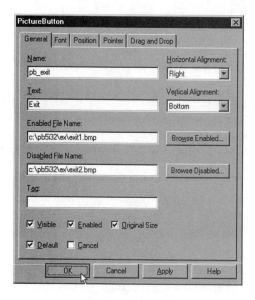

Along with property sheets properties found in the command button property sheet, a Picture Button property sheet allows you to define the following properties:

Enabled File Name The Enabled File Name is the name of the bitmap file that is displayed when the picture button is enabled.

Disabled File Name The Disabled File Name is the name of the bitmap file that is displayed when the picture button is disabled.

Original Size Clicking Original Size indicates that you want the bitmap to be displayed in its original size.

Horizontal Alignment   Horizontal Alignment is the alignment (left, right, or center) of the text inside the picture button.

Vertical Alignment   Vertical Alignment is the alignment (top, center, or bottom) of the text inside the picture button.

N O T E You may consider not placing any text inside a picture button. Often, complicated pictures can make the text unreadable. If you need a picture and words, make sure the picture is small enough so the text you type can be viewed. ▨

 Single-Line Edits   To put a single-line edit control on your window, click the Single-Line Edit icon and then click where you want the single-line edit to go in the window you are defining (see fig. 4.36).

FIG. 4.36

Use the Single-Line Edit dialog box to put a single-line edit in a window you are defining.

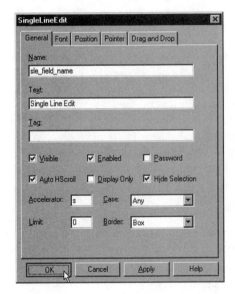

Single-line edits are data-entry fields that you can put in a window to enter a single line of text. Single-line edit controls usually aren't used because most data entry is done on a DataWindow.

Many of the single-line edit properties are common in controls discussed earlier in this section. The following single-line edit properties have not yet been described:

Password   The Password property describes whether or not any entry into the single-line edit is masked, like a password. The default is FALSE.

Auto HScroll   The Auto HScroll property allows the control to automatically scroll to allow the user to enter text that is wider than the length of the control. The default is TRUE.

Part

I

Ch

4

Display Only	Display Only protects the single-line edit from data entry at the user level. (However, the developer can change the contents of the single-line edit with PowerScript.) The default is TRUE.
Hide Selection	Hide Selection tells if the selected text of the control remains highlighted when the focus switches to another control. The default is FALSE.
Accelerator	An Accelerator allows the user to set focus on a field when a specific key is clicked. The default is no accelerator.
Case	Case allows the user to select upper, lower, or any to indicate the case allowed upon entry. The default is Any!.
Limit	Limit describes how many characters can be entered. A value of 0 indicates that an unlimited number of characters can be entered. Valid values are 0 to 32767.
Border	Border describes how the border appears on a single-line edit.

Multi-Line Edits   To put a multi-line edit control on your window, click on the Multi-Line Edit icon and then click where you want the multi-line edit to go in the window you are defining (see fig. 4.37). Unlike single-line edits which only allow one line of text to be entered or viewed, multi-line edits are controls that allow several lines of text to be entered by the user. Multi-line edits are often used for free-form comments. With many editing features built in (such as cut and paste and arrow movement), multi-line edits are indispensable when entering large amounts of data in a field. However, multi-line edit controls are often not used since enhanced functionality can be achieved through a DataWindow column or through a rich text edit control (discussed later in this chapter).

Properties for multi-line edits not previously discussed are as follows:

HScrollBar	Clicking HScrollBar places a horizontal scroll bar on your control. The default is FALSE.
VScrollBar	Clicking VScrollBar places a vertical scroll bar on your control. The default is FALSE.
Auto VScroll	The Auto VScroll property allows the control to automatically scroll to allow the user to enter text that is wider than the length of the control. The default is FALSE.
Alignment	Alignment specifies whether text is aligned left, center, or right. The default is Left!.
Tab Stop	The TabStop[ ] property allows you to define several tab stops in your multi-line edit. The default is empty (no tab stops were defined).
Ignore Default Button	Clicking Ignore Default Button allows the end user to use ENTER for a carriage return when the control has focus. When Ignore Default Button is FALSE, any button set as default is executed when the ENTER key is pressed. The default is FALSE.

FIG. 4.37

The General properties for a Multi-Line edit control allow you to set the properties for a multi-line edit.

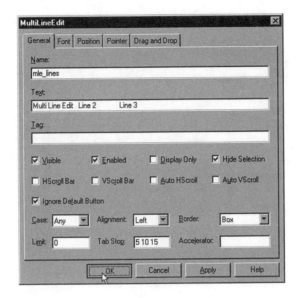

Part

I

Ch

4

Edit Masks   To put an edit mask control on your window, click the Edit Mask icon and then click where you want the edit mask to go in the window you are defining. Edit masks are a type of single-line edit that allow you to specify the formatting required upon entry. Like single- and multi-line edits, edit mask window controls are often not used since enhanced functionality is provided by DataWindows.

As you can tell by figure 4.38, all the edit mask general properties have been discussed in previous sections.

However, the Mask tab of the property sheet, as seen in figure 4.39, contains several innovative edit mask properties. These properties are defined as follows:

Mask	Masks are characters that act as place holders for the field that the user is entering. For instance, a four-digit year field would have an edit mask of ####, or a Social Security number would have a mask of ###-##-####, or a dollar field would have a mask of ###,##0.00.
Type	Type indicates the data type of a control. Different data types allow different masks. For instance, strings have different masks allowed than numbers.
Spin Control	Spin Control places an up and down arrow on your column. These arrows allow your user to use a mouse to select between proper values, or to scroll at a given increment.
Auto Skip	Clicking Auto Skip indicates that you automatically want to go to the next field when the maximum number of characters has been entered in an edit mask.

FIG. 4.38
The general properties
of an edit mask are
common to many
window controls.

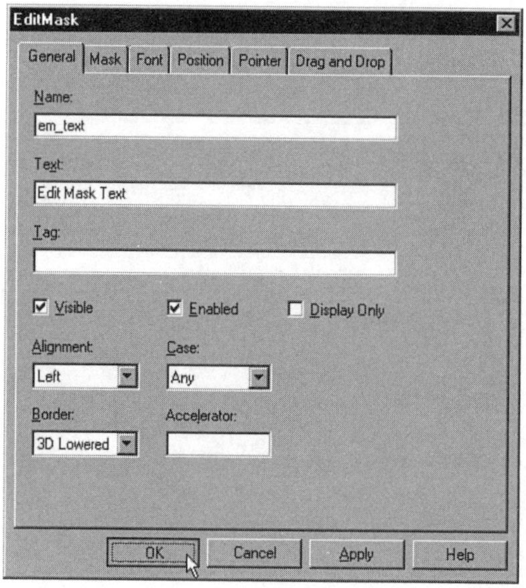

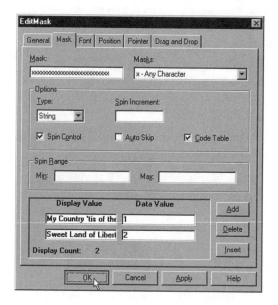

FIG. 4.39
The Mask properties
of an edit mask allow
the developer much
flexibility when
accepting a value
from an end user.

If you choose Spin Control, you can use the following edit mask properties:

Spin Increment	Spin increment determines how much your spin increases or decreases the value in your field.

Code Table   Code tables can be used to interpret a certain value into a code. Code tables can be handy for interpreting Yes, No, True, False, Y, or N questions to give a consistent value to the program.

Min   Min is the minimum amount that can be scrolled to in a scroll table.

Max   Max is the maximum amount that can be scrolled to in a scroll table.

Static Text   Static text is a phrase or description displayed on your window. To put a static text control on your window, click on the Static Text icon and then click where you want the static text to go. By clicking on the static text, you can type the text you want displayed in the window you are defining.

Static text is handy for describing controls (such as pictures or picture buttons), or for using multiple lines on controls (such as a checkbox) that only allow a single line of descriptive text to be displayed.

 Checkbox   To put a checkbox control on your window, click on the Checkbox icon and then click where you want the checkbox to go in the window you are defining.

Checkboxes are yes-no questions that can be clicked on or off. Internally, a code table describes the data value returned when a checkbox is clicked on or off. Like many other window controls dealing with data entry, checkbox window controls are often not used since enhanced functionality is provided by DataWindows.

Left Text on the property sheet (see fig. 4.40) allows you to place the text on the left side of the checkbox rather than the right side.

N O T E   You can also place a checkbox into a third state by clicking on the Three State property on the property sheet as seen in figure 4.40. (To default to the third state upon opening, click on Three State and Third State.)

Although three-state checkboxes are possible, they are often confusing to the end user. If you have more than two possible answers to a question, you may want to consider using a radio button or dropdown listbox. ■

  Radio Buttons and Group Boxes   To put a radio button on your window, click on the Radio Button icon and then click where you want the radio button to go in the window you are defining. To put a group box control on your window, click on the Group Box icon and then click where you want the group box to go in the window you are defining.

A radio button is a type of checkbox. Several radio buttons are grouped together inside a group box. These radio buttons, like checkboxes, are either on or off, but only one radio button inside a group box can be clicked at one time.

Part

I

Ch

4

FIG. 4.40

The CheckBox property sheet allows three state and third state attributes.

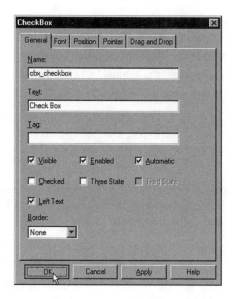

Listbox and Drop-Down Listbox   Listboxes are a type of multiple choice control that gives the user several choices for the right answer. Drop-down listboxes (DDLBs) allow only one choice, and the choices are accessed by clicking on the down arrow of the DDLB. Scroll bars can be used if there are a lot of choices that can be made. Like many other window controls dealing with data entry, listbox window controls are often not used since enhanced functionality is provided by DataWindows.

The general properties of a listbox are seen in figure 4.41:

Sorted	If Sorted is checked, the items will be sorted.
Disabled Scroll	If Disabled Scroll is checked, then the scroll bar will always be visible, but will be disabled when all the items can be accessed without scrolling. If not checked, then the scroll bar will be displayed only if necessary based on the number of items and the height of the listbox.
Multi Select	Multi Select indicates that more than one item can be selected.
Extended Select	Extended Select indicates that more than one item can be selected, and items may be selected by clicking and dragging the mouse pointer over the items. (If Multi Select and Extended Select are both clicked, Extended Select takes precedence.)

The properties of a drop-down listbox, as seen in figure 4.42, are slightly different than a listbox. Since only one item can be selected, Extended Select and Multi Select are both not allowed on a drop-down listbox. The following attributes can be chosen for a drop-down listbox:

Allow Editing	Allow Editing lets the user type in an item that is not on the selection list.

Always Show List   If Always Show List is checked, then the DDLB list of choices is always displayed. Otherwise, it is displayed only when the DDLB has focus.

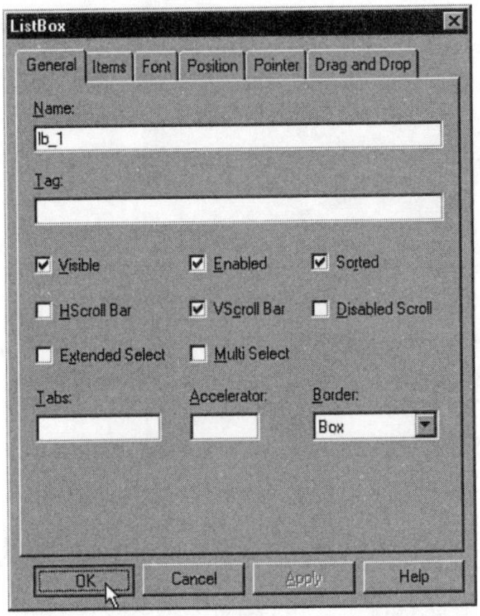

FIG. 4.41

The general properties of a listbox control can be accessed through the ListBox property sheet.

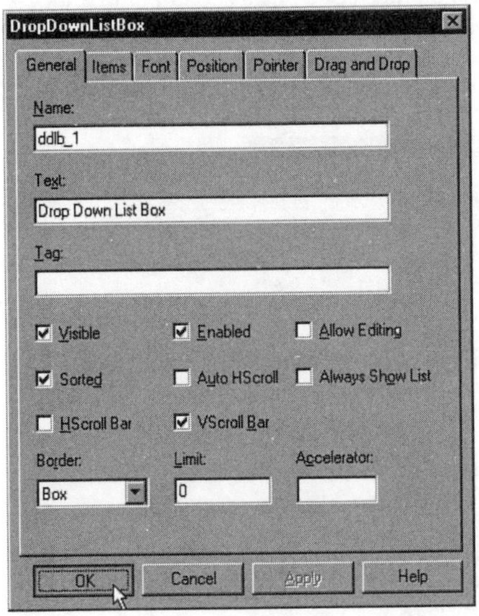

FIG. 4.42

The property sheet of a drop-down listbox control differs slightly from the standard listbox control.

Both listboxes and DDLBs allow you to specify a list of choices. This is done using the Items tab, as seen in figure 4.43. Using the Items tab of the property sheet, you can populate your listbox.

FIG. 4.43
DDLBs and listboxes allow you to specify the items in your list using the Items tab of the ListBox property sheet.

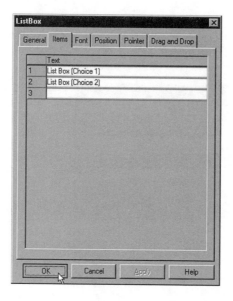

Pictures   Pictures are controls that reference bitmaps to be displayed in a window. Like static text, pictures are only used for displaying information (except in the form of pictures, not words). Usually, nothing more is done with these.

The general properties for the picture control, as seen in figure 4.44, are similar to other control attributes already discussed. You can also specify Invert Image, which will give you a "negative" image of your picture.

FIG. 4.44
Picture attributes allow you to invert your picture's image.

N O T E   Although not commonly used this way, picture objects can be used as buttons. When you code for the clicked event, picture objects behave identically to buttons except they don't give the appearance of being pressed down. Usually, if you want to press on a picture, you use a picture button as opposed to a picture object. ▣

Scroll Bars   Scroll bar controls can be placed on your window as well. Often these controls are not necessary, since you can specify that your window (and many window controls) are to contain scroll bars. However, sometimes a scroll bar will be necessary to indicate progress or placement through some process.

CAUTION

Unlike the scroll bars that you place on your window and controls, scroll bar controls themselves are a little harder to use. You have to control how your scroll bar looks at all times. If a user clicks on your scroll bar control, nothing will happen until you code for the scroll bar clicked event.

Properties of scroll bars not discussed before are:

Max Position	Specifies the value of the Position attribute when the scroll box is at the right edge (horizontal) or bottom edge (vertical) of the control.
Min Position	Specifies the value of the Position attribute when the scroll box is at the left edge (horizontal) or top edge (vertical) of the control.
Position	A value between MinPosition and MaxPosition specifying the position of the scroll box when the window is opened.
Standard Height/Width	If standard measurements are used, PowerBuilder uses the standard window height (for horizontal scroll bars) or width (for vertical scroll bars).

Part

I

Ch

4

FIG. 4.45

The Scroll Bar property sheet allows you to specify how your measurements will be used in the scroll bar.

Drawing Controls Drawing controls for windows include ovals, lines, rectangles, and round rectangles. These drawing controls have few properties compared to other controls. Some properties, as seen in figure 4.46, include:

Line Style	Line Style is the thickness of the line used in the drawing control.
Line Color	Line Color is the color of the line in the drawing control.
Fill Pattern	Fill Pattern is the pattern used to fill in the control.
Fill Color	Fill Color is the color used to fill in the control.
Corner Width/Height	Corner Width and Height are used to specify the "roundness" of a round rectangle. A small width and height make the round rectangle look squarish. A large width and height make the round rectangle look circular.

FIG. 4.46
Drawing objects, like a round rectangle, have different attributes than other controls.

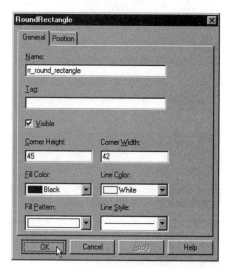

OLE Control OLE (Object Linking and Embedding) controls allow you to actually place one program inside another. In the example in figure 4.30, a Microsoft Excel spreadsheet was placed inside my PowerBuilder window. This is not that difficult to accomplish, and can add a lot of versatility to your PowerBuilder program.

When you first click on the OLE icon, PowerBuilder will ask you what OLE-compliant program you want to use. (As you can see in figure 4.47, I picked Microsoft Excel.)

Then you merely click where you want the OLE link to appear, and a resizable OLE link will be placed where you click your mouse.

The properties of an OLE control, as seen in figure 4.48, are as follows:

Contents	Contents allow you to specify the contents of your OLE link. Valid values are Any, Embedded, and Linked.

Display Type Display Type governs how your OLE control appears in your application. You can either display your OLE with contents or as an icon.

Link Update Your window control can be updated automatically or manually through PowerScript.

Activation You can activate the OLE program by using a double-click, when the OLE control gets focus, or manually through PowerScript.

FIG. 4.47
Immediately after clicking OLE, PowerBuilder will prompt you for your OLE-compliant application.

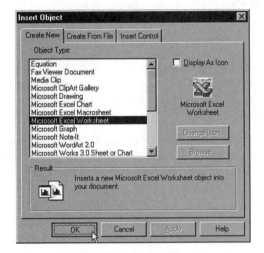

FIG. 4.48
OLEs are easy to set up and configure using the OLE property sheet.

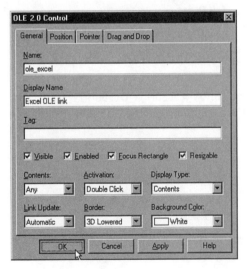

 DataWindow DataWindows are PowerBuilder's answer to data entry screens. DataWindows are very handy to use when trying to tie your application to a database, and are integral to

Part

I

Ch

4

development in PowerBuilder. Also, DataWindows have several advanced editing features. DataWindows are discussed at length in the chapters listed in Part III, "Using DataWindows."

N O T E Usually you won't use single-line edits, multi-line edits, edit masks, listboxes, drop-down listboxes, checkboxes, radio buttons, or group boxes in a window. Instead, you'll find it easier to use a DataWindow with these type of controls and attach the DataWindow to your window through a DataWindow control. Database fields can then be directly linked to your window through the DataWindow control. You'll find out how to use DataWindows and these controls in Part III, "Using DataWindows." ■

Tab Order

You can use the keyboard instead of the mouse. To move between controls, the user must press the Tab key. However, the tab order of the window controls defaults to the order in which those controls were added.

To change the tab order in a window, open Design and choose Tab Order (see fig. 4.49), which displays the tab order of each control, incremented by 10. To change the tab order, simply renumber your controls. Then choose Design, Tab Order again to turn off the tab order.

N O T E When you pull up the tab order, PowerBuilder automatically renumbers the tabs by 10 for you. For example, assume that when you pull up tab orders, you have the following buttons with the following tab orders:

Button	Tab Order
BUTTON_1	10
BUTTON_2	30
BUTTON_3	20

With this tab order, you go from BUTTON_A to BUTTON_C to BUTTON_B. If you want to change the order to BUTTON_A, BUTTON_B, and BUTTON_C, change the BUTTON_B tab order to 15. Now you have the following tab orders:

Button	Tab Order
BUTTON_1	10
BUTTON_2	15
BUTTON_3	20

Now your buttons are numbered 10, 20, and 15. If you leave tab order and get back in, you'll see that PowerBuilder renumbered the buttons by 10 so you'll have the following tab order:

Button	Tab Order
BUTTON_1	10
BUTTON_2	20
BUTTON_3	30

As you can see, PowerBuilder keeps the tab orders numbered for you with enough space between numbers so you can easily reorder your tabs. ■

FIG. 4.49
By choosing Design, Tab Order, you can change the order when tabbing through your window.

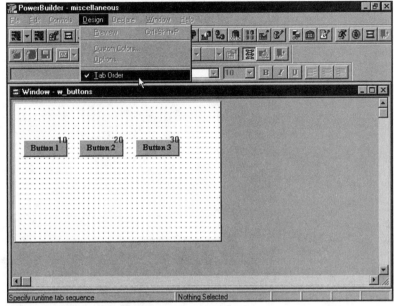

Starting a Data Entry Window

Now, you are going to add another window, but you need to define a prototype for the data entry windows. This prototype is called an ancestor. First, create a new window as you did in chapter 1. Make the window type main and the window color silver, as shown in figure 4.50. Then add a tab control using the Tab Control icon.

▶ **See** "Adding an About Window," **p. 428**
▶ **See** "Associating DataWindow Controls with a DataWindow Object," **p. 303**

N O T E Eventually, each tab page of your tab control will contain a DataWindow. Most data entry DataWindows take up the whole window, so expand your tab control to cover almost the entire window. For a good effect, leave a little room around the edges as shown in figure 4.51. This gives your tab control a three-dimensional look. ■

Now all other windows that use this data entry window ancestor will contain a tab control.

Now save this window in the ancestor.pbl, as shown in figure 4.52. (I called it w_tab_ancestor.) Because this window is a prototype for other windows, save it as w_tab_ancestor in the ancestor.pbl by clicking ancestor.pbl under Application Libraries.

FIG. 4.50
When defining a window ancestor, make sure that all colors, fonts, etc., are how you wish them to appear in the descendant.

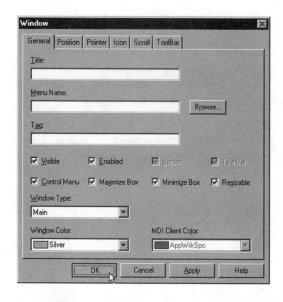

FIG. 4.51
Make sure your tab pages of your tab control can eventually contain a data entry DataWindow.

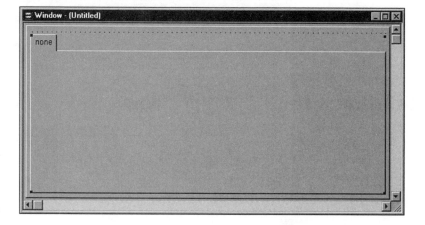

FIG. 4.52
This window will now be a prototype for other data entry windows.

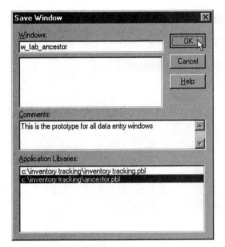

Implementing Window Inheritance

Inheritance is the way we use our prototypes in PowerBuilder. By using inheritance, the child object takes all the controls, PowerScripts, and properties from the ancestor object. Any further changes to the ancestor object are automatically made in the child object. The child object can then add to or modify what it has inherited. Windows and menus can be inherited.

N O T E   Only windows, menus, and user objects can be inherited. You can find more about menus in chapter 5, and more about user objects in Part V: "User Objects and Object-Oriented Development." ■

To inherit a window, click the Window icon on the PowerBar. This pulls up the Select Window dialog box. However, instead of clicking New as before, click Inherit, as shown in figure 4.53.

The Inherit From Window dialog box appears, as seen in figure 4.54. Click the ancestor.pbl, choose w_tab_ancestor, and click OK. (Ancestor.pbl and w_tab_ancestor may be selected already by PowerBuilder.)

Notice that this pulls up a window that looks exactly like the w_tab_ancestor window, as seen in figure 4.55. This is because the new window has been inherited from w_tab_ancestor.

You now have the opportunity to customize your window. In w_item, we can use tab pages to allow data entry for the Item, Warehouse, and Supplier tables. In figure 4.56, you can see this customization by added tab pages to the tab control and changing the text on the tab control as was discussed earlier in this chapter.

Part
I

Ch
4

FIG. 4.53

To inherit from a window, pull up the Select Window dialog box and click on Inherit.

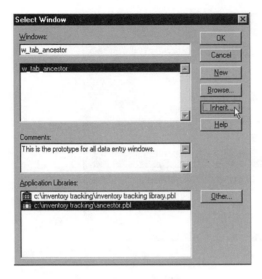

FIG. 4.54

Use the Inherit From Window dialog box to tell PowerBuilder what window you want to inherit from.

FIG. 4.55

When you first start developing a child window, it is identical to its ancestor.

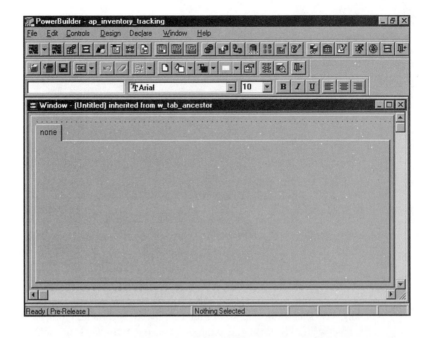

FIG. 4.56

A descendant window can be customized to perform its own functionality, yet still use constructs developed in the ancestor window.

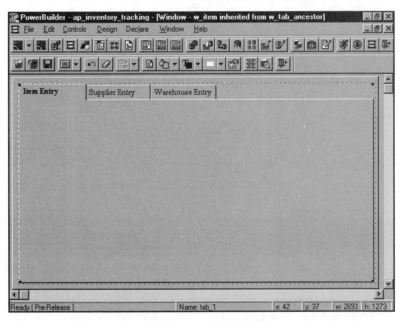

Now pull up the window property sheet for your new window, as seen in figure 4.57, by double-clicking the window you are defining (but not the tab control). Because you need to enter items in an inventory system, you can name this the Item Entry window. You can also attach m_ancestor to the window until you make other menus.

FIG. 4.57

Using the Window Style dialog box, you differentiate it from other "children."

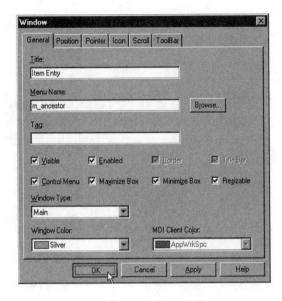

Finally, save this window as w_item in the Inventory Tracking.pbl, as seen in figure 4.58. (Because w_item is not an ancestor, don't save it in the ancestor.pbl.)

FIG. 4.58

Now save your window as w_item in the Inventory Tracking.pbl.

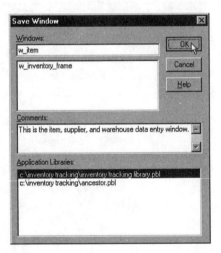

N O T E Now repeat the steps you used to create w_item to create your other windows. You will also need a w_invoice window created with an Invoice entry and Customer entry tabs.

Right now, the w_item and w_invoice windows will be identical except for different tab pages. Eventually, we will add different menus to these windows and then attach different DataWindow objects to each tab page. ■

Opening a Window Sheet

This chapter discussed window frames and sheets, and you learned how to open a window frame. To open a sheet within a window, you use the OpenSheet command, typically in the open event of the frame window, as shown in figure 4.59. To get to the open event, open the window and click the Script icon. (As an added bonus, the MicroHelp has been set to welcome the user to your system.)

FIG. 4.59

As you code the open event for w_inventory_frame, OpenSheet is used to open a window sheet inside the frame window, and SetMicroHelp sets the MicroHelp.

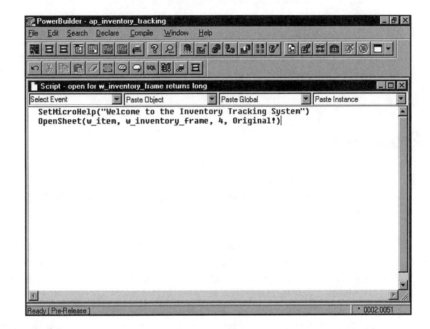

Part

I

Ch

4

N O T E The OpenSheet function uses the following syntax:

OpenSheet(sheet,{window_name},frame,{position{, arrangeopen}})

OpenSheet opens a sheet window within a frame.

- sheet is the window name of the sheet.
- window_name (optional) is a string containing the name of the window type you want opened. For our purposes, window_name is not needed.
- frame is the window name of the MDI frame.
- position is the menu item in which all open sheets are displayed. You can read more about this item in chapter 5, "Designing Menus."
- arrangeopen is a PowerBuilder enumerated data type that tells you how you want the sheet opened. Valid values are:

    Cascaded! (default). Cascade the sheet when it is opened.

    Layered!. Layer the sheet when it is opened.

continues

continued

Original!. Open the sheet in its original size and cascade it.

Note the exclamation points on the arrangeopen parameter. All PowerBuilder enumerated data types end in an exclamation point. ▨

▶ **See** "Listing Open MDI Sheets," **p. 182**

N O T E The SetMicroHelp function uses the following syntax:

MDIFrame.SetMicroHelp(helpstring)

SetMicroHelp sets the MicroHelp on an MDI frame window. MDIFrame is the name of the frame containing the MicroHelp. If this command is done within an MDI frame window event (as this one was), MDIFrame is not needed and is assumed to be the MDIFrame containing the event. helpstring is the string you want displayed in the MicroHelp. ▨

From Here...

In this chapter, you've seen different types of windows and different types of window controls. You have learned about inheritance and how an MDI application can look. The importance of windows can't be understated in a PowerBuilder application. Windows are the cornerstone of an application and how the application interfaces with the end user.

N O T E Once more, you can run your application. With a full-screen MDI frame and an open sheet inside it, you can see the development toward a professional Windows application (see fig. 4.60). Have you noticed how you've added so easily onto existing work? This is one aspect of PowerBuilder's easy iterative design. ▨

Further information on windows and window controls can be found in the following chapters:

- Chapter 1, "Introducing PowerBuilder," introduces windows and the window painter. It's a must-read for the beginning PowerBuilder developer.

- Chapter 5, "Designing Menus," shows how to define menus for your window and how to associate a menu with a window.

- Chapter 7, "Programming in PowerScript," discusses window events and how to program for windows and controls. You also see how inheritance affects programming for windows.

- Chapter 9, "Creating DataWindows," teaches you how to create a DataWindow object to place on your tab pages inside w_item and w_invoice.

FIG. 4.60

With a full-screen MDI frame and a sheet inside the frame, it's looking a lot more like a professional Windows application.

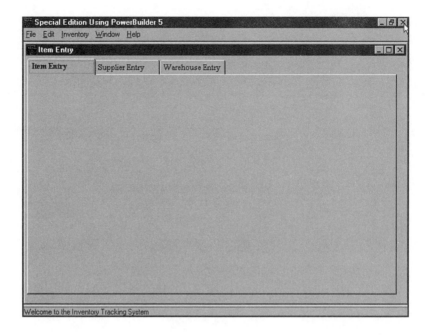

Designing Menus

by Charles A. Wood

Menus are an important part of any Windows application. Menus issue commands, trigger events, and control the flow of an application.

You've already been exposed to menus somewhat when m_ancestor was created in chapter 1. Now you can increase your understanding of menus in this chapter. ∎

Understand menu design.

Some menu design is helpful before actually starting to develop a menu in PowerBuilder. This chapter shows you how to lay out a menu before beginning menu development.

Use the menu painter to develop a menu.

The menu painter in PowerBuilder is a powerful tool for developing menus. This chapter will show you how to use the menu painter.

Use inheritance to build a menu.

As with windows, inheritance can greatly reduce the amount of code that a system needs for menus. This chapter shows you how to inherit a menu and the benefits of menu inheritance.

Use toolbars with a window.

In PowerBuilder applications, toolbars are linked with the menu. This chapter shows you how to build a toolbar from menu elements.

Associate a menu with a window.

Every main, pop-up, or MDI window can have a menu associated with it. This chapter shows you how to attach a particular menu to a particular window.

Planning Your Menu

Before you design your menu, it's important to have an idea of what you want your menus to look like. Using a spreadsheet, a word processing table, or a piece of paper, sketch what you want contained in all your menus. It may be helpful to look at other Windows applications to see what they have in their menus.

To keep your menus consistent, develop one menu with all of your menu options instead of designing several different menus. (As you'll soon see, it's also a lot easier to maintain and code if you use a consistent layout.) This master menu (called m_ancestor) will be used as a prototype for other menus. The menu design you'll be using for the Inventory Tracking system is shown in table 5.1.

Table 5.1 Menu Prototype (m_ancestor) for Inventory Tracking System

File	Edit	Inventory	Window	Help
New	Undo	Item Entry...	Tile	Table of Contents...
-	-	Invoice Entry...	Cascade	Search...
Print	Cut		Layer	-
Print Setup...	Copy		Arrange Icons	Introduction...
-	Paste		-	-
Close	-		Toolbars...	About...
Exit	Insert		[Top]	
	Delete		[Bottom]	
			[Left]	
			[Right]	
			[-]	
			[Hide Toolbar]	
			[-]	
			[Show Text]	
			-	
			{Open Sheets}	

You'll notice in the menu that there are several dividing lines (-) within menu bar options. Most Windows menus use these to group related menu bar options. Also notice the ellipsis (...) at the end of several menu bar options. Added by the developer, this tells the user that another screen or menu will pop up if this option is chosen. The {Open Sheets} entry under Window is where you list all open sheets within the MDI frame. Finally, brackets ([ ]) indicate that these options are part of a cascading menu that pops up when the menu bar option above them is chosen.

Developing Your Menu Using the Menu Painter

In Chapter 1, you started your ancestor menu, which serves as the prototype for all menus in the Inventory Tracking system. To enhance what was already begun in the m_ancestor menu, click on the Menu icon to pull up the Select Menu dialog box, shown in figure 5.1. Click ancestor.pbl, and then click m_ancestor. Finally, click OK to pull up the menu painter.

FIG. 5.1
Use the Select Menu dialog box as the first step toward creating new menus or editing existing menus.

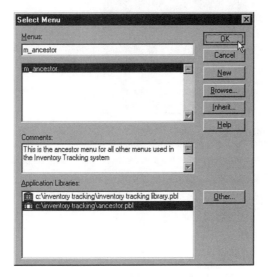

In the first chapter, only Save, Close, and Exit were added to the menu. Now you will make a complete menu for your Inventory Tracking system, which will serve as a prototype for all other menus in the Inventory Tracking system.

Part
I

Ch
5

Adding Options

As you saw by the design in table 5.1, you need to add several items to your menu structure. PowerBuilder gives you the following three tools to do that:

Icon	Name	Description
Insert	Insert	Insert a new menu option between two other menu options.
Move	Move	Move an option or menu bar item to another position.
Delete	Delete	Delete menu bar items and menu options.

You can add to the rest of your menu by using these icons or using the Enter key to add menu options to the bottom of the list. When you're done with File, continue with Edit, Inventory, and so on, until the rest of the menu items are added.

To add the separator lines, use a hyphen (-) as the option name. Several separators will cause PowerBuilder to display the Invalid Menu Item Name dialog box, as seen in figure 5.2. This is telling you that you have two menu items (but in this case, menu separators) with the same name, and that PowerBuilder is automatically renaming one of them. Click OK to continue.

FIG. 5.2
Often, the Invalid Menu Item Name dialog box appears when you add separators to a menu.

NOTE   Placing an ampersand (&) before a menu bar item allows the user to access that menu bar item with Alt + the letter after the ampersand. (This is called a hot key or shortcut key.)

An ampersand before an option under a menu bar item allows the end user to press the letter after the ampersand to execute that option if the menu bar item is pulled down. (This is called an accelerator.) ■

Using General Properties

Unlike other objects in PowerBuilder, the menu property sheet is always displayed. General properties that you can specify, as seen in figure 5.3, include the following:

Menu Item Name   The menu item name is how you access the individual menu items later in your application. It is automatically built when you define your individual menu items unless Lock Name is checked.

Lock Name   Lock Name indicates if the name can change. After a newly created menu item loses focus for the first time, Lock Name is automatically checked.

MDI Microhelp   MDI Microhelp is the text that displays in Microhelp when your menu item (or corresponding toolbar item, discussed later in this chapter) is defined.

Tag   The tag is a value that the developer can place on this menu item for identification. Although it doesn't affect PowerBuilder, tags can be used internally by the developer.

CAUTION
Often, tags are used by frameworks packages. If you use a frameworks package, using tags may interfere with the execution of the framework or the framework may overwrite any tag you use.

FIG. 5.3

General properties can
be seen when you open
the menu painter.

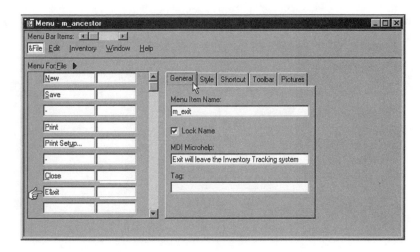

Using Shortcut Keys

To make your application easier to use, PowerBuilder gives you the ability to assign a shortcut
key to a menu option. As shown in figure 5.4, in the Shortcut tab of the menu properties you
can assign any key combination using the Alt, Ctrl, and Shift keys (and any letter) to execute
a menu option. In figure 5.4, Alt+X executes the Exit menu option.

FIG. 5.4

Alt+X executes the Exit
menu option.

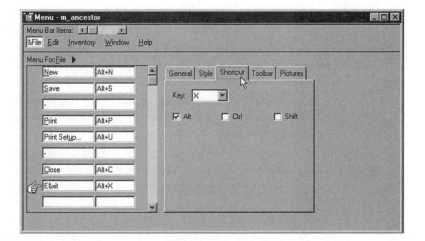

Part

I

Ch

5

You can even use function keys, Ins, and Del to act as shortcut keys. In figure 5.5, Alt+Ins
executes the Insert option; Alt+Del executes the Delete option.

Using shortcut keys is a must for any quality program. Not only do they allow the user to avoid
using a mouse when desired, they can also be much faster—the user can use a quick key combination instead of going through the menu.

FIG. 5.5
You can also use the function keys, Ins, and Del to act as shortcut keys.

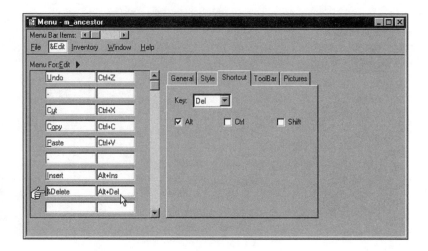

CAUTION

Be sure not to mask over one of your menu bar items or one shortcut key with another shortcut key. For example, because Alt+I pulls down the Inventory menu bar, assigning another Alt+I to an option as a shortcut key disables the quick keyboard access to your menu bar. It's also very confusing to the end user.

N O T E Most developers allow you to run their Windows applications without ever using a mouse. At first, this may seem ridiculous to some of you. ("You can't run Windows without a mouse, can you?") Actually, you can! There are several reasons for allowing this:

- Some end users actually prefer using a mouse as little as possible, especially those that learned DOS pretty well.

- Sometimes using a mouse is inconvenient or annoying. This is particularly the case with some laptops. A mouse or trackball can also become difficult or impossible to use if dust and dirt get into the tracking mechanism of the mouse.

- In a desire to save space, some laptops have excluded a mouse or have substituted a pointing device (such as a trackball, trackpoint, or trackpad) that mouse users may not like. Also, the placement of many trackballs sometimes makes them almost painful to use!

- On some laptop LCD (Liquid Crystal Display) screens, a mouse pointer is easy to lose (the gray-scale, lower-quality displays of some laptops cause users to lose track of the mouse pointer). An alternative way of moving around would be useful.

- It is a good idea to have an alternate way of conveying information, especially for exiting an application. This comes in handy if your mouse is acting up.

Because of this, try to make your application completely usable with or without the mouse. Always assign Alt keys to your menu items and command buttons, and make sure the tab order of your fields makes sense. You'll be happier with fewer complaints, and your end users will admire your talents even more than before! ▪

N O T E So what's the difference between a shortcut key and an accelerator? A shortcut key allows the user to execute the menu function immediately without accessing the menu at all (for example, press F1 for help, or Alt+X for exit). To access the menu bar using the keyboard, you always use a shortcut key (for example, Alt+F opens the File menu bar item).

An accelerator key is implemented when the user is in the menu list already. Pressing a key will highlight or execute the option with that accelerator key. For instance, when you have the File menu bar pulled down, pressing C will execute the Close function. ▪

Using Cascading Menus

Sometimes, you want your menu options to pull down other menus. These pull-down menus are called cascading menus. To form a cascading menu, click the option you want to cascade and then click the Next Level icon on the painter bar. This brings up a new menu list in which you enter your menu choices. Also, notice that the Menu For: statement at the top of the painter (where the mouse is pointing in figure 5.6) shows the parent menu item.

FIG. 5.6
You can tell how far a menu cascades by the Menu For: statement at the top of the menu items.

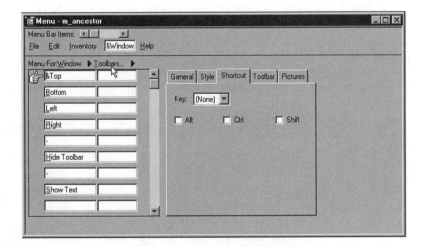

By clicking the Prior Level icon, you return to the first drop-down level under your menu bar. As seen in figure 5.7 (where the mouse is pointing), Toolbars has a right arrow displayed right next to it. This denotes that there is a cascading menu under Toolbars.

Part
I

Ch
5

FIG. 5.7

Returning to Toolbars from the cascaded menu, you see the right arrow right next to Toolbars, denoting that it has a cascading menu beneath it.

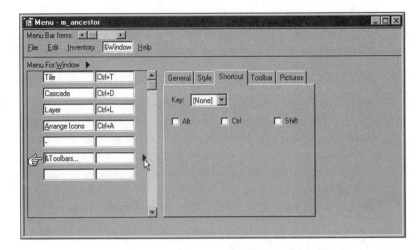

 TIP You can add a shortcut key before defining a menu item as a cascading menu, but the key will not function. You cannot define it as cascading and then add a shortcut key.

Previewing Your Menu

You can preview your menu while you're working on it or after you're finished by clicking Design, Preview (see fig. 5.8). You can check out your work, as seen in figure 5.9.

FIG. 5.8

To preview your menu, click on Design Preview, or press Ctrl+W.

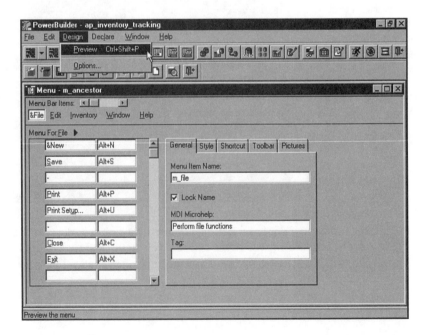

FIG. 5.9

A cascading menu appears in the menu preview.

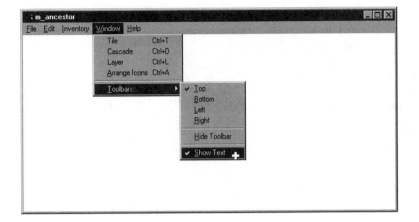

 T I P The MicroHelp and shortcut keys are not implemented in a preview. They will show when the program is run.

Implementing Menu Inheritance and Toolbars

▶ **See** "Implementing Window Inheritance," **p. 157**

Like windows, menus can be inherited from other menus and changed somewhat. This is especially useful for menus because every menu in a system is usually similar to every other menu in the system. Having one parent menu allows the developer to go to just one place to find the code for all the menus.

Using Toolbars and Inheritance

Menu inheritance and toolbars are discussed together because you will be using a toolbar ancestor menu that inherits from m_ancestor. A toolbar is a set of icons that (usually) appear at the top of your MDI Frame window. In PowerBuilder, these toolbars correspond to menu entries.

Similar to the PowerBuilder environment, an MDI application can have two toolbars—one toolbar for the frame window and one for the sheet window. All menus in the Inventory Tracking system are inherited from m_ancestor. If you use a toolbar with the MDI frame menu, you unnecessarily duplicate your toolbar icons.

Here comes the confusing part. In the inventory tracking system, you really won't use enough toolbar items to justify two toolbars. Because you don't want to duplicate your toolbar icons, two ancestors are implemented: m_ancestor and m_ancestor_toolbar. The frame menu will inherit from m_ancestor; the sheet menus (or system menus) will inherit from m_ancestor_toolbar. Actually, m_ancestor_toolbar is inherited from m_ancestor, thereby making m_ancestor the "grandparent" of the system menus. This is shown graphically in figure 5.10.

FIG. 5.10

The system menus get all the benefits of the m_toolbar_ancestor, as well as the m_ancestor through inheritance.

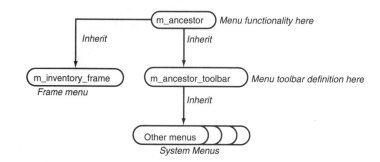

Implementing Inheritance

To inherit a new menu from an existing menu, click on the Menu icon to pull up the Select Menu dialog box, as shown in figure 5.1, and click Inherit.

N O T E You don't need to choose an existing menu in the Select Menu dialog box before clicking on Inherit. The menu you inherit from is chosen from the Inherit From Menu dialog box, shown in figure 5.11. ■

Clicking on the Inherit button pulls up the Inherit From Menu dialog box, shown in figure 5.11. Choose the PBL and the menu you wish to inherit from. When you've made your choice, click OK.

FIG. 5.11

The Inherit From Menu dialog box is used to choose which menu you're inheriting from.

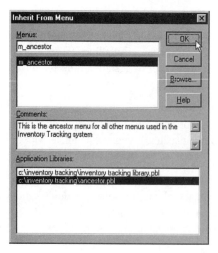

Now you're in the menu painter again. Notice on the title bar that the menu is inherited from m_ancestor. Also notice that this menu seems to be a copy of m_ancestor. Inheritance fills up the new menu with the entries in m_ancestor, but any future changes to m_ancestor will automatically be reflected in this menu.

Making a Toolbar

Now you need to add a toolbar by assigning pictures to each menu item you want displayed on the toolbar. On the menu property sheet, click the Toolbar tab, as seen in figure 5.12.

FIG. 5.12

In the Toolbar tab of the menu property sheet, you can enter information about your toolbar.

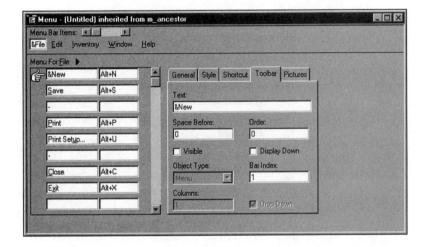

Here you can enter the following information about your toolbar:

Text   Text is the text that appears on your toolbar button for this menu item.

 TIP Make sure you don't use too much text for your menu bar or it won't all fit on the button. Use Microhelp for large text.

Space Before   Space before indicates how much space should appear before this toolbar button on the toolbar.

Order   Order specifies the order of the buttons on the toolbar. If order is not specified, the order of the toolbar buttons will be the same as their order on the menu.

Visible   Visible is checked to indicate that this toolbar picture will be visible.

Display Down   Display Down is checked to indicate that the toolbar button should appear to be pressed down when the toolbar is opened.

Part
I

Ch
5

To choose a picture for your toolbar, you click the Pictures tab, as seen in figure 5.13. You can define two pictures for your toolbar:

Picture Name Picture name is the name of the picture on the toolbar button. It can be a stock picture or an external bitmap.

Down Picture Name Down Picture Name is the name of the picture that displays on the toolbar button when the button is being pressed. If no Down Picture Name is specified, the Picture Name is used.

FIG. 5.13

The Pictures tab of the menu property sheet allows you to define pictures for your toolbar.

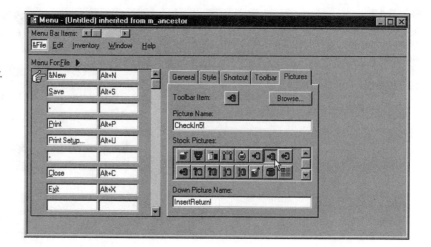

 Similar to the menu bar, you can use an ampersand (&) before a letter on the toolbar to underline the letter that corresponds to the hot key.

 Repeat the process of selecting toolbars for all items that will have an icon. Table 5.2 lists the pictures that were selected for the Inventory Tracking system.

You are now finished with this menu; it will be the ancestor to all system menus. When exiting the menu painter, save this menu as m_ancestor_toolbar, as seen in figure 5.14. Be sure to save it in the ancestor PBL.

FIG. 5.14

You have created the m_ancestor_toolbar—as your second ancestor menu.

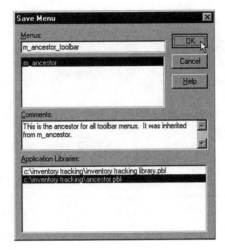

Inheriting Menus

Now that the ancestor menus have been defined, we need to inherit them for the customized menus in the Inventory Tracking system:

- We need to build the frame menu by inheriting from m_ancestor.
- We need to build toolbar menus for all the sheet windows (w_item, w_customer, w_warehouse, w_invoice, and w_supplier).

  ▶ **See** "Implementing Window Inheritance," **p. 157**

N O T E If you have not yet defined all your sheet windows, see "Implementing Window Inheritance" in chapter 4. In this section, you will see how to define w_item. There is also a note at the end of the section asking you to repeat the process for the rest of the sheet windows. ■

Inheriting the Frame Menu Remember that you only wanted one toolbar appearing at the top of the frame window. To do this, each sheet within a frame has a specialized menu with a toolbar, but a frame that contains multiple sheets has a specialized menu without a toolbar. Hence, the menu for the w_inventory_frame window inherits from m_ancestor; the system menus on each sheet inherit from m_toolbar_ancestor.

Click the Menu icon to create a new menu, and click Inherit to open the Inherit From Menu dialog box. Choose the ancestor.pbl and m_ancestor, and click OK (refer to fig. 5.11). Now you are in the menu painter with a new menu inherited from m_ancestor, as shown in figure 5.15.

The frame menu will be active only when no sheets with menus are open. You aren't allowed to delete ancestor members from your inherited menu. To suppress and hide options that make no sense from the frame, deselect the Enabled and Visible options, as shown in figure 5.15.

Part
I

Ch
5

FIG. 5.15

Disabling and making invisible are good ways to customize your inherited menu.

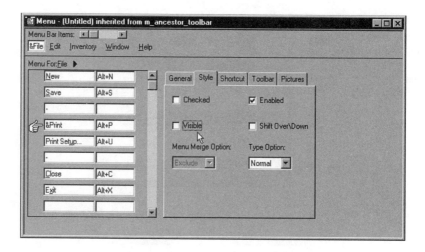

For the new inventory frame, you only need Close and Exit (under File). Because you can't cut, copy, or paste anything from here, you can't inherit or delete from here, and you can't undo anything from here, the entire Edit menu bar selection has been disabled and made invisible. Because no sheet windows are open, there is no need for sheet window manipulation, so the entire Window menu bar selection has been disabled and made invisible. The rest of the options will stay. After you're done disabling options you don't want, save this menu as m_inventory_frame (in the inventory.pbl).

Inheriting the Sheet Menus

For each sheet, the entire menu will stay except for the menu option, which calls up the sheet. (How can you pull up your sheet if it already has been pulled up?) You will need to make the following changes:

- In w_item's case, w_item's menu will be identical to m_toolbar_ancestor, except that there will be no Ite&m Entry option under Inventory. Inherit m_toolbar_ancestor, disable Ite&m Entry and make it invisible, as seen in figure 5.15. Save it out as m_item.

- Inherit m_toolbar_ancestor, disable In&voice Entry, and save it out as m_invoice.

Unlike previous inheritance, you must also make the toolbar item invisible if you want to avoid displaying a toolbar icon for your disabled menu option. To disable a toolbar icon, click the Toolbar tab of the menu property sheet. Deselect visible, as seen in figure 5.16, for any menu items that are disabled (Ite&m Entry on m_item, In&voice entry on m_invoice, etc.).

FIG. 5.16

You must make a toolbar button invisible to avoid displaying it even if you have already disabled the menu item.

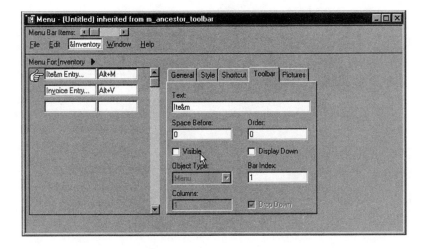

Table 5.2 lists the attributes for the m_ancestor and m_ancestor_toolbar menus.

N O T E For those of you following along on your computer, table 5.2 lists all menu bar items and attributes in the Inventory Tracking system. ▪

Table 5.2   Inventory Tracking Menu Bar Items and Attributes

Menu Bar Item	Option Name	Menu Item Name	Picture*	Toolbar Text*	Shortcut Key
&File		m_file			Alt+F
	&New**	m_new	CheckIn!	&New	Alt+N
	&Save	m_save	Custom008!	&Save	Alt+S
	-	m_-			
	&Print	m_print	Print!	&Print	Alt+P
	Print Set&up	m_printsetup	Custom074!	Print Set&up	Alt+U
	-	m_-1			
	&Close	m_close	Custom041!	&Close	Alt+C
	E&xit	m_exit	Exit!	E&xit	Alt+X
&Edit		m_edit			Alt+E
	&Undo	m_undo			Ctrl+Z
	-	m_-2			
	&Cut	m_cut			Ctrl+X
	C&opy	m_copy			Ctrl+C
	&Paste	m_paste			Ctrl+V
	-	m_-3			
	&Insert	m_insert	Insert!	&INSert	Alt+Ins
	&Delete	m_delete	Clear!	&DELete	Alt+Del

continues

Table 5.2 Continued

Menu Bar Item	Option Name	Menu Item Name	Picture	Toolbar Text	Shortcut Key
&Inventory			m_inventory UserObject!		Alt+I
	Ite&m Entry	m_itementry		Ite&m	Alt+M
	In&voice Entry	m_invoiceentry	ScriptYes!	In&voice	Alt+V
&Window		m_window			Alt+W
	&Tile	m_tile			Ctrl+T
	&Cascade	m_cascade			Ctrl+D
	&Layer	m_layer			Ctrl+L
	&Arrange Icons	m_arrangeicons			Ctrl+A
	-	m_-5			
	&Toolbars...	m_toolbars			Alt+T
	&Top	m_top			
	&Bottom	m_bottom			
	&Left	m_left			
	&Right	m_right			
	-	m_-4			
	&Hide Toolbar	m_hidetoolbar			
	-	m_-6			
	&Show Text	m_showtext			
&Help		m_help			Alt+H
	&Table of Contents	m_tableofcontents		Help!	
Help (F1)					
	&Search...	m_search			Shift+F1
	-	m_-7			
	&Introduction	m_introduction			Ctrl+I
	-	m_-8			
	&About	m_about			Alt+A

Associating a Menu with a Window

You've completed the first step of forming your menus; now you need to attach them to your windows. This way, every time you switch sheets, the menu and toolbar will automatically switch.

 TIP Only Main, Pop-up, and MDI window types are allowed to have a menu associated with them.

▶ **See** "Defining Window Types," **p. 118**

Attaching Your Menu to a Window

To attach a menu to a window, open the window (w_inventory_frame) in the window painter. Double-click on the window; the window property sheet appears. Click Browse. The

Select menu dialog box opens, as seen in figure 5.17. Attach the inventory frame menu (m_inventory_frame) to the inventory frame window (w_inventory_frame). After you choose the appropriate menu, save your choices and exit the window painter. Repeat this process for the item menu (m_item) and the item window (w_item) and for the invoice menu (m_invoice) and the invoice window (w_invoice).

FIG. 5.17

You can select which menu belongs to your window with the Select Menu dialog box.

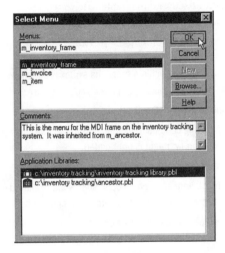

Running Your Application with a Toolbar

Click the Run icon on the PowerBar to run your application. Look at the improvements you made. In figure 5.18, you can see the Item Entry dialog box activate with a set of toolbar icons at the top of the frame.

Part

I

Ch

5

FIG. 5.18

When running your program, the toolbar(s) display at the top of the frame window.

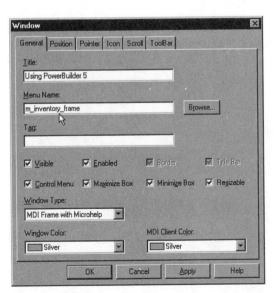

Listing Open MDI Sheets

In figure 5.19, notice that all your open sheet windows are listed. (In this case, Item Entry is currently the only open sheet.) With an MDI application, PowerBuilder appends the name of the open sheets to the next-to-last menu item in the menu bar. A check mark appears next to the current active sheet. You can control which menu option the open sheets appear under by using the OpenSheet command (discussed in chapter 3).

▶ **See** "Using the Windows Property Sheet," **p. 116**

▶ **See** "Enumerated Data Types Quick Reference," **p. 723**

N O T E   OpenSheet opens a sheet window within a frame. Its syntax is as follows:

```
OpenSheet(sheet {, window_name}, frame,{position{, arrangeopen}})
```

- *sheet* is the window name of the sheet.
- *windowname* is a string containing the name of the window type you want opened. For our purposes, window_name is not needed.
- *frame* is the window name of the MDI frame.
- *position* is the menu item in which all open sheets are displayed. If omitted, PowerBuilder lists open sheets in the next-to-last menu bar item.
- *arrangeopen* is a PowerBuilder enumerated data type that tells the way you want the sheet opened. Valid values are as follows:

  Cascaded! Cascade the sheet when it is opened.

  Layered! Layer the sheet when it is opened.

  Original! Open the sheet in its original size and cascade it

Note the exclamations on the arrangeopen parameter. All PowerBuilder enumerated data types end in an exclamation point.   ■

Finally, notice in figure 5.20, that with all the sheets closed, the menu is scaled down reflecting the change from m_item to m_inventory_frame. Notice also that the toolbar disappears, since m_inventory_frame was inherited from m_ancestor rather than m_ancestor_toolbar, and therefore does not have any toolbar defined.

FIG. 5.19
Using the OpenSheet command, you can control where the open sheet windows are displayed.

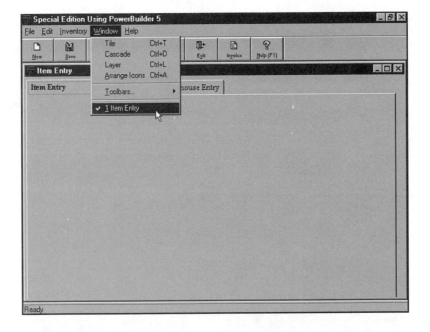

FIG. 5.20
The menu is scaled down now, and the toolbar disappears.

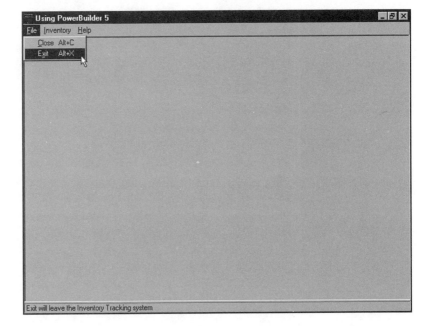

Part

I

Ch

5

From Here...

From this chapter, you should have learned how to create, edit, and display menus. You also examined menu inheritance and toolbars. If you need to review what was already discussed, or you want to discuss menus further, refer to the following chapters:

- Chapter 1, "Introducing PowerBuilder," is a must for beginners and introduces menus and menu programming.

- Chapter 6, "Using Events, Functions, and the PowerScript Language," teaches you how to implement PowerScript within your events. Menu programming is covered extensively.

Using PowerScript

Using Events, Functions, and the PowerScript Language

by Charles A. Wood

As the programming language of PowerBuilder, PowerScript controls the flow of a program, updates databases, displays information and error messages, and ends the program.

It's important that the PowerBuilder developer have a good working knowledge of PowerScript. ∎

Have a complete understanding of events.

Event programming is vital to Windows development. This chapter will give you a complete understanding of events as they relate to PowerBuilder.

Understand the PowerScript language.

The PowerScript language supports structures, objects, controls, and variable scope. This chapter will explain the PowerScript language and how to use it.

Use the PowerBuilder script painter.

The script painter has been enhanced in PowerBuilder 5 to include color coding, multiple level undos, and automatic indentation. The PowerScript painter is a great tool to use when coding PowerScript. This chapter will show you how to become proficient with the PowerScript painter.

Understanding Events

Event programming is a relatively new concept in software development. Traditional programming is sequential in nature—every function can be traced to a previous statement. However, in the real world, most business functions are event-driven instead of sequential.

Event-driven functions are functions that don't follow a logical sequence. Rather, certain events cause the functions to be executed. (For example, you order new supplies when your inventory is low, you play solitaire when you double-click the solitaire icon, and so on.) Consequently, software development was difficult because programmers tried to map the event-driven world onto their sequential programs.

PowerBuilder codes for events. For example, if you click an icon, certain PowerScript in an event is executed. If a window loses focus (a new window pops up), other PowerScript in another event is executed. Event programming is better suited to the way an end user will use your application. Event programming is one of the many strengths of PowerBuilder.

Entering the PowerBuilder Script Painter

A PowerBuilder object is an entity you develop usually by using the PowerBar. Windows, menus, DataWindows, and applications are all examples of objects.

PowerBuilder controls are constructs that attach to objects. Command buttons, pictures, and DataWindows are all examples of controls.

▶ **See** "Associating DataWindow Controls with a DataWindow Object," **p. 303**

N O T E There is a difference between DataWindow objects and DataWindow controls. It is discussed in chapter 9, "Creating DataWindows." ▉

Each control and each object can have PowerScript (also called script). To code script for an object or control, follow these steps:

1. Choose the control that needs PowerScript in its events. In this case, start with the w_tab_ancestor window.

2. Click the Window icon, click ancestor.pbl, and pull up w_tab_ancestor.

3. Now click the Script icon to pull up the script painter, as shown in figure 6.1.

4. Now you can type any PowerScript commands you want for the open event of w_tab_ancestor.

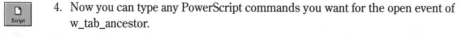

N O T E If an object or control has no script written for it yet, a "blank paper" script icon appears on the painter bar. If a script has been written for an object or control, a "written page" script icon appears on the painter bar. ▉

FIG. 6.1

The script painter appears every time you click the Script icon.

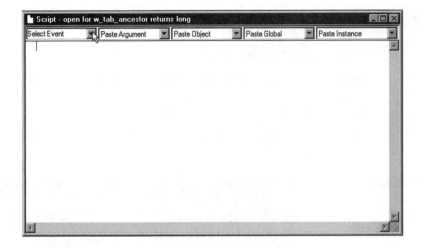

Using the Event List Box

Each object and control has many different events for which you can code. By clicking Select Event in the upper left corner of the painter window (see fig. 6.2), you see the event list box. Using the event list box, you select which event you want to code for that window (open, close, activate, and so on).

Whenever the event you code for is triggered, the script you've written for that event is executed. This is vastly different from traditional programming techniques, in which code always has to be written to check for events as well as react to the event.

FIG. 6.2

The script painter automatically opens for the first time in the open event.

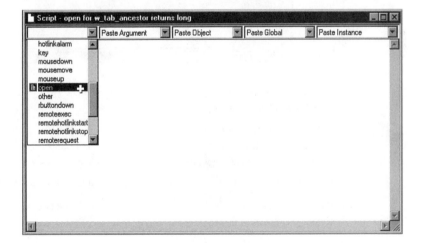

Part

II

Ch

6

Implementing User-Defined Events

▶ **See** "Using Event Arguments," **p. 234**

▶ **See** "Posting Functions and Events," **p. 438**

PowerBuilder does an excellent job predetermining what events you'll need to code for. However, you may need to define your own events if a special event is needed that PowerBuilder has not provided for. To define your own events, follow these steps:

1. On the menu bar, click Declare, User Events, as shown in figure 6.3. The Events dialog box appears.

FIG. 6.3
To declare a user event, open Declare and choose User Events.

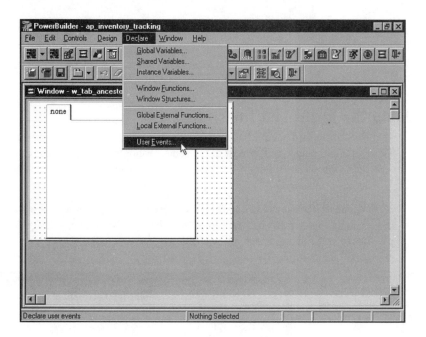

2. Enter a unique event name. As you can see in figure 6.4, three events were added to your normal event list: print, save, and retrieve.

3. Click the Args button for each event. This will display the Event Declaration dialog box. We will discuss how to use arguments with events in chapter 7, but for now, you probably want to change the return value of your event to (None), as seen in figure 6.5.

4. After you're done adding events, click OK to save it and return to your painter.

Now when the event list box displays in the painter, you can see the new events are added alphabetically, as shown in figure 6.6.

FIG. 6.4
In the Events dialog box, you can add customized events.

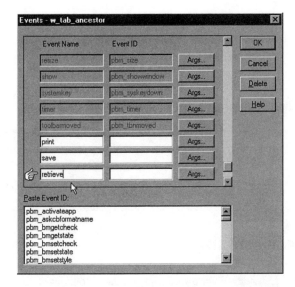

FIG. 6.5
You can define arguments and return values to your events using the Event Declaration box.

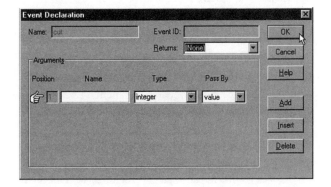

FIG. 6.6
Any new events are listed alphabetically in the event list box.

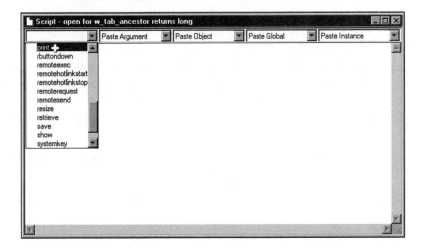

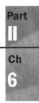

N O T E   In earlier PowerBuilder versions, you had to declare an event id for each user event. With version 5, you no longer need to. In fact, declaring an event id will force a default set of return datatypes and arguments. ▣

Discussing the PowerScript Language

You saw some examples of the PowerScript when you opened w_inventory_frame and w_item. There's a lot more to PowerScript, however—it is a fully functional language.

 T I P   In this example, user events are added to the window; you can add them to any window or window control by using this method.

PowerScript Fundamentals

It seems that every computer language treats comments, white space, and multi-line statements differently. Before coding PowerScript, you need to know some fundamental information about the language that will resolve these issues.

Comments   Comments are an important part of any development. Comments are not executed or compiled, but serve as notes to future developers about what a script is doing, who wrote a script, why a script is needed, and so on. Well-commented PowerScript will save hours (or longer!) in future maintenance.

A double slash (//) makes the rest of the line comments. Enclosing a set of text (even several lines) in /* and */ also works well for commenting.

In the following example, notice how you can use a // to comment a line after a command:

```
a = b      // This part after the double slash is a comment
```

Now you can see how a comment can span several lines (without the need for continuation characters) by using /* and */ to enclose the comment:

```
/*  This is
also a long series
of contiguous comments */
```

Continuation Character   Sometimes a line continues off the window, which can make debugging, printing, or viewing the PowerScript difficult. You can type in the continuation character & (ampersand) at the end of the line to tell PowerBuilder to continue on to the next line.

The following example uses the continuation character:

```
string Gaddress
Gaddress = "Four score and seven years ago our fathers brought" &
+ " forth, upon this continent, a new nation, conceived in" &
+ " Liberty, and dedicated to the proposition that all men" &
+ " are created equal...."
```

White Space White space, or spaces between variables, constants, and commands, is ignored in PowerScript except inside a string variable. You can put as many spaces between commands as you like.

TIP Remember, the Enter key (a carriage return) is not considered white space. Carriage returns are only ignored when inside of comments.

Using Variables

As with any language, PowerScript allows you to use variables to hold values. Some of these variables you declare; others are declared for you by PowerBuilder.

Data Types Every variable has a data type, which tells the developer what kind of information is stored in the variable, and tells PowerBuilder the amount of storage to set aside and how to handle the variable. The following is syntax for a variable declaration:

```
data type variable_name
```

For example, to declare the integer loop_counter, you use the following statement:

```
int loop_counter
```

Table 6.1 lists commonly used data types, their ranges, and a short comment on their uses.

Table 6.1 Commonly Used Data Types

Data Type	Range	Comments
Boolean	TRUE or FALSE	Often used as a return value from a function.
Character	Single Character	Can be abbreviated as char.
Date	01-01-1900 through 12-31-3000	Date is in mm-dd-yyyy format. Blanks are not allowed.
DateTime	01-01-1900 00:00:00:0000 23:59:59:9999	Usually used as a database timestamp holder.
Decimal	Up to 18 digits (all significant)	The decimal point can occur anywhere within the 18 digits. The sign and decimal point are not counted as digits. Can be abbreviated as dec.
Integer	-32,768 through 32,767	Can be abbreviated as int.

Part

II

Ch

6

continues

Table 6.1   Continued

Data Type	Range	Comments
Long	-2,147,483,648 through 2,147,483,647	
String	Up to 60,000 characters	All ASCII characters.
Time	00:00:00:0000 - 23:59:59:9999	Time is incremented in milliseconds.

Some data types are not commonly used, but PowerBuilder gives you access to them. These data types are listed in table 6.2.

Table 6.2   Data Types Not Commonly Used

Data Type	Range	Comments
Blob		Unbound data type that stands for binary large object. Usually used to hold pictures in a database.
Double	2.23E-308 through 1.78E+308 —15 digits of precision	
DragObject		Contains the dragged object type. Values include all draggable objects with controls (but no drawing objects).
Object		Contains the enumerated type of a PowerBuilder object. Values include all windows and controls.
PowerObject		Any PowerBuilder object including structures. Usually used with the OpenWithParm commands.
Real	1.18E-38 to 3.40E+38 —	6 digits of precision.
UnsignedInteger	0 through 65,535	Can be abbreviated as unsignedint or uint.
UnsignedLong	0 through 4,294,967,295	Can be abbreviated as ulong.

> **CAUTION**
>
> All number data types (variables) include ranges for that data type. Also, some number data types include digits of precision (or significant digits). If you do a calculation that loses significant digits, PowerBuilder won't tell you, so be careful!
>
> Also, if you exceed the data type's range, rollover occurs. Rollover happens when a number exceeds one range and starts over at the other side of the range. For example, if you stored 32,766 in an integer and added five, the integer would contain –32,765 in the field. (In other words, you rolled over by four.) Now you have a corrupt value in your integer. No error message will occur if this happens.

Variable Scope   In old languages, such as COBOL and BASIC, every variable could be accessed everywhere in the application. Now, most languages support the concept of variable scope. Scope describes where a variable can be used.

The concept of variable scope is important. Scope allows one user to write a function or event without writing over the variables in another area of the application, even if the variables have the same name. There are four levels of scope in PowerBuilder: Local, Instance, Shared, and Global.

Local Scope   Local scope variables (or just local variables) are variables you declare inside your script. Most user-defined variables you use are local variables, which exist only inside the event or function in which they are declared.

For example, you can declare int loop_counter in the window open event and also declare int loop_counter in the window close event. Now you have two versions of loop_counter; each is separate from the other. If you increment loop_counter in the open event, loop_counter in the close event is not affected.

Furthermore, no other event or function has access to the loop_counter variables. For instance, you can't access either loop_counter variable from the activate event.

TROUBLESHOOTING

I set a local variable in a script, but every time I go back into the script, the value is reset to 0 or "". What can I do? Local variables go out of scope when their function or event is finished. When a variable goes out of scope, no function or event has access to it any more, and the memory where the variable was stored is freed up for other functions and variables to use. If you re-enter the event or function later, all local variables will be reset.

If you want to keep a value in a script, try using an instance, shared, or global variable.

Instance Scope   Instance variables are variables that the entire object has access to. If you declare a variable to be an instance variable of an object, then every event, function, or control of that object has access to the variable.

To declare an instance variable, click Declare, Instance Variables, as seen in figure 6.7.

FIGURE 6.7

To declare an instance variable, click Declare, Instance Variables...

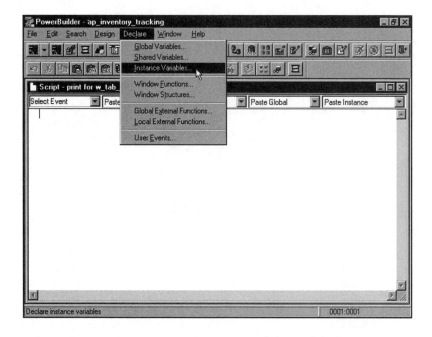

Type in your instance variable's data type and name, as shown in figure 6.8. When you're finished, click OK.

FIG. 6.8

In the Declare Instance Variables dialog box, you declare the instance variable used in your object.

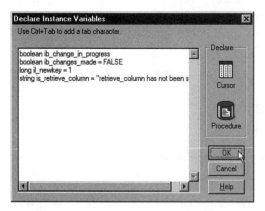

Instance variables go out of scope when their control is closed, and get reset if the control is reopened.

Shared Scope With an MDI application, you can open more than one window of the same type. (In other words, two w_item windows can be open at the same time.) These multiple versions of the same window are called instances of that window. Shared variables are variables that are allowed to be shared by every event, function, and control of every instance of an object.

To declare a shared variable, click Declare, Shared Variables. Then type in your shared variables.

Global Scope   Global variables are accessed by the entire application. They never go out of scope until the application is closed.

You should not use global variables if another variable type will do. Using a lot of global variables violates the principle of encapsulation. In other words, if you set a global variable in an event, another event can reset it without your event knowing it.

To declare a global variable, click Declare, Global Variables. Then type in your global variables.

Encapsulation   Encapsulation is a term used often in object-oriented programming. When a function or event is encapsulated, it means that it stands alone. The encapsulated function can't have its variables changed from outside itself. The encapsulated function also does not access variables outside of itself.

The beautiful part of encapsulation is that a function, object, or control can be used in many systems without modification! You should keep encapsulation in mind while you develop any system.

▶ **See** "Using Naming Conventions," **p. 759**

CAUTION

Local, instance, shared, and global variables can all share the same name. However, if you access a variable that shares its name with a variable of another scope, you may not be able to anticipate the results.

To search variables, PowerBuilder follows this series of procedures:

1. First, PowerBuilder looks for a local variable with the name you're using.
2. If PowerBuilder can't find a local variable, it searches for an instance variable with the name you're using.
3. If PowerBuilder can't find a local or instance variable, it searches for a global variable with the name you're using.
4. Finally, if PowerBuilder can't find any other variable scope with the name you're using, it searches for a shared variable with the same name.

This is different than the variable search path that most languages (such as C++ and Smalltalk) use, so be careful! By the way, none of this needs to concern you if you use the naming conventions outlined in Appendix A.

Part

II

Ch

6

Encapsulation is a matter of degrees. To encapsulate a system as much as possible, follow these tips:

■ All your variable declarations should be local, if possible, because this is the best way to encapsulate your data from corruption by other functions and events. At this highest level of encapsulation, a function or event can be placed in any object and still work properly.

- If a local variable won't work because you need to preserve a value or access the variable from other areas in your object, try an instance variable or (if that won't work) a shared variable. In PowerBuilder, other events and functions can access your instance and shared variables, so any degree of protection from other developers is lost. However, many developers will resist setting an instance or shared variable in a different object. At this level of encapsulation, a window, menu, or user object can be moved to another system and still function properly.

- If no other course of action is possible, try a global variable. Global variables can be altered or redefined by any object or function in an application, so you have to assume that your global variable can be changed at any time. At this level of encapsulation, when you copy any script or object to another application, you must also copy the global variable to the new area.

- The very lowest form of encapsulation is when an object accesses one instance or shared variable of another object. Not only can this set a variable "owned" by another object, but now your objects must travel together. At this level, reusability is lost.

N O T E If you need to set an instance variable in another object, try writing a function or user defined event in one object for the other object to access. For example, instead of setting object B's variable from object A like this:

```
B.variable = NEW_VALUE          // Don't set variables this way
```

instead, try writing a function inside object B to set the variable and access it from object A by passing the NEW_VALUE like this:

```
B.set_variable(NEW_VALUE)       // Set variables this way
```

This way, although these two functions still must travel together, you at least leave object B in full control of its own variables. Any future maintenance to B will not involve looking at A. ■

▶ **See** "Implementing User-Defined Functions," **p. 226**

TROUBLESHOOTING

I set a variable and it gets reset somehow but is NOT going out of scope. How does that happen?
Your variable probably is declared as an instance, shared, or global variable, and another script or function that you invoke in the middle of your function is resetting your variable.

When you use a variable type that another script can access, you violate the principle of encapsulation.

Using Objects and Controls   Often, you'll need to refer to one control from within another control. (For example, the open event of the application object issued a command to open the w_inventory_frame window object.) You also need to be able to tell one object or control to perform a function, or to set an attribute of one object or control from within another object or control.

Every control and object has attributes, or variables that control the functionality and appearance of an object or control. You access the attributes of an object or control with dot notation:

```
control.attribute
object.attribute
```

 TIP TRUE and FALSE are Boolean constants provided by PowerBuilder to set or test other Boolean variables.

Setting Attributes with Dot Notation   To set an attribute, you simply refer to the control or object the attribute is in, followed by a dot (period) and the attribute name. For example, most objects and controls have a Boolean attribute called visible that sees whether the object or control can be seen on the screen. To set this for your tab control (tab_1) in the w_item window, use the following notation:

```
w_item.tab_1.visible = FALSE
```

Through inheritance, you have many tab controls called tab_1. w_item that tells which window tab_1 is in. In this case, the entire name (also called the fully qualified name) of the control is w_item.tab_1. The visible attribute is set to FALSE using this statement, which makes the tab control invisible.

You can also check to see if something is visible by using the following if statement:

```
if w_item.tab_1.visible then
       {perform some function}
end if
```

N O T E   This section discusses some PowerScript that you may not have seen before, although you've probably seen it in other languages:

- Visible is an attribute on most objects and controls. It determines and describes whether or not a control or object can be seen.

- The If statement tests a condition. If the condition is true, a command or set of commands is executed. ElseIf is always accompanied by an If. ElseIf tests a condition if all previous If and ElseIf conditions have failed. If the tested condition is true, a command set is executed. Else executes a command set if all previous If and ElseIf conditions have tested false. Finally, End If ends an If statement. ■

```
If condition-1
       command-set-1
ElseIf condition-2
       command-set-2
ElseIf condition-3
       command-set-3
.
.
.
Else
       command-set-n
End If
```

Part
II

Ch
6

Executing a Function with Dot Notation   You also use the dot notation to execute functions. Every object and control has a set of functions that can run within it. Some functions (such as open for opening a window) don't need to be qualified with an object or control name.

The Hide function is shared by most controls and objects, and it sets the visible attribute. To hide the tab_1 tab control by using a function instead of an attribute, use the following function:

```
w_item.tab_1.hide()
```

N O T E   Using a function to set another object's attributes is considered more object-oriented than actually setting the attribute. For instance,

```
w_windowname.command_button.visible = FALSE      // Not very encapsulated
```

is not as encapsulated as

```
w_windowname.command_button.hide( )              // More encapsulated
```

The idea behind encapsulation is to let each object set its own variables.

Using Dot Notation with Menus   Menus have a unique structure. To access a menu item, you need to give the menu name, followed by the tree structure of the menu. For instance, to use the TriggerEvent function to make PowerBuilder "pretend" that the user opened the Window menu and chose Display, Tile in the m_item menu, you use the following syntax:

```
m_item.m_window.m_display.m_tile.TriggerEvent(Clicked!)
```

T I P   For more information, refer to chapter 28, "Enumerated Data Types Quick Reference."

▶ **See** "Enumerated Data Types Quick Reference," **p. 723**

Using Structures   Structures are used to create your own data type. Structures contain several different related variables of different types and group them under a single name. Structures allow you to move data around and refer to the data under a single name instead of using several names.

Creating a Structure   To create a structure, follow these steps:

1. Click the Struct icon. This will pull up the Select Structure window shown in figure 6.9.
2. Click New to start creating a new structure. The structure painter appears (see fig. 6.10).
3. Type in your variable names and data types. When you're finished, click OK.
4. After you define your structure, PowerBuilder asks if you want to save your work (see fig. 6.11). Pick a PBL (PowerBuilder Library), type in a name, and click OK.

Developing Local Structures   So far, the structures that have been discussed are global structures, which, like global variables, can be used by any event or function in your application. PowerBuilder also allows you to declare local structures, which can only be accessed in the object where they were created.

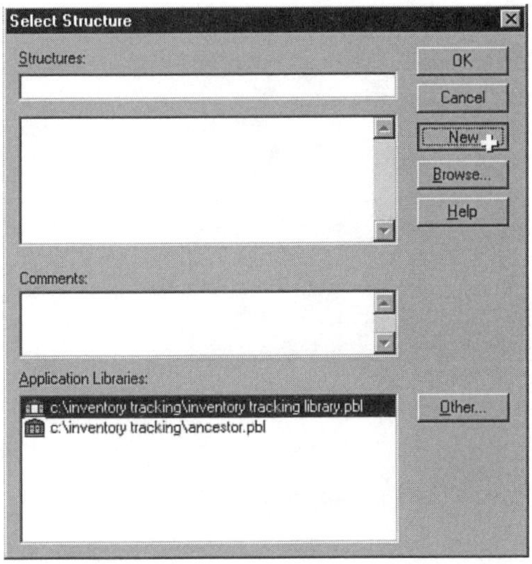

FIG. 6.9

By clicking the Struct icon, you pull up the Select Structure window. Click New to start a new structure.

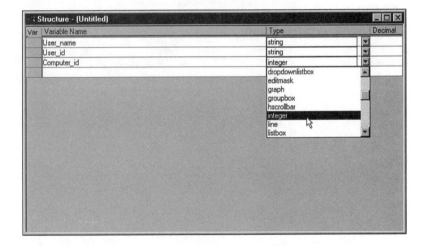

FIG. 6.10

Using the structure painter, you can define your structure by typing in structure variable names and their data types.

Part
II

Ch
6

To create a local structure for a window, pull up one of your windows and click Declare, Window Structures, as seen in figure 6.12.

This pulls up the Select Structure in Window dialog box (seen in fig. 6.13). This dialog box is identical in function to the Select Structure dialog box, except that it only selects or creates local structures.

Now you will see the structure painter with your existing structure displayed (if updating an existing structure) or a blank structure (if creating a new structure).When you're finished creating a new structure, the Save Structure in Window dialog box appears, as seen in figure 6.14, which enables you to save your local window structure.

FIG. 6.11

After you define your structure, the Save Structure dialog box allows you to save your work in a PBL.

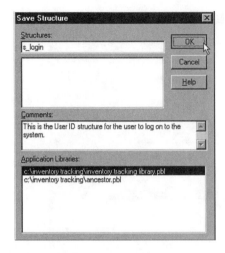

FIG. 6.12

Click Declare, {objectname} Structures to declare a local structure inside a PowerBuilder object.

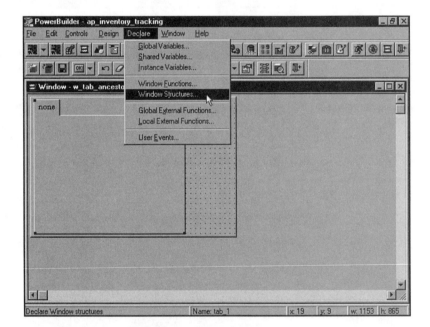

FIG. 6.13

The Select Structure in Window dialog box appears if you want to modify or create a local window structure.

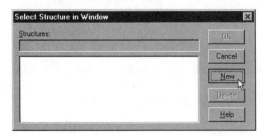

FIG. 6.14

The Save Structure in Window dialog box allows you to save your structure work.

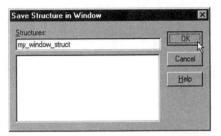

You just created a local window structure. You can also create a local structure for most PowerBuilder objects (menus, applications, and so on) by using the same technique.

Accessing a Structure You're done creating your structure, but remember that a structure is a data type—not a variable. You still have to declare variables using your structure, and then use dot notation to access the variables within a structure. Listing 6.1 assigns values to your structure:

Listing 6.1 Using a Structure

```
string name            // name is a variable of type string
s_login login_info     // login_info is a variable of type s_login

name = "C Wood"                  // Assign a value to name
login_info.user_name = name      // Assign user name to name
login_info.user_id = 123-45-6789 // Assign a constant to user_id

 login_info.computer_id = 12  // Assign computer number to computer_id
```

Notice in listing 6.1 how you have to declare login_info, just as name is declared. After a variable is declared for the structure, you can access the structure's variables using dot notation.

N O T E The Inventory Tracking system doesn't use any structures—although when dealing with a group of variables, there are several cases in which using structures dramatically decreases workload (for example, sorting groups of different variables or moving a group of variables). ▨

Enumerated Data Types   Enumerated data types are constants that PowerBuilder provides which are related to certain functions and usually act as parameters or attribute values. TRUE and FALSE are examples of enumerated constants.

With the exception of TRUE and FALSE, enumerated constants end in an exclamation point (!). Clicked! is an example of an enumerated data type. All enumerated data types are listed in chapter 28, "Enumerated Data Types Quick Reference."

Arrays   Arrays are series of indexed variables of the same data type. Think of an array as a numbered variable.

You declare an array by putting a number in brackets behind a data declaration. In figure 6.15,

you see that declaring an integer sets up a single integer cell in memory. By adding [10] to the integer declaration, you now have declared 10 integers. Arrays can be accessed using the array name, followed by a bracketed number.

FIG. 6.15

By declaring an array, you create a group of like variables of a single data type, as opposed to a single variable.

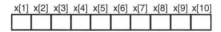

If you use the following statements, 15 cells of x are reserved, and the number 1492 is placed in cell 5:

```
int x[15]
x[5] = 1492
```

Multi-Dimensional Arrays   Multi-dimensional arrays are also hard to understand. If an array declaration has more than one set of numbers following it, a multi-dimensional array has been declared.

A good example of a multi-dimensional array is a program that keeps track of bowling scores (tracking every frame of every match). Suppose, for example, you have five bowling matches per season. You can store all the bowling scores in a 5–10 multi-dimensional array, as shown in figure 6.16.

FIG. 6.16

You can see the difference in storage between single- and multi-dimension arrays.

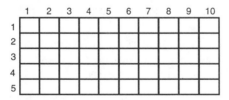

Listing 6.2 shows how to code a multi-dimensional array:

Listing 6.2   Multi-dimensional arrays

```
int bowling_season[5, 10]      // Declare a multi-dimensional array
int score = 200                // Set a score
```

```
int match = 3                    // Declare the game counter
int frame = 7                    // Declare the frame counter
// Set the bowling array to the score for the given frame and match
bowling_season[match, frame] = score
```

The code in listing 6.2 puts a score of 200 into row 3, column 7 of the bowling season array.

> **CAUTION**
>
> You can do more than two dimensions in an array, but be careful. Nothing grabs available memory more than a huge multi-dimensional array. It can cause your Windows application to fail.
>
> For example, suppose you want to keep bowling scores for your entire high school team for a four-year period. There are 20 members on your bowling team, and they bowl 10 frames per match, five matches a night, 50 times per year. Your four-dimensional array declaration looks like this:
>
> ```
> // Declare 20 team members for 4 years, 50
> // nights per year, 5 matches per night, 10
> // frames per match.
> int bowling_life[20, 4, 50, 5, 10]
> ```
>
> Because an integer takes up two bytes, you have just declared 400,000 (2 * 20 * 4 * 50 * 5 * 10) bytes of storage with this declaration. That alone may cause Windows to send an application error.

Variable Arrays   Variable arrays are arrays whose size is not set upon declaration. To declare a variable array, leave the number out of the brackets when declaring your array. The size of the array is set with the largest access to that array. The following code shows the use of the variable array:

```
string months[ ]                 // Setting up a variable array

// Set the upper array bound to 12 (so far) and fill it in
months[12] = "December"
```

Object Data Types (Instances)   The objects you declare are themselves a data type. These special kinds of data types are called instances of your object (not to be confused with instance variable scope).

The main use of instance variables is to open multiple versions of the same window in an MDI frame. For instance, if you wanted to open two w_item windows, you could use the following code:

```
w_item window1           // Declare the first instance of w_item
w_item window2           // Declare the second instance of w_item

Open (window1, w_item)
Open (window2, w_item)
```

The previous syntax opens two windows. You can navigate between them by using the window list in the Window menu. Also, because Close (in the File menu) closes the parent window to the menu, you really don't need any special coding from here to use your windows.

The hard part of multiple windows arises when you have another set of windows coming from the multiple windows. (For instance, you open the supplier of each item.) Now you must keep track of which window was opened from where. This can get quite confusing.

You also have the problem of both windows trying to update the same database, and perhaps the same row, at the same time. The questions that arise are who gets to update and who doesn't?

TIP   If you try to open a window that is already open, the window will simply appear. No new window will be opened.

N O T E   In the Inventory Tracking system, multiple versions of the same window are not opened by using instances. It's much easier to navigate through windows if only one version of that window is open at a time. However, instances definitely have their place in MDI applications. If you are designing an MDI application, you should consider whether or not you want multiple copies of the same window open at one time. ■

Naming Convention   It's important to follow naming conventions when writing your scripts, especially with instance variables, shared variables, and global variables that are not part of the script.

Do yourself and all your coworkers a favor: Implement the naming conventions suggested in Appendix A, or develop your own. This saves time and trouble later during debugging.

Using Operators

There are four types of operators: arithmetic, string, logical, and grouping. Arithmetic operators are used for mathematical calculations. Logical operators are used for testing conditions. String operators perform functions on string variables. The only grouping operators are parentheses, which affect the order in which your operators will be executed.

Arithmetic Operators   Arithmetic operators can be divided into three categories: binary operators, unary operators, and combination operators.

Binary operators require two operators. (Operators are variables or constants.) The PowerBuilder binary operators are listed in table 6.3.

Table 6.3   Binary Arithmetic Operators

Symbol	Name	Example	Description
^	Exponential	a ^ b	Raises a to the bth power.
+	Addition	a + b	Adds a and b.
−	Subtraction	a − b	Subtracts b from a.
*	Multiplication	a * b	Multiplies a and b.

Symbol	Name	Example	Description
/	Division	a / b	Divides a by b.
=	Equals	a = b	Places the value of b into a.

Unary operators require one operator. The PowerBuilder unary operators are listed in table 6.4.

Table 6.4   Unary Arithmetic Operators

Symbol	Name	Example	Description
-	Negative	- a	Symbolizes the negative value of a.
+	Positive	+ a	Symbolizes the positive value of a. (This is never needed.)
++	Increment	a ++	Increments a by one.
—	Decrement	a —	Decrements a by one.

N O T E   In PowerBuilder, the subtraction (-), unary negative (-), and decrement (—) operators must be surrounded by spaces. ■

C and C++ programmers will be happy to know that combination operators are included in PowerBuilder. Combination operators are binary operators that combine the functionality of two operators, equals and either addition or subtraction. Because combination operators are binary, they require two operators. The PowerBuilder combination operators are shown in table 6.5.

Table 6.5   Combination Operators

Symbol	Name	Example	Description
+=	Plus Equals	a += b	Sets a equal to a + b.
-=	Minus Equals	a -= b	Sets a equal to a – b.
*=	Times Equals	a *= b	Sets a equal to a * b.
/=	Divide Equals	a /= b	Sets a equal to a / b.
^=	Power Equals	a ^= b	Sets a equal to a ^ b.

String Operators   The only string operator PowerBuilder uses is a plus sign (+) for concatenation. The following PowerScript shows how this is done:

```
string s1 = "Hi "
string s2 = "Mom!"
```

```
string s3
s3 = s1 + s2
```

The resulting value in s3 is "Hi Mom!"

Logical Operators   Logical operators test for a condition to be true or false. There are two types of logical operators: relational operators and conjunction operators.

Relational operators are always binary, and therefore require two operators. The PowerBuilder relational operators are seen in table 6.6.

Table 6.6   Logical Operators

Symbol	Name	Example	Description
=	Equal	a = b	Returns TRUE if a is equal to b.
>	Greater than	a > b	Returns TRUE if a is greater than b.
<	Less than	a < b	Returns TRUE if a is less than b.
>=	Greater than or equal	a >= b	Returns TRUE if a is greater than or equal to b.
<=	Less than or equal	a <= b	Returns TRUE if a is less than or equal to b.
<>	Not equal	a <> b	Returns TRUE if a is not equal to b.

Any relational operator that does not return TRUE returns FALSE.

CAUTION

In PowerBuilder, relational operators always try to evaluate both operands as numbers. However, if an operand can't be evaluated as a number, PowerBuilder treats it as text and performs a string comparison. For example, the following is evaluated as TRUE because 2 is less then 10.

```
2 < 10
```

The following statement, however, is treated as FALSE because "Paragraph 10" comes alphabetically before "Paragraph 2."

```
"Paragraph 2" < "Paragraph 10"
```

Conjunction operators have relational expressions as their operands. (Relational expressions are expressions using relational operators.) PowerBuilder's three conjunction operators are two binary operators, AND and OR, and one unary operator, NOT. Their functions can be seen in the truth table in table 6.7.

Table 6.7 Conjunction Operators

a	b	a AND b	a OR b	NOT a
TRUE	TRUE	TRUE	TRUE	FALSE
TRUE	FALSE	FALSE	TRUE	FALSE
FALSE	TRUE	FALSE	TRUE	TRUE
FALSE	FALSE	FALSE	FALSE	TRUE

The first row can be read as "If a is TRUE and b is TRUE, then a AND b is TRUE, a OR b is TRUE, and NOT a is FALSE."

Precedence and Parentheses Certain operations take precedence over each other. For instance, you may (incorrectly) think that the following equation evaluates to 27 because 5 + 4 = 9 and 9 multiplied by 3 is 27.

```
5 + 4 * 3
```

In actuality, this equation is evaluated to 17 because multiplication (*) takes precedence over addition (+). Therefore, 4 * 3 is evaluated first to 12, and then 5 is added to the result to make 17.

Parentheses change all that. Parentheses are the only grouping operators. To evaluate the statement to 27, group it as follows:

```
(5 + 4) * 3
```

Parentheses cause 5 + 4 to be evaluated first before multiplying by 3.

You can also nest parentheses. (Nesting means putting one inside of another.) The following expression evaluates the 7 + 3 first (because it's in the deepest nested parentheses) to 10:

```
NOT (8 > ((7+3)*12))
```

This is multiplied by 12 to get 120. Because 8 is not greater than 120, NOT (8 > 120) evaluates to TRUE.

Table 6.8 shows the order of operations (or precedence) in PowerBuilder.

Table 6.8 Precedence of Operators

Operator	Use
( )	Grouping
^	Raising a number to a power
* /	Multiplication and division of numbers
+ −	Addition and subtraction of numbers and concatenation of strings

continues

Part

II

Ch

6

Table 6.8 Continued

Operator	Use
< > <= >= =	Logical operation for numbers and arithmetic
<> += -= *= ^= /*	assignment
NOT	Negation of relational statements
AND	Logical AND
OR	Logical OR

If a statement has two operators with the same precedence, the statement is evaluated from left to right.

Equivalent Statements   In English, there are several ways to say the same thing. In PowerBuilder, too, there are several ways to code the same logical or arithmetic statement, and have it mean the same thing. Table 6.9 lists some equivalent statements.

Table 6.9 Equivalent Logical and Arithmetic Statements

Statement	Equivalent Statement
a = a + 1	a ++
a = a – 1	a --
a = a + b	a += b
a = a – b	a -= b
a <> b	NOT (a = b)
a <= b	NOT (a > b)
a < b	NOT (a >= b)
a = b	NOT (a <> b)
NOT a AND NOT b	NOT (a OR b)
NOT a OR NOT b	NOT (a AND b)

 TIP For future maintenance, try to pick the "easiest" way to state your operation. (For instance, use a < b as opposed to NOT (a >= b).)

Using PowerBuilder Commands

The PowerScript Language contains two types of statements: built-in functions and commands. Although there are lots of built-in functions, there are only three major types of commands:

assignment commands, which assign a value to a variable, decision structures, which consist of If statements and Choose Case statements, and iterative (or looping) structures, which consist of Do loops and For_Next loops.

Using Decision Structures Decision structures are commands that evaluate variables. PowerBuilder supports two types of decision structures: the If_ElseIf_Else_End If structure (or just the If structure) and the Choose Case structure.

Using the If Structure The If statement evaluates variables. Based on that evaluation, the If statement takes some form of action. Listing 6.3 is an example of the simplest form of an If statement:

Listing 6.3   Simple If statement

```
If a < b Then // First evaluate a logical expression
      // Commands if expression is true
      {a command or set of commands}
End If                          // End the If statement
```

As you can tell by the comments in listing 6.3, a logical expression is first evaluated. If that logical expression is true, then a set of commands is executed. Now we have a more complicated If statement. In listing 6.4, the If statement contains an Else clause.

Listing 6.4   Simple If-Else statement

```
If a < b Then                 // First evaluate a logical
// expression
      command set 1           // Commands if expression is TRUE
Else
      command set 2           // Commands if expression is FALSE
End If                        // End the If statement
```

With this If decision structure, one of the command sets gets executed, depending on the value of a and b.

Listing 6.5 adds an ElseIf statement to the If structure to evaluate another condition.

Part
II

Ch

6

Listing 6.5   If-Else-ElseIf-End If Structure

```
If a < b Then                 // First evaluate a logical expression
      command set 1           // Commands if expression is TRUE
ElseIf a < c Then             // Commands if previous expression is
// FALSE
      command set 2           // and this expression is TRUE
Else                          // Commands if all previous expressions
// are FALSE
      command set 3
End If                        // End the If statement
```

The If decision structure in listing 6.6 is a fourth If statement, which contains two ElseIfs:

Listing 6.6   If-Else-ElseIf-ElseIf-End if Structure

```
If a < b Then              // First evaluate a logical expression
        command set 1         // Commands if expression is TRUE
ElseIf a < c Then          // Commands if previous expression is
// FALSE
        command set 2          // and this expression is TRUE
ElseIf a < d Then          // Commands if all previous expressions
        command set 3          // are FALSE and this expression is TRUE
Else                       // Commands if all previous expressions are
        command set 4          // FALSE
End If                     // End the If statement
```

You can have as many ElseIfs in an If statement as you want.

Using the If decision structure is a powerful way to control the flow of your program based on existing information.

Using the Choose Case Structure   In the above example, we were comparing **a** to several other variables. In a situation such as this, you would be better off to use a Choose Case statement. The Choose Case statement is good for evaluating a single variable in several different ways. The format for the Choose Case statement can be seen in listing 6.7.

Listing 6.7   Choose Case structure

```
Choose Case test_variable
     Case expression1
           command set 1     // Commands if expression1 is TRUE
     Case expression2     // Commands if expression2 is TRUE
           command set 2      //            and previous expressions are FALSE
           ...
     Case expression3     // Commands if expression3 is TRUE
           command set 3      //            and previous expressions are FALSE
     Case Else
           command set 4     // Commands if all expressions are FALSE
End Choose
```

In the Choose Case decision structure, the `test_variable` is the variable you want to run several tests on. Each Case statement performs a test on the `test_variable`. At least one CASE clause is required.

Each expression can test many different situations. An expression can be a single value (such as variable 2 or 5), a list of values separated by commas, a TO clause (such as 10 to 20) or a relational operator preceded by Is (such as Is < 50).

Listing 6.8 is a Choose Case statement that could be used at the Las Vegas blackjack tables (with a little more work, of course):

Listing 6.8 Blackjack Choose Case Structure

```
Choose Case card_total
     Case is > 21
          busted = TRUE
     Case 3 To 16
          hit_me = TRUE
     Case 21
          black_jack = TRUE
     Case 17, 18, 19, 20
          stick = TRUE
     Case Else                    // Only 2 is left
          double_down = TRUE
End Choose
```

As you can tell, a Choose Case statement is easier to write, easier to read, and more efficient to run than the equivalent If...ElseIf...Else...End If statement, but not as versatile.

 TIP Typically, a Choose Case command is more efficient than an equivalent If...ElseIf...Else...End If command.

Using Iteration (Looping) Structures   Looping structures are constructs that cause a series of commands to be executed a number of times. PowerScript has two looping structures: the Do Loop structure and the For_Next structure.

Using the Do Loop Structure   The Do Loop structure in PowerScript is a powerful way to implement a loop. Following are four different types of Do Loops and their functions.

Listing 6.9 Pretest While Loop

```
Do While condition1  // Executes command set 1 While condition1 is
    command set 1     // TRUE
Loop
```

Listing 6.10   Pretest Until Loop

```
Do Until condition2  //  Executes command set 2 Until condition2 is
    command set 2     // TRUE
Loop
```

Listing 6.11   Posttest While Loop

```
Do                   // Executes command set 4 at least once
    command set 4     // while condition4 is TRUE
Loop While condition4
```

Listing 6.12   Posttest Until Loop

```
Do                      // Executes command set 3 at least once
    command set 3       // until condition3 is TRUE
Loop Until condition3
```

Suppose you want to search for the first space in an instance variable string named is_full_name. Use the logic found in listing 6.13:

Listing 6.13   String Search

```
int count                      // Declare your string counter

count = 1                      // Initialize your count to one
// Now search the string using Mid. Notice the continuation character
Do Until Mid(is_full_name, count, 1) = " " and &
              count <= len(is_full_name)
        count++
Loop
```

Using the For_Next Structure   The other type of loop construct is the For_Next loop, which combines iteration with incrementing a counter. It has the following format:

```
For numeric_variable = start  To  end { Step increment }
    command set
Next
```

In the above For command, numeric_variable is a variable (usually an integer) to be incremented during the loop. start To end tells what the numeric variable is to be initialized with and where it's supposed to go to until the loop ends. Step increment allows you to increment your loop during each iteration. If this step is skipped, 1 is assumed. Next symbolizes the end of the loop.

TIP   Often, Step -1 is used with the For_Next statement to force the loop to decrement instead of increment.

CAUTION

Any variable you use for incrementing during your loop will have its value altered.

Here's a For Next example of a For_Next loop that resets an array:

Listing 6.14   For Next Loop

```
int a          // Loop Counter
int b[100]     // Array to be reset
.
```

```
  . .         Additional processing here
  .
// To reset your array, set a to go from 1 to 100
For a = 1 to 100
     b[a] = 0;     // Reset your array
Next               // End loop
```

Nested Loops and Loop Statements   No discussion of PowerBuilder loops would be complete without mentioning the statements Continue and Exit. Continue is used to skip down to the bottom of the loop for another iteration; Exit is used to leave the loop completely.

Nested loops are loops inside of each other. Exit only leaves the current loop. Listing 6.15 is the traditional (and a little inefficient) bubble sort, which is used to sort an array using a nested loop.

Listing 6.15   Bubble Sort

```
int sort_array[100]   // Declare an array to be sorted
int loop1             // loop counter 1
int loop2             // second loop counter
int last_chg          // check up to this number + 1
int hold_number       // holder for the sort
int hold_last_chg     // holder for last change
boolean changes_made  // Flag to see if changes were made
// .
// . Commands fill the array with values
// .
// Now begin the bubble sort
last_chg = 99        // Check the entire array
for loop1 = 1 to 99  // Go through the entire array
     changes_made = FALSE                // Reset changes_made
     for loop2 = 1 to last_chg           // loop2 is nested
         if sort_array[loop2] < sort_array[loop2+1] then    // Check values
             continue                    // Iterate loop2 again
         end if
         changes_made = TRUE             // set changes_made
         hold_last_chg = loop2 - 1       // Go this far next loop2
         hold_number = sort_array[loop2]        // Swap array numbers
         sort_array[loop2] = sort_array[loop2 + 1]
         sort_array[loop2 + 1] = hold_number
     next           // End loop2
     if NOT changes_made then
         exit       // Exit if sort is done
     end if
     last_chg = hold_last_chg            //set how far loop2 should go
next               // End loop1
```

Part

II

Ch

6

The previous example used a nested loop to perform a sort. You also can employ a Continue statement to skip to the next iteration of loop2. Finally, if the array is sorted, you can exit the loop.

Using Built-in Functions

In its PowerScript, PowerBuilder gives you a lot of built-in functions (such as the Mid function). Built-in functions are already declared and ready for use.

Also, every control and object has functions of its own. All built-in functions are listed in chapter 25, "Function Quick Reference."

Using Context-Sensitive Help

If you have any question about a command or PowerBuilder construct, PowerBuilder comes with an excellent online help. By pressing F1, you see the table of contents. By placing the cursor on a script command, and pressing Shift+F1, you'll pull up help for that command.

Using the PowerBuilder Script Painter

The PowerScript language comes with a very handy script painter. Properly used, this painter makes your job as a developer much easier.

Using the Undo Function

 You'll find that the Undo function will save you lots of time. When you've done something in a script that you shouldn't have, click the Undo icon and put your script back the way it was.

N O T E   You can also access the Undo function by pressing Alt+Backspace or by clicking Edit, Undo. ■

 PowerBuilder 5 supports a multi-level undo. This is a great feature that can undo several previous changes to your PowerScript.

Selecting Text

 Often you'll find you need to select text before you can perform other actions, like commenting, cutting, or pasting text. There are many ways you can select text:

- ■ To select all your text, click the Select All icon.
- ■ To select part of your text:

    1. Position your mouse pointer to the start of your selection.
    2. Press and hold the left mouse button.
    3. Move your mouse pointer to the end of your selection.
    4. Release the mouse button.

N O T E   You can also select text with the keyboard with the following steps:

1. Position your cursor at the beginning of your selection.

2. Hold down the Shift key while you use your arrows to move to the end of your selection.

3. Release the Shift key. ▒

Commenting and Uncommenting

To comment or uncomment your text, click the Comment or Uncomment icon. Clicking these icons will add (or take away) the double slash (//) at the beginning of each line selected (or the current line, if no lines are selected). It's just a faster way to comment out a lot of code.

> **N O T E** PowerBuilder won't let you leave the script painter if you have any errors in your script. However, there are times you may want to leave your script painter anyway. ▒

To leave your painter with errors in the code, click the Select All icon and then the Comment icon. This comments out all your code and allows you to leave your script.

When you return, click the Select All icon again and then the Uncomment icon. Your code will be as you left it. ▒

Copying, Clearing, and Cutting Text

After you've selected text, copy to the Windows Clipboard by clicking the Copy icon. If you click the Clear icon, the selected text is deleted out of your script. Cutting text is a combination of the copy and clear functions. If you click the Cut icon, the selected text is copied to the Clipboard and then deleted out of your script.

Pasting Text

If you have anything in the Windows Clipboard, you can paste it into your text by clicking the Paste icon.

> **N O T E** In PowerBuilder, you can pull up any text file on your hard drive by pressing Shift+F6. Using the same icons, you can cut, copy, or paste from any file to any other file. ▒

Pasting Statements

To paste a statement in your script painter, click the Paste icon which has what looks like a flow chart on it. This pulls up the Paste Statement dialog box (see fig. 6.17).

From here, click the function you want, then click OK. This pastes the syntax for the PowerBuilder statement, as shown in figure 6.18.

Now change the words surrounded in less-than and greater-than signs to appropriate syntax.

Part

II

Ch

6

FIG. 6.17

You can paste the syntax for a PowerBuilder statement using the Paste Statement dialog box.

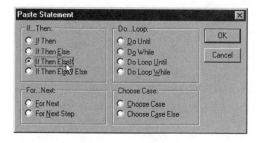

FIG. 6.18

This is the result of using the Paste Statement dialog box.

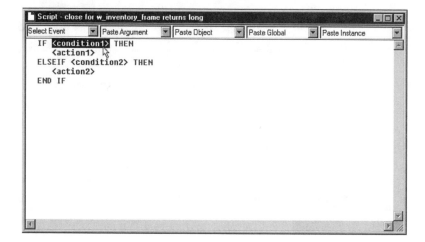

Pasting Functions

 You can also paste functions by using the function painter. Click Edit and choose Paste Function (see fig. 6.19).

Now you should see the Paste Function dialog box, as shown in figure 6.20.

In the Paste Function dialog box, click the function you want to paste (see fig. 6.21).

Now the function you've chosen is pasted onto the script painter. You'll notice that none of the arguments are included when you paste your function. You have to fill these in for yourself.

Using the Paste List Boxes

On the top of your script painter, you can see three paste list boxes, which allow you to quickly paste variables and objects that you often use while coding your script.

The Paste Instance list box, as shown in figure 6.22, pulls down all instance variable declarations. By double-clicking an instance variable, it is pasted in your script.

FIG. 6.19
Use the PowerBuilder menu to access the Paste Function dialog box.

FIG. 6.20
The Paste Function dialog box allows you to choose a function and paste it back to your script painter.

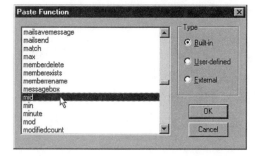

FIG. 6.21
Now the function name is pasted in your window.

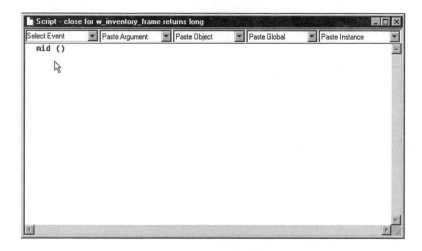

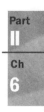

FIG. 6.22

The Paste Instance list box allows you to paste instance variables into your script.

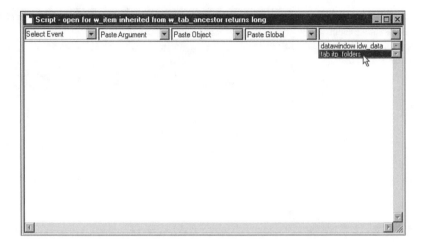

The Paste Global list box, as shown in figure 6.23, allows you to paste any global variable (and system global variable) into your script.

FIG. 6.23

The Paste Global list box allows you to paste global variables into your script.

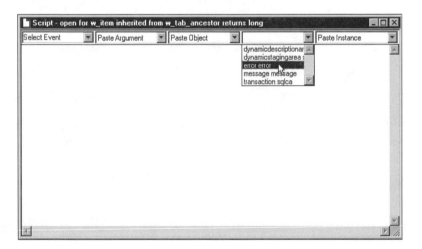

Finally, the Paste Object list box allows you to paste objects that are related to the script you are writing. As you can see in figure 6.24, the tab control name (tab_1) and the window name (w_item) are in the Paste Object list box.

TIP Shift+Del cuts your selected text. Shift+Ins pastes your script. Cut, copy, and paste can also be accessed by Ctrl+X, Ctrl+C, and Ctrl+V, respectively.

FIG. 6.24

The Paste Object list box allows you to paste related object names into your script.

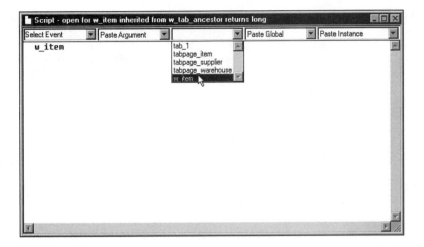

Using the Object Browser

Sometimes, you need to go outside what is provided in the paste boxes for areas in your script. However, keeping track of all the objects, their attributes and functions, and all the instance variables and events for each object can be mind-boggling.

To meet this need, PowerBuilder developed the Object Browser, which enables you to browse into any object, enumerated data type, function, or control. To get into the Object Browser, click the Browse icon.

In the Object Browser (see fig. 6.25), click the object type you want (in this case, Application), and choose the paste category of what you want to paste (in this case, Properties). You'll then be given a list of paste values. Pick one, and click OK to paste that value into your script painter.

As you can see in figure 6.26, the highlighted variable gets pasted into your script. Furthermore, the variable is fully qualified. Now just finish the statement and you're finished.

FIG. 6.25

You can scan all the properties of your inventory_tracking application.

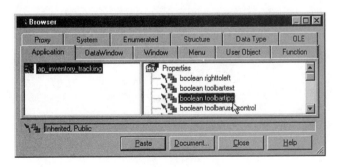

Part

II

Ch

6

FIG. 6.26

The Browse Objects pastes the appropriate name into your script painter.

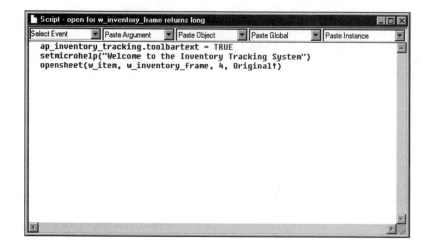

From Here...

In this chapter, you learned a lot about the PowerScript language and PowerBuilder's script painter. As with any language, the best way to learn PowerScript is to practice it.

You can find more discussion on PowerScript in this book by reviewing the following chapters:

- Chapter 7, "Programming in PowerScript," describes the best way to implement PowerScript from within your application.

- Chapter 8, "Using SQL in PowerBuilder," shows you how to access your database effectively within PowerScript.

- Chapter 25, "Function Quick Reference," lists all the functions allowed in PowerBuilder.

- Chapter 26, "Event Quick Reference," lists all the events used by PowerBuilder objects and controls.

Programming in PowerScript

by Charles A. Wood

In the last chapter, you learned the basics on how to program in PowerScript. Now you get to apply your knowledge using the Inventory Tracking system.

In this chapter, much of the PowerScript coding for the Inventory Tracking system is complete. It is designed to give you a hands-on feel for PowerScript. ■

Define a database transaction.

Database transactions are how PowerBuilder "talks" to your database. This chapter shows you how to use database transactions.

Use the PowerScript language.

This chapter delves into practical applications for the PowerScript language.

Program for PowerBuilder events and functions.

You'll need to know how to program for certain events and functions inside PowerBuilder. This chapter shows you how.

Understand Function and Event arguments.

Now PowerBuilder allows you to use Event arguments. You can also post functions. This chapter shows how this is done.

Avoid certain programming practices.

Certain programming practices are to be avoided. This chapter details what to look out for when programming.

Understanding Database Transactions

Transaction objects are used by PowerBuilder to communicate with a database. Before you use a database, you must define it in the transaction object. Although you can define your own transaction variable, PowerBuilder provides one for you: the SQLCA.

Exploring PowerBuilder's Transaction Objects

A transaction object (or structure) such as SQLCA has 15 fields. Ten of these fields need to be filled in by the developer; the other five are used for a return area after you make SQL calls. The structure is defined in tables 7.1 and 7.2.

 Instead of trying to define your own transaction object, you should probably use the SQLCA transaction that is already defined.

Table 7.1 shows the elements of the SQLCA transaction object that are defined by the user.

Table 7.1 User-Defined Transaction Variables

Attribute	Data Type	Description
DBMS	String	The name of the database type (for example, ODBC for Watcom).
Database	String	The name of the database to which you are connecting. In Watcom, use the file-name prefix (INVENTRY).
UserID	String	The UserID connecting to the database ("dba" in Inventory Tracking).
DBParm	String	DBMS-specific. (In Watcom, this is the connect string.)
DBPass	String	The password that will be used to connect to the database ("sql" in Inventory Tracking).
Lock	String	The isolation level (often not needed).
LogId	String	The name or ID of the user who will log on to the server (often not needed).
LogPass	String	The password used to log on to the server (often not needed).
ServerName	String	The name of the server on which the database resides (often not needed).
AutoCommit	Boolean	The automatic commit indicator. TRUE commits automatically after every database activity. FALSE (default) does not commit automatically.

Table 7.2 shows the elements of the SQLCA transaction object that are returned to the user by the database the user is working with. These values then can be accessed to give information about the previous SQL call, particularly to tell if the SQL code worked or what error occurred.

Table 7.2   Database Transaction Return Variables

Attribute	Data Type	Description
SQLCode	Long	The success or failure code of the most recent SQL operation: 0—Success 100—No result set returned −1—Error (use SQLDBCode or SQLErrText to obtain the details)
SQLNRows	Long	The number of rows affected. The database vendor supplies this number; therefore, the meaning may not be the same in every database.
SQLDBCode	Long	The database vendor's error code.
SQLErrText	String	The database vendor's error message.
SQLReturnData	String	DBMS-specific return data.

CAUTION

Before you can use the default transaction object (SQLCA) or any other transaction object, you must assign values to the attributes that will be used.

The user-defined transaction structure variables may vary from database to database.

Using Your Transaction in the Application Open Event

Probably the best place to code your database connection is in the application that is open. The code in listing 7.1 is added before the w_inventory_frame open statement in the application open event.

Listing 7.1   Connecting to the Database

```
// − − − Define the parameters necessary to connect to the database.
SQLCA.DBMS      = "ODBC"
SQLCA.Database  = "INVENTRY"
SQLCA.UserID    = "dba"
SQLCA.DBPass    = "sql"
SQLCA.DBParm    = "Connectstring='DSN=INVENTRY;UID=DBA;PWD=SQL'"
```

continues

Listing 7.1 Continued

```
// ——— Once transaction object parameters are defined,
// ——— try connecting to the database
CONNECT USING SQLCA;

If SQLCA.SQLCode <> 0 Then
MessageBox ("Database Connect", &
"Unable to connect to the Inventory Database.~r~n" &
+ "DB Error Code: " + String (SQLCA.SQLDBCode ) &
+ "~r~n" + "DB Error Message: " + SQLCA.SQLErrText, &
StopSign!, OK!, 1 )
Halt
End If

open (w_inventory_frame)
```

As you can see, you didn't have to code every transaction variable. Now you are ready to start using SQLCA and your database in your application.

Always test the SQLCode (usually SQLCA.SQLCode) after making any SQL call. You'll want to know if it worked. Most databases don't display error messages automatically; instead, they return codes for the developer to test.

TIP To check the syntax of your script, press Ctrl+L or choose Compile, Script.

NOTE CONNECT is an SQL statement used to connect to the database using your transaction object. If you don't include a USING statement, the transaction object defaults to SQLCA. ■

Implementing User-Defined Functions

In addition to user-defined events, PowerBuilder also lets the developer write user-defined functions. A *user-defined function* can either be *global* (every object in the application has access to the function) or *local* (only the object in which the local function is defined has access to that function).

Using the PowerBuilder Global Function Painter

To create a global function, click the Function icon. The Select Function dialog box appears, as shown in figure 7.1.

Click New in the Select Function dialog box. The New Function dialog box appears (see fig. 7.2).

FIG. 7.1

The Select Function dialog box appears when you click the Function icon.

FIG. 7.2

The New Function dialog box is where you start defining your new function.

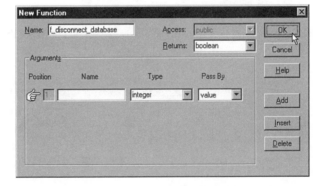

The following fields are available in the New Function dialog box:

- The Name field is where you type in the name of the function (the name other objects use to access your function).

- The Access field tells who has access to this function. There are three types of access: public, private, and protected. *Public access* means that anyone can access the function. *Private access* means that only the object that the function is defined in has access to the object. *Protected access* means that only the object the function is defined in (and all the descendants of that object) have access to the function.

    Global functions are only allowed to have public access because global functions aren't defined within an object. (You'll probably be using public access almost exclusively anyway.) Private or protected access are for those destructive, monetary, or secretive information functions that you don't want every developer calling from their object.

Part

II

Ch

7

■ The Returns field tells what data type of variable is returned by this function to the calling function. Valid values for a Boolean variable are TRUE and FALSE. Boolean variables usually make excellent return variables if you want to indicate to the calling program whether the function succeeded or failed.

■ Arguments fields allow you to pass arguments to your function. You can type in the name of your argument and choose the data type. You can also choose to pass the argument by value (which tells PowerBuilder that any changes you make to the argument won't be reflected in the calling script) or by reference (which tells PowerBuilder that any changes made to the argument variable during the function will be reflected in the calling script).

TIP When calling a function with a large structure, it's more efficient to pass it by reference as opposed to value, even if you don't intend to change the values in the structure.

N O T E Your first function will be a function to disconnect the database when you leave the application. This function will be called by the close event and any other function that wants to disconnect the database. ■

When you're done defining your function, click OK. This will pull up the function painter, as seen in figure 7.3.

FIG. 7.3
The function painter
is used to type
PowerScript into
a function.

```
Function - f_disconnect_database returns boolean

Paste Argument                          Paste Global

// f_disconnect_database

if NOT gb_disconnecting then
    gb_disconnecting = TRUE
else
    return FALSE                // Already disconnected
end if

DISCONNECT USING SQLCA;
If SQLCA.SQLCode <> 0 Then
    MessageBox ( "Database Disconnect", "Unable to disconnect from the " +&
        "database.~r~n" + &
        "DB Error Code: " + String (SQLCA.SQLDBCode ) + "~r~n" + &
        "DB Error Message: " + SQLCA.SQLErrText, StopSign!, OK!, 1 )
    halt
End If
return TRUE                     // Disconnect was successful
```

The function painter is just like the script painter except for the paste list boxes. Because functions don't have events, there is no Paste Event list box. However, there is a Paste Argument list box that pastes any arguments you have defined. Global functions have no instance variable or objects they are attached to, so the function painter for global functions does not include these paste list boxes.

Type in your function script, and then save your function by choosing File, Save or by clicking the close button in Windows 95 (or by double-clicking the painter Control menu box in Windows 3.x) and clicking Yes when PowerBuilder asks if you want to save your changes.

 TIP Always put the name of your function or event in comments at the top of your script. That way, when you print the function or event, you know which function or event it came from.

The source code for f_disconnect_database is shown in listing 7.2.

Listing 7.2   f_disconnect_database

```
// f_disconnect_database

if NOT gb_disconnecting then
     gb_disconnecting = TRUE
else
     return FALSE                        // Already disconnected
end if

DISCONNECT USING SQLCA;
If SQLCA.SQLCode <> 0 Then
     MessageBox ( "Database Disconnect", &
          "Unable to disconnect from the " +&
          "Database. ~r~n" + &
          "DB Error Code: " + String (SQLCA.SQLDBCode ) + "~r~n" + &
          "DB Error Message: " + SQLCA.SQLErrText, StopSign!, OK!, 1 )
     halt
End If
return TRUE                             // Disconnect was successful
```

N O T E   When you try to save the above script, you'll notice some errors were detected in your script, as seen in figure 7.4. Whenever you try to save your script, PowerBuilder will check its syntax.

You have an error because the global variable, *gb_disconnecting*, has not yet been declared. You have to add a Boolean global variable, *gb_disconnecting,* for this script to work. To do this, click Declare, Global Variables, as seen in figure 7.4.

This will pull up the Declare Global Variables dialog box, as seen in figure 7.5. Here, you will enter the definition of all global variables that will be used in your system. ■

Using the PowerBuilder Local Function Painter

You can also use *local functions* (functions tied to a specific PowerBuilder object). You can have local functions in applications, menus, and windows. (You can also have them in user objects, but user objects are beyond the scope of this book.) To access a local function painter, choose Declare and pick *objectname* Functions, in which *objectname* is the type of object function you're declaring (Application, Menu, or Window). This can be seen in figure 7.6.

Part

II

Ch

7

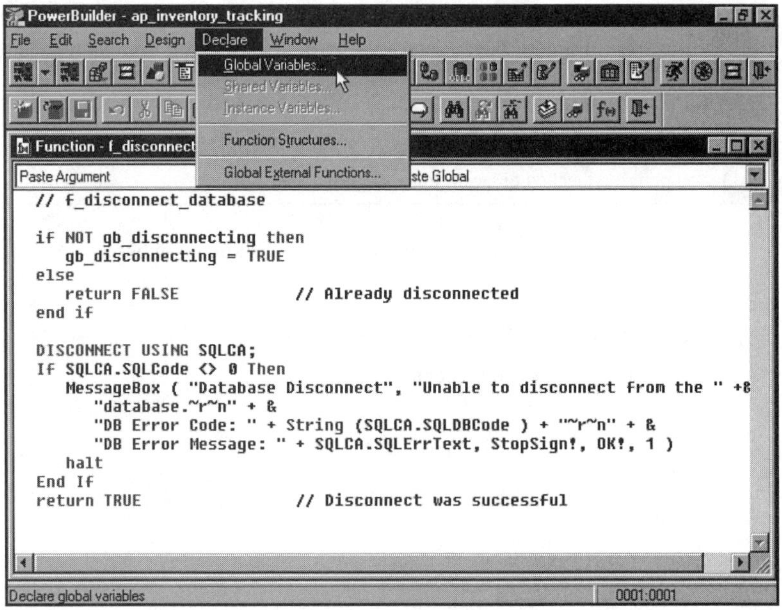

FIG. 7.4

PowerBuilder will display compiler errors when you try to save your PowerScript.

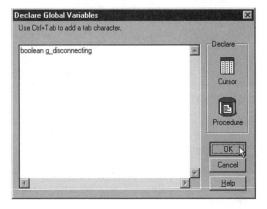

FIG. 7.5

Use the Declare Global Variables dialog box to define variables accessed throughout your system.

Assume the object you're working on is a menu. The local Select Function in *{objectname}* (in this case, Select Function in Menu) dialog box appears, as seen in figure 7.7.

Click New to pull up the New Function dialog box. This dialog box, shown in figure 7.8, is identical to the one seen in figure 7.2.

FIG. 7.6
To get into a local function painter, choose Declare, {objectname} Functions for the object you're in.

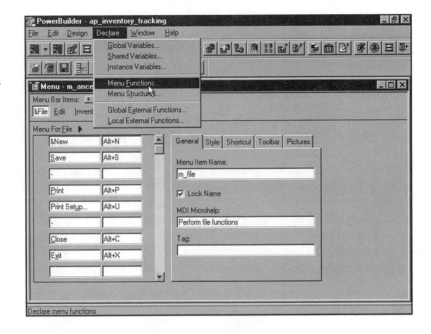

FIG. 7.7
The local Select Function in Menu dialog box allows you to modify an existing local function or create a new local function in a menu object.

Deciding Between a Function and an Event

The line between functions and user-defined events is starting to blur with PowerBuilder 5.0. Events now support functions, and functions can now be posted due to new techniques keywords that PowerBuilder has introduced.

Using Function Arguments

In figure 7.8, an argument is added to the local function you are declaring. Now, every script calling this function must also pass a character argument.

> **N O T E** mf_set_toolbar will be used to manipulate the toolbar position in the Inventory Tracking system. ■

FIG. 7.8

The New Function dialog box is the same for local functions as it is for global functions.

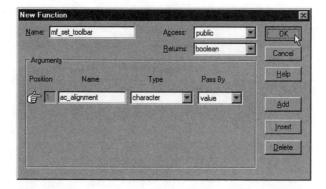

After you're done declaring your function, click OK. This will pull up the local function painter, which is identical to the global function painter except there's a Paste Instance window and a Paste Object window on the local function painter. (This is understandable—global functions have no instance variables or connected objects like local functions have.)

Because you declared an argument in figure 7.8, you can access the Paste Argument list box, as seen in figure 7.9.

FIG. 7.9

To paste your argument into your function painter, access the Paste Argument list box.

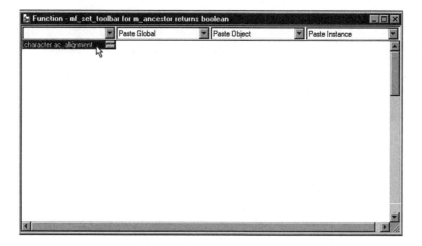

Figure 7.10 shows the completed local function. When you're done, exit the painter. Although PowerBuilder will ask you if you want to save, because this is a local function, you can't specify a PBL or comments as in a global function.

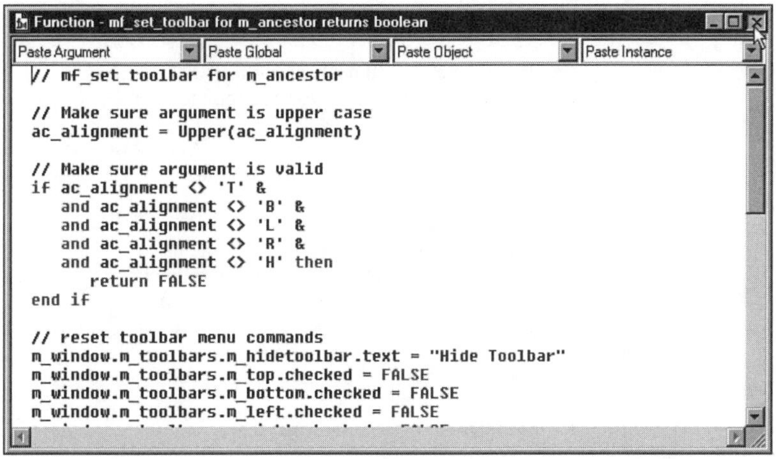

FIG. 7.10

Here's the finished local function to adjust the toolbar.

```
// mf_set_toolbar for m_ancestor

// Make sure argument is upper case
ac_alignment = Upper(ac_alignment)

// Make sure argument is valid
if ac_alignment <> 'T' &
    and ac_alignment <> 'B' &
    and ac_alignment <> 'L' &
    and ac_alignment <> 'R' &
    and ac_alignment <> 'H' then
        return FALSE
end if

// reset toolbar menu commands
m_window.m_toolbars.m_hidetoolbar.text = "Hide Toolbar"
m_window.m_toolbars.m_top.checked = FALSE
m_window.m_toolbars.m_bottom.checked = FALSE
m_window.m_toolbars.m_left.checked = FALSE
```

N O T E The mf_set_toolbar function handles all of your toolbar needs. The complete PowerScript listing is shown in listing 7.3 (note that ib_visible_toolbar is a Boolean instance variable.). ▪

Listing 7.3 mf_set_toolbar

```
// mf_set_toolbar for m_ancestor

// Make sure argument is upper case
ac_alignment = Upper(ac_alignment)

// Make sure argument is valid
if ac_alignment <> 'T' &
        and ac_alignment <> 'B' &
        and ac_alignment <> 'L' &
        and ac_alignment <> 'R' &
        and ac_alignment <> 'H' then
     return FALSE
end if

// reset toolbar menu commands
m_window.m_toolbars.m_hidetoolbar.text = "Hide Toolbar"
m_window.m_toolbars.m_top.checked = FALSE
m_window.m_toolbars.m_bottom.checked = FALSE
m_window.m_toolbars.m_left.checked = FALSE
m_window.m_toolbars.m_right.checked = FALSE
choose case Upper(ac_alignment)
     case 'T'
         Parentwindow.ToolBarAlignment = AlignAtTop!
         m_window.m_toolbars.m_top.checked = TRUE
     case 'B'
         Parentwindow.ToolBarAlignment = AlignAtBottom!
         m_window.m_toolbars.m_bottom.checked = TRUE
     case 'L'
```

Part

II

Ch

7

continues

Listing 7.3 Continued

```
            Parentwindow.ToolBarAlignment = AlignAtLeft!
            m_window.m_toolbars.m_left.checked = TRUE
    case 'R'
            Parentwindow.ToolBarAlignment = AlignAtRight!
            m_window.m_toolbars.m_right.checked = TRUE
    case 'H'
            if ib_visible_toolbar then
            parentwindow.toolbarvisible = FALSE
            m_window.m_toolbars.m_hidetoolbar.text = "Show Toolbar"
            ib_visible_toolbar = FALSE
            return TRUE                      // Don't execute the rest of the code
    else
            // Minor league recursion to set toolbar on top if it was hidden and
            // now should be shown.
            mf_set_toolbar('T')
    end if
    end choose

    ib_visible_toolbar = TRUE
    parentwindow.toolbarvisible = TRUE
    return TRUE
```

Using Event Arguments

▶ **See** "Implementing User-Defined Events," **p. 190**

PowerBuilder 5 now supports event arguments. You must declare any user-defined event arguments when you first declare the event. Click Declare, User Events (as seen in the previous chapter). Type in your event name and click Args, as seen in figure 7.11.

FIG. 7.11
You must click Args to choose arguments for your user-defined event.

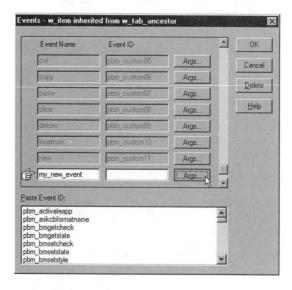

Now you should see the Event Declaration dialog box, as seen in figure 7.12. Here, you define the arguments needed for your event just like you would with a function. You can also define a return argument for testing.

TROUBLESHOOTING

I'm trying to declare arguments for my user-defined event, but PowerBuilder won't let me. What's wrong? Unlike previous versions of PowerBuilder, you are not allowed to choose an event ID for user-defined events unless you want that event ID's default arguments and return value. Normally, you would leave the event ID blank. Otherwise, PowerBuilder will assign arguments based on the event ID you've chosen.

FIG. 7.12

You can define arguments and return arguments for events in the Event Declaration dialog box.

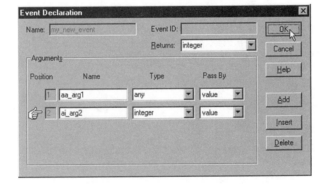

After you're done deciding the arguments you need, click OK to return to the Events dialog box, and click OK again to return to the window painter.

Now you can use the arguments you declared in your event using the Arguments drop down list box, as seen in figure 7.13.

FIG. 7.13

Arguments you declared are now available for use in your event script.

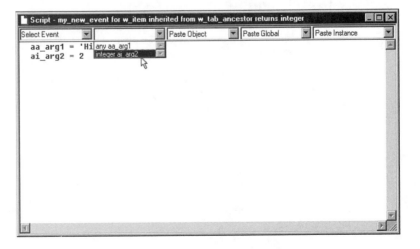

Part

II

Ch

7

Triggering and Posting Events and Functions

 Calling events with arguments and posting functions are new features of PowerBuilder 5. These tasks are accomplished with the new keywords, POST and TRIGGER. To call an event with arguments, you must use these new keywords. For instance, to call the event we declared in figures 7.11 through 7.13, you would use the following syntax:

```
TRIGGER EVENT my_new_event(la_any_variable, li_integer)
```

Posting the event with arguments to run after the current PowerScript is done running is similar:

```
POST EVENT my_new_event(la_any_variable, li_integer)
```

Using similar syntax, you can now post a function to run after the current PowerScript is done running:

```
POST FUNCTION my_function( )
```

You can also use TRIGGER FUNCTION, but that's identical to simply calling the function. The statements:

```
TRIGGER FUNCTION my_function( )
```

and

```
my_function( )
```

are identical. Most developers will prefer the second syntax since there's less typing involved, but both are acceptable.

Programming for Specific Events

Now that you've declared and written some functions, you need to code for some application events and the myriad of menu events, and also declare and program for some window events.

Programming for Application Events

You have seen the programming for the open event of the application. As was mentioned before, unless you code for the open event of the application, nothing will happen in your application. Now you can program for other application events.

Coding for the Application Close   You should disconnect from the database upon exit, which can be done in the close event of the application. Fortunately, you've already written a global function to disconnect from the database. So, the entire code for your event consists of two comments and one function call:

```
// Close event of the Inventory Tracking system.
// Before application closes, disconnect database.

f_disconnect_database ( )
```

Although you've written functions, this is the first time you've called a user-defined function. See how easy it is?

System Errors   The systemerror event on the application is triggered when PowerBuilder encounters an error in a script it is executing. If it can, PowerBuilder will then call the systemerror event of the application.

You may want to format your messages a little differently than PowerBuilder formats them. You also may want to give an option to continue. The code in listing 7.4 can accomplish this.

Listing 7.4   Systemerror Event

```
// Systemerror event in Inventory_tracking

int answer

answer=MessageBox("System Error","A system error has occurred."+&
"~r~n~r~n    Powerbuilder error number: "+String(error.number)+&
"~r~n    Error Message:         " + error.text + &
"~r~n    Window/Menu in error: " + error.windowmenu + &
"~r~n    Object in error:       " + error.object + &
"~r~n    Event in error:        " + error.objectevent + &
"~r~n    Line of error:         " + string(error.line) + &
"~r~n~n Do you wish to continue?", StopSign!, YESNO!, 1 )

if answer <> 1 then
close (w_inventory_frame)
halt close
end if
```

In the above event, a message box appears with a yes or no question, telling the user about the error and asking the user if he or she wants to continue. If the answer isn't yes, the frame window closes and issues a halt close statement.

Programming for Menu Events

The need for PowerScript is most apparent with menus. For every menu option or every toolbar button you click, some PowerScript needs to be executed. In this section, you'll program for every menu option except those options under Help.

▶ **See** "Adding Help for Inventory Tracking," **p. 428**

Most event coding consists of one or two lines. Therefore, you can see each event script, in table form, listed in the following sections.

Using Window Inheritance with PowerScript   As said before, you probably want to do all of your coding in the ancestor menu and then inherit all the code to all other menus. This way, you have one place to go to add a menu item, and one place to modify the code.

Triggering Windows Events   Because you are using generic functions in your menu, you probably don't want to specifically name a sheet window in your processing. Therefore, all references to windows will use ParentWindow as the window name.

Part

II

Ch

7

Because you are using ParentWindow as your window name, you can't access DataWindows or other window controls. Therefore, you'll delegate functions that need access to a window control to the windows themselves by declaring user-defined window events and then triggering them from your window.

▶ **See** "Understanding Events," **p. 188**

Table 7.3 and 7.4 list all the scripts in the File and Edit menu bar items of m_ancestor. Therefore, they will be inherited to all menus in the Inventory Tracking system. (For brevity, comments were left out of the table.)

N O T E   Notice that we had to declare user events in w_tab_ancestor. These events will be triggered when the user clicks the appropriate menu item. The user events needed are:

- new—Triggered when the user clicks File, New.
- save—Triggered when the user clicks File, Save.
- print—Triggered when the user clicks File, Print.
- undo—Triggered when the user clicks Edit, Undo.
- cut—Triggered when the user clicks Edit, Cut.
- copy—Triggered when the user clicks Edit, Copy.
- paste—Triggered when the user clicks Edit, Paste.
- newrow—Triggered when the user clicks Edit, Insert.
- delrow—Triggered when the user clicks Edit, Delete.

User-defined events are a great way for a descendent menu to trigger an event in a descendent window. It also allows all windows coding to be contained inside a window rather than split between a menu and a window. ■

Table 7.3   Menu Script for Items in the File Menu

Menu Option	PowerScript for Menu Option
&New	ParentWindow.TriggerEvent("new")
&Save	ParentWindow.TriggerEvent("save")
&Print	ParentWindow.TriggerEvent("print")
PrintSet&up	PrintSetup()
&Close	Close(ParentWindow)
E&xit	Halt Close

Table 7.4 Menu Script for Items in the Edit Menu

Menu Option	PowerScript for Menu Option
&Undo	ParentWindow.TriggerEvent("undo")
C&ut	ParentWindow.TriggerEvent("cut")
C&opy	ParentWindow.TriggerEvent("copy")
&Paste	ParentWindow.TriggerEvent("paste")
&Insert	ParentWindow.TriggerEvent("newrow")
&Delete	ParentWindow.TriggerEvent("delrow")

N O T E Of course, now all of those events that have been triggered need to be defined. These windows events will be discussed later in this chapter. ▨

Using OpenSheet Commands   In the Inventory menu bar item, all the commands relate to opening windows. The OpenSheet command is used for each option, as seen in table 7.5.

Table 7.5 Menu Script for Items under Inventory

Menu Option	PowerScript for Menu Option
Ite&m Entry	opensheet(w_item, w_inventory_frame, 4, Layered!)
Cust&omer Entry	opensheet(w_customer, w_inventory_frame, 4, Layered!)
Supp&lier	opensheet(w_supplier, w_inventory_frame, 4, Layered!)
In&voice Entry	opensheet(w_invoice, w_inventory_frame, 4, Layered!)
Wa&rehouse Entry	opensheet(w_warehouse, w_inventory_frame, 4, Layered!)

Arranging Sheets and Icons   Table 7.6 shows that most of the menu items in this category share the same command. Each of these commands arranges your window a little differently, depending on the enumerated variable passed to the windows function ArrangeSheets.

N O T E You can actually name the window in this category since the window is a frame window. ▨

Table 7.6 Menu Script for Items under Window

Menu Option	PowerScript for Menu Option
&Tile	w_inventory_frame.ArrangeSheets (Tile!)
Casca&de	w_inventory_frame.ArrangeSheets (Cascade!)

continues

Table 7.6 Continued	
Menu Option	**PowerScript for Menu Option**
&Layer	w_inventory_frame.ArrangeSheets (Layer!)
&Arrange Icons	w_inventory_frame.ArrangeSheets (Icons!)
Toolbars_	Not applicable because Toolbars is a cascaded menu.

Changing the Toolbar Remember the long mf_set_toolbar function? Here's where that pays off. Because of writing one function, you can coordinate all functions that affect the appearance of the toolbar—all with a single call to that function.

Table 7.7 shows the commands needed to write each toolbar function now that you have mf_set_toolbar.

Table 7.7 Menu Script for Items under Toolbars	
Menu Option	**PowerScript for Menu Option**
&Top	mf_set_toolbar('T')
&Bottom	mf_set_toolbar('B')
&Left	mf_set_toolbar('L')
&Right	mf_set_toolbar('R')
&Hide Toolbar	mf_set_toolbar('H')

&Show Text	if checked = FALSE then
	checked = TRUE
	inventory_tracking.toolbartext = TRUE
	else
	checked = FALSE
	inventory_tracking.toolbartext = FALSE
	end if

Now you have a menu script more than one line long. Remember that mf_set_toolbar is a user-defined function.

Programming for Window Events

Developing applications by using PowerBuilder windows events makes your windows programming easier than with any other windows development tool. Remember all those events you typed in while programming your ancestor menu? Well, now you have to declare them, as seen in figure 7.14. This is best done, again, in w_datawindow_ancestor. That way, the PowerScript extends down to the individual windows as it did with the menus.

FIG. 7.14
You have to declare many events because of the way the menus were created.

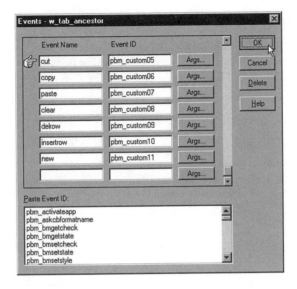

Again, PowerScript makes programming for events fairly easy. Tables 7.8–7.10 list events and the script (without comments) that goes with each event in the w_tab_ancestor window.

Table 7.8   Events in w_tab_ancestor

Window Event	PowerScript for Window Event	Syntax Description
clear	idw_data.clear()	Calls the DataWindow clear function of the current DataWindow.
copy	idw_data.copy()	Calls the DataWindow copy function of the current DataWindow.
cut	idw_data.cut()	Calls the DataWindow cut function of the current DataWindow.
delrow	idw_data.triggerevent ("delete_row")	Triggers the delete_row event (see below) of the current DataWindow.
paste	idw_data.paste()	Calls the DataWindow paste function of the current DataWindow.
insertrow	idw_data.triggerevent ("insert_row")	Triggers the insert_row event (see below) of the current DataWindow.

Part
II

Ch

7

continues

Table 7.8   Continued

Window Event	PowerScript for Window Event	Syntax Description
new	idw_data.triggerevent ("new_datawindow")	Triggers the delete_row event (see below) of the current DataWindow.
open	wf_set_datawindow()	Sets the current DataWindow and triggers the retrieve event.
	if message.doubleparm <> 0 then	
	triggerevent("retrieve") end if	
print	idw_data.triggerevent ("print_datawindow")	Triggers the print_ datawindow event of the current DataWindow.
retrieve	long retrieval_argument	Retrieves the current DataWindow based on the argument passed to the window (via an OpenWithParm function).
	retrieval_argument = message.doubleparm	
	idw_data.retrieve (retrieval_argument)	
save	idw_data.triggerevent ("update_datawindow")	Triggers the current update function.
undo	idw_data.undo()	Calls the DataWindow undo function of the current DataWindow.

Table 7.9   Events in w_tab_ancestor's Tab Control

Window Event	PowerScript for Window Event	Syntax Description
SelectionChanged	Int li_control_num = 1	
	WindowObject hopeful_datawindow	
	Do While IsValid(&	
	control[selectedtab].control	
	[li_control_num])	
	If control[selectedtab].control[&	
	li_control_num].typeof() =&	

Window Event	PowerScript for Window Event	Syntax Description
	DataWindow! Then	When the tab selection changes, this routine resets the current DataWindow so that all the events that are required to act on the current DataWindow can function.
	hopeful_datawindow = &	
	control[selectedtab].control[&	
	li_control_num]	
	Exit	
	End If	
	Loop	
	If IsValid(hopeful_datawindow) Then	
	idw_data = hopeful_datawindow	
	Else	
	SetNull(idw_data)	
	End If	

Table 7.10   Events in u_datawindow_inventory_entry

Window Event	PowerScript for Window Event	Syntax Description
after_change	Retrieve(GetItemNumber(getrow(), & is_retrieve_column))	Retrieves the current row when a new key has been chosen.
constructor	triggerevent("new_datawindow")	Triggers the new_datawindow (see below) event.

delete_row	if messagebox("Delete Row", &
	
	 "Are you sure you want to delete this row?",&
	
	 STOPSIGN!, YESNO!, 2) = 1 then
	  deleterow(0)
	end if
	if getrow() = 0 then
	  triggerevent("insert_row")
	end if
		Deletes the current row and inserts a new row if there are no more rows on the DataWindow.

insert_row	insertrow(0)	Inserts a new row on the DataWindow.

Part

II

Ch

7

continues

Table 7.10 Continued

Window Event	PowerScript for Window Event	Syntax Description

itemchanged	gb_ask_about_update = TRUE
	
	if is_retrieve_column = '' then
	
	MessageBox ('Retrieve Column Not Set', &
	  'The column needed to generate a new ' + &
	  'retrieve has not been set in ' +&
	  'Constructor event of the Datawindow ' + &
	  dataobject)
	elseif GetColumnName() = &
	    is_retrieve_column then
	  // Save out if necessary
	  if uf_ask_to_save() = FALSE then
	Return 2 // Make the itemchange event fail
	   else
	PostEvent("after_change")
	end if
	end if
		Check if the key has changed, and if it has, see if the user wants to save out the current row before selecting a new row.

new_datawindow	if uf_ask_to_save() = FALSE then
	
	Return 2 // Event fail
	else
	  reset () // Clear DataWindow
	  triggerevent("insert_row") // Make blank row
	end if
		Sees if the user wants to save the current information, and if so resets the DataWindow and inserts a blank row.

print_datawindowprint()		Prints the DataWindow
update_datawindow update()		Saves the contents of the current DataWindow.

N O T E In the retrieve event, you first need to convert the doubleparm to a string and then to a long. PowerBuilder has no facility for converting decimals to longs. ■

Programming for Treeviews

Although the Inventory Tracking system does not need to treeviews, treeviews can be implemented when a breakdown or subdivision of a category is needed. For instance, an organization chart program or a process decomposition program can be implemented using treeviews. Windows uses treeviews for directory and subdirectory diagramming of your hard drive.

Treeviews can be a little tricky to implement. First, you must define the pictures you are going to use in the treeview properties sheet, as seen in figure 7.15. (Of course, a text-only treeview does not need to contain or use pictures, but pictures add a professional touch.)

FIG. 7.15

You must define any pictures you use for a treeview.

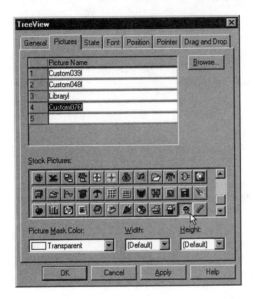

N O T E The code for this example can be found in the miscellaneous PBL included on your CD. ■

Next, you must code PowerScript to add nodes to your treeview. This is probably best done with a function so that this PowerScript only needs to be coded once. As you can see in figure 7.16, I passed the treeview, the label (that is displayed), the data (that is returned to the program), and the window handle of the parent node to this function.

There are three functions written used to process a treeview. The first, f_add_to_treeview (seen in listing 7.5) declares a treeviewitem, which is a node on a treeview. Then it fills in that item and adds it to the treeview using the InsertItemLast treeview function.

Part

II

Ch

7

FIG. 7.16

A separate function is a good idea to add nodes to a treeview.

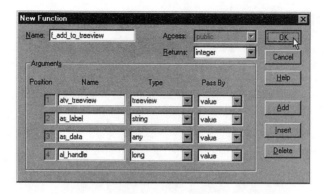

Listing 7.5 f_add_to_treeview

```
treeviewitem ltvi_new
long ll_newhandle

ltvi_New.Label = as_label
ltvi_New.Data = aa_data
ll_newhandle = atv_treeview.InsertItemLast(al_handle, ltvi_New)
If ll_newhandle < 1 Then
        Messagebox('TREEVIEW ERROR', &
                'Insertlastitem error on in the wf_add_person '+ &
                'function of w_treeview')
End If
return ll_newhandle
```

If a handle of another node is passed to the treeview, InsertItemLast adds the new node as a subdivision of the handle's node. If a 0 is passed as a handle, InsertItemLast adds the new node as a root node (with no parent).

In the w_treeview window, the window function, wf_buildtree, calls f_add_to_treeview to build the treeview, as seen in listing 7.6.

Listing 7.6 wf_buildtree

```
long    ll_company_handle
long    ll_office_handle

ll_company_handle = f_add_to_treeview(tv_1, "Make More Money, Inc.", 1, 0)
ll_office_handle = f_add_to_treeview(tv_1, "East Coast Division", 1,
➡ll_company_handle)
f_add_to_treeview(tv_1, "Jack Horner", 1, ll_office_handle)
f_add_to_treeview(tv_1, "Mary Q. Contrary", 3, ll_office_handle)
ll_office_handle = f_add_to_treeview(tv_1, "West Coast Division", 1,
➡ll_company_handle)
f_add_to_treeview(tv_1, "L. Bo Peep", 4, ll_office_handle)
f_add_to_treeview(tv_1, "I. John Henry", 4, ll_office_handle)
ll_office_handle = f_add_to_treeview(tv_1, "International Division", 1,
```

```
➥ll_company_handle)
f_add_to_treeview(tv_1, "K. Cole", 2, ll_office_handle)
f_add_to_treeview(tv_1, "Ali Babba", 4, ll_office_handle)
f_add_to_treeview(tv_1, "Santa Clause", 4, ll_office_handle)
tv_1.SetLevelPictures(1, 2, 1, 0, 0)
tv_1.SetLevelPictures(2, 3, 1, 0, 0)
tv_1.SetLevelPictures(3, 4, 4, 0, 0)
```

Now, the treeview will look like figure 7.17.

To capture any data changes in your treeview, use the SelectionChanged event. Here, you can tell when a user has changed the current selected node. Some example code for the SelectionChanged event can be seen in listing 7.7.

FIG. 7.17

A finished treeview built by wf_buildtree and f_add_to_treeview.

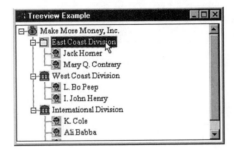

Listing 7.7   SelectionChanged Event of a Treeview

```
// In Selectionchanged event of a treeview,
// oldhandle and newhandle are argument events

treeviewitem ltvi_olditem
treeviewitem ltvi_newitem
string level_name[] = {"Company", "Sales office", "Employee"}
string ls_message

getitem (oldhandle, ltvi_olditem)
getitem (newhandle, ltvi_newitem)

if ltvi_olditem.level > 0 Then //First time through
        messagebox ("Treeview Change", &
                "Old Selection:" +&
                "~r " + level_name[ltvi_olditem.level] + " Name: " +
➥ltvi_olditem.label +&
                "~r " + level_name[ltvi_olditem.level] + " ID: " +
string(ltvi_olditem.data) +&
                "~r~rNew Selection:" + &
                "~r " + level_name[ltvi_newitem.level] + " Name: " +
➥ltvi_newitem.label +&
                "~r " + level_name[ltvi_newitem.level] + " ID: " +
string(ltvi_newitem.data))
end if
```

Part

II

Ch

7

The oldhandle and newhandle variables are arguments passed to the SelectionChanged event. With the above code, a messagebox opens every time the treeview changes nodes with a message that can be seen in figure 7.18.

FIG. 7.18
You can take action when a treeview node is selected, as seen by this messagebox.

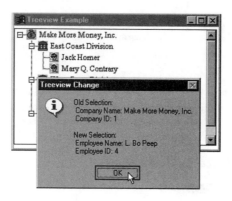

Avoiding Trouble

PowerBuilder has incorporated many tools to help you develop your applications. Behind every one of these tools, PowerScript controls the flow of control and the implementation of the design. Following are some tips to help you prevent problems while coding in PowerScript:

- Use comments generously. Often, a developer thinks his or her code is self-documenting. When other developers start to work on this code or when the developer comes back to the code after a year, sometimes several days can be wasted as the flow of the code is deciphered.

- A well-placed comment, especially on a tricky or "really neat" piece of code, can help future developers maintain your code.

- Avoid bad coding constructs. A poorly written SQL SELECT statement or a deep, complicated nested loop can bring an application to its knees. If you find your application running slowly, try looking at your SQL SELECT statements and your loops to see if there's a way to improve them.

- Avoid excessive coding in PowerScript. PowerScript is necessary in PowerBuilder for every application. However, usually only a few lines of PowerScript are necessary for each event and menu item. If you find yourself coding scripts that are several pages in length (especially if no SQL or database-initialization calls were used), then you're *probably* being inefficient and/or using older COBOL-like and BASIC-like experience to code your PowerBuilder.

- Try reviewing the code to see if there is any way to not code in PowerScript or to code less PowerScript to achieve the same ends. One of the major benefits of PowerBuilder is that it does a lot of work for you if you let it.

From Here...

This chapter shows you much about how to program for events and functions. If you need further help, consult the PowerBuilder online help. You can also read further in these areas:

- Chapter 6, "Using Events, Functions, and the PowerScript Language," describes basic PowerScript programming. It's a must for the beginner.

- Chapter 14, "Putting It All Together in an Application," discusses inheritance, online help, and how to make your Inventory Tracking system ready to deliver.

- Chapter 15, "Debugging Your Application," reminds you that no programming is finished until it's been fully tested and debugged. Here, PowerBuilder expert Blaine Bickar shows how to debug an application.

- Part VII, "References," serves as an excellent reference resource when you need to look up a function, an enumerated data type, an attribute, or an event.

Part
II

Ch
7

Using SQL in PowerBuilder

by Charles A. Wood

SQL (Structured Query Language) is a common language found in many databases. SQL was designed to give developers a common method for updating and retrieving data from tables on a database. SQL allows you to access your database from your PowerScript. There are many concepts common to most SQL implementations. Most of these commands (except the cursor commands) can be entered through the Database Administrator in the database painter.

This chapter discusses what you can do with SQL inside PowerBuilder. Notice all of the cautions in this chapter—when dealing with SQL, your application can either be accelerated or grind to a complete halt. SQL is a powerful tool, but be aware of its pitfalls. ■

Understand the SQL syntax of several SQL commands.

SQL syntax occurs throughout PowerBuilder development. This chapter can give you a handle on those complex SQL commands.

Using SQL transaction objects.

Transaction objects are used to talk to the database from PowerBuilder. This chapter describes transaction objects like SQLCA and how to use them.

Understand the way databases handle NULLs.

NULLs are a complex database topic. This chapter discusses NULLs and tells when and how they are used.

Use the SQL painter and the cursor painter.

The SQL painter can paint a complex SQL statement with a few mouse clicks. This chapter shows you how to paint your SQL statements rather than coding them from scratch using the SQL painter.

Implement an SQL cursor.

Cursors are some of the most complex SQL structures. This chapter shows you how to implement an SQL cursor in PowerBuilder.

TIP Don't confuse *all* SQL with *Sybase SQL Anywhere* SQL. There is a Sybase SQL Anywhere SQL appendix with tips, notes, cautions, and utilities that are unique to SQL Anywhere. PowerBuilder's implementation of SQL works on any database PowerBuilder supports.

Understanding SQL Syntax

You'll first learn the SQL syntax that you are likely to run into when inside PowerBuilder's script painter. You can also view SQL syntax when painting a DataWindow. Understanding some basic SQL is important to any client-server development in PowerBuilder.

SELECT

SELECT is the command that lets you read from your tables. It is one of the most complex SQL commands. Its format is the following:

```
SELECT     { DISTINCT } ¦ select-list ¦
 ¦    *    ¦
INTO host_variable_list
FROM table_list
{ WHERE search_condition }
{ GROUP BY column_name }
{ HAVING search_condition }
{ ORDER BY  field_list {DESC }};
```

The components of the SQL SELECT command are as follows:

- DISTINCT. If DISTINCT is specified, all duplicate rows are eliminated. Otherwise, all rows are returned.

CAUTION

Remember, DISTINCT only eliminates rows that are exact duplicates of each other. This is not the same as only selecting one row. If any columns are different between two rows, DISTINCT will report both rows.

Embedded SQL can only retrieve one row at a time. Reporting more than one row could cause an SQL run-time error.

Also, using DISTINCT takes a lot of time. If possible, avoid using it.

- select-list. The select-list is the list of column names you want selected. An asterisk (*) in the place of the select-list will cause all columns to be selected.

CAUTION

Although coding an * for your select-list is much easier than typing every column in a table, if columns are added, deleted, or change order, your select statement may no longer work. It's better to bite the bullet and code in all of the field names.

■ INTO host_variable_list. The host_variable_list is a list of variables in your application that will hold the retrieved columns.

N O T E The INTO clause of the SELECT statement is required when you embed SQL into your PowerScript. However, the INTO clause is not allowed any other time, as with the Database Administrator in the database painter. Host variables cannot be declared or used in the Database Administrator. With no host variables, you can't make the host_variable_list required for the INTO clause. ■

CAUTION

Remember, not all database data types are the same as PowerBuilder data types. For instance, the Sybase SQL Anywhere integer has a range of –2,147,483,647 to 2,147,483,647; PowerBuilder's integer only has a range of –32,768 to 32,767. There's a lot of room for overflow when the two transact with each other. When overflow of this nature occurs, no error message is given, and your PowerBuilder integer has a corrupted value! Any overflow errors have to be caught during run-time testing!

 T I P (If you are reading in a Sybase SQL Anywhere integer datatype, store it into a PowerBuilder long datatype and everything will be OK.)

■ FROM table_list. The FROM clause allows the developer to specify which tables to SELECT data from.

■ WHERE search_condition. The WHERE clause filters the incoming data based on the search_condition specified.

■ GROUP BY column_list. The GROUP BY clause groups together multiple rows from the database, based on unique values found in your column_list.

■ HAVING search_condition. The HAVING clause must be accompanied by a GROUP BY clause. The search_condition of the HAVING clause filters the SELECT much like the WHERE clause, but unlike the WHERE clause, the HAVING clause is applied to the group data.

■ ORDER BY field_list {DESC}. The ORDER BY clause allows you to arrange the resulting columns of SELECT in a certain order, defined by field_list. The order is ascending unless DESC is specified.

Some SQL SELECT examples are shown in table 8.1.

Table 8.1 SQL SELECT Examples

SQL SELECT Statement	Description
SELECT * FROM customer;	This selects all columns and rows from the customer table.
SELECT name, address, sales FROM customer WHERE purchase > 1000 ORDER BY sales;	This selects the name, address, and sales from the customer table for all customers whose purchases are over 1,000. It puts these customers in sales order.
SELECT territory, SUM(sales) INTO :sales_territory, :sales_total FROM customer GROUP BY territory HAVING COUNT(*) > 10;	This sums the sales by territory for those territories with more than 10 customers. It puts these values into host variables sales_territory and sales_total.
SELECT supplier.name, item.name, item.cost FROM item,supplier WHERE item.cost > 100 AND supplier.supplier_number = item.supplier_number;	This joins the item and supplier table by supplier number and selects supplier name, item name, and item cost for all items priced over $100.

N O T E A host variable is a variable previously declared in PowerScript. These can be used inside most SQL commands. Notice in table 8.1 that they are always preceded by a colon (:). This indicates to your database that they are host variables and not table columns. ■

INSERT

INSERT puts additional rows into a table. Its format is the following:

```
INSERT INTO table_name {column_list} ¦ VALUES values_list    ¦
¦ SELECT command          ¦
```

The parts of the INSERT command are as follows:

- ■ table_name. This is where you are going to insert new rows. It can be as fully qualified as your database allows.

- ■ column_list. This is a list of columns that you are going to fill with your INSERT. If omitted, the INSERT command assumes all fields will be entered in the order they appear on your table.

CAUTION

Although column_list is not required in an INSERT command, you should be careful about omitting it. If you try to save some typing by not adding it and someone later adds fields to your table, your SQL statement may no longer work.

- values_list. This is a list of values (either constants or host variables) that you want to insert.
- SELECT_command. This is a SELECT command that returns values in the same order as the column_list.

Some examples of the INSERT command are shown in table 8.2.

Table 8.2   SQL INSERT Examples

SQL INSERT Statement	Description
INSERT INTO customer (name, address) VALUES ('Joe Schmoe', :working_address);	This inserts a row into the customer table with "Joe Schmoe" as the name and the contents of the host variable working_address as the address.
INSERT INTO customer (name, address, phone) VALUES (SELECT prospect_name, :working_address, '555-5555' FROM prospect_table WHERE prospect_id = :new_client_id);	This inserts all rows from the prospect table into the customer table using the prospect_name as the name, the host variable working_address as the address, and a constant "555-5555" as the phone number.

N O T E   Notice how you can mix host variables, constants, and table variables on the INSERT command when you use a SELECT command to retrieve your INSERT information. ■

UPDATE

The UPDATE command is used to update existing rows on a table with new data. Its format is as follows:

```
UPDATE table_name
SET    column_name1 = expression1,
column_name2 = expression2,...
WHERE search_condition;
```

The table_name is the name of the table you wish to update. The search_condition in the WHERE clause is the same as in the SELECT statement. The column_name is a name of a column, and expression is the constant or host variable whose value will be placed inside the column.

Some examples of the UPDATE statement are shown in table 8.3.

Table 8.3   SQL UPDATE Examples

SQL UPDATE Statement	Description
UPDATE my_table SET inactive_switch = 'Y';	This sets inactive_switch to 'Y' for all rows in my_table.
UPDATE my_table SET inactive_switch = 'Y', inactive_date = :todays_date WHERE last_name = "SMITH";	This sets inactive_switch to 'Y' and inactive_date to the host variable :todays_date for all rows in my_table whose last_name is SMITH.

DELETE

The DELETE command is used to delete existing rows from a table. Its format is as follows:

```
DELETE FROM table_name
{WHERE search_condition};
```

The table_name is the name of the table in which you can delete rows. The search_condition in the WHERE clause is the same as in the SELECT statement.

Some examples of the DELETE statement are shown in table 8.4.

Table 8.4   SQL DELETE Examples

SQL DELETE Statement	Description
DELETE FROM my_table;	This deletes all rows from my_table.
DELETE FROM my_table WHERE last_name = "SMITH";	This deletes all rows from my_table whose last name is SMITH.

CONNECT and DISCONNECT

The CONNECT command connects the database transaction (*SQLCA*) to your application. The DISCONNECT command releases the database and frees up system resources used to keep the database connected to your application. The format for the two commands is as follows:

```
CONNECT {USING transaction};
```

```
DISCONNECT {USING transaction};
```

The transaction is usually SQLCA, although you can define new transactions in PowerBuilder. Table 8.5 shows some examples of CONNECT and DISCONNECT.

Table 8.5   SQL Connect and Disconnect Examples

SQL Statement	Description
CONNECT;	This connects to the database defined by SQLCA.
CONNECT USING my_transaction;	This connects to the database defined by my_transaction.
DISCONNECT;	This disconnects from the database defined by SQLCA.
DISCONNECT USING my_transaction;	This disconnects from the database defined by my_transaction.

N O T E   If you don't use the SQLCA transaction, you must add a USING clause every time you use a SQL statement. Most developers simply use SQLCA to avoid additional coding. Although this will work, PowerSoft suggests you always code the transaction to avoid ambiguity. ■

COMMIT and ROLLBACK

When you make changes to your table, the changes are not permanent until you use COMMIT to commit them to the table. If you later decide against keeping the data (in your application), you issue a ROLLBACK statement to erase all changes to the database since the application started or since the last COMMIT statement. Table 8.6 shows examples of COMMIT and ROLLBACK.

Table 8.6   SQL Commit and Rollback Examples

SQL Statement	Description
COMMIT;	This commits all work since the last COMMIT.
ROLLBACK;	This erases all work since the last COMMIT.

Using SQL Transactions and Testing Your SQLCode

▶ **See** "Understanding Database Transactions," **p. 224**

Depending on your database and how it's defined, not committing your work will eventually cause a slowdown in database performance. This is because the disk space and memory space that the database sets aside for non-committed work can grow to a size larger than what the database creators have optimized for. It's not a bad idea to commit your work every time you have a successful SQL function, thereby keeping the buffer organized and efficient.

To see if you have a successful SQL function, you should check SQLCode every time you access the database. If SQLCode is not 0, then you know you have a database error and can act on it. For example, the following code checks for errors that occurred during the CONNECT and COMMIT statements:

```
CONNECT;
If SQLCA.SQLCode = 0 Then
 COMMIT;
End If
If SQLCA.SQLCode <> 0 Then
   { error processing goes here }
End If
```

TROUBLESHOOTING

My program works fine on my system, but I can't CREATE, DROP, or ALTER anything on my SQL Anywhere database after I distribute. Why is that? Certain SQL commands (such as CREATE commands, DROP command, and ALTER command) work fine inside your PowerBuilder environment, but don't work with the run-time version of SQL Anywhere and your compiled program. The incompatibility between the developer and run-time versions will cause your application to work inside the PowerBuilder environment, but cause your application to fail upon distribution. Unfortunately, incompatibilities between the Watcom SQL development version and the SQL Anywhere run-time version are only discussed in the Deployment and Development Kit that comes with PowerBuilder. (By the time you read the PowerBuilder documentation, some massive recoding may be necessary.)

If you are using the Sybase SQL Anywhere database, refer to Appendix B, "Using the SQL Anywhere Database and SQL Anywhere," for some commands not seen inside the PowerBuilder documentation and for some distribution tips.

▶ **See** "Comparing the Run-Time Version and the Developer's Version," **p. 775**

▶ **See** "Listing ISQL Commands," **p. 775**

Understanding NULL

One of the most difficult concepts in databases is the concept of NULL. When a database field has a value of NULL, that means that nothing was entered into the field. NULL is not zero, nor is it an empty string—it means that nothing was entered.

Several SQL statements (such as SELECT) can cause hard-to-track errors if they encounter a NULL. Updates can also fail with a NULL in a field if the field was defined to have no NULLs allowed.

Part

II

Ch

8

Using the SQL Painter

If you haven't guessed by now, SQL statements can be a pain to write. Not only do you have to know SQL syntax, but you have to know the columns of the tables you want to access.

PowerBuilder answers these concerns with its SQL painter. If you go into either a script painter or into the Database Administration painter, you can enter the SQL painter by choosing the SQL icon. The SQL Statement Type dialog box appears (see fig. 8.1).

FIG. 8.1

Clicking on the SQL icon displays the SQL Statement Type dialog box.

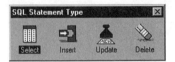

Although you can paint other SQL commands, in this example, the SELECT statement is chosen. In the SQL Statement Type dialog box, choose Select. The Select Tables dialog box, shown in figure 8.2, appears. Select both item and supplier, and choose Open.

FIG. 8.2

The first step in using the SQL painter is to choose the table(s) you want to access through the Select Tables dialog box.

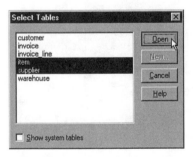

Now the painter pulls up the tables and shows you the two tables and how they are related, as shown in figure 8.3. Using the icons in the SQL painter PainterBar, you can choose any part of the SQL statement. Choose the tab, also shown in figure 8.3, to specify a WHERE clause in your SELECT statement.

FIG. 8.3

After choosing the item and supplier tables to SELECT from, the SQL painter appears.

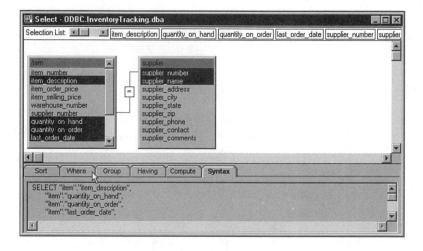

The Where Criteria tab now appears, as shown in figure 8.4. Here you can choose an SQL function or field, and then compare it to an expression (which would be a constant or host variable).

FIG. 8.4

In the Where Criteria tab, you can define the criteria for your WHERE statement.

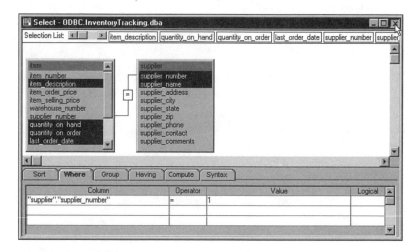

Finally, exit the SQL painter. PowerBuilder then asks you if you want to paste your changes to your script or database administration. Click Yes, and the PowerScript painter in figure 8.5 pops up. Now you have a relatively complicated SQL statement on-screen.

This is easier than coding it yourself (unless you're a fast typist, you happen to be an SQL genius, and you're completely familiar with your database).

▶ **See** "Using the SQL Toolbox," **p. 351**

FIG. 8.5

Now you have a finished, flawless SQL statement.

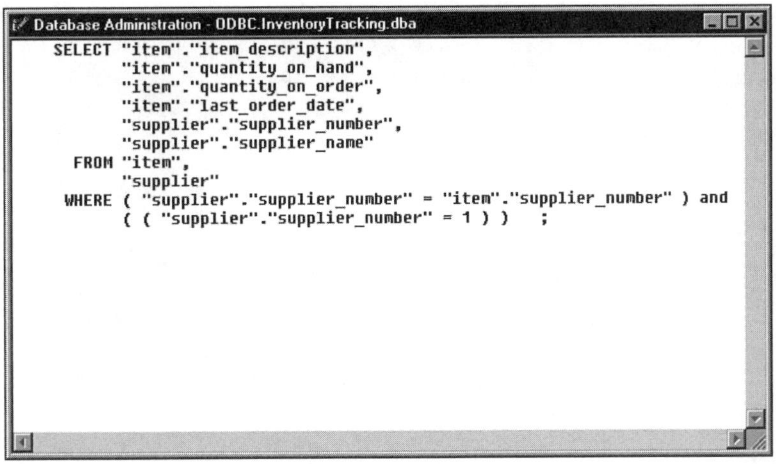

```
Database Administration - ODBC.InventoryTracking.dba

SELECT "item"."item_description",
       "item"."quantity_on_hand",
       "item"."quantity_on_order",
       "item"."last_order_date",
       "supplier"."supplier_number",
       "supplier"."supplier_name"
  FROM "item",
       "supplier"
 WHERE ( "supplier"."supplier_number" = "item"."supplier_number" ) and
       ( ( "supplier"."supplier_number" = 1 ) )   ;
```

Using Cursors

In embedded SQL, you'll receive a SQL error if you try to retrieve more than one row from a table. However, there are times when you want to retrieve many rows that meet certain criteria. If this is the case, you need to use a cursor. A cursor is a temporary table set up by SQL that brings in all rows that meet certain criteria. These rows can then be accessed one row at a time. Unlike previous SQL commands, you will examine all cursor commands and then see syntax examples for them.

DECLARE

Before you use a cursor, you must first DECLARE it. The syntax for declaring a cursor is as follows:

```
DECLARE cursor_name CURSOR FOR select_statement;
```

With this syntax, the cursor_name is any valid PowerBuilder name, and the select_statement is any valid SELECT statement, except that it can't have an INTO clause. (The INTO clause is used for the FETCH statement, which is described in the following sections.)

The CURSOR Painter

As you recall, the SQL statement for the cursor is fairly lengthy. You can enter the Select SQL painter by entering the Declare Instance Variables dialog box from an event or function, and double-clicking Cursor, as shown in figure 8.6. This puts you into an SQL painter so you can paint a SQL cursor statement as seen in the earlier figures. Your cursor now becomes an instance variable, a variable that PowerBuilder initializes with its default datatype when you open an object and ceases to exist when the object closes.

FIG. 8.6

Using the Declare
Instance Variables
dialog box, you can
paint your SQL cursor.

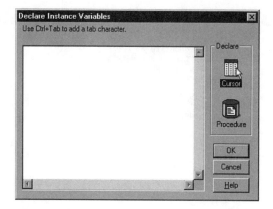

OPEN

After you DECLARE your cursor, you must OPEN it. The OPEN applies the SELECT criteria
and builds your temporary table with your rows in it. Its syntax is as follows:

```
OPEN cursor_name;
```

> **T I P** You might not like having SQL in your instance variables. You can use the Edit menu bar item to Cut
> and Paste your cursor to the script in which you use it. This changes your cursor into a local variable.

FETCH

After you are OPEN, you FETCH each row. FETCH allows you to sequentially process each
row. Its syntax is as follows:

```
FETCH cursor_name

INTO host_variable_list;
```

The INTO clause is identical to the INTO clause used in the SELECT statement.

CLOSE

When you are done with your cursor, you CLOSE it. Closing your cursor frees up any memory
taken up by the temporary tables, or allows you to reopen your cursor with new criteria. Its
syntax is as follows:

```
CLOSE cursor_name;
```

UPDATE and DELETE (Positioned)

You can issue update or delete commands on a FETCHed row by using what are called positioned cursor commands. While you are fetching your rows, you can issue a positioned DELETE to the current row by the command:

```
DELETE {table_name} WHERE CURRENT OF cursor_name;
```

cursor_name is the name of the cursor defined in the declare statement. table_name is optional, but used most often with multiple-table cursors.

The positioned UPDATE command is very similar to the normal UPDATE command mentioned earlier. You can also issue a positioned UPDATE to the current row by the command:

```
UPDATE table_name
SET    column_name1 = expression1,
column_name2 = expression2.
WHERE CURRENT OF cursor_name;
```

Example of a Cursor

In an event or function, table 8.7 shows how you would use a cursor.

Table 8.7 SQL CURSOR Examples

SQL CURSOR Statement	Description
DECLARE my_cursor CURSOR FOR SELECT name, address FROM customer;	This statement tells the cursor to SELECT the name and address from the customer table of all the customers when the cursor is OPENed.
OPEN my_cursor;	This statement applies the SELECT described in the DECLARE statement. It builds a temporary table to store the results.
FETCH my_cursor INTO :name, :address;	This statement retrieves one row into the host variable's name and address. Now the processing begins until the next FETCH statement.
CLOSE my_cursor;	This statement closes my_cursor and frees all the resources needed for the cursor.

From Here...

In this chapter, you've become familiar with several SQL commands and have learned how to work with them in PowerBuilder. This chapter has also shown you how databases handle NULLs, one of the most difficult concepts in databases. You've also examined all cursor commands and seen syntax examples for them.

SQL is necessary in PowerBuilder to do those tasks which are out of the ordinary. If you want to learn more about SQL, refer to the following chapters:

- Chapter 11, "Manipulating Data Using DataWindows," shows how SQL can be used to define a DataWindow. In this chapter, you learn more about the SQL toolbox and the SQL syntax behind a DataWindow.

- Appendix B, "Using SQL Anywhere Database and SQL Anywhere," shows how you can use SQL Anywhere to implement your application. Also covered in this appendix are SQL Anywhere SQL functions and SQL commands not allowed inside the PowerBuilder environment.

 Don't confuse *all* SQL with *SQL Anywhere* SQL. There is an SQL Anywhere SQL appendix with tips, notes, cautions, and utilities that are unique. PowerBuilder's implementation of SQL works on any database PowerBuilder supports.

Using DataWindows

Creating DataWindows

by Charles A. Wood

One of PowerBuilder's strongest features is DataWindows. DataWindows are data-entry screens that link a window to a database. They include several types of controls found on PowerBuilder windows.

The difference between DataWindows and data window screens found in other development environments is that DataWindow fields can be treated as individual columns or as single entities that consist of several rows. This makes updates to and retrieval from the database easier.

This chapter describes several DataWindow development techniques. You follow this by creating three DataWindows to use in your Inventory Tracking system. You then learn how to hook your DataWindows to your application. ■

Use the DataWindow Painter.

The DataWindow painter is a powerful tool for creating data entry windows. This chapter will show you how to use the painter.

Set and change default options for your DataWindow.

There are many options that can be set before you start developing your DataWindow. Setting these options before development can save you time later.

Differentiate between different data sources.

DataWindows can receive and update data from many different sources.

Differentiate between different presentation styles.

DataWindows can present data in many different formats, from graphs and crosstabs to tabular and freeform formats.

Use DataWindow controls.

Like windows, DataWindows have their own set of controls. This chapter describes each of the DataWindow controls.

Associate your DataWindow with a window or tab control.

After building your DataWindow, you'll need a way to tie it to a window or tab control. This chapter shows you how.

Using the DataWindow Painter

To get into the DataWindow painter, follow these steps:

1. Click the DataWindow PowerBar icon. The Select DataWindow dialog box, shown in figure 9.1, appears.

FIG. 9.1
Click on the
DataWindow icon; the
Select DataWindow
dialog box appears.

2. You can instruct PowerBuilder to either create a new DataWindow or modify an existing DataWindow. For now, click New to create a new DataWindow. The New DataWindow dialog box appears (see fig. 9.2).

FIG. 9.2
In the New DataWindow
window, choose your
data source and
presentation style.

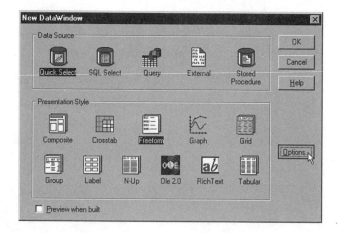

3. In the New DataWindow dialog box, you can define the Data Source, the Presentation Style, and the Generation Options, as discussed in the following sections.

In figure 9.2, Quick Select is chosen, which tells PowerBuilder to only use one table to create the DataWindow, and Freeform is chosen to tell PowerBuilder that you want a full screen with a single row represented. This also gives you the freedom to position the fields (columns) where you want them on the window.

N O T E   Notice in figure 9.2 that the Preview when built check box is deselected. Choosing to Preview when built only displays the DataWindow as PowerBuilder built it if there is data on the table chosen. You have no data on your tables, so choosing this only displays a confusing blank window. (Often you won't have any data on your tables when first creating your DataWindows because you'll probably use DataWindows to populate your tables.) ■

Understanding DataWindow Options

By clicking the Options button in the New DataWindow dialog box, the DataWindow Options window appears. DataWindow options are used to set initial defaults on DataWindows. These options are separated into three groups: general options, zoom options, and generation options.

Using General Options

General options, as seen in figure 9.3 are how DataWindows are displayed while in the painter. The following options can be set using the General tab of the DataWindow Options window:

- *Snap to Grid*. If clicked, then DataWindow controls snap to the grid when you place or move them in the window.
- *Show Grid*. If clicked, PowerBuilder shows the grid when it displays the DataWindow workspace.
- *Show Ruler*. If clicked, PowerBuilder shows the ruler when it displays the DataWindow workspace.
- *X*. X is the width of each cell in the grid in pixels.
- *Y*. Y is the height of each cell in the grid in pixels.

FIG. 9.3

General options for DataWindows can be specified using the General tab of the DataWindow Options window.

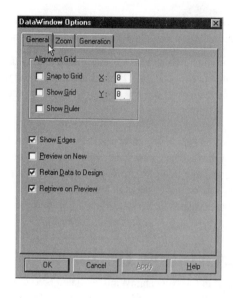

Using Zoom Options

Zoom options (see figure 9.4) let you zoom out (or in) of your DataWindow. This is often used in reports, where a sheet of paper will hold more than a screen.

FIG. 9.4

Zoom can be controlled using the Zoom tab of the DataWindow Options window.

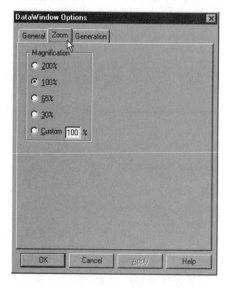

Using Generation Options

Generation options are default options that are used when a DataWindow is created. The following options can be set using the DataWindow Options dialog box, seen in figure 9.5:

- *Presentation Style.* Presentation style is the style of DataWindow initially chosen. Valid choices are tabular, form, grid, label, nup, crosstab, and group. These different presentation styles will be covered in the *Determining Presentation Style* section later in this chapter.

N O T E Notice that OLE 2.0, graph, rich text edit, and composite are not valid choices for initial presentation styles. This is because these formats are not your typical DataWindows in that they are mainly for viewing only and do not allow updates. ▓

- *Background Color.* This is the color of the DataWindow with no data on it.
- *Text Border.* This is the border of each field. Border choices are None, Underlined, Box, Shadowbox, 3D Raised, and 3D Lowered.
- *Text Color.* This is the color of any text on the DataWindow.
- *Column Border.* This is the border of each data entry field (column) on the DataWindow.
- *Column Color.* This is the color of each column on the DataWindow.
- *Wrap Height.* Wrap height allows the developer to start a new column after a given number of inches of fields have been placed on a free form DataWindow. Wrap height allows easier placement of columns on a DataWindow.

FIG. 9.5

The DataWindow Options window lets you set default options for all DataWindows.

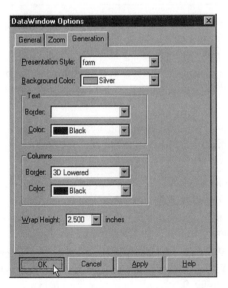

TIP A wrap height of 2.5 inches will wrap your DataWindow so that all columns can be seen without scrolling.

Understanding Data Sources

The *data source* is the database table (or tables) that you want to use to populate fields in your DataWindow. You can later change your mind on what your data sources are with little difficulty. This chapter discusses the main data sources used in PowerBuilder: Quick Select and SQL Select.

Quick Select

Choosing Quick Select as your data source tells PowerBuilder that you want your DataWindow to retrieve from and write to a single table or a set of related tables.

SQL Select

Choosing SQL Select as your data source tells PowerBuilder that the information on your DataWindow comes from multiple tables.

 TIP You may want to use Window Background and Window Text as your options for color. That way, the user can adjust the application's colors through Windows without you having to write a special setup module.

Determining Presentation Style

The *presentation style* tells PowerBuilder the way you want to present your data. Once chosen, the presentation style is hard to change. (You'll probably want to recreate your DataWindow if such a change is needed.)

The following lists the various types of presentation styles, why they should be chosen, and how to format them. Following the list are examples of DataWindows used in the Inventory Tracking system.

- *Freeform.* Freeform DataWindows are used for data entry screens of primary entities (such as Item, Warehouse, Supplier, Customer, and so on). Usually, freeform DataWindows show only one row at a time, and have no headers or summary information. You can see a completed freeform DataWindow in figure 9.22, later in the chapter.

- *Tabular.* Tabular DataWindows typically show several rows of information at once. Usually, tabular DataWindows have a header row (instead of prompts as seen in the freeform DataWindow in fig. 9.10) and often have summary rows. An invoice is an excellent example of a tabular DataWindow. An invoice shows many rows (invoice lines) at once, and has header information (company and customer name and address, date, and so on), as well as summary information (tax and total amount owed).

■ *Grid.* The best example of a grid DataWindow is a spreadsheet. Grids force the developer to keep detail entries on one line. They can have headings and summary information, but headings and summary information are part of the grid. Grids are best used for retrieval screens and when spreadsheet functionality is called for.

■ *Label.* Label DataWindows are used for printing mailing labels (instead of data entry).

■ *N-Up.* Like labels, N-Up DataWindows are usually not for data entry. N-UP DataWindows are typically used for reporting multiple rows across a report.

■ *Groups and Crosstabs.* Groups allow you to group data for displaying, sorting and summarizing. Crosstabs allow you to compare and contrast data values as they relate to two different columns. Groups and crosstabs are complicated subjects. They will be explained later in the book.

■ *Graphs.* Graphs graphically represent your data on a DataWindow. They will be covered in chapter 12, "Creating Reports."

■ *Rich Text.* Rich Text DataWindows are used to include formatted text on a DataWindow. Often, they are used for form letters. They will be covered in chapter 12, "Creating Reports."

■ *OLE 2.0.* You can use an OLE 2.0 compliant application as a DataWindow presentation style. Simply choose your table or tables that you want for your data source. PowerBuilder will then open the Insert Object dialog box to ask you which application you want to use, as seen in figure 9.6.

FIG. 9.6
Microsoft Excel Worksheet was chosen as the OLE object type in the Insert Object dialog box.

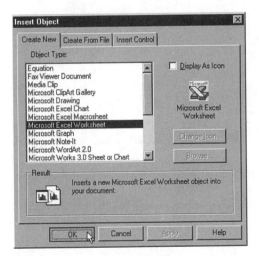

Simply choose the OLE object type application and click OK. Your object application will then open and allow you to do data entry, as seen in figure 9.7.

FIG. 9.7
Microsoft Excel opens to
allow customization of
the OLE object.

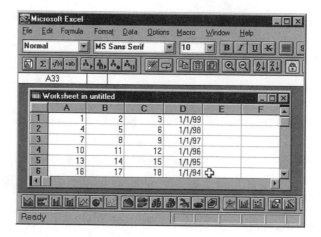

When you are finished, close out the application. You will then be asked if you want to update your application. Click Yes, and your new object will appear in your DataWindow, as seen in figure 9.8.

FIG. 9.8
Microsoft Excel is now
an OLE DataWindow
object.

	A	B	C	D
1	1	2	3	1/1/99
2	4	5	6	1/1/98
3	7	8	9	1/1/97
4	10	11	12	1/1/96
5	13	14	15	1/1/95
6	16	17	18	1/1/94
7	19	20	21	1/1/93
8	22	23	24	1/1/92
9	25	26	27	1/1/91
10	28	29	30	1/1/90
11	31	32	33	1/1/89
12	34	35	36	1/1/88

■ *Composite.* Composite DataWindows are DataWindows whose sole purpose is to contain other DataWindows. Composite DataWindows have no SQL, and are often used for reporting purposes. They are covered in chapter 12, "Creating Reports."

CAUTION
Composite DataWindows are easy to build. After they are built, however, they have no links to your database and therefore may seem hard to use. Remember, *DataWindows can contain nested DataWindows just like a composite DataWindow.* By using freeform or tabular DataWindows to contain other DataWindows, you'll be able to nest DataWindows as well as use standard DataWindow features.

▶ **See** "Using Crosstabs," **p. 367**

▶ **See** "Creating Graphs," **p. 396**

Creating a Quick Select/Freeform DataWindow

The type of DataWindow you'll probably use most often is the quick select/freeform DataWindow. This DataWindow is commonly used for single-table single-row data entry. Most of our DataWindows in the Inventory Tracking system will be this type.

Making the Item DataWindow

The first DataWindow you will create is the Item DataWindow. When you choose Quick Select and Freeform (refer to fig. 9.2), the Quick Select dialog box appears, as shown in figure 9.9.

FIG. 9.9

Populate your DataWindow by clicking the columns you want represented or use the Add All button.

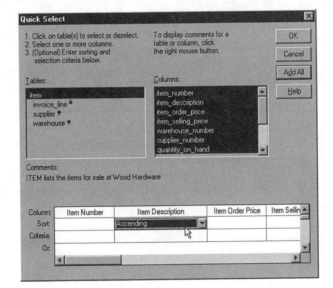

Hooking Your DataWindow to a Table   In the Quick Select dialog box, first select the table you want to use (in this case, the item table).

After choosing your table, you can choose the fields you want on the DataWindow. You can choose one field at a time or add all of them with the Add All button. You can also choose the sort criteria or selection criteria. *Sort criteria* are the order you want your data appearing on a retrieval. Sort criteria are entered in each column in the Sort row. *Selection criteria* act as a filter for unwanted rows. You enter selection criteria in the Criteria row, and any additional criteria in the Or rows that follow. A sort is added in figure 9.9 to the DataWindow to sort by Item Description. When you've added all of the fields, and sort and selection criteria you desire, click OK or press Enter.

Part
III

Ch
9

Formatting Your DataWindow   After clicking OK, the DataWindow painter appears. Initially (with freeform presentation style), all columns are displayed with their prompt beside them in a single column, as shown in figure 9.10 (or multiple columns if you use enough columns or reset the wrap height to 2.5, as shown in figure 9.5). Using the mouse, simply drag the fields to where you want them to appear within the DataWindow.

FIG. 9.10

Because you picked Freeform in the New DataWindow dialog box, you now can move the columns and text around.

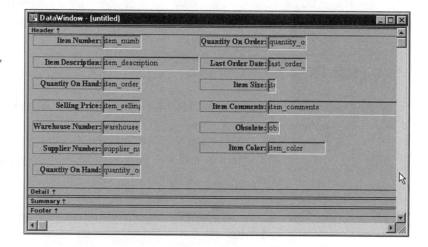

Notice how hard it is to line up fields and prompts next to each other, and how difficult it is to evenly space between them using a mouse. Also, notice the way the size height of fields sometimes varies. PowerBuilder makes it easier by providing a way to align objects, evenly space between objects, and size objects identically. To format your DataWindow, perform the following steps:

 When moving selected items around your DataWindow, you can drag with your mouse for speed or use the arrow keys for more control.

1. Customize the properties of your DataWindow. Although it's easier to set many of the DataWindows properties when the DataWindow is created as seen in figures 9.2, 9.3, 9.4, and 9.5, you may wish to make modifications. To change DataWindow properties, double-click any blank area in the DataWindow to pull up the DataWindow property sheet.

   The DataWindow property sheet consists of three tabs:

   - *General.* The General tab, as seen in figure 9.11, allows you to change the way your DataWindow measures graphics, how often the timer event is executed in the DataWindow, and the background color.

   - *Pointer.* The Pointer tab (fig. 9.12) allows you to choose what the mouse pointer will look like when it's over your DataWindow. The default is to use the same pointer that is used for the window where the DataWindow resides.

FIG. 9.11

By double-clicking the DataWindow (outside of any columns), you open the DataWindow property sheet.

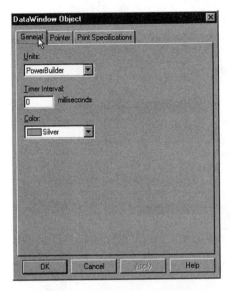

FIG. 9.12

You can choose your DataWindow's mouse pointer from a variety of stock cursors or from a .cur file

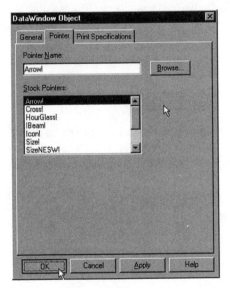

- *Print Specifications.* DataWindows can be printed using the *datawindow.print( )* function. The Print Specifications tab (fig. 9.13) allows you to specify the document name of your printout, the margins, the paper orientation, size, and source, and the column width. You can also force a prompt before you print your DataWindow.

FIG. 9.13

The Print Specifications tab allows you to specify print characteristics for your DataWindow.

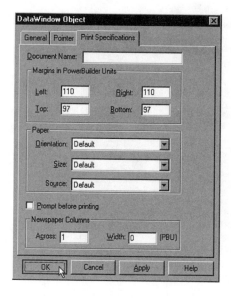

2. Select one or more objects (to select an object, click that object). A selected object has a dot in each corner. There are many different ways to select several objects at once; some of the most popular ways are listed as follows:

- Hold down the left mouse key and drag the mouse pointer to "box" or "lasso" your objects in.

- Click your first object, and then hold down the control button while clicking on all other objects you want to select.

- Open Edit and choose Select. This activates a menu that allows you to select several different types of objects. For instance, to select every column, click Edit and choose Select, and then click Select Columns, as shown in figure 9.14.

3. Now that all the columns are selected, you can change the background color of each column, text, or control on your DataWindow. First, select the controls that you want to alter. (In figure 9.15, all the columns were selected.) Then click the drop-down icon box and choose the appropriate color, as shown in figure 9.15.

FIG. 9.14

Select all columns by clicking Edit, Select, Select Columns.

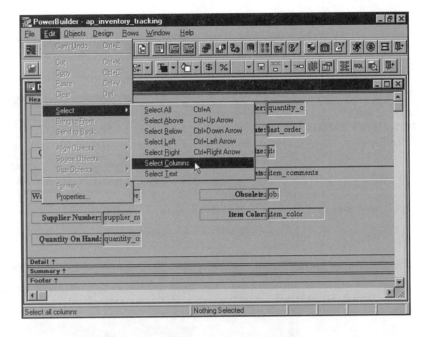

FIG. 9.15

Changing color is easily accomplished using the color drop-down icons.

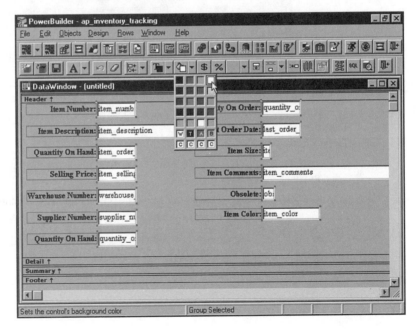

4. To further set your columns apart from your text, you can set the border of all selected columns. To do this, use the border drop-down icon, as seen in figure 9.16, and choose the border you wish to use.

FIG. 9.16

Border can now be controlled with a drop-down icon.

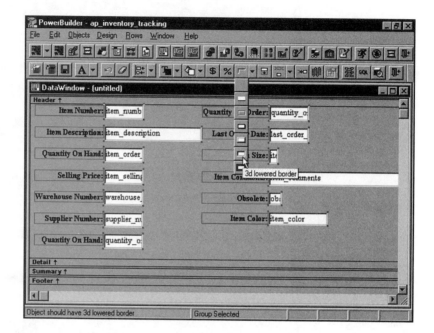

TIP The border and background color drop-down icons are on the style bar. Because of space limitations, you may want to remove some items from your style bar or move these icons to your PainterBar so you can access them.

5. After selecting objects, open the Edit menu and choose the formatting action you want to accomplish:

- Click Edit, Align Objects to line all the objects up (as shown in fig. 9.17).
- Click Edit, Space Objects to evenly space between objects (see fig. 9.18).
- Click Edit, Size Objects to make all selected objects either the same height or the same width (see fig. 9.19).

FIG. 9.17
Click Edit, Align Objects to be given the alignment choices for your selected items on your DataWindow.

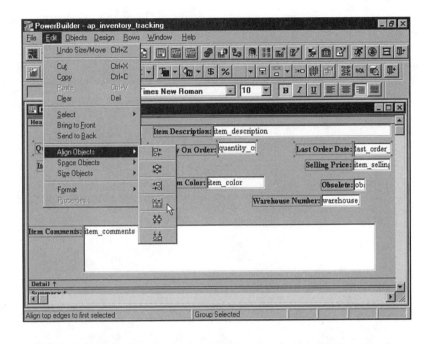

FIG. 9.18
Click Edit, Space Objects to adjust the spacing of your selected items on your DataWindow.

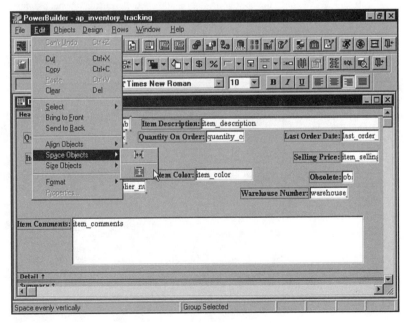

FIG. 9.19

You can size objects to be the same height or width using the Edit, Size Objects menu selection.

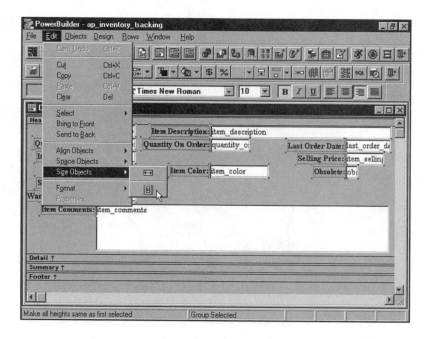

N O T E Although not on your original icon list, you can customize your painter bar to add a drop-down icon to control size, spacing, and alignment. This way, you can adjust the formatting of your DataWindow using icons, as seen in figure 9.20, rather than using menu items. ■

FIG. 9.20

You can use the formatting drop-down icon to format fields in your DataWindow.

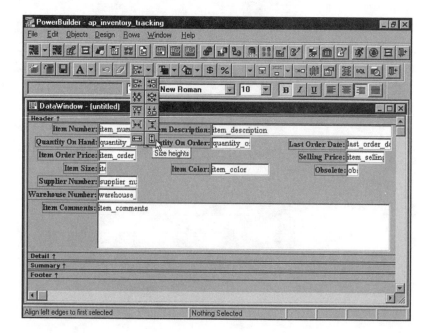

- If you select numeric fields, you can also format them to be currency or percent by choosing Edit, Format.

6. Now you have finished formatting your screen. However, all the field moving has affected the order that you tab through your DataWindow. Open Design and choose Tab Order to put your DataWindow in Tab Order mode. Click the red number above each field to set the tab order to flow with the layout of the DataWindow.

   You won't be able to perform any other actions to your DataWindow until you leave tab order mode. When you're done ordering fields, choose Design, Tab Order again to leave the tab order mode so you can save your DataWindow (see fig. 9.21).

Part

III

Ch

9

FIG. 9.21

Setting the tab order should be the last order of business before saving your DataWindow.

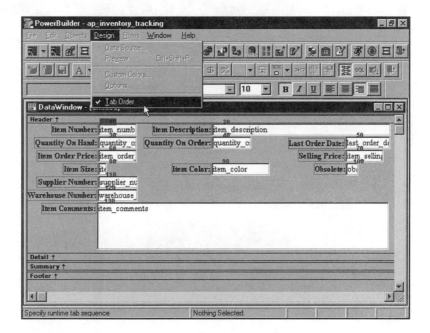

You've finally finished your DataWindow (see fig. 9.22). Now you need to save your work. Double-click the painter Control menu box. PowerBuilder will ask you if you want to save. Click on Yes. This pulls up the Save DataWindow dialog box shown in figure 9.23. Like other Save windows, click on the PBL where you want to store this DataWindow (inventry.pbl), and type in your DataWindow name (d_item). You'll continue defining DataWindows for the major entities in your Inventory Tracking system.

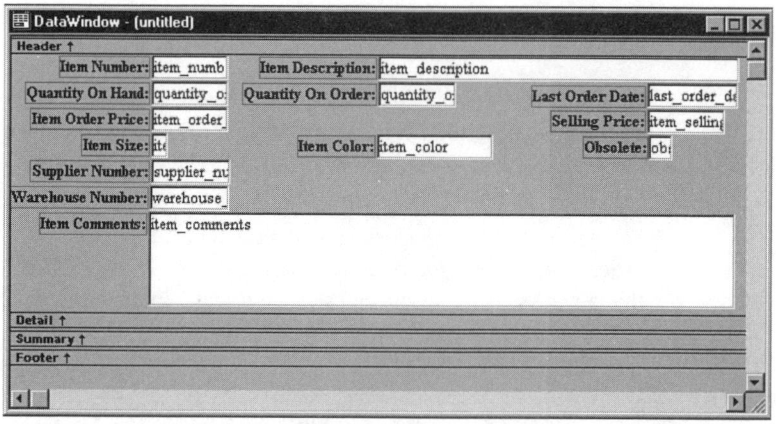

FIG. 9.22

After you're done formatting, your Item DataWindow should look like this.

FIG. 9.23

Close the DataWindow by double-clicking the painter Control menu box, and save the DataWindow in the Save DataWindow dialog box.

Making the Customer DataWindow

Now you should make some of your other DataWindows. Click the DataWindow icon to start working with the Customer DataWindow. Activate the Select DataWindow dialog box by clicking the DataWindow icon.

Click the New button to activate the New DataWindow dialog box. Choose your options and click Quick Select, Freeform, and then OK. Like before, the Quick Select window displays. This time, instead of choosing Item, select Customer (because this is the Customer DataWindow). Then select all the columns to be added to the DataWindow.

Next, format and align the DataWindow the way you want to see it. After you're done, set the tab order. You should now have a DataWindow that looks like figure 9.24. Notice how the customer_comments column is stretched out into a multi-line edit.

TIP Instead of changing the DataWindow column color and border later, use the Generation Options menu (seen in fig. 9.5).

FIG. 9.24

Here is a sample of the Customer DataWindow.

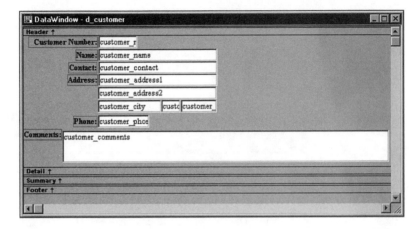

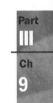

Part

III

Ch

9

Save your finished Customer DataWindow to d_customer in your inventry.pbl. You've now finished your work on the Customer DataWindow.

Making the Warehouse and Supplier DataWindows

Now create the Warehouse DataWindow, shown in figure 9.25, and the Supplier DataWindow, shown in figure 9.26, just as you made the Item and Customer DataWindows. Save these DataWindows to d_warehouse and d_supplier.

FIG. 9.25

Using the same process you used with Item and Customer, develop the Warehouse DataWindow.

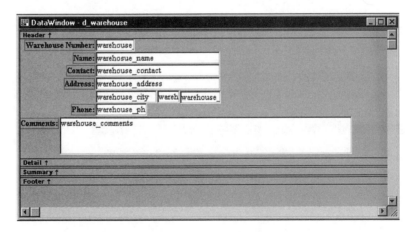

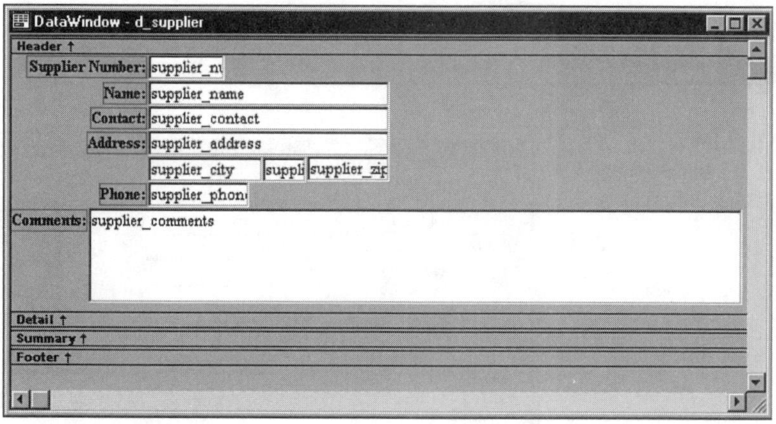

FIG. 9.26
Using the same process
as with Item, Customer,
and Warehouse, develop
the Supplier
DataWindow.

Reviewing Invoice Design

Most of your data entry DataWindows will be Quick Select/Freeform. Quick Select/Freeform DataWindows are useful for single-table DataWindows that don't require much processing, but sometimes more complicated processing is needed.

A typical invoice has several components:

- *Header information.* Usually found at the top of the invoice, this information consists of invoice number, date, customer name and address, and headings for the invoice lines.

- *Detail information.* Consists of the line number, the item description, the quantity ordered, the unit price, and the total price. There can be several lines per invoice, each referring to a different order.

- *Footer information.* This information usually consists of some comments, miscellaneous charges, sales tax, freight, and a total amount owed.

To enter, display, or print an invoice, three DataWindows (d_invoice_header, d_invoice_detail, and d_invoice_footer) need to be involved. Also, the DataWindows must be made to be a little more complicated than a straight single-row data entry.

Making d_invoice_header and d_invoice_footer

d_invoice_header and d_invoice footer use the same table information in that their combined data forms the invoice database table. Because of this, we are (eventually) going to share these two DataWindows.

N O T E *Sharing DataWindows* is a technique allowed by PowerBuilder that allows two different DataWindows with the same number of columns and same column types to share their data. Sharing the d_invoice_header and d_invoice_footer DataWindows will make processing easier in that you can populate DataWindows from one database retrieval, update with one *datawindow.update ( )* function, etc.

Shared DataWindows will be discussed more in chapter 11, "Manipulating Data Using DataWindows." It will also be discussed in detail in chapter 23, "Using ShareData Functions" as expert Dave O'Hearn discusses the many uses for shared DataWindows. For now, just understand that all invoice columns will be added to both d_invoice_header and d_invoice_footer. ■

For both d_invoice_header and d_invoice_footer, use a Quick Select Freeform window as you have used previously, and add all columns to each DataWindow. This will add all columns to the SQL select statement that drives each DataWIndow. Then delete the columns you don't use off the DataWindow display. The result of this is that both DataWindows will retrieve and update all the columns, but will only display the columns relevant to each DataWindow.

Making d_invoice_header   Like the window painter, the DataWindow painter allows you to add several different types of controls. Every column or static text (prompts) are considered controls. (You'll add some more controls to your Invoice DataWindow.)

Text Controls   After you're finished moving your prompts and columns where you want them, add a company name and address to the title invoice by clicking the Text icon. Now, highlight any prompts and columns that seem out of place and delete them by pressing the *Delete* key or clicking the Clear icon. Finally, click the Text icon again to add appropriate prompts to your system. When you're finished to this point, your d_invoice_header DataWindow should look like figure 9.27.

FIG. 9.27
Using the style bar and text controls can make a DataWindow look professional.

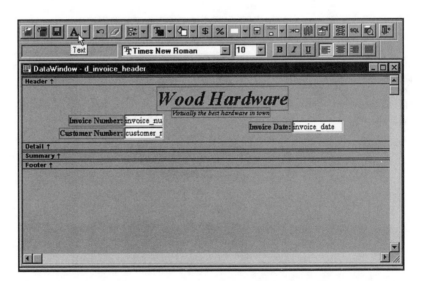

Picture Controls   By clicking on the Picture icon and answering the appropriate questions, a bitmap is added to your DataWindow (see fig. 9.28).

Before the bitmap is added to the DataWindow, the picture property sheet appears, as seen in figure 9.29. Clicking Browse allows you to select an existing bitmap to add to your PowerBuilder application.

FIG. 9.28
By selecting the Picture icon, you can choose a bitmap picture to add to your DataWindow.

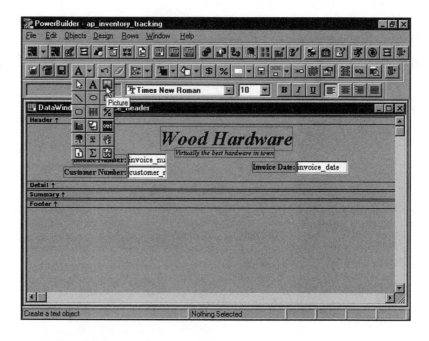

FIG. 9.29
The Picture property sheet allows you to enter picture properties. Browse allows you to choose an existing .BMP file to add to your DataWindow.

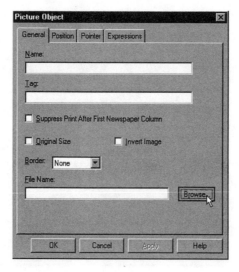

You should then see the Select Picture dialog box (fig. 9.30). The Select Picture dialog box allows you to pick which .BMP file you wish to add to your DataWindow.

When you're finished with your d_invoice_header DataWindow, it should look like the DataWindow shown in figure 9.31.

FIG. 9.30

The Select Picture dialog box can be used to add pictures, like a hammer or a screw-driver, to your DataWindow.

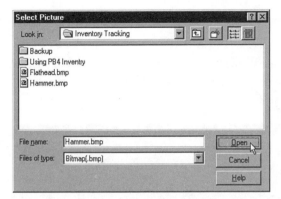

FIG. 9.31

The final d_invoice_header DataWindow.

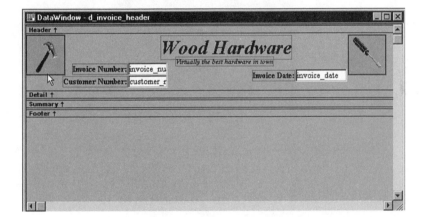

Making d_invoice_footer   When you create d_invoice_footer, you must still add all the columns of the invoice table. d_invoice_footer is shown in figure 9.32.

FIG. 9.32

The final d_invoice_footer DataWindow.

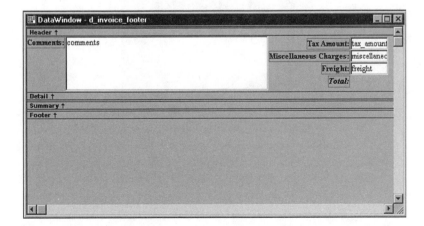

Making d_invoice_detail Using a SQL Select/Tabular DataWindow

To start making your d_invoice_detail DataWindow, click on the DataWindow icon. As before, the New DataWindow dialog box appears. This time, select SQL Select and Tabular as your Data Source and Presentation Style, and choose OK (see fig. 9.33).

FIG. 9.33

To make a multiple-table DataWindow, choose SQL Select for the Data Source. A Tabular Presentation Style places the headings at the top of the DataWindow.

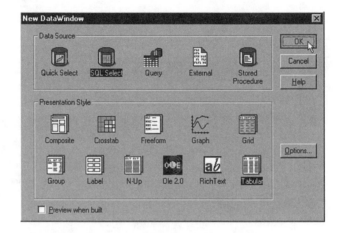

Choosing and Joining Tables   Now, the Select Tables dialog box appears. Choose all the tables that you need to make your DataWindow by clicking on them, as seen in figure 9.34. For an invoice, you need invoice and invoice_line. You also have customer and item information on the invoice, so those tables should be chosen also. When you are finished choosing all the tables you need for a DataWindow, click Open.

FIG. 9.34

The Select Tables dialog box appears when using the SQL Select Data Source. Choose all the tables for your DataWindow, and click OK.

After you've picked your tables, the DataWindow SQL toolbox appears, as shown in figure 9.35. This painter lists all your tables and the way they are joined together (via the foreign keys you set up earlier). Pick the columns you want to be displayed as fields on your DataWindow. When you're done, click the SQL icon on the PainterBar to return to the DataWindow painter.

FIG. 9.35
In the DataWindow SQL toolbox, you choose which columns will appear on your DataWindow.

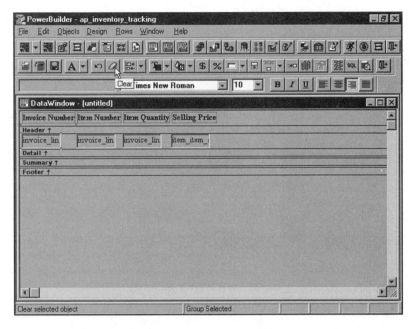

Formatting an Invoice Using DataWindow Bands   Now you are in the DataWindow painter. PowerBuilder has done something different this time. Instead of all the information being displayed in one area on the screen (in the Detail area) with a tabular presentation style, the prompt information is now in the Header area; the column information is in the Detail area, as shown in figure 9.36. These areas are called *bands*.

FIG. 9.36
With the tabular presentation style, prompts appear in the header band; column information appears in the detail band.

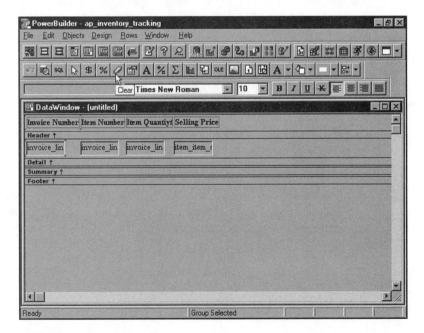

There are four bands to each DataWindow (although seldom are all used in one DataWindow). They are as follows:

T I P Be sure to choose the primary keys for all tables you will be updating from your DataWindow.

- *Header band.* This band appears at the top of your DataWindow. All fields that you want displayed only once per window go here.
- *Detail band.* The detail band is the second band. All repetitive information is stored here. The DataWindow displays as many detail bands on a DataWindow as it can, given the window space that you allocate for it.
- *Summary band.* In this third band, you summarize (usually via computed fields) the information in the Detail band. You can also move entry columns that you want at the end of your detail information to this band.
- *Footer band.* Fields and prompts in the footer band are displayed at the bottom of each DataWindow. On single-window or single-sheet DataWindows, often the footer band is used to display summary information at the bottom of the page. This is also a good place for page numbers, recurring footnotes, and so on.

N O T E invoice_number was deleted from the DataWindow (as seen in figure 9.36). You will need to retrieve a primary key for updating your information later, and invoice_number is part of the primary key. However, since invoice_number is already displayed in the invoice_header, there is no need to also display the invoice_number on every line of the invoice. ■

N O T E Although tabular presentation style places all of your columns in the detail band, don't be afraid to move them to other bands. For example, you may want a multi-line detail area that needs a text prompt for the second line. In fact, the only difference between a tabular DataWindow and a freeform DataWindow is how the DataWindows look when they are first formed. ■

Using Computed Fields   The Invoice layout is still incomplete. Although it lists quantity ordered and selling price, you still need to list the total amount owed for each invoice line (and the total amount owed for the entire invoice). These fields aren't stored on a table—they are *computed fields.*

To show a computed field on your DataWindow:

1. Click the Compute icon on the PainterBar.
2. Click the place where you want the computed field to go. This activates the Computed Object property sheet, shown in figure 9.37. Here, you can enter an expression used to return a value to your computed field.

FIG. 9.37
The Computed Object property sheet allows you to enter a computed field for your DataWindow.

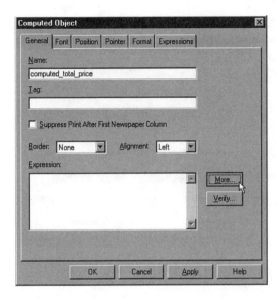

3. By clicking More, as shown in figure 9.37, you open the Modify Expression dialog box shown in figure 9.38. Although PowerBuilder gives you many functions to choose from, you only need a simple equation to calculate your line total. Click the invoice_line_item_quantity field in the Columns area. Then press the multiplication symbol (*). Finally, click the item_item_selling_price and then click OK.

FIG. 9.38
The Modify Expression dialog box is helpful when creating the equation behind a computed field.

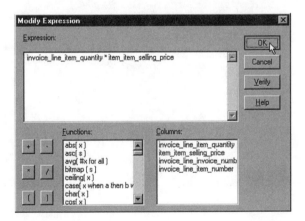

N O T E You should specify the format of your computed field, especially when using numeric computed fields. You can specify the format of your computed field by clicking the Format tab of the Computed Object property sheet, as seen in figure 9.39. ■

FIG. 9.39

Using the Format tab of the Computed Object property sheet allows you to make your computed fields look more readable, polished, and professional.

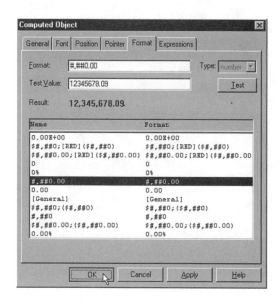

4. The computed field of invoice_line_item_quantity * item_item_selling_price will then appear on your DataWindow. Don't forget to add the appropriate prompt to the heading band, as shown in figure 9.40.

FIG. 9.40

Your computed field can now be part of the DataWindow.

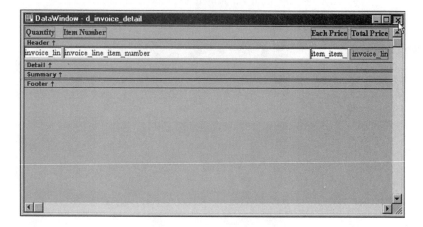

Summation is the most common computed field. The Invoice subtotal is a summation of all line totals. Click the total amount computed field. Then click the Sum icon. A computed sum will appear in the summary band. Then supply the appropriate prompt. You can see a layout of the invoice in figure 9.41.

Most summations are placed in the footer or summary bands, since several detail rows can then be summarized. If you place a summation in a detail line, only one detail row can be summarized at a time.

Revisiting Tab Order   Now you can set the tab order of your DataWindow, as you did for the Item DataWindow, by opening Design and choosing Tab Order command. However, the Invoice DataWindow is different from all previous DataWindows because there are some fields that are display-only.

N O T E   By setting the tab order to zero, you make a column display-only. The end user can't tab to or click on a column with a zero tab order (refer to fig. 9.41). ■

FIG. 9.41
The tab order is set to zero on item selling price, making the column display-only. Computed fields don't have tab orders—they are always display-only.

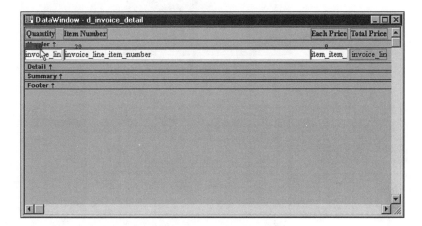

Specifying Update Characteristics   The last step to complete a DataWindow with an SQL Select data source is to specify the update characteristics. Because you are pulling from several tables, PowerBuilder doesn't know which table to update. Open Rows and choose Update Properties, as seen in figure 9.42.

FIG. 9.42

To change the update characteristics, open Rows and choose Update Properties.

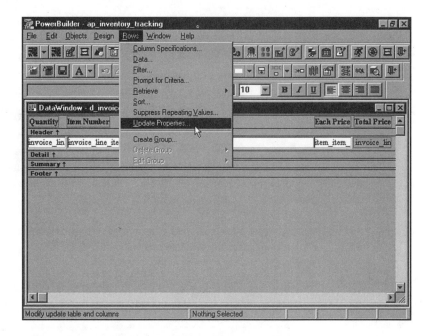

The Specify Update Properties dialog box appears (see fig. 9.43).

FIG. 9.43

The Specify Update Properties dialog box tells PowerBuilder which table to update with this DataWindow.

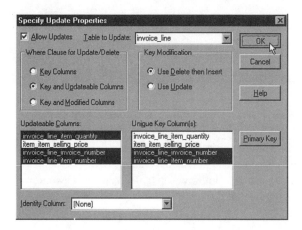

First, click Allow Updates to allow this DataWindow to update a table. Then choose the table you want to update. You probably want to update two tables with this DataWindow (invoice and invoice_line) instead of one. Because you can only choose one table for the DataWindow to automatically update, it is better to update the detail table (invoice_line).

N O T E   You will use SQL to update the Invoice table later. You should update the detail table because multiple rows are more complicated to update than single rows using PowerScript and SQL. ■

Next, click the columns you want to update in the table you have chosen.

You also can choose the Where clause that the DataWindow will use for your updates and deletes from the DataWindow. This is useful in a multi-user situation, in which several users are updating a single set of tables at once. Clicking Key and Updatable Columns or Key and Modified Columns enhances security—one user can't write over another user's table. This way, if a row gets updated by one user while another is also attempting an update, one update will fail.

Under Key Modification, you have the options of issuing a Delete and Insert, or an Update to update the key if a user modifies a key. This can be useful (or problematic) in cascading updates and cascading deletes that some databases support. Using an Update to change the key is faster.

Finally, pick which key the table will be using. If you have already chosen your table, you can click Primary Key and let PowerBuilder pick your update key for you.

Click OK to return to the DataWindow painter. Now save your DataWindow under d_invoice_detail and exit the DataWindow painter.

N O T E Because the invoice_line table was chosen as the table to update, you want the invoice_line_number, the item_number on the invoice, and the quantity ordered to display. Now pick the primary key of the line number and the invoice_number as the key. ■

CAUTION

You won't be able to update any tables using an SQL Select or Query data source unless you use the Specify Update Characteristics dialog box (refer to fig. 9.43). This dialog box tells PowerBuilder which tables to update, and flags the DataWindow as updatable.

Using Other Data Sources

There are other data sources than SQL Select and Quick Select. These other data sources aren't as popular since SQL Select and Quick Select are so versatile and meet most needs. However, you may find yourself using or running into them some day.

Queries

Using a *query* is a lot like creating a permanent SQL Select—even the windows are laid out the same way. The only difference between the two is that you can use queries as the predefined data source for several different DataWindows instead of recoding your SQL Select every time.

Queries aren't that popular because a change to a query is not reflected in the DataWindow that uses it. In fact, when you use a query for a data source, it is immediately converted to an SQL Select. If you only plan to use a query once, you should save yourself some time and space by using an SQL Select.

Queries are gaining acceptance with certain third-party software packages—they are being produced to use with PowerBuilder. Like many alternative development techniques, it's a matter of preference.

▶ **See** "Using Queries," **p. 782**

External Data Sources

When you use an external data source for your DataWindow, you populate the DataWindow using PowerScript. When you start building your DataWindow using an external data source, the Result Set Description dialog box will appear. You can determine which fields are to be used and what their data type and length are, as shown in figure 9.44. You can then continue to build your DataWindow as if you were using a Quick Select as your data source.

FIG. 9.44

Using an external source allows you to make a DataWindow, but you must populate the fields with a PowerScript statement after describing your fields.

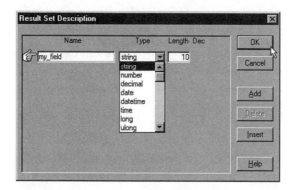

With the exception of stored procedures, external data sources are not popular, and with good reason. By taking away the database table from the DataWindow, you take away much of its functionality. Working with the data becomes extremely tedious. Your life will probably be easier if you instead consider using a temporary database table for your DataWindow.

Stored Procedures

Stored procedures are extremely popular for display-only DataWindows that you can use if your database supports them. Some databases have extremely efficient stored procedures. You can often improve the speed of your application by doing some of your SQL statements inside a stored procedure.

N O T E Every database differs on how to declare a stored procedure, and not all databases support stored procedures. To find out if your database supports stored procedures, review your database documentation or contact your Database Analyst (DBA). ▪

Using DataWindow Control User Objects

After you are done creating the DataWindow *objects*, you must use DataWindow *controls* to display them in a window. We are using several DataWindows throughout the Inventory Tracking system. Much of the PowerScript and SQL would be identical for each DataWindow. PowerBuilder allows you to create *user objects* that allow you to *encapsulate* or join a window control with functions and events that would be common to several similar objects. Unlike "normal" window controls, user objects can then be inherited so that all common functionality is defined only once.

Part
III

Ch
9

> **N O T E** There is often some confusion about terminology when discussing DataWindows. Here is a
> list of DataWindow terms that may clear up some ambiguity:
>
> - A DataWindow object is what we've been painting using the DataWindow painter.
>   DataWindow objects are not useful until connected to a window object. DataWindow
>   objects are often refered to as DataWindows.
>
> - A window DataWindow control is the control on a window that links a DataWindow
>   object to a window object or a tab control on a window object. These are also called
>   DataWindows and DataWindow Controls. Window DataWindow controls are not useful
>   unless linked to a DataWindow object.
>
> - A DataWindow user object is a DataWindow Control that is defined as a user object.
>   These are also called DataWindows or DataWindow controls.
>
> - Controls on DataWindows are text, columns, pictures, and so on that are added to a
>   DataWindow. These are also called controls or DataWindow Controls.
>
> As you can see, there is a lot of overlap in terms when discussing DataWindows. You'll often need to
> view the context of the rest of the sentence to understand what is being described when discussing
> DataWindow objects, window DataWindow controls, and controls on a DataWindow. ■

> **N O T E** This book has added an entire section to user objects and object-oriented development
> (part V, "User Objects and Object Oriented Development"). This section includes chapter
> 17, "Understanding Object-Oriented Concepts," chapter 18, "Understanding User Objects," and chapter
> 19, "Specialized User Objects."
>
> This section is targeted toward the intermediate to advanced user and covers topics and concepts that
> can make system development much easier. ■

Creating a DataWindow Control User Object

To create a DataWindow user object, click the User Object icon. That will open the Select User Object dialog box. Click New, as shown in figure 9.45.

FIG. 9.45

The Select User Object dialog box allows you to edit an existing user object or create a new user object.

Now you will see the New User Object dialog box. Click the Standard icon in the Visual group box, as seen in figure 9.46, and click OK. This will tell PowerBuilder that you want to create a window control as a visual user object.

FIG. 9.46

The New User Object dialog box allows you to declare what kind of user object you will be creating.

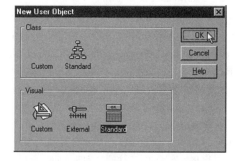

The Select Standard Visual Type dialog box appears. In the Select Standard Visual Type dialog box, you choose the window control you want to define. Choose datawindow, as seen in figure 9.47.

FIG. 9.47

The Select Standard Visual Type dialog box is used to choose which window control you want to define as a visual object.

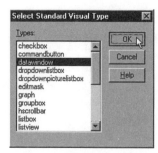

Then save your user object using the Save User Object dialog box, as seen in figure 9.48. You can then use this user object anytime you have need for a DataWindow.

FIG. 9.48
The Save User Object dialog box allows you to select the name and PBL where you want your user object stored.

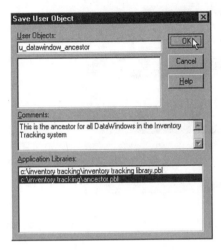

N O T E My ancestor DataWindow was named *u_datawindow_ancestor*.

Hooking a DataWindow to an SQL Transaction

Before going further, you must tell PowerBuilder which database you want all your DataWindows to access. By putting the following code in the constructor event of the DataWindow control, you ensure that all your DataWindows are hooked up to SQLCA:

```
SetTrans(SQLCA)
```

N O T E The constructor event is executed whenever a window control is created, or constructed. It is similar to the Open event in a window object.

The SetTrans(transaction) function added to the constructor event associates your DataWindow with the database defined by a transaction like SQLCA. This way, your DataWindow knows where to go to retrieve and update data. This is a DataWindow function—not an SQL statement. Although this is a DataWindow function, you'll usually see it inside the open event of your window.

Inheriting a DataWindow User Object

Now you can inherit the DataWindow you created for use in your entire Inventory Tracking system. To inherit a user object, click the User Object icon. This will bring up the Select User Object dialog box, as seen in figure 9.45. Instead of clicking New, click Inherit. This will allow you to inherit a DataWindow user object from an ancestor user object. The Inherit From User Object dialog box will then open, as seen in figure 9.49.

FIG. 9.49

The Inherit From User Object dialog box allows you to create a new DataWindow from a prototype DataWindow.

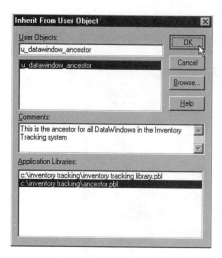

I added the following code to my Constructor event in the new DataWindow:

```
// Extend constructor from ancestor
insertrow(0)
```

N O T E   InsertRow(rownum) inserts a new row on your DataWindow. In the case of freeform
DataWindows, InsertRow(0) inserts a blank "screen" for the user to enter another row to
the database. ■

Now, when this DataWindow user object is constructed, the ancestor constructor event is executed first:

```
SetTrans(SQLCA)
```

Followed by the code in the descendent constructor event:

```
// Extend constructor from ancestor
insertrow(0)
```

Now, whenever this new DataWindow user object is created, the transaction will be assigned to SQLCA and a new, blank row will be inserted in the DataWindow. You can now save the DataWindow as *u_datawindow_inventory_entry* as seen in figure 9.50. This new DataWindow will be the prototype for all data entry DataWindows in the Inventory Tracking system.

FIG. 9.50
You can now save the new, inherited DataWindow using the Save User Object dialog box.

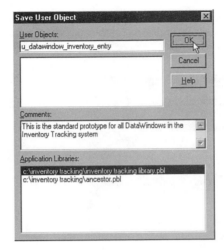

Associating DataWindow Controls with a DataWindow Object

Now that you have defined your DataWindow objects and defined the DataWindow control user object prototype, you can now start using the DataWindow control user object as a link between your windows or tab controls and your DataWindow objects.

To add the DataWindow object d_item to your item tabpage, open w_item. Then choose the user object control from the drop-down icon list as seen in figure 9.51.

FIG. 9.51
To add a user object control to a window, you need to select the user object from the drop-down icon list.

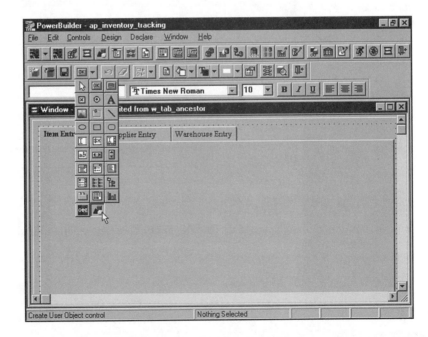

Immediately, the Select User Object dialog box will open. Here, you can choose the user object you want to place into your tab page. (In this case, that would be u_datawindow_inventory _entry, as seen in figure 9.52.)

FIG. 9.52

The Select User Object dialog box allows you to choose the user object to be associated with your window.

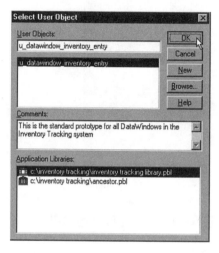

Then click where you want the user object you've chosen to go. In figure 9.53, the DataWindow user object went inside the Item Entry tab page.

FIG. 9.53

The DataWindow user object can be placed inside a window or tab page.

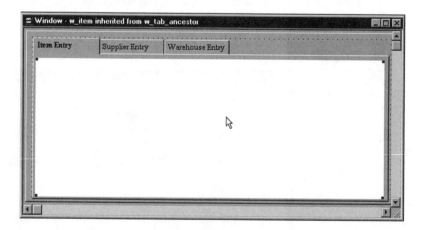

 Double-clicking the user object or selecting the user object and clicking the properties icon will open the DataWindow control property sheet, as seen in figure 9.54. You should change the name to something appropriate (like dw_item). Then set your DataWindow Object Name by clicking Browse.

N O T E The property sheets of standard visual user objects always mimic the control behind the user object. In this case, the DataWindow user object uses a DataWindow property sheet when you attach the user object to a window. ■

FIG. 9.54
A DataWindow user object shares the DataWindow control property sheet.

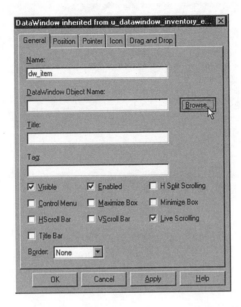

The Select DataWindow dialog box then appears, as shown in figure 9.55. Here, you can choose the DataWindow you want to correspond to DataWindow user object.

FIG. 9.55
You can select the DataWindow object that is related to your DataWindow control or DataWindow user object using the Select DataWindow dialog box.

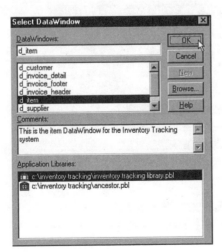

As you can see in figure 9.56, the d_item DataWindow object is now showing in the dw_item DataWindow user object control.

FIG. 9.56

The DataWindow you've chosen in the DataWindow control property sheet is now shown in your DataWindow user object control.

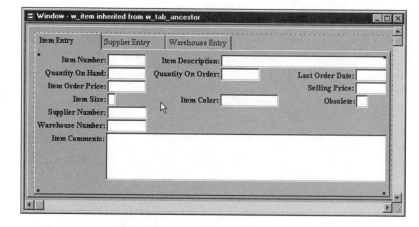

The same task done with d_item and the item entry tabpage should also be done with d_supplier—supplier tabpage and d_warehouse—warehouse entry tabpage in the w_item window. Also, in the w_invoice window, d_customer should be associated with the customer entry tabpage.

You need to place three DataWindow user objects on the invoice tab page: d_invoice_header, d_invoice_detail, and d_invoice_footer. The finished product can be seen in figure 9.57.

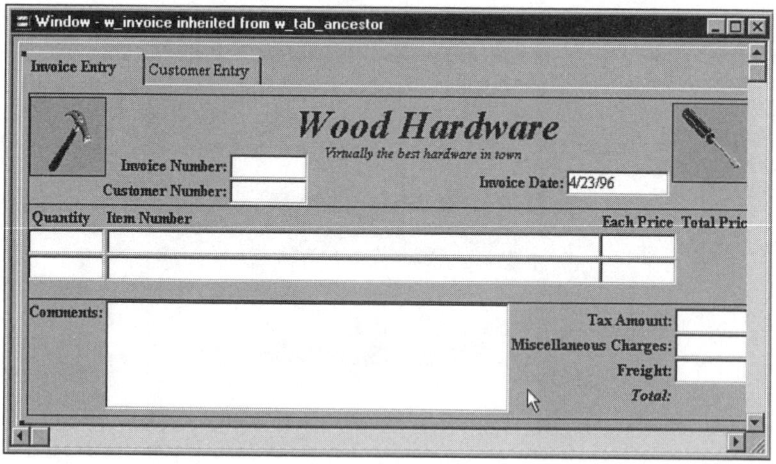

FIG. 9.57

In the invoice tabpage, three DataWindow controls are needed to link three DataWindow objects to one tab page.

Notice in figure 9.57, the totals on the d_invoice_footer don't align exactly with the totals in d_invoice detail. PowerBuilder allows you to pull up any DataWindow object in the DataWindow painter from the window where the DataWindow object is referenced. Right-click the DataWindow, and a pop-up menu appears. Choose Modify DataWindow to open the DataWindow painter with the appropriate DataWindow object. You can then adjust your DataWindows to meet the display needs of your window (see figure 9.58).

FIG. 9.58
You can pull up a DataWindow object in the DataWindow painter directly from the window painter by right-clicking a DataWindow control.

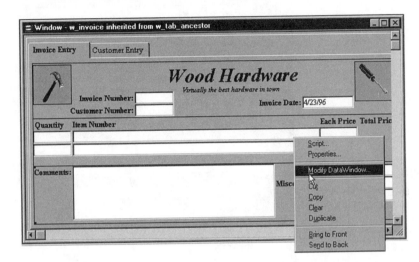

N O T E On freeform DataWindows, all the information is put in the detail band. Although it's not necessary, most developers keep the information in the detail band. You must be careful not to size your DataWindow so that more than one row appears on your DataWindow (unless you have designed it that way). Otherwise, you'll have a multi-row DataWindow when you wanted a single-row DataWindow. ■

Running Your Application

 Now click the run icon to run your application. You will then see w_item open with the d_item DataWindow displayed, as seen in figure 9.59.

 Notice that if you click the Warehouse Entry tabpage, as seen in figure 9.60, the item information disappears and d_warehouse is displayed. This is faster than creating a new window for each DataWindow, as was often done before PowerBuilder 5.

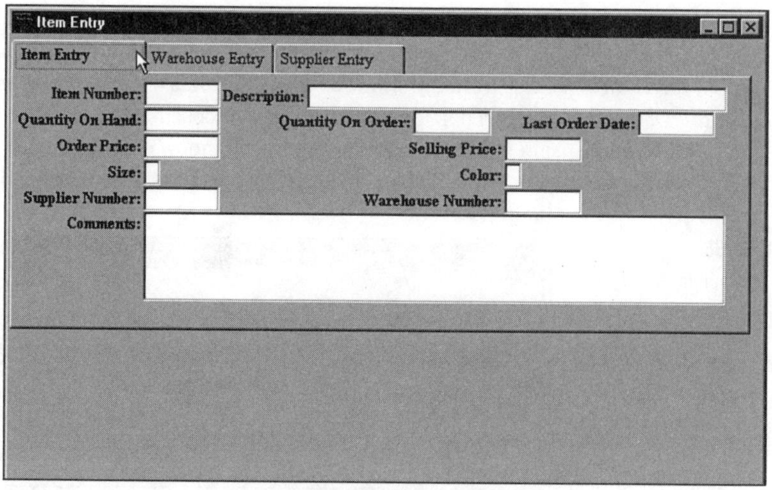

FIG. 9.59

The Inventory Tracking system looks like this when it first opens.

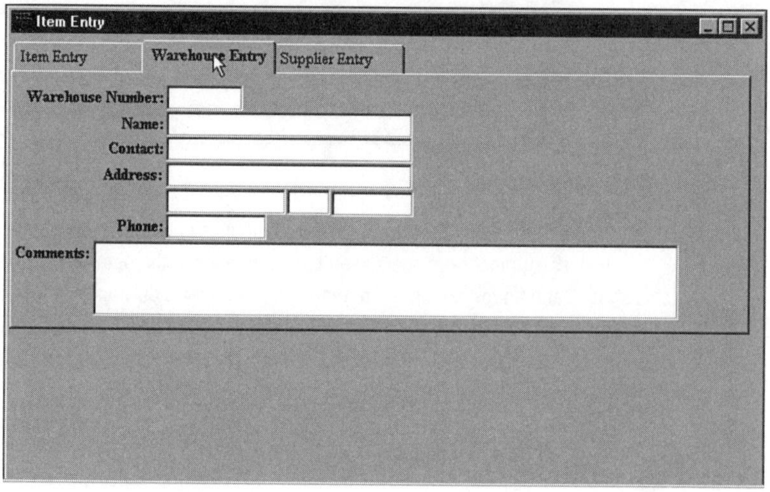

FIG. 9.60

Clicking a different tab page hides the old tab page information and displays the clicked tab page information.

Finally, if you click the Invoice toolbar item (seen in the toolbar in figure 9.60), the w_invoice window is opened. Notice that the d_invoice_header, d_invoice_detail, and d_invoice_footer DataWindows are displayed, but look like they are only one DataWindow. This way, the end user is insulated from the complexities of entering both header and detail information at the same time.

FIG. 9.61
Multiple DataWindows can appear to look like a single DataWindow.

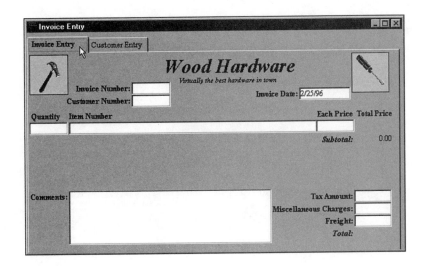

From Here...

In this chapter, you learned how to create a DataWindow and how to hook a DataWindow object to a DataWindow control. If you want to find out more information, refer to the following chapters:

- Chapter 10, "Enhancing DataWindows," goes beyond creating DataWindows and delves into field manipulation and edit styles, like radio buttons and drop-down DataWindows.

- Chapter 11, "Manipulating Data Using DataWindows," describes how to use a DataWindow to convey information to and from a database.

- Chapter 12, "Creating Reports," shows how to use your DataWindows as reports. This chapter also describes grouping and graphing data, as well as some new PowerBuilder 5 features.

- Chapter 14, "Pulling It All Together in an Application," describes the final steps needed to finalize your application.

Enhancing DataWindows

by Charles A. Wood

In the last chapter, you learned how to create
DataWindows. Now you will see how to modify, enhance,
and use your DataWindow. ■

Use edit styles.

Edit styles range from edit masks to
radio buttons and check boxes. This
chapter shows you how to define
edit styles for your DataWindow
columns.

Use display formats.

Sometimes you need to format your
data after it's been entered. This
chapter shows you how to use
display formats to accomplish this
task.

Use validation rules.

Older computer languages forced
you to go through lengthy edit
processes to validate data. Using
validation rules, you can make data
entry validation a snap. This chapter
shows you how.

**Set default values for your
columns in the database
painter.**

Sometimes you'll want the user to
see default values in the
DataWindow columns. This chapter
shows you how to easily set them.

Use conditional expressions.

One of the more powerful features
of DataWindows is conditional
expressions. This chapter shows
you how to implement them.

Using Edit Styles

So far, you have been shown all columns as entry fields on the DataWindow. This section will show you how to enhance your DataWindow to include other edit styles such as drop-down lists, radio buttons, check boxes, and edit masks. You'll also learn how to include a DataWindow within a DataWindow.

To define or review an edit style, double-click the DataWindow column you want to modify or review. This will open the column property sheet. Click the Edit tab. This will display the current edit style defined for your column. As you can see by the Style drop-down list box shown in figure 10.1, you can choose which edit style you want to use with your column.

FIG. 10.1

The Edit tab lets you view or modify the edit style chosen. Edit is the default edit style.

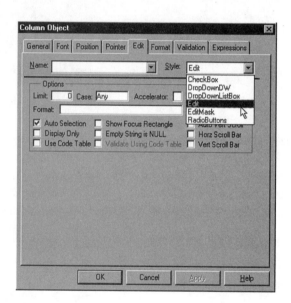

Edit

Edit is the default edit style. By choosing Edit as the edit style in the Edit tab of your DataWindow column property sheet, you can define many aspects of your edit field (see fig. 10.2).

Name You can design your own edit styles from the database painter. Also, some edit styles (especially for numeric fields) are defined for you. If you want to use a predefined edit style, you put the name of the edit style here.

▶ **See** "Defining Your Own Edit Styles," **p. 330**

Limit The Limit box is where you specify how many characters can be entered. If you specify 0, you can enter an unlimited amount of characters.

FIG. 10.2

The Edit tab allows you to set properties on your field relating to this edit style.

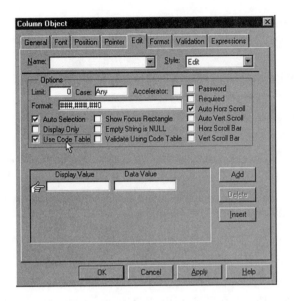

Case You can specify upper- or lowercase in the Case box. The default is any case.

Accelerator The Accelerator key allows you to define a key or key sequence that will set focus on the column you are defining. (Remember, to set focus on a field or control means to bring the cursor to that field.)

 T I P As with menus, if you define an accelerator key for your DataWindow, underline the letter associated with the Accelerator key by placing an ampersand (&) before the letter.

Format The Format box is usually used for numeric fields. Formatting allows an edit mask to be applied to the field after the field has been entered. For instance, if you typed $#,### in the Format box and the user typed 1234 in the field, as soon as the field lost focus, 1234 would be converted to $1,234.

Auto Selection The Auto Selection check box, when clicked, tells PowerBuilder to highlight the column when it receives focus. Since the entire field is now selected, anything you type will take the place of the current contents of the field. If Auto Selection is not selected, the cursor will go to the beginning of the field when that field receives focus.

Show Focus Rectangle Clicking the Show Focus Rectangle check box makes PowerBuilder display a faint rectangle around the field if it has focus.

Display Only To mark a field as Display Only, click the Display Only check box. The default allows the user to edit the field. (You could also set a field to Display Only by using the Tab Order, as discussed in chapter 9, "Creating DataWindows.")

Part
III

Ch
10

Empty String is NULL   An empty string is not normally considered a NULL. If the Empty String NULL check box is selected, PowerBuilder converts any empty string entered into a NULL.

Password   The Password check box tells PowerBuilder to place asterisks (*) when the user types in this column (similar to a password).

Required   The Required check box does not allow the field to lose focus unless a value is entered.

Auto Horz Scroll   If you type past the end of a data entry column, the Auto Horz Scroll check box automatically scrolls horizontally. The default is checked.

Auto Vert Scroll   To allow a column to automatically scroll vertically when needed, click the Auto Vert Scroll check box. The default is not checked.

Horz Scroll Bar   Clicking the Horz Scroll Bar check box places a horizontal scroll bar on the field.

Vert Scroll Bar   Clicking the Vert Scroll Bar check box places a vertical scroll bar on the field.

Use Code Table   A Use Code Table in the Edit style tells PowerBuilder to convert a specific value entered into another value. For instance, you can click the Use Code Table check box and then enter the following:

Display Value	Data Value
Indiana	IN
In	IN
indiana	IN
in	IN

If the user entered one of the display values, the field would be converted to IN internally.

Validate Using Code Table   Validate Using Code Table forces the user to enter one of the display values or data values. If the user enters something else, he or she will get an error message saying that what they entered for this column did not pass the validation test.

Drop-Down List Box

A list box is a box that has a list of choices. To make a choice in a list box, simply click on that choice. PowerBuilder employs a drop-down list box. This is a column whose list box doesn't appear until that column has focus. To make a column a drop-down list box, choose DropDownListBox from the Style drop-down list box in the Edit tab of the column property sheet as shown in figure 10.1. You'll notice in figure 10.3 that many of the options for the list box style are the same for the edit style. The different properties are as follows:

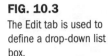

FIG. 10.3

The Edit tab is used to define a drop-down list box.

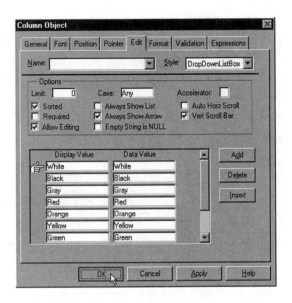

Sorted　Clicking the Sorted check box shows the Display Values in ascending order.

Allow Editing　Sometimes you'll want to give the user a set of choices, but other times you'll want the user to be able to type in his or her own choice. Clicking the Allow Editing check box allows the user either to select a choice from the list box or to type in a new choice. If the Allow Editing check box is not selected, the user must fill the field by choosing from the list box.

 TIP　If you click on the Allow Editing check box, a gap is placed between the arrow and the field boxes. If the Allow Editing check box is not selected, the arrow box is flush against the field box.

Always Show List　Always Show List converts the drop-down list box into a list box. By clicking the Always Show List check box, the list box is always displayed. If the Always Show List check box is not selected, the column's list box then will drop down when the column has focus.

Always Show Arrow　Always Show Arrow shows the arrow that pulls down the list box at all times. If the Always Show Arrow check box is not selected, the arrow is shown only when the field has focus.

Unlike the edit code table, the code table for the drop-down list box is used to display choices. Any choice made is then translated to the proper data value.

You can see in figure 10.4 what this does to your field. Since you added an arrow, an arrow appears in the DataWindow painter. Notice that the arrow is set off from the field. This is because this drop-down list box is editable as opposed to strictly multiple-choice.

FIG. 10.4
Item Color shows what a drop-down list box looks like in the DataWindow painter.

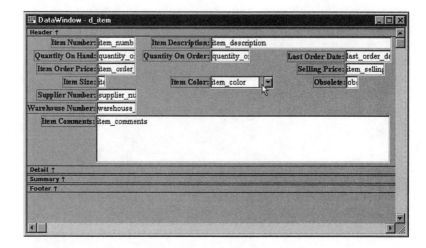

Figures 10.5 and 10.6 show how this drop-down list box looks while running. Notice that the user can quickly choose a common value but also can enter a not-so-common value if needed. Speeding data entry while allowing flexibility is a big benefit when using a drop-down list box.

FIG. 10.5
Using a drop-down list box, the user can quickly choose an option.

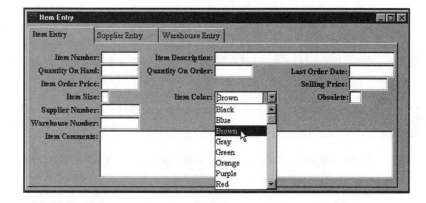

FIG. 10.6
Since this drop-down list box allows edits, the user is allowed the flexibility to enter a value not on the list.

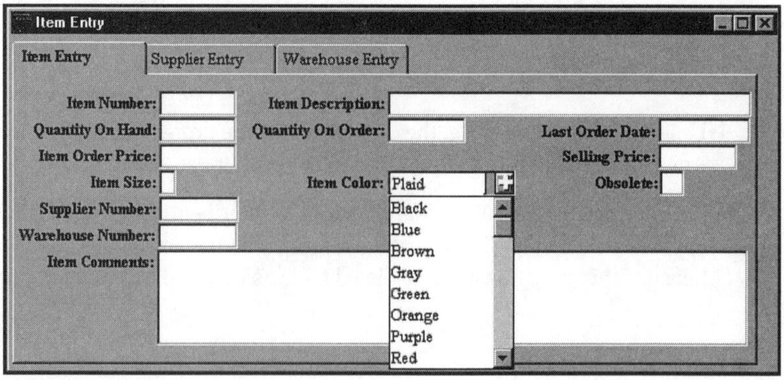

N O T E You can either allow edits or not allow edits with a drop-down list box. Allowing edits adds to flexibility (as shown in figs. 10.5 and 10.6), yet keeps the advantage of the list of commonly used values for the column.

However, sometimes such flexibility is not desired. By not allowing edits, you easily limit the valid values for the column without a lot of difficult coding to test for the proper values, displaying error messages, re-entering the column, and so on.

For each column, you must decide whether you want to allow the user as much flexibility as possible, or if you want to limit the choices of a column to a select set of answers. ▪

Radio Button

Radio buttons, like drop-down list boxes, are a multiple-choice of sorts for the user to quickly select the value for a column. To make a column into a radio button, choose RadioButtons from the Style drop-down list box in the Edit tab of the column property sheet as shown in figure 10.1. The Radio Button Edit tab appears, as shown in figure 10.7.

Part III

Ch 10

FIG. 10.7

The Radio Button Edit tab enables you to define your radio button column.

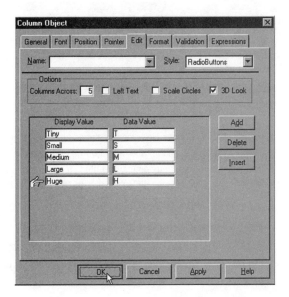

In the Radio Button Edit tab, you define your radio button column with the following properties.

Columns Across   The Columns Across box controls the number of columns displayed across.

Left Text   The Left Text check box tells PowerBuilder to put the text on the left side of the radio button. If this is not clicked, the text will be placed on the right side of the radio button.

Scale Circles   Scale Circles tells PowerBuilder to scale the radio buttons to the size of the field.

3D 3D gives radio buttons a lowered appearance. This usually is a good look for a radio button.

The code table used is similar to the drop-down list box. If you click a display value, the data value is returned to the program. You can see how the radio button you defined in figure 10.7 looks when completed in figure 10.8.

FIG. 10.8

Radio buttons shown in the Size DataWindow column are quick ways of entering multiple-choice questions.

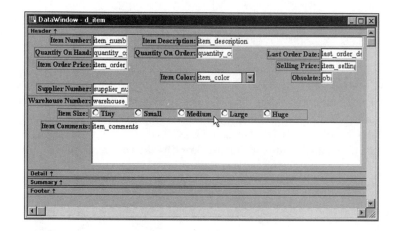

PowerBuilder doesn't mark any button if an invalid value is in the field. This aids in run-time testing and execution.

N O T E Radio buttons are very fast to enter. However, you should limit the number of radio buttons in a column before making the column a no-edit drop-down list box. Too many radio buttons clutter a screen and slow down data entry as the user hunts for the right button. (Anything over six radio buttons in one column typically becomes difficult to use, but it's a matter of preference.) ▪

Check Box

Check boxes are yes-no boxes that are clicked on or off. To make a column into a check box, choose CheckBox from the Style drop-down list box in the Edit tab of the column property sheet as shown in figure 10.1. The Check Box Edit tab appears, as shown in figure 10.9.

In the Check Box Edit tab, you define the properties of your check box. The following are properties specific to check boxes only.

Text Text is the prompt that is shown on one side of the check box.

Data Value For The Data Value For attribute allows you to define what values are returned for each state of the check box. Usually, this is just Y or N.

Scale Scale is similar to the Scale Circle used with radio buttons. Scale makes the square box as large as the defined field will allow.

FIG. 10.9

The Check Box Edit tab defines your check box column.

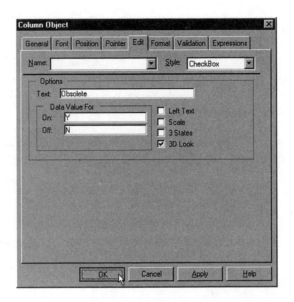

3 States   Check boxes don't always have to be yes or no. Windows (and PowerBuilder) allow for a 3 State check box. This is usually checked, not checked, or grayed-in. If 3 States is checked, an Other: option will be added to the Data Value For list, as shown in figure 10.10.

FIG. 10.10

3 State check boxes allow an Other: option to be added to the possible choices of a check box.

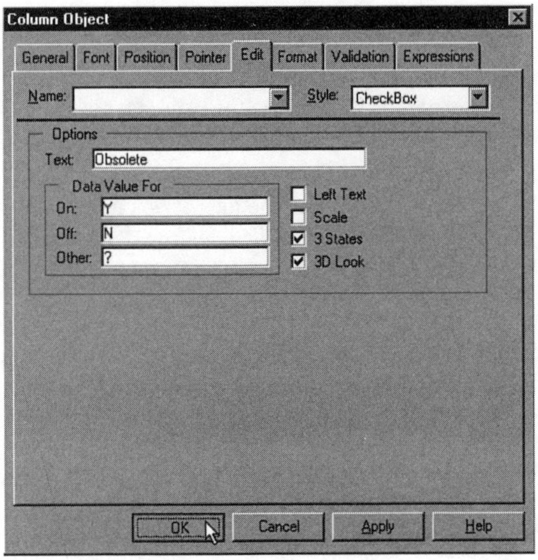

Part
III

Ch
10

TIP 3 State check boxes can be confusing. Although it's a matter of preference, try using three radio buttons instead.

Returning to Your DataWindow with a Check Box When you're finished defining your check box, click OK, as shown in figure 10.9. Your DataWindow will now be formatted with a new check box, as seen in figure 10.11.

FIG. 10.11
This is how the Obsolete check box looks when implemented in the DataWindow painter.

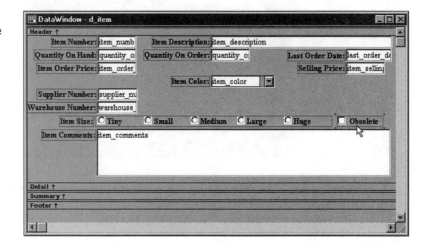

Edit Masks

Edit masks are used for formatted input while the user is typing in a column. For instance, if you declared an edit mask of ##,### for a field, PowerBuilder would only allow numeric input (# is numeric). Also, using an edit mask inserts the appropriate markings (such as commas) during entry as opposed to after entry like the format box in the default edit style. To make a field an edit mask, choose EditMask from the Style drop-down list box in the Edit tab of the column property sheet as shown in figure 10.1. The Edit Mask Edit tab appears, as shown in figure 10.12.

The Edit Mask Edit tab enables you to define the properties of the column by using the edit mask. Some of these properties are the same as the ones used for the default edit style. New attributes used for edit mask are as follows.

Name Name is used to choose a predefined edit mask. However, unlike other edit styles, PowerBuilder has predefined edit masks available. User-defined edit masks will be discussed later in this chapter.

Mask Mask is the format you define for your field. For instance, a social security number might have the format of "###-##-####." A phone number might have the format of "(###) ###-####."

FIG. 10.12
The Edit Mask Edit tab is used to define the properties for the edit mask column.

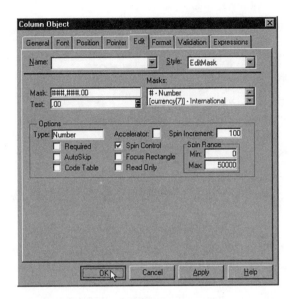

Test After you define your Mask, Test lets you type in the field to see how your Mask works.

Masks The Masks box allows you to choose a predefined or user-defined mask.

Type Usually, the Type box is set as Display Only. The only time you are allowed to change the type is if PowerBuilder cannot determine what type the field in question is. (For example, a computed field would allow you to choose the type.)

Autoskip The Autoskip attribute skips over this field when you use Tab.

> **N O T E** Autoskip is not often turned on. In fact, if you were to use this attribute, you would probably do so with PowerScript during execution as opposed to setting Autoskip as the default. More than likely, you would set the Tab Order to 0 to skip the field entirely. ■

Spin Control Spin Control allows the user to use the mouse to increment or decrement the edit mask value by placing an up-arrow button and a down-arrow button within the edit mask box. By clicking on Spin Control, you can enter attributes used for Spin Control, as shown in figure 10.12. The mouse pointer in figure 10.13 is pointing to an example of what Spin Control on a field looks like in a DataWindow.

Spin Increment, Spin Range, Code Table, and Code Table options are properties that are related to Spin Control.

Part
III

Ch
10

FIG. 10.13
You can see the use of
Spin Control now
present in the d_item
DataWindow.

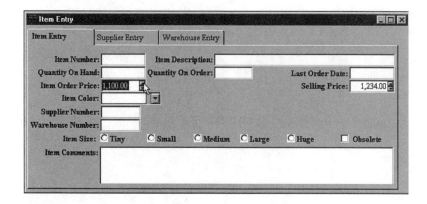

N O T E It's very important to give some keyboard alternatives to the user who doesn't like to use a
mouse. Conversely, Spin Control is nice for the user who doesn't like to let go of the mouse
and hates the keyboard. In figure 10.13, Spin Control is placed on order price and selling price. ▪

Spin Increment   Spin Increment is the increment (or decrement) that you can click to
increase (or decrease) the current value in the edit mask box. Each time you click the Spin
Control arrows, the increment increases or decreases. For instance, if you have a spin
increment of 100, and you have 0 in your edit mask box, clicking the up arrow once will place
100 in the box, twice will place 200, and so on.

Spin Range   The Spin Range area allows you to specify a minimum and a maximum for your
spin increment.

Code Table and Code Table Options   This Code Table is defined exactly as the code tables
you've seen before in the default edit style, the radio button style, and the drop-down list box.
However, when an edit mask uses a Code Table, as seen in figure 10.14, the Spin Control
transverses through the code table values instead of incrementing and decrementing the value
in the edit mask box.

Clicking on Read Only forces the user to change the value in the edit mask box by using the Code Table
and Spin Control only, and doesn't allow users to type in the Spin Control edit mask box.

FIG. 10.14
Code tables can be
used with spin controls
in place of spin
increments.

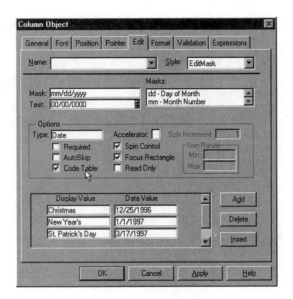

Using Drop-Down DataWindows (DDDWs)

Often, you'll need to hook the entry in one DataWindow to an entry in another DataWindow. For example, figure 10.13 includes both the supplier and the warehouse in the d_item DataWindow. Although it's necessary for the users to enter these fields, it's unreasonable to assume that they know the numbers for all the warehouses and all the suppliers. More likely, they know the name of the suppliers and the description of the warehouses.

It's also unreasonable to force every user to type in the name of the supplier or the description of the warehouse exactly the same as every other user. Allowing the users to type in names instead of numbers also becomes a PowerScript editing nightmare.

These problems are answered by Drop-Down DataWindows. Drop-Down DataWindows are a type of drop-down list box. Instead of using constant display values that are translated into internal data values, a Drop-Down DataWindow (or DDDW) uses two values from an existing DataWindow, making a DDDW a DataWindow-within-a-DataWindow.

To add a DDDW to an existing DataWindow, you must first create a new DataWindow to define what you want to display. Although any type of DataWindow will work, the most used for a DDDW is a tabular or free form quick-select DataWindow.

First, you must add the field you want to display and the field you want to be translated to the program. In the supplier number's case, you probably want the user to choose the supplier name and return the supplier number, so these two fields should be added to your DataWindow, as shown in figure 10.15.

Part
III

Ch
10

FIG. 10.15
To make a DDDW, start by defining a DataWindow with the field that you want to display and the field that you want to return.

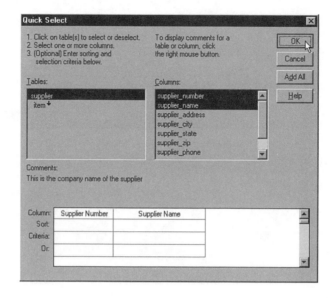

When you arrive at the DataWindow painter, delete all the headings and all the fields you do not want to display. Since you only want to display the supplier name, that should be the only field shown (see fig. 10.16).

 T I P Drop-Down DataWindows (DDDWs) are sometimes called child DataWindows.

FIG. 10.16
Delete all non-display fields and all headings from the DataWindow painter when defining a DDDW, leaving only the field you want to display.

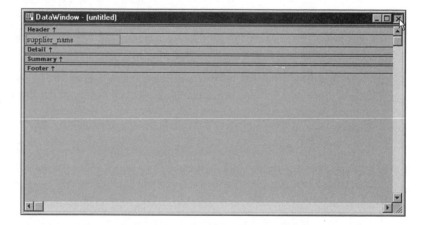

N O T E Even though you deleted a field out of the DataWindow painter, the field is no longer displayed but still remains and is internally processed. ▨

Save this DataWindow. It's probably a good idea to include a DDDW somewhere in the name if this DataWindow is used only for DDDWs. (I called this DDDW dddw_supplier.) Now return to your DataWindow that you are adding your DDDW to (d_item). Select DropDownDataWindow for the style.

Now you will see the DropDownDataWindow Edit tab. Choose the DataWindow that you want to associate with this column (see fig. 10.17). In this case, that would be dddw_supplier.

FIG. 10.17
To make a column a DDDW, you must choose the DataWindow you want associated with that column.

After you choose your DataWindow for the DDDW, click on the column from the DDDW that you want to display. Now also choose the Data Column from the DDDW. This is the value that is returned to the DataWindow when a display value is chosen.

Now fill in the rest of your DDDW properties. These correspond to the list box properties. (This probably isn't surprising to you, since a DDDW is a type of list box.) Click on OK. To run the DDDW, enter data in the Supplier table. To do this, use the database painter as shown in figure 10.18.

Now you're ready to run. Click the Run icon and open your application. Since the Item window is pulled up first, you can see the supplier DDDW. Click the down arrow to view and choose a supplier, as seen in figure 10.19.

The supplier number will be stored in the d_item DataWindow supplier_number column after you choose the supplier name.

FIG. 10.18
You can use the database painter to enter data into your table to test your DDDW.

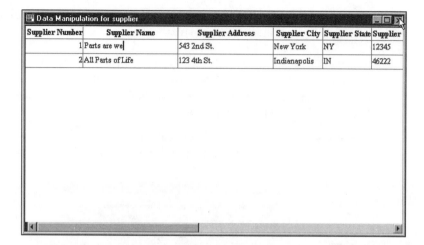

FIG. 10.19
Click on the displayed value in the DDDW, and a data value will be returned.

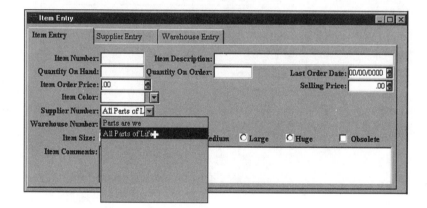

Using Display Formats

Display formats are a lot like edit masks. The main difference is that display formats are applied to a field after entry, while edit masks are applied to a field during entry. To define a format for a field on your DataWindow, click the format tab of a column property sheet, as seen in figure 10.20.

FIG. 10.20
You can define formats
using the column
property sheet in the
DataWindow painter.

The Display String Formats dialog box opens, and all existing formats for this data type are displayed. From here, you can define the format for your field and test the result. In figure 10.20, the format for a phone number is defined.

TROUBLESHOOTING

I'm using '#' in my format string, but the numbers aren't printing. All that's showing is the actual # sign. With a string column, the at sign (@) is used to tell PowerBuilder to allow any character. In a numeric column, the pound sign (#) is used to allow any number. However, you cannot use '#' in a string format unless you want '#' to appear in your string column.

With a numeric format, you can define different formats for positive and negative numbers by defining two formats separated by a semicolon. A format of

`#,##0.00;[red]#,##0.00`

will turn your number red if it is negative.

When you actually enter a format string, your type looks normal, as seen in figure 10.21. However, as soon as the column you're typing in loses focus, the format style is applied (see fig. 10.22).

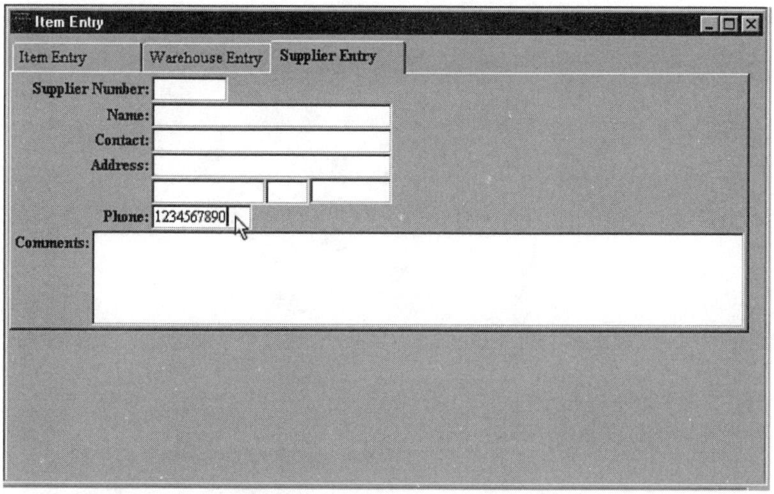

FIG. 10.21

Unlike edit masks, format styles are not applied to the column until after the column loses focus.

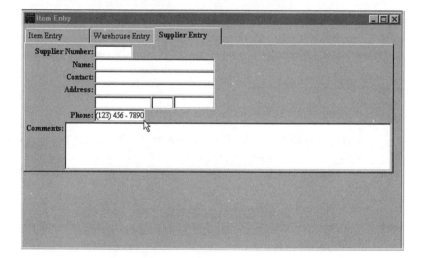

FIG. 10.22

As soon as a column loses focus, any format style is applied to the display.

Using Validation Rules

Validation rules don't allow your column to lose focus if the value entered does not meet the criteria you defined for that column. For example, the order price can't be negative. If the user enters a negative number, you want to stop right there and make him or her correct the entry. To define a validation rule for a column, click the Validation tab of the column property sheet in the DataWindow painter, as shown in figure 10.23.

FIG. 10.23

The Validation tab of the column property sheet is used to define a validation rule for a column.

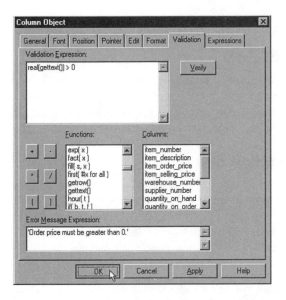

As seen in figure 10.23, you type in the rule you want to define using PowerScript functions (like abs( )) and relativities (like < and >). Here, you use GetText( ) to return the string value of the current column, convert it to a real number, and make sure that the number is not negative.

 TIP GetText( ) returns the value of the current column in string format. Real converts a string into a real number.

As you can see in figure 10.24, an error message box appears when a validation rule has been violated. Validation rules make coding for exceptions and invalid situations easier.

FIG. 10.24

An error message is displayed if what the user entered violates the validation rule for that column.

TROUBLESHOOTING

I'm using a validation rule, but my column allows me to enter an invalid entry occasionally. Other times, I get an error message when the incorrect value has been fixed. What gives? Validation rules are first checked before the entered value is stored in the column. If you use the column name in your validation rule, you may experience a "lagging effect," where the column is checked before the value in the column is changed. Try using the GetText() function as seen in figure 10.23 to get the current string shown in the column and convert it to a value you can test with.

Part

III

Ch

10

Using the Database Painter to Define Different Column Properties

You are able to define many column properties that are often used in the database painter. For instance, if you use a Yes-No check box often, you may want to define a Yes-No check box. If you use phone numbers, you might want a phone number edit mask. If many of your strings need to be numeric, you might want to define a numeric validation rule.

Defining Your Own Edit Styles

To define your own edit styles, get into the database painter and choose Design, Edit Style Maintenance, as shown in figure 10.25. This pulls up the Edit Styles dialog box, shown in figure 10.26. As you can see, many edit styles (mostly for date and DateTime data types) have been defined for you. PowerBuilder also lets you define new drop-down list boxes and drop-down data window, check box, radio button, default edit, and edit mask edit styles. To create a new edit style, click New, as seen in figure 10.26.

The Edit Style dialog box appears, as shown in figure 10.27. From here, you can define all edit styles just as you would for a DataWindow column. The only difference is that you need to name the edit style so that many columns can use it. In figure 10.27, we create an edit mask.

You can also define other edit style types. If you choose CheckBox for the style in figure 10.27, a CheckBox Edit Style dialog box pops up allowing you to define a default check box, as seen in figure 10.28.

FIG. 10.25

To define an edit style, open Design in the DataWindow painter and choose Edit Style Maintenance.

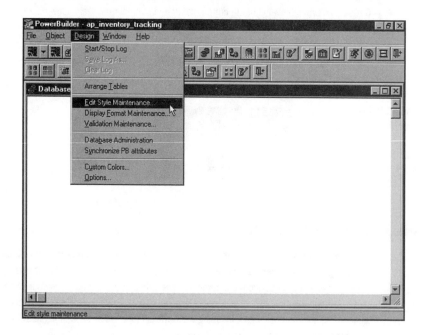

FIG. 10.26
The Edit Styles dialog
box will let you edit or
create edit styles used
with DataWindow and
database columns.

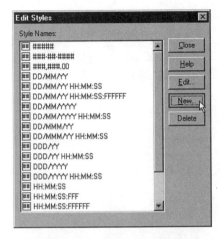

FIG. 10.27
The Edit Styles dialog
box in the database
painter is identical to
the property sheet Edit
tab in the DataWindow
painter except you can
enter a name in the
database painter.

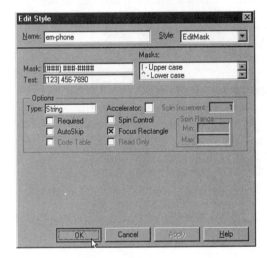

When you return to the Edit Styles dialog box, you can see the new edit styles you defined, as
seen in figure 10.29. These styles can be used in the name field of all the column edit style
property sheets in the DataWindow painter.

FIG. 10.28

You can define a default check box in the CheckBox Edit Style dialog box.

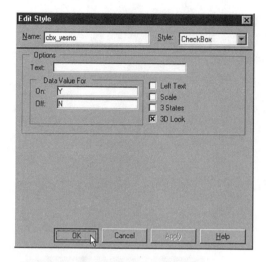

FIGURE 10.29

All user defined edit styles are displayed in the Edit Styles dialog box.

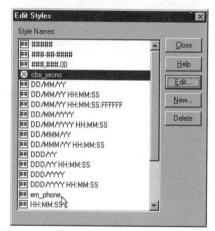

N O T E Notice how the name of the edit mask definition began with em_ and the name of the check box definition began with cbx_. Naming prefixes will group all your defined edit masks together with those of the same type and will let other developers know that this is a user-defined edit mask. Similarly, you should prefix your other defined edit styles with the appropriate prefix (for example, use rb_ for radio button, cbx_ for check box, ddlb_ for drop-down list box, and ed_ for edit). ▇

Defining Your Own Display Formats

To define your own display formats, get into the database painter and choose Design Display Format Maintenance. The Display Formats dialog box appears, as shown in figure 10.30. As with edit styles, there are several display formats defined. However, all predefined formats are for numeric fields.

FIG. 10.30

The Display Formats dialog box is used to edit or create display formats for use in the database painter and the DataWindow painter.

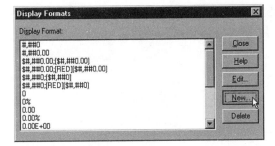

To define your own display format, click New in the Display Formats dialog box. This pulls up the Display Format Definition dialog box (see fig. 10.31).

FIG. 10.31

The Display Format Definition dialog box is used to define a format for use in the database and DataWindow painters.

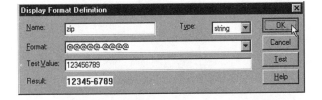

The Display Format Definition dialog box shown in figure 10.31 allows you to define a display format for use in the DataWindow and database painters. When you have defined your display format, it appears in the Display Formats dialog box, as shown in figure 10.32.

FIG. 10.32

All user-defined formats are displayed in the Display Formats dialog box.

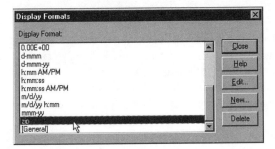

Defining Your Own Validation Rules

To define your own validation rules, get into the database painter and choose Design, Validation Maintenance. The Validation Rules dialog box appears, as shown in figure 10.33.

Unlike edit styles and display formats, there are no predefined validation rules. To define a validation rule, click New in the Validation Rules dialog box (refer to fig. 10.33). The Input Validation dialog box appears, as seen in figure 10.34.

Part
III

Ch
10

FIG. 10.33

The Validation Rules dialog box is where you first define and then later edit validation rules.

FIG. 10.34

The Input Validation dialog box lets you define the name, rule, and error message of a validation rule.

As with the Validation Rules dialog box used in the DataWindow painter (refer to fig. 10.33), the Input Validation dialog box shown in figure 10.34 allows you to use PowerScript functions to define your edit rule. Unlike the Validation Rules dialog box, the Input Validation dialog box forces you to use the @col variable at least once in your validation rule. The @col variable is a variable used in the Input Validation dialog box denoting the current column.

N O T E You must refer to the current column at least once in a validation rule. This makes using GetText() impractical. Because of this, you would probably define your validation rules at the DataWindow level rather than the database level. ■

Once you're done defining your rule, click OK. This will return you to the Validation Rules dialog box, and your new rule will be listed there, as seen in figure 10.35.

FIG. 10.35
After you define a validation rule, it's listed in the Validation Rules dialog box.

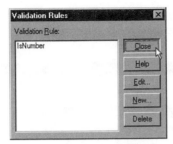

Setting Different Column Defaults

You can set default edit styles, display formats, validation rules, and values for your columns in either the database painter or the DataWindow painter.

Setting Defaults in the Database Painter   To set column defaults in the database painter, open the table whose columns you want to set and double-click on the table. The Alter Table dialog box opens, as shown in figure 10.36.

FIG. 10.36
You can assign an edit mask, display format, or validation rule to a field in the Alter Table dialog box.

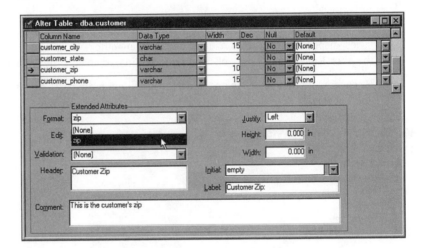

N O T E   The Create Table dialog box used for creating new tables and the Alter Table dialog box used for updating existing table definitions are almost identical. Information about setting defaults in the Alter Table dialog box also applies to the Create Table dialog box. ■

Assign the zip format display for the customer_zip. In a similar way, you could also set the validation rule in the Alter Table dialog box by choosing a column and then choosing the appropriate validation rule.

You also can set a default (empty string) in the zip code column. Here, you are allowed to set defaults for field values.

As seen in figure 10.37, you can also change default values in the database painter by right-clicking on a field displayed in a table and choosing Properties.

FIG. 10.37
By right-clicking on a column in the database painter, you can pull up a database column property sheet.

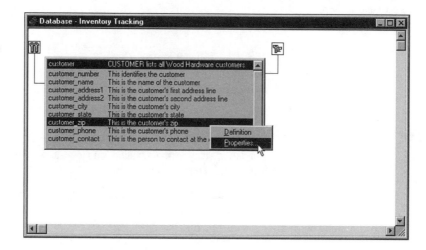

The column property sheet in the database painter allows you to define default values, edit styles, display formats, or validations, and to change the column comments. You can also enter the Alter Table dialog box by clicking on Definition, or change the table header.

By clicking the validation tab on the database column property sheet, as seen in figure 10.38, you can change the validation rule (or create a new rule) or change the initial (default) value.

FIG. 10.38
The column property sheet in the database painter allows you to change various aspects about the database column, including the default validation rule.

CAUTION

When you add default definitions to your database, they only apply to DataWindows you will create, not to DataWindows you already have created. For those DataWindows, you'll either need to redefine the fields in the DataWindow painter or delete the DataWindow and re-create it.

Setting Defaults Using the Rows Column Specifications   You can also set defaults for columns in your DataWindow by choosing Rows, Column Specifications, as seen in figure 10.39. The Column Specifications dialog box appears, as shown in figure 10.40.

FIG. 10.39

To define default values for your DataWindow columns, choose Rows, Columns Specifications.

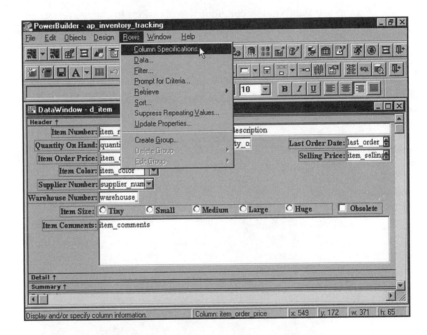

Part
III

Ch
10

FIG. 10.40

You can set the defaults and validation rules for your DataWindow columns in the Column Specifications dialog box.

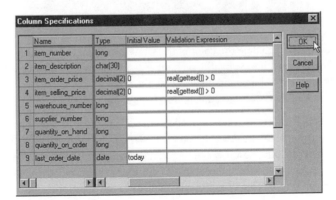

In the Column Specifications dialog box, you can set the initial value, validation expression, validation message, and database column relating to the DataWindow column. Using the Column Specifications dialog box is one of the easiest ways to manipulate you default values.

 T I P   To avoid confusion, be sure to initialize all your check box and radio button variables. That way, what the user looks at will be what is represented in the program.

Using Conditional Expressions

You can use DataWindow conditional expressions to change properties of a DataWindow column based on a conditional expression. To define a conditional expression for a column on your DataWindow, click the Expressions tab in the column property sheet in the DataWindow painter, as seen in figure 10.41.

FIG. 10.41

The Expressions tab of the column property sheet in the DataWindow painter allows you to conditionally change attrributes of your DataWindow columns.

Say you wanted to change the color of the Quantity on Hand column on the d_item DataWindow to red if the quantity on hand was less than 10. Pull up the Expressions tab of the Quantity on Hand column and double-click the color attribute, as seen in figure 10.41. This will pull up the Modify Expression dialog box seen in figure 10.42.

In figure 10.42, an If( ) function is used to change the color of the Quantity on Hand column if the Quantity On Hand field was less then 10. Otherwise, the black color is returned. You can see the color attribute now is set to be red if the Quantity On Hand is less than 10; otherwise the attribute is black. When you return to the Expressions tab, the rule you just coded in the Modify Expression dialog box is displayed next to the appropriate attribute, as seen in figure 10.43.

FIG. 10.42

The Modify Expression dialog box allows you to use DataWindow painter functions to conditionally modify an attribute of a DataWindow column.

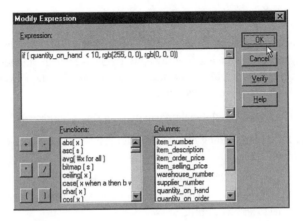

FIG. 10.43

All conditional expressions for a column are reflected in the Expressions tab of the column property sheet in the DataWindow painter.

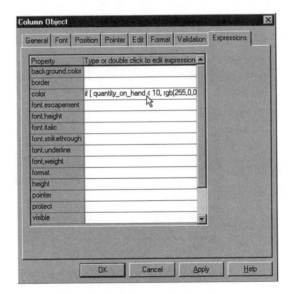

N O T E   The syntax for the If ( ) function is as follows:

```
If(expression, if-true return value, if-false return value )
```

The If( ) function is available only in the DataWindow painter, and not in PowerScript. It allows you to test an expression and return a value based on whether the expression evaluated to be TRUE or FALSE. In addtion to using an If( ) function inside the Expressions tab of the column property sheet, If( ) functions are often used inside computed columns. ■

Part

III

Ch

10

From Here...

This chapter teaches you how to make your DataWindows more useful to the end user. It also shows you ways to avoid long and lengthy editing scripts by using the tools that Powersoft provides with PowerBuilder. More information can be found in the PowerBuilder User's Guide in chapter 15, "Displaying and Validating Data."

Refer to these chapters for additional information on DataWindows and databases:

- Chapter 2, "Understanding Analysis, Design, and Databases," gives a detailed description of the database painter and setting up tables in your database.
- Chapter 9, "Creating DataWindows," describes how to define your DataWindows.
- Chapter 11, "Manipulating Data Using DataWindows," shows how to use your DataWindow to access your database.

Manipulating Data Using DataWindows

by Charles A. Wood

Now that you've seen how to format a DataWindow, you can start using it. This chapter doesn't discuss the format of the DataWindow, but rather how to manipulate data through your DataWindow. ■

Suppress, filter, and sort data.

After retrieving data, you can manipulate it so it may or may not be visible to the user. You can also sort and group the data.

Modify your data source.

Sometimes modifications require you to change where you get your data from, and how much data you get.

Retrieve from and update your database from your DataWindow.

The DataWindow is the doorway between your application and your database. This chapter shows how to retrieve and update database information using a DataWindow.

Specify retrieval arguments and retrieve data from a database.

Sometimes you only want to retrieve certain rows from your database to place on your DataWindow.

Work with crosstabs.

Crosstabas are pretty complex. You can learn about crosstabs in this chapter.

Access data in a DataWindow.

PowerBuilder 5 now lets you directly access your DataWindow columns and attributes.

Filtering

Sometimes you'll want to limit the access your DataWindow has to your data either for security considerations or to make the DataWindow easier to use for the end user. You can achieve this by using a filter. To specify a filter in the DataWindow painter, open Rows and choose Filter, as seen in figure 11.1.

FIG. 11.1
To establish a filter for a DataWindow, open Rows and choose Filter.

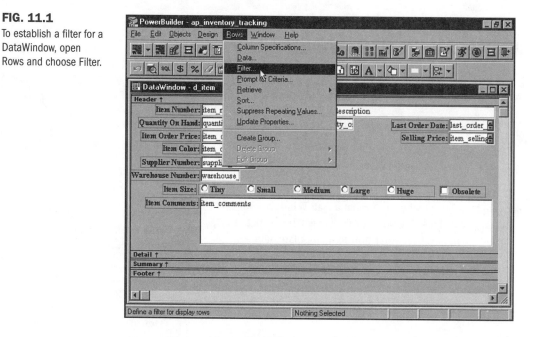

Now you'll see the Specify Filter dialog box, where you enter the condition you want all rows to meet. PowerBuilder gives you a list of functions to choose from and a list of columns in the DataWindow. Figure 11.2 shows all the obsolete items eliminated from the DataWindow.

FIG. 11.2
In the Specify Filter dialog box, you enter the condition you want all rows to meet in the DataWindow.

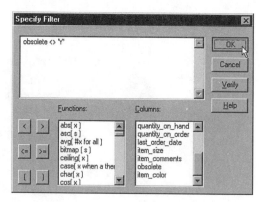

The filtered data is not deleted from the DataWindow entirely. (Indeed, deleted rows are not deleted off the DataWindow entirely.) PowerBuilder establishes buffers for primary data, filtered data, and deleted data. Ordinarily, your DataWindow automatically uses the primary buffer. However, several DataWindow functions allow you to access the other buffers or even change their state so that they return to the primary buffer (see fig. 11.3).

FIG. 11.3
Although the primary buffer is used to populate columns on the DataWindow, DataWindow functions have access to all filtered and deleted rows.

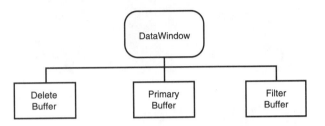

Sorting

You'll almost always want to establish a sort criteria for your DataWindow. This can be done two ways. The harder (but more efficient) way is to code an order by clause in the DataWindow SQL (covered later in this chapter in the "Using the SQL Toolbox" section). The other way is to establish a sort column in your DataWindow painter.

N O T E Just because a table has a primary key does not necessarily put the table's rows in primary key order. If you want to view the table in any order, you'll have to either specify a sort criteria or add a sort/order by clause to your DataWindow's SQL. ▓

▶ **See** "Creating Tables," **p. 76**

To establish a sort through the DataWindow painter, perform the following steps:

1. Click Rows, Sort from your DataWindow painter.
2. The Specify Sort Columns dialog box appears. Here, you select the column from the Source Data area and move it to the Columns area, as seen in figure 11.4.

N O T E The Ascending check box is automatically selected. To have the field selected in descending order, unselect the check box. ▓

 If you notice that you are sorting the fields in the wrong order, simply click on the field you need to move and drag it to the new location.

Part
III

Ch
11

FIG. 11.4
The Specify Sort Columns dialog box allows you to specify the sort order by dragging the columns you want sorted from the Source Data area to the Columns area.

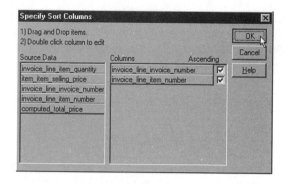

Modifying Your Data Source

   The data source is where the data for the DataWindow comes from. By clicking the SQL Select icon, you go into PowerBuilder's SQL Toolbox, as seen in figure 11.5.

FIG. 11.5
Clicking the SQL Select icon puts you into the SQL Toolbox.

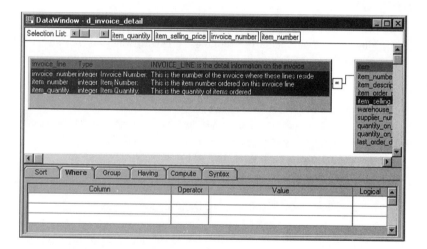

Customizing Your Data Source Viewing Area

PowerBuilder has several options that can control the viewing area of your database data source for a DataWindow. These options, discussed in this section, are saved when you exit the SQL Toolbox.

Using Show   Under Design, PowerBuilder adds Show, as shown in figure 11.6. Show allows you to customize your display by toggling on and off your data type display, labels display, comments display, and SQL toolbox.

FIG. 11.6

You can toggle on or off what you want to display by opening Design and choosing Show.

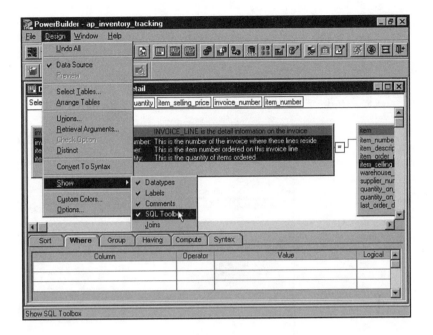

Resizing, Arranging, and Dragging Your Database Windows   After choosing what you want to display, you can resize your database windows to an appropriate size. At any time during this process of showing only the options you want to see and resizing your database windows, you can also arrange your database windows much like you would arrange icons by opening Design and choosing Arrange Tables.

If you drag your table windows around and turn off all the table information displays, you can end up with the screen shown in figure 11.7.

FIG. 11.7

You can drag your table windows around for a better display.

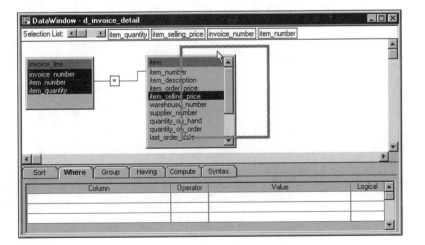

Displaying Columns vs. Displaying Joins   Columns are automatically joined by foreign keys, and you can define your own (as seen later in this chapter). To display the joined fields, click the Joins icon (see fig. 11.8). This will highlight only the columns that are joined to other tables. To re-highlight the columns selected for the DataWindow, click the Join icon again to turn joins off.

▶ **See** "Creating Tables," **p. 76**

FIG. 11.8
Clicking the Joins icon will only display those columns that are joined together.

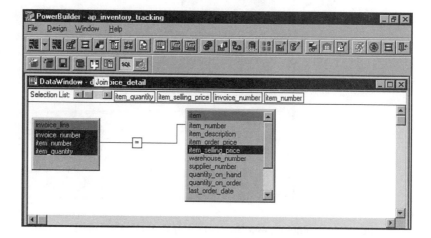

Converting to SQL Syntax or Graphics   You can also modify SQL statements that are used to retrieve data into your DataWindow. This is done by choosing Design, Convert To Syntax, as shown in figure 11.9.

FIG. 11.9
You can see and modify the SELECT syntax behind a DataWindow by clicking Design, Convert To Syntax.

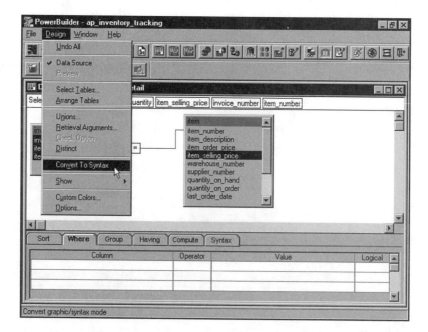

If you were in the d_invoice_detail DataWindow, the painter now shows you the SQL syntax behind the d_invoice_detail DataWindow, as shown in figure 11.10. To return to Graphics mode, choose Design, Convert To Graphics.

FIG. 11.10
When you convert to SQL, the select painter shows the SQL syntax that lies behind the DataWindow.

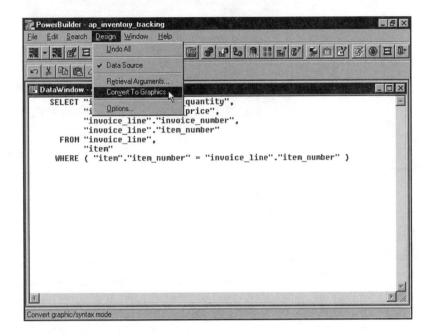

Changing Your Data Source

Often you will find that you need additional information on a DataWindow, or that you don't need all the tables and/or columns that you originally specified. In this case, you can change the data source that you originally specified.

> **CAUTION**
> Changing your data source will affect your DataWindow. You may see an additional field or some fields missing in your DataWindow painter after using the select painter.

Modifying Joins Joins are how tables relate to each other. When you select the columns for your DataWindow, joins are automatically set up for all foreign-primary key matches. You can add new joins and delete or modify existing joins in the select painter.

 To add a new join, click the join table icon and then click the two columns from the two different tables that you want to join. This will establish a join between the two tables when the two clicked columns are equal.

To modify an existing join, click the join box. (The join box is on the line connecting two tables.) Usually the join box contains an equal sign (=).

When you click the join box, the Join dialog box appears, as seen in figure 11.11.

FIG. 11.11
The Join dialog box is
used to select join type
or delete a join.

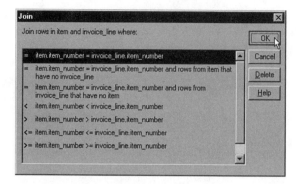

 Make sure that you click the Join icon off to start selecting columns for your DataWindow again.

Here you can specify whether a table join is an exact match to another table's column, or if it's
some other relationship.

TROUBLESHOOTING

**When I add a table to my DataWindow's data source, a join line appears between two columns,
but these two columns are not how I want my data joined. What do I do?** PowerBuilder will
automatically try to join any tables you add to a DataWindow first by column name and then by key
relationship. If you have two tables that have the same name for a column (i.e., "comments," "type," or
"name"), PowerBuilder will try to establish a join for those columns *even if you wouldn't want to join
the tables that way*!

Simply delete the join by clicking the join box and then the delete key. Then you can establish a new
join between your new table and an existing table.

Changing a DataWindow's Columns   When you open the select painter from the
DataWindow painter, all the relevant tables are displayed. To add or remove a column, simply
click one of the columns. In figure 11.12, item_number was clicked off. This removed it from
the selection list at the top of the painter. Reclicking item_number will put it back on the list.

FIG. 11.12
Clicking a column in the select painter will toggle a column on and off the selection list.

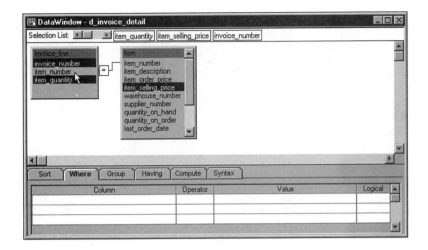

Changing a DataWindow's Tables   Adding or removing a column or table from your DataWindow is relatively easy. You also have the option of starting over with a new query for your tables, but this means you have to start your definition over and have a query defined.

▶ **See** "Using Queries," **p. 782**

 To add columns from another table to your DataWindow, you must first add that table to your DataWindow. This is done by clicking the Tables icon and selecting the table you wish to add to your DataWindow. In figure 11.13, the customer table is added to the d_invoice_header DataWindow. After you add the table, the table appears in your SQL Toolbox, as seen in figure 11.14. You can choose columns from your newly added table that you want to manipulate in your DataWindow.

FIG. 11.13
The customer table is added to the d_invoice_header DataWindow.

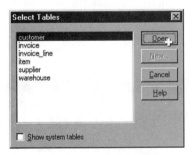

FIG. 11.14

You can now access the newly added table by adding columns to your DataWindow or by adding new joins or adjusting the joins that may have been automatically placed.

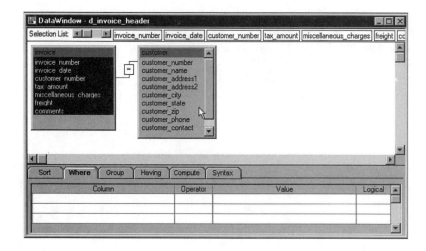

CAUTION

After selecting new columns to add to your DataWindow and clicking the SQL button to return to your DataWindow painter, you may be tempted to click the column icon to add your new columns. PowerBuilder has already added them for you at the top of the detailed section and to the right of the last field.

N O T E To add new columns to your DataWindow, first select the new columns and then click the SQL icon. The new column will automatically be added to the right side of the Detail section of your DataWindow. ■

You can remove a table by right-clicking the table header. Here, you will have the option of closing the table, as seen in figure 11.15. Choosing Close will remove the table from your DataWindow.

FIG. 11.15

By right-clicking the table header, a pop-up menu appears. By choosing Close, you can remove the customer table from your DataWindow.

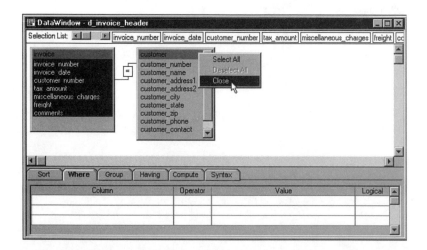

Using DISTINCT

A DISTINCT SELECT SQL statement eliminates all duplicate rows from the result of the SELECT statement. To place DISTINCT in the SQL statement, choose Design, Distinct, as seen in figure 11.16. This will put a check mark beside Distinct to let future developers know that you have selected this option.

FIG. 11.16
Clicking Design, Distinct removes any duplicate rows from your DataWindow SELECT.

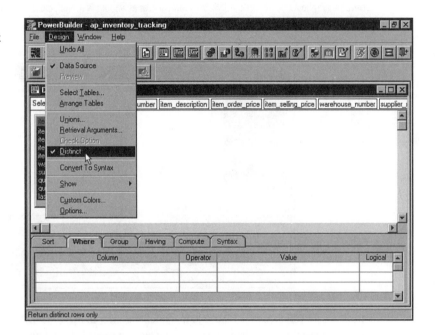

> **NOTE** DISTINCT can slow down an application, since every row retrieved is compared against existing rows selected. In the above case, DISTINCT was added to a SELECT that by its nature would never return a duplicate row since the primary key was part of the SELECT. Therefore, the DISTINCT option is turned off when you look at the application.
>
> DISTINCT also eliminates duplicate rows. If a row has similar columns but is not entirely the same as another row, it is not eliminated. ■

Using the SQL Toolbox

The SQL toolbox, as shown in figure 11.17, is a handy way to review all facets of the SQL behind your DataWindow. Using the toolbox, you can view and modify all aspects of the SELECT statement needed to retrieve database information in your DataWindow.

Sort   To establish an SQL sort, first click the Sort tab, and then click and drag a column from the list of columns to the list of columns to be sorted, as seen in figure 11.17. This statement puts an ORDER BY clause in the SELECT statement. Therefore, this sort is different than the Rows, Sort selection in the DataWindow Painter.

Part
III

Ch
11

This sort should be used instead of the Rows, Sort selection whenever possible. The limitation of this sort is that you can't sort on computed columns. Other than that, this sort is usually faster than the equivalent sort inside the DataWindow painter.

> **CAUTION**
>
> Never issue the same sort in the DataWindow painter as you have in the select painter. This has the effect of performing two of the same sorts on the same data. In other words, it will slow you down.

FIG. 11.17
To establish an ORDER BY clause, drag a column from the column list to the sort list.

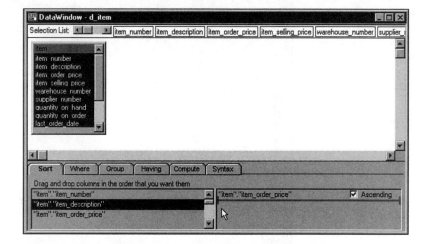

Where   The WHERE SQL clause joins tables together in SQL. WHERE can also be used to filter out unwanted records or to select only certain records based on a retrieval argument.

Establishing Retrieval Arguments   A retrieval argument (or arguments) forces the user to pass an argument (or arguments) in the Retrieve() PowerBuilder function. To establish a retrieval argument, choose Design, Retrieval Arguments, as seen in figure 11.18.

The Specify Retrieval Arguments dialog box appears, as seen in figure 11.19. Here, type the argument Name and choose the Type of the argument. If there is more than one argument, click the Add button or the Insert button and add more arguments.

Now every time you issue a Retrieve statement in a PowerScript statement for this DataWindow, you'll need to pass these arguments.

N O T E   The Retrieve( ) function gets information from the database tables and populates the columns of the DataWindow. Arguments (if any) are necessary to correspond to the retrieval arguments specified for this DataWindow. ■

FIG. 11.18
Clicking Design,
Retrieval Arguments
allows you to set
retrieval arguments
in a DataWindow.

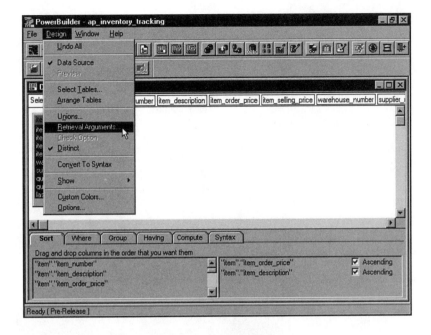

FIG. 11.19
In the Specify Retrieval
Arguments dialog box,
you choose the
argument name and the
type of your retrieval
arguments.

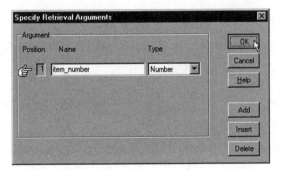

Using the Where Tab in the SQL Toolbox   By clicking the Where tab in the SQL toolbox, you
can use your retrieval argument to specify which row will be retrieved from the database into
the DataWindow. You can also use Where to act as a type of filter, as seen in figure 11.20.

N O T E   Once you screen out obsolete records, you can no longer retrieve those records. Hence, the
row screening out obsolete records was for discussion purposes only and will not be saved
in the Inventory Tracking system.

continues

Part
III

Ch
11

continued

However, the retrieval argument (item_number) is necessary to use this DataWindow as a data entry as well as a data retrieval DataWindow. In fact, you should also create the following retrieval arguments with an integer data type:

d_customer	customer_number
d_invoice_header	invoice_number
d_invoice_detail	invoice_number
d_invoice_footer	invoice_number
d_item	item_number
d_supplier	supplier_number
d_warehouse	warehouse_number

FIG. 11.20

You can use the retrieval argument and also add a filter (of sorts) to screen out any obsolete records.

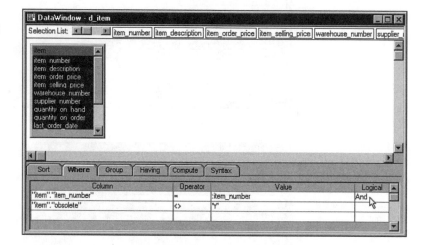

Comparing the Where Clause and the DataWindow Filter   You can use the WHERE SQL clause to filter out unwanted data much like the DataWindow filter. The major difference between the DataWindow filter and the WHERE SQL clause is that the DataWindow filter still pulls in the data and puts it into the filter buffer. The WHERE SQL clause does not.

> **CAUTION**
> Don't use the WHERE SQL clause as a filter and then repeat the same filter using a DataWindow filter. This performs the same task twice. If you don't need to access the Filter! buffer, a Where clause is more efficient.

Group The Group tab establishes a GROUP BY SQL clause in your SELECT statement. To group by a column, move that column from the column list to the group by list, as seen in figure 11.21.

FIG. 11.21
You can drag columns from the SELECT column list to be used with the GROUP BY clause.

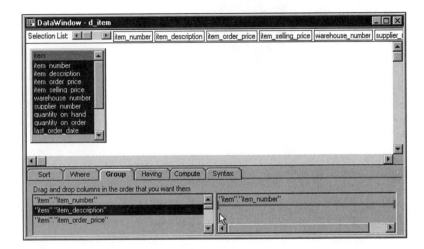

Grouping your data allows aggregate SQL functions (like MIN and AVG) to affect a segment of related rows instead of the whole database. Unfortunately, when you GROUP BY a column or columns, you can only use those GROUP BY columns and aggregate SQL functions in your SELECT. Using aggregate functions forces many of your retrieved columns to be SQL computed columns, thereby not allowing their update.

N O T E The changes adding a GROUP BY are not saved to the final system. The GROUP BY was added for discussion only. ■

▶ See "DataWindow," **p. 290**

Having The Having tab generates an SQL HAVING clause. The HAVING clause is a type of filter for GROUP BY clauses. As you see in figure 11.22, you can use an aggregate function to SELECT only those groups with an above average order price.

N O T E The DataWindow Painter also allows you to establish groups. However, these groups are radically different than the groups set up by an SQL GROUP BY statement.

The DataWindow groups allow you to display detailed information and then subtotal and total the information in different bands. Conversely, the SQL GROUP BY statement only returns summary information, and returns it into (mainly) computed columns.

For DataWindows, the use of a GROUP BY clause is limited. However, if you're only interested in summary information, use the SQL GROUP BY clause. If you're interested in seeing the detailed information that makes up the summary information, use the DataWindow Group. DataWindow groups are covered more in the next chapter on reports. ■

Part
III

Ch
11

FIG. 11.22
A HAVING clause is generated by selecting only those groups with an above average order price.

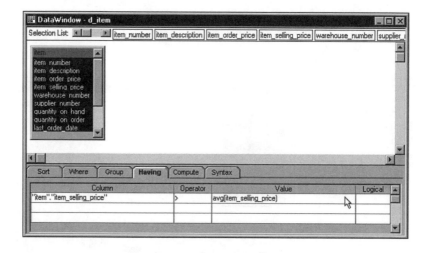

HAVING is only valid for use on SELECT statements that only retrieve aggregate functions or in SELECT statements with a GROUP BY clause. Since the use of aggregate functions and GROUP BY is limited, the use of HAVING is also limited.

SQL Computed Columns Instead of establishing a computed column in the DataWindow painter, you could add a computed column with the SQL statement using the Compute tab (see fig. 11.23).

FIG. 11.23
Using the Compute tab, you can enter your own computed column.

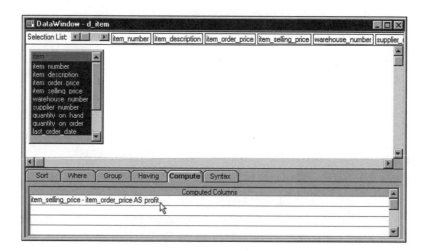

TIP Always use the AS clause to rename your computed columns to something meaningful. If you have several computed columns, you could get lost determining which one you want.

The SQL computed column is reflected in the SQL SELECT syntax. If you convert to syntax, you can see the computed column added to the bottom of your SQL, as seen in figure 11.24.

FIG. 11.24

SQL computed columns
are reflected in the
SQL syntax of a
DataWindow.

```
DataWindow - d_item                                      _□×
    SELECT DISTINCT "item"."item_number",
                   "item"."item_description",
                   "item"."item_order_price",
                   "item"."item_selling_price",
                   "item"."warehouse_number",
                   "item"."supplier_number",
                   "item"."quantity_on_hand",
                   "item"."quantity_on_order",
                   "item"."last_order_date",
                   "item"."item_size",
                   "item"."item_comments",
                   "item"."obsolete",
                   "item"."item_color",
                   item_selling_price - item_order_price AS profit
      FROM "item"
     WHERE ( "item"."item_number" = :item_number ) AND
           ( "item"."obsolete" <> 'Y' )
  GROUP BY "item"."item_number"
    HAVING ( "item"."item_selling_price" > avg(item_selling_price) )
  ORDER BY "item"."item_order_price" ASC,
           "item"."item_description" ASC
```

The SQL computed column is added to your DataWindow. Figure 11.25 shows the column after some reformatting.

FIG. 11.25

SQL computed columns
can be reflected in the
DataWindow.

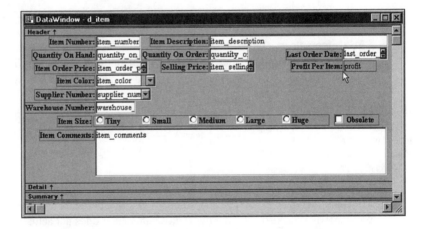

N O T E If you want your field on your DataWindow to constantly change based on what is entered in other columns, an SQL computed column will not work. An SQL computed column is evaluated based only on the data that was retrieved from the database. A DataWindow computed column bases its value on the current displayed columns in the DataWindow.

If your DataWindow is static (as in a report) or the fields used in the computation don't change, an SQL computed column edges out a DataWindow computed column in performance. However, the DataWindow computed column has more functionality that is quite useful at times. ▪

N O T E Because profit can change during data entry, it is better to use a DataWindow computed column rather than an SQL computed column to display the profit per item. ▪

SQL Syntax   Many developers like to see the effects of their actions on the SQL statement behind that DataWindow. This SQL statement can be modified only by choosing Design, Convert To Syntax, as discussed previously. However, you can view the SQL syntax as PowerBuilder sets it up by clicking the Syntax tab, as shown in figure 11.26.

FIG. 11.26

By clicking the Syntax tab, you can view the SQL syntax as PowerBuilder sets it up.

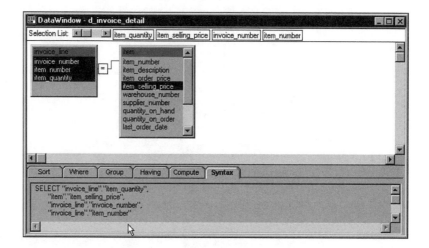

SQL Statements vs. DataWindow Setup   You have found out how to set up your DataWindow through the DataWindow painter or through SQL in the select painter. The basic flow of data from the database to the DataWindow can be seen in figure 11.27.

FIG. 11.27

The SQL statements can eliminate data before the DataWindow processes it.

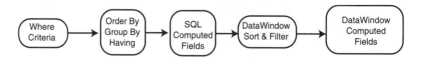

The basic rule in PowerBuilder is the sooner you isolate the data you need, the faster your program will run. Also note that the DataWindow filter does not actually remove data from the DataWindow like a WHERE statement would, but rather moves it to the filter buffer.

DataWindow commands are much more versatile than SQL commands. However, if SQL commands can process the data for you, it's a good idea to let them. That way, your program will run faster, and you may save some development and maintenance work in the process.

Updating Your Database with Your DataWindow

The *update( )* function can update a DataWindow. However, as a system developer, you may want to know how to update a DataWindow from a menu command. Although there are many different ways to accomplish this task, the Inventory Tracking system uses the following steps:

1. In the m_ancestor File, Save menu item, add the following code:

   ```
   parentwindow.triggerevent("save")
   ```

   This will allow each window to customize its own saves. This is all the code you need to accomplish updates in the Inventory Tracking menus.

2. In the w_datawindow_ancestor window, you need to make some changes:

   - Add a user-defined Save event by clicking Declare, User Events. This event will be triggered when the user clicks Save from the menu or toolbar.

   - Add a DataWindow instance variable by typing the following line in the instance variable dialog box:

     ```
     datawindow idw_data
     ```

   - Add this line to the Save event that you just created:

     ```
     idw_data.triggerevent("update_datawindow")
     ```

3. In your tab control, add the code found in listing 11.1 to the SelectionChanged event.

Part III

Ch 11

Listing 11.1   SelectionChanged Event of tab_1 in w_tab_ancestor

```
Int li_control_num = 1
WindowObject hopeful_datawindow

Do While IsValid(control[selectedtab].control[li_control_num])
     If control[selectedtab].control[li_control_num].typeof() =&
               DataWindow! Then
          hopeful_datawindow = control[selectedtab].control[li_control_num]
          Exit
     End If
Loop

If IsValid(hopeful_datawindow) Then
     idw_data = hopeful_datawindow
Else
     SetNull(idw_data)
End If
```

What this code will do is find a DataWindow control on any tab and assign it to the idw_data instance variable defined in step 2.

4. Now open the u_datawindow_inventory_entry user object. Create a user defined event called *update_datawindow* and put the following command inside:

   ```
   update()
   ```

Although this may seem a little complicated to update a DataWindow, now all your DataWindows in your Inventory Tracking system can be updated *without any additional coding.* Our code is powerful enough to allow any number of DataWindows to be updated when they receive focus by clicking the Save toolbar item. Now when you click the Save toolbar item, your changes will be saved.

Verifying Actions Before Losing Data

It's probably a good idea to verify the user's actions often. Before any retrieval or insertion that wipes out existing data, you will want to see if the user would like to save or not. Also, when you exit, you'll want to check if the user wants to save. All of this is done with a user object function in the u_datawindow_inventory_entry user object. This function is called uf_ask_to_save, and can be seen in listing 11.2.

Listing 11.2 uf_ask_to_save

```
// uf_ask_to_save for w_datawindow_ancestor by Chuck Wood
// This function checks to see if any changes have been made to dw_data.
// If changes were made, uf_ask_to_save asks the user if he or she wants
// to save before retrieving a row or creating a new row. uf_ask_to_save
// returns a TRUE if the user answers yes or no, and a FALSE if the user
// cancels.
int answer

if ModifiedCount() > 0 or DeletedCount() > 0 then
    if gb_ask_about_update then
        answer = Messagebox("You're about to lose your changes!", &
                        "You have made unsaved changes. " &
                        + "Would you like to save now before proceding?", &
                        STOPSIGN!, YESNOCANCEL!, 1)
    elseif gb_automatic_update_or_not = TRUE then
        answer = 1
    else
        answer = 2
    End if
    if gb_set_update_without_asking then
        gb_ask_about_update = FALSE
        gb_set_update_without_asking = FALSE
        gb_automatic_update_or_not = FALSE
    end if
    Choose Case answer
        Case 1
            Update()
            if gb_set_update_without_asking then
                gb_automatic_update_or_not = TRUE
            end if
        Case 3
            Return FALSE
    End Choose
End If
Return TRUE
```

TIP Variables with a gb_ prefix are global boolean and should be declared in the Global Variable dialog box.

Now you can call uf_ask_to_save whenever the users risk losing changes that have been made to your DataWindow. For instance, in the ItemChanged event of the u_datawindow_inventory_entry user object, listing 11.3 can be added when the user changes the primary key (thereby retrieving a new record).

Listing 11.3   ItemChanged Event of u_datawindow_inventory_entry

```
gb_ask_about_update = TRUE
if is_retrieve_column = '' then
    MessageBox ('Retrieve Column Not Set', &
    'The column needed to generate a new retrieve has not been set in ' +&
    'Constructor event of the Datawindow ' + dataobject)
elseif GetColumnName() = is_retrieve_column then
    // Save out if necessary
    if uf_ask_to_save() = FALSE then
        Return 2                                    // Make the itemchange
event fail
    else
        PostEvent("after_change")
    end if
end if
```

Finally, you make uf_ask_to_save() function calls in the destructor event of the u_datawindow_inventory_entry user object. These precautions protect you from exiting without saving your data.

Retrieving Data from a DataWindow

The *datawindowname.Retrieve()* PowerBuilder function clears your DataWindow of all existing rows and populates your DataWindow with information on your database tables.

Using a DDDW for Retrieval

To make life easy, you can add a primary key number field to each of the DataWindows. These fields will be drop-down DataWindows that are filled in automatically on an insert as well as used for retrieving existing clients.

Figure 11.28 shows how you can add a customer number DDDW to the d_customer DataWindow.

This DDDW is defined, as shown in figure 11.29. You'll notice that the display column and data column are displayed on the DDDW, but both are filled in with customer_number. The customer name is displayed. Since the customer name is larger than the customer number, you can change the width of the DDDW to 200 percent of the width of the customer number field.

Part

III

Ch

11

To enable the DDDW to retrieve data for use, you have to code for the itemchange event on dw_data in u_datawindow_inventory_entry with the PowerScript seen in listing 11.4.

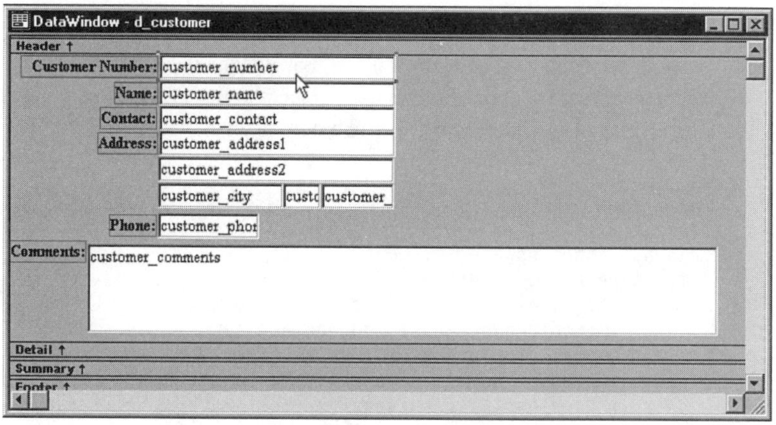

FIG. 11.28

A DDDW was added to retrieve existing customers on the d_customer DataWindow.

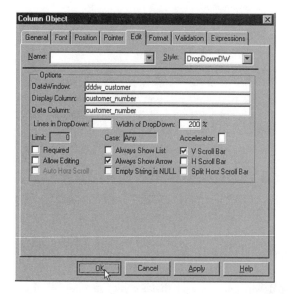

FIG. 11.29

You can use the same column for both the display and data columns, and end up updating a different column altogether.

Listing 11.4   ItemChanged Event of u_datawindow_inventory_entry

```
if GetColumnName() = is_retrieve_column then
// Save out if necessary
      if uf_ask_to_save() = FALSE then
            SetActionCode(2)        // Make the itemchange event fail
            Post Event reset_key( )
```

```
        else
                PostEvent("after_change")
        end if
    else
        ib_changes_made = TRUE
    end if
```

N O T E   The primary key string variable, is_retrieve_column, is set in the open event of each
Window. ■

The itemchange event tests to see if the column retrieved is the key column set up in the open
event of each window. If it's the key column, the itemchange event calls the uf_ask_to_save
function. With a YES or NO response from uf_ask_to_save, the itemchange event posts an
event to run after the itemchange event is complete. This posted event (after_change) is a user-
defined event with the following line of code in it.

```
Retrieve(GetItemNumber(getrow(), is_retrieve_column))
```

If the Cancel button is pressed in uf_ask_to_save, the key column is reset in the user-defined
reset_key event with the following PowerScript command:

```
settext(string(getitemnumber(getrow(), is_retrieve_column)))
```

In figure 11.30, you can see how the DDDW is now used to select an existing customer. When
the selection is complete, the entire row is filled in (see fig. 11.31).

Part

III

Ch

11

FIG. 11.30

Along with identifying
the primary key number,
the DDDW is also used
for retrieving data.

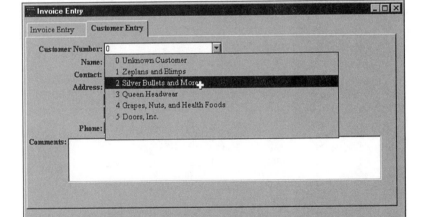

FIG. 11.31

As you can see, the name is converted into a number while the rest of the row is displayed.

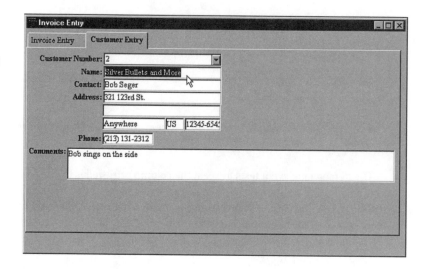

Retrieving Data Inside a DDDW

Normally, a DDDW does not require any special processing to function. However, if the DataWindow behind the DDDW contains a retrieval argument, you must retrieve the DDDW with a valid retrieval argument before retrieving the rest of your DataWindow. DDDW retrievals are usually done in the window open event before retrieving the rest of the DataWindow.

Assume you have a state field and a city field on your window. Your city field requires a state code as a retrieval argument, and the DDDW will list all the cities for that state. The code in listing 11.5 could be used to retrieve your city DDDW before retrieving your parent DataWindow.

Listing 11.5 ItemChanged Event of u_datawindow_inventory_entry

```
DataWindowChild dwc
// Assign the warehouse to a DataWindow child.
dw_data.GetChild("city",dwc)
dwc.SetTransObject(SQLCA)
dwc.Retrieve("IN")      // IN is a valid state

// Now retrieve the parent data window
dw_data.retrieve

// If you want, you can now reset the city field list to be blank
dwc.retrieve(" ")
```

Now, as seen in listing 11.6, you'll need to code the itemchange event in your DataWindow to retrieve a new city list every time a new state is entered.

Listing 11.6 DataWindowChild Retrieval

```
// Assign the warehouse to a DataWindow child.
if GetColumnName() = "state" then
     DataWindowChild dwc
     string state
     state = Getext()
     GetChild("city",dwc)
     dwc.Retrieve(state)      // retrieve state
end if
```

TIP

DataWindowChild is a data type used in PowerBuilder. The DataWindowChild data type is used for DataWindows within DataWindows, like DDDWs.

TIP

GetColumnName() returns a string containing the column name that has focus in a DataWindow.

TIP

The itemchange event is executed just before an item changes value. To get the text of the current column that is being changed, use the GetText() function.

TIP

GetChild() associates a DataWindowChild variable with a DataWindow column.

Now every time you enter a new state in the state field, city will retrieve the valid cities for that state.

Inserting Rows and Clearing Your Window

Insert can take two forms. The insertrow user-defined event simply inserts a row into the DataWindow with the dw_data.InsertRow(0) function call. This method is used to insert an invoice line onto the invoice.

However, most of the DataWindows only display one row at a time. All of the DataWindows allow the user to clear out all data and start over by clicking the New toolbar item, which accesses the new user-defined event. The new event is coded in listing 11.7.

Listing 11.7   The New Event

```
if uf_ask_to_save() = FALSE then
    Return 2                   // Make the new_datawindow event fail
else
    reset ()                   // Clear DataWindow
    triggerevent("insert_row")     // Make blank row for new entry
end if
```

 TIP   Reset( ) deletes all the rows on a DataWindow. These deletions *are not* reflected in the database during a datawindow.update( ) command.

As you can see, before clearing out all data, Inventory Tracking makes a call to uf_ask_to_save to make sure this is okay. Then the new event triggers the insert_row event, which simply uses an insertrow(0) command to insert a new row onto the database.

Deleting Rows and Clearing Your Window

It's important to verify before deleting a row. The delete_row event (called by the Edit, Delete from the menu and the delrow event from the w_datawindow_ancestor) is coded in listing 11.8.

Listing 11.8   The delete_row Event

```
if messagebox("Delete Row", "Are you sure you want to delete this row?", &
        STOPSIGN!, YESNO!, 2) = 1 then
    deleterow(0)
end if
if getrow() = 0 then
    triggerevent("insert_row")
end if
```

Not only can you verify before deleting, but also you can access the new event used for inserting a row if you delete all the rows.

Every time you insert a row, you need to add a new key. PowerScript similar to the code in listing 11.9 must be added to *each* DataWindow except d_invoice_detail and d_invoice_footer (d_item, d_invoice_header, d_customer, d_supplier, and d_warehouse).

Listing 11.9 Insert_row Event in All Datawindows

```
// Extend ancestor
long item_number

SELECT max(item_number)+1
    INTO :item_number
    FROM item
    USING SQLCA;
if isnull(item_number) or item_number < 1 then
    item_number = 1
end if
setitem(getrow(), "item_number", item_number)
```

CAUTION

The code in listing 11.9 will not work too well in a multi-user environment. This is because if two users are on the system at the same time, more than one user will eventually try to insert a row onto the table using the same primary key.

In a multi-user environment, you could do one of the following:

- Use a datetime stamp. Often, you can get your datetime stamp down to one millionth of a second. This will minimize the chance that two users will update at exactly the same time with the same primary key.

- Use an autoincrement column. Most databases support them. This way, your database does the work for you.

- Use a sequence in the database and a database trigger that automatically adds the new key to the record before it is added to the database. That way, the program does not have to worry about adding the key because the database does it automatically.

Part
III

Ch
11

(This SELECT varies from table to table, the only difference being the primary key that is SELECTED reflects the primary key of the other table.)

The new event then deletes all existing rows by resetting the DataWindow and frees it from all database calls, does an insert, and puts the new primary key into the primary key field.

Using Crosstabs

Crosstabs are a special type of display that take a lot of data and condense it down into a grid, spreadsheet, or chart format. To make a Crosstab DataWindow, click Crosstab when creating your DataWindow, as seen in figure 11.32. Then you choose the tables you want to be referenced by the Crosstab, as seen in figure 11.33.

FIG. 11.32

To create a Crosstab, click on Crosstab when creating your DataWindow.

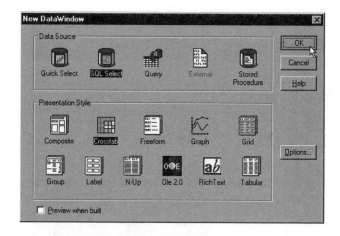

FIG. 11.33

As with any DataWindow, you need to select the tables you want referenced by your Crosstab.

Choose the fields you want to include and click the SQL button. After this is where crosstabs diverge from other DataWindows. After selecting the fields you want as shown in figure 11.34, the Crosstab Definition dialog box appears, and you are asked to take the source data you defined and divide it into one of three areas. The table column is either a row on the Crosstab, a column on the Crosstab, or a data value on the Crosstab. Notice how data values are automatically computed when moved in to the values box, as seen in figure 11.35.

When you're done, click OK, and the DataWindow painter appears with your Crosstab definition. From here, you can define the Crosstab like other DataWindows, as shown in figure 11.36.

Although there are no crosstabs in the Inventory Tracking system, Crosstabs are a good way to make sense of a lot of numbers. The User's Guide has a very comprehensive chapter on crosstabs. It may be useful to you or your organization someday.

FIG. 11.34
Crosstabs require the same type of column selection as other DataWindows.

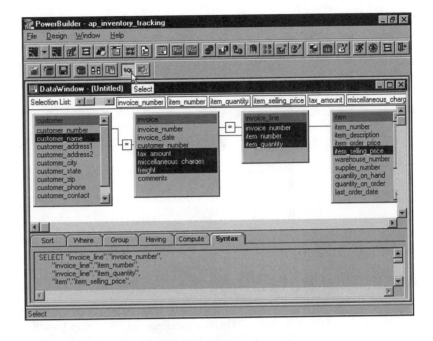

FIG. 11.35
In the Crosstab Definition dialog box, you must move your source data to one of the three other categories.

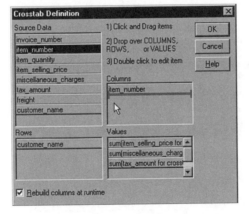

FIG. 11.36
Although it looks slightly different, the DataWindow painter can modify and enhance your Crosstab.

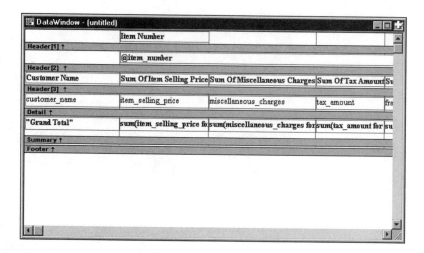

Accessing DataWindow Columns

PowerBuilder 5 now allows you to directly access DataWindow columns and attributes. Examples of this are on the CD in the miscellaneous PBL under DataWindow example. In the miscellaneous PBL, there is a developed window that is divided into two parts, as seen in figure 11.37.

FIG. 11.37
This window accomplishes the same tasks using older coding methods and newer direct DataWindow access.

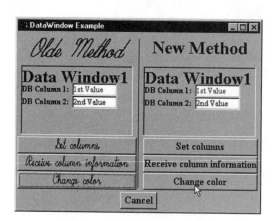

Each part of the window in figure 11.37 performs 3 tasks:

1. The Set columns buttons set the column information in the DataWindow to a default.
2. The Receive column information buttons retrieve column information from the DataWindow.
3. The Set color buttons change DataWindow attributes to set DB Column 1 to red.

Setting Column Information from a DataWindow

In previous versions of PowerBuilder, you had to use the SetItem function to set column information in your DataWindow. The code behind the "Olde" Set columns button in figure 11.37 used the SetItem() function:

```
dw_1.setitem(dw_1.getrow(), "database_column_1", "1st Value")
dw_1.setitem(dw_1.getrow(), "database_column_2", "2nd Value")
```

This is not that difficult to code or understand. Contrast this with direct DataWindow access method found behind the "New" Set columns button in figure 11.37:

```
dw_2.object.database_column_1[dw_2.getrow()] = "1st Value"
dw_2.object.database_column_2[dw_2.getrow()] = "2nd Value"
```

Using *datawindow.object.columnname[row] = columnvalue* may be a little more intuitive than *datawindow.SetItem(row, columnnamestring, columnvalue)*. The direct access method also fits more closely with accessing other variables using PowerScript. Both methods, however, are acceptable in PowerBuilder 5.

Retrieving Column Information from a DataWindow

Retrieving column information has also changed. The "Olde" Receive column information command button in figure 11.37 used the GetItemString () function to retrieve column information:

```
string column1_info
string column2_info

column1_info = dw_1.getitemstring(dw_1.getrow(), "database_column_1")
column2_info = dw_1.getitemstring(dw_1.getrow(), "database_column_2")
messagebox ("values",          "Column 1 is " + column1_info +&
                    "~rColumn 2 is " + column2_info)
```

Contrast this method with the "new" Receive column information's method of directly accessing DataWindow data:

```
string column1_info
string column2_info

column1_info = dw_2.object.database_column_1[dw_2.getrow()]
column2_info = dw_2.object.database_column_2[dw_2.getrow()]
messagebox ("values",          "Column 1 is " + column1_info +&
                    "~rColumn 2 is " + column2_info)
```

Once more, retrieving information using the *columninfo = datawindow.getitemstring(row, columnamestring)* may be a little less intuitive than *columninfo = datawindow.object .columnname[row]*. Both methods are still supported by PowerBuilder 5.

Change DataWindow Attributes

▶ **See** "Using Conditional Expressions," **p. 338**

One theme seen in recent PowerBuilder upgrades is the attempt to allow complex PowerBuilder applications without the use of the Modify() and Describe() functions.

Part

III

Ch

11

Conditional expressions, introduced in PowerBuilder 4, allow you to set DataWindow attributes conditionally without the need for PowerScript. In PowerBuilder 5, you no longer need Modify to change your DataWindow attributes.

The Change color buttons in figure 11.37 both change DB Column 1 to red. The "Olde" method uses the Describe ( ) function:

```
string color

color = string(rgb(255,0,0)) //Red
dw_1.modify("database_column_1.color = "+ color)
```

The new method uses a much more intuitive approach:

```
dw_2.object.database_column_1.color = rgb(255,0,0)        //Red
```

As you can see, changing variables using the direct DataWindow access method found in PowerBuilder 5 is much clearer and easier than the old Describe( ) function. However, both are still supported in PowerBuilder 5.

From Here...

DataWindows are the heart of PowerBuilder—they're what makes PowerBuilder so unique and easy to develop in. Using DataWindows, you can generate user-friendly, easy-to-develop windows to access and update the data on your database.

In this chapter, you learned how to choose the data you want to display and modify, how to join tables through the DataWindow painter, and how to use the SQL toolbox to customize your DataWindow.

If you want to read more about DataWindows, refer to the following chapters:

- Chapter 7, "Programming in PowerScript," shows how to write script that will be behind all DataWindow objects.
- Chapter 8, "Using SQL in PowerBuilder," can help you manipulate data that is beyond the scope of DataWindows.
- Chapter 9, "Creating DataWindows," shows how to choose and create the DataWindow you want.
- Chapter 10, "Enhancing DataWindows," describes how to define fields and validation rules, display formats, and edit styles.
- Chapter 12, "Creating Reports," shows you even more uses for DataWindows as reports.
- Chapter 25, "Function Quick Reference," can be helpful when reviewing available DataWindow functions.
- Chapter 26, "Event Quick Reference," overviews the events available to a DataWindow.
- Chapter 27, "Property Quick Reference," describes the attributes a DataWindow can have.

Creating Reports

by David J. O'Hearn

When you create an application, it's inevitable that you will create reports as well. In PowerBuilder, creating reports is very easy. In fact, you already know how! That's because reports are almost identical to DataWindows, and you already know how to create DataWindows. ■

How to create reports using the report painter.

Learn to use the report painter in both Run mode and Edit mode.

How to include the Report Painter icons on the PowerBar.

Customize your PowerBuilder Toolbar by adding one or both Report Painter icons.

How to create a grouped report.

Learn how to create a report using the Group Presentation style.

How to use the features of the Group Presentation style.

Learn how to include these features: page break, page number reset, header and trailer bands, page orientation, subtotals and grand totals, nested groups, sorting, and suppressing duplicate values.

How to add a graph to a report.

Find out how to use a graph object to display different types of graphs using data from a report.

How to create labels.

Find out how to use the Label Presentation style.

How to include another report or DataWindow in your report.

Learn to make complex reports using the Nested Report Object.

Understanding PowerBuilder Reports

A PowerBuilder report is the result of an SQL Select statement, formatted and organized in a particular way. The principle use of a report is to print them out on paper.

Similarities Between Reports and DataWindows

Reports can be created using all the same presentation styles and all the same data sources as DataWindows.

To create a report, you go through the same steps you would to create a DataWindow; you start with the SQL Select area to define your data source, and then move into the design area to format the report however you want. The options available in the design area for a report are the same as for a DataWindow (for example, borders, colors, and fonts).

N O T E Since reports have a lot in common with DataWindows, you may want to see some other chapters in this book: chapter 9, "Creating DataWindows," and chapter 10, "Enhancing DataWindows." ■

Differences Between Reports and DataWindows

The major difference between DataWindows and reports is that reports are not able to be edited by the user, while DataWindows certainly can. Because of this, a report has no tab order (all columns have a zero tab order, actually), and therefore, the user cannot get to an individual column to edit it. Since reports are not editable, there would be no need to allow them to update the database, nor would there be a need for any validation rules.

Using the Report Painter

When bringing the report painter from PowerBuilder, you have two choices. You can bring up the report painter in Edit mode or in Run mode. The Edit mode of the report painter is where you create and modify reports. The Run mode of the report painter only allows you to bring up reports to preview them.

Adding the Report Painter Icons to the Toolbar

The easiest way to launch the report painter, either in Edit mode or Run mode, is from the PowerBar. By default, however, the report icons do not appear on the PowerBar. To add them, follow these steps:

1. Right-click the PowerBar and choose Customize from the pop-up menu (see fig. 12.1).

FIG. 12.1

By right-clicking while the pointer is on the toolbar, you will see a pop-up menu that allows you to make changes to the toolbar.

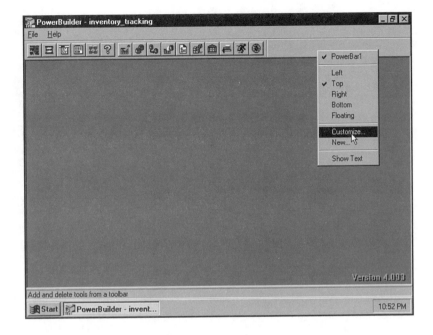

2. In the Customize dialog box, drag the Run Report Painter icon to the Current Toolbar area (see fig. 12.2). Place the icon wherever you want it to appear amid the existing icons.

FIG. 12.2

The Customize window allows you to add, move, or remove icons from your PowerBar.

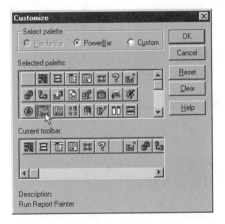

3. Repeat the preceding step to add the Report Painter (Run mode only) icon.

4. Click OK. The Customize window closes, and your toolbar appears similar to the one shown in figure 12.3.

Part

III

Ch

12

FIG. 12.3

If you forget which Report button is which or if you have a monochrome monitor, the PowerTips show you the name of each icon when the mouse comes over the top of the icon.

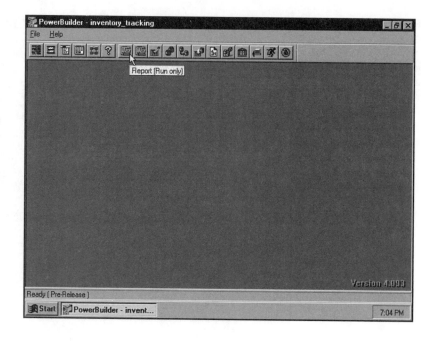

Launching the Report Painter in Run Mode

To open the report painter in Run mode, follow these steps:

1. Click the Report (Run only) icon on the PowerBar. The Select Report dialog box appears (see fig. 12.4).

FIG. 12.4

Just as with the other painters, the first thing you do when you start up the report painter is select an existing report to preview.

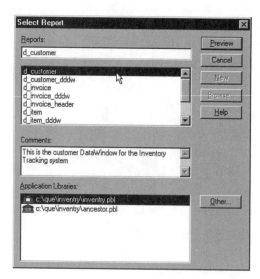

2. Select a library from the Application Libraries list, and then select the report you wish to preview. Both DataWindows (objects whose names start with d) and reports (objects whose names start with r) will appear in this list.

N O T E If you open a DataWindow object inside the report painter, the DataWindow will act like a report. This is good because you do not have to create a report that does the same thing as an existing DataWindow, but rather you can simply use the DataWindow as a report. ■

3. When you have found the report you want, click Preview. The report automatically retrieves the data specified by the report's SQL Select statement and displays it in the preview window (see fig. 12.5).

FIG. 12.5

This is the preview of the d_invoice DataWindow as a report.

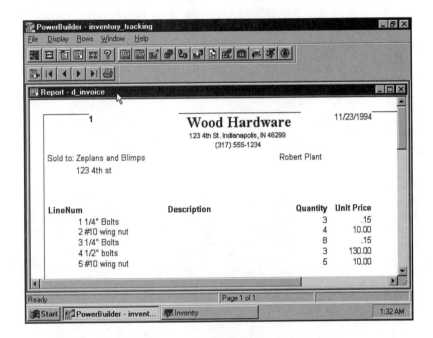

This window looks a lot like the DataWindow preview window. All the things you can do from the DataWindow preview window can be done from here, with only a few small differences:

■ Reports are not updateable; therefore, the icons that represent insert, delete, and update are not on this preview window.

■ Because this is a report in Run Only mode, there is no menu choice for returning to the design area to modify the look of the report.

■ The report preview shows a border around it, as if it were on a piece of paper. This makes sense, as most reports will ultimately end up in hard copy.

The report preview window is the only window available for the report painter in Run mode.

Part

III

Ch

12

Launching the Report Painter in Edit Mode

To report a new report or to change to the Edit mode, click the Report icon on the PainterBar. The Select Report dialog box appears. This dialog box is identical to the one that appears in Run mode, except that the New button now is available.

To create a new report, it isn't necessary to look through the lists of existing reports and libraries; just click New. To edit an existing report, select the library you want and the report you want to work on, and then click OK.

Creating a Grouped Report

In this section, you create a Customer Order History Report, which is a report of all invoice activity grouped together by the customer placing the order. The following steps show you how to create such a report:

1. To create a new report from the Select Report dialog box, click New. (If you are already in the report painter, select File, New.) The New Report dialog box appears, as shown in figure 12.6.

   This dialog box is just like the New DataWindow dialog box, where you must select a data source and a presentation style. All the same data sources and presentation styles are available.

FIG. 12.6
You must select one
Data Source and one
Presentation Style from
this dialog box to begin
creating a new report.

2. Since you are building a group report, select the Group presentation style. You must also select a data source. For this report, choose SQL Select as your data source, and then click OK. The Select Tables dialog box appears (see fig. 12.7).

3. Just as with DataWindows, you must set up the SQL Select statement. First, decide which tables to use. For this example, use the Customer, Invoice, and Invoice_line tables. After you make your selections, click Open.

FIG. 12.7

The Select Tables dialog box displays the list of tables in the database. Select the tables you wish to use for this report by clicking them once.

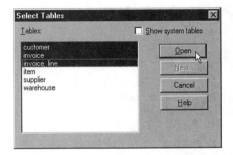

4. Next, decide which columns from these tables you want to use (see fig. 12.8). Since this report is for all the orders placed for a customer, you would want the customer_name and phone_number columns from the Customer table, as these fields help describe the customer for the report. You also want the invoice_comments column from the Invoice table and the item_number and quantity from the Invoice_line table.

For this example, you do not need to do anything else at the SQL Select level. You might decide to limit the amount of data this report produces by specifying some kind of Where clause; however, the goal of this unit is not so much to discuss the possibilities of an SQL Select as it is to show you how to create a report. As you can see already, creating reports is similar to creating DataWindows. You might be thinking, since you want this data grouped by customer, you need to add a Group By clause to the SQL Select statement. As you will soon see, for a group report (or a group DataWindow, for that matter), the grouping is not done in the SQL statement.

FIG. 12.8

The SQL Select window of the Report Painter is used for setting up the SQL Select statement. Click the desired column once to select columns for the report.

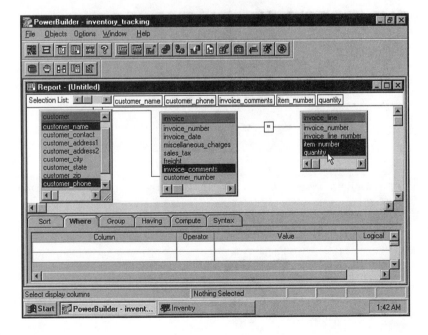

Part
III

Ch
12

5. If you are done with the SQL Select level, it's time to move on to the design level. To do that, choose File, Design.

6. The Group Report dialog box contains two tab pages. The Definitions tab page asks how you want to group the data. It lists all the columns that you have selected for retrieval. You must select which column(s) from this list that you want to group. You should group together all information for one customer. The customer_name column is a unique name for each customer; by using this field to group by, you can be sure that you will not get more than one customer's data mixed together.

7. To select customer_name as the column to group by, drag it from the list on the left to the list on the right (see fig. 12.10).

N O T E You can select more than one column to group by from the Group Report dialog box; simply repeat the steps to put the customer_name column in the list. For example, you might want to group by all orders for a date for a customer, instead of only by customer. ■

8. If you want to have your report perform a page break when a new group is encountered, click New Page on Group Break to enable this feature.

FIG. 12.9

The Definitions tab page of the Group Report dialog box is the way to designate which column or columns should be used for grouping the resulting report.

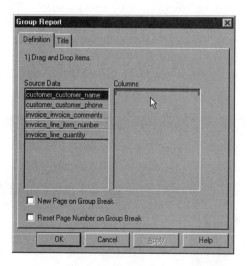

 This is a handy feature, since a fresh page for each customer makes it easier to read, and allows them to make a copy of the report for that customer without showing another customer's information.

9. If you want each new group to begin at page 1, click the Reset Page Number on Group Break check box. This feature is useful if you are printing a report that groups information by department, and you must give a copy of the report to each department. You could use this feature and give each department only its portion of the report. The fact that each department's portion of the report would start on page 1 would minimize confusion for the recipient.

10. To supply a title for this report, click the Title tab control to access the Title tab page. The title is a concatenation of all the tables used by this report with the word `Report` thrown in at the end. Hence, the default name for this report is `Customer Invoice Invoice Line Report`. Usually, this default title is not sufficient, so you have the opportunity to put in your own title. How about `Customer Order History Report`?

FIG. 12.10

The Title tab page on the Group Report dialog box allows you to modify the title for this report.

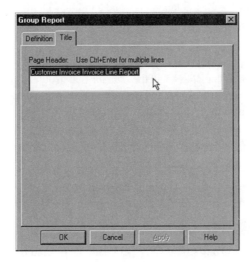

N O T E Although you are asked to change the title of the report here, this is not your last chance to do so. You can change the title at any time during the design level, since the title is actually nothing more than a static text field. ▨

11. After you have selected the column to group by, decided upon your page breaks and page numbering, and changed the title, click OK. Finally, you see the initial design of the report (see fig. 12.11).

FIG. 12.11

The default design of the group report shows the title you created for the report, as well as all the columns chosen for the report.

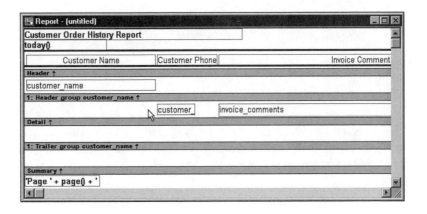

Again, this window looks almost exactly the same as the design window in the DataWindow painter. The only differences are that there are no menu choices for tab order or for update, since these do not apply for reports.

Understanding the Bands of a Group Report

In addition to the "normal" header, detail, footer, and summary bands, all grouped reports (and grouped DataWindows as well) have two more bands to them than tabular and freeform reports:

- The group band appears at the top of every group. This band is typically used to display general information that applies to all the data for that group. In the example, you see that the customer_name column is (by default) in the group header band, while the other columns (those that are not used to group by) are in the detail band.

- The trailer group band appears once at the end of every group. Since this band prints at the end of the group, it is ideal for displaying subtotal information for numeric data, such as the total for the quantity column for a customer.

It is possible (and not uncommon) to have more than one group for a report, that is, having a group inside another group. For example, you might want a group by customers, and then for each customer, a group for each separate invoice. You would then have a header and trailer band for each group. The outermost group (in our example, the customer) would be called group 1, and the innermost group (the invoice per customer) would be called group 2. You can see this in figure 12.11, where the header and trailer bands for the customer_name group start with 1:.

The next step in creating this report is to preview the report. Report preview works the same way that DataWindow preview does. It executes the underlying SQL Select statement, retrieving all rows that match the select statements' criteria.

> **CAUTION**
>
> You might be inclined to dive right into arranging the design of the report to suit your tastes, but that might not be smart. First, you should preview the report to make sure that it is using the correct data. Otherwise, you will be wasting your time making it look pretty.

To preview the report, select Design, Preview. A preview of the report you are working on appears in figure 12.12.

Generally, when creating a new report, the first thing to do when previewing is to determine if this is the correct data. Then and only then do you worry about what it looks like and how to arrange it. In this case, however, you will not be able to determine if the data is correct until you rearrange the design at least a little.

When PowerBuilder creates the report, it automatically puts a border around the entire report to represent the edges of a piece of paper. The way that this report is designed right now, all of the columns do not fit within this border. You must go back to design to fix it.

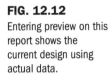

FIG. 12.12

Entering preview on this report shows the current design using actual data.

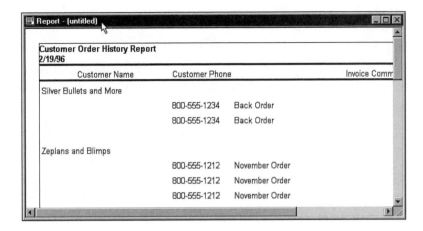

To return to design from preview, select Display, Design. Just as in the DataWindow painter, you are free to change the look, color, border, and size of the columns on a report.

The problem with the Customer Order History Report is that it's too wide to fit on a page. To make it narrower, change the invoice_comments column from one long field to a field half as wide, but tall enough to display on two lines instead of one. You should also shorten the length of the corresponding label for this field in the header band (see fig. 12.13).

FIG. 12.13

Changing the size of the invoice_comments field involves selecting the field, and then making it both taller and narrower.

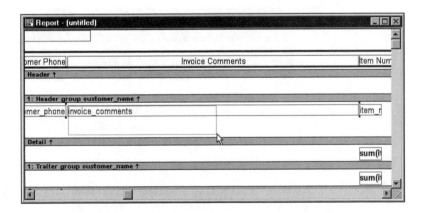

Part
III

Ch
12

Now that you have shortened the comments field, you have a lot of space between that field and the next field. You could move the item number and the quantity fields to the left so that they are next to the comment field. In fact, you can move the columns, labels, and subtotals and grand total fields together as a unit. (The computed fields at the bottom of the screen are the subtotals and grand total fields, which are discussed later in more detail.) To select all eight of these fields together, click once on one of the fields, and while holding down the Ctrl key, click the other seven fields. Now release the Ctrl key.

T I P   Be sure to make the detail band taller first, so that it can hold the taller invoice_comments field.

As you do this, you will notice that each one of the fields gets selected; you can tell this because their corners are highlighted. After selecting them, click any one of those fields and drag to the desired position (see fig. 12.14).

> **CAUTION**
>
> If you accidentally click (without the Ctrl key depressed) somewhere else on the window, your previous selections will be lost, and you will have to repeat the process of selecting fields.

Now, the total of all the columns require a lot less width than they did at first.

FIG. 12.14
After selecting each field to be moved, dragging any one of them will drag them all to a new location, closer to the invoice_comments field.

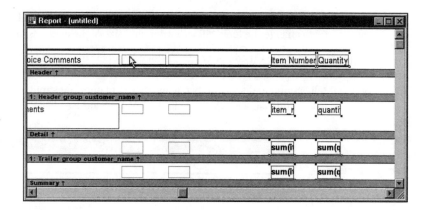

Before going back into preview to see the results of these changes, it would probably be a good idea to save what you have so far. To save the report, choose File, Save As, and name the report r_order_history. Don't forget to put in a comment describing r_order_history. Save this report to your inventry.pbl library.

N O T E   To save the report, you must be in the Report Design window. The Save command is not available during preview nor while working with the SQL Select statement. ■

Next, go into preview again to see the results of the changes. The data now fits within the border that represents the piece of paper.

N O T E   Can you think of another way to solve the problem of fitting all the data within the paper's border? You could have shortened the width of the report in this example, but couldn't you have also just changed the size of the paper? Well, not exactly, but you could have changed the orientation of the paper. If this report were printed landscape (or sideways), it would be wider.

To change the page orientation, choose Design, Properties from the menu and then select the Print Specifications tab page from the Report Object dialog box (see fig. 12.15). Simply change Orientation to Landscape. The next time you preview the report, the page border is much wider. ■

FIG. 12.15
The Print Specifications tab allows you to designate how that report should print on hard copy.

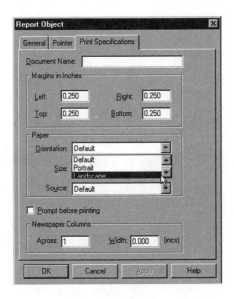

Working with Grand Totals and Subtotals

Part
III
Ch
12

Grand totals and subtotals were mentioned earlier, and now it's time to examine them more closely. As you recall, subtotal and grand total are defined as the following:

- A subtotal is a summation for all occurrences within a group.
- A grand total is a summation for all occurrences for the entire report.

When you create a group report, PowerBuilder will, by default, create both a subtotal and a grand total for all columns whose data is numeric. Also, by default, subtotals appear in the group trailer band, which will display once for every group; therefore, each groups' subtotals display as the group is completed. Grand totals appear in the summary band, which will display once at the end of the report.

In the Customer Order History Report, there are two numeric fields: item number and quantity. PowerBuilder has created totals for both of these fields. It should be obvious to you, however, that a summation of the item numbers is not meaningful information. On the other hand, a summation of the quantity might very well be. This would not be obvious to PowerBuilder, however, because it sees that both fields are numeric.

You should remove the totals for item number from the report. To do this, you simply click once on the field, and then click Clear; or you can press the Delete key on the keyboard.

Modifying Computed Fields

The total fields were created as computed fields. You can modify them just as you can any computed fields that you create yourself.

Although the fields are displaying the correct information (for example, correct subtotals and grand totals), how is the recipient of this report going to know what these numbers stand for? Like any other piece of information on a report, it is not useful without some kind of label identifying the field.

Working with the Subtotal   To modify a computed field, you can double-click the field or right-click the field and select Properties from the pop-up menu (see fig. 12.16). Select the subtotal field for the quantity column.

FIG. 12.16

Right-clicking a field brings up a pop-up menu that allows you to modify the field selected (in this case, the subtotal for quantity). To change the computed expression, select Properties.

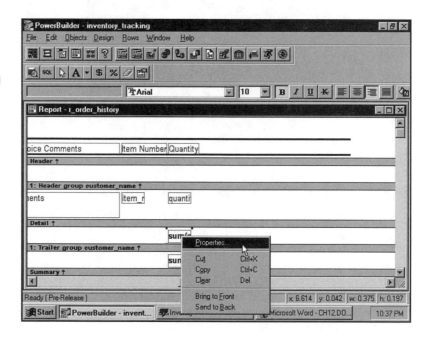

The Computed Object dialog box opens with the General tab page on top, as shown in figure 12.17. Notice that the existing formula for the calculation is displayed in Expression field; sum(quantity for group 1). Totals would, of course, be summations, but what makes this a subtotal is the for group 1 clause. Remember that groups are numbered, the first (outermost) group being group 1. If a formula says for group x, then that formula would be applied to all rows from that group only. In the example, group 1 is a customer, so the summation is total quantity for one customer.

What this computed field needs is a label. You can accomplish this in one of two ways. You could create a static text field on the report saying "Total for customer" and place it right next to the computed field. This is a simple way of doing things, but it can be tiresome to line everything up and assure that the spacing between the static text and the computed fields is proper.

FIG. 12.17

The Computed Object dialog box shows you the current expression and allows you to change it.

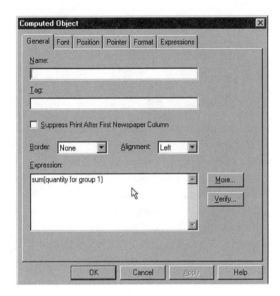

The other way of doing this is to add the static text right into the computed field. To do this, follow these steps:

Part

III

Ch

12

1. Click on the More command button. The Modify Expression box appears, displaying the subtotal formula.

2. Place your cursor at the beginning of the formula.

3. Type (including the quotation marks) "Total for" + .

4. While leaving the cursor right where it is, click customer_name in the Columns list box. This places the field customer_name right inside the computed field, too. Since the customer_name is a string, the + sign will be taken to mean string concatenation between the static text "total for" and the customer_name field from the database.

5. Your cursor should be right after customer_name and just before sum(). Add another + sign to add one more string concatenation in the actual total amount. At this point, your computed field should look like figure 12.18.

FIG. 12.18

This is how your computed field for the subtotal of quantity should look (be sure you have the plus signs and the quotes in the appropriate places).

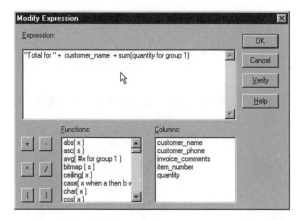

6. Before you click OK, you must turn the total field into a string. (At this point, you would be mixing data types, since you have a string + a string + a number.) To do this, type string(right after the second plus sign and before sum( ). Go to the end of this formula and add a closing parenthesis) to balance out the parentheses. The string( ) function that you just used converts a number into a string. It takes one argument inside the parentheses—a number. Your computed field should now look like figure 12.19. When finished, click OK in the Modify Expression dialog box and OK in the Computed Object dialog box.

FIG. 12.19

The computed field is completed after using the string function, so that the entire expression is considered a string.

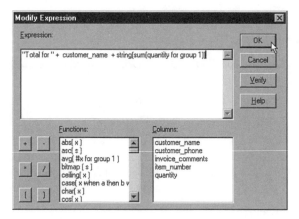

TROUBLESHOOTING

When I clicked OK, I got the error message Expression is not valid. When you click OK, PowerBuilder tries to make sense out of the expression. If you have forgotten the plus signs or left out the quotation marks, PowerBuilder cannot understand the expression. Correct the problem, and click OK again.

6. Before you go back to preview to check it out, you need to make the field a little wider to display all this information. In the Report Design window, stretch this field out to the left to make it wider.

Now, go back into preview and see the results of your changes (see fig. 12.20). As you can see, the field wasn't stretched quite wide enough—the left part of the expression is truncated.

N O T E The reason why the left is truncated and not the right is that this field has been designated as right-justified. ▪

FIG. 12.20
A preview of the order history report shows the subtotals with their labels.

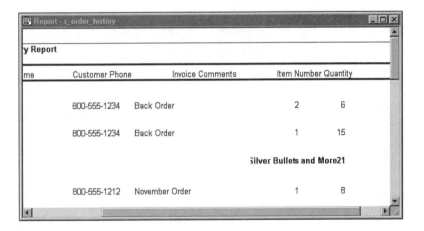

Also, there is no space in between the customer name and the quantity total. To fix these problems, go back to design, stretch the field out some more (although yours might already be stretched wide enough) and double-click the computed field.

You should add one space (inside of quotes) and another plus sign after the customer_name column and before the total, as shown in figure 12.21.

TIP Preview often while making changes, because one seemingly small change can have a big impact on your report.

Part III
Ch 12

Preview the report once again. It should look much better (see fig. 12.22).

You might have noticed a pattern as you work on reports. You change one or two things, then preview, change one or two things, and then preview.

FIG. 12.21

To correct the fact that the label and the data are running together, place a blank (one space) in between the label and the data.

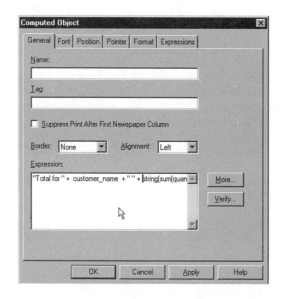

FIG. 12.22

Now that the subtotal field is wide enough and there's a space between the customer name and the subtotal, the report looks much better.

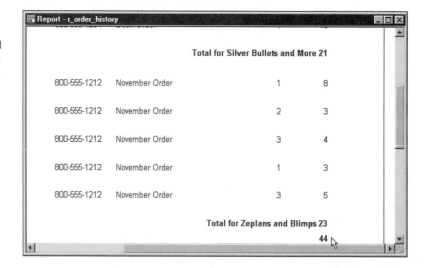

Working with the Grand Total   Notice in figure 12.22 the number 44 right next to the pointer. Do you know what that number is? Do you think the recipient of this report would know what that number is? It is the grand total quantity for all customers. In order for the readers to know that, this field needs a label similar to the label you just built for subtotals. The difference would be that you would not be including a customer name in this computed field, since this number applies to all customers.

To create the label, double-click the grand total field (it's in the summary band). The Computed Object dialog box appears again, this time for the grand total. Notice that the formula is the same (for example, sum), but that this time it says for all. The for all clause means all rows of data retrieved, which is exactly what a grand total is supposed to do.

For the grand total, the formula will be a little simpler than for subtotals since the customer_name field is not involved. It should read something like the text in figure 12.23. You can modify the expression on the right of the General tab page of the Computed Object dialog box or, you can click the More command button and change the formula in the Modify Expression dialog box. Do not forget the plus sign in between " and the string() around the summation. When you are done, click OK.

FIG. 12.23
Here you add a label for the grand total of quantity, as well as a string function to make the entire expression a string.

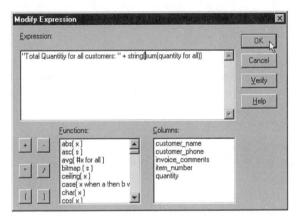

Your report should look a lot better than it did when you first started. There are many other things you can do to a report (and all of this applies for DataWindows as well). For instance, as mentioned earlier, you can have more than one group within a group report.

Adding Another Group

It is very common to want more than one group in a report. For example, you might want to group some information by state, and within state by county. In this example, state would be the outermost group (group 1) and county would be the innermost group (group 2).

In our Customer Order History Report, you will be grouping by invoice number within customer. Each invoice's information will be grouped together for that customer.

At this time, the report does not retrieve the invoice number. In order to group by the invoice number, however, it must be one of the columns retrieved from the database. Therefore, you must change your SQL Select statement to include the invoice number field.

To change the SQL Select statement, go back to the SQL Select dialog box. Include invoice_number from the invoice table by clicking that column once, as shown in figure 12.24.

FIG. 12.24
From the SQL Select window, click the field once to add another column to the report.

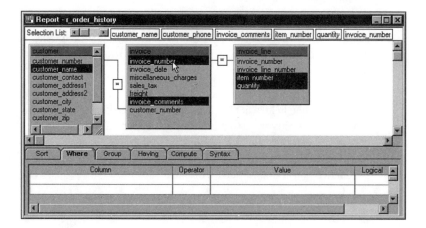

Now that you have done that, it's time to return to design. Click the Design icon from the toolbar. When you return to design, PowerBuilder adds the new column to the report, but you cannot see this new field right away. You will find this new field in the detail band to the far right (you will probably have to scroll the screen to the right to see it). However, you should leave it alone for now.

Now that you have included this column, you can group your data by it. To create another group, select Create Group. When you do, you will see the Band Object dialog box with the Definition tab page on top just as you did for the first group you created. And, like for the first group, you click the column (or columns) you want to group by from the list on the left and drag them to the list on the right. When you have selected all the columns you want for this second group (which would be only the invoice_number column), click OK.

When you return to the Report Design window, you can see that two new band areas have been created: a header band for group 2 and a trailer band for group 2. As mentioned earlier, all groups have their own header and trailer bands. These bands will print once for each new group 2 occurrence. In this case, you will see a group 2 header and trailer once for every invoice in the database.

Since there are now two groups, you might want to have two subtotals, a total quantity for each invoice, and a total quantity for the customer (which was already created by PowerBuilder), as well as the grand total quantity for all customers (which was also already done by PowerBuilder). It makes sense that you would want the total quantity for each invoice to display at the end of the invoice, which would be in the group 2 trailer.

There are two ways to create a summation field in PowerBuilder. There's the hard way and there's the easy way. The hard way is to pull down the group 2 trailer band to make room for a column, then select Objects, Computed Field, click the report where you want to place the computed field, then type in sum (quantity for group 2), and then click OK.

Whew! That's a lot of work! Now, the easy way: Click once on the Quantity column in the detail band to select it, and then select Objects, Sum - Computed Field.

That's all there is to it. Wasn't that a whole lot easier? PowerBuilder automatically makes room for it in the group 2 trailer band and places the exact same computed field just described in that band (see fig. 12.25).

FIG. 12.25
The Sum - Computed Field provides an easy way to get summary information into a trailer band.

```
┌─────────────────────────────────────────────────────────────────────────────┐
│ 🔲 Report - r_order_history                                      _ □ ✕         │
├─────────────────────────────────────────────────────────────────────────────┤
│ ┌──────────────────────┐                                               ▲      │
│ └──────────────────────┘                                                      │
│   │Customer Phone│        Invoice Comments        │Item Number│Quantity│      │
│ Header ↑                                                                      │
│ ┌─┐                                                                           │
│ └─┘                                                                           │
│ 1: Header group customer_name ↑                                               │
│ 2: Header group invoice_invoice_number ↑                                      │
│     │customer_phone│invoice_comments              │item_r│    │quanti│        │
│                                                                               │
│ Detail ↑                                                                      │
│                                                              │sum(q│          │
│ 2: Trailer group invoice_invoice_number ↑                                     │
│                          "Total for " +  customer_name  + " "       ▼         │
│ ◄│       ▮                                                      ►│   /         │
└─────────────────────────────────────────────────────────────────────────────┘
```

Now, just fix that subtotal to include a description of what is being totaled, as you did for the other subtotal and for the grand total.

Before previewing this report, there is something else that must be done in order for the second group to work correctly. You see, the data must be sorted in the same order as the grouping or you might get more groups than you thought.

If you have one row from invoice #4, followed by one row from invoice #7, followed by another row from invoice #4, and it is not sorted, that's three groups. You can see that it should be only two groups since there are only two invoices represented. If, however, the data was sorted by invoice number, you would see only two groups, one for each invoice.

You might be saying to yourself, "I didn't have to do that with the first group, and it worked OK." That is because PowerBuilder does the first group for you automatically. With any other groups you create thereafter, you're on your own to sort them correctly.

Part
III

Ch
12

Setting the Sort Order

To set up the report's sort order, select Specify Sort Columns dialog box. As you can see from figure 12.26, the customer_name column is already in the sort order as the outermost sort column.

To add the invoice_number column to the sort order, drag the invoice_number column from the list to the right. If you wish to sort in ascending order, leave the ascending selected. If you wish to sort in descending order, click the Ascending check box to deselect it. When you have done this, click OK.

FIG. 12.26

The Specify Sort
Columns dialog box
allows you to modify the
sort order for this report.

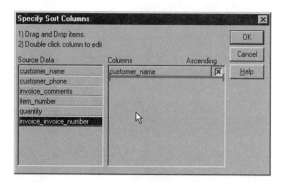

TROUBLESHOOTING

I forgot to set up my sort order before previewing the report. You can go back at any time to change
the sort order. Simply follow the steps outlined before while in the Report Design window.

Now, preview the report. The only thing left to do (besides maybe add some color, change a
few borders, and other cosmetic things) would be to show the invoice number somewhere on
the report. (The invoice number is on the report now; it is just too far to the right to be seen
within the piece of paper's border.) You should move the invoice number to where it can be
seen. In fact, you should put it in the group 2 header band instead of the detail band so that it
appears only once for an invoice that has more than one item on it.

To do this, follow these steps:

1. Make room in the group 2 header band. From the Report Design window, move the
    mouse on top of the group 2 header band. You will see the pointer change to a double-
    arrow pointer. Click and drag the band down until there's enough room in between the
    group 1 header band and the group 2 header band.

2. Find the invoice number field; it should be to the far right. Drag it into the group 2
    header band and to the left so that it appears in the same general area as the other fields.

3. Add a label for the field so that the reader will know what that number stands for.

To see how this looks, refer to figure 12.27.

FIG. 12.27

The label and the invoice_number field have been placed in the group 2 header, so that they will appear once for every invoice.

```
Report - r_order_history                                    _□X
Customer Order History Report
today()
        Customer Name        Customer Phone      Invoice Comments      Item Num
Header ↑
customer_name
1: Header group customer_name ↑
    Invoice Number: invoice_invoice_number
2: Header group invoice_invoice_number ↑
                        customer_phone invoice_comments         item_r
Detail ↑
                                            "Total for invoice number
2: Trailer group invoice_invoice_number ↑
```

Suppressing Duplicated Information

You might also want to move the invoice_comments column into the group 2 header band, since this comment is the same for each item in any given invoice (for example, there is only one comment for an invoice, and that's the comment you see repeatedly in the detail area of the report). While you are at it, the phone_number column should be moved to the group 1 header band, since this is the customers' phone number, which is the same for every invoice for a given customer.

This is one way to get rid of duplicated information—by moving the information into a band other than the detail band, it will not print each time there is a row retrieved from the database. However, moving things from one band to another also affects where that information is displayed on the report. All header bands are above the detail, and all trailer bands are below the detail. If you want to get rid of duplicated information from the detail line, but leave the data in the detail band, you can follow these steps:

1. Select Suppress Repeating Values from the Rows menu. The Specify Repeating Value Suppression List dialog box appears (see fig. 12.28).

FIG. 12.28

The Specify Repeating Value Suppression List dialog box allows you to designate a column or columns to display only once when the same information is repeated.

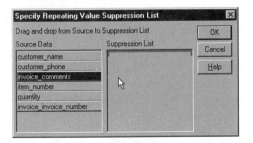

2. Select the columns that, when they repeat, you want to be suppressed. Drag and drop them to the list on the right side of this window. When you have selected all the columns you want, click OK.

So there you have it—a group report with two groups! And of course, you could have as many groups as you'd like. Each group gets its own header and trailer band, whether you use them or not. Keep in mind that when you create a new group, you must set up the sort order in the same order you grouped by, in order for the grouping to be effective.

N O T E Be sure to save your report again so that all the changes you made are not lost. In fact, it's a good idea to save all PowerBuilder objects frequently when modifying them. ▦

The next thing to do is add a graph to the report. While you can create an entire report that is a graph itself (since graph is one of the presentation styles to select from when creating a new report), you can also inlay a graph on a report.

Creating Graphs

A graph is basically the same as any other report, except that instead of displaying data to users as raw numbers, the data is presented in a graphical format. To create graphs, there are some terms that must be understood. In a graph, you will have categories, values, and series.

- The category is the independent data. It can include things such as departments, months, quarters, years, and states.
- The value is the dependent data. This information will typically vary by category, such as number of employees (per department), total sales (per quarter), and number of counties (per state).
- The series is the set of data points for the graph.

When you create a graph, you must decide what your categories and values will be. The series will "fall out" of the graph based upon the categories and values. The categories will typically be a column in the SQL Select statement. The value might also be a column, but it is more likely that it will be data derived from a column—that is, a summation, a count, or an average of some column from the data.

With this information in mind, you can add a graph to this report. For this example, you will graph the total quantity for each customer. This information is already available in the report, but sometimes it helps to see such information in graphical format, particularly when it comes to doing comparisons. This graph will make it easy to tell which customers are purchasing in heavy volumes.

To add a graph to an existing report, you simply select Objects, Graph from the menu, and then click the report where you would like to place the graph. The Graph Object dialog box appears with the Data tab page on top (see fig. 12.29).

FIG. 12.29

The Data tab page of the Graph Object dialog box allows you to designate the Category, Value and Series for the graph.

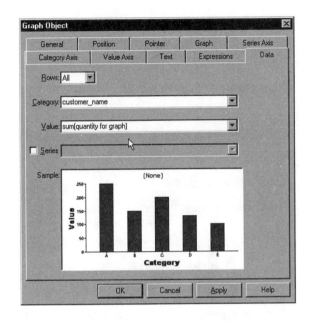

From the Data tab page, you select the Category and Value. Each of these is a drop-down list box.

The list box for the category contains all the columns that are part of the SQL Select statement for this report. You should select customer_name as the category.

The Value list box for the value contains more possibilities than the Category list box. It lists all the columns from the SQL Select statement, such as the Category list box, but it also includes a count for all the non-numeric fields, such as customer_comments (to count the number of comments) and a summation for all the numeric fields, such as item_number (to add up the item numbers). You can pick from this list or you can create your own value. For instance, you might want to use the average for the quantity, and not the sum of the quantity. In this example, however, you should select sum (quantity for graph).

When you have selected both the category and value, click OK. PowerBuilder places a small graph on your report (see fig. 12.30). The default type for the graph is a 2-D column graph. This graph also has, by default, a resizeable border. You might want to make the graph a little larger so that its information is legible when the report is created. Also, notice that the graph does not sit inside any bands. The graph is in the foreground of the report, which means that it does not belong to any band.

A discussion of the different types of graphs that are available is found later in this chapter.

Part

III

Ch

12

N O T E   Graphs are, by default, in the foreground layer, but can be placed into a band. As a matter of fact, any object on a report, including columns and static text, can be placed in the foreground, background, or the band layer. To change the layer of an object, right-click the object and select Properties from the pop-up menu, and then select the Position tab page. You can then change the layer from the Layer drop-down list box, which gives you the choice of foreground, band, or background.

FIG. 12.30

The graph that is added to the existing report can be moved around and resized. This graph is not part of any layer; it's in the foreground of the report.

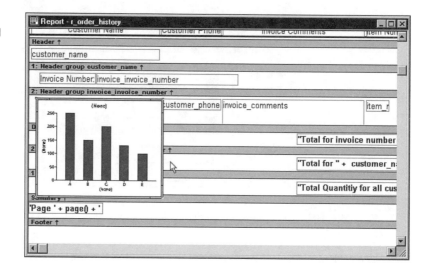

Before doing anything else, preview the report to see what the graph looks like. Notice that the initial size of the graph is probably too small to be useful. However, since this graph is in the foreground and is resizeable, the user can both move the graph and change its size at run time. In figure 12.31, the graph is larger and is moved a little so that the data in the graph becomes more legible.

Since this graph is in the foreground, it does block the data that it is on top of, so it is a good thing that the graph can be moved around on-screen. (Of course, once it is printed out on paper, it cannot be moved around!)

Remember that this is a graph of the quantity by customer. This graph needs some labels so that the user will know this, too. You need to go back to design (when you do, notice that the graph that was resized retains this new size back in design) and make some changes to the graph.

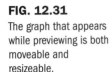

FIG. 12.31
The graph that appears while previewing is both moveable and resizeable.

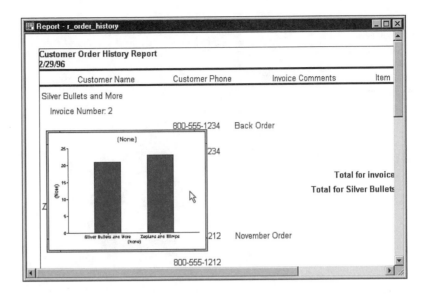

Modifying a Graph

To change a graph, you can do one of two things: Double-click anywhere on the graph or right-click on the graph, bringing up a pop-up list to choose from; then select Properties.

From this dialog box, you can modify a number of things. (In general, graphs have a great many options and attributes available to them, most of which will not be covered in the book.) The things to be concerned about are adding labels to the graph.

First, give this graph a title. In figure 12.32, you see a field labeled Title. The default is (None). Type in a new title to read something like Quantity by Customer.

N O T E If you want to change other aspects of the title, such as the font or point size, select the Text tab page and choose Title from the Text for: listbox as seen in figure 12.33. ■

Next, label the categories and values axis. At this time the category label is category and the value label is value. To change these labels, you must select a different tab page. To change the category label, select the Category Axis tab page; for the value label, select the Value Axis tab page. Figure 12.34 shows the Category Axis tab page. Both the Category Axis tab page and the Values Axis tab page have all the same information, each dealing with their respective axis. They each have a lot of information to them. This information deals with the tick marks, the major and minor divisions, and so on. For more information on these items, see the PowerBuilder online help or the PowerBuilder manuals.

Part
III

Ch
12

FIG. 12.32

The Graph Object dialog box allows you to change various information about how the graph should be displayed, including the Title of the graph.

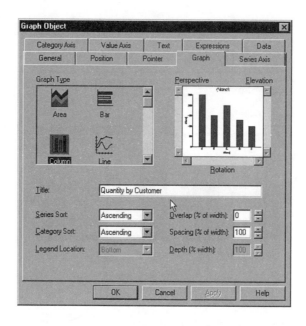

FIG. 12.33

Choosing Title from the Text for: listbox allows you to modify characteristics about the title, such as font type and point size.

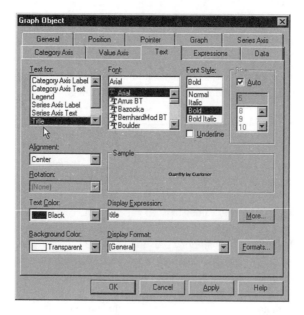

FIG. 12.34
The Category Axis tab page allows you to modify how the category data should be graphed.

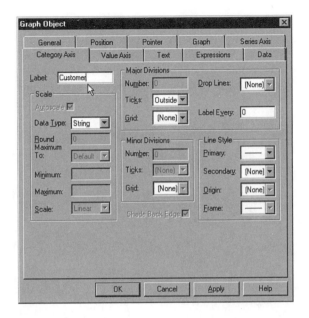

The item you are interested in is the Label. You will find that on the left side of either tab page. Change category to Customers for the category. Then select the Value Axis tab page and change the default label value to Quantity Purchased. This way, the user of this graph will know that they are looking at a graph of quantity purchased by customer.

N O T E To change other aspects of the labels, such as the font and point size, click the Text tab page and choose the Category Axis Label or Value Axis Label from the Text For: listbox. ■

You now return to the Graph tab page. You can see the new labels reflected in the Graph window's mock-up of your graph. From the Graph Object dialog box, click OK to clear that dialog box from the screen. Your changes will now be reflected in the report.

Selecting a Different Kind of Graph

The graph you are building—a comparison of each of the customers and the quantity they purchased—might be better served by using a pie chart. Pie charts are useful for comparisons of how much of the overall amount is attributed to each category. The column chart you are using now shows the total quantity for each customer. As discussed previously, this information is already available on your report. To show that information in a different way, you could use the pie chart.

To change the type of graph you are using, once again you would double-click the graph, bringing up the Graph Object dialog box as seen in figure 12.32. By scrolling through the Graph Type listbox, you can see all the available graph types in PowerBuilder. While this is not the most exhaustive list of graphs, it is pretty comprehensive, particularly for business graphing applications.

Part
III

Ch
12

The column graph type is currently highlighted since it's the default graph. Select the 3-D Pie graph by clicking on it. You will then see the mock-up change to reflect that you are now using a pie chart (see fig. 12.35). If you select the Category Axis or Value Axis tab pages again, you will see that the Label field is now disabled since they do not apply for pie charts. You might also notice that the scroll bars around the graph mock-up on the Graph tab page are now enabled. These allow you to change the perspective, elevation and rotation for 3D graph types.

FIG. 12.35

Now that the graph is a 3D Pie chart, the Perspective, Elevation, and Rotation Scroll bars are enabled.

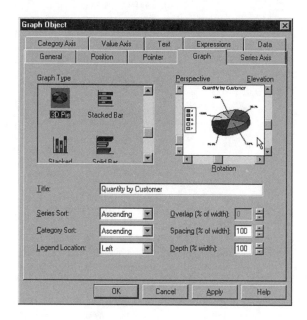

From the Graph Object dialog box, click OK to return to the report window. You then will see that your graph has changed to a Pie chart. Preview the report at this time to see the difference that the Pie chart makes.

N O T E   Notice there was no change in the information that the graph uses, only the type of graph that it is. If you wanted to change the data, you would double-click the graph object to open the Graph Object dialog box and select the Data tab page. ■

You should save your report again at this point, so that the effort you have just put forth is not lost. Next, preview your report, observing the pie chart on your report. Notice that in the case of a pie chart, each customer is represented as a different colored slice of the pie, and that the percentage of the grand total that each customer is responsible for appears.

Creating Label Reports

A label report is a report that is designed to create labels, usually by using label paper. Label is one of the presentation styles that's available for a new report.

As an example, you can create a customer mailing label report. This label report will use only one table, the Customer table. The Customer table contains all the information about a customer that is necessary to mail something to that customer, such as an invoice.

To create the label report, click the Report icon, and then choose New in the Select Report dialog box. You then see the New Report dialog box. Since the labels use only one table, select Quick Select as the data source and Label as the presentation style, and then click OK.

The next thing you see is the Quick Select dialog box. Select `customer` as the table, and when the list of columns from the customer table appears, select the following fields: `customer_name`, `customer_address1`, `customer_address2`, `customer_city`, `customer_state`, and `customer_zip` (see fig. 12.36). When you have done this, you might also want to set up a sort order so that the labels are in some kind of order. When completed, click OK.

FIG. 12.36
Using a quick select for the customer table only, select the fields from the customer table that handle address information.

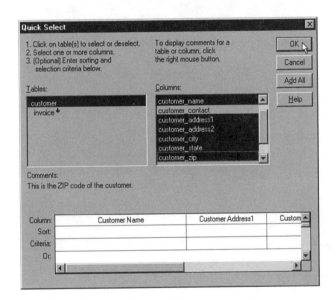

Since this is a label report, the next dialog box you see is the Specify Label Specifications dialog box. You use this dialog box to determine the dimensions of your labels, as well as how the labels are laid out on the label paper. After all, the principle reason for creating a label report is to print it on label paper and use the individual labels. If you have not laid out your labels correctly, when you print them on paper you will not get a one-to-one correspondence between your labels and each row of data.

CAUTION

You can select from the drop-down list box of predefined labels. In doing so, PowerBuilder will fill in all the information on this dialog box, based upon your selection. Each of these fields can be edited. However, you should exercise caution in making changes to these settings since you might be messing up something that is already layed out nicely.

Part
III

Ch
12

In this dialog box, you must also decide whether the paper to be printed on is Continuous Feed or Sheet Feed, and whether the labels should print Left-to-Right or Top-to-Bottom.

For this example (which won't be printed anyway), you can select whatever predefined labels you want. I have selected Laser Address 1 X 2.63, 3 labels across, 10 down, which will fit the customer information nicely (see fig. 12.37). After making your selection, click OK.

N O T E If you make a selection here that does not work out for you, you can always change these settings later by right-clicking the label in the Report Design window and selecting Properties. When Report Object Dialog box appears, select the Definitions tab page. ■

FIG. 12.37
The Specify Label Specifications dialog box allows you to designate the size and arrangement of your labels.

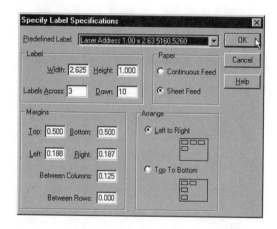

You then see the design window for your label report, with the outline of your label and the columns you selected during Quick Select within the label (see fig. 12.38). It almost seems as though the label height of one inch is not enough to display all the fields.

Making Adjustments

Before going to the Report Object dialog box and changing the height of the label, take another look at figure 12.38. Although the last two fields do not fit vertically, do you really want them in that position anyway? Those last two fields are customer_state and customer_zip. They should be moved up next to the customer_city field. When you do that, everything fits inside the border of the label.

N O T E It is important that everything fit within the border of the label, so that when it is printed out on label paper, all the information needed for each label appears on the label. ■

Before you do anything else, you should save this report. Select Save As from the File menu. Name this report r_customer_labels and provide a description of the report in the Comments area.

FIG. 12.38
The initial design of
your labels shows all
the fields you selected
and an outline of the
label size you specified.

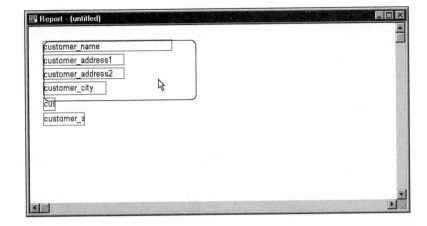

Now, preview this report. Click the Preview icon on the Report Painter toolbar. All of the customers from your customer table will have a label (see fig. 12.39). This looks pretty good so far, but there a couple of things you can do to improve this report.

First of all, the City, State, and Zip columns are lined up properly, but there is a big gap in between most of the data. The City field is pretty wide to allow for cities with many letters; therefore, the State field cannot be any closer than it is. To solve this problem, you need to create a computed field.

Normally, when you think of computed fields, you probably think of calculations to be performed. However, you can use a computed field simply to do string concatenation.

After getting back into Design mode, the first thing you must do is remove the City, State, and Zip fields from the report. Highlight each one of them and click the Clear icon. Now, in their place you will create a computed field.

Part

III

Ch

12

FIG. 12.39
Previewing the label
report shows how the
actual data fits within
the borders of a label.

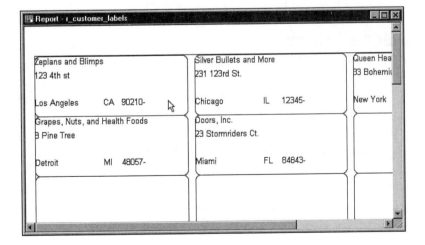

To create the computed field, select Objects, Computed Field from the menu, and then click on the report where you want this field to be placed. When the Computed Object dialog box appears, click the More command button to bring up the Modify Expression dialog box. Figure 12.40 shows you what the expression should look like. To create this expression, click once on customer_city in the Columns list box, and it will be pasted into the expression wherever your cursor is. Watching for the needed quotes, place a comma and a space between the City and State fields, and just a space between State and Zip. When you have completed this, click OK and OK again, which takes you back to the Report Design window.

FIG. 12.40

The computed field, in this case, is nothing more than several string fields concatenated together (don't forget the plus signs in between each string).

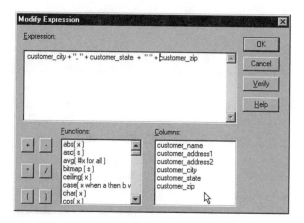

When you are back in the Report Design window, you see the computed field just created. It will probably need to be stretched out to make sure that it is wide enough to display all three fields. It might also need to be aligned and spaced properly to fit in with the other fields.

When you are finished, preview the report again. Notice how the City, State, and Zip are all nicely spaced! Be sure to test that the width of your field is adequate by including in your test data the city that has the most letters in it.

Sliding a Column

The report looks better but is still not complete. As you can tell, the customer_address2 column is not always used. You have to include it here in your labels in case it is used for some customers. It would be nice if you could leave room for it, but not have that gap when there is no data.

PowerBuilder has a feature called a sliding column. Each column in a report (and in a DataWindow) can be set up as a slider. What is meant by sliding is that if there is no data in the designated direction (either to the left or above), this column will slide in to fill the gap.

It's very easy to designate a column as a slider. You just right-click on top of the column (here, you want the computed column to be the slider) and select Properties. When the Computed

Object Dialog box appears, select the Position tab page (see fig. 12.41). On this page is the Slide Group box. In the group box is a drop-down list box labeled Up. In this list box, you must decide between All Above or Directly Above. The difference between these two is that with All Above, all the fields that make up the line above must be emptied before it can slide up; Directly Above means only the fields that are directly overhead must be blank. In this case, however, there is only one field overhead (customer_address1), so either choice will do. Once you have made your selection from the list box, click OK to close the Computed Object dialog box.

FIG. 12.41

Designating a column as a slider means that if there is no data in the designated direction, that data will slide to fill in the gap.

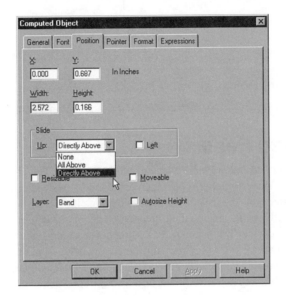

N O T E The field to slide into (for example, customer_address2) must have no data in it for the other column to slide into its place. Anything in there, even one space, would not be considered blank. ▪

There is one more thing you must do before this can work. You must make sure that the Autosize Height attribute is turned on for the column that might be blank (in this case, the customer_address2 column). Autosize Height assures that the column has a specific height that the sliding field can utilize for its repositioning.

You turn on Autosize Height for the customer_address2 field by right-clicking that column and selecting Properties. When the Column Object dialog box appears, select the Position tab page again. On this page is a check box labeled Autosize Height. If it is not already checked on, click it now to do so. Remember to click OK to close the dialog box when you're done. Now, preview the report again (see fig. 12.42). Notice that for any customer who did not have address2 field information, the City, State, and Zip fields moved up to appear directly below the address1 field.

FIG. 12.42
With the city-state-zip computed field designated as a slider, the computed field slides up to fill in the gap when there is no address2 information.

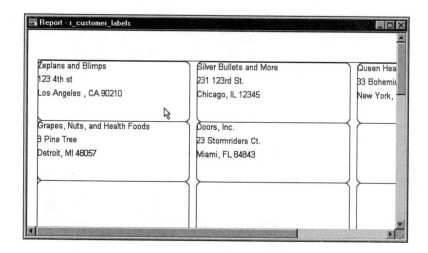

Creating Nested Reports

In PowerBuilder, you can put a report inside of another report. (This works for DataWindows, as well.) A report inside of another report is referred to as a nested report. Although the Inventory Tracking system you are creating here does not lend itself to nested reports very well, you could do something like change the Customer Order History Report created in this chapter to include the customer DataWindow (d_customer) created in an earlier chapter. If you were to do this, of course, you would probably delete the fields from the customer table that you included in the report initially (at least pull them off-screen, but you would still need the customer_name column to be retrieved because you grouped this report using that field).

To add a nested report in the Customer Order History Report, open r_order_history in the report painter. To do this, click the report painter from the PowerBar and scroll through the list of reports until you find r_order_history. Click it once, and then click OK.

Delete (from the screen only) the customer_name and customer_phone columns. (To do this, click each one once, and then click the Clear icon on the Report Painter toolbar.)

Now, select Objects, Report from the menu, and then click on the screen where you want the nested report to go. (You should click in the header for group 1 band, as this is where you were displaying the customer_name column.)

Next, you see the Report Object dialog box with the Select Report tab page on top (see fig. 12.43), where you see a list box of all the reports and DataWindows in your application. Select the one you want (d_customer) by clicking it once, and then click OK.

FIG. 12.43

The Report Object dialog box allows you to choose which report (or DataWindow) you wish to nest into your report.

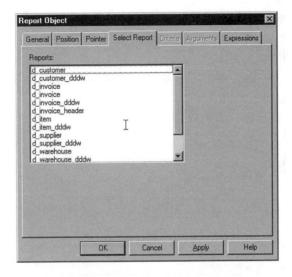

You then see a rectangular object on your report that is labeled d_customer (see fig. 12.44). This represents the nested report. You cannot see any of the details for this report, such as the columns or their labels; all you ever see of d_customers from here is this rectangle. You must resize the rectangle so that all of the data from d_customer would fit within its border. This can only be accomplished by good ol' fashioned trial-and-error. Size it up and preview the report; if it doesn't quite fit, size it up and preview again, and so on (see fig. 12.45).

FIG. 12.44

The nested report shows up in your report as an empty rectangle during design. It must be sized up appropriately so that when the report is previewed, all the data from the nested report will fit.

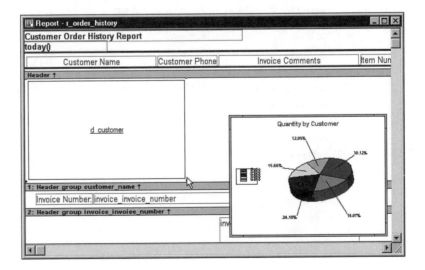

Part
III

Ch
12

FIG. 12.45

The results of the nested report are shown here while previewing the reports.

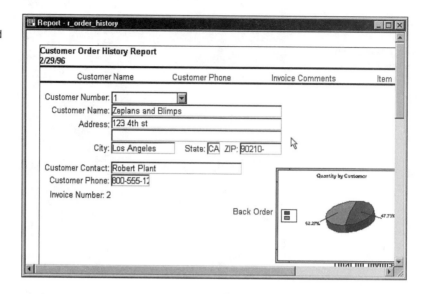

From Here...

In this chapter, you learned how to create grouped reports, graphs, labels and reports within reports. Along the way, you used computed fields in innovative ways.

You saw that reports (and DataWindows) are a very powerful means of displaying data. For more on what DataWindows can do, refer to the following chapters:

- Chapter 9, "Creating DataWindows," describes several DataWindow development techniques. You learn how to create three DataWindows and hook your DataWindows to your application.

- Chapter 10, "Enhancing DataWindows," shows you how to modify, enhance, and use your DataWindow.

- Chapter 11, "Manipulating Data Using DataWindows," shows how SQL can be used to define a DataWindow. This chapter covers the SQL toolbox and the SQL syntax behind a DataWindow.

Delivering the Final Product

CHAPTER 13

PowerBuilder Libraries

by Charles A. Wood

PowerBuilder libraries (PBLs) are where PowerBuilder stores all of its objects. Most developers use the library painter method to navigate through their systems. ■

Use the library painter.

The library painter is a very powerful tool. You can use the library painter to pull up different painters, and to move, copy, and delete library entries.

Search through your Library Entries.

You can use the library painter to search through your PowerBuilder application for a string of text. This can be very helpful, especially when working on large applications in a team environment.

Use system regeneration from the library.

You can regenerate your entire system from the library painter. This chapter shows you how.

Use the library painter to manage multi-developer projects.

The library painter is key to managing multi-developer projects. This chapter shows how you can make multi-developer projects a little less painful.

Export your library entries to text.

Sometimes it may be necessary to export your library entries to text. This chapter shows you how.

Using the Library Painter

The library painter is how most developers navigate through their system. To pull up the library painter, click the Library icon. Along with pulling up the library painter, this shows you all the objects in the PBL containing the application you're working on. If you've been coding the Inventory Tracking system so far, your library should look something like what is shown in figure 13.1.

FIG. 13.1
The library painter as it first appears.

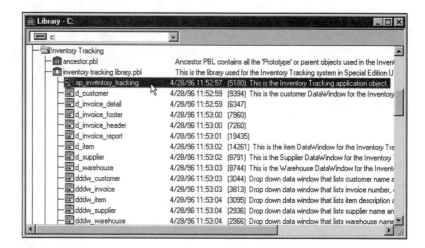

Jumping to a Painter

One of the library painter's best features is its capability to jump to a painter and pull up an entry for you. This saves you the time of going through the long process of selecting the painter, PBL, and then the module you want to update.

With the library painter, simply find the entry you want and double-click it. This automatically brings up the proper painter, with the module you clicked already open inside the painter.

 When you first bring up the library painter, it displays only the PBL that contains the application. You can display or stop displaying other directories by double-clicking them.

Selecting Entries

Most library painter functions require you to select one or several PBL entries first. There are several different ways to select a single PBL entry or a set of PBL entries:

- To select a single PBL entry, click it with the mouse.
- To select every entry in a PBL, click that PBL, then click the Select All icon. All your entries are now selected, as seen in figure 13.2.
- To select several entries, you can click an entry and then Shift+click on another entry. All library entries will be selected between the two entries already clicked.

FIG. 13.2

To select all of your entries in a PBL, click that PBL and then click the Select All icon.

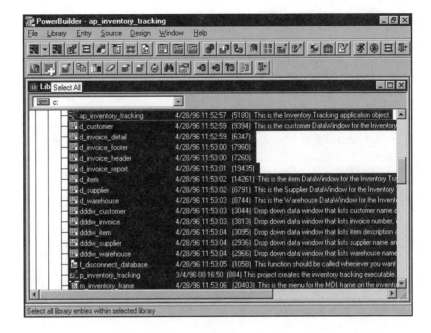

- To select additional non-contiguous entries after you already selected entries, hold down the Ctrl key while clicking your additional entry.

- To select several entries—even across PBLs—make sure all entries you want to select are displayed and not hidden behind a PBL or directory. You can then hold down the mouse button across entries (similar to a "drag" motion, except nothing is being dragged). All entries that the mouse passes over while "dragging" will be selected. To select into another PBL, click the Ctrl key down when you click the second PBL, as seen in figure 13.3.

FIG. 13.3

By "dragging" your mouse pointer across library entries, you select those library entries. To select more entries in another PBL, Ctrl+click those entries.

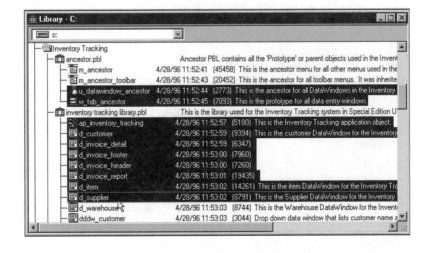

Copying or Moving Selected Entries

To copy or move a library entry or entries to another library, select the entry(ies) you want to copy, and click the Copy icon or the Move icon. This opens the Select Library dialog box, seen in figure 13.4. Click the proper directory and the proper PBL, and then click OK. Your entry is copied or moved to the new PBL.

FIG. 13.4
The Select Library dialog box allows you to copy or move entries from one PBL to another.

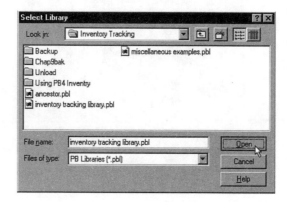

Deleting Selected Entries

To delete a library entry or entries, select the entry(ies) and click the Delete icon. PowerBuilder then asks if you are sure you want to delete this library entry, as seen in figure 13.5. Click Yes (if you're sure); the entry is deleted.

FIG. 13.5
PowerBuilder always verifies before you delete a library entry.

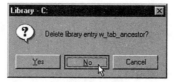

Understanding Regeneration

Regeneration is important during the development of your PowerBuilder application. *Regeneration* realigns all your objects and internal object calls, and regeneration updates descendants of a window. Often, your PowerBuilder application will halt for no apparent reason. This happens if the internal calls no longer match the existing structure; it usually can be solved by regeneration.

To regenerate, select the entries you want regenerated (usually all of them in an application) and click the Regeneration icon. This regenerates all selected entries.

Searching Library Entries

Often, you will want to find out where you declare or use a variable, or all occurrences of an object, and so on. To search through your entries:

1. Select the entries and then click Entry, Search, as seen in figure 13.6. This opens the Search Library Entries dialog box, seen in figure 13.7.

FIG. 13.6

To search library entries for the occurrence of a string, select the library entries you wish to search and click Entry, Search.

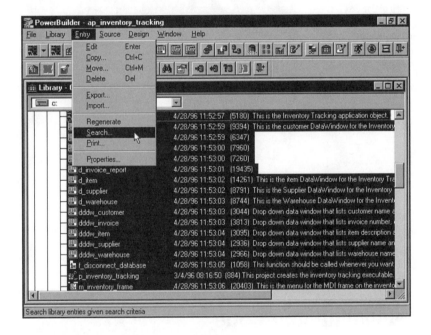

FIG. 13.7

The Search Library Entries dialog box allows you to search through entries for the occurrence of a variable or text.

Part

IV

Ch

13

2. In this dialog box, type in what you want to search for. You can choose to match case and which entries to display. You can also choose where to search in the entries you've chosen.

3. When you've decided what to search for and the search criteria, click OK. All selected entries are searched, based on the criteria you've chosen. When the search is finished, the Matching Library Entries dialog box appears, as seen in figure 13.8. This displays the criteria you've selected in the Search Library Entries dialog box.

FIG. 13.8
The Matching Library Entries dialog box displays the results of your search described in the Search Library Entries dialog box.

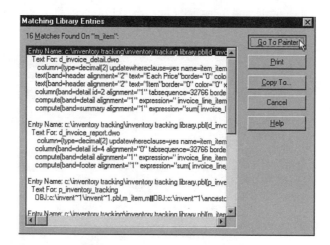

4. From the Matching Library Entries dialog box, you can print the results of your search by clicking Print, or copy the results of your search to a text file by clicking Copy To_, or you can immediately pull up the painter of the entry where the search string is located by clicking Go To Painter.

Rebuilding Your Code

Often when you're developing, you'll need to regenerate those pieces of code affected by changes made to an ancestor. Also, you may have inadvertently made changes to a global variable that is being accessed by a library member.

PowerBuilder allows you to regenerate those areas of your application affected by changes. To completely rebuild your application, click Utilities, Full Rebuild, as seen in figure 13.9. To only regenerate those members with changes, and their decendants, click Utilities, Incremental rebuild of current application.

FIG. 13.9
Clicking Utilities allows you to fully or incrementally rebuild your current application.

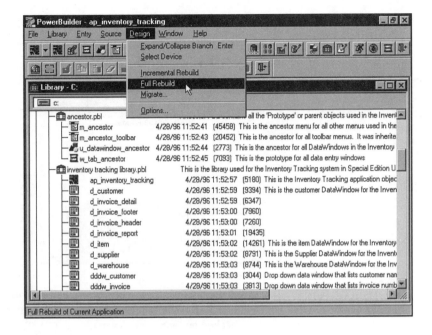

Managing Multi-Developer Projects

Several people may be working on a project at once. The PowerBuilder library painter has tools to help manage multi-developer projects.

Checking Out an Entry

PowerBuilder enables any developer to "check out" an entry from the library. If this is done, no other person can update or delete that entry until that entry is "checked in."

To check out an entry, click the Check Out icon. This opens the Set Current User ID dialog box, as seen in figure 13.10. The Set Current User ID dialog box lets you specify who you are. Be reasonably descriptive so that other developers really do know who checked out the entry.

FIG. 13.10
This dialog box lets you check out an entry and specify a User ID.

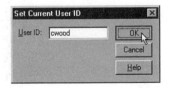

After you enter your User ID, PowerBuilder asks you which PBL to copy your entry to, as seen in the Check Out Library Entries dialog box in figure 13.11. Choose your work PBL, and the entry is copied there.

FIG. 13.11

You specify which PBL to copy your entry to in the Check Out Library Entries dialog box.

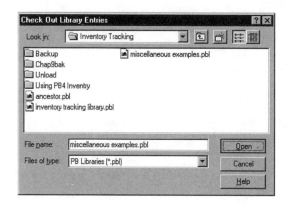

Now that the entry is checked out, no one can modify the original copy until the entry is returned. If you try to open the entry, a warning message appears, as seen in figure 13.12. However, you can still open the checked out entry for viewing.

FIG. 13.12

A warning message appears if you try to open an entry that is checked out.

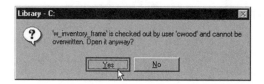

If you try to make changes and save them over the checked-out entry, an error message appears telling you that the entry is checked out and cannot be overwritten, as shown in figure 13.13.

FIG. 13.13

You get an error message if you try to overwrite an entry that has been checked out.

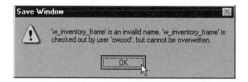

If another developer tries to check out your entry, PowerBuilder stops him or her with another error message stating that the entry is already checked out to someone else, as seen in figure 13.14.

FIG. 13.14
Only one developer is allowed to check out an entry at a time.

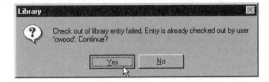

Listing the Status of an Entry

When an item is checked out, a "disk lock" icon appears next to the library entry, as seen in figure 13.15.

FIG. 13.15
Checked-out library entries are denoted by a "disk lock" icon.

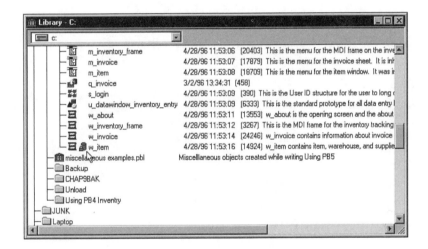

To list the status of all entries, click Source, View Check Out Status, as seen in figure 13.16. The View Entries Check Out Status appears, showing the check out status of all selected entries, as seen in figure 13.17.

FIG. 13.16
Source, View Check Out
Status allows you to see
the status of all checked
out library entries.

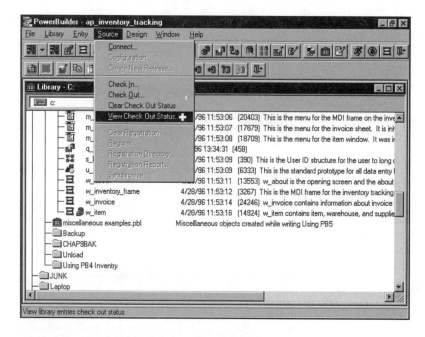

FIG. 13.17
The View Entries Check
Out Status dialog box
shows the check out
status of all selected
entries.

Checking In an Entry

After you're done with an entry, select it and click the Check In icon. The entry then automatically overwrites the older version.

If you try to check in an entry that wasn't checked out, you get an error message, as seen in figure 13.18.

FIG. 13.18
You can't check in an entry that hasn't been checked out.

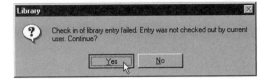

Clearing the Check Out Status

Finally, there are times when you need to clear the check out status of an entry. (Suppose there was a hard drive crash where the checked out version was, or the developer who checked the entry out left the company and took the hard drive.)

To clear the check out status of an entry, choose Source, Clear Check Out Status, as seen in figure 13.19. This allows you to update that entry.

FIG. 13.19
To clear the check out status of an entry, choose Source, Clear Check Out Status.

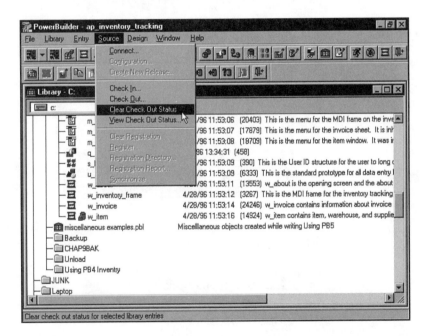

CAUTION
Make sure you have a good reason for clearing the check out status. Otherwise, you'll have two developers overwriting each other's changes!

Part
IV

Ch
13

Working with PVCS

There are other third-party packages available (such as PVCS, available for PowerSoft) that allow version control. Version control saves old versions and can be very handy if you've over-written or deleted something you need later.

Exporting and Importing Library Entries

You can export and import library entries into a PowerBuilder command text file. This is typically not needed with normal PowerBuilder development, but is often useful for both debugging your application and for viewing your application like PowerBuilder views it.

 To export an entry, select that entry and click the export icon. This will open the Export Library Entry dialog box, as seen in figure 13.20. Here, you can choose which folder (directory) will contain your exported PowerBuilder library entry.

FIG. 13.20
The Export Library Entry dialog box allows you to choose the receiving folder of your export.

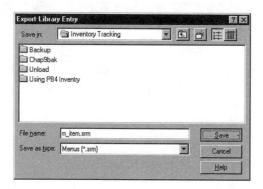

In listing 13.1, you can see an example of the m_item exported file. As you can see, the coding is very complex compared to the normal PowerBuilder graphical environment.

Listing 13.1 Exported Menu Code

```
$PBExportHeader$m_item.srm
$PBExportComments$This is the menu for the item window. It was inherited from
m_ancestor_toolbar
forward
global type m_item from m_ancestor_toolbar
end type
end forward

global type m_item from m_ancestor_toolbar
end type
global m_item m_item
```

```
on m_item.create
m_item=this
call m_ancestor_toolbar::create
end on

on m_item.destroy
call m_ancestor_toolbar::destroy
end on

on m_undo.create
call m_ancestor_toolbar`m_undo::create
this.Text="&Undo~tCtrl+Y"
this.Shortcut=345
end on

on m_insert.create
call m_ancestor_toolbar`m_insert::create
this.Visible=false
this.Enabled=false
this.ToolBarItemVisible=false
end on

on m_delete.create
call m_ancestor_toolbar`m_delete::create
this.Visible=false
this.Enabled=false
this.ToolBarItemVisible=false
end on

on m_itementry.create
call m_ancestor_toolbar`m_itementry::create
this.Visible=false
this.Enabled=false
this.ToolBarItemVisible=false
end on
```

 You can also import PowerBuilder command text files. To do this, click the Import icon. This will open the Select Import Files dialog box. Here, choose which files you want to import into your current PowerBuilder application.

FIG. 13.21
The Select Import Files dialog box allows you to indicate which PowerBuilder command text file you wish to import.

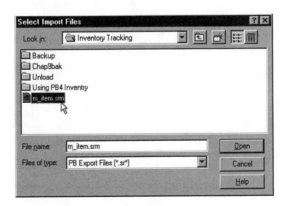

Finally, you should see the Import File into Library Entry dialog box. From here, you can choose where you want to place the imported library entry.

FIG. 13.22

The Import File into Library Entry dialog box allows you to select the receiving library for your import.

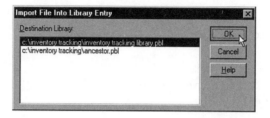

From Here...

You learned how to manipulate the library in this chapter. If you want to know more about what you can do with libraries, refer to the following:

- Chapter 1, "Introducing PowerBuilder," introduces windows, menus, libraries, and painters. It's a must-read for the beginning PowerBuilder developer.

- Appendix F, "The Windows API and Third-Party Products (What's on the CD?)," shows you what is included on the CD-ROM.

CHAPTER 14

Pulling It All Together in an Application

by Charles A. Wood

The Inventory Tracking system is almost complete. There are only a couple of things you need to pull together before running through the system. ▪

How to go about making and showing a help file.

You'll often need a help file to include with your application. This book shows how to access a help file within PowerBuilder.

How to use and override inheritance.

Inheritance is an extremely powerful tool. This chapter continues the inheritance discussion and shows when and how to override inheritance.

How to form a report and place it on a window to be used.

Although you can now track inventory, you still don't have the finished Invoice report. This chapter shows you how to develop one and add it to the window.

How to add the finishing touches to an application.

You still have not finished the Inventory Tracking system. There are some finishing touches needed to make the complete application.

How to run the Inventory Tracking system.

When the Inventory Tracking system is complete, this chapter takes you through the application and shows the features you've added throughout this book.

Adding Help for Inventory Tracking

Every Windows application should have some form of online help, especially when Windows does most of the work for you in a help file. Unfortunately, PowerBuilder and Windows have no method of generating a help file without additional third-party support.

To generate a help file, you need a help compiler. The Windows Software Developer's Kit comes with a help compiler, or you can write your own. Most developers, however, use a third-party help compiler because writing your own help compiler is very difficult and time-consuming.

N O T E   I used RoboHelp from Blue Sky Software for my online help file, INVENTRY.HLP. ▦

You use the ShowHelp() command for displaying help files. In the Inventory Tracking system, the Help menu item still needs to be coded for all options except About (which is covered in the next section). The following choices are coded as follows:

Menu Option	Command	Description
Table of Contents	ShowHelp ("INVENTRY.HLP," INDEX!)	Displays the table of contents of the help file.
Search	ShowHelp ("INVENTRY.HLP," KEYWORD!)	When you use a keyword, the Windows help system opens a search with those letters in it. An empty string opens a search at the beginning of the help file.
Introduction	ShowHelp ("INVENTRY.HLP," KEYWORD!, "Introduction")	Pulls up the introduction help topic.

Adding an About Window

You now need to make an About window. This About window is displayed whenever the user chooses Help, About. The About window, also called a "Splash" window, is also displayed while the Inventory Tracking system starts to execute.

The About window consists of static text, bitmaps, and an OK command button. The script behind the OK command button is:

```
Close(Parent)
```

You can see the About window in figure 14.1.

FIG. 14.1

The About window conveys information about the system to the end user.

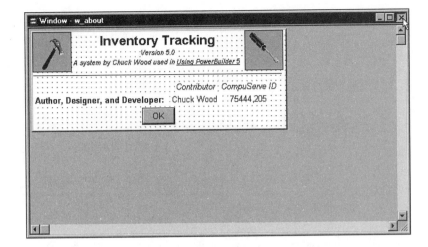

To access the About window through PowerBuilder, choose Help, About, as seen in figure 14.2. This opens the w_about window. Click the OK command button to close your window.

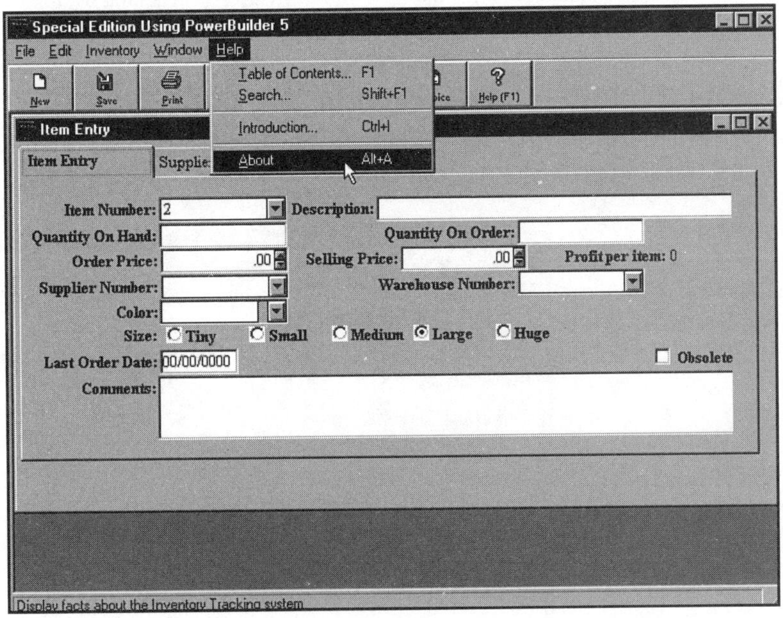

FIG. 14.2

To display the About window, click Help, About.

The About window has other uses as well. It often takes quite a while to start a Windows application; however, the About window, while conveying information, gives the illusion of a faster start up to your application because the user is too busy reading the About window to notice the time he or she is waiting. On the application open event, code the PowerScript found in listing 14.1.

Listing 14.1   The Application Open Event

```
Open(w_about)          // Open the w_about window
w_about.cb_OK.hide()   // Disable the button to close the window
.
.       // The body of the application open event goes here.
.
Close (w_about)
```

This opens and closes your w_about window in your application open event.

Adding to Inheritance

Inheritance has become a big part of the Inventory Tracking system. However, sometimes you want to add on to or overwrite what the ancestor does in order to customize your object.

Handling Ancestor Events from the Child Event

From any script, you can view what the ancestor has coded by choosing Design, Display Ancestor Script, as seen in figure 14.3.

FIG. 14.3
To view what an ancestor has written, choose Design, Display Ancestor Script.

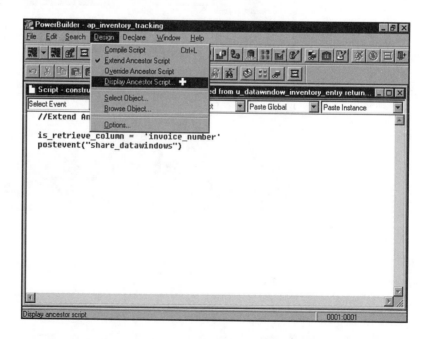

This displays the ancestor of your event, as seen in figure 14.4. Inheritance can be more than level deep; therefore, if the Ancestor button is enabled, that signifies there is yet another ancestor script. Although you can't modify the ancestor script from the child script, you can copy the contents if you wish. This may come in handy if you need to make only minor modifications to the event.

FIG. 14.4

The Display Ancestor Script dialog box allows you to view the contents of the ancestor of the current event you are working on.

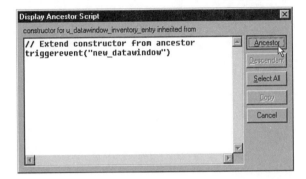

By clicking the Ancestor button, as shown in figure 14.4, you can move up and down the ancestor list. Figure 14.4 shows the constructor event in u_datawindow_inventory_entry. By clicking the Ancestor button, the Display Ancestor Script dialog box then continues "up the ancestral line" to show the code in u_datawindow_ancestor, as seen in figure 14.5.

FIG. 14.5

The Display Ancestor Script dialog box can display the "ancestor of an ancestor" PowerScript as well.

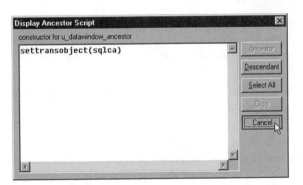

When coding a script that already has an ancestor script coded, you have two choices for handling the ancestor script. You can extend the ancestor script (which is the default), thereby adding the child script to the end of the existing ancestor script. You also can override the ancestor script, thereby making the child script ignore the ancestor script.When you choose to extend or override the ancestor script, choose Design, Extend Ancestor Script or Override Ancestor Script, as seen in figure 14.6.

FIG. 14.6
Choosing Design,
Override Ancestor Script
allows your descendant
to ignore ancestor script
in favor of its own script.

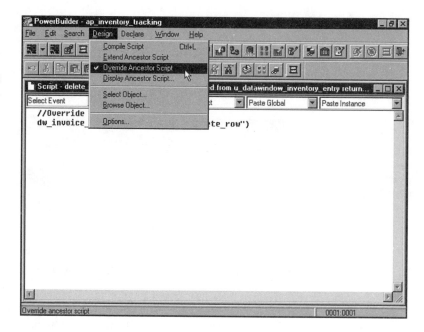

TROUBLESHOOTING

I have overridden my ancestor script as you indicated, but it still looks like it's being executed.
Why? For the descendant event to override the ancestor event, you must have at least one line of code
in the descendant event. I always put a comment in the descendant event:

`// Override Ancestor`

whenever I override the ancestor script. This not only satisfies the one line of PowerScript requirement,
but also lets others know that the ancestor was overridden.

As you can see in figure 14.7, you have three different types of marks on your events. The first
mark of a half-purple, half-white Script icon next to your event name indicates that you have an
ancestor script and have written a child script for your event. An all-purple Script icon indicates
that only an ancestor script exists for this event. An all-white Script icon indicates that only a
child script exists for this event. The different shaded Script icons should tip you off to look at
the code in the ancestor before adding and/or modifying any code in the current script.

FIG. 14.7

The Script icon next to the event names indicates where code for the event is located.

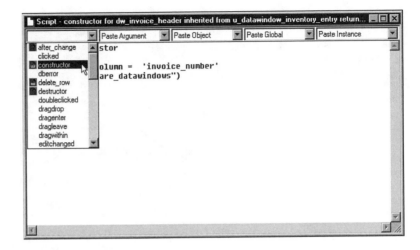

Updating a Multiple-Table DataWindow

The Invoice_detail DataWindow is different than all other DataWindows in the Inventory Tracking system, since you need to update multiple tables in your database when updating your DataWindow.

The best way to do this is with the following steps:

1. Choose Rows, Update Properties in your DataWindow painter.

2. In the Specify Update Characteristics dialog box shown in figure 14.8, select the table to update and the unique key columns. In the Updatable Columns section, select all of the columns that are updated in the detail section of the DataWindow.

3. Update the rest of the information by overriding the save and insert row events in your w_invoice window and the itemchanged event in the dw_data DataWindow control of your w_invoice window. Use SQL and PowerScript to update the nondetail columns if needed.

 TIP Always check the update characteristics of your DataWindows before completing your project.

FIG. 14.8
The Specify Update
Characteristics dialog
box allows the user to
specify what table and
columns to update with
a DataWindow.

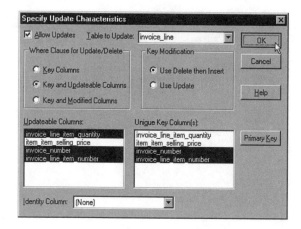

> **CAUTION**
>
> If you need to update multiple rows from within your table, you should use SQL within PowerScript to hard-code the update. However, your program design should avoid this if possible. Hardcode SQL updates lead to modifications every time the user adds, deletes, or changes a column on a DataWindow.
>
> Sometimes hardcode SQL updates are unavoidable, but the attempt should be made to resolve multiple-table updates from one DataWindow.

Adapting the Invoice Tab on the w_invoice Window

The Invoice tab on the w_invoice_window is different than all the other tabs in the Inventory Tracking system. In this tab, we actually have three DataWindows designed to look like one DataWindow. Furthermore, two of the DataWindows are shared (d_invoice_header and d_invoice_footer) so that information on the footer DataWindow is populated whenever an update or retrieve occurs on the header DataWindow.

Adding Script for dw_invoice_header

The invoice header controls much of what occurs on the Invoice tab. Most of the control is passed through the dw_invoice_header control.

The constructor and share_datawindows Events   The constructor event has been extended from d_datawindow_inventory_entry to include the following lines of code:

```
//Extend Ancestor

is_retrieve_column = 'invoice_number'
postevent("share_datawindows")
```

The share_datawindows event has been posted to share data between the dw_invoice_header DataWindow and the dw_invoice_footer DataWindow. The code for the share_datawindows event is as follows:

```
ShareData(dw_invoice_footer)
```

> **CAUTION**
>
> Make sure that the SQL Select statements are identical for d_invoice_header and d_invoice_footer. Otherwise, the ShareData command will not allow the d_invoice_footer to be displayed during runtime.

The delete_row and insert_row Events   It really does not make sense to delete a row in the dw_invoice_header DataWindow. The following code has been added to ensure that only the dw_invoice_detail control is triggered when the dw_invoice_header delete_row event is called:

```
//Override
dw_invoice_detail.triggerevent("delete_row")
```

Similarly, the insert_row event also defers to the dw_invoice_detail control:

```
//Override
dw_invoice_detail.triggerevent("insert_row")
```

The ItemChanged Event   The ItemChanged event is extended from the ancestor to assign the current invoice number to il_current_invoice_number:

```
//Extend Ancestor
if GetColumnName() = is_retrieve_column then
    il_current_invoice_number = long(gettext())
end if
```

> **N O T E**   GetColumnName ( ) retrieves the columnname of the current column that has focus.
> GetText( ) retrieves the text of the current field. GetText is often used in the ItemChanged event to retrieve the text of any change before the change actually takes place. ■

The new_datawindow Event   The new_datawindow event has been overridden simply to trigger the new_datawindow event in the dw_invoice_detail DataWindow, as seen in listing 14.2.

Listing 14.2   The new_datawindow Event

```
//Override
if uf_ask_to_save() = FALSE then
    Return 2                     // Make the new_datawindow event fail
else
    reset ()                     // Clear DataWindow
    insertrow(0)
    SELECT max(invoice_number)+1
        INTO :il_current_invoice_number
```

continues

Listing 14.2   Continued

```
            FROM invoice
            USING SQLCA;
      if isnull(il_current_invoice_number)&
            or il_current_invoice_number < 1 then
         il_current_invoice_number = 1
      end if
      setitem (getrow(), "invoice_number", il_current_invoice_number)
      dw_invoice_detail.triggerevent("new_datawindow")
end if
```

CAUTION

The code in listing 14.2, while functional in a single-user environment, can cause problems in a multi-user environment. If two people try to add an invoice at the same time, an error will result since the primary key will no longer be unique.

There are many ways to get around possible errors in a multi-user environment:

- Of course, the best way to handle this is with an auto-increment column on your database table if your database supports auto-increment columns. That way, the database can take care of multi-user access.

- You can avoid the use of sequence numbers and instead use date-time stamps. This often can result in acceptable performance; however, the keys may be a little hard to use outside of the PowerBuilder application you're developing.

- You could set table locks on updates so that no other user can access the next number at the same time as you before the update. (However, this may cause other users to be locked out of the database.)

- You can trap the error that's returned and try to insert again if the row already exists. This may result in long updates if several users update the table at the same time.

The reason this script simply could not have been extended to add the one trigger is that if the user clicks cancel, the detail trigger event should not be executed.

The RetrieveEnd Event   The RetrieveEnd event is executed whenever a DataWindow is finished with a retrieve. In the dw_invoice_header RetrieveEnd event, corresponding invoice information from the dw_invoice_detail DataWindow is retrieved. If no corresponding information is found, a blank row is inserted, as seen in listing 14.3.

Listing 14.3   The RetrieveEnd Event

```
int invoice_number

invoice_number = getitemnumber(getrow(), "invoice_number")
if dw_invoice_detail.retrieve(invoice_number) < 1 then
    dw_invoice_detail.insertrow(0)
end if
```

The update_datawindow Event   The update_datawindow event is triggered by the developer to update a DataWindow. dw_invoice_header extends this script to also update the dw_invoice_detail DataWindow, as seen in listing 14.4.

Listing 14.4   The update_datawindow Event

```
// Extend

int number_of_rows
int loop_counter

number_of_rows = dw_invoice_detail.rowcount()
for loop_counter = 1 to number_of_rows
    dw_invoice_detail.setitem(loop_counter, 'invoice_number',
il_current_invoice_number)
next
dw_invoice_detail.update()
```

Adding Script for dw_invoice_footer

Since dw_invoice_footer is shared with dw_invoice_header, all data, updates, retrieves, and inserts done to dw_invoice_header are reflected in dw_invoice_footer. Consequently, when using dw_invoice_footer, you'll always want to override your events and possibly trigger the events in dw_invoice footer.

The constructor and destructor events are simply overridden with a comment:

```
// Override
```

The delete_row, insert_row, ItemChanged, new_datawindow, print_datawindow, and update_datawindow all trigger the corresponding dw_invoice_header events. For instance, the new_datawindow event in the dw_invoice_footer control overrides the ancestor and contains the following script:

```
//Override
dw_invoice_header.triggerevent("new_datawindow")
```

Adding Script for dw_invoice_detail

Similar to dw_invoice_footer, dw_invoice_detail defers to dw_invoice_header for the new_datawindow and print_datawindow events. For instance, the print_datawindow event in dw_invoice_detail overrides the ancestor and contains the following script:

```
//Override
dw_invoice_header.triggerevent("print_datawindow")
```

However, other events are needed for dw_invoice_detail to function properly.

The insert_row Event   The insert_row event has been extended to make sure the current invoice number is set on every new row on the DataWindow with the following script:

```
// Extend ancestor
setitem(getrow(), "invoice_number", il_current_invoice_number)
```

Part
IV

Ch
14

Posting Functions and Events   The post_itemchanged event has been added to dw_invoice_detail. Select dw_invoice_detail in the window painter and click Declare, User Events. The Events for dw_invoice_detail dialog box should appear. Type in the event name (post_itemchanged) and click on Args, as seen in figure 14.9.

 TROUBLESHOOTING

I've named my event and have clicked on the Args button just like you said, but PowerBuilder appears to already have assigned arguments to the event, and I can't change them. What's going on? You must assign arguments before you assign an Event ID to your user-defined event. Otherwise, PowerBuilder will use the default arguments for that Event ID.

If you've already assigned an Event ID, delete it, change the arguments to the arguments you want, and then reassign the Event ID.

The Event Declaration dialog box should appear. This is similar to the Function Declaration dialog box that you've seen before. Here, declare ai_row and as_column arguments for your event.

The ItemChanged event has now been overridden to call the post_itemchanged event with the current row and columnname. The reason that we are retrieving the row and columnname now is that after the item changes, the row and columnname might also change.

```
//Override Ancestor
EVENT POST post_itemchanged(row, getcolumnname())
```

 N O T E   PowerBuilder has added keywords that allow you to pass arguments to events or to post functions. These keywords are TRIGGER, POST, EVENT, and FUNCTION. The syntax for the keywords are as follows:

```
TRIGGER EVENT eventname(arguments...)
POST EVENT eventname(arguments...)
POST FUNCTION functionname(arguments...)
TRIGGER FUNCTION functionname(arguments...)
```

Using the TRIGGER keyword or the POST keyword followed by the EVENT or FUNCTION keyword followed with either the allows you to trigger or post an event or function with arguments.

You can even switch the order of the keywords. For instance, EVENT POST and POST EVENT have the same effect. However, POST EVENT may seem a little more readable than EVENT POST. ■

Now the post_itemchanged event will set the subtotal column every time the item changes with the Powerscript found in listing 14.5.

FIG. 14.9
You can now set arguments for your PowerScript events.

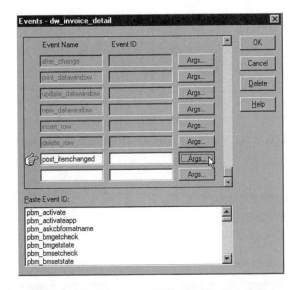

FIG. 14.10
The Event Declaration dialog box lets you define arguments for your events.

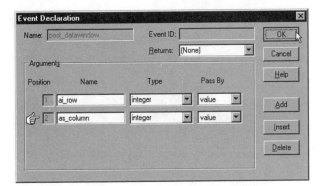

Listing 14.5 The update_datawindow Event

```
decimal item_price
long item_number
decimal {3} subtotal

if as_column = 'invoice_line_item_number' then
    item_number = getitemnumber(ai_row, 'invoice_line_item_number')
    SELECT item.item_selling_price
   INTO :item_price
   FROM item
  WHERE item.item_number = :item_number;
    setitem(ai_row, 'item_item_selling_price', item_price)
end if
subtotal = getitemdecimal(ai_row, 'subtotal')
dw_invoice_footer.setitem(dw_invoice_footer.getrow(), "subtotal", subtotal)
```

Part
IV

Ch

14

Adding the Inventory Report

 The major requirement not yet met by the Inventory Tracking system is the actual Inventory report. There are two ways you can add a report to a window:

1. The first way involves placing a DataWindow control on the window and making it invisible. This way is often used, and is the major way reports were added prior to PowerBuilder 5.0. (Several of your earlier PowerBuilder systems will use this method.)

 2. The more efficient way is to use DataStores. DataStores are new to PowerBuilder 5.0, and are more efficient than actually placing an invisible control on a window.

Using Invisible DataWindows

To create the DataWindow used for the Inventory report, click the DataWindow icon on the PowerBar to create a new DataWindow. Then choose SQL Select and Freeform as your data source and presentation style (see fig. 14.11).

FIG. 14.11
The Inventory report
should use SQL Select
and Freeform.

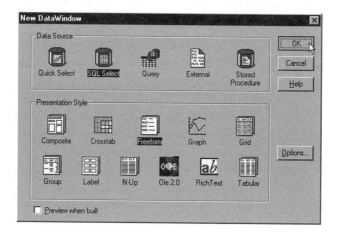

Choose Customer, Invoice, Invoice_line, and Item as your tables. Then choose all the columns you'll need for the Invoice report, as seen in figure 14.12.

This gives you the unformatted DataWindow shown in figure 14.13. Obviously some reformatting is needed to get the proper report.

After reformatting, moving columns to the appropriate bands, and adding computed columns and pictures, your Invoice DataWindow should look like figure 14.14.

 Use either a DataWindow control by clicking the DataWindow icon or a DataWindow user object by clicking the user object icon to add the DataWindow to your w_invoice window.
 There's no need to add it to a tab control, so you should place it somewhere on the window outside the tab control.

FIG. 14.12

These are the tables and columns needed for the Invoice report.

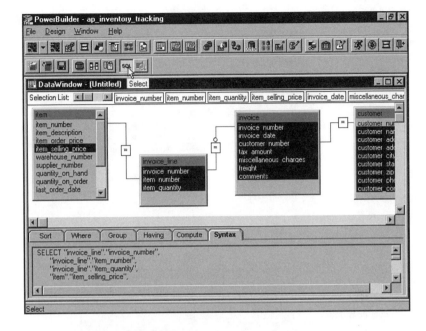

FIG. 14.13

The columns first appear on the DataWindow in an unformatted arrangement.

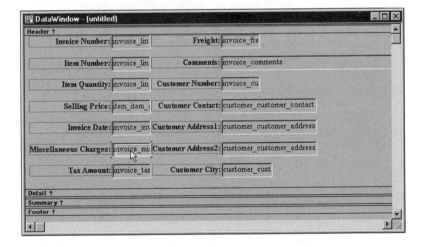

The properties for the Invoice report can be seen in figure 14.15. Notice that visible is clicked off. This is because the end user should not view the report before it's printed.

Unfortunately, since we marked invisible, we can no longer view the Invoice report on the w_invoice window. To view invisible items, click Design, Options as seen in figure 14.16. This displays the Options dialog box. Here, you can click Show Invisibles to see what is hidden, as seen in figure 14.17.

Part
IV

Ch
14

FIG. 14.14

The final Invoice report uses columns from the database as well as computed columns and bitmaps.

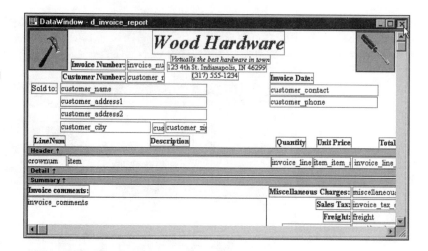

FIG. 14.15

Many times, printed reports are kept invisible on the window.

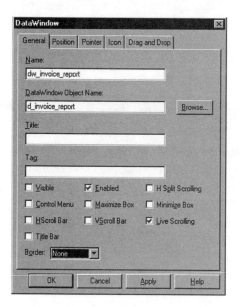

In figure 14.18, you can then see the invoice report as it appears on the w_invoice window. Notice that it does not have to be kept to full height and width. In fact, keeping a full report displayed would be quite burdensome. We can keep the control small since we are printing it, and not viewing it.

Now we need to add the code needed for printing the invoice. In the print_datawindow event of the d_invoice_header DataWindow, you need to override the ancestor script and add the PowerScript found in listing 14.6:

FIG. 14.16
Click Design, Options to change viewing options on a window.

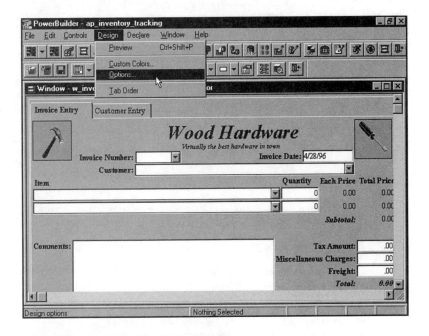

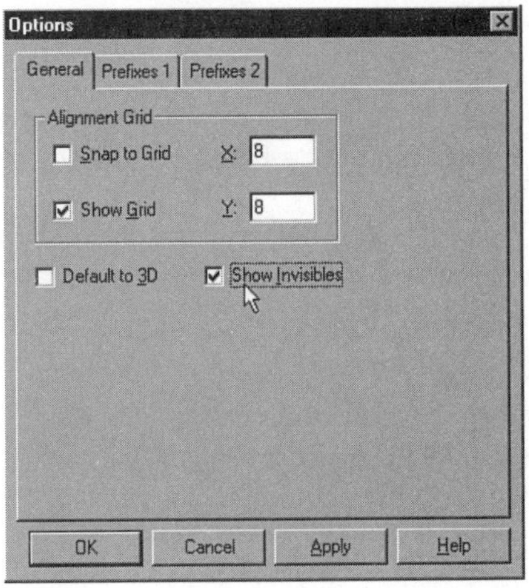

FIG. 14.17
Among other things, the Options dialog box allows you to show invisible window controls.

FIG. 14.18
Although it's still invisible to the end user, you can now view the Invoice report on the w_invoice window.

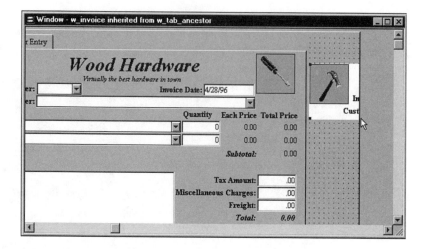

Listing 14.6   The print_datawindow Event Using Invisible DataWindows

```
//Override
long invoice_number

//Make sure the window is updated and get the invoice number
triggerevent("update_datawindow")
invoice_number = getitemnumber(getrow(), "invoice_number")

// Retrieve data into the report and print it
dw_invoice_report.retrieve(invoice_number)
dw_invoice_report.print()
```

N O T E   The PowerScript in listing 14.6 is not actually in the Inventory Tracking system. Rather, DataStores were used. DataStores are discussed in the next section. ■

Instead of printing just the d_invoice_header DataWindow, the print_datawindow event will now retrieve and print the invoice report.

Using DataStores

As was mentioned earlier in this section, invisible controls still require a lot of resources. PowerBuilder and Windows still treat the invisible control as a control, thereby allowing you to turn an object visible and invisible without much overhead.

However, with a control that always stays invisible, such as a report, using invisible controls slows down a system, especially if that system only uses that control some of the time. DataStores are new to version 5.0, and are the answer to this inefficiency. You can use DataStores as invisible DataWindow controls without the control overhead.

In the previous example, we built the invoice report (figures 14.11 through 14.14). This still needs to be done. However, instead of adding an invisible DataWindow control to the w_invoice window (as seen in figures 14.15 through 14.18), we simply add the code found in listing 14.7 to the print_datawindow event.

Listing 14.7   The print_datawindow Event Using DataStores

```
//Override
long invoice_number

//Make sure the window is updated and get the invoice number
triggerevent("update_datawindow")
invoice_number = getitemnumber(getrow(), "invoice_number")

// Create the DataStore used by this example
datastore lds_invoice_report
lds_invoice_report = Create DataStore
lds_invoice_report.DataObject = "d_invoice_report"
lds_invoice_report.settransobject(sqlca)

// Retrieve data into the report and print it
lds_invoice_report.retrieve(invoice_number)
lds_invoice_report.print()

// Destroy the DataStore
Destroy lds_invoice_report
```

Using DataStores, you can avoid the hassle of using invisible DataWindow controls on your window. As you can see in listing 14.7, there are only two sections of code added when using DataStores:

- The create DataStore section where you declare the datastore, allocate memory to the DataStore by using the Create statement, then assign a DataWindow object (d_invoice_report) and transaction object (SQLCA) to the report.
- The Destroy DataStore section where you deallocate the DataStore memory when you're finished using the DataStore.

CAUTION

Be sure to use a Destroy statement everytime you use a Create statement. Create will allocate memory, but will not deallocate it even when the window containing the Create statement is closed. Destroy will release the memory used in a Create statement.

If you do not use a Destroy statement every time you use a Create statement, your application will experience "memory leak." Memory leak is when an application reserves more and more memory until finally the application and Windows locks up.

When using DataStores with a report-intensive system, you'll notice a big improvement in speed. The amount of time it takes to open a window will noticeably decrease.

Last-Minute Cleanup of Your System

When you think you're finished with your system (until testing, of course), there are *always* two steps you should take. First, go into every DataWindow and choose Rows, Update Properties as before. This opens a dialog box similar to the one seen in figure 14.8.

Here, make sure the update characteristics of your tables and fields are defined as you like them. Throughout development, you add fields and tables. These new fields and tables may not have the update characteristics you want, and it's a good idea to check them. If you add a field to a DataWindow, it will not be automatically selected as an updatable field.

Also, check and set the tab order on all your fields and windows. Again, since you've added columns and objects to your windows and DataWindows, you'll need to make sure the tab order is what you want. There's nothing more annoying than trying to tab to the next field and losing your cursor to a field at the bottom of the screen.

Running Through the Inventory Tracking System

Thanks to inheritance from w_datawindow_ancestor, the Inventory Tracking system requires only five lines of code for every window except the w_invoice window. This is a pretty amazing feat for a development language.

A quick run-through of the Inventory Tracking system can show you what you've created. When the system first comes up, you see the Item Entry tab displayed, as seen in figure 14.19. Here you add and modify items.

FIG. 14.19

The Item Entry tab is the first entry window displayed in the Inventory Tracking system.

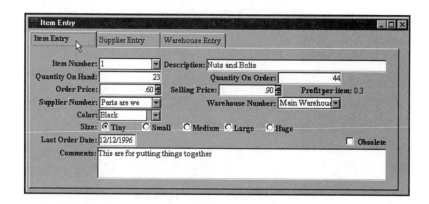

Clicking the Warehouse tab opens the Warehouse Entry DataWindow, seen in figure 14.20. Here, you add and modify warehouses.

Clicking the Supplier tab opens the Supplier Entry DataWindow. Here, you enter and change supplier information, as seen in figure 14.21.

The Invoice Entry tab is where you can edit the invoice information (see fig. 14.22). This window allows you to add and modify invoices and invoice lines. It also can be printed to give the invoice report to the customer.

Clicking the Customer tab opens the Customer Entry DataWindow. Here, you can add and modify customers, as seen in figure 14.23.

FIG. 14.20

The Warehouse Entry tab is where you add and update warehouses.

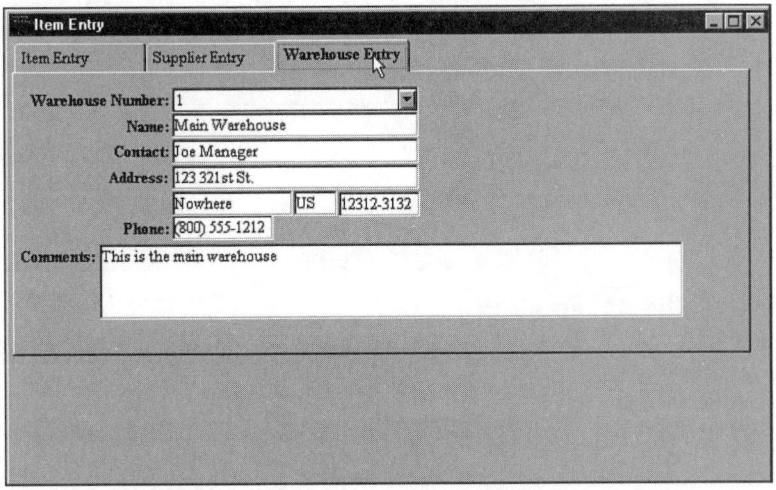

FIG. 14.21

The Supplier Entry tab is where you add and modify suppliers.

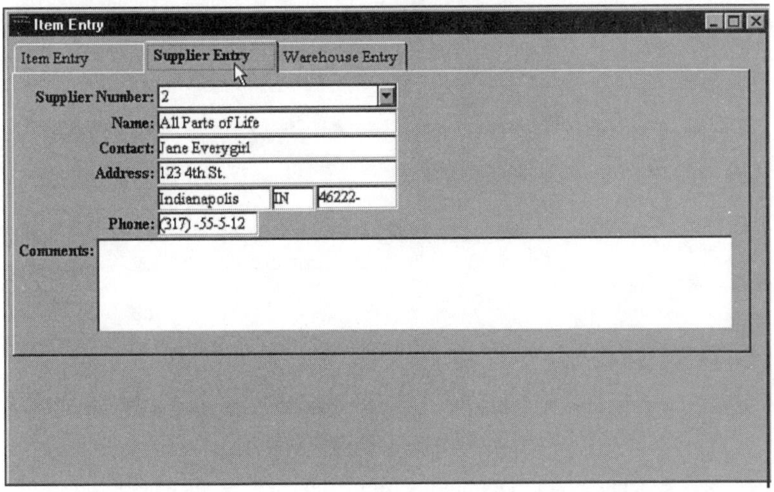

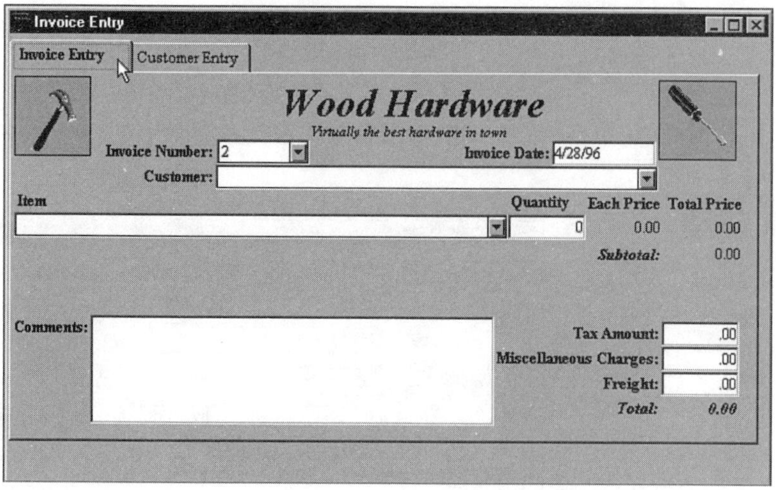

FIG. 14.22
The Invoice Entry dialog box allows you to update invoices and invoice lines.

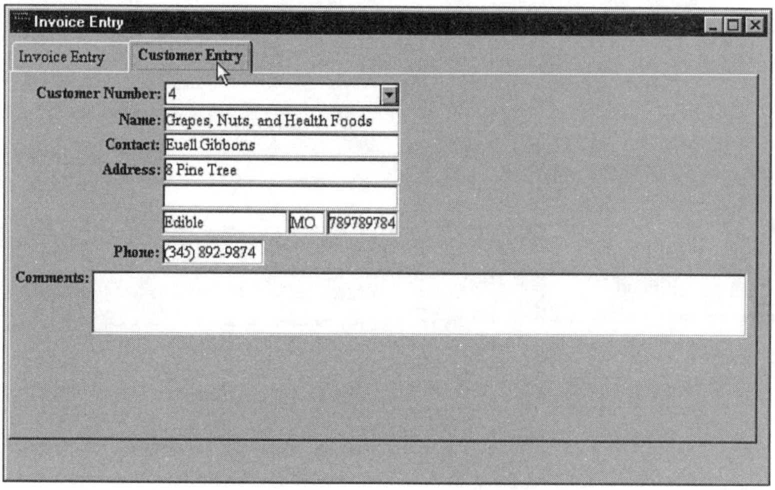

FIG. 14.23
The Customer Entry tab is where you add and modify customers.

From Here...

Now you need to debug your application and deliver the executable version of your program. To do this, refer to the following chapters:

- Chapter 15, "Debugging Your Applications," is where you can find out how to debug an application.

- Chapter 16, "Delivering an Executable," describes how to compile the application you developed and how to distribute the compiled application.

Debugging Your Applications

by Blake Coe

As you may be well aware, after you develop an application, often someone might go into your application and add erroneous code that causes unexpected problems. These errors have been appropriately termed *bugs*.

What better way to find bugs in an application than by using a debugger? The debugger allows you to step through your function and event scripts and inspect variable values. This is very useful in determining why a program is not working the way you intend it to.

Starting the debugger.

Look here to find out how to start your application running in debug mode.

Setting break points.

Look here to learn how to get your application to suspend processing so you can inspect your code and variables.

Stepping through code.

This section tells you how to execute your code one line at a time.

Examining and changing data values.

Being able to see the current information in your variables and attributes is very important in determining problems in your code. Look at this section to learn how.

Running Your Application in Debug Mode

The PowerBuilder debugger lets you step through your code as it is executed to evaluate the current value of variables. This is a very useful tool to determine if your code is executing as expected and if data values are being set appropriately.

Starting the Debugger

PowerBuilder has an appropriate icon to symbolize the debugger—a bug with the NO symbol stamped on it.

 To start the debugger, click on the bug-buster icon. If you currently have a painter open with unsaved modifications, you will be prompted to save changes before the debugger starts.

Setting Stops

When you start the debugger, the Edit Stops dialog box, shown in figure 15.1, will appear if you have previously established break points. If no break points are established, the Select Scripts dialog box will appear.

FIG. 15.1

The Edit Stops dialog box.

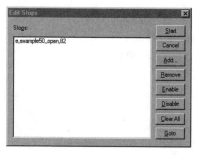

Stops are lines of code that you select for the debugger to suspend the running of an application. The terms stops and break points are used interchangeably in this book.

The Edit Stops dialog box will list all the break points that have been set. The following list describes the use of each command button on the dialog box:

- The Start button runs the application.
- The Cancel button exits the debugger without running the application.
- The Add button opens the Select Scripts dialog box.
- The Remove button removes the highlighted break point from the list of stops.
- The Enable button enables the highlighted break point.
- The Disable button disables the highlighted break point.
- The Clear All button removes all of the break points from the list.
- The Goto button takes you to the debug workspace for the highlighted break point.

If no break points exist when you start the debugger, or if you click the Add button from the Edit Stops dialog box, the Select Script dialog box in figure 15.2 will appear.

FIG. 15.2

The Select Script dialog box.

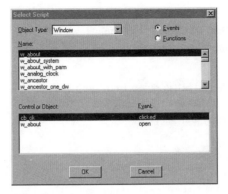

From the Select Script dialog box, select the script where you want to establish break points. To select a script for establishing break points:

1. Select the object type from the drop-down list box. The list of all the objects in the application of the selected type will appear in the Name area.

2. Select the script type by clicking either the Event or the Function radio button. All of the scripts for the selected script type and the selected object appear in the lower window.

3. Select the object for which you want to select a script by clicking the object name.

4. Select the control that contains the script you wish to add break points by clicking the name of the script.

5. Click the Okay button.

After you have selected the script, the debug workspace (see figure 15.3) for that script will appear.

FIG. 15.3

The debug workspace.

```
Debug - open for example50
0078: // Get the current environment for cross-platform issues
0079: GetEnvironment(ge_Environment)
0080:
0081: // Set DBMS connection
0082: li_RC = f_get_profile("sqlca", "dbms", sqlca.dbms)
0083: If li_RC = -1 Then
0084:     If (ge_Environment.OSType = windows! And ge_Environment.OSMajorRevision = 4) Or &
0085:         ge_Environment.OSType = windowsnt! Then
0086:         // Using registry, set default values
0087:         sqlca.dbms = "ODBC"
0088:         sqlca.dbparm    = "ConnectString='DSN=Powersoft Demo DB V5;UID=dba;PWD=sql'"
0089:     Else
0090:         If ge_Environment.OSType = macintosh! Then
0091:             MessageBox("Cannot find example.ini","The .ini file used by The code examples v
0092:                 " Not found.  Please ensure that it is in your System:Prefrences folde
0093:                 " folder containg PowerBuilder, or The folder containing The code exam
0094:         Else
0095:             MessageBox("Cannot find example.ini","The .ini file used by The code examples v
0096:                 " Not found.  Please ensure that it is in The same directory as The ex
0097:                 "libraries And that This is your current directory.",StopSign!)
0098:         End If
0099:         Halt Close
0100:         Return
0101:     End if
0102: End If
```

Now you can scroll through the script and add break points by double-clicking the lines of code. The lines of code that you marked as break points will be identified by a stop sign on the left-hand side of the code. You can remove a break point by double-clicking a line of code with a break point.

You can select more scripts to add break points to by reopening the Select Script dialog box. Just select the Select Script option from the Debug menu. You may also edit your stops while your application is suspended by a break point.

Stepping Through Your Code

 To start the application running from the Edit Stops dialog box, click the Start button. From the debug workspace, click the Start picture button to start the application.

Your application will run, assuming no errors occur, until a script with a break point is executed. The application will be suspended at the break point, and the debug workspace will appear.

> **N O T E** The highlighted line of code in the debug workspace has not yet been executed. It is the next line of code to be executed once the processing is resumed. ■

 There are two ways to continue running your application. You can click the Continue button, and the application will run until completion or until another break point occurs.

 The second option is to step through the code one line at a time. You can do this by clicking the Step button.

This will execute the next line of code and allow you to step through your script to determine exactly in what order your code is executed.

Working with Variables in Debug Mode

As well as being able to determine how your code is executed, you will want to know how your code affects the value of variables.

Evaluating Variables

 When you run your application in debug mode and reach a break point, you can view the current value of your variables. To view the variables, click the Variable button.

The debug workspace will now be split into two sections: Script and Variables. To hide the variable section, click the Variable button again.

The variables are grouped into five categories, shown in figure 15.4: This, Parent, Global, Shared, and Local. If there is a plus sign in the yellow box next to a listed item, you can double-click that item to view the variables and structures for that item. After you double-click an item (e.g. double-click Local to view local variables), all the variables and their current values will be listed. For objects and structures, you will need to double-click to get down to the variable level.

FIG. 15.4
The variable workspace displays variables and their current values.

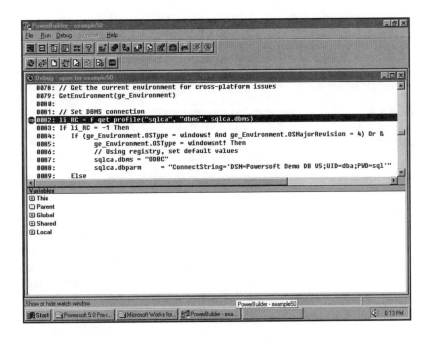

```
0078: // Get the current environment for cross-platform issues
0079: GetEnvironment(ge_Environment)
0080:
0081: // Set DBMS connection
0082: li RC = f_get_profile("sqlca", "dbms", sqlca.dbms)
0083: If li_RC = -1 Then
0084:     If (ge_Environment.OSType = windows! And ge_Environment.OSMajorRevision = 4) Or &
0085:         ge_Environment.OSType = windowsnt! Then
0086:         // Using registry, set default values
0087:         sqlca.dbms = "ODBC"
0088:         sqlca.dbparm       = "ConnectString='DSN=Powersoft Demo DB V5;UID=dba;PWD=sql'"
0089:     Else
```

Variables
- ⊞ This
- ☐ Parent
- ⊞ Global
- ⊞ Shared
- ⊞ Local

N O T E As shown in figure 15.4, the PowerBuilder 5 debugger has been enhanced to directly access "this" and "parent" objects. ■

Now that you can see your variables and their values, you can step through your code to see how their values change.

Working with the Watch List

It is very useful to see the values stored in your variables and watch how they are affected by your code. You may not be able to see all the variables that you want to watch without scrolling through the variable list. To make it easier to observe the variables and their values, you can select watch variables. Click the Watch button to display (or hide) the Watch variable workspace.

To add variables to the Watch workspace:

1. Click the variable in the Variable workspace.
2. Click the Add Watch button.

To remove variables from the Watch workspace:

1. Click the variable in the Watch workspace.
2. Click the Remove Watch button.

Modifying Data Values

In the previous section, you learned how to view the values of your variables. You may also make changes to these values. To change a variable's value:

1. Double click the variable whose value you wish to change. The Modify Variable dialog box will appear (fig. 15.5).

2. Enter the new value into the New Value field, or click the Null box to set the value to null.

FIG. 15.5

The Modify Variable dialog box.

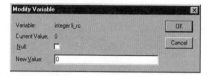

3. Click the OK button.

Now why would you ever want to change a variables value? You learned about PowerScript constructs (IF..THEN, Loops, CHOOSE CASE) in chapter 6. The decisions that are made through constructs are based on the values of variables. If you want to test all the possible paths that your constructs can lead you down, you can take advantage of the debugger's ability to change variables. The following "pseudo" PowerScript is for determining income tax based on pay range.

```
CHOOSE CASE gross_pay
    CASE id_range_1_start TO id_range_1_end
        //calculate income tax
    CASE id_range_2_start TO id_range_2_end
        //calculate income tax
    CASE id_range_3_start TO id_range_3_end
        //calculate income tax
    CASE id_range_4_start TO id_range_4_end
        //calculate income tax
    CASE IS> id_range_4_end
        //calculate income tax
END CHOOSE
```

If you wanted to evaluate each tax calculation through debug mode, you can change the gross_pay value to force the execution of the appropriate block of code.

From Here...

In this chapter, you learned how to work with PowerBuilder's Debugging facility; from setting up stop points to walking through a running application.

You learned how to set up the Watch list to narrow down all the variables and attributes available to the ones you care about, as well as how to modify the values of some variables during execution. For more on PowerBuilder applications, refer to the following chapters:

- Chapter 14, "Pulling It All Together in an Application," shows you how to finalize your application before you compile.

- Chapter 16, "Delivering an Executable," describes how to compile the application you developed and how to debug at run time.

Delivering an Executable

by Charles A. Wood

Now that you've wrapped up development, you need to deliver your executable. This involves building your executable (EXE) file and distributing it with the right DLLs. ■

Understand what is needed before compiling.

Some steps are needed if you want to get a clean compile every time.

Use the project painter and project objects to compile your application.

PowerBuilder project objects are a neat way to make sure the right code gets compiled every time.

Understand PowerBuilder Dynamic Link Libraries (DLLs and PBDs) and PowerBuilder Resource Files (PBRs).

Some concepts, like DLLs, PBRs, PBDs, machine code, and so on. are important to understand before delivering the compiled version of your PowerBuilder application.

Deliver an executable with the PowerBuilder Development and Deployment Kit (DDK).

To run a PowerBuilder application on a machine that isn't running PowerBuilder, you need to use the PowerBuilder Development and Deployment Kit with your executable.

Learn various techniques for debugging at run time.

Although not the easiest way to debug, PowerBuilder allows you to trace through your executable at run time.

Understanding What to Do Before Compiling

Before you begin a compile, you need to optimize your system. This first involves regenerating your entire application. To begin, follow these steps:

1. Back up your application. If you haven't backed up yet, do so. This may save you much grief later on, especially if your hard drive crashes or a PBL gets corrupted.

   ▶ **See** "Using the Library Painter," **p. 414**

2. Get into the library painter, open all PBLs, and then select all PBL members. Click the Regen icon, as shown in figure 16.1.

FIG. 16.1

Regeneration of all your PBLs should be the first step in building an executable.

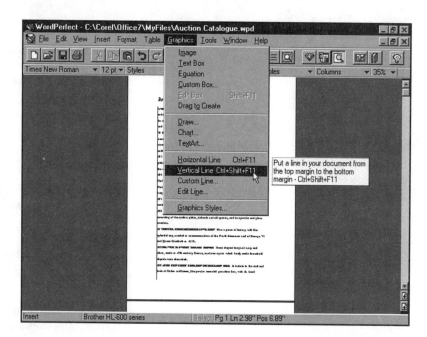

3. Next, you need to optimize your libraries. This is done by selecting the library you want to optimize and clicking Library, Optimize, as seen in figure 16.2.

4. Repeat this procedure for every PBL in your application.

5. Make sure you've defined an icon in the application painter property sheet, as was discussed in chapter 3.

FIG. 16.2
Use Library, Optimize to optimize every PBL in your application before creating your executable.

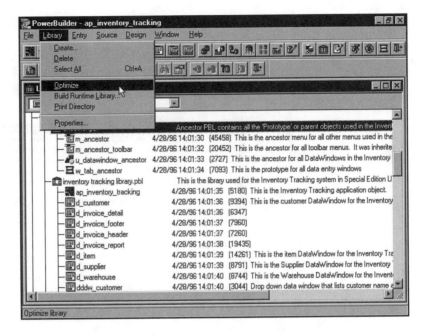

Using PowerBuilder Dynamic Libraries (DLLs)

As an application increases in size, it may become difficult to distribute and may take a long time to load. These problems can be resolved by using Dynamic Link Libraries, or DLLs.

By using DLLs, you decrease the size of your application to a shell and then make calls to your DLLs. Also, if one DLL changes, you can redistribute those changes in a DLL without releasing the entire application.

To create a DLL, follow these steps:

1. Open the library painter, select a PBL, and choose Library, Build Runtime Library. This opens the Build Runtime Library dialog box (see fig. 16.3).

2. From here you specify the whether you want native or 16-bit code (for Windows 3.x executables) and whether you want to optimize for speed or size. When you're finished, click OK.

3. Do this for all PBLs you want to convert to DLLs.

FIG. 16.3

The Build Runtime Library dialog box lets you specify information about your DLL.

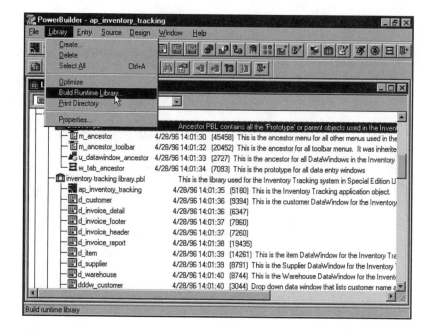

NOTE Converting a PBL into a DLL does nothing to the original PBL. When you are done converting, you'll have your original PBL and a new DLL file. ■

TROUBLESHOOTING

I'm using Windows 3.x with PowerBuilder, but cannot compile into a DLL. Why not? PowerBuilder only supports machine code executables in 32-bit environments like Windows NT or Windows 95. If you're still running Windows 3.x, you must compile using interpreted code and PowerBuilder Dynamic Libraries (PBDs) rather than DLLs. Your executables will also run slower because they are interpreted rather than machine code.

My advice is to get Windows 95 or Windows NT and compile using those environments.

 Remove all objects that aren't used from your PBL before creating a PBD or executable. These unused objects take up space and slow down the load of your executable or the search through your PBD.

Using Project Objects

Project Objects are an easy way to manage and compile a project, especially if you are responsible for multiple projects. To use the project painter, do the following steps:

1. Click the Project Painter icon. This opens the Select Project dialog box (see fig. 16.4).

2. Click New to pull up the project painter.

3. Immediately you will be asked for the executable name in the Select Executable File dialog box, seen in figure 16.5. Choose the executable drive, path, and file name, and click OK.

FIG. 16.4
You can edit a new project or create a new project from the Select Project dialog box.

FIG. 16.5
The Select Executable File dialog box lets you choose what EXE is to be created in the project painter.

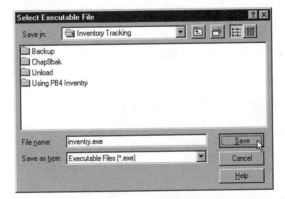

▶ **See** "Understanding Regeneration," **p. 416**

4. Now you will be able to enter information in the project painter, as shown in figure 16.6. Here you can enter resource names and libraries. You also can specify whether or not to regenerate, and whether or not to convert each PBL into a PBD.

FIG. 16.6
Define your project in the project painter.

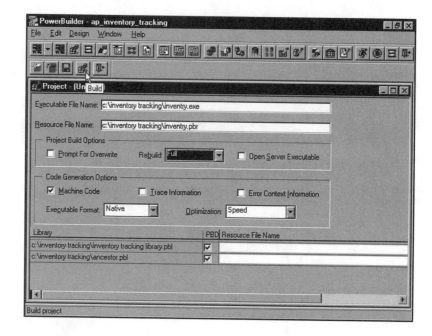

5. After your executable is defined in the project painter, click the Build icon. This will create your EXE file.

After you're finished, every time you use the Project Painter to recompile, the Project Painter regenerates, converts libraries to DLLs, pulls in all desired resources, and compiles your application into a Windows EXE.

You can then save your project into a PBL. When you tell PowerBuilder to save your project, the Save Project dialog box appears (see fig. 16.7).

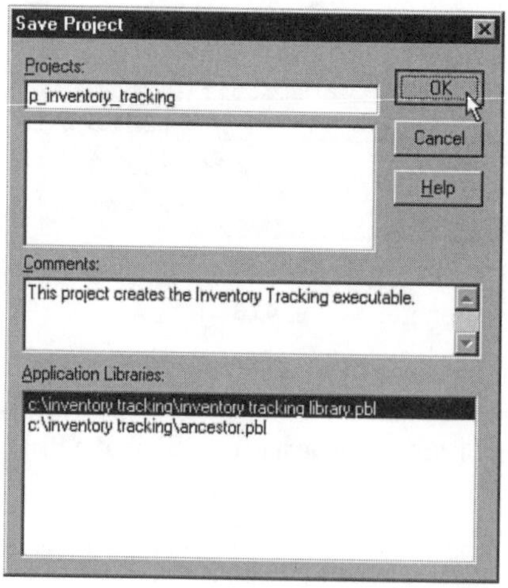

FIG. 16.7
To save your project, enter the name, comments, and PBL of your new project and click OK in the Save Project dialog box.

Projects are a big time saver, and they prevent bad executables or mismatch executables and libraries from being delivered.

Using Resources and PowerBuilder Resource Files (PBRs)

Often, you'll want to include other resources in your executable. A resource is any icon (ICO file), picture (BMP and RLE files), pointer (CUR files), or DataWindow object that you use in your program. For example, you may use a specific icon when a window is minimized, a bit map picture on a DataWindow, or a special mouse pointer for an object. You also may want to switch DataWindow objects of a DataWindow control during run time.

All of these take resources not found in your PBLs. You can have PowerBuilder search the path of the application to try to find them, or you can specify them in a PowerBuilder resource file (PBR).

Building a PowerBuilder Resource File (PBR)

To avoid forcing the user to have these resources in a path, you can make a PowerBuilder resource file. A PBR is an ASCII text file that provides the locations of your resources. For instance, on the d_invoice DataWindow, use bit maps are declared. These bit maps must be present on every computer that runs the Inventory Tracking system. To avoid putting bit maps everywhere, you could just make a resource file before compiling called INVENTRY.PBR. Inside INVENTRY.PBR are the following lines:

```
c:\invent~1\FLATHEAD.bmp
c:\invent~1\HAMMER.bmp
c:\quote\Usingpb5.ico
```

Now reference the resource file either when you compile your INVENTRY.PBD or when you compile your application.

N O T E The two bit maps used were taken from PowerBuilder Version 3. PowerBuilder Version 5 no longer has these bit maps, although several other bit maps are included. ■

You can include resource files in PBDs as well as executables. To include a PBR, type the name of the PBR in the Resource File Name field in the Build Dynamic Runtime Library dialog box (refer to fig. 16.6).

N O T E You may wonder how to decide whether or not to include your resource file in a PBD or in the application. If you include it in the application, the resource is compiled with the application. If you include it in the PBD, the resource is not loaded into memory until it is needed.

If you seldom use the objects that access the resource, then you can compile your resource with the object's PBD. This saves time because the resource is loaded into memory when it's needed.

However, if you use the objects that compile the resource throughout your application, you should compile the resource file with the application. This saves time because the resource only needs to be loaded into memory once and not every time a new PBD is accessed. ■

Adding DataWindow Resources

Sometimes you'll want to change the DataWindow objects of a DataWindow control. For example, if you sold hardware and food, you would want different information about the inventory of each type of product.

To change a DataWindow object during run time, you simply assign the DataObject of the DataWindow control to the new DataWindow Object with the following command:

```
datawindow.DataObject = 'new name'
```

So, if you had a new DataWindow object called "d_item_food" to assign in the place of d_item in the w_item window, you would use the following command:

```
w_item.dw_data.ObjectName = "d_item_food"
```

You would then have to add d_item_food to the resource file with the following line:

```
c:\book\inventry\inventry.pbl(d_item_food)
```

Delivering the Right DLLs Using the Development and Deployment Kit

PowerBuilder offers a Development and Deployment kit. This allows the developer to distribute his or her new executable. To deliver your executable, include the following:

- The EXE
- All DLLs (or PBDs if you're using Windows 3.x) that are used with your EXE
- All resources that are not in an included resource file
- All Database and Database Log files needed for your application
- All DLLs that PowerBuilder includes in its Development and Deployment kit

TROUBLESHOOTING

I distributed my executable, but I still can't connect to my database. Why not? This is always a tricky problem. Here are a few solutions:

1. You did not install the run time version of Sybase SQL Anywhere or your current database when you installed your program.

   ▶ **See** "Using SQL Anywhere," **p. 766**

2. You installed Sybase SQL Anywhere, but did not change the DBENG50 to RTDSK50 or DBENG50W to RTDSK50W and DBENG50S to RTDSK50S for Windows 3.x) for your startup program on your database. Because you are using the run time version, you'll need to do this.

3. You installed your database, but do not have a path set to it in the AUTOEXEC.BAT file (in Windows 3.x) or Registry (in Windows '95 or Windows NT). (For more registry help, consult one of the several Windows '95 books available, such as Special Edition Using Windows '95, from QUE publishing.)

4. You do have the proper path set to the programs in the AUTOEXEC.BAT file, but you haven't rebooted since installing your database to make that path change take effect. (In Windows '95 or Windows NT, this will occur when using older databases or databases designed to work with Windows 3.x.)

5. You didn't include a database log file with your executable.

This is always tricky at first. Play around with the database and make sure that it's pointing to files in their right location, using the right driver, and so on.

Debugging at Run Time

By the time you release your product, it should be flawless. Unfortunately, sometimes bugs creep into a delivered executable. If you included a string of a column on a DataWindow that doesn't exist, or tried to access a window after it was closed, you will receive a system error describing where the error took place. (This is especially true if you coded the system error application event.)

N O T E There is a list of PowerBuilder system messages in chapter 29, "Message Quick Reference." ■

Sometimes, however, the error bypasses the system error event and causes a Windows error. In this case, you may try running your program compiled with the trace checkbox clicked (fig 16.6). This action traces your application by telling you which lines are executed and lets you know exactly where the error occurred. Then, if you run your PowerBuilder program with a /pbdebug switch in the command path, all of your PowerBuilder calls are also placed in a DBG file with the same name as your program.

CAUTION

Use the debug trace as a last resort. Turning on the trace with /pbdebug, entering the Inventory Tracking system, and immediately exiting can generate 504 lines of debug code. Even a simple event with a simple script causes a lot of debug trace statements. If you were to run through an entire program, the result could be more than you're equipped to handle!

Still, there are some errors that debug finds. However, if you can solve your problems without resulting to tracing, you'll be happy you did.

From Here...

This chapter provided information about delivering your executable. You can also consult your PowerBuilder User's Guide on delivering an executable. For related information, consult the following chapters:

- Chapter 14, "Pulling It All Together in an Application," shows you how to finalize your application before you compile.

- Chapter 15, "Debugging Your Applications," demonstrates the debugging process. You'll need to debug your application before compiling.

- Appendix B, "Using SQL Anywhere Database and SQL Anywhere," discusses the differences between the run time and developers' versions of SQL Anywhere. If you're distributing with a SQL Anywhere database, you really should review this chapter carefully.

User Objects and Object-Oriented Development

CHAPTER 17

Understanding Object-Oriented Concepts

by Bill Heys

In this chapter we help you understand the concepts and terminology of object-orientations and how they are used with PowerBuilder. Here are some of the topics that will be covered in this chapter:

Object-orientation is a methodology and approach for developing software. Some goals of object-orientation include increased code reuse, and reduced software maintenance. Object-orientation is not a revolutionary concept. Many aspects of object-orientation build upon earlier methodologies, such as structured design and structured programming.

Object-oriented development promises to increase code reuse and reliability while reducing the cost of software maintenance. It is important to put these promises into perspective. Initially, it may take you longer to design and implement a set of robust, reusable objects. However, if these objects are well designed, carefully implemented, and thoroughly documented, you will be able to use some of them again in future projects.

We often refer to object-oriented development as component-based development. One goal is to improve how we develop software—to the point where we can assemble new systems from existing, pre-engineered components, rather than coding everything from scratch.

Basic object-oriented terminology.

We begin by describing the important terms and concepts of object-orientation.

Defining object attributes and methods.

Look here to see how to construct objects in PowerBuilder.

Differences between functions and events.

Here we illustrate many of the important differences between PowerBuilder functions and events. We help you decide between functions and events when implementing object methods. We also introduce many significant enhancements to using events and functions in PowerBuilder 5.

Understanding inheritance, encapsulation, and polymorphism.

Look here to understand how these important object-oriented features are implemented in PowerBuilder applications.

Object creation and object referencing.

We present many important tips and techniques to avoid memory leaks and orphans in your application.

Classes, Objects, and Instances

PowerBuilder often uses the terms "object" and "class" interchangeably when describing the development process. In this section, we will chart a path through the wilderness by providing some more traditional definitions of important object-orientation terms.

Class

A class is a description or definition of an object or group of similar objects. Classes are templates or blueprints used for building objects. A class defines the data contained in an object and the processing done by an object.

You may have been told that you develop objects in the PowerBuilder painters, and save these objects in a PowerBuilder library (PBL). From an object-oriented perspective, you are actually defining classes in the PowerBuilder painters, and storing these classes in your PowerBuilder libraries.

Most people build PowerBuilder applications primarily by defining visual classes: windows, window controls, menus, and DataWindows. In the user object painter, you can also define standard and custom visual classes.

PowerBuilder offers a number of system classes, including powerobject, graphicobject, window, message, error, transaction, and many more.

In this chapter and the next, we will show you how you can build nonvisual classes in the user object painter.

Objects

An object is a software package containing data and processing that works with or is closely related to the data. Objects are the basic building blocks or components of object-oriented development.

Objects communicate with each other by sending messages. In PowerBuilder, an object sends a message by calling a function, triggering an event, or posting an event in another object. In PowerBuilder 5, it will be possible to trigger functions as well as events.

The object sending the message acts as a client, and the object receiving the message acts as a server. For this reason, object-oriented applications fit nicely into the world of client-server, message-based computing.

Instance

Instances are objects created from classes at run time. You can think of an object as a run-time instance of a class. It is possible to create many objects from the same class. Let's say you define a new window class in the window painter called w_employee_maint. You can create an instance of this class by opening the window at run time. For example:

```
Open (w_employee_maint)
```

Classes Versus Instances

Each object created from a class contains the same attributes and has the same methods. However, values assigned to an object's attributes may be different for each instance of the class.

Where I live in New England, it is common to see housing developments where all the houses on the street look identical. Think of an architect's blueprint as a class definition, and houses built from the blueprint as objects or instances of the class. After they are constructed, individual houses may be painted different colors or decorated differently. The houses may each be a different color, but they are all structurally the same.

Object Components

Since a class is a description or definition of an object, it is in the class that you define the components of an object. In this section we describe object components and show how they are implemented in the classes you create with PowerBuilder.

Part
V

Ch
17

Attributes

Attributes are data values or variables stored in an object. In PowerBuilder, use instance variables to define attributes for your class. For example, let's say you have a w_customer_list window requiring an attribute for customer id. In this window, define a long instance variable called il_customer_id.

 TIP Our naming convention has a variable prefix indicating both variable scope and datatype (il for instance scope and long datatype).

Each time you open a new instance of w_customer_list, PowerBuilder allocates memory from the instance memory pool to hold values assigned to the object's instance variables.

Services and Operations

Services and operations are the processing performed by a class. A class may provide one or more services to other classes on request. Classes may also have internal operations not accessible to other classes. An object's behavior consists of its services and operations implemented in its class.

Methods

A method is an implementation of an operation or service in a class. In PowerBuilder, you can implement a class method as an object function or event. The event can be either a PowerBuilder-defined event such as Constructor or Destructor, or a user-defined event in the class.

To print your w_customer_list window, you would define a print method in the w_customer_list class.

Functions

One choice would be to implement the print method in your window as a window function, wf_print ( ). You could print your customer list window from another object by calling the function using dot notation (instance-name . function-name):

```
lw_customer_list2 . wf_print ()
lw_customer_list3 . wf_print ()
```

Events

Alternatively, you could implement the print method in your window as a user-defined event, we_print. You would then invoke printing by triggering or posting the event:

```
lw_customer_list2 . TriggerEvent ( 'we_print' )
lw_customer_list3 . PostEvent ( 'we_print' )
```

Inheritance

Inheritance is the ability to define new classes from existing classes. A descendant class inherits all of the attributes and methods defined for its ancestor class. Inheritance is a way of incorporating, without copying, ancestor class characteristics into the definition of a new class.

You can define new attributes and methods in the new class. The descendant class can also extend or add to the behavior of inherited methods, or alternatively, can provide replacements to override inherited methods. Inheritance is sometimes also called subtyping or subclassing.

In PowerBuilder you can have many levels of inheritance, but at any level, a class can have only one ancestor class. This is called single inheritance. Some languages support multiple inheritance, where a class can have more than one direct ancestor. Multiple inheritance is often difficult to use when there are conflicting attributes or methods defined in the ancestor classes.

All visual classes have a common ancestor, the PowerBuilder graphicobject system class. Because windows, menus, and window controls are visible classes, they inherit attributes from the graphicobject class to define their visible properties. These attributes include: x and y (for positioning), height and width (for size), color, visible, and so on.

You can also create standard, custom, or C++ nonvisual classes in the user object painter. We will introduce you to the user object painter in the next chapter.

PowerBuilder itself provides a robust set of system classes. The system classes have a very high level of reuse because they are used as ancestors for all classes defined by PowerBuilder developers. Now you can see how object-oriented development can achieve high levels of code reuse.

Encapsulation

One of the key features of object-oriented development is the ability to encapsulate objects behind a public interface. Encapsulated objects are more independent of each other. Object independence leads to more reusable objects and less software maintenance. In this section we describe encapsulation and how it is implemented.

What Is Encapsulation?

Encapsulation begins when we group data and operations together into a software package known as an object. Encapsulation is also a form of information hiding, where an object hides its internal implementation details from view.

All classes should be encapsulated. Classes should restrict or control access to their internal attributes. A class may also have internal methods that other classes cannot access. In this chapter we will illustrate some techniques for hiding the implementation details of an object.

Part

V

Ch

17

I often use the following analogy to explain encapsulation. When I was a young child, I received a vacuum tube radio for my bedside table as a birthday present. The radio encapsulated its circuitry inside a hard plastic case for my protection. To operate the radio, I could slide the on-off switch, turn the volume knob, and spin the tuning dial. These three controls constituted my public interface to the radio.

Several years later I was given a newer, transistorized radio. The new radio had the same public interface as the older radio: on-off switch, volume knob, and tuning dial. The internal circuitry was more compact and energy-efficient. I noticed that the transistor radio was cooler than the vacuum tube radio. I didn't have to learn a new interface or change how I operated the radio in order to take advantage of more up-to-date electronics.

Narrow, clearly defined object interfaces are an important benefit of encapsulation. As long as the public interface to an object does not change, the internals of the object can change without impacting users of the object. In PowerBuilder, we encapsulate an object by making its attributes private, or protected. The object's public interface is implemented by defining public events or functions in the class.

Variable Scope

In order to encapsulate your object's attributes, you must define variables of the proper scope and access. PowerBuilder has four levels of scope for variables: global, local, instance, and shared. The scope of a variable determines its life span in memory.

Global variables have application-wide scope, meaning they are allocated in memory when the application starts up, and remain in memory until the application shuts down. Global variables can be defined in the script painter from any object, and have a broader scope than shared, instance, or local variables.

Local variables are variables declared inside a specific script. PowerScript allocates memory for local variables when the script begins executing, and removes them from memory when the script finishes executing. Local variables have narrower scope than global, shared, or instance variables. Since local variables never exist outside a single script, I often describe them as temporary variables.

Instance variables are defined in a class and exist for each object or instance of a class. When an object is created, memory is allocated for all its instance variables. When an object is destroyed, its instance variables are removed from memory. Each instance of a class has a separate set of instance variables. Class attributes are usually defined as instance variables.

Shared variables are sometimes called class variables. All instances of a class share a common set of shared variables. Memory for shared variables is allocated when the first instance of a class is created. Once allocated, shared variables retain their values in memory until the application shuts down.

N O T E Class attributes can be encapsulated in an object only if they are defined with instance or shared scope. ■

Public, Private, and Protected Access

The first step in encapsulating any object is to restrict access to the object's attributes. You should specify an explicit access right when you define instance variables. Your access right choices are public, private, or protected. You may specify access rights only for instance variables and object functions. Private instance variables and private shared variables are visible only to other scripts defined in the same class. This is the most restrictive access right.

Public instance variables are part of an object's public interface. Any script in any object can directly access public attributes or change their values. This is the least restrictive access right.

Protected instance variables are visible only to scripts defined in the same class or descendants of the class. Unrelated classes are unable to directly access protected attributes in another class.

 T I P Since public variables are not encapsulated, make all class attributes either private or protected.

It is much easier to broaden the access restriction than it is to narrow it after you make an attribute part of the public interface to a class. When in doubt, begin by making all attributes private. Then broaden access to protected if necessary. Never make class attributes public. Instead, define public methods in the class for accessing or updating its attributes.

To fully understand access rights, consider the following:

■ Access rights are enforced by the PowerScript compiler.
■ Shared variables are always private and cannot be made public or protected.

- Since global variables are not contained in any object, they are always public and cannot be encapsulated or made private or protected.

- Local variables exist only for the duration of a single script execution, therefore access restrictions are not defined for local variables.

There are two ways of specifying access rights when you define instance variables (see figs. 17.1 and 17.2):

- The grouping approach

- The individual, line-by-line approach

FIG. 17.1
The Declare Instance Variables dialog box, showing access rights specified for groups of variables.

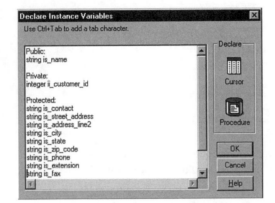

FIG. 17.2
The Declare Instance Variables dialog box, showing access rights specified for each variable.

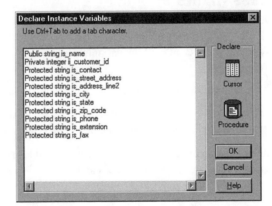

The library entries browser allows you to search selected entries in your PowerBuilder libraries for matching string values. Figure 17.3 shows the result of searching several library entries for variable names beginning with "is_."

TIP Specify the access right on each variable declaration so the library entries browser will display it when you do a search on the variable name.

FIG. 17.3
The library entries browser displays this Matching Library Entries dialog box, showing access rights specified on each variable declaration.

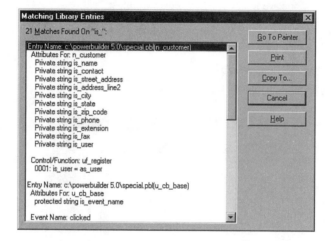

Private and protected class attributes are now encapsulated and hidden from direct manipulation by other objects. You now need to provide a public interface to allow other objects to access or change attribute values.

Read and Write Access Rights

In PowerBuilder 5, you will also be able to define read and write access rights in addition to an overall access-right. For a specified access right, you control access with modifier keywords. The modifiers specify which scripts can read the variable's value and which scripts can change it. The syntax is:

```
{ access-right } { ReadAccess } { WriteAccess } datatype variablename
```

The *ReadAccess* modifier is an optional keyword for instance variables restricting the ability of scripts to read the variable's value. ReadAccess can be either ProtectedRead or PrivateRead.

The *WriteAccess* modifier is an optional keyword for instance variables restricting the ability of scripts to change the variable's value. WriteAccess can be either ProtectedWrite or PrivateWrite.

If specified, ReadAccess and WriteAccess must be more restrictive than the variable's overall access-right. For example, if a variable's access-right is public, you can give it a ReadAccess of ProtectedRead or PrivateRead and a WriteAccess of ProtectedWrite or PrivateWrite. If the variable's access-right is protected, you can only specify ReadAccess of PrivateRead and WriteAccess of PrivateWrite. If a variable's access-right is private, you cannot specify either ReadAccess or WriteAccess. Here are some examples:

```
public integer ii_public
public protectedread protectedwrite integer ii_protread_protwrite
public protectedread privatewrite integer ii_protread_privwrite
public privateread protectedwrite integer ii_privread_protwrite
public privateread privatewrite integer ii_privread_privwrite
public protectedread integer ii_protread
public protectedwrite integer ii_protwrite
public privateread integer ii_privread
public privatewrite integer ii_privwrite

protected integer ii_protected
protected privateread privatewrite integer ii_prot_privread_privwrite
protected privateread integer ii_prot_privread
protected privatewrite integer ii_prot_privwrite

private integer ii_private
```

You can have a variable with public access that can only be read or written by the owner object and, possibly, by its descendants.

```
public ProtectedRead ProtectedWrite integer ii_count
public PrivateRead PrivateWrite integer ii_reserved
```

By defining overall access-rights as public, you can reserve the variable name preventing descendant objects from defining another variable with the same name. The compiler will also generate a warning if you define a local variable with the same name in the object or in its descendants.

Defining the Public Interface

For read-only access to a private or protected attribute, define a public function to return the value of the attribute. For update access to a private or protected attribute, define a public function with an argument for passing a new value of the attribute. Public functions become part of an object's public interface.

Here is an example. Create a custom class business object called n_customer. Define the attributes of customer as private or protected instance variables (see fig. 17.4).

FIG. 17.4
This dialog box shows the attributes of a custom class defined as private instance variables.

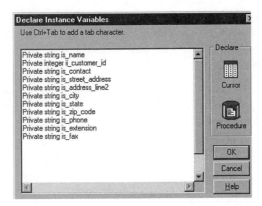

Now define public functions to return the values of some of your object's attributes, for example:

```
public function long uf_get_l_customer_id ()
Return il_customer_idpublic function string uf_get_s_street_address ()
Return is_street_address
```

Next, define public functions to allow other objects to change some of the values of your customer attributes.

```
public Subroutine uf_set_s_customer_name (string as_name)
is_name = as_name
```

This may seem like a lot of extra work. You might be asking: Why not simply make the attributes public? It would make your life much simpler!

In the short term, it certainly may seem a lot easier to make your object attributes directly accessible. However, your object will be less reusable and less independent of other objects. When you properly encapsulate your object, changes to your object will be less likely to cause unnecessary maintenance of other objects in your application.

Here are some more reasons why you should encapsulate your attributes:

■ Your object is notified when other objects access or change its attributes.

■ You have more control over access and changes to your instance variables.

■ You can implement security on both read and update functions.

■ You can implement validations in your update functions.

■ You can provide read-only access to an attribute without providing update access.

By defining a public `uf_get_xx ( )` function without defining a `uf_set_xx ( )` function for an attribute, the attribute becomes read-only to other objects using the class.

When you make your instance variables public, they become part of the public interface to a class. As we said earlier, it is very difficult to make access more restrictive once development begins. Whenever you change the public interface to an object, you need to determine the impact of the change on other objects.

Suppose your application needs special processing for senior citizens. You define a public attribute, ii_age in your customer class. For the purpose of this example, let's also assume you have implemented a function to update the customer's age on an annual basis, based on another attribute, id_birthdate.

Since it is a public attribute, any other object could directly access the customer's age attribute; for example:

```
int li_age
c_customer ic_customer
ic_customer = create c_customer
li_age = ic_customer . ii_age
```

By defining ii_age as a public attribute, you will be unable to prevent other objects from changing a customer's age directly. Your object won't even be notified when another object changes its customer age. You will not be able to rely on the value in age being accurate.

Therefore, you should define age as a private instance variable. Define a public function giving other objects read-only access to customer age. Now your customer class can control when and how customer age is changed. The example from above now becomes:

```
int li_age
c_customer ic_customer
ic_customer = create c_customer
li_age = ic_customer . uf_get_i_age ()
```

When you store a customer's age, you have to update its value on an annual basis on the customer's birthdate. Instead of storing age as an attribute, you could calculate age on request. Your method, instead of simply returning the value of a customer's age, can be changed to calculate age using today's date and the customer's birthdate. The function, uf_get_i_age ( ) changes only internally. You can eliminate the age attribute altogether.

What will be the impact of this change on other objects? As long as the public interface remains the same, other objects will be unaware of the change. The public function uf_get_i_age ( ) still returns a customer's age, but calculates age on request instead of returning a stored value.

Compared to objects that allow uncontrolled public access to their attributes, properly encapsulated objects are more independent of other objects. Code in encapsulated objects will be more reusable. If you change the internal implementation of a class, without changing its public interface your changes will not impact other objects. Lower software maintenance will result.

 TIP Since it is easier to loosen restrictions than it is to tighten them up later, it is much better to start out by encapsulating too much rather than too little.

Functions Versus Events

Developers are often uncertain whether to implement class methods as functions or as events. In this section, we describe some of the key differences between functions and events.

PowerBuilder 5.0 will eliminate many of the distinctions between functions and events. Using new keywords you will be able to call events with arguments like functions, post functions and events for later execution, and specify run-time type checking of events and functions (static vs. dynamic binding).

Message Timing

Message timing determines when an object will receive a message sent to it. Messages are either synchronous or asynchronous. Triggered events and called functions execute synchronously. The sender of the message waits while the triggered event in the receiving object executes. Control returns to the invoking script.

Part
V

Ch
17

PowerBuilder 5 introduces the ability to post functions as well as events. Posted events and posted functions execute asynchronously. Posted messages are placed onto a queue. The sending script finishes executing before the posted message executes.

Information Passing

Information passing determines how you pass information as part of a message. In PowerBuilder 5, with both functions and events, you can now pass explicit named arguments.

In prior versions of PowerBuilder, when you trigger or post events, you often do not pass explicit arguments to the event. There are, however, two optional parameters (word and long) on the `TriggerEvent ( )` and `PostEvent ( )` functions. PowerBuilder uses the message object to pass this information to events. It will store the value passed in the word parameter in the WordParm attribute, and value passed in the long parameter in LongParm attribute of the message object.

In PowerBuilder 5, you will be able to define named arguments on user-defined events for passing values when they are triggered. We have traditionally preferred functions over events primarily for the ability to pass named arguments and get back return values when they are called. Defining named arguments to a function or event helps to document the message interface.

Typing

Strongly typed languages will not permit you to compile references to a class unless the class has already been defined. Since PowerBuilder is a strongly typed language, calls to object-level functions and references to object instance variables are checked at compile time. The compiler ensures that a function or variable has been properly defined before you can reference it in a script.

On the other hand, user-defined events are weakly typed in PowerBuilder. Weak typing means the compiler will not check to see if a posted or triggered event actually exists in the receiving object at compile time. At run time, the `TriggerEvent ( )` or `PostEvent ( )` function will simply return a -1 if the event does not exist, or if no script exists for the event in the target object. No run-time failure will occur.

PowerBuilder 5 will introduce optional strong typing of events and weak typing of functions. Two new keywords, "static" (for compile-time checking) and "dynamic" (for run-time checking) are now options when calling functions or triggering events.

Method Encapsulation

Object-level events are always public and cannot be hidden or encapsulated inside the object. Since events cannot be made private or protected, they are always part of an object's public interface.

Object-level functions, on the other hand, can be hidden by specifying private or protected access. Public functions, like events, however, will be part of the object's public interface.

TIP Internal operations are operations that are only accessible to other scripts in the same class. To implement an internal operation, define a private or protected function.

Ease of Discovery

The script painter shows all events defined for the object in the paste event drop-down listbox. All events, whether defined in the descendant or inherited from the ancestor, appear in this list. In addition, this listbox shows which events have scripts defined, and whether the scripts are defined in the ancestor, descendant, or both.

The script painter, on the other hand, doesn't show any inherited functions when you open the declare function painter. It is also much more difficult to determine whether an ancestor function contains script or is simply defined as a stub. For this reason, ancestor functions are much harder to discover than ancestor events.

PowerBuilder 5 now has an improved object browser that makes it easier to see ancestor functions inherited by class (see fig. 17.5).

Part

V

Ch

17

FIG. 17.5

The object browser dialog box, showing the functions defined for the powerobject system class.

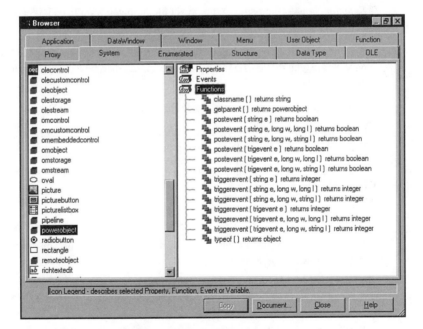

New PowerBuilder Syntax for Events and Functions

There are several keywords that control how object functions and events are called. The new syntax can be used in place of the TriggerEvent and PostEvent functions found in prior versions of PowerBuilder:

```
{ objectname.} { type } { calltype } { when } functionname ( { argumentlist } )
```

Objectname is the name of the object where the function is defined or the descendant of that object.

Type is an optional keyword specifying whether you are calling a function or event. Values are FUNCTION (Default) and EVENT.

Calltype is an optional keyword specifying whether PowerBuilder does compile-time or run-time type checking of the event or function. Values are STATIC (Default) and DYNAMIC. When Static is specified, PowerBuilder checks for the existence of the function or event when the code is compiled. If it isn't found, you get a compiler error. When Dynamic is specified, PowerBuilder will not check for the existence of the event or function until run time. At that time, if it doesn't exist, you get a run-time error.

When is an optional keyword specifying whether the function or event should execute immediately or after the current script is finished. Values are: TRIGGER (Default) and POST. A Triggered function or event executes immediately (synchronously). A Posted event or function is put into the object's message queue and will execute after other pending messages have executed (asynchronously).

FunctionName is the name of the object function you want to call. It can be a PowerScript function or a user-defined function belonging to the class of *objectname*.

Argumentlist specifies the values you want to pass to *functionname*. Each value in the list must have a data type that corresponds to the declared data type in the function or event definition or declaration.

The *type, calltype*, and *when* keywords can be in any order after the dot.

Calls can be cascaded using dot notation. Each function call must return an object type that is the appropriate object for the following function.

To post a user-defined event, we_retrieve, in window w_customer with run-time type checking, use one of the following:

```
w_customer . PostEvent('we_retrieve') // familiar syntax
w_customer . EVENT DYNAMIC POST we_retrieve( ) // new syntax
```

To trigger a user-defined event, we_retrieve, in window w_customer with run-time type checking, use one of the following:

```
w_customer . TriggerEvent('we_retrieve') // familiar syntax
w_customer . EVENT DYNAMIC TRIGGER we_retrieve( ) // new syntax
w_customer . EVENT DYNAMIC we_retrieve( ) // new syntax with defaults
```

To trigger a user-defined event, we_retrieve, in window w_customer with compile-time type checking, use one of the following:

```
w_customer . EVENT STATIC TRIGGER we_retrieve( ) // new syntax
w_customer . EVENT we_retrieve( ) // new syntax with defaults
```

To call a user-defined function, wf_retrieve, in window w_customer with compile-time type checking, use one of the following:

```
w_customer . wf_retrieve() // familiar syntax
w_customer . FUNCTION STATIC TRIGGER wf_retrieve( ) // new syntax
```

To post a user-defined function, wf_retrieve, in window w_customer with compile-time type checking, use one of the following:

```
w_customer . FUNCTION STATIC POST wf_retrieve( ) // new syntax
w_customer . POST wf_retrieve() // new syntax with defaults
```

From a window control, to call a user-defined function in the parent window, use one of the following:

```
Parent . wf_retrieve( ) // familiar syntax using defaults
Parent . FUNCTION STATIC TRIGGER wf_retrieve( ) // alternative syntax
```

The preceding statements are equivalent because FUNCTION, STATIC, and TRIGGER are the defaults. PowerBuilder will check for the existence of the function at compile time, and will call the function synchronously.

In the next example, the clicked event of a DataWindow control triggers the doubleclicked event for the same control. The arguments passed to clicked event from the system are passed through to the doubleclicked event.

```
This. EVENT DoubleClicked(li_xpos, li_ypos, ll_row, ldw_datawindow)
```

This statement posts (asynchronously) the same event:

```
This. EVENT POST DoubleClicked(li_xpos, li_ypos, ll_row, ldw_datawindow)
```

In the next example, a menu script calls a window function, wf_print, using a reference variable for an ancestor window, w_base_sheet. Since the function is not defined in the w_base_sheet class, the DYNAMIC keyword is specified so that the script will compile.

```
w_base_sheet iw_base_sheet
iw_base_sheet = w_frame . GetActiveSheet()
iw_base_sheet. DYNAMIC wf_print( )
```

At run time, the actual window opened will be a descendant of w_base_sheet containing a definition of wf_print. A reference to that window is assigned to iw_base_sheet and the call to wf_print succeeds.

Overriding and Extending Methods

Ancestor events can easily be overridden or extended in the descendant object with a simple compile-time selection. To override an ancestor object's functions, add an implementation of the function to the descendant object. The ancestor function and descendant function should have the same signature (function name, number, and types of parameters). They should also both return the same datatype.

It is harder to extend a function inherited from an ancestor class. The descendant function needs explicitly to call the ancestor's function. For this purpose, use the reserved word, Super, in place of a direct reference to the ancestor object's name with the :: navigation operator:

```
ancestorobject :: { type } { when } functionname ( { argumentlist } )
```

Ancestorobject is the classname of the object whose function or event you want to execute. The pronoun *Super* provides the appropriate reference when ancestorobject is the immediate ancestor of the current object.

```
Super :: uf_init ()
Call Super :: ue_init ()
```

The navigation operator on the CALL statement provides the ability to call an event of a control in the ancestor window. The event will always be triggered, and you cannot specify arguments for the event. For example, in the clicked event of cb_retrieve on window w_customer (which is a descendant of w_base_sheet) you can call the ancestor's clicked event:

```
CALL w_base_sheet ' cb_retrieve :: clicked
```

Object Coupling

In addition to passing named arguments to a function, you can also share information between objects implicitly in a variety of ways.

Some developers use global variables to share information between objects. There are many problems with global variables. Global variables have the effect of creating dependencies among all your objects. These dependencies are a type of object coupling. The more global variables you have, the more coupling exists between objects.

If one object needs a value in a global variable, you have to do a lot of research to see how other objects set the value. If you want to change the value of a global variable, you need to assess the impact of this change on other users of this variable. For global variables, potentially every script in every object uses the variable. Impact analysis for global variables is time-consuming.

To reduce object coupling, the sender of a message should explicitly pass only the values needed by the receiver of the message. The communication interface between the caller of a function and the receiver of the function can be more narrowly defined using named parameters. A message with explicit arguments is better documented than a message which relies on global variables for passing values between objects. This approach succeeds only if by convention, mutual agreement, or decree, all developers understand this issue, and explicitly pass all needed values as message arguments from the sender to the receiver.

When objects are coupled, they become more intertwined. Changes to one object are more likely to affect other objects coupled with it. An important goal of object-orientation is to minimize object coupling and maximize object independence.

Defining Message Interfaces

There are many techniques for defining message interfaces. In this section, we will compare various techniques for passing arguments to functions or events. We want to choose a technique that minimizes unnecessary coupling between objects. We also want the interface to be self-documenting.

In this section we will explore the question: When we have many values to pass as arguments to a function or event, should we pass them as individual named arguments, attributes of a structure, or attributes of an object?

Passing Named Arguments

In this approach, all information is passed as explicit named arguments to the function or event. Only necessary information is passed with the message. For example, define a function as:

```
Public Function boolean f_validate_dates ( date ad_entry_date,  &
    date ad_trade_date, date ad_settlement_date)
```

An advantage with this approach is that the argument names help to document the interface. Object coupling is reduced, because no unnecessary data is passed with the message. Both the author of the calling script and the author of the called function have a clear idea of the meaning of each parameter. Fewer misunderstandings and bugs result.

A disadvantage with this approach is the effort required to add or remove a parameter from the interface. The function declaration must be changed, and all of the calling scripts must also be changed. It is unlikely, however, that you can ever change the interface to a message without also changing the calling scripts.

Part
V
Ch
17

Passing Structures

Some developers prefer to pass structures in place of long lists of arguments. It is acceptable to pass a structure to a function as long as all the attributes of the structure are used by the function.

Anytime you pass to a function a structure containing attributes the function doesn't need or use, you unnecessarily increase the dependency between the calling and receiving objects. This type of dependency is sometimes called stamp coupling.

 TIP

When you use structures as arguments to a function, there is a tendency to define a single generic structure for all message passing. The result is that the structure may contain attributes that are not needed for a given message. In order to avoid passing unneeded attributes, define a separate structure for each message interface.

An advantage of using structures is that when you add or remove attributes from the message interface, both the sending and receiving objects will change together. You will minimize the possibility that a calling script sends arguments different from those the function expects to receive.

A disadvantage with structures is that they cannot be inherited from existing structures. I often characterize structures as objects that are inheritance- and function-impaired. It is difficult, therefore, for class libraries to define a generic approach for message processing without defining in advance all of the arguments one object would ever need to pass in a message to another object.

Some commercial class libraries use a generic structure for passing parameters. In the application framework libraries distributed with previous versions of PowerBuilder, a global structure, str_parms, is used for passing information between objects. In figure 17.6 it contains arrays of simple datatypes.

FIG. 17.6

This is the definition of global structure, str_parms, from the PowerBuilder 4.0 application library.

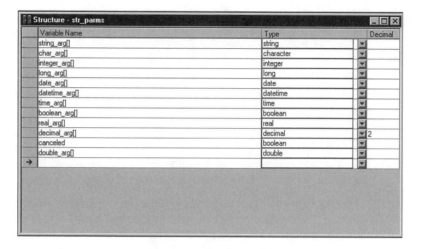

When you look at str_parms, you can't tell anything about the meaning of the actual arguments passed in it to a function. If you are writing a script that passes str_parms to a function, you can't simply look at the function declaration to know how to initialize str_parms before passing it to the function. Without examining the function script itself, you can't tell which array elements are used and how they are used.

Suppose you are developing a mutual fund trade entry system, and need to pass a security trade date, entry date, and settlement date as arguments to a function. Using str_parms, the sending script might put the trade date into date_arg[1], entry date into date_arg[2], and settlement date into date_arg[3]. By looking at the str_parms in the debugger, can you tell which entry in the array is the trade date? Probably not. What if the function expected trade date in date_arg[2] and entry date in date_arg[1]? You will have a bug that is hard to find. The generic structure interface is not self-documenting.

Passing Objects

We recommend using custom classes instead of structures in most situations. It is almost as easy to define a new custom class as it is to define a structure with the same attributes.

An advantage of using custom classes is that you can define a common ancestor or base custom class. A class library can now define a generic message-passing approach using the base class as an argument. At run time, an instance of a descendant class can be passed when the function or event is called.

Let's say you have a function for opening sheets in your application. You want to pass multiple arguments to a sheet when it is opened. A class library does not need to know in advance exactly what arguments you want to pass to a specific sheet. So you define a generic window-level function in the MDI frame, w_frame:

```
Public Function Integer wf_opensheet(window aw_window, & n_base_class
an_base_class)
```

For a specific sheet such as w_order_entry, define a custom class, n_order_entry, which is a descendant of n_base_class. The custom class will have instance variables for each of the arguments you want to pass to the sheet. When you open w_order_entry, create and initialize the attributes of an instance of n_order_entry:

```
n_order_entry ln_order_entry
ln_order_entry = create n_order_entry
// initialize attributes here
w_frame. wf_opensheet ( w_order_entry, ln_order_entry)
```

The custom class combines all the advantages of structures with the reusability of inheritance.

Function Overloading

Function Overloading allows you to define more than one version of a function within the same class. Overloaded functions have the same name and return type. They differ only in the number or types of arguments defined.

To see an example of an overloaded PowerScript function, go into the library painter and bring up the object browser. From the menu, select Utilities, then Browse Objects. You will now see a tab display of class (object) types. Click the System tab (see fig. 17.7).

Part
V

Ch
17

FIG. 17.7

The object browser dialog box, showing how the TriggerEvent() function is overloaded in the powerobject system class.

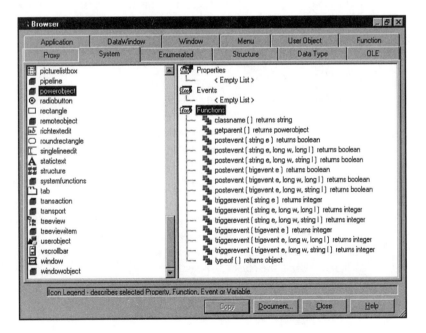

The System tab has two panes. The left pane displays a list of PowerScript system classes, and the right pane has a tree object with folders to display class properties and class functions. Scroll through the list of PowerScript system classes in the left pane, and select the powerobject class. You can view the list of powerobject functions by double-clicking the Functions folder in the right pane.

Notice that both the PostEvent and TriggerEvent functions are overloaded within the power-object class. The TriggerEvent function has six different implementations or overloaded versions. Each version of the function has the same name and returns the same datatype. Overloaded functions can differ only with respect to the number or types of arguments.

For example, you can trigger an event in an object by calling the TriggerEvent function and passing a string in the first argument containing the name of a user-defined event:

```
w_customer . TriggerEvent ('ue_retrieve')
```

You can also trigger an event in an object by passing an enumerated value of the trigger event datatype specifying a PowerScript-defined event:

```
w_customer . dw_1 . TriggerEvent ( Clicked! )
```

A benefit of overloading is being able to have optional arguments for a function. PowerScript will invoke the correct implementation of a function based on the number and types of arguments passed when you call the function.

PowerScript has overloaded its implementation of the string function. You can pass a date, datetime, integer, double, float, time, or decimal value as the first argument to the string function.

Until PowerBuilder version 5, it was not possible for you to overload user-defined functions. The PowerScript compiler would not allow you to define more than one function with the same name in the same class.

To overcome this limitation, many developers used inheritance to implement a form of function overloading. Start by defining an object function in a class. Using this class as an ancestor, create a descendant class and define a different implementation of the same function. Be sure to use the same function name and return data type. Using this second class as an ancestor, define another descendant class with a different implementation of the function. For each overloaded version of the function, you must define a new level of inheritance in the class hierarchy.

Many developers find it cumbersome and inefficient to create new levels of inheritance simply to achieve the benefits of function overloading. PowerBuilder 5 will now allow you to define your own overloaded functions within the same class. You can see the various implementations of a function using the object browser (see fig. 17.8)

FIG. 17.8

This dialog box shows several definitions of an overloaded function, uf_register, within the same class.

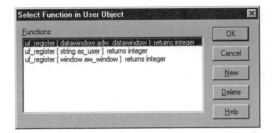

Polymorphism

Polymorphism is derived from a Greek word meaning many forms. In object-oriented software, it means different objects are able to respond differently to the same message.

For example, if you send an update message to a customer-form window, it knows to update the customer table. If you send an update message to an employee form, it knows to update the employee table. In this example, the message name is the same: update. The implementation of update is different in the two objects.

The primary benefits of polymorphism are that a sender of a message (client) does not need to know the specific type of receiving object (server) in order to be able to send messages to it. Regardless of the server object type, the client object sends the same message, update.

Message Binding

Message binding determines when a specific implementation of a message is selected and bound to the sender of the message. Some languages bind all messages at compile time; some bind messages at link-edit time; still others wait until run time to bind a message to its sender.

Static binding requires the sender of a message to identify the type of object receiving the message at compile time or link edit time. An advantage of static binding is that there will be fewer run-time errors caused by an inability to find a suitable implementation of a message.

Dynamic binding allows the sender of a message to identify the actual object receiving a message at run time. Most object-oriented languages support dynamic binding as a way of providing polymorphism. Smalltalk is a pure object-oriented language that uses dynamic binding for all messages sent between objects. Dynamic binding tends to offer greater flexibility during development at the risk of more run-time errors.

PowerBuilder uses a combination of dynamic binding and inheritance to implement function overloading and polymorphism. PowerBuilder will bind to or select a function only if its signature matches the actual parameters passed on a function call. A function's signature consists of the function name and the number and data types of each of the function's arguments.

Part
V

Ch
17

Reference Variables

When you declare a variable in PowerBuilder, you define its scope, access, and datatype. In PowerBuilder, a variable's datatype can be:

- Standard
- Enumerated
- Structure
- Class

Standard datatypes include integer, string, date, double, and so on. PowerBuilder does not allow you to define new standard datatypes.

Enumerated datatypes are like designer datatypes. Enumerated datatype variables can contain only a value from a list of predefined values for that datatype. PowerBuilder today does not permit you to define your own enumerated datatypes, nor add to the predefined list of values for a PowerBuilder-defined enumerated type.

User-defined structures can be either global structures or object-level structures. Global structures are defined in the PowerBuilder structure painter.

NOTE A global structure is a template. While the definition of the structure is global, not all instances of the structure must have global scope. Any object can declare an instance of a global structure with local, instance, or shared scope.

Instances of a global structure can have any scope. The scope of the instance is determined by the scope of the structure identifier. For an object-level structure, instances of the structure can be defined only in the same class or descendant classes.

Class variables can be defined for Powersoft system classes such as PowerObject, Window, Menu, or DragObject. Class variables can also be defined for user-defined classes. User-defined classes are defined in a painter such as window, menu, or user object. When you define a user object, you are defining a new class or type.

A class variable has the name of a class as a datatype. It can contain a pointer or reference to an instance of its declared class or one of its descendants. Since the variable contains a pointer, not an actual object, it is also called a reference variable. If you define an array of class variables, it is an array of pointers or references. An array of window variables is simply an array of pointers to window instances.

When you assign an object reference to a reference variable, you are only copying a pointer to an object from one reference to another. In PowerBuilder, objects themselves are not copied during reference assignment.

Constants

Starting with PowerBuilder 5, you will be able to define constants in your applications. Any identifiers of standard or enumerated data type that can be assigned an initial value can be defined as a constant. Constants have any scope (global, shared, instance, or local). Use the new keyword, CONSTANT, in the variable declaration. A constant is initialized to a value when it is declared. The value is assigned at compile time and cannot be changed at run time by any script. A constant must be initialized to a value in the declaration. Here are some examples of local constants (caps are for emphasis only):

```
CONSTANT string ls_name = "William B. Heys"
CONSTANT real lr_pi = 3.14159265
```

Object Creation

Class variables are different from standard datatype and structure variables. When you declare an identifier for a standard data type or structure instance, memory is allocated when the identifier comes into scope, and is released when the identifier goes out of scope. Class variables require memory explicitly allocated to a class instance. If a class variable does not point to a valid instance of its class or descendant class, it is considered to be an invalid or null object reference.

Instances of visual classes can be created at run time using a form of the PowerBuilder Open ( ) function. The following script opens an instance of the w_customer_list class by specifying the classname of the window to open:

```
Open ( w_customer_list )
```

To create multiple instances of the w_customer_list class, you need explicitly to declare reference variables to point to each instance:

```
w_customer_list lw_customer_list2, lw_customer_list3
Open ( lw_customer_list2 )
Open ( lw_customer_list3 )
```

You can also create nonvisual objects using the Create statement. For example, SQLCA is the instance name assigned to the default global transaction object that PowerBuilder creates for you.

You can create multiple instances of the nonvisual PowerBuilder transaction system class:

```
transaction SQL_trans_one, SQL_trans_two
SQL_trans_one = Create transaction
SQL_trans_two = Create transaction
```

PowerBuilder 5 will introduce dynamic creation of objects, where the class is not known at compile time. For example:

```
string ls_classname
ls_classname = 'n_customer'
CREATE USING ls_classname
```

Part
V

Ch

17

The using expression can be a string constant, a string variable, an "any" variable, or an expression that returns a string or an "any."

Passing Arguments by Value, Reference, or Readonly

A function's definition determines how its arguments are passed. In PowerBuilder 5 the choices are to pass an argument by value, by reference, or readonly. If a function expects an argument to be passed by reference, you must call the function using a variable, not a literal. You can pass variables to a function by value or by reference, but you can pass literals only by value.

When passing an argument to a function by value, PowerBuilder creates a temporary variable in memory and copies the value into the temporary variable. The function sees only a copy of your value. If the function changes the value of this argument, the calling program will not see the change. A variable, when passed by copy to a function, cannot have its value changed by the function.

When you pass a variable to a function by reference, PowerBuilder passes a pointer containing the memory address of your variable to the function. The function can now change the value in your variable.

When you pass a variable to a function by readonly, PowerBuilder passes a pointer similar to passing by reference, but prevents the function from changing the value of the variable. Since it is not necessary to copy the variable's value to a temporary variable, readonly combines the protection of passing by value with the efficiency of passing by reference.

N O T E   Standard or enumerated datatype variables can be passed as arguments by value, by reference, or readonly. ■

When you pass a reference variable to a function, you pass a pointer to an object, not the object itself. This is true whether the reference variable itself is passed by value or by reference. When passing an object by value, PowerBuilder passes a copy of the reference variable, not a copy of the object.

N O T E   Whenever you pass an object's reference as an argument to a function, you should be careful to encapsulate the object properly. Encapsulation is your best protection against unwanted changes being made to your object by the called function. ■

Unlike objects, structures, when passed by value, are copied in their entirety to temporary structures in memory.

Reference Typing

All variables are given a data type when they are declared. The data type of a reference variable is the name of its declared class. The data type of a reference variable can change at run time, based upon the actual data type of an object it is associated with or pointed to.

In a strongly typed language like PowerBuilder, all data types are validated at compile time. PowerScript will not implicitly convert data types for you. The compiler will prevent you from using mixing data types in assignments and certain expressions.

For example, you cannot assign an integer value directly to a string variable. You must explicitly convert the integer to a string value using the string () function before assigning it to a string variable.

Static Type   The static type of a reference variable is its declared data type or classname. A reference variable can point to an object of its own class or to descendants of its class.

For example, a reference variable of type window, the Powersoft system class, can point to any window. To illustrate this, in the window painter create a new window class called w_sheet. Your w_sheet window class is inherited from Powersoft's window class. Now create a second window, w_customer, by inheriting from w_sheet. In your application, open an instance of w_sheet and an instance of w_customer.

A variable of type window can reference (point to) an instance of either w_sheet or w_customer. A variable of type w_sheet can also reference an instance of either w_sheet or w_customer. However, a variable of type w_customer cannot point to an instance of w_sheet.

Dynamic Type   When you use a reference variable of a given class, and point it to an object of a descendant class, PowerBuilder changes the run-time type of the reference variable. This is called dynamic typing. The static type of the variable (as known by the compiler) remains its declared class, but the dynamic type of the variable changes to the class of the object it is pointed to. Note that you cannot point to an object outside your class hierarchy, nor to an ancestor object.

Functions and attributes are strongly typed by default in PowerBuilder. This means that if you have a reference variable of a given class, the compiler will prevent you from referencing a function or attribute that is not already defined in that class (or inherited from its ancestor class). The compiler does type checking based on the static type of a variable. What is allowed at run time, however, is based on the dynamic type of the variable.

The compiler will permit you to assign a reference variable of a given class to a reference variable of an ancestor class, the same class, or a descendant class. To illustrate this, let's say you have defined three custom classes. Figure 17.9 shows the hierarchy of these custom classes.

Part

V

Ch

17

FIG. 17.9

The object browser dialog box, showing the hierarchy of custom class user objects.

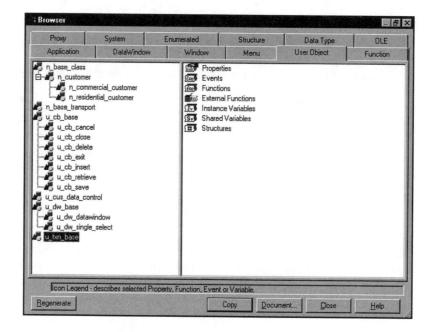

Study the following four code examples:

1. Assigning a class reference to a variable of the same class:

```
n_commercial_customer in_commercial_customer_1
n_commercial_customer in_commercial_customer_2
in_commercial_customer_1 = Create n_commercial_customer
in_Commercial_Customer_2 = in_Commercial_Customer_1
```

The compiler will accept the assignment, because the two reference variables have the same static type (n_commercial_class). The assignment will also work at run time. The reference to in_commercial_customer_1 is copied to in_commercial_customer_2. Both reference variables now point to the same object. The static type and dynamic type of both reference variables are the same after the assignment.

2. Assigning a descendant class reference to an ancestor class variable:

```
n_commercial_customer in_commercial_customer
n_customer in_customer
in_commercial_customer = Create n_commercial_customer
in_Customer = in_Commercial_Customer
```

The compiler will accept the assignment, because it allows a descendant reference to be assigned to an ancestor reference variable. The assignment will also work at run time because an ancestor reference variable can point to an instance of a descendant class.

The reference to in_commercial_customer is copied to in_customer. Both references now point to the same object. The second reference (in_customer) is dynamically retyped as n_commercial_customer. Both references now have the same dynamic type, although they continue to have different static types.

3. Assigning an ancestor class reference to a descendant class variable without prior dynamic retyping:

```
n_commercial_customer in_commercial_customer
n_customer in_customer
in_customer = Create n_customer
in_Commercial_Customer = in_Customer
```

The compiler will accept the assignment, because it allows an ancestor reference to be assigned to a reference variable of a descendant class. The assignment will not work at run time, because a reference variable whose dynamic type is descendant class cannot point to an instance of an ancestor class.

You will get a run-time error. The compiler accepts the assignment, however, because it is possible that you will retype the target reference variable before the assignment (see below).

4. Assigning an ancestor class reference to a descendant class variable after dynamic retyping of the target variable:

```
n_commercial_customer in_commercial_customer
n_customer in_customer
in_customer = Create n_commercial_customer
// note in_customer is now dynamically retyped as
// n_commercial_customer
in_Commercial_Customer = in_Customer
```

The compiler will accept the assignment, because it allows a descendant class reference to be assigned to an ancestor class reference variable. The assignment will also work at run time, because the target reference variable (in_customer) had previously been dynamically retyped to n_commercial_customer.

Avoiding Orphans

When you copy an object reference to a reference variable already pointing to another object, you lose the reference to the second object. If there is no other reference to this object it will be orphaned. An orphan is an object in memory with no reference. There is no way to reestablish a reference to an orphan. Without a reference, you cannot access the object nor destroy it.

This illustrates another important concept: the scope (life span in memory) of an object and the scope of its reference variable may be entirely different. By scope, we are referring to the time between when an object or variable is created and when it is destroyed. Note that when something is in scope it exists in memory, but it is not always visible or accessible. Scope and access are different concepts.

Consider this example using a custom class, n_employee:

```
n_employee in_employee_1, in_employee_2
in_employee_1 = Create n_employee
in_employee_2 = Create n_employee
```

At this point, you have created two instances of the n_employee class, and you have a reference to each (in_employee_1, and in_employee_2). What happens when you assign one reference to the other?

```
in_employee_1 = in_employee_2
```

You have now lost your reference to the first instance of n_employee. It is now orphaned, and there is no way to regain a reference to it in order to use it or destroy it. You have created a memory leak.

To avoid creating orphans, you need to be careful when you do reference assignment. If, when doing reference assignment, you are about to lose your last reference to an object, then destroy the object prior to the assignment:

```
n_employee in_employee_1, in_employee_2
in_employee_1 = Create n_employee
in_employee_2 = Create n_employee
if IsValid (in_employee_1) then
destroy in_employee_1
end if
in_employee_1 = in_employee_2.
```

By destroying an object before it becomes an orphan, you will avoid memory leaks.

There are many ways objects can be orphaned inadvertently. We often define reusable reference variables for creating multiple instances of a window or sheet. A reusable window reference variable is a local window variable used to open a sheet. At the end of the script, the reference variable is destroyed, although the window remains open. For example:

```
w_customer_list lw_sheet
opensheet (lw_sheet, w_frame, 0, Original!)
```

This script causes a new instance of the w_customer_list window to be opened as a sheet. The reference variable, lw_sheet, is destroyed when the script ends.

Why aren't we concerned about orphans when we use reusable reference variables to open sheets? PowerScript gives a set of functions to reestablish a reference to an open sheet. These functions include GetActiveSheet ( ), GetFirstSheet ( ), and GetNextSheet ( ). Each of these functions returns a reference to a sheet. We can thus reestablish a reference to a sheet by using one of these functions and assigning the returned value to a new reference variable.

Unfortunately, PowerBuilder doesn't give us an easy way to reestablish a reference to an orphaned nonvisual object. We have to be careful when we assign references to reference variables.

It is possible to destroy an object without destroying its reference variable. When the object is destroyed, its reference variable is no longer valid. If you use this reference variable, you will get a run-time null object reference. It is also possible to destroy a reference variable without destroying the object it points to, causing an orphan.

From Here...

This chapter has introduced some basic object-oriented terminology and described some techniques for incorporating object-orientation in your application development. By using these techniques, your PowerBuilder objects will become more independent of each other and more reusable. You will be able to spend more time building new applications and less time doing unnecessary software maintenance.

For more introductory information on inheritance, PowerScript, and objects, see the following chapters:

- Chapter 4, "Exploring Windows," has more information on window inheritance.
- Chapter 5, "Designing Menus," contains more information on menu inheritance.
- Chapter 6, "Using Events, Functions, and the PowerScript Language" contains information on variables in PowerScript.
- Chapter 18, "Understanding User Objects," has more information on custom classes and other user objects.

Part
V

Ch
17

Understanding User Objects

by Bill Heys

In order to fully exploit the object-oriented features of PowerBuilder, it is important to take advantage of PowerBuilder's User Objects. User Objects are visual and nonvisual classes used to define objects or building blocks for PowerBuilder Applications.

In this chapter, we introduce the User Object painter, describe each of the types of User Objects, and give examples of their uses. ■

How to build Visual User Objects in PowerBuilder.

As you build collections of reusable Visual User Objects, you will be able to develop new applications by assembling predefined objects, and spend less time rewriting the same code.

How to incorporate OLE 2.0 controls (OCX) into your application.

OLE controls replace Visual Basic Controls (VBXs), supported in earlier versions of PowerBuilder. Here you will learn how to register an OLE control, place an OLE control on a window, and then add behavior to the control.

How to define Standard and Custom Classes.

Learn how these non-visual user objects can increase the flexibility and reusability of your application.

How to use DataWindows with Business Objects.

Here you will learn how business objects and DataWindows can work together.

How to use Distributed PowerBuilder.

Learn how to implement an n-tier architecture and reduce the "fat client" by partitioning your application using custom classes as distributed objects.

Visual User Objects

Visual User Objects are reusable window controls. In this section, we will introduce several types of visual user objects:

- Standard
- External
- Custom
- OLE 2.0 Controls

Standard Visual User Objects

Table 18.1 lists the standard window controls from which Standard Visual User Objects can be created.

Table 18.1   Standard Visual Controls

Control	Description
CheckBox	CheckBoxes are small square boxes used to set independent options. Two-state CheckBoxes are either on or off. Three-state CheckBoxes have a third state, unknown.
CommandButton	CommandButtons are used to initiate an action.
DataWindow	DataWindow controls are used in a window to display and control DataWindow objects.
DropDownListBox	DropDownListBoxes combine the features of a ListBox and SingleLineEdit into a single control.
DropDownPictureListBox *	DropDownPictureListBoxes are special DropDownListBoxes where each item in the list can be associated with a picture.
EditMask	EditMasks are similar to MultiLineEdits with built-in text formatting.
Graph	Graphs visually represent a series of data values.
GroupBox	GroupBoxes are used to group a set of related controls.
HScrollBar	HScrollBars are horizontal bars containing a scroll box and arrows at either end.
ListBox	ListBoxes are used to select from a set of available options or values.
ListView *	ListView controls display lists that contain more information than can be found in a text-only list. The available views are: Large Icon, Small Icon, List, and Report.
MultiLineEdit	MultiLineEdits are boxes for entering and editing more than one line of text.

Control	Description
OLEControl	OLEControls contain objects such as spreadsheets or word processing documents created by other applications.
Picture	Pictures are bitmap images (BMP, RLE, or WMF format).
PictureButton	PictureButtons combine CommandButtons with pictures and are used to initiate an action.
RadioButton	RadioButtons are small circles used to turn an option on or off. When used in a group of other RadioButtons, selecting one RadioButton turns off all others in the group.
PictureListBox *	PictureListBoxes are special ListBoxes where each item in the list can be associated with a picture.
RichTextEdit *	A RichTextEdit control contains a document, which it displays as formatted text. It can include input fields that are linked to a DataWindow.
SingleLineEdit	SingleLineEdit boxes are for entering and editing only one line of text.
StaticText	StaticTexts are display-only text fields.
Tab *	A Tab control contains tab pages, which are User Objects that contain controls. Tab pages can be defined within the Tab control or they can be defined in the User Object painter and inserted into the Tab control.
TreeView *	TreeView controls incorporate expanding and collapsing tree nodes with bitmap and text representations for each node.
VScrollBar	VScrollBars are vertical bars containing a scroll box and arrows at either end.

*Part V
Ch 18*

* Indicates new window control for PowerBuilder 5

Defining a New Standard Visual User Object   On the PowerBar, click the User Object icon. Figure 18.1 shows the Select User Object dialog box.

From the Select User Object dialog box, you can choose one of the following options:

- OK—to view or change an existing User Object
- Cancel—to cancel a request and leave the User Object painter.
- New—to build a new User Object
- Browse—to do a text search on User Objects in your PBL.
- Inherit—to inherit a new User Object from an existing User Object
- Help—to bring up the Select User Object dialog box.
- Other—to bring up a Select Other Library dialog box to change libraries.

FIG. 18.1

The Select User Object dialog box in the User Object painter.

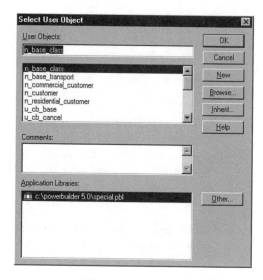

Click the New button. Figure 18.2 shows the New User Object dialog box.

FIG. 18.2

The New User Object dialog box.

On the New User Object dialog box, select the Visual Standard icon, and click the OK button. Next you must select a window control type from the list displayed in the Select Standard Visual Type dialog box (see fig. 18.3).

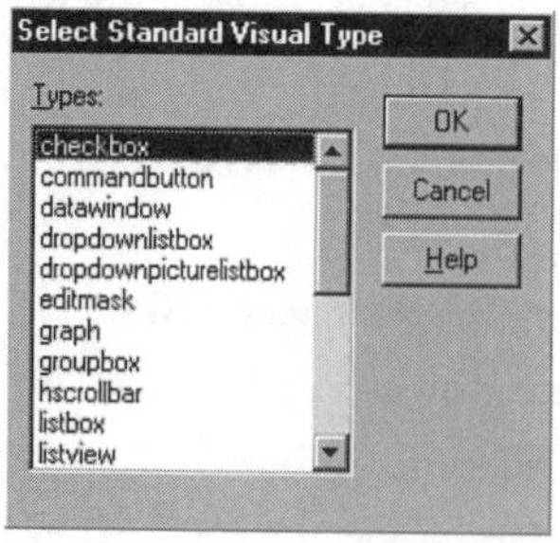

FIG. 18.3

The Select Standard Visual Type dialog box.

Let's begin by defining a generic ancestor CommandButton called u_cb_base. Highlight the CommandButton choice, and click the OK button (or double-click the CommandButton choice). Figure 18.4 shows the basic CommandButton window control.

FIG. 18.4
A CommandButton
Standard Visual User
Object.

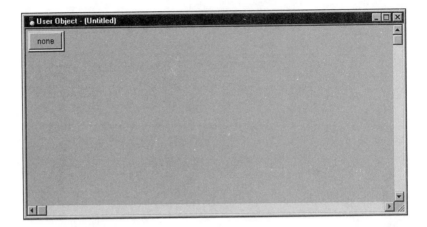

Note how this looks just like a CommandButton when you paint one on a window. The text attribute is initially set to display "none" as a button label. Select File from the menu, then Save As. Save this User Object with the name u_cb_base. It will be an ancestor for all CommandButtons used anywhere in your application.

You can now customize your CommandButton User Object by adding event scripts, defining instance variables for attributes, or defining object-level functions. You can also change the properties of your User Object by bringing up the Properties dialog box.

Defining Attributes Start by defining a protected attribute as an instance variable. From the menu, select Declare, then Instance Variables. Define the following variable and then click OK:

```
protected string is_event_name
```

The is_event_name attribute will be used by every CommandButton User Object to specify the name of an event to be triggered when the button is clicked. The event itself will be triggered in the object containing the button, usually a window.

Adding Event Scripts Point to the CommandButton with your mouse and click your right mouse button. From the pop-up menu, select script, to open the script painter. From the script painter, click the arrow for the select event drop-down listbox. Figure 18.5 shows the pre-defined events for a command button.

Enter the following script for the clicked event:

```
//The following script is for the clicked event
Parent. TriggerEvent (is_event_name)
```

This is the only script in the u_cb_base User Object. Click the Return icon in the PainterBar to return to the User Object painter.

FIG. 18.5

Script painter for a CommandButton Standard Visual User Object, showing the predefined events for a CommandButton.

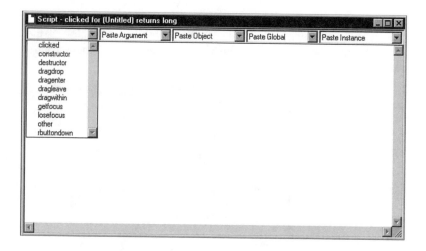

 TIP   A window control should never refer to the window containing it by name. A control should always use the parent pronoun as a generic reference to its container. By using only generic references, the User Object will be more reusable.

 TIP   Never put any business logic into a CommandButton. When clicked, a CommandButton should trigger a window event that defines the actual processing to be performed when the button is clicked. By having a CommandButton serve simply as a triggering mechanism, it becomes more reusable.

Using the Properties Dialog Box   Point to the CommandButton with your mouse and click your right mouse button. From the pop-up menu, select Properties, to open the properties dialog box. For Standard Visual User Objects, the properties listed are based on the type of window control the User Object is built from. In figure 18.6, we see properties for a CommandButton.

Since we are building a generic ancestor CommandButton, clear the Text attribute for your User Object. Click OK to return to the User Object painter. We have now completed our first visual User Object, u_cb_base. Close the User Object painter, and save your changes.

Using Inheritance with Standard Visual User Objects   Next, we will build some additional Standard Visual User Objects using u_cb_base as the ancestor. On the PowerBar, click the User Object icon. From the Select User Object dialog box, click the Inherit Button. Figure 18.7 shows the Inherit From User Object dialog box.

Select u_cb_base and click OK (or double-click u_cb_base). The new User Object looks just like u_cb_base. We need to do only two things to customize any CommandButton Standard Visual User Object.

First, point to the CommandButton with your mouse and click your right mouse button. From the pop-up menu, select Properties, to open the Properties dialog box. Change the Text attribute to "&Retrieve." Click OK to return to the User Object painter.

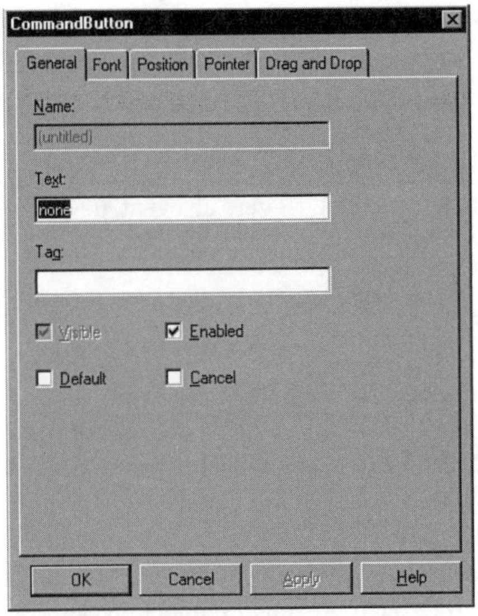

FIG. 18.6
The Properties dialog box for a Command-Button Standard User Object.

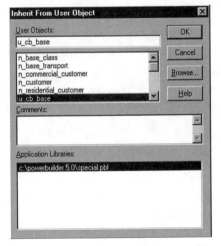

FIG. 18.7
The Inherit From User Object dialog box.

Next, enter the following script for the constructor event:

```
//The following script is for the constructor event
is_event_name = 'ue_retrieve'
```

Finally, save this new CommandButton. Select File from the menu, then Save As. Save this User Object with the name u_cb_retrieve.

Anytime you need a CommandButton in your application, follow this same process:

- Inherit a new Standard Visual User Object from u_cb_base.
- Change the text attribute to display the appropriate button label.

- Add a one-line script to the constructor event to initialize the inherited instance variable, is_event_name.
- Save the control as u_cb_xxxxxxxx.

You might want to create several reusable buttons at this point. For example:

- An update button, u_cb_update, that triggers an event, ue_update.
- An insert button, u_cb_insert, that triggers an event, ue_insert.
- A delete button, u_cb_delete, that triggers an event, ue_delete.
- A close button, u_cb_close, that triggers an event, ue_close.

Next, let's build an ancestor class for all DataWindow controls. On the PowerBar, click on the User Object icon. From the Select User Object dialog box, click the New Button. On the New User Object dialog box, select the Visual Standard icon, and click the OK button. Highlight the DataWindow choice, and click the OK button (or double-click the DataWindow choice). Select File from the menu, then Close. Save this User Object with the name u_dw_base. It will be an ancestor for all DataWindows used anywhere in your application. Right now, you may not have any scripts to add to the base DataWindow. You might identify some generic process to add later.

 TIP It is much easier to define an ancestor class at the outset than it is to add an ancestor to dozens of existing classes.

Next, we will build a DataWindow control that does single-row selection using u_dw_base as the ancestor. On the PowerBar, click the User Object icon. From the Select User Object dialog box, click the Inherit Button. Select u_dw_base and click OK (or double-click u_dw_base).

Next, enter the following script for the RowFocusChanged event:

```
//The following script is for the RowFocusChanged event
This. SelectRow (0, false)
This. SelectRow (this . GetRow() , true)
```

Finally, save this new DataWindow control. Select File from the menu, then Save As. Save this User Object with the name u_dw_single_select.

External Visual User Objects

External Visual User Objects are custom controls created using the Windows Software Development Kit (SDK). They are deployed as Windows Dynamic Link Libraries (DLLs).

In this section, we will describe the process of creating an External Visual User Object, and then placing the control on a window. Finally, we will add behavior to the control in the script painter.

 TIP Refer to the vendor's documentation for your specific external control to understand how to integrate it into the PowerBuilder environment.

For this example, we will use CPALLETE.DLL, which comes with PowerBuilder. This DLL contains several classes, each of which defines a 3-D Windows control.

The documentation for CPALLETE.DLL (available from the vendor) lists the registered classes contained in the DLL. We will be using the 3-D CheckBox class called cpCheckBox. Unlike the standard Powerbuilder CheckBox, cpCheckBox displays a blue check mark rather than an *x* when checked.

Along with the class name, we need to know the appropriate style bit setting for the class. Style bits for the 3-D controls are the same as the Windows SDK style bits for normal window controls. The style setting for cpCheckBox is defined as BS_AUTOCHECKBOX (which in the SDK has a value 0x00000003L, or Decimal 3).

Each custom control class can also define message interfaces for communicating with the control. The messages are used to bring about an action or to get a value for the control. For cpCheckBox, there are two messages corresponding to the SDK messages for normal CheckBox controls: BM_GETSTATE (which is message id WM_USER + 2, or Decimal 1026), and BM_SETSTATE (which is message id WM_USER + 3, or Decimal 1027).

BM_GETSTATE returns the current state (0 for unchecked or 1 for checked). BM_SETSTATE takes an integer as an argument (0 changes the state to unchecked and 1 changes the state to checked).

Finally the control issues a notification message when it is clicked. The notification message corresponds to the notification message issued by standard controls, BN_CLICKED (which is 0).

Defining an External Visual User Object   On the PowerBar, click the User Object Icon. On the Select User Object dialog box, click the New Button. On the New User Object dialog box, click the Visual External icon. This brings you to a Select Custom Control DLL dialog box (see fig. 18.8).

FIG. 18.8
The Select Custom
Control DLL dialog box.

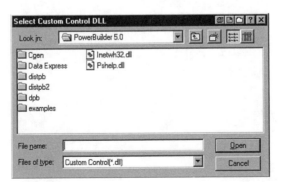

Locate CPALLETE.DLL in its appropriate subdirectory (for example, c:\pbn\example). Highlight the DLL Name and click the Open Button. This brings you to the External User Object style dialog box.

Specifying the Class and Style Settings Verify that the correct DLL name appears in the top of the dialog box. Enter the appropriate class name. For the 3-D CheckBox, the class name is cpCheckBox. At the bottom of the dialog box, enter the appropriate style bit setting for the control. In our example, enter 3 (for BS_AUTOCHECKBOX). Figure 18.9 shows the Style dialog box settings for the 3-D CheckBox in CPALLETE.DLL.

FIG. 18.9

The External User Object style dialog box.

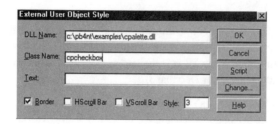

Define the Windows Notification Event Define a user-defined event triggered by the CheckBox notification message, BN_CLICKED. Notification messages are different from standard Windows messages. Notifications are sent by Windows in the wParm parameter to the parent of the control, using the WM_COMMAND message.

PowerBuilder maps external User Object notification messages 0 through 24 to its own event ids, pbm_uonexternal01 through pbm_uonexternal25, respectively.

In the User Object painter, click the Declare menu, then User Events. This brings up the Events dialog box. Enter a new event name, ue_clicked, and associate this with the BN_CLICKED event id (0), pbm_uonexternal01 (see fig. 18.10).

FIG. 18.10

The Events dialog box with ue_clicked user-defined event.

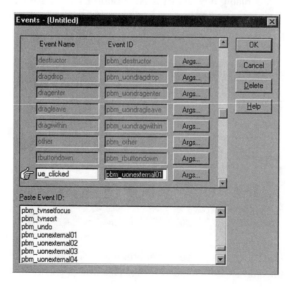

Defining the Public Interface to the External User Object   Define two public object-level functions in the User Object as wrappers for the two messages defined for cpCheckBox. These will make the User Object easier to use, since object function names are easier to remember than the cryptic message numbers specified in the documentation: WM_USER + 3 (1026) and WM_USER + 3 (1027). Each function will call the PowerBuilder Handle() function to obtain a Windows handle for the control. Using the Windows handle, PowerBuilder can send messages to the control.

From the User Object painter, click the Declare menu item, then User Object Functions. This brings up the Select Function in the User Object dialog box. Click the New Button. Define the function in the New Function dialog box.

The name of the first function is uf_GetState. It will be a public function and will return an integer. It is not necessary to pass any arguments to the uf_GetState function. Figure 18.11 shows the definition of uf_GetState.

FIG. 18.11

The New Function dialog box with definition of uf_GetState object function.

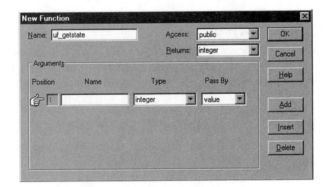

Enter the script in listing 18.1 for the uf_GetState function.

Listing 18.1   uf_Get State Function

```
// Script for uf_GetState
integer li_ReturnValue
// Send a message to the control test the state ( WM_USER + 2 )
li_ReturnValue = Send( Handle( this ), 1026, 0, 0 )
// Return it to the calling script
Return li_ReturnValue
```

The name of the second function is uf_SetState. It will be a public function with no return value. There is one argument passed to uf_SetState. Figure 18.12 shows the definition of uf_SetState.

Enter the following script for the uf_SetState function:

```
// Script for uf_SetState
// Send a message to the control with a new value to set ( WM_USER + 3 )
Send (Handle(this), 1027, ai_newstate, 0 )
```

FIG. 18.12
The New Function dialog box with definition of uf_SetState object function.

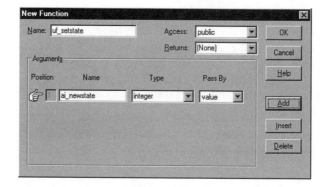

Saving the External User Object   Save the User Object as u_ext_3d_CheckBox and close the User Object painter. From the File menu, click Close.

Custom Visual User Objects

Custom Visual User Objects are User Objects containing more than one window control or Standard Visual User Object. They are similar to Windows in that they are container objects. Each of the controls contained in a custom control can have scripts defined in the User Object painter.

N O T E   Individual controls become encapsulated inside a custom User Object. When the custom control is placed on a window, it is not possible to see or code scripts for the individual control events. ■

The User Object itself has its own events defined:

- Constructor
- Destructor
- DragDrop
- DragEnter
- DragLeave
- DragWithin
- Other
- RButtonDown

Defining a New Custom Visual User Object   On the PowerBar, click on the User Object icon. From the Select User Object dialog box, click on the New Button. On the New User Object dialog box, select the Visual Custom icon and click the OK button. At this point, the Custom Visual User Object painter resembles the window painter (see fig. 18.13).

FIG. 18.13
The Custom Visual User Object painter.

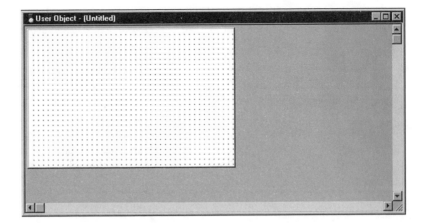

Adding Controls to a Custom Visual User Object   Controls are painted in a Custom Visual User Object in exactly the same way they are painted in a window. The User Object painter toolbar in PowerBuilder 5 has the same drop-down toolbar for window controls that you see in the window painter. Click this window control drop-down toolbar and select the desired window controls or User Objects. You can also select Controls from the menu and then pick the desired controls or visual User Objects.

For our example, let's add several standard command button visual User Objects to the custom User Object: u_cb_retrieve, u_cb_insert, u_cb_delete, u_cb_update, and u_cb_close. Let's also add a standard DataWindow visual User Object, u_dw_single_select. Figure 18.14 shows the resulting Custom Visual User Object.

FIG. 18.14
The Custom Visual User Object containing a DataWindow and several CommandButtons.

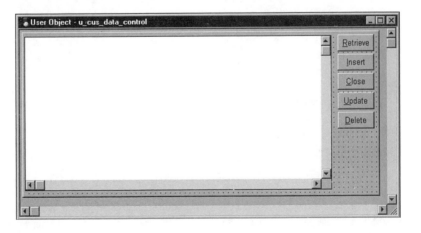

> **N O T E**   Custom Visual User Objects are container objects. They can contain any number or combination of standard window controls, Standard Visual User Objects, External Visual User Objects, or other Custom Visual User Objects. ■

Part
V

Ch
18

Scripting Custom Visual User Objects   You may define scripts for any of the events for individual controls inside the custom User Object. You may also add user-defined events for any of the individual controls.

In our example, each of the CommandButtons in the User Object has been scripted to trigger a specific event in its parent. The Custom Visual User Object is considered the parent of each of the controls it contains. We will define events on the Custom Visual User Object corresponding to each of the events which can be triggered by the individual CommandButtons. The container events will each be triggered by a control event. Then these events will simply trigger the appropriate event in their container (perhaps a window, perhaps another Custom Visual User Object). The container's events are simply pass-through events.

Define the following user-defined events for the container (one for each CommandButton): ue_retrieve, ue_insert, ue_delete, ue_update, and ue_close. Figure 18.15 shows these events.

FIG. 18.15

The Events dialog box for the Custom Visual User Object with pass-through events defined.

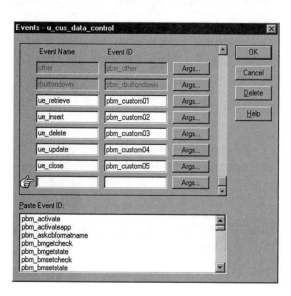

Each of the pass-through events will trigger the same event in its parent:

```
//Script for ue_insert
Parent . TriggerEvent ('ue_insert')

//Script for ue_retrieve
Parent . TriggerEvent ('ue_retrieve')
```

TIP   In many class libraries, you will often see user-defined event names in a window with a prefix of we_, in a menu with a prefix of me_, and in User Object ue_. We are recommending a slightly different naming convention. All user-defined events in any type of object will have a prefix of ue_. Likewise, all object-level functions will start with uf_. If, in all your objects, you give the same functions and events the same name, they will be more generic and polymorphic.

Saving the Custom Visual User Object   Save the User Object as u_cus_data_control and close the User Object painter. From the File menu, click Close.

Adding Visual User Objects to a Window

Once you have defined a Visual User Object, add it to a window like any other window control. Click the window control drop-down toolbar and select the User Object control. Or you can select Controls from the menu and then User Object. This brings you to the Select User Object dialog box (see fig. 18.16).

FIG. 18.16
The Select User Object dialog box.

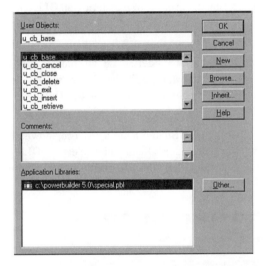

Select the appropriate User Object from the list and click OK. Now point and click on the window where you want the control to be painted (see fig. 18.17).

FIG. 18.17
A window with a CommandButton Standard Visual User Object.

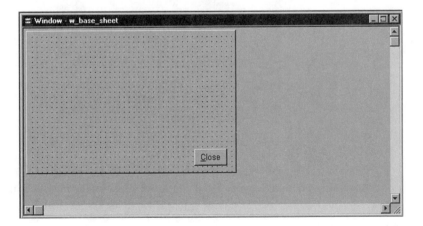

Part
V

Ch
18

OLE 2.0 (OCX) Controls

OLE controls are OLE 2.0 Controls created in the Window Painter. OLE controls replace Visual Basic Controls (VBXs), supported in earlier versions of PowerBuilder. VBX controls were defined as a type of visual User Object in the User Object painter. Once defined, a VBX control can be placed on any window in the window painter. In PowerBuilder 5, OLE controls are now registered to PowerBuilder in the window painter. Once registered, an OCX can be painted as a control on any window. The PowerBuilder 5 User Object painter no longer supports VBX controls.

In this section, we will describe the process of registering an OLE control to PowerBuilder, placing an OLE control on a window, and then adding behavior to the control in the script painter.

Registering an OLE Control to PowerBuilder   OLE 2.0 controls are distributed as specialized Dynamic Link Libraries (DLLs) known as OCX files. Before you can add an OLE 2.0 control to a window, the OCX file must be registered to PowerBuilder. Complete the following steps to register an OCX file.

The window painter toolbar in PowerBuilder 5 has a new drop-down toolbar for window controls. Click the window control drop-down toolbar and select the OLE 2.0 control. Or you can select Controls from the menu and then OLE 2.0. This brings you to the OLE 2.0 Insert Object dialog box (see fig. 18.18).

FIG. 18.18
The OLE 2.0 Insert Object is a tabbed dialog box for inserting new or existing OLE 2.0 objects or OLE 2.0 controls into a window.

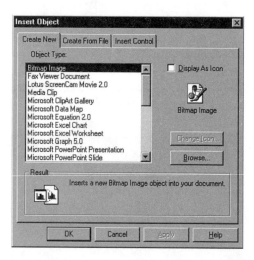

On the Insert Object dialog box, click the Insert Control tab. This tab displays a list of all registered OLE control types. If you have not yet registered any OCX files to PowerBuilder, there will be no control types listed. Figure 18.19 shows the Insert Control tab.

FIG. 18.19

The Insert Control tab of the OLE 2.0 Insert Object dialog box.

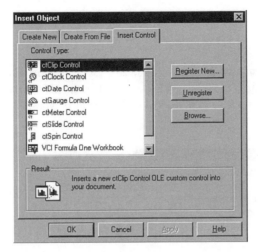

On this tab, you can:

- Register a new OLE control
- Unregister an existing OLE control
- Invoke the OLE object Browser

To register a new OLE control, click the Register New... button. You will now see the standard PowerBuilder File Browse dialog box. You may browse for OLE control files having a file type of OCX. PowerBuilder 5 comes with a component gallery containing several OLE controls. They are usually located in the Compglry subdirectory of your PowerBuilder 5 directory. Figure 18.20 shows the sample OLE controls from the PowerBuilder 5 component gallery.

FIG. 18.20

The Browse dialog box showing the sample OCX files in the PowerBuilder 5 component gallery.

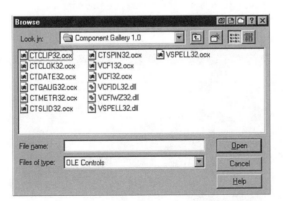

Register the date control from the component gallery. Select CTDATE32.OCX file name and click the Open button. The selected control will now appear in the list of control types.

T I P If you are using PowerBuilder for Windows 3.x, you should use 16-bit DLLs. If you are using PowerBuilder for NT you should use 32-bit DLLs.

Placing an OLE Control on a Window   To add an OLE control to a window, click the window control drop-down toolbar and select OLE 2.0 control. In the Insert Object dialog box, click the Insert Control tab to view a list of registered OLE 2.0 control types. Figure 18.21 shows an example list of registered OLE controls.

FIG. 18.21

The Insert Control tab from the Insert Object dialog box.

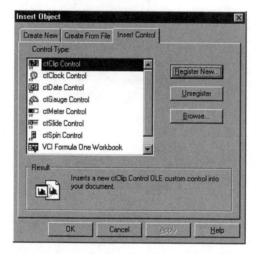

Select the name of an OLE control from the control type list, then click the OK button. You should now be back in the window painter. Simply click anywhere on the window to place your selected control. You should now see the control on the window. Figure 18.22 shows a window with several OLE controls.

FIG. 18.22

A window containing several OLE 2.0 controls.

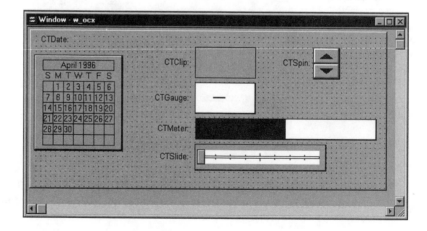

Viewing the Properties of an OLE Control   To view the properties of an OLE control, click the window control drop-down toolbar and select OLE 2.0 control. In the OLE Insert Object dialog box click on the Insert Control tab to view a list of registered OLE 2.0 control types. Select a control from this list and click on the Browse button.

The OLE Object browser is a tree list display of methods (functions), events, and properties (attributes) of your selected OLE control. Figure 18.23 shows the properties of the ctDate Control.

FIG. 18.23
The PowerBuilder OLE Object Browser dialog box.

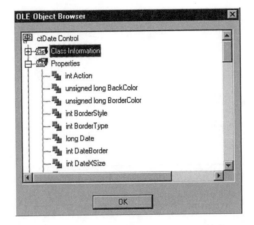

The ctDate OLE control has several predefined methods or functions:

- AboutBox( )
- ClearDays( )
- LastDay( )
- LastMonth( )
- LastYear( )
- NextDay( )
- NextMonth( )
- NextYear( )
- Today( )

There are also several predefined events:

- Click( )
- DateChange( )
- DblClick( )
- KeyDown( )
- KeyPress( )

Part
V

Ch
18

- KeyUp( )
- MouseDown( )
- MouseMove( )
- MouseUp( )

There are also several properties, including:

- Month (integer)
- Year (integer)
- Day (integer)
- FirstDay (integer)
- Date (long)
- Action (integer)
- DayHeader (string)
- MonthButtons (boolean)
- MonthNames (string)

TIP Refer to the vendor's documentation for your specific OLE control to understand the meaning of each property, event, and function contained in the control.

Adding Script to an OLE Control   Write a script to display a messagebox displaying the selected date. Code this script for the DateChange event. In PowerBuilder 5, you can now pass arguments to an event. The DateChange event in the ctDate OLE control has four arguments, all integers passed by reference. They are:

- ndow—Day of Week for the selected date (a number from 1 to 7).
- nday—Day portion of the selected date.
- nmonth—Month portion of the selected date.
- nyear—Year portion of the selected date.

```
//Script for DateChange event
date ld_date
ld_date = date(nyear, nmonth, nday)
MessageBox ('Selected Date', string (ld_date))
```

Next, add a button to the window, and add a script to the button's clicked event to send a message to the date control, telling it to scroll to the prior month.

```
//Script for Clicked Event on cb_prior_month
ole_1. Object . LastMonth()
```

N O T E   LastMonth is an object function defined in the OCX for the ctDate OLE control. The syntax for calling this function is ControlName. Object. FunctionName. In this syntax, Object is a keyword. ■

Classes (Nonvisual User Objects)

Standard Classes

Standard classes are nonvisual classes created from existing PowerBuilder system classes. Table 18.2 lists the standard system classes from which standard classes can be created.

Table 18.2   Standard System Classes

Control	Description
Connection *	A Connection Object specifies the parameters that a distributed PowerBuilder client application uses to connect to a PowerBuilder server application.
DataStore *	A DataStore object is a nonvisual DataWindow.
DynamicDescriptionArea	The DynamicDescriptionArea object is used to store information about the input and output parameters used in Format 4 of dynamic SQL.
DynamicStagingArea	The DynamicStagingArea is used with dynamic SQL to store the following information for use in subsequent statements: the SQL statement in your PREPARE statement, the number of parameters, and the Transaction object.
Error	The Error object is used to record run-time errors.
MailSession	The MailSession object contains the session id and message used for mail-enabled applications.
Message	The Message object is used to process non-PowerBuilder-defined events and to communicate parameters between Windows when they are opened and closed.
OLEObject	The OLEObject acts as a proxy to interface with a remote OLE Object.
OLEStorage	The OLEStorage object acts as a proxy to interface with an open OLE storage.
OLEStream	The OLEStream object acts as a proxy to interface with an OLE Stream.
Pipeline	The Pipeline system object manages execution of a data Pipeline (painted in the Pipeline painter).
Transaction	The Transaction object manages a connection between PowerBuilder and a database.

* Indicates new for PowerBuilder 5

Part

V

Ch

18

Standard Transaction Class   Transactions objects are used to manage database connections. Many developers create standard transaction classes for each DBMS they connect to. For example you might define a transaction for connecting to Sybase SQL Anywhere using ODBC called n_txn_sql_anywhere, one for connecting to Oracle 7 called n_txn_oracle7, and one for connecting to Sybase System 10 called n_txn_system10.

Start by defining a common ancestor for your transaction classes. On the PowerBar, click on the User Object Icon. On the Select User Object dialog box, click the New Button. On the New User Object dialog box, click on the Standard Class icon. On the Select Standard Class Type dialog box, select transaction from the list. Save this as your ancestor transaction class, n_txn_base.

Next, define a transaction for connecting to a Sybase SQL Anywhere database. On the PowerBar, click the User Object Icon. On the Select User Object dialog box, click the Inherit Button. On the Inherit From User Object dialog box, select n_txn_base, and click OK. Add an object-level function, uf_connect, for establishing a connection to a Sybase SQL Anywhere database (see listing 18.2).

Listing 18.2   uf_connect for SQL Anywhere Database

```
public function integer uf_connect ()
this.DBMS = "ODBC"
this.DbParm =ProfileString("PB.INI","Database","DbParm", " ")
transaction lt_trans
lt_trans = this
Connect Using lt_trans;
If this.SQLCODE = -1 Then
        Messagebox("Connect","Unable to connect to SQL Anywhere database")
End IF
Return this.sqlcodethis
```

Save this class as n_txn_sql_anywhere.

Next, define a transaction for connecting to Sybase System 10. Follow the same steps as before. Since different attributes are used for connecting to Sybase System 10, uf_connect in n_txn_System10 might look like listing 18.3.

Listing 18.3   uf_connect for Sybase System 10 Database

```
public function integer uf_connect ()
this.DBMS = "SYC"
this.Database =ProfileString("PB.INI","Database","Database", " ")
//this.LogID =ProfileString("PB.INI","Database","LogId", " ")
//this.LogPass =ProfileString("PB.INI","Database","LogPass", " ")
this.ServerName =ProfileString("PB.INI","Database","ServerName", " ")
this.DbParm =ProfileString("PB.INI","Database","DbParm", " ")
transaction lt_trans
lt_trans = this
Connect Using lt_trans;
```

```
If this.SQLCODE = -1 Then
      Messagebox("Connect","Unable to connect to Sybase System 10 database")
End IF
Return this.sqlcodethis
```

Save this as n_txn_system10.

You might consider adding additional functions to your transaction classes for error handling. Each transaction class could be set up to check for specific database error codes, such as duplicate primary key on insert. Each transaction class would check for vendor-specific error codes. The differences between one database vendor's error code and another vendor's error code would be encapsulated inside your transaction classes. Simply plug the appropriate transaction class into your application.

Standard Message Class   The Message object is used to process non-PowerBuilder-defined events. It is also used to communicate parameters between windows when you open and close them. Any optional parameters passed to TriggerEvent or PostEvent functions are passed using attributes of the Message object.

You can also customize your own version of the Message class by defining a class user object inherited from standard Message class. Message classes have two events: Constructor and Destructor.

Start by defining a common ancestor for your Message classes. On the PowerBar, click the User Object Icon. On the Select User Object dialog box, click the New Button. On the New User Object dialog box, click the Standard Class icon. On the Select Standard Class Type dialog box, select message from the list. Save this as your ancestor message class, n_msg_base.

Next, define your own message class with additional attributes such as sending object, or user name. On the PowerBar, click the User Object Icon. On the Select User Object dialog box, click the Inherit Button. On the Inherit From User Object dialog box, select n_msg_base, and click OK. Add private instance variables for each new attribute:

```
Private powerobject ipo_sending_object
Private string is_user_name
```

Next provide functions for accessing the attribute in listing 18.4.

Listing 18.4   n_msg_message Class

```
Public function uf_get_s_user_name () Returns string
Return is_user_name

Public function uf_get_po_sending_object () Returns powerobject
Return ipo_sending_object

Public function uf_set_s_user_name (string as_user_name)
is_user_name = as_user_name
```

continues

Listing 18.4   Continued

```
Public function uf_set_po_sending_object &
        (powerobject apo_sending_object)
ipo_sending_object = apo_sending_object
```

Save this class as n_msg_message.

Standard Error Class   The Error object is used to record information about execution-time errors. In the application's SystemError event, you can access attributes of the Error object to learn which error occurred and where it occurred.

You can also customize your own version of the Error object by defining a standard class inherited from the Error system class. The Error class has two events: Constructor and Destructor.

Start by defining a common ancestor for your Error classes. On the PowerBar, click the User Object Icon. On the Select User Object dialog box, click the New Button. On the New User Object dialog box, click the Standard Class icon. On the Select Standard Class Type dialog box, select message from the list. Save this as your ancestor Error class, n_err_base.

Next, define your own Error class with a function to display the attributes of the Error object in a window or datawindow. On the PowerBar, click the User Object Icon. On the Select User Object dialog box, click the Inherit Button. On the Inherit From User Object dialog box, select n_err_base, and click OK. Add a public function to display a user-friendly system error message window.

Save this object as n_err_error.

Changing the Application's Default Global Variable Types   PowerBuilder creates five global standard class objects for every application. Their names and datatypes are:

- Error, a type of Error object
- Message, a type of Message object
- SQLCA, a type of Transaction object
- SQLDA, a type of DynamicDescriptionArea object
- SQLSA, a type of DynamicStagingArea object

You may have defined your own standard class types for PowerBuilder to create in place of the default types. For example, you may have defined a transaction class, n_txn_sql_anywhere, for connecting to SQL Anywhere ODBC data sources. You can tell PowerBuilder to associate SQLCA with an instance of your class, n_txn_sql_anywhere, instead of the default transaction class.

In the application painter, select the Properties icon from the painterbar. Select the Variable Types tab. Enter your class names: n_txn_sql_anywhere, in place of the transaction class name associated with global identifier SQLCA, n_msg_message, in place of the message class name associated with global identifier Message, and n_err_error, in place of the Error class name associated with the global identifier Error (see fig. 18.24).

FIG. 18.24

The Application dialog box showing variable types.

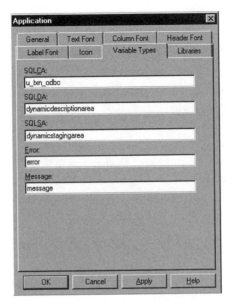

Custom Classes (Nonvisual User Objects)

PowerBuilder custom classes used to be called Nonvisual User Objects (NVOs). To build a custom class, go into the User Object Painter, Select New, then Custom Class.

The custom class painter resembles the window painter or the Custom Visual User Object painter. The painterbar has a window control drop-down toolbar. You also see a box in the painter that looks like a window. Don't be alarmed. The box has no significance, and the drop-down toolbar icons are all disabled. Figure 18.25 shows the custom class User Object painter.

FIG. 18.25

The custom class User Object painter.

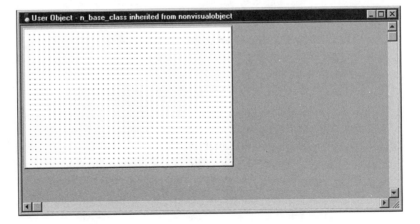

Start by defining a common ancestor for all custom classes. On the PowerBar, click the User Object Icon. On the Select User Object dialog box, click the New Button. On the New User Object dialog box, click the Custom Class icon. Save this as your ancestor custom class, n_cc_base.

Next, let's create a Customer class. On the PowerBar, click on the User Object Icon. On the Select User Object dialog box, click the Inherit Button. On the Inherit From User Object dialog box, select n_cc_base, and click OK. Save this class with the name n_customer.

Defining Attributes for a Custom Class Custom class attributes are defined as instance variables. From the custom class menu, select Declare and then Instance Variables. Define an instance variable for each attribute. For a customer, we might define:

```
Private string is_name
Private integer ii_customer_id
Private string is_contact
Private string is_street_address
Private string is_address_line2
Private string is_city
Private string is_state
Private string is_zip_code
Private string is_phone
Private string is_extension
Private string is_fax
Private decimal {2} idec_acct_bal
```

Defining Methods or Operations for a Custom Class Custom class methods are defined as user-object functions or user-events. To define a user-object function, from the custom class menu, select Declare and then User Object Functions. Define an object function to return the value of a customer's account balance:

```
Public Function uf_get_dec_acct_bal () Returns decimal {2}
Return idec_acct_bal
```

To define a user-object event, select Declare and then User Events. Custom class user-defined events are defined in the same way as any object's user-defined events.

Using Custom Classes as Service Delegators Did you ever wish you could inherit from the PowerBuilder Application Object? Are you trying to eliminate global variables, but find you need a variable that stays around for the duration of the application? In this section, we will describe how to use a custom class as a service delegator.

Every application requires an application object. Global variables and global external function declarations are stored in your application object, regardless of where they are declared. In many applications, the MDI frame window is opened and a connection to the database is established in the application open event. The application disconnects from the database in the close event.

You would like to reuse the application object in many projects, but PowerBuilder doesn't allow you to inherit your application object from an ancestor. You end up copying your application object every time you start a new project. Suddenly you have dozens of copies of the application object all over the place.

Later you may want to change the way your applications connect to the database. Or, heaven forbid, you may want to add a global variable to your application. Unfortunately, you can't make a simple change to your application code in one place. You need to make the same change to all your application objects.

Next, we will design a service delegator custom class, n_base_application, to replace most of the functionality of the PowerBuilder application object. We will move all code normally placed in the application to this custom class called n_base_application. Global variables, if needed, will become encapsulated instance variables of the custom class.

Define four user-defined custom events in n_base_application. These events will have similar names and will be triggered by the four built-in events of the PowerBuilder application:

- ue_open assigned event id PBM_Custom01
- ue_idle assigned event id PBM_Custom02
- ue_systemerror assigned event id PBM_Custom03
- ue_close assigned event id PBM_Custom04

Next, define another custom class inherited from n_base_application. Save this new class as n_application.

In the open event of the "real" application object, create an instance of the n_application class. The instance identifier, n_application, is a default global variable created by PowerBuilder with a datatype of n_application:

```
n_application = Create n_application
```

Next trigger the ue_open event in n_application from the "real" application open event:

```
If IsValid (n_application) then
      n_application . TriggerEvent ('ue_open')
end if
```

In each of the other events of the "real" application, trigger the associated user-defined event in n_application.

Finally, in the close event of the "real" application, you will need to destroy the custom class object, n_application. Do this as the last thing in the script, after triggering the ue_close event in n_application.

Your "real" application object now delegates all of its services to the custom class, n_application. Any changes made to n_base_application can be made in one place and will be, in a sense, inherited by all "real" application objects. The application will only ever have one global variable, n_application, which is a reference or pointer to the instance of n_application created in the application open event.

The scripts in the "real" application object never need to be changed. Yet because they delegate their services to a custom class object, their behavior can change.

Part
V

Ch
18

This is but one example of an object delegating services to another object. In this example, we are able to get around a frustrating limitation of PowerBuilder and, in effect, implement inheritance with the application object where PowerBuilder does not directly support it.

Managing Your Objects

Object management involves:

- Deciding who should have responsibility for destroying an object (the creator or the last user).
- How to pass that clean-up responsibility to some other object.
- How to avoid orphaning an object or destroying an object you create but which is used by some other object.
- How to make sure you clean up after yourself before your application shuts down (for example, avoiding memory leaks).

As a general rule, the creator of an object should be responsible for destroying any objects it creates. For example, if a window creates an object or instance of a custom class when it is opened, it should usually destroy this object before the window is closed.

There are, however, some situations where this approach is too simple. Suppose you have a customer list window and a customer detail window. The user double-clicks on a row in the list to see the details about the selected customer. The customer list window needs to pass the customer id of the selected customer to the detail window. There may be other values you want to pass from the list window to the detail window (first name, last name, and so on).

How do you pass values to a window when you open it. In the early days of PowerBuilder, this was a big reason for defining global variables. Now you can open another window using OpenWithParm( ) or OpenSheetWithParm( ). This gives you the ability to pass either a single numeric value, a single string value, a structure of values, or an object.

Passing a structure is easy. PowerBuilder applications do not need explicitly to create or destroy the memory associated with a structure. In this respect, structures are like simple datatypes. You simply define a structure variable, and PowerBuilder takes care of allocating memory for the structure and cleaning up memory when the structure goes out of scope or the application ends.

We recommend using custom classes instead of structures. Define a custom class containing instance variables for each of the attributes. The object at this point might be only a collection of attributes, like a structure, but you can add functions or events if you wish. You can inherit new custom classes from existing custom classes. You cannot inherit new structures from existing structures. You can add behavior (methods or functions) to a custom class. You cannot add behavior to a structure.

So, given a choice of a defining structure of attributes, or a custom class containing the same attributes, we prefer custom classes because they offer greater flexibility and reusability.

However, you are responsible for managing the memory of your own objects. If you create an instance of a custom class, you should assume responsibility for that object, and destroy it when you no longer need it.

Back to the example of the customer list and customer detail Windows. Rather than passing a single value or a structure of values from the list window to the detail window, create a custom class object. Define a custom class called n_customer. In the list window, when it opens the detail window, create an instance of this class. First, define the reference variable as a protected instance variable of the customer list window:

```
protected n_customer in_customer
```

Then in the double-clicked event of the list DataWindow, create the custom class object, initialize its attributes, and pass it to the detail window:

```
in_customer = create n_customer
...
initialize other attributes of in_customer
OpenSheetWithParm (w_customer_detail, in_customer, 0, Original!)
```

Both the customer list and the customer form share this object. Although we have created the object in the list window, we may not want to destroy it here. One problem is knowing when to destroy an object. Another problem is making sure all objects are destroyed to avoid memory leaks.

First, add an attribute as a private instance variable to a custom class base object, n_base_class. All custom classes we define will inherit from this base class.

```
Private integer ii_use_count = 0
```

Next, define two public functions in the base custom class. They are uf_acquire( ) and uf_release( ). The first function, uf_acquire( ), is called by any user of a custom class object gaining a reference to the object. In the uf_acquire( ) function, the ii_use_count attribute is incremented.

```
Public Function uf_acquire() Returns Integer
        ii_use_count ++
        Return (ii_use_count)
```

The second function, uf_release( ), decrements the ii_use_count attribute and returns its current value. The release function is called by any user of an object to release its reference to the object.

```
Public Function uf_release( ) Returns Integer
        ii_use_count --
        if ii_use_count < 1 then
                destroy this
        end if
        Return (ii_use_count)
```

This allows the users of objects to know when they can delete an object without affecting other users of the same object. Here is an example of its use:

Part

V

Ch

18

Since the use count is initialized to 1, the creator of an object doesn't need to call the object's uf_acquire( ). By default, the creator is the object's first user.

If you have created an object in a window, call the object's uf_release( ) function prior to closing the window.

The double-clicked event of the customer list DataWindow now looks like this:

```
integer ii_use_count
in_customer = create n_customer
if IsValid (in_customer) then
        // Increment the use count
        ii_use_count = in_customer . uf_acquire()
end if
...
// initialize other attributes of in_customer
OpenSheetWithParm (w_customer_detail, in_customer,0, Original!)
```

The closed event of the customer list window looks like this:

```
integer ii_use_count
if IsValid (in_customer) then
        // Decrement the use count
        ii_use_count = in_customer . uf_release()
        // If no other users of this object, then destroy it
        if ii_use_count < 1 then
                Destroy in_customer
        end if
end if
```

Whenever you are passed a reference to an object, call the uf_acquire( ) function in that object and then, prior to closing, call the objects uf_release( ) function.

The open event of the customer detail window looks like this:

```
// Get the object passed to the window
in_customer = Message.PowerObjectParm
if IsValid (in_customer) then
        // Increment the use count
        ii_use_count = in_customer . uf_acquire()
end if
```

The close event of the customer detail window looks like this:

```
integer ii_use_count
if IsValid (in_customer) then
        //Decrement the use count
        ii_use_count = in_customer . uf_release()
end if
```

We suggest maintaining a use count as a private instance variable in every object. With this approach, it is easy to share an object with multiple users.

Each new user, when it gains a reference to another object, calls the object's uf_acquire( ) function to increment its use count. And each user, when it no longer needs a reference to the object, calls the object's uf_release ( ) function to decrement its use count. If proper procedures are followed, an object's use count always indicates how many users have an active reference to the object. The object destroys itself whenever the use count drops to zero.

Custom Class Example, an Object Manager   Next we will design an object manager custom class. This object will be responsible for knowing about all the custom class instances your application creates, and making sure they are destroyed before your application shuts down.

The object manager is actually a very simple object. It maintains an array of PowerObject datatypes. It has a public function, uf_register( ), and a Destructor event. The essential elements of the object manager are shown in listing 18.5.

Listing 18.5   n_object_manager

```
n_object_manager

// Instance variables follow
private PowerObject ipo_object_array[]
private integer ii_max_object = 0

public function uf_register (PowerObject apo_object) Returns integer
string ls_classname
if IsValid (apo_object) then
        ii_max_object ++
        ipo_object_array [ ii_max_object ] = apo_object
end if
return ii_max_object

// Destructor event script follows
integer li_sub = 0
FOR li_sub = 1 TO ii_max_object
        if IsValid ( ipo_object_array [ li_sub ] ) then
                Destroy ipo_object_array [ li_sub ]
        end if
NEXT
```

The n_object_manager object will be created during the application open event process, and destroyed during the application close event process, giving it application-wide scope.

Every other custom class object will register itself to the object manager when it is created. A call to the object manager uf_register( ) function is made from the constructor event for all custom classes:

```
// Script for the constructor event of n_base_class
if IsValid (n_object_manager) then
        n_object_manager . uf_register (this)
end if
```

We recommend defining a common ancestor for all your custom classes. Place the preceding script into the constructor event of this ancestor. It will now be inherited by all your descendant custom classes.

Part

V

Ch

18

The registration process is now automatic. You do not have to rely on each developer remembering to register every custom class object with the object manager when it is created.

By the same token, when the application shuts down and the object manager is destroyed, the object manager's Destructor event ensures that any remaining custom class objects are destroyed before they are orphaned, avoiding a memory leak.

It is not the responsibility of the object manager to create custom class objects for you. These are created by other objects whenever they are needed. The primary responsibility for the object manager is to know about all the custom class objects that the application creates, and to destroy any remaining objects before the application shuts down.

Now that you have an object manager, it is possible to add more functionality to it. You can use the object manager to "broadcast" a message to all active custom class objects.

You could also implement a "primary key" field in all of your custom classes. You could ask the object manager to search for a particular type of object having a specific primary key value. Each custom class would be responsible for maintaining its own primary key. The object manager simply loops through the array of PowerObjects. For each valid entry in the array, it could ask the object for its primary key value. When it finds a match, it could return a reference to the object.

We have designed a very simple object manager. You are limited only by your imagination when it comes to defining all the features you might want in an object manager. Good riddance to memory leaks in your applications.

Business Objects

Business objects are objects from the business world or problem domain. Most objects are comprised of three main components: class name, attributes, and operations or processes. These components are defined in the class definition or template for an object.

In PowerBuilder, we construct business objects by creating custom classes in the User Object Painter.

The name we assign to the custom class User Object when we save it to our PBL becomes the class name. This is what you will get back when you send the classname( ) message to an object created from the class.

Object attributes are defined as instance or shared variables. Each object we create from the class (class instance) will contain its own set of instance variables. Each object has its own distinct values for instance variables. All instances created from a class share the same set of shared variables.

Business Objects and DataWindows

Let's say you have a business class for a customer, implemented in PowerBuilder as a custom class. You need to display a list of customers in a DataWindow. Where should you put your database access: in the DataWindow or the business object?

In this section, our recommended solutions to this question are based on Powersoft's class, Object-Oriented PowerBuilder Development.

One Class Instance for Each Database Row (Array of Business Objects) Each instance of the customer class contains attributes for only one customer. The application will create a separate instance of this class for every row in the database. An array of reference variables will be defined to manage the customer object instances. To retrieve a list of customers, a method (function) in the application will define a database cursor, and will use embedded SQL to access the customer table. As each row is fetched, the method will create a new instance of the customer class and add it to the array of customer objects. This method will display customer attribute values in the list DataWindow using SetItem( ) functions.

A benefit of this approach is that the class can encapsulate its attributes. The resulting classes, therefore, are more reusable. Other objects (clients) can easily access the attributes of a customer object using traditional methods (for instance, uf_set_xx( ) and uf_get_xx( )).

Some disadvantages of this approach are: the application must create many instances of the class, using up a lot of Windows memory; the inherent capabilities of a DataWindow, such as efficient database access for update and retrieval, are not used; updating and accessing data in a DataWindow, using GetItemxx( ) and SetItem( ) functions, will be much slower; database access, no longer provided by the DataWindow, is not entirely provided by the business object either; and the database cursor processing and object instantiation will be done outside the class.

Single Business Object Instance with an Array of Attributes The customer class will contain an array of attributes for several customers. The application will create one object from the customer class. To retrieve a list of customers, a method (function) in the customer object will define a database cursor and will use embedded SQL to access the customer table. As each row is fetched, the script will add it to the array of customer attributes in the customer object. The object will still display the customer attribute values in the list DataWindow using SetItem( ) functions.

A benefit of this approach, like the preceding approach, is that the class can still encapsulate its attributes. Other objects (clients) can easily access the attributes of a customer object using traditional methods (for instance, uf_set_xx( ) and uf_get_xx( )).

Some disadvantages of this approach are: the application creates only one instance of a class, but this class contains an array of attributes for many customers; the inherent capabilities of a DataWindow, such as efficient database access for update and retrieval, are still not used; updating and accessing data in a DataWindow, using GetItemxx( ) and SetItem( ) functions, are still necessary and will be much slower; database access, no longer provided by the DataWindow, is not entirely provided by the business object either; and the database cursor processing is still located outside the class.

Single Business Object Instance Using DataWindows for Attributes The customer attributes will be stored in a DataWindow rather than as attributes of the class. The class will contain an array of DataWindow reference variables. The application will create one customer object from the customer class. To retrieve customer data, the application will "register" a

DataWindow by passing it to a method in the customer class, causing it to be added to the object's array. A method (function) in the customer object will retrieve the DataWindow. The application could "register" multiple DataWindows with the object to display customer data in different formats (for instance, list, free-form data entry, and so on).

The benefits of this approach include: the built-in DataWindow database access capability is retained; it is no longer necessary to use SetItem() functions to display the attribute values in a DataWindow; changes to the database will primarily impact the DataWindow, not the class; the DataWindows are more independent from the class; and much less memory will be needed than in either of the two preceding options.

The disadvantages of this approach include: the attributes of the object are encapsulated longer; it is more difficult to control or restrict access to these attributes; and the class requires a DataWindow to hold its attributes.

On balance, the last option, using one or more DataWindows in place of defining attributes for an object, will probably be more efficient in a two-tier architecture with the current DataWindow architecture.

Mapping Business Objects to Relational Databases

Let's say we are designing a customer billing system for a gas or electric energy utility. We might identify the following business objects (not a complete list): Commercial Customer, Residential Customer, Premises (location where energy service is provided), Account (to bill a customer for the gas and electricity you provide to the customer's premises), and Meter (representing the point where gas or electricity consumption is measured).

When you develop an initial object model, you will see some common attributes and duplicated processing in both the Commercial Customer and Residential Customer. Abstract these common elements to a generalized Customer class. Both the Commercial Customer class and the Residential Customer class will be specializations or subclasses of the generic Customer class.

The relationship between these three customer classes is known as a generalization/specialization (gen/spec) relationship. Gen/spec relationships occur whenever we have one class described as being a type of another class.

In PowerBuilder, we use custom classes to define business objects. We use inheritance to implement gen/spec relationships within our custom classes. Our commercial customer and our residential customer are both types of customers. Figure 18.26 shows our customer class hierarchy.

Inheritance relationships can also be characterized as supertypes and subtypes. The generic class, n_customer is the supertype, and both n_commercial_customer and n_residential_customer are subtypes of n_customer.

How does an inheritance hierarchy map to a Relational Database (RDBMS)? Usually you will build a logical data model at the same time as you build your object model. Each class in your object model often maps to an entity or table in your normalized logical data model.

FIG. 18.26

The customer class hierarchy.

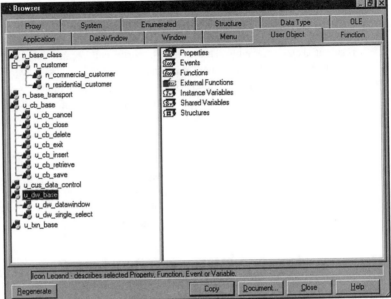

During physical database design, you evaluate and modify your normalized data model to enhance performance. During this denormalization process, you generally have three ways of representing a class hierarchy in a relational database.

Separate Database Tables for the Ancestor Class and Each Descendant Class

First, you could define a separate table for each class. With this approach, you would have three tables corresponding to the three customer classes: generic customer table, commercial customer table, and residential customer table. The customer table will contain all the attributes common to both commercial customers and residential customers. The commercial customer table, therefore, will contain only attributes needed for only commercial customers, and likewise for the residential customer table.

To obtain values for all attributes for a commercial customer, it is necessary to join a row from the commercial customer table with a row from the generic customer table. To retrieve a residential customer, you must join a row from the residential customer table with a row from the generic customer table. Since all customers will be either a commercial customer or a residential customer, it will always be necessary to join two tables to retrieve all the attributes for a particular customer. For performance reasons, you might choose an alternative denormalized approach.

Merge the Descendant Classes into the Table for the Ancestor Class

Another approach merges all three tables into one. The two descendant tables are eliminated. Each row in the customer table, therefore, contains certain attributes that are not filled in (null). For example, commercial customers will have null values in columns (attributes) that pertain only to residential customers. The benefit of this approach is that you never need to join two tables in order to select all of the columns for a particular type of customer.

Part

V

Ch

18

Merge the Ancestor Class into the Tables for Each of the Descendant Classes   The third approach eliminates the ancestor table (customer). The attributes (columns) defined in the customer table will now be redundantly defined in both the commercial customer table and the residential customer table. This approach works well because any given customer is going to be either a residential customer or a commercial customer (we never have simply a generic customer and the same customer will never be both residential and commercial). It is not necessary to join two tables to read all the attributes for a given customer. We will not define any unneeded columns in either table. All columns in the commercial customer table will pertain to commercial customers, and so on.

It is not possible to choose the proper alternative without knowing more about the specific data being stored, and how that data will be accessed and updated. You should look at table sizes (number of columns and rows), access frequencies, and so on. Any one of these approaches may be viable for your situation. Which approach you choose for a given situation depends. "It depends"; that is the answer to every design question.

Golden Rules for Object-Oriented PowerBuilder Development

We have a set of golden rules for object-oriented PowerBuilder development. By using these rules as guidelines, you can become a more productive PowerBuilder developer. You will be able to exploit more fully the object-oriented capabilities of PowerBuilder. Understanding User Objects is a key to object-orientation.

The golden rules are:

- Every window in your application should be inherited from an ancestor window (for instance, w_ancestor_sheet).
- Put your ancestor Windows into a common framework class library.
- Every window control should be painted from a Standard Visual User Object. For example, use u_cb_retrieve whenever you need a retrieve button, or u_dw_single_select whenever you need a DataWindow control with single-row selection.
- Every Standard Visual User Object in your application should be inherited from an ancestor Standard Visual User Object. For example, all command buttons are inherited from u_cb_base, and all DataWindows are inherited from u_dw_base.
- Put your ancestor Standard Visual User Objects into a common framework class library.
- Buttons and menu items never contain business rules. Buttons and menus trigger events in other objects containing the business rules.
- Put your business rules into business objects (custom classes).
- Every custom class in your application should be inherited from a common ancestor. For example, n_customer and n_employee are inherited from n_base_class.
- Put your ancestor custom classes into a common framework class library.

- As you develop your application, make your ancestor classes more robust while keeping them generic.
- Every application should use a class library. You should either Build, Buy, Beg, or Borrow a class library (the four Bs).

Introduction to Distributed PowerBuilder

In the past, most PowerBuilder applications relied upon the powerful database access capabilities built into the DataWindow. In addition to providing the user interface to the database, the DataWindow is often responsible for generating the SQL sent to the database for data retrieval and updating. DataWindows also can contain some of the application's business rules in the form of data validation rules associated with columns in the DataWindow.

This approach is often called the 2-tier architecture or fat client design. All of the application's processing is implemented on the client side, which is the first tier. The second tier is the database, typically residing on a database server connected to the client workstation using a Local Area Network (LAN). The client application sends SQL requests to the database server for retrieval and updating. The database server processes the client requests and returns data to the client in the form of result sets, or performs the requested updates. The database itself does little of the actual processing for the application.

In those databases that support them, stored procedures provide a means of partitioning the application by moving some of the business rules and data access out of the client to the server. Unfortunately, most databases use a proprietary language for coding stored procedures. If an application needs to be portable across a variety of back-end databases, it is necessary to avoid stored procedures, or at least convert them from one language to another. Since stored procedures reside in the back-end database, we still have a 2-tier architecture. We have turned our fat client design into a fat server design.

While these very powerful features of PowerBuilder's DataWindow help developers to be very productive building client/server applications, these same features make it difficult to partition the application or to exploit 3-tier or n-tier architectures.

One approach for application partitioning uses Remote Procedure Calls (RPCs). An RPC would be developed in a language such as C or C++ and deployed on an application or function server. The remote procedure is made to appear to the PowerBuilder application as if it was an external function in a local Dynamic Link Library (DLL). Software known as middleware, would allow you to define the function interface using an Interface Definition Language (IDL). The middleware would generate a stub DLL for the client side of the application and a stub for the remote side of the application. The two stubs would communicate using a protocol such as TCP/IP and would be responsible for dealing with the hardware differences between the client platform and the remote procedure platform. The PowerBuilder application would invoke the RPC by calling an external function in the local stub DLL. The local DLL in turn would pass the message to the corresponding stub on the remote platform. Finally the remote stub would pass the message to the actual remote procedure.

Needless to say, there are many challenges to implementing 3-tier architectures using remote procedure calls. RPCs cannot be written in PowerBuilder. Companies have to have developers who can code in C or C++ (or some other 3/GL language). The middleware can be an expensive additional software purchase that may also incur a significant learning curve. Finally, since the DataWindow cannot call a remote procedure directly, it is necessary to implement an efficient mechanism for getting data returned by a remote procedure into DataWindow buffers.

Distributed PowerBuilder is intended to provide an easier path to 3-tier and n-tier application architectures. Using the custom class feature of PowerBuilder, it will be possible to separate application processing from the client and deploy it on a remote server. A developer can take any custom class (non-visual user object) and easily distribute it onto an application server. The client application simply instantiates the custom class and calls its functions. It will not be necessary to code the remote process in a 3/GL like C or C++. It will also not be necessary to purchase, install, and learn special middleware to generate the client-and server-side stubs. The learning curve for distributed PowerBuilder will be a lot less than that for implementing RPCs.

A distributed PowerBuilder object can be both a server (to the client application) as well as a client of another service object. This is where the term n-tier comes about. There can be any number of logical or physical layers to the application. It is also not necessary to have a physical separation between the layers. It is possible to implement a distributed object and test it on a local machine, and then distribute it to an application server later.

There are several advantages to n-tier applications. First, you can take advantage of the faster processing speeds available on an application server compared to client workstations. Moving most of the application processing out of the client side of the application may give you better overall performance without having to upgrade the memory and CPUs of all the client workstations.

A second advantage of distributed processing is easier management of software changes. Changes to application processing can now be deployed to the application server instead of each of the individual client workstations.

A third advantage of distributed processing is tighter database security. When the client application communicates directly with the database, the user must be granted privileges for accessing or updating tables in the database. However, there is no way to prevent a user from accessing or updating the database outside of the application, such as by using an interactive SQL tool. Using such a tool a user can bypass the application's built-in validations and integrity rules. By moving data access out of the application, the user can be granted access to the remote process without being granted direct access to the database.

With Distributed PowerBuilder (DPB), there is now the concept of a server application as well as a client application. The server application contains custom classes (NVOs) whose services (functions) are invoked by one or more client applications. When deployed as part of a server application, these custom classes become known as remote objects.

When PowerBuilder 5 is released for the windows platforms, a DPB server application can be deployed on either a Windows NT 3.51 or Windows 95 platform. A DPB client application can reside on either Windows 3.x, Windows NT 3.51, or Windows 95. When PowerBuilder 5 is released for the UNIX and Macintosh platforms, there will be support for those platforms. Depending on the combination of client and server platforms, the appropriate communications driver must be selected. Table 18.3 lists the available choices of communications protocols.

Remote objects can be invoked across process boundaries, which are separate executables running on the same machine, or across computer boundaries connected by a network.

Table 18.3   Distributed PowerBuilder Communications Protocols

Platform	Communications Driver	Server	Client
Windows 3.x	NamedPipes	No	No
	Sockets	No	Yes
	OpenClientServer	No	Yes
Windows NT 3.51	NamedPipes	Yes	Yes
	Sockets	Yes	Yes
	OpenClientServer	Yes	Yes
Windows 95	NamedPipes	No	Yes
	Sockets	Yes	Yes
	OpenClientServer	No	Yes
PowerBuilder UNIX	N/A		
PowerBuilder Mac	N/A		

Part
V

Ch
18

Developing Distributed PowerBuilder Clients and Server Applications

A DPB server application can be a separate PowerBuilder client application running locally, a remote server application, or a remote client to another PowerBuilder server application. A DPB client application is one that invokes services from remote objects.

To support distributed objects, PowerBuilder 5 introduces some new non-visual classes:

```
nonvisualobject
      connectionobject (new)
             connection (new)
             transport (new)
      remoteobject (new)
structure
      connectioninfo (new)
```

Creating the DPB Proxy Object

When a custom class object is distributed to a remote server, PowerBuilder builds a proxy object to serve as the client-side replacement for the remote object. Creating a proxy object for an existing custom class is very easy. Simply set the proxy name for the custom class in the custom class painter.

Suppose you have a customer business object called n_customer. Open n_customer. Right-click on the object in the user object painter. From the pop-up menu, choose Set Proxy Name. In the proxy field type in "p_customer", and click the OK button. Finally, save the user object. PowerBuilder will create the proxy object for you. The custom class object, n_customer, will be moved to a PBL for the DPB server application, while the proxy object, p_customer, is moved to a PBL for the DPB client application.

Creating the DPB Server Application

The transport class is a standard non-visual class used by a DPB server application to listen for and process client requests for its services. The transport object is set up to use a specific communications protocol, and contains a method, Listen ( ), to accept client requests for services using the specified communications protocol.

Define a main window, w_server_main, for the DPB server application to open. In the open event of the application, open this window:

```
open (w_server_main)
```

The next step in building a DPB server is to create an instance of the transport class. Do this in the open event of w_server_main:

```
protected transport itrnsp_transport   // Defined as an instance variable
itrans_transport = Create transport
```

Next, initialize the attributes of the transport object. Since our example will use Windows 95 for both the client and server platform, we will use the Sockets communications driver:

```
itrnsp_transport.driver = "winsock"
itrnsp_transport.location = "."
itrnsp_transport.options = ""
itrnsp_transport.application = "11111"
```

Finally, have your DPB server listen for client requests:

```
rc = itransp_transport.listen()
if rc <> 0 then
        Messagebox ("DPB Server", "Error Code = " + &
                string(itransp_transport.errcode) + "   Error Text = " &
                + itransp_transport.errtext)
        halt close
end if
```

Creating the DPB Client Application

The connection object is a standard non-visual class used by a DPB client application to connect to a DPB server application. The connection object is also set up to use a specific communications protocol. Once created and initialized, the client application invokes a method in the connection object, ConnectToServer ( ), to establish a communications channel between the DPB client and the DPB server applications.

Define a main window, w_client_main, for the DPB client application to open. In the open event of the application, open this window:

```
open (w_client_main)
```

The next step in building a DPB client is to create an instance of the connection class. Do this in the open event of w_client_main:

```
protected connection iconn_connection   // Defined as an instance variable
iconn_connection = Create connection
```

Next, initialize the attributes of the connection object. Since the DPB server application will be running on the same machine as the DPB client, we will use "localhost" for the connection location. For a remote DPB server, specify the IP address of the server:

```
iconn_connection.application = "11111"
iconn_connection.options = ""
//iconn_connection.location = "199.93.182.000"
iconn_connection.location = "localhost"
iconn_connection.driver = "winsock"
```

Next establish a connection between the DPB client and server applications:

```
int rc
rc = iconn_connection.ConnectToServer()
if rc <> 0 then
        Messagebox ("DPB Client", "Error Code = " + &
                string(iconn_connection.errcode) + "   Error Text = " &
                + iconn_connection.errtext)
        halt close
end if
```

Next, create the proxy for the remote object, and tell it to use the established connection:

```
protected p_customer ip_proxy_customer // defined as an instance variable
ip_proxy_customer = CREATE p_customer
ip_proxy_customer.SetConnect (iconn_connection)
```

You should now be able to call a function in the remote object from the client application:

```
string ls_address
ls_address  = ip_proxy_customer . uf_get_s_address ()
```

Implementing Distributed PowerBuilder Applications

Distributed PowerBuilder (DPB) emphasizes the importance of application partitioning. If you have already moved your application's business logic out of the interface elements of your application (windows, menus, DataWindows, and window controls) into custom class business objects (NVOs), you will be able to easily exploit the features of Distributed PowerBuilder. Your business objects can easily be remotely distributed when you migrate to PowerBuilder 5

Part

V

Ch

18

Distributed PowerBuilder does not provide any additional security features beyond the built-in security provided by your network.

A DPB server application cannot call a DPB client application. The server application must be activated and then it waits for requests from the client application.

The initial implementation of Distributed PowerBuilder in release 5.0 is only a first step. It will not provide asynchronous processing or multithreading of remote objects. Each connection to a remote object will require a separate thread.

Each DPB client application will have its own program variable space. Data from one client application will not be shared with other clients connected to the same or different application servers.

From Here...

This chapter has introduced you to the PowerBuilder User Objects. User Objects are essential to exploiting fully the object-oriented features of PowerBuilder. As you build robust, reusable sets of User Objects, you will be able to build new applications by assembling predefined objects, and spend less time writing the same code over and over inside every window. You will then be able to spend your time understanding and developing solutions to specific business problems.

- For more information on windows and window controls, see chapter 4, "Exploring Windows."

- For more information on object-orientation, see chapter 17, "Understanding Object-Oriented Concepts."

- For more on inheritance, see chapter 22, "Exploiting the Power of Inheritance."

CHAPTER 19

Specialized User Objects

by Raghuram Bala

PowerBuilder 5 facilitates large-scale client-server development with two specialized objects called Data Pipelines and Proxy Objects.

In large enterprises, it is common to find many heterogeneous data sources, and often there are conversion projects to move data from one database to another. Usually such a task is accomplished by writing scripts in arcane database 4GLs, e.g., SQLLoader for Oracle. If there are more than two databases involved, the complexity of such an undertaking increases in order of magnitude. With the data pipeline object in PowerBuilder, this task is simplified tremendously with a standard method of converting and moving data from one database to another.

When developing large-scale client server projects where transaction volume is high, there is usually a need for the application to be scalable. This means that the application should not falter if transaction volumes increase over time. The only way to safeguard against this is to partition an application in such a way that most of the heavy processing logic is placed in a highly scalable environment. In a two-tier client server environment using PowerBuilder, most of the processing logic is placed on the desktop environment running Windows 3.x or Windows 95, which

Learn how to create and use a data pipeline.

Transfer large amounts of data from one database to another with a data pipeline. The pipeline can also be used for other functions, including a distributed data network.

Understand the concept of a data warehouse.

Data pipelines can be used to administer a data warehouse. A *data warehouse* is a read-only storage area. This storage area can be periodically updated from remote areas where the data is maintained.

Understand how to implement a pipeline inside an application using a user object.

You can execute a data pipeline in the PowerBuilder environment, but you could also put a pipeline into an application using User Objects.

Learn how to develop and implement a Distributed PowerBuilder application.

In a distributed application built with PowerBuilder 5, the client has the ability to invoke methods on a remote object on an application server as if it were local. The client and the application server can reside on the same machine or on different machines.

are not very scalable environments. Increases in transaction volumes will also require a massive upgrade of hardware throughout the organization. In a three-tier or N-tier client server environment, performance bottlenecks are isolated and placed on platforms such as Windows NT or Unix, which support heavy transaction loads. ■

Using the Data Pipeline

Using data pipelines, you can transfer large amounts of data from one database to another. These databases don't even have to use the same driver. For example, you could transfer data from a Watcom SQL 4.0 database to an Oracle 7.1 database.

Although the idea of transferring data is appealing, especially if you are switching from one database to another, the pipeline can be used for other functions, including a distributed data network.

Creating and Using a Data Pipeline in PowerBuilder

To create a data pipeline, click the Pipeline icon. This will open the Select Data Pipeline dialog box seen in figure 19.1. Click New.

FIG. 19.1
Use the Select Data Pipeline dialog box to edit or create a data pipeline.

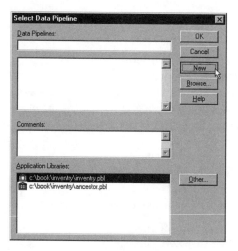

When you create a data pipeline, you must choose both a source connection and a destination connection. The source connection is where the data and table definitions currently reside. The destination connection is where the data and table definitions will be transferred. The source and destination connections are chosen in the New Data Pipeline dialog, as seen in figure 19.2. This dialog box automatically opens when you're creating a new data pipeline.

FIG. 19.2

The New Data Pipeline dialog box is used to define your source and destination connections, and data source for a data pipeline.

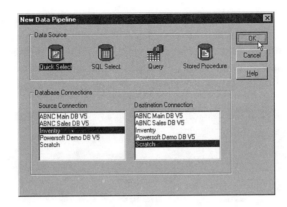

You have four possible data sources for a new pipeline, namely:

- **Quick Select**—Select a single table from your Source Connection, and select fields from that table for the data pipeline.
- **SQL Select**—Construct a complex query using one or more tables from your Source Connection.
- **Query**—Choose an existing query and use its output for the data pipeline.
- **Stored Procedure**—Select a stored procedure in the Source Connection and use its output for the data pipeline.

Selecting tables and fields for a data pipeline is similar to defining DataWindows. Here, we shall create a pipeline using the Quick Select data source.

The Quick Select dialog box opens inside the select painter, as seen in figure 19.3. (You've seen the select painter before when you defined DataWindows.) Choose the tables and fields you want to process and click OK.

Part

V

Ch

19

FIG. 19.3

The Quick Select dialog box lets you choose the tables and fields you want to process.

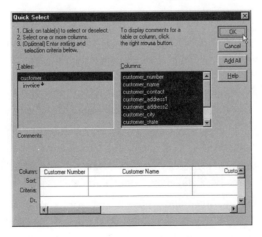

As with DataWindows, you can use the select painter to choose which columns you want to transfer. You can also control what data you transfer by using the Where tab, as seen in figure 19.4. By allowing you to choose the columns and order of the columns that are transferred, as well as allowing you to filter data with a Where SQL statement, the data pipeline is more efficient than a simple export/import combination.

FIG. 19.4

The select painter lets you choose which columns to transfer as well as which data.

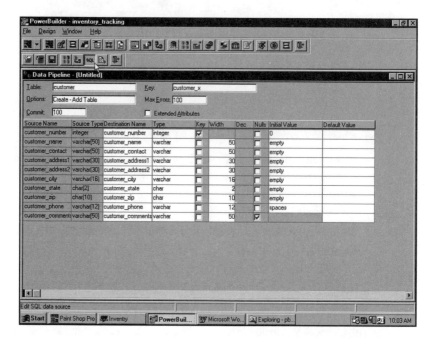

When you've defined the tables, columns, and Where criteria to be used in the data pipeline transfer, click the Design icon. This opens the data pipeline painter, as seen in figure 19.5.

The data pipeline painter contains many fields that must be filled in before the transfer takes place:

- Table allows you to name the table you are creating with the data pipeline. Usually, this will be the same table name as the source database's table.

- Key allows you to name your primary key of the destination table. Usually, this is the same key that is used in the source database's table.

- Options allow you to describe how you want the data transfer to take place. Valid options from which you can choose using the drop-down list box are:

  - Create—Add Table allows you to create a new table. The data pipeline will fail if this table already exists on the destination database.

  - Replace—Drop/Add Table drops the table from the destination database if that table exists, and then creates a new table with the source database's information.

  - Refresh—Delete/Insert Rows keeps the destination database in place, but makes all the rows match the source database by using SQL Deletes and Inserts.

- Append—Insert Rows allows you to insert rows that do not exist on the destination database. Any duplicate keys will not be appended and will receive an error.

- Update—Update/Insert Rows inserts rows that do not exist on the destination database, as well as updates those rows that do exist with new information from the source database.

■ Max Errors lets you determine how many errors your transfer can receive (for example, duplicate key) before halting. Valid values are No Limit, 1, 10, 100, 200, 300, and so on, up to 1,000.

FIG. 19.5

The data pipeline painter lets you define how the data will be received by the destination database.

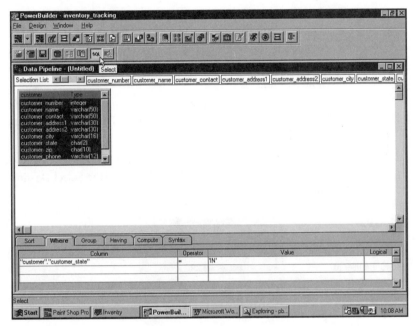

NOTE When setting Max Errors, you should determine how error prone you can be. For instance, if you are using the Replace-Drop/Add Table option, you should not receive any errors, and should mark Max Errors to reflect this.

If, on the other hand, you're using the Append-Insert Rows option and expect a lot of duplicate rows, you should mark this at a high setting so that your data transfer goes through. ■

TIP You cannot change the Source Name or Source Type columns in the data pipeline painter.

■ Commit allows you to choose how many SQL statements get executed before committing. Commits usually take a lot of time. When doing bulk transactions (as is done with the data pipeline), it may be better if the database were committed at the end of the pipeline processing.

Part
V

Ch
19

- You may try to commit as many as possible, especially with a low Max Error count, before rolling back your transaction.

- Destination Name lets you change the name of the column on the destination table.

- Type allows you to change the data type (for example, from an integer to a float) of the column on the destination table.

- Key lets you indicate which fields will be part of the primary key on the destination database.

- Width lets you resize the field on the destination database.

- The Dec column allows you to enter the number of decimals for a field.

- The Nulls column indicates which fields are allowed to be NULL.

- Initial Value sets the default value on the new database if the end user tries to update a column with a NULL value. You cannot have an Initial Value if you allow a column to contain NULL.

- Default Value allows the user to define a default value on a field if the user attempts to update a column in an existing row with a NULL value. You cannot have a Default Value if you allow a column to contain NULL.

When you're finished defining your pipeline, click the Pipeline Profile icon to make sure the destination profile setup is correct. This will pull up the Select Destination Profile dialog box seen in figure 19.6.

FIG. 19.6

The Select Destination Profile dialog box allows the user to redirect the output of a pipeline to another data source.

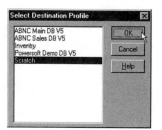

The Select icon will return you to the select painter with the SQL toolbox. The select painter and the Select Destination Profile dialog box are useful if you want to use the same pipeline to populate different databases using different Where criteria.

Finally, save the data pipeline using the Save Data Pipeline dialog box, as shown in figure 19.7, by choosing File, Save.

Click OK and then click the Execute icon to start the transfer.

Using a Data Pipeline in an Application

You can execute a data pipeline in the PowerBuilder environment, but you could also put a pipeline into an application using User Objects.

First, declare a user object by clicking the User Object icon. This opens the New User Object dialog box. Choose the standard class type of user object, as seen in figure 19.8.

FIG. 19.7

The Save Data Pipeline dialog box is used to save the data pipeline into a PBL.

FIG. 19.8

Data pipelines must be used as standard class user objects.

PowerBuilder then opens the Select Standard Class Type dialog box to ask you what type of user object you want to declare. Click pipeline, as seen in figure 19.9.

FIG. 19.9

Click on pipeline in the Select Standard Class Type dialog box.

Now use the code in listing 19.1 in the constructor event of your user object:

Listing 19.1   Source Code for Data Transfer from the INVENTRY Database to the SCRATCH Database

```
DataObject = "l_inventry_to_scratch"

// Define database transactions
transaction Source
transaction Destination
```

continues

Part
V

Ch

19

Listing 19.1   Continued

```
// Define datawindow for process
DataWindow customer

// — Define the parameters necessary to connect to the database.
Source.DBMS             = "ODBC"
Source.Database         = "INVENTRY"
Source.UserID           = "dba"
Source.DBPass           = "sql"
Source.DBParm           = "Connectstring='DSN=INVENTRY;UID=DBA;PWD=SQL'"

// — Define the parameters necessary to connect to the database.
Destination.DBMS        = "ODBC"
Destination.Database    = "SCRATCH"
Destination.UserID      = "dba"
Destination.DBPass      = "sql"
Destination.DBParm      = "Connectstring='DSN=SCRATCH;UID=DBA;PWD=SQL'"

start ( Source, Destination, customer )
```

Save your user object. (The user object in the example is named u_inventry_to_scratch.)
Finally, start your pipeline with the following user object declaration. Put this line of code
behind a command button or in your application open event:

```
u_inventry_to_scratch start_this          // start the pipeline
```

The pipeline attributes are listed in table 19.1.

Table 19.1   Pipeline Attributes

Attribute	Data Type	Description
Anchor	Long	N.A.
RowsInError	Long	The number of rows the pipeline found in error (for example, rows containing a duplicate key).
RowsRead	Long	The number of rows read by the pipeline.
RowsWritten	Long	The number of rows written by the pipeline.
DataObject	String	The name of the pipeline object (the object created in the data pipeline painter).
Syntax	String	The syntax used to create the pipeline object (the object created in the data pipeline painter).

Pipeline events are listed in table 19.2.

Table 19.2   Pipeline Events

Event	Occurs
Constructor	When the user object is created.
Destructor	When the user object is destroyed.
PipeEnd	When Start or Repair is completed.
PipeMeter	After each block of rows is read or written. The Commit factor specified for the pipeline determines the size of each block.
PipeStart	When a Start or Repair is started.

Pipeline functions are listed in table 19.3.

Table 19.3   Pipeline Functions

Returned Data Type	Function	Description
Cancel()	Long	Stops execution of a pipeline.
ClassName()	String	Returns the name assigned to the user object.
GetParent()	PowerObject	Returns the parent object of a pipeline object.
PipeCreate()	Long	N.A.
PipeDestroy()	Integer	N.A.
PostEvent(event_name)	Boolean	Runs the event after the function or event currently running is finished.
Repair(transaction)	Integer	Updates the transaction database with corrections that have been made in the pipeline user object's Error DataWindow.
Start(src, dest, dw)	Integer	Executes a pipeline.
TriggerEvent(ename)	Boolean	Runs the event immediately.
TypeOf()	Object	Returns the type of the user object.

Part
V

Ch

19

Understanding Data Warehouses

Data pipelines can be used to administer a data warehouse. A *data warehouse* is a read-only storage area. This storage area can be periodically updated from remote areas where the data is maintained.

For example, say you are running a company. Your company has offices all over the country, and each remote office is responsible for maintaining its own data. You would like a copy of the data at the home office to run reports, process information, and complete other tasks.

Each remote office could process the data relevant to them (say, by region or state) and on a daily basis, use the data pipeline to transmit data to you over the wide area network (WAN) data warehouse.

What is described here is a type of distributive database, where one central store of data can be populated by remote sites without too much "traffic" over the WAN.

The pros of using a data pipeline to implement a distributive database are as follows:

- Not much line traffic is involved, so your WAN or LAN (local area network) won't be overloaded.

- Any WAN line traffic can be controlled, so large data transfers can occur at light periods of WAN or LAN use.

- Remote sights are responsible for their own data, so the burden of data control is taken off the home office.

- The home office still can access the data warehouse for reports or to copy the data.

The cons of using a data pipeline to implement a distributive database are as follows:

- Remote sites are responsible for their own data, so the burden of data control as well as database management is added to their tasks.

- The data in the data warehouse must be read-only, or else there's a chance that some updates to the data will be overwritten. This limits the processing available.

- Huge bulk data transfers are necessary periodically. During these transfers, the LAN or WAN access will slow down.

If needed, the home office can pipeline data "the other way" to populate read-only data on the remote sites, or to update remote sites after processing. This must be used judiciously to avoid overwriting changes at the remote sites. You could use this technique to send back a compilation of data from all sites so that each individual site could see how they compare.

If the pros of this situation appeal to you and the cons don't concern you too much, you could implement a distributed data network using data warehouses and remote sites with the data pipeline.

Using Distributed PowerBuilder

What we have seen up to now are capabilities of PowerBuilder in a two-tier client/server environment. With PowerBuilder 5, we can now scale our applications to a three-tier client/server architecture. In a two-tier client/server architecture, traditionally, presentation and business logic reside on the client tier, while data is stored in the database management system that makes up the second tier. See figure 19.10.

FIG. 19.10
Two-tier client/server architecture.

Two-tier Client/Server Architecture

Although such an architecture is adequate for most departmental applications, it has its limitations when used in large enterprises. Two common limitations are:

- Lack of Scalability—In large organizations, the transaction volume generated by an application may be very high. In order for such an application to run, it requires powerful hardware capable of handling heavy transaction loads, and operating systems built for multi-user environments. Windows NT and Unix machines are geared towards multi-user environments and have the capability to handle large transaction loads better than single-user operating systems such as MacOS or Windows 3.x.

- Poor Performance—When transaction volumes are high and because all transaction management is handled on the client tier, poor performance is exhibited. Performance can be improved by partitioning the application differently.

The three-tier client/server architecture solves the problems of scalability and performance by introducing a new tier. This way, the client tier in the two-tier architecture is now split into the presentation layer and application layer. The presentation layer takes care of the user interface components, while the application layer consists of the business logic and handles transaction management. The presentation layer would normally reside on a PC, and the application layer on a high-performance Windows NT or Unix machine (also known as the application server). See figure 19.11.

Part
V

Ch
19

 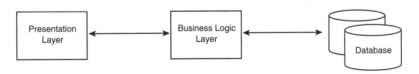

FIG. 19.11
Three-tier client/server architecture.

Three-tier Client/Server Architecture

Developing with Distributed PowerBuilder

In a distributed application built with PowerBuilder 5, the client has the ability to invoke methods on a remote object on an application server as if it were local. The client and the application server can reside on the same machine or on different machines. The client can communicate with the application server using one of three methods:

- *Named pipes.* An interprocess communication mechanism that opens a channel for passing data between two processes. This channel is treated as if it were a file, and one can read, write, open, and close a named pipe.

- *Winsock*. The Windows standard implementation of sockets. Sockets are used by TCP/IP stacks for interprocess communication.

- *OpenClientServer*. A Sybase customer server that enables applications to communicate with one or more Sybase database servers.

Three objects used by Distributed PowerBuilder for interprocess communication are:

- *Connection Object*. Used to establish a connection from the client to the application server. This object is instantiated on the client.

- *Transport Object*. Instantiated on the server and listens for client requests.

- *ConnectionInfo Object*. Used by a client to retrieve information about its connection to a particular server. A client with CONNECTWITHADMIN! privileges can retrieve information about all clients connected to a particular server.

Before implementing a Distributed PowerBuilder application, you have to design the interface specification for the remote object. An interface specification consists of all the methods that are exposed to the external entities wanting to use the remote object.

Implementing with Distributed PowerBuilder

You are now ready to build Distributed PowerBuilder applications. Building a distributed application is a two stage process. In the first stage, you build the server application and in the second stage you build the client application. The client and server applications can reside on two separate machines or on the same machine. It is prudent to test them on the same machine before introducing the complexity of a LAN or WAN, network protocols, and communications.

You can create a simple Distributed PowerBuilder application in which a client program invokes a method on a remote object on an application server to multiply a number. This application consists of three PBLs. The client program consists of CLIENT.PBL and COMMON.PBL, while the server consists of SERVER.PBL and COMMON.PBL. The COMMON.PBL contains a proxy object that makes it appear to the client that the remote object resides locally when in fact it resides on the application server (see fig. 19.12).

CAUTION

In order to use Distributed PowerBuilder, you must have the run-time DLLs on your client machine and your application server. When using Winsock for connectivity ensure that TCP/IP is installed on your machine. On Windows 95 and NT, TCP/IP comes with the operating system.

The Server Program   First, you create a server application in the usual way, and create a Class UserObject as seen in figure 19.13.

Next, you define the userobject functions that the client would invoke as seen in figure 19.14.

The uf_mult function in the remote object multiplies the argument received from the client by two and returns the result, as seen in figure 19.15.

FIG. 19.12
Architecture for Distributed PowerBuilder sample application.

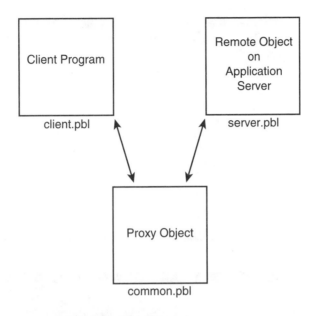

Client Program

client.pbl

Remote Object on Application Server

server.pbl

Proxy Object

common.pbl

FIG. 19.13
Remote object creation.

FIG. 19.14
Definition of multiplication function in Remote object.

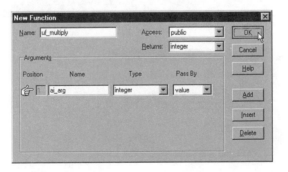

Once you have completed creating the necessary userobject functions, the next step is to define the proxy object. This is done simply by clicking the right mouse-button as shown in figure 19.16.

Name the proxy object appropriately as this will be used in the client program later. See figure 19.17.

FIG. 19.15

Multiplication function in Remote object.

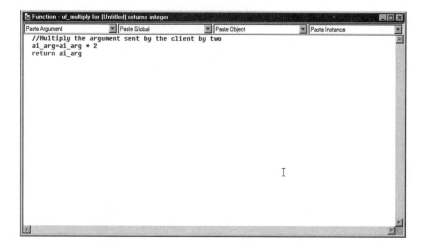

FIG. 19.16

Defining a proxy object.

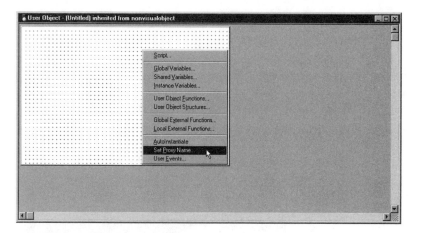

FIG. 19.17

Naming the proxy object.

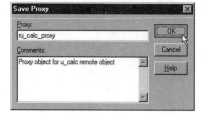

Finally, save the user object as u_calc, as seen in figure 19.18.

When you do this, notice that PowerBuilder creates a new object called ru_calc_proxy within SERVER.PBL, as shown in figure 19.19. Recall that this was the name of the proxy object. The proxy object is a special object which acts as a conduit between the client and the remote object. It cannot be edited using any of the PowerBuilder painters.

FIG. 19.18
Saving the remote
object.

FIG. 19.19
Proxy object created in
SERVER.PBL.

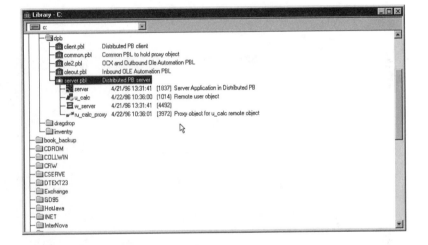

The proxy object needs to be shared by both the client and server programs. Hence, you should create a new PowerBuilder library called COMMON.PBL and move the proxy object to this new PBL as shown in figure 19.20. Add COMMON.PBL to the library list of the the server program.

You then create a simple server window, w_server, as seen in figure 19.21, to invoke the server process. This window consists of the *Listen* and *Exit* commandbuttons.

When the Listen commandbutton is clicked, it establishes the server program as a service handler and puts it into a listening mode. While in a listening mode, the server awaits requests from client programs. You should define an instance variable for w_server as shown in figure 19.22.

The code for the Clicked event of the Listen commandbutton is shown in listing 19.2.

FIG. 19.20

Move proxy object to COMMON.PBL.

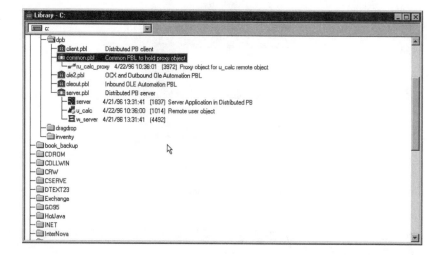

FIG. 19.21

w_server window.

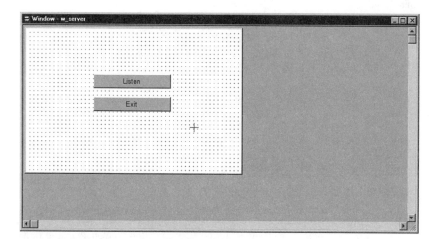

FIG. 19.22

Instance variable in w_server.

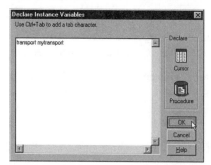

Listing 19.2 The Code for the Clicked Event of the Listen Commandbutton

```
// Clicked event of Listen commandbutton
//1      Create a transport object
mytransport = create transport

//2      Specify the transport driver
mytransport.driver = "winsock"

//3      Specify the server application name
mytransport.application = "12345"

//4      Activate the remote object listener
mytransport.Listen()
```

When the Listen button is clicked, it creates a transport object and specifies the transport driver and application name. The connection driver in the client program must be the same as the transport driver on the server. This is the protocol used by the two programs to communicate with one another. The application name indicates the name by which the server program is referred to by client programs.

The *Exit* commandbutton closes the window and ends the server program.

```
// Clicked event of Exit commandbutton
DESTROY mytransport
close(parent)
```

The Client Program The client program will be a separate application from the server, and the COMMON.PBL declared earlier needs to be in its library list. The client program will consist of a single window as shown in figure 19.23.

FIG. 19.23
w_client window.

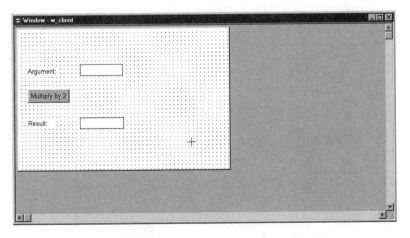

The client window, w_client, has two instance variables, namely, myconnect and ruo_calc, as shown in figure 19.24. The former is used for establishing a connection with the server while the latter maintains a handle to the remote object.

FIG. 19.24

Instance variable in Client program.

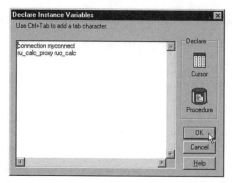

The open event of w_client creates a connection object and establishes a connection with the server program. In order to do this, a connection object is instantiated, and its driver and application attributes are set to that of the transport object in the server. Next, the machine in which the server resides is identified via the location attribute of the connection object. In listing 19.3, the location attribute is set to *localhost* which indicates that both client and server reside on the same machine.

N O T E Consult your Network Administrator if you are unsure of the server machine's name. ▪

Listing 19.3 Code for Establishing a Connection with the Server Program

```
// Open event of w_client
//1     Create a connection object
myconnect = create connection

//2     Specify the connection driver
myconnect.driver="winsock"

//3     Specify the server machine name
myconnect.location = "localhost"

//4     Specify the server application
myconnect.application="12345"

//5     Connect to the server application
myconnect.ConnectToServer()

//6     Create a local proxy for the remote object
ruo_calc = create ru_calc_proxy

//7     Instantiate the object on the server
ruo_calc.setconnect(myconnect)
```

Once connection to the server process is established, you need to get the handle to the remote object. This is done by instantiating a copy of the proxy object, and invoking the `setconnect` function as shown above.

Having done this, you are now ready to invoke the `uf_multiply` method on the remote object as though it were a local user object. Listing 19.4 shows the code for the *Multiply by 2* commandbutton.

Listing 19.4 Code for the Multiply by 2 Commandbutton

```
//     Invoke remote user object method
int result,arg

arg=Integer(sle_arg.text)
result=ruo_calc.uf_multiply(arg)
sle_result.text=String(result)
```

Notice that the syntax for calling the user object function, `uf_multiply`, is the same as calling a local user object function.

Finally, you need to destroy the instance variables in the Close event of the window.

```
//Close event of w_client
DESTROY ruo_calc
DESTROY myconnect
```

Testing the End-Product You can now test the client and server programs to see Distributed PowerBuilder in action. PowerBuilder 5 on Windows 95 allows one to start up multiple instances of PowerBuilder. Hence, you can test the client and server in runtime mode without compilation.

Part

V

Ch

19

CAUTION
If you are compiling your client and server programs, then the `COMMON.PBL` library containing the proxy object must be compiled as a Dynamic Library using the Library Painter.

First invoke your server program and click on the *Listen* commandbutton. Next, invoke the client and it will establish connection with the server. Next, enter an integer value in the *argument* field in the client window. Click on the *Multiply* button. This should invoke the remote object on the server and call the `uf_multiply` method. The `uf_multiply` method will return a value twice that of the argument and this will be displayed in the *result* field. See figure 19.25.

FIG. 19.25
Distributed PowerBuilder
in action.

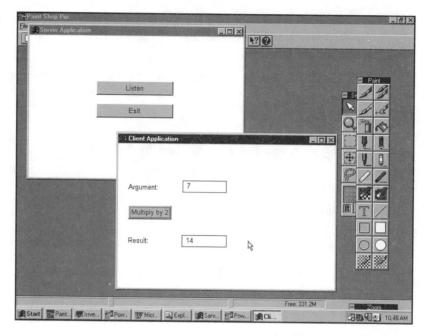

From Here...

This chapter has demonstrated some of PowerBuilder's advanced features geared toward large-scale client-server development.

In the world of object-oriented software development, the hottest catch-phrase for the next several years is "distributed objects." This phenomena has much to do with the limitations of traditional two-tier client-server development. It is also fueled by the ever-increasing popularity of the Internet where information resources are distributed globally. PowerBuilder has taken the step in the right direction by enabling application partitioning which enables code to be distributed across platforms.

Information on other advanced features of PowerBuilder 5 can be found in:

■ Appendix C, "Implementing Advanced Procedures," will show you how to add OLE, DDE and Drag-Drop to your applications. ●

Techniques from the Pros

CHAPTER 20

Using Modify and Describe to Get the Most Out of DataWindows

— *by Blake Coe*

The DataWindow in PowerBuilder is often described as the most powerful feature of the tool. DataWindows porvide you with the ability to create a powerful yet easy-to-use interface between the user and the database.

PowerBuilder has several funcitons to manipulate a DataWindow control (the DataWindow cotnrol appears on the window of user object). To manipulate the data object (which resudes inside the DataWindow control and which you create using the DataWindow painter), you use the Modify and Describe functions.

Why Do I Need to Use Describe and Modify?

As a software developer, you know that to be successful you need to customize your applications to suit your users' needs. While you can certainly do a lot with DataWindows without ever using these functions, using Modify and Describe will give you the ability to develop applications that exactly meet your users' requirements. Properly utilized, these functions can reduce the amount of code you need to write, improve performance, and make your application easier to maintain.

For example, let's say you developed a DataWindow to display employee information such as employee ID, first name, last name, social security number, date of birth, and salary (see fig. 20.1). Your boss has been using this DataWindow for a while, but now she wants to delegate the maintenance of the data to her assistant. She asks you to set it up so that the assistant can view and update all of the data except the salary column. How do you accomplish this?

FIG. 20.1

Manager's view of the DataWindow with the salary column visible.

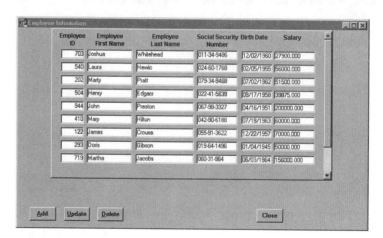

One way would be to create another DataWindow with the same data, but omitting the salary column. This seems like a lot of work, and now you have doubled your maintenance requirements. If you need to add more columns in the future, you would need to add them to both DataWindows.

A better solution would be to use the Modify function, and display or hide the salary column based on the user id. With a few lines of code, you save yourself from having to create another DataWindow, and you still have only the one DataWindow to maintain.

Place this code in the open event for the window:

```
IF sqlca.logid <> 'manager' THEN
    dw_1.Modify("salary.visible=0")
    dw_1.Modify("salary_t.visible=0")
END IF
dw_1.SetTransObject(sqlca)
dw_1.Retrieve()
```

FIG. 20.2

Nonmanager's view of the DataWindow with the salary column hidden.

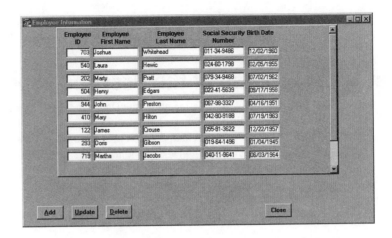

Your nonmanager users now see the same DataWindow, but the salary column is not visible when they run the application (see fig. 20.2).

What Else Can I Change on My DataWindow Using Modify?

You can change just about anything! Using Modify, you can add, delete, and move columns, rename a header, change the column tab sequence, background color, and so on.

Look at the Modify function and its syntax:

```
DataWindowname.Modify(modstring)
```

Parameter	Description
DataWindowname	The name of the DataWindow control or child DataWindow you are modifying.
modstring	A string containing the specifications for the modification.

You can use three types of statements in *modstring* to modify a DataWindow object:

Statement Type	How It's Used
CREATE *object*	Add objects such as columns, drawing objects, text, bit maps and computed fields to the DataWindow object.
DESTROY *object*	Remove objects from the DataWindow object.
Attribute *assignments*	Dynamically set attributes such as background color, font size, and tab sequence.

All PowerBuilder functions return a value. Modify returns an empty string if it's successful; otherwise it returns an error message. For simplicity, the examples here do not always check the return value, but it's important that you check the return value after each modify function call, and act accordingly.

What Is the Purpose of the Describe Function?

You can use Describe to get information about the DataWindow. You might want to modify the where clause of your SQL Select Statement. To do this, you would use Describe to get the select statement and use Modify to change it. You might want to know the first visible row on your DataWindow. Again, you use the Describe function to return the first row on page attribute.

Take a look at the Describe function and its syntax:

```
DataWindowname.Describe(syntax)
```

Parameter	Description
DataWindowname	The name of the DataWindow control or child DataWindow.
syntax	A string containing a blank-separated list of attributes.

Describe returns a string value that can be one of three things:

- A description of the object and attributes requested.
- An exclamation point (!) if an illegal item is found.
- A question mark (?) if there's no value for the attribute.

Can I Update More Than One Table Through a DataWindow?

Let's say you have a DataWindow with columns from more than one table, and you need to be able to update all of the columns. But the DataWindow Painter will only allow you to specify one table for update. Can you get around this?

Yes, but it can be a little tricky. The SQL standard allows you to update only one table at a time. PowerBuilder enables you to create a DataWindow from joined tables, but the DataWindow will allow you to update only one of those tables automatically. To get around this, use the Modify function.

Listing 20.1 shows an example of updating two tables from one DataWindow:

Listing 20.1   Code to Update Multiple Tables in One DataWindow

```
integer li_rc //Return code from Update function

li_rc = dw_1.Update(TRUE,FALSE)
```

```
//If the update against customer is successful, modify the update
//characteristics of the DataWindow object to point to the next table.
IF li_rc = 1 THEN
     //Turn off the update for customer columns
     dw_1.Modify("customer_custnum.Update = No")
     dw_1.Modify("customer_name.Update = No")
     dw_1.Modify("customer_address.Update = No")
     dw_1.Modify("customer_custnum.Key = No")

     //Make cust_order table updateable.
     dw_1.Modify("DataWindow.Table.UpdateTable = ~"cust_order~"")

     //Turn on update for desired cust_order columns.
     dw_1.Modify("cust_order_custnum.Update = Yes")
     dw_1.Modify("cust_order_ordnum.Update = Yes")
     dw_1.Modify("cust_order_duedate.Update = Yes")
     dw_1.Modify("cust_order_balance.Update = Yes")
     dw_1.Modify("cust_order_custnum.Key = Yes")

     //Update the cust_order table.
     li_rc = dw_1.Update()

     IF li_rc = 1 THEN
          dw_1.ResetUpdate()
          COMMIT USING SQLCA;
          MessageBox("Status","Update completed successfully")
     ELSE
          MessageBox("Status","Update of cust_order table failed.  Changes
          ➥rolled back.")
          ROLLBACK USING SQLCA;
     END IF
ELSE
     MessageBox("Status","Update of customer table failed.  Changes rolled
     ➥back.")
     ROLLBACK USING SQLCA;
END IF
```

Make sure you reset your customer columns (see listing 20.2) so that they can be updated the next time this script is performed.

Listing 20.2 Code to Reset Attributes for Subsequent Update

```
//Turn off update for cust_order table.
dw_1.Modify("cust_order_custnum.Update = No")
dw_1.Modify("cust_order_ordnum.Update = No")
dw_1.Modify("cust_order_duedate.Update = No")
dw_1.Modify("cust_order_balance.Update = No")
dw_1.Modify("cust_order_custnum.Key = No")

//Turn on the update for customer columns
dw_1.Modify("customer_custnum.Update = Yes")
dw_1.Modify("customer_name.Update = Yes")
dw_1.Modify("customer_address.Update = Yes")
```

continues

Listing 20.2   Continued

```
dw_1.Modify("customer_custnum.Key = Yes")

//Make cust_order table updateable.
dw_1.Modify("DataWindow.Table.UpdateTable = ~"customer~"")
```

Can I Temporarily Delete Columns from a DataWindow?

If you don't want to remove columns permanently and don't want to hide them, you can destroy them using Modify. The syntax is:

```
<DW Control Name>.Modify( &
"destroy <optionally specify the keyword 'column'> <Columnname>")
```

Here's an example:

```
dw_1.Modify("destroy column salary")
```

Or you can try this:

```
dw_1.Modify("destroy salary")
```

The difference in using Destroy rather than Hide is that the Destroy command will remove the column from the DataWindow, not merely make the column invisible. If you use the keyword "column," the column is removed from the DataWindow and the result set retrieved from the database. Without the keyword "column," the column is removed from the DataWindow, but the data remains in the result set.

Adding a Column to a DataWindow at Run Time

Again, the Modify function lets you create the column and a heading or label for it.

Listing 20.3 shows an example of the attributes you can set using the Modify function to create a column:

Listing 20.3   Code to Dynamically Add a Column to a DataWindow

```
<DW Control Name>.Modify ( &
"create column(band=detail id=1 alignment='1' tabsequence=10 border='5' " + &
"color='0' x='412' y='24' height='65' width='165' format='[general]' " + &
"Name=id edit.limit=0 edit.case=any edit.focusrectangle=no edit.autoselect=yes "
➥+ &
"edit.autohscroll=yes font.face='Arial' font.height='-10' font.weight='400' " +
➥&
"font.family='2' font.pitch='2' font.charset='0' background.mode='1' " + &
"background.color='536870912')")
```

You won't have to set all these attributes, but you could. This should give you an idea of the power and flexibility available in DataWindows.

Changing the SQL Select Statement

You can set the Table.Select attribute using Modify:

```
<DW control Name>.Modify("DataWindow.Table.Select='string containing the SQL
➥select source of the DW>'")
```

If you want dynamically to add a WHERE clause for the salary example, so that only employees making less than $25,000 a year are selected, complete the code as shown in listing 20.4:

Listing 20.4   Code to Dynamically Change the WHERE Clause

```
string ls_rc, ls_orig_sql, ls_mod_sql, ls_where_clause // Declare local
variables

dw_1.SetTransObject(sqlca)

ls_orig_sql = dw_1.Describe("DataWindow.Table.Select")
ls_where_clause = "Where employee.Salary < 25000"
ls_mod_sql = "DataWindow.Table.Select~"" + ls_orig_sql + ls_where_clause + "~""
ls_rc = dw_1.Modify(ls_mod_sql)
IF ls_rc = "" THEN
    dw_1.Retrieve()
ELSE
    MessageBox("Status","dwModify Failed " + ls_rc)
END IF
```

Finding the Display Value

If you're using a column with a code table and need to find out what the display value is, but all you seem to get is the data value, you need to make use of the Describe, Evaluate, and LookupDisplay functions. The following example retrieves the name of the state from the code table based on the state id selected.

```
string ls_data_value, ls_row
ls_row = string(dw_1.GetRow())
ls_data_value = dw_1.Describe ("evaluate('lookupdisplay(sate_id)',"+ls_row+")")
```

How Can I Incorporate the Data Manipulation Grid into My DataWindows?

Some people like the way the data manipulation grid in the Database Painter shows the range of rows visible in the DataWindow and how many rows were retrieved. Many developers want to incorporate this feature into their applications. You can accomplish this by using the Describe and RowCount functions. Basically, you use the attributes DataWindow.FirstRowOnPage and DataWindow.LastRowOnPage to display the range of rows visible on the page (see listing 20.5), and use RowCount function to display the total number of rows retrieved, as shown in figure 20.3.

FIG. 20.3

Rows visible and total rows retrieved.

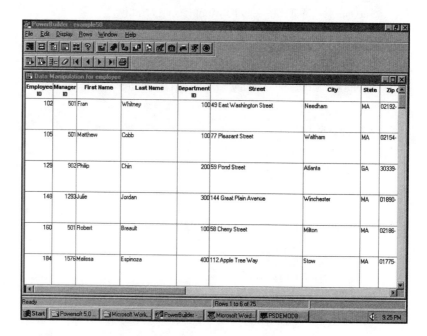

Listing 20.5   Code to Display Visible and Total Rows Retrieved

```
long ll_first_row, ll_last_row, ll_row_count
string ls_rows_information
ll_first_row = dw_1.Describe("DataWindow.FirstRowOnPage")
ll_last_row = dw_1.Describe("DataWindow.LastRowOnPage")
ll_row_count = dw_1.RowCount()
ls_rows_information = "Rows " + string(ll_first_row) + " to " + &
string(ll_last_row) + " of " + string(ll_row_count)
```

For efficiency, create a custom user event for this code on your DataWindow control, and trigger it from the RetrieveEnd and RowFocusChanged events.

Will a Lot of Modify Statements Impact Performance?

Yes, if you have a DataWindow with a lot of columns from multiple tables and you want to update them as you did previously, you might notice a decrease in performance. There's a way around this. You can concatenate your Modify statements into one Modify function call. This will result in a significant performance increase.

> **CAUTION**
>
> Concatenate your Modify statements only after you have debugged them. It's hard enough trying to debug a Modify function call with a single Modify statement. When you combine several Modify statements, the task becomes nearly impossible.

You can combine multiple Modify statements into one Modify function using embedded tab characters. Use the tilde (~) and the letter *t* to accomplish this (~t).

So from our previous example, this:

```
dw_1.Modify("customer_custnum.Update = No")
dw_1.Modify("customer_name.Update = No")
dw_1.Modify("customer_address.Update = No")
dw_1.Modify("customer_custnum.Key = No")
```

would look like this:

```
dw_1.Modify("customer_custnum.Update = No ~t &
    "customer_name.Update = No ~t &
    "customer_address.Update = No ~t &
    "customer_custnum.Key = No")
```

N O T E You removed the quotes around each update statement, so now you have only two quotes, one to start the Modify string and one to end it. ■

It's easy to understand how calling a function once instead of four times will result in performance improvements.

Guidelines for Using Quotes and Tildes

Many developers have trouble with this when they first start using Modify and Describe. You can avoid this trouble if you remember a couple of rules:

- To embed a string within a string, single quotes are recognized as separate from double quotes.
- A single quote represents a ~".

There's a string parser in PowerBuilder used to evaluate your string. The tilde is used to tell the parser that the following character should be taken as a literal.

You have already read about embedding tabs with ~t. You also can embed a carriage return and a new line by using ~r~n.

```
dw_1.Modify("subtitle.Text='The quick brown fox~r~njumped over the lazy dog's
➥back.'")
```

Can I Conditionally Change Things at Run Time?

These functions sound great if you know what you want to Modify or Describe when you're writing code, but sometimes, you may not know what you want to do until run time. You can use expressions in most Modify and Describe statements. For example, say you wanted to highlight a column if the value was higher than an amount specified by the user. Since you don't know what that amount will be when you are creating your application, you will need to do something like this:

```
string ls_mod_string, l_error
ls_mod_string = "salary.color= '0~tif (salary >" + sle_amount.Text + ",255,0)'"
l_error = dw_1.Modify(ls_mod_string)
```

In the above example, you are taking the value entered by the user in sle_amount.Text and embedding it in your modification string.

How Do You Keep Track of All the DataWindow Attributes?

You will really want to take advantage of the online help available in PowerBuilder. You can set up bookmarks in Help to allow you to quickly reference help information about DataWindow attributes (see fig. 20.4).

- Valid attributes for Describe and Modify.
- Attributes of a DataWindow control.

FIG. 20.4

Help Bookmark Set showing the valid attributes for Describe and Modify.

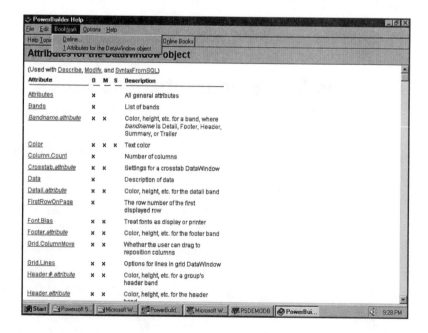

These will be a great help as you begin using the Modify and Describe functions. The bookmarks will still be a useful reference even after you become a pro at using Modify and Describe.

From Here...

Practice, practice, practice! Another thing, you don't want to start out with something too complicated because you will only wind up frustrated. Add complexity as you go along. When it comes to customizing your DataWindows, you are limited only by your own imagination.

In this chapter, you learned how to change the characteristics of your DataWindow at run time. For more on what DataWindows can do, refer to the following chapters:

- Chapter 9, "Creating DataWindows," describes several DataWindow development techniques. You learn how to create three DataWindows and hook your DataWindows to your application.

- Chapter 10, "Enhancing DataWindows," shows you how to modify, enhance, and use your DataWindow.

- Chapter 11, "Manipulating Data Using DataWindows," shows how SQL can be used to define a DataWindow. This chapter covers the SQL toolbox and the SQL syntax behind a DataWindow.

DataWindows Tips and Tricks

— *by Victor Rasputnis and Anatole Tartakovsky with Chuck Boudreau*

Over the course of several application development efforts, it is easy to find yourself coding the same Powerscript over and over. This is particularly true regarding DataWindow controls. You select rows, create search and print option response windows, and put DataWindow objects in query mode time and again. Wouldn't it be great to have a DataWindow control with the smarts to do most of these routine tasks? Imagine the savings in time and energy.

This chapter introduces a DataWindow user object control called u_DataWindow. It has a lot of built-in functionality. It is a simplified version of an object found in the CTI PowerBase Class Library on the CD-ROM.

In the process of introducing u_DataWindow, you learn how to extend the basic behavior of a control via a user object. This is a key concept in beginning to master PowerBuilder.

Useful Features of a DataWindow User Object

Imagine that you want to give application users the ability to customize reports or data entry forms in a standard way. Adding this functionality to a DataWindow user object makes these features available to any DataWindow control in your application. Clicking the right mouse button on your DataWindow control displays these features in a pop-up menu in your application.

The standard features of u_DataWindow include:

- Filtering and sorting report data
- Dynamic grouping of report data
- Searching for data
- Printer and page setup
- Print preview, rulers, and zoom
- Selective printing of specific pages or highlighted rows
- Enhanced query mode

The report features of u_DataWindow lets users work with meaningful names for their data rather than the cryptic database column names displayed by a normal DataWindow.

This set of features makes u_DataWindow useful in many applications just as it is. To add or remove features from the menu, create a new DataWindow user object by inheriting from u_DataWindow. Then supply it with a modified or inherited menu like the one shown in figure 21.1.

FIG. 21.1
A pop-up menu for u_DataWindow edit control can be accessed by right-clicking the control.

Additional features you might consider adding to u_DataWindow include:

- Multiple selection of rows—Program Manager style
- Automatic scrolling, resizing, and focusing synchronization

- Logging of DataWindow errors
- Drag-and-drop capabilities
- Clipboard support

Selective Printing

Users of graphical operating environments expect applications to provide selective printing and Clipboard support. The bad news is that it normally takes effort on our part to include such standard facilities in every report or data entry form in our application. The good news, however, is that u_DataWindow contains most of this functionality and thereby eliminates a lot of effort. These functions are implemented through user events or user object functions.

To add printing functionality to u_DataWindow, begin by creating a visual component for users to interact with. Create a response window w_DataWindow_print (see fig. 21.2) to allow users to select printing options.

FIG. 21.2

A Print function dialog box is used as a basic print functionality for the generic DataWindow.

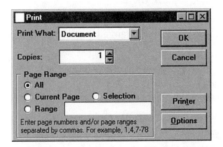

N O T E Other printing features introduced in PowerBuilder 4 (such as printer name, collate copy, print to file options, and so on) can be added to the Print dialog box to enhance functionality. Developers upgrading from versions earlier than PowerBuilder 4 should consider problems that can arise with support compatibility to previous releases of PowerBuilder. ■

In addition to the visible controls in figure 21.2, w_DataWindow_print contains an invisible DataWindow control named dw_print. This control implements all print functionality through functions and events. Therefore, the original u_DataWindow user object does not require any modifications.

When the user selects the Print menu item from the pop-up menu, its clicked event opens w_DataWindow_print. u_DataWindow is passed as a parameter. This makes it accessible to w_DataWindow_print via the PowerObjectParm attribute of the Message object. As the following code segment shows, the open event of w_DataWindow_print assigns the parameter that references u_DataWindow to idwSource.

```
idwSource= Message.PowerObjectParm
...
em_copies.Text = idwSource.Describe("DataWindow.Print.Copies")
IF (trim(em_copies.Text) = "") THEN em_copies.Text = "1"
.....
```

w_DataWindow_print contains the DataWindow instance variable idwSource. idwSource serves as a reference variable for the events and functions of w_DataWindow_print to access the data and format of u_DataWindow.

Once w_DataWindow_print displays, the user sets the print parameters and clicks OK. The cb_ok clicked event tests the checked attribute of rb_current_page (see listing 21.1). If this boolean attribute is TRUE, printing begins from the page associated with the current row of u_DataWindow. This is done by setting isPrintSelection, an instance variable of w_DataWindow_print of type string, to the result string from the Describe function listed below.

A Modify function assigns the print range for dw_print to use. If the user did not specify a range, isSelectPrint contains an empty string. This causes dw_print to default to printing all the rows. The dw_print DataWindow then prints using the Print function. The ShareDataOff function turns off sharing between the two DataWindows (u_DataWindow and dw_print).

Listing 21.1   Clicked Event for cb_ok

```
dw_print.Create(idwSource.Describe("DataWindow.syntax")) //
... // Additional code to eliminate unwanted bands, place comments, etc.
isPrintSelection = ""
IF rb_selection.Checked THEN
//Only selected rows have to be moved to different dw
//Copy rows using RowsCopy
idwSource.uf_Copy_Selected_Rows( wPrint.dw_print )
dw_print.Print()
ELSE
idwSource.ShareData(dw_print)
dw_print.Modify("DataWindow.print.preview=yes")
IF rb_current_page.Checked THEN
long lRow
string sRowNumber
lRow = idwSource.GetRow()
sRowNumber = string( lRow )
isPrintSelection = &
dw_print.Describe( "evaluate('Page()',"+ sRowNumber + ")" )
ELSEIF rb_range.Checked THEN
isPrintSelection = sle_selection.text
ELSEIF rb_page_range_all.Checked THEN
// Standard DataWindow Print will do it
// all parameters are already set
END IF
dw_printd.Modify("DataWindow.print.page.range='"
+isPrintSelection+"'")
dw_print.Print()
dw_print.ShareDataOff()
END IF
close(Parent)
```

Print Preview

Application users often want to view a report as it looks formatted for printing. To implement print preview mode in all of your DataWindows, consider using a Preview Options response window. Ths window switches u_DataWindow between the normal screen mode and print preview mode. It also controls the percentage of reduction or enlargement of the text (Zoom), and the display of the Print Preview rulers.

To implement print preview functionality in u_DataWindow, begin by creating a visual component for users to interact with. Create the w_print_preview response window (see fig. 21.3) to allow users to manipulate the preview options. When the user selects Print Preview from the pop-up menu, the clicked event of the menu item opens w_print_preview, passing the u_DataWindow control as a parameter. The following event scripts must be coded to make this window functional.

1. First, code the open event for w_print_preview (see listing 21.2). Just like the open event for w_DataWindow_print, u_DataWindow is passed as a parameter and assigned to the DataWindow instance variable idwSource. The edit controls on w_print_preview (em_zoom, rb_rulers_on, rb_rulers_off, rb_preview_on, and rb_preview_off) are set to their corresponding values found in idwSource. The Describe function queries idwSource for specific information, setting the initial values of each edit control.

Listing 21.2   The w_print_preview Event

```
idwSource = Message.PowerObjectParm
em_zoom_level.Text =
      idwSource.Describe("DataWindow.Print.Preview.Zoom")
IF (Trim(em_zoom_level.Text)="") THEN em_zoom_level.Text = "100"
IF idwSource.Describe("DataWindow.Print.Preview.Rulers") = "yes" THEN
rb_rulers_on.Checked=TRUE
ELSE
rb_rulers_off.Checked=TRUE
END IF
IF idwSource.Describe("DataWindow.Print.Preview") = "yes" THEN
rb_preview_on.Checked=TRUE
ELSE
rb_preview_off.Checked=TRUE
END IF
```

2. Next, code an event for each w_DataWindow_print control to set the corresponding print preview value in idwSource.

N O T E   As an example, the following code segment lists the clicked event for the rb_preview_on control. It tests the value of rb_preview_on.checked. If it is TRUE, the Modify function sets PrintPreview to Yes. If it is FALSE, the PrintPreview value is set to No. The other edit controls need similar events. Also, the cb_ok clicked event needs to close the w_print_preview window.

The following is the clicked event for rb_preview_on:

```
idwSource.Modify("DataWindow.Print.Preview=yes")
```

FIG. 21.3

The w_print_preview dialog box (Preview Options) allows the user to control the print preview display of u_DataWindow.

Sorting and Filtering

Application users often want to sort and filter their data. The traditional way to provide these capabilities in a DataWindow is through the SetFilter and SetSort functions. However, the windows displayed by these functions show cryptic DataWindow column names to the user when specifying sort and filter criteria.

An alternative to this is to create filter and sort response windows like the one in figure 21.4. It looks like the normal DataWindow filter window. However, it uses a data dictionary which allows users to see meaningful names for data elements. It is easier to use because it does not display the internal DataWindow column names.

FIG. 21.4

A Specify Filter dialog box can be used as a more user-friendly replacement for the default filter window.

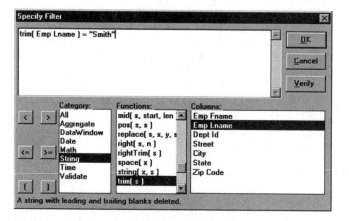

Building a General Purpose Search Engine

Many PowerBuilder applications provide search capabilities within a DataWindow control. Rather than creating a general purpose search engine, developers often take the low road by creating application-specific search facilities from scratch. The following section discusses approaches for building a general purpose search engine, and the coding problems behind it.

Understanding the Issues

In designing a general purpose search engine, the first issue you must address is: What is the subject of the user's search?

How Does a User Select Columns to Search By?   The process of searching begins with a user looking for rows where columns match some specific values. But what is a column from the search perspective? At first glance, any DataWindow column is a candidate to search by. You might be inclined to provide a way for the user to select from a list of all columns in a DataWindow object. But a few concerns arise:

- What if a DataWindow column is not visible to the user? Users might be confused by seeing a column that they are unfamiliar with. What if that column is not a part of any band in the DataWindow object? When you delete a column from the DataWindow canvas, it is set to invisible. However, it is still retained as a result set column. In either case, the user is unable to verify that the row found contains the specific value.

- What if the DataWindow column is a computed column and is not specifically named? It has an Expression attribute, but it is doubtful that the user is comfortable using it.

As you can see, a plain column list does not work for two reasons. First, it violates a what-you-see-is-what-you-get (WYSIWYG) principle by allowing the user to search on columns that are not displayed on the DataWindow. Second, it may not meet basic implementation problems of manipulating expressions using the PowerBuilder Expression Painter.

Now look at an alternative solution. If you confine a search to the visible set of columns in the detail band, the user may point to the column(s) to search in. So there is no need to display the list of column names.

How Many Columns Are Involved in the Search?   The next issue concerns the scope of the search capabilities you intend to provide. Are you providing a search on a column-by-column basis (one column at a time), or on complex criteria (a combination of columns)?

Theoretically, everything that can be found by the Find function can also be found by the SetFilter and Filter functions. When the data is sorted in the order of the search criteria, searching the data using the filtering functions achieves the same result as using the Find function. However, when the data is not sorted in the order of the search criteria, Find allows the user to see the search record surrounded by its neighboring records—a significant advantage over filtering.

How Should the Process Work?   From a design perspective, it is important to consider which search processes make the user interface most effective. Should users be forced to compose search expressions every time they wish to search data? Or would a visual approach, allowing users easily to choose the search criteria, be more effective?

Considering all of this, it is desirable to develop a more visual point-and-click-driven search engine. This allows the user to search one column at a time. This intuitive approach eliminates the problems associated with a column list method, and allows the user to view the matching rows with the neighboring rows. Complex, multicolumn searches do not have to be incorporated into the search engine, since the Filter function can process these.

Implementing the Search Engine

Once you have determined to allow searching on a column-by-column basis and that the user has a way to point to a search column, you are ready to develop your search engine with the following features:

- Search on any column regardless of datatype
- Interactive access to any column for the search
- Search by column display or code table value

Remember that some DataWindow columns may contain "hidden" lookups, depending on the edit style. Columns using edit display styles, drop-down DataWindows, and listboxes can all use code tables to change the displayed data. Naturally, the user prefers (at least initially) to search the data the same way it appears.

Figure 21.5 shows a simple search engine from the PowerBase Class Library. It implements searching in a pop-up menu item.

FIG. 21.5

The search window displayed at the bottom of the window allows the user to search the DataWindow. The highlighted column is the current search column.

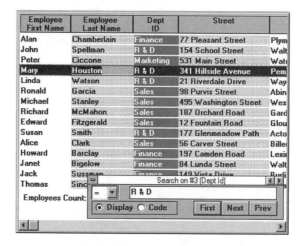

The Search response window provides users the following functionality:

- Select which column to search on by clicking the arrow buttons. The Dept ID column is in this example.
- Switch between the code table data and display values of the DataWindow columns by clicking the Display and Code option buttons.
- Specify search expressions by using the drop-down list, which contains conditions such as = and < .

■ Move between matching rows for the search by using the First, Next, and Previous push buttons.

Two functions play a key role in the implementation of the search engine. The first function is uf_prepare_dwFind (see listing 21.3). It prepares a search string based on the column number to be searched (argument piCol) and the user-specified search value (argument psItem). It determines the column's datatype using the Describe function, assigning it to the string sColumnType. By testing sColumnType in several IF statements, the proper syntax is built depending on the search column's datatype.

The second function, wf_search, is the primary search function (see listing 21.4). This function builds the search syntax for the Find function and then processes it. The Search response window (fig. 21.5) passes start and end rows to this function. It retrieves other search data entered and selected by the user from the controls on the dialog box and DataWindow. After verifying that valid data exists, it assembles the search string into the sModel string variable. It then uses the Find function to search the DataWindow.

Listing 21.3   Function uf_prepare_dwFind

```
uf_prepare_dwFind (string psItemText, int piColumn)
// Part of U_DataWindow
string sColumnType, sModel
sModel = ""
sColumnType = Describe("#" + String(piColumn) + ".ColType")
IF (sColumnType<>"!") AND (sColumnType<>"?") THEN
IF Pos(sColumnType, "char") <> 0 THEN
sModel = "'" + psItemText + "'"
ELSE
IF Pos(sColumnType, "decimal") <> 0 THEN
sModel = "Dec('" + psItemText+ "')"
ELSE
CHOOSE CASE sColumnType
CASE "date"
sModel = "Date('" + psItemText + "')"
CASE "time"
sModel = "Time('" + psItemText + "')"
CASE "datetime"
sModel = "Datetime('" + psItemText + "')"
CASE "number"
sModel = psItemText
END CHOOSE
END IF
END IF
END IF
return sModel
```

Listing 21.4 Function wf_search

```
wf_search (long plStartRow, long plEndRow)
//Actual search
long        lFoundRow
long        lRowCount
string      sColumnName,    sColumnType,    sModel,    sSearchKey
pointer     poOldPointer
poOldPointer = SetPointer(HourGlass!)
IF iiSearchColumnID  <>0 THEN
lRowCount =  idwSearch.RowCount()
// We'll check for possible absence of data at all
IF lRowCount > 0   THEN
sSearchKey = sle_search_value.text
sColumnType = idwSearch.uf_Get_Column_Type(iiSearchColumnID)
// Check if current search column has "Code Table"
// Translate Code/Display value to appropriate value
sSearchKey =
idwSearch.uf_Convert_To_Code_Text(sSearchKey,iiSearchColumnID)
sModel = idwSearch.uf_Prepare_dwFind(sSearchKey, iiSearchColumnID)
sModel = "#" + String( iiSearchColumnID) +
ddlb_operator.Text + sModel
lFoundRow = idwSearch.Find(sModel, plStartRow, plEndRow)
IF lFoundRow > 0 THEN
ilCurrentRow = lFoundRow
idwSearch.ScrolltoRow(ilCurrentRow)
idwSearch.SetRow(ilCurrentRow)
ELSE
Beep(1)
END IF
END IF
END IF
SetPointer(poOldPointer)
```

Dynamic Grouping

Dynamic grouping is the most advanced feature of the u_DataWindow user object. It addresses one of the biggest limitations of the DataWindow control: that it does not allow modification of existing groupings. The Describe or Modify function cannot access DataWindow grouping expressions.

Therefore, you cannot create a new DataWindow group dynamically via Powerscript. In most cases, this means that you must pre-design the same DataWindow with different groupings, and let the user choose among them. This approach leads to complicated maintenance of additional DataWindows, and limited functionality.

The only way to change the grouping is to recreate the DataWindow object with a modified syntax. However, when you change the grouping, you must consider some complications:

- Group headers must be changed to reflect new grouping titles.
- Total and aggregate functions must be placed in the trailer band for each group.
- The sort order needs to reflect the new grouping.
- Page control (page breaks, numbering, and so on) might need changes.

u_DataWindow provides the user with the ability to specify grouping at run time. Such user-defined groups can maintain standard headers, provide replication of summary fields at the group level, and automatically update the sorting order in accordance with the group definition. All of these options are available via the Grouping Editor (see fig. 21.6).

FIG. 21.6

The Grouping Editor dialog box allows the user to add or change grouping controls on the DataWindow at run time.

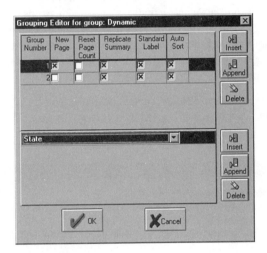

> **N O T E** u_DataWindow provides the ability to attach and detach the data in the DataWindow so that you can reconnect your data after you recreate your DataWindow object. This is important when using the Grouping Editor, because the editor destroys and recreates the DataWindow object when changing group controls. ■

Using the Grouping Editor

The Grouping Editor accomplishes its work by completing the following steps:

1. Destroy previous groups or bands.
2. Define new groups or bands.
3. Replace the original DataWindow object with a new one from new syntax.
4. Create new headers for each group.
5. Replicate the summary band through all group trailers.

A custom class user object called the u_group_description_scanner contains some of the code used by the Grouping Editor dialog box to dynamically change group information. The code segment below contains the syntax that PowerBuilder uses to create this user object. It shows you several functions along with the constructor event.

The first of these functions is uf_get_group_count. It is a simple function that returns the upper bound of the isGroupByList instance string array.

The second function, uf_get_group_expression, returns the string isGroupExpression based on the piGroupID integer passed to it. If this integer is valid, it is used as an index to look up the correct Group Expression from the isGroupExpressionList array. The uf_get_group_by function is very similar to the uf_get_group_expression function. It returns a string from isGroupByList array based on the index of the passed integer, piGroupID.

The rest of the code segment displays the constructor event for the u_group_description_scanner user object. It is executed just after the user object is created. It retrieves the syntax for the DataWindow that was passed to it via the Message.PowerObjectParm, and then proceeds to search and extract the group control information from the DataWindow syntax. As each group level is found, the control data is stored in instance arrays, using the group level as the index. These arrays are then used to populate the Grouping Editor dialog box.

Listing 21.5 shows the source code of the custom class user object u_group_description_scanner. It was created by exporting the user object to an operating system file using the Library Painter.

Listing 21.5   User Object u_group_description_scanner

```
$PBExportHeader$u_group_description_scanner.sru
global type u_group_description_scanner from nonvisualobject
end type
global u_group_description_scanner u_group_description_scanner
type variables
string isGroupBYList[]
string isGroupExpressionList[]
end variables
public function integer uf_get_group_count()
return UpperBound(isGroupBYList)
end function
public function string uf_get_group_expression (integer piGroupID)
string sExpression
sExpression = ""
IF NOT (piGroupID > uf_Get_Group_Count() or piGroupID <=0) THEN
sExpression = isGroupExpressionList[piGroupID]
END IF
return sExpression
end function
public function string uf_get_group_by (integer piGroupID)
string sGroupBY
sGroupBY = ""
IF NOT (piGroupID > uf_Get_Group_Count() or piGroupID <=0) THEN
sGroupBY = isGroupBYList[piGroupID]
END IF
return sGroupBY
end function
```

TECHNIQUES FROM THE PROS

```
on constructor
string sdwSyntax
long iGroupCnt, iPosCntlong, iPosCnt1
DataWindow pdwSource
pdw_source = Message.PowerObjectParm
sdwSyntax = pdwSource.Describe("DataWindow.syntax")
iPosCnt = 1
DO
iPosCnt = Pos( sdwSyntax , "group(", iPosCnt+1)
IF iPosCnt <> 0 THEN
iPosCnt = Pos( sdwSyntax , "by=(",        iPosCnt ) + 4
iPosCnt1 = Pos( sdwSyntax , ")",        iPosCnt )
iGroupCnt++
isGroupBYList[iGroupCnt]  &
=Mid(sdwSyntax,iPosCnt,iPosCnt1-iPosCnt)
END IF
LOOP WHILE iPosCnt <> 0

string sCurrentColumn, sNormalHeader, sSummaryField, sFormat
int ij , ii

FOR ii = 1 TO iGroupCnt
ij = 1
sNormalHeader = ""
DO WHILE ij > 0
ij = f_get_token( isGroupBYList[ii], " ", ij, sCurrentColumn )
if Mid(isGroupBYList[ii], ij, 1) = " " and ij > 0 THEN ij++
sCurrentColumn = Trim(sCurrentColumn)
IF sCurrentColumn > "" THEN
// Create Standard Header
IF   sNormalHeader<>"" THEN    &
sNormalHeader=sNormalHeader+"+~" ~"+"
IF pdw_source.Describe(sCurrentColumn+".coltype") = "!"        ÂOR &
pdw_source.Describe(sCurrentColumn+".coltype") = "?"                    ÂTHEN
MessageBox("Unknown Datatype", "Column:"+sCurrentColumn+ ":"+&
pdw_source.Describe(sCurrentColumn+".coltype"))
END IF
IF Pos(pdw_source.Describe(sCurColumn+
.coltype"),"char")>0 THEN
sNormalHeader = sNormalHeader + sCurrentColumn
ELSE
sFormat = pdw_source.Describe(sCurrentColumn+".format")
IF sFormat ="?" OR sFormat ="!" OR sFormat="[general]"              ÂTHEN
sNormalHeader=sNormalHeader+ "string ("+sCurrentColumn+')'
ELSE
sNormalHeader=sNormalHeader+"string("+sCurrentColumn+&
",~~~""+sFormat+"~~~")"
END IF
END IF
END IF
LOOP
isGroupExpressionList[ii] = sNormalHeader
NEXT
end on
```

Demonstrating the Power of Dynamic Grouping

The Outliner Demo window in figure 21.7 demonstrates the power of dynamic groupings. It contains a user object inherited from the Microsoft OUTLINER.VBX object and an extended DataWindow control. Any information provided in the DataWindow is reflected in the outliner, such as the File Manager directory tree.

FIG. 21.7

The left side of the Outliner Demo window shows the structure of the group bands on the right.

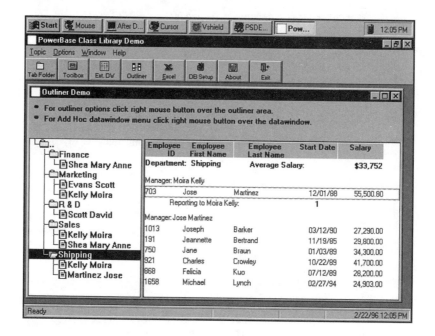

This window creates a group expression that is placed in the outliner object to identify each group break. In turn, the value from the outliner is used to filter all the records that belong to this group. When the DataWindow is populated with data, the outliner is also populated. When a user clicks a particular item in the outliner, the automatic filter is created and applied to the DataWindow.

Listed in the code segments below are the ue_create_tree user event (see listing 21.6) and the wf_sync_views functions (see listing 21.7). This code is taken from the Outliner Demo window. Displaying the outliner, DataWindow triggers the ue_create_tree event. It leads the user step-by-step through the data in the DataWindow and builds the group hierarchy tree from it. The wf_sync_views function keeps the levels of group information on the outliner DataWindow in sync.

Listing 21.6   ue_create_tree User Event

```
on ue_create_tree
string sBand, sExpression
string sTag
long lGroupBreak, l, lGroupStart, lCurrentInOutliner
```

TECHNIQUES FROM THE PROS

```
int j, k, m
dw_data.SetFilter("")
dw_data.Filter()
s_Group_Start_Stop strGroupStartStop[]
lCurrentInOutliner = 1
FOR j = 1 To dw_data.uo_group.uf_Get_Group_Count()
strGroupStartStop[j].lStartRow = 1
strGroupStartStop[j].lEndRow = 0
NEXT
uo_tree.DeleteItem(1)
lCurrentInOutliner = 1
uo_tree.Indent[ lCurrentInOutliner ] = 1
uo_tree.List[ lCurrentInOutliner ] = ".."
FOR l=1 TO dw_data.RowCount()
FOR j = 1 TO dw_data.uo_group.uf_Get_Group_Count()
IF l > strGroupStartStop[j].lEndRow THEN
lCurrentInOutliner ++
uo_tree.Indent[ lCurrentInOutliner ] = j + 1
uo_tree.List[lCurrentInOutliner]=dw_data.Describe("evaluate('"+&
dw_data.uo_group.uf_get_group_expression(j)+&
"',"+string(l)+")")
IF j = dw_data.uo_group.uf_Get_Group_Count() THEN
uo_tree.PictureType[ lCurrentInOutliner ] = 2
ELSE
uo_tree.PictureType[ lCurrentInOutliner ] = 0
END IF
strGroupStartStop[j].lStartRow = l
strGroupStartStop[j].lEndRow = dw_data.uf_FindGroupChange(l,j)
IF strGroupStartStop[j].lEndRow < 0 THEN
strGroupStartStop[j].lEndRow = dw_data.RowCount()
END IF
NEXT
NEXT
uo_tree.ListIndex = 1      // Start at the root
uo_tree.Expand[1] = 1   // and expand it
end on
```

Listing 21.7 Function wf_sync_views

```
public function int wf_sync_views (long plindex)
string sFilter
int j
IF plIndex >=1 THEN
sFilter = "~"..\~""
FOR j = 2 TO uo_tree.Indent[plIndex]
sFilter=sFilter+"+"+ &
dw_data.uo_group.uf_get_group_expression(j-1)+"+~"\~""
NEXT
sFilter = sFilter + "='" + uo_tree.FullPath[plIndex] + "\'"
dw_data.SetFilter( sFilter )
dw_data.Filter()
ELSE
dw_data.SetFilter( "" )
```

continues

TECHNIQUES FROM THE PROS

Listing 21.7   Continued

```
dw_data.Filter()
END IF
return 1
end function
```

From Here...

This chapter introduced the DataWindow user object control called u_DataWindow, which allows you to extend the basic behavior of a control via a user object. For more information about DataWindows, check out the following chapters:

- Chapter 9, "Creating DataWindows," describes several DataWindow development techniques.

- Chapter 10, "Enhancing DataWindows," shows you how to modify, enhance, and use your DataWindows.

- Chapter 11, "Manipulating Data Using DataWindows," explains how to suppress, filter, and sort data, as well as how to retrieve information from and update a database using DataWindows.

- Chapter 20, "Using Modify and Describe to Get the Most Out of DataWindows," details how to customize your DataWindows.

- Chapter 23, "Using ShareData Functions," describes how you can make your DataWindow control objects share the same data.

CHAPTER 22

Exploiting the Power of Inheritance

— by Ron Cox with Chuck Boudreau

Perhaps the greatest promise of object-oriented software development tools is that of productivity gains through code reusability. Code reusability has been an elusive goal of developers for decades. Whether it's copy books, run-time linking, or simply copying and pasting code, none of the previous methods used by developers matches the enormous potential for reusability found in inheritance.

With inheritance, you can develop a new object class by building on a previously developed object class. The new object class, the descendant, "inherits" the properties, events, and functions of the ancestor object class. You can then add to the new object class whatever is specific about it, building on the more generic aspects of the ancestor.

One of the many good things about PowerBuilder is that it does not force you to use any of the object-oriented features it has. It is possible to write production-quality applications without giving a single thought to object-oriented programming (OOP). But if you're looking for pro-ductivity gains through code reuse, you owe it to yourself to understand how to take advantage of inheritance.

Understanding the Benefits of Inheritance

Exploiting the power of inheritance can help you obtain several of the following benefits:

- Increased code reuse
- Improved programming productivity
- PowerScript coding standardization and consistency
- Improved ease of maintenance

The number of objects in a PowerBuilder application can grow to be quite large. It's not un-usual for an application to contain over a hundred windows. Each window, in turn, may contain a menu, command buttons, DataWindow controls, as well as other controls. With a procedural, non-object-oriented software development tool, you'd likely end up with more repetitive code than you'd care to maintain.

For example, every window with an updatable DataWindow control on it requires functionality to have that DataWindow update the database. Other common functionality might include data validation, error handling, and committing or rolling back the transaction. So if your application has 20 windows with updatable DataWindows, that type of functionality is required for all 20 of those windows.

An experienced software developer might attempt to address this by putting that update func-tionality into PowerScript functions that each of those twenty windows could call. Thus, the amount of repetitive code would be reduced, but certainly not eliminated. This is because every one of those 20 windows would need the code to invoke the function calls.

Any way you look at it, that's a lot of repetitive PowerScript when you code in a procedural, non-object-oriented way. For instance, you might develop one window to the point where it works exactly to your liking. This might become your master template window. After saving it into a PowerBuilder library, you might choose "File/Save As…" to create a new functional window. Then you modify the new window. This method of "code cloning" is widespread. When working with development tools lacking OOP features, this may be a familiar method. But this method has considerable weaknesses.

Developing a template window perfectly the first time is a big task, and generally an impossible one. So a change to the update functionality later produces a tremendous impact. It requires that you change the template window and all of the windows cloned from it. This is not exactly an ideal scenario from a productivity perspective.

And don't forget maintenance. At some point, either you, the developer, or someone else is going to have to maintain that application. A change to the update functionality in one window may mean modifying all 20 of those windows, and testing all 20 modifications—another strike against productivity.

You need to add one more aspect into this potentially bleak picture. Suppose the application is being developed by a team. If those 20 different updatable windows are being developed by multiple members of the team, what level of standardization do you suppose you'll get?

Now imagine that you could write and test that code once, and every window that needed it would have it. And the functionality would be consistent across all those windows, no matter how many different developers were working on the project. And when it was time to modify the code, you only had to modify it once. These are the benefits of inheritance.

Identifying Inheritable Objects

In PowerBuilder, you can use inheritance to build three types of objects:

- Windows
- Menus
- User objects

N O T E   At first glance, having only three types of inheritable objects may seem to be a little restrictive. Just three types of objects? What about all the rest of the objects you use in PowerBuilder? Keep in mind that the user object is a very flexible tool. A standard user object can be made from any of the controls that can be placed on a window. A custom user object can be made from groups of those controls. In PowerBuilder, the User Object Painter is your method of creating custom controls. And you can use inheritance to use those custom controls over and over again. ■

Inheritance with Windows

Without a doubt, windows are most often the objects you inherit from. Because PowerBuilder applications are generally online, interactive applications, they center around windows. Developing with a library of window object classes enables you to realize significant productivity gains through reusability.

Inheritance with Menus

How useful you find inheritance with menus depends on how heavily you use menus in your application. Normally every window has a menu. For that reason, inheriting from menus is just as desirable as inheriting from windows. You might consider having a menu object class corresponding to every window object class.

Inheritance with User Objects

Inheritance with user objects is a very powerful tool. In the case of those 20 windows with updatable DataWindow controls, it is possible that those DataWindow controls could be inherited from a common DataWindow user object. This would provide a way to eliminate that redundant code. You could build a DataWindow user object class that has all of the database update functionality required. Then you could place that DataWindow user object on each of those 20 windows.

Employing Object Class Design

The benefits of using inheritance are plentiful—build an object class and then inherit from it over and over again. What could be easier? The inheriting part of it is easy. Building the object class, on the other hand, can be challenging.

Building an object, a window for example, by inheriting from an ancestor provides a foundation to build on. The base functionality and attributes you need for that window are already there; they were inherited from the ancestor. All you need to do with the new window is to add whatever functionality is specific to it.

Designing an object class that you intend to inherit from can be a complicated process. It takes a lot of thought to look at the big picture and visualize what windows in your project can be built on a common foundation. What generic functionality and attributes will the descendants need? It's also important to look ahead to future projects. Designing generic object classes now—classes that can be used over and over again in future projects—provides you with untold productivity gains. Object class design is a skill in its own right. Good design of your class library is absolutely essential in order for you to get any real benefits from inheritance.

Different windows need different functionality and attributes. The same is true for menus and user objects. Is it possible to design an object class that is all things to all descendants? It depends on your particular project and what the descendants need to inherit from the ancestor. The answer is almost assuredly, "No." In this case, what you need is an object class hierarchy.

NOTE PowerBuilder does not allow you to delete controls from a descendant that were defined on the ancestor. However, it is possible to make them invisible. Similarly, functionality in the ancestor that you don't want in the descendant can be overridden or simply ignored, depending on how it's implemented. But if you find yourself continually performing this kind of "negative inheritance," inheriting from an ancestor object and then taking away the inherited features you don't want, then the ancestor object probably wasn't designed quite right. In this case, it's best to reevaluate the design of the object class. ■

An object class hierarchy is like a tree. You start with a base ancestor, and then branch out from there. When designing a class hierarchy it's best to start with very generic functionality and attributes in the base ancestor, and then develop more specific ones in the descendants. It's common to get several levels deep before you have an object class that you will inherit from to build a production object class. In such a case, the first couple of levels of ancestors serve as foundations for their descendants, which in turn are the foundations for their own descendants.

> **TIP**
> An object class you inherit from, but never directly use, is sometimes called a *virtual class*. A class you use directly, such as a window that you open in an application, is known as a *production class*.

> **CAUTION**
> While there are no defined limits to how many levels a class hierarchy can have, there are practical limits. If you go beyond six levels, you may begin to encounter a performance degradation.

Analyzing the Case Study

To illustrate the value of inheritance and the process of designing an object class hierarchy, the rest of this section will focus on a case study. Though fictitious, the case study is representative of the kind of real-world issues PowerBuilder developers encounter on every project.

The Premise

Suppose that you have just been hired to build a new system for the customer service division of a small firm, Sample, Inc. The new system will be used by the customer service representatives who answer questions from both customers and company employees.

Project Requirements

After the analysis and design phases, the project team develops a project plan that includes building a front end to the database tables.

The team has also come up with a basic design philosophy for development of the new system. The new system is to be developed with a focus on what the team has termed *business objects*. Business objects are what the users visualize when they think about the customer service business function.

Based on a study of how the users work and the database design, the project team has identified three business objects:

- Customer
- Product
- Employee

Because the customer service representatives need easy access to information in order to answer questions, each business object needs to be developed to have at least two types of functionality: *search functionality* and *detail functionality*. The search functionality will give users the ability to query the database and locate the record(s) they need. It must display enough discriminating information for the users to determine when they've found the record(s) they're looking for. The detail functionality must display the detail of the information the users found.

Already, you can see the potential for using inheritance during the project. There are only two basic categories of windows: search and detail. Fantastic. Two object classes, and you're all set, right? Well, almost. The team has identified different functionality required for the windows for the different objects, as described in table 22.1.

Table 22.1   Required Window Functionality

Window	Description
Customer Search	Multiple record display
Customer Detail	Single record display
Product Search	Multiple record display
Product Detail	Single record display
Employee Search	Multiple record display plus a display of the detail of the currently highlighted record

In addition to the requirements listed in table 22.1, it has been decided that each window will have the company name (Sample, Inc.) in a *window label*, a text box placed across the top of the window. In addition, each window will have a micro help text box across the bottom of the window.

Of course you can develop these five windows individually, and be done with it. But with a little effort in constructing an object class hierarchy, you can reap the benefits inheritance has to offer.

 TIP   Adopt an object-naming convention at the beginning of your project to ensure a consistent look and feel to the application, even though many developers may be working on it. It makes maintenance much easier.

First of all, you have a situation where all windows have two things in common: the window label text box, and the micro help text box. This leads you to develop your first object class from which all the other windows will be inherited, called *w_ma_base*.

w_ma_base

The w_ma_base object class is exactly what the name implies. It's the base for all other windows in the project. In this object class, you define a window with static text controls for the window label and micro help. Code the PowerScript in the window resize event required to resize the window label and micro help text boxes. Next, write a window function to place text in the micro help text box. In addition to functionality, set attributes that you want to carry forward to all descendants, such as a gray window background to facilitate implementation of the 3-D look.

w_ma_base is your first object class. It provides your first opportunity to use your object-oriented design skills. You'll want to ensure that you're taking advantage of inheritance to build a generic object class to use on other projects. When developing object classes, it's always in your best interest to attempt to design them in such a way that they're *portable*—not specific to the current project. Of course, with some object classes that may not be possible. But it's possible with w_ma_base.

A static text box was placed on the window for the company name. The text attribute was set equal to the company name. All it takes to make this window object class generic is to program the functionality to set the text attribute of the window label text box dynamically at run time. But how does the window know what the text is supposed to be? There are several ways of handling this. In this example, you decided to pass a string parameter to the window which is displayed in the text. You can make the parameter a structure, so you can add other elements to it later on if you need to.

The initial evaluation of required object classes holds true to some extent. There are definitely two basic categories of windows for this application: search and detail. In looking at the project requirements, you assume that all search windows will share some basic features. This leads you to develop the w_ma_search object class.

w_ma_search

You can develop the w_ma_search object class by first inheriting it from the w_ma_base object class. The new window class inherits the functionality for the window label and the window micro help. You can then add what you need for a generic search window. Additions include a DataWindow control, static text control to display the record count, and command buttons for search, query, and opening a detail window. Query-by-example functionality is programmed, as is some basic DataWindow behavior. You can extend the script in the window resize event to size the DataWindow control to the maximum width of the window and the maximum height allowed, without changing its Y coordinate or overlaying the window's micro help text box.

Of course, a DataWindow control needs a transaction object if you're going to have any database access with it. Should you set the transaction object in this class? Not if you want it to be generic. If this is a virtual class, and you intend to inherit from it not only during this project but in future projects as well, you can't guarantee that all descendants will use the same transaction object (SQLCA, for example). You could modify the u_str_open_window structure and add a transaction to it. Then a descendant of this class could use whatever transaction is passed to it. How's that? Pretty good. But, you can't guarantee that every descendant will use a transaction that exists when the window is opened. Some search windows may create their own transaction (maybe they connect to different databases). The best thing for you to do is allow the descendant to deal with setting the DataWindow's transaction object.

w_m_customer_search Our First Production Class!

The requirements for the Customer Search window are fairly straightforward. They can be satisfied with the features you've put into the w_ma_search object class. First, develop the

DataWindow object needed for the Customer Search window. Then develop the Customer Search window by inheriting from w_ma_search. You can change the title of the window to "Customer Search." Next, associate the DataWindow object you just developed with the DataWindow control on the window. There's only one more thing to do—set the transaction object for the DataWindow.

> **NOTE** Detailed coverage of creating a DataWindow object and associating it with a DataWindow control is given in chapter 9, "Creating DataWindows." ■

w_m_product_search

That last window was easy to develop, so another search window won't be difficult. The Product Search window has the same basic requirements as the Customer Search window; you can develop it through exactly the same process:

1. Develop the DataWindow object.
2. Develop the window by inheriting from w_ma_search.
3. Change the window title to "Product Search."
4. Associate the DataWindow object with the DataWindow control.
5. Set the transaction object for the DataWindow.

That's all there is to it! Inheritance gives the capability to develop a fully functioning search window like this in five easy steps.

You just developed two search windows with minimal effort by taking advantage of the power of inheritance. The only real work you had to do was developing the DataWindow objects. Imagine the productivity gain if you had 20 of these windows to develop!

w_m_employee_search

The requirements for the Employee Search window are a little more demanding. In addition to the search capability you've already developed, this window requires an additional DataWindow control that displays the detail of the record currently highlighted in the original search DataWindow. The Employee Search window is the only window in the project that requires this kind of Search/Detail display. Fortunately, it still needs the same search functionality that is provided by w_ma_search. Inheritance will provide you with an excellent starting point.

You can develop this new object class by inheriting from w_ma_search. Then develop another DataWindow object for the detail. Next, add another DataWindow control to the window for the detail. Extend the window's open event by adding the ShareData function required to share data between the search DataWindow and the detail DataWindow. You can then extend the search DataWindow's rowfocuschanged event to keep the detail DataWindow in synch with it. Now you have only one task left: modify the window's resize event to handle resizing the two DataWindows.

You've had PowerScript in the window resize event since you first developed w_ma_base. That script was extended in w_ma_search. Can you extend it here to make the modifications you need? Unfortunately, you cannot. The technique you're using to resize the first DataWindow control—the search DataWindow—is inappropriate for this new window object class. You could override the ancestor's resize script, but there's other resizing code in there that you still need (for the window label and the micro help). So the best option is to modify the w_ma_base object class to give you a "hook" for resizing the DataWindow controls in the descendants. The new event won't have any PowerScript in it in w_ma_base. The script will be added in the descendants. That gives you a path for different search window object classes to do whatever resizing they need.

You can accomplish this by creating a custom user event named "ue_resize_dw" in w_ma_base. You then add the PowerScript to w_ma_base's resize event to trigger the ue_resize_dw event. Next, open the w_ma_search object class and move the DataWindow resizing script from the window's resize event to the new ue_resize_dw event. In the final step required to finish development of the new w_m_employee_search object class, you need to override the "ue_resize_dw" event's ancestor script with the new script to resize the two DataWindow controls in a way appropriate for this window class.

w_ma_detail

You've already figured out that this project needs two basic categories of windows object classes: search and detail. You've developed the search window object classes. Now it's time to develop the detail window object classes.

You need two detail windows: one for Product and one for Customer. (The Employee business object doesn't require one, because the detail is shown on the Employee Search window.) The good news is that the two detail windows appear to have exactly the same requirements, so you'll be able to develop one detail window object class, and then inherit from it to develop the two production detail windows.

You can develop the w_ma_detail window object class by inheriting from w_ma_base. You then add what is specific to this object class. Add a DataWindow control, which will hold the detail DataWindow objects in the descendants. Next, add the script to the ue_resize_dw event to size the DataWindow to use the maximum amount of window space available.

You have one final task. In this case, you will want the detail windows to display only the record the user selected. That means your detail DataWindow objects will have a retrieval argument. But how will the detail window know which record to retrieve? To meet this requirement, change your u_str_open_window structure to include two retrieval arguments: one that's a long data type, and one that's a string. You need both, since you don't know what the descendant detail windows will need. When the detail window is opened (by the corresponding search window), you'll pass to the detail window the value it needs in order to retrieve the right record from the database. No modification of the w_ma_base open event is needed to capture the retrieval arguments, as it captures the entire structure passed to it.

That's all there is to developing the detail ancestor object class. Now you can develop your two detail windows by inheriting from this class.

w_m_product_detail

The requirements for the Product detail window are very straightforward. Simply display a detail of the record selected in the corresponding search window. First you develop the Product detail DataWindow object. This DataWindow object needs a retrieve argument so that you can retrieve only the record you want. Since the unique key for the product table is the product ID, you make a retrieval argument of type number.

You can develop the w_m_product_detail object class by inheriting from w_ma_detail. Then you associate the new DataWindow object with the window's DataWindow control. You can add script to the ue_addl_open event to make the DataWindow read-only, and to set the transaction object. Next, you add script to the ue_post_open event to retrieve the record from the database by using the retrieve_arg_long element in the u_str_open_window structure passed to the window upon opening.

To implement the w_m_product_detail object class, you modify the ue_detail event in the w_m_product_search class to open an instance of the detail window, passing it the product ID of the selected record to be used as the retrieve argument for the detail data window. You now have a detail window for Product.

> **N O T E** If your users are complaining that windows are opening too slowly, try the following technique. The w_ma_base object class has an event named "ue_post_open," which is executed from the window's open event using the PostEvent function. The significance of this is that the event is placed at the end of the event queue, because it is posted rather than triggered. Therefore, the window finishes painting before the ue_post_open event fires. By placing the DataWindow retrieve function in this event, you can realize a gain in what is often termed *perceived performance*. The user sees the window before the record is retrieved, rather than after.

w_m_customer_detail

The requirements for the Customer detail window are exactly the same as those of the Product detail window. You need to follow the same steps to develop it:

1. Develop the detail DataWindow object.
2. Develop the new window object class by inheriting from w_ma_detail.
3. Associate the DataWindow object with the DataWindow control.
4. Add the required PowerScript to w_m_customer_detail and w_m_customer_search.

Examining the Results

And you're done! You now have a fully developed window class hierarchy that contains both ancestor and production object classes. Because you were careful to develop the ancestor classes, they're not specific to the application you were working on. They're fully reusable on other projects.

Do you see opportunities for more reusability? Perhaps the search/detail window class developed for w_m_employee_search has the potential to be made into a virtual class of its own, named w_ma_search_detail. The w_m_employee_search window would then be inherited from it, as would other windows requiring the same kind of functionality.

Inheritance is a powerful tool in the set of object-oriented features in PowerBuilder. The productivity gain you'll get from building reusable object classes will far outweigh the effort required to build them.

From Here...

Messages are important to check during any system error or DBError event, and return codes should *always* be checked after using embedded SQL. For more information about checking messages, check out the following chapters:

- Chapter 17, "Understanding Object-Oriented Concepts," explains the concepts and terminology of object-orientations and how they are used with PowerBuilder.
- Chapter 18, "Understanding User Objects," introduces the User Object painter, describes each of the types of User Objects, and gives examples of their use.
- Chapter 19, "Specialized User Objects," shows you how to incorporate C++ into your PowerBuilder code for maximum efficiency.
- Chapter 24, "Implementing MDI Applications," demonstrates a practical approach to creating database apps with an MDI interface.

Using ShareData Functions

— by Blake Coe

I have a 2 and a half year-old son whom my wife and I are trying to teach that sharing with his younger brother is a good thing. He has not quite grasped the cost effectiveness and efficiency of sharing. His favorite function, which was not implemented in PowerBuilder 5, is the "Mine( )." In this chapter, we are going to cover the benefits of sharing.

Understanding ShareData Functions

There are actually two Sharedata functions: ShareData, which allows DataWindow control objects to share the same data; and ShareDataOff, which causes the DataWindow control objects to stop sharing data. When sharing DataWindow controls, the primary DataWindow shares its data buffers (primary, delete, and filter) with the secondary DataWindow. Any function calls on the secondary DataWindow that change the data (for example, Retrieve or SetItem) will affect the primary DataWindow's data buffers and will appear in both DataWindows. If initial field values, a sort order, or filter statements are set in the DataWindow painter for the secondary DataWindow, they are ignored. Both DataWindows must have result sets for their data source. This means that the same number of fields must be selected in each data source and each field in the select list must have the same field type and length. For example, if Emp_ID was Numeric(10) and SSN was Numeric(9), they could not share. Other features, such as Where clauses in SQL and retrieval arguments, can also be different.

NOTE dwprimary.ShareData(dwsecondary)

DataWindowName.ShareDataOff()

The ShareData function is used in PowerBuilder scripts to share data between two or more DataWindows. dwprimary and dwsecondary must be DataWindows, and their data source result sets must match. dwsecondary has no data buffers, but points to dwprimary's data buffers.

The ShareDataOff function causes the DataWindow DataWindowName to stop sharing. DataWindowName can be the dwprimary DataWindow. ■

NOTE The functions dwShareData and dwShareDataOff in PowerBuilder 4 have been changed to ShareData and ShareDataOff in PowerBuilder 5. ■

Understanding the Benefits of Using ShareData

The benefit of sharing DataWindows is that they can have completely different formats. This allows the same data to be displayed and/or edited in many different ways. Data can be shared between tabular and freeform formats, summary and detail DataWindows, display and printed reports, and even grids and graphs. The DataWindows also can appear on the same window or different windows (as long as both windows exist). Costly retrieves or tedious coding to move data from one DataWindow to another can be avoided.

Examining Some Working Examples

To illustrate the benefits of the ShareData functions, some examples from a sample application will be explained. Even with these examples, it is apparent that the ShareData functions can be a useful and innovative tool to PowerBuilder developers and can help create more efficient and effective applications.

Example #1: Sharing Like DataWindows

Figure 23.1 is an example of the same DataWindow object being displayed in two DataWindow controls on the same main window. The upper DataWindow control (dw_data) is the primary, and the lower DataWindow control (dw_alternate) is the secondary. Because both controls use the same DataWindow object, they meet the criteria for having the same result set. Both DataWindows share the same data, so all the data displayed is the same (except for the Department field, which will be explained later in this chapter).

FIG. 23.1

Two DataWindow controls sharing the same data buffers display the same data. The Department field doesn't match because the drop-down child DataWindow that populates this field has not been shared from the primary DataWindow to the secondary.

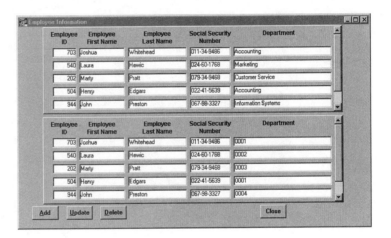

The code in listing 23.1 is contained in the open event of the main window (w_employee):

Listing 23.1   Code to Share Data Between Two DataWindows

```
//Set the transaction object for the primary dw
dw_data.SetTransObject(sqlca)

//Share the primary dw with the secondary dw
dw_data.ShareData(dw_alternate)

//Retrieve the primary dw
dw_data.retrieve()
```

First the transaction object is set for the primary DataWindow (dw_data), and then the ShareData function is used to share the secondary DataWindow(dw_alternate) with the primary. When the retrieve function executes for the primary, both DataWindows are populated.

N O T E dwprimary.ShareData(dwsecondary)

The ShareData function could also be coded after the retrieve function without changing the results. Only a slight timing difference might be noticeable when first displaying the DataWindows. ■

Example #2: Using ShareDataOff

The next example, figure 23.2, shows how the same DataWindows looks when the sharing function is turned off. Using ShareDataOff is often unnecessary, because the sharing of the DataWindows usually ends when the Window that contains either DataWindow is closed. The following script turns off the data sharing:

```
//Turn off data sharing for Primary dw
w_employee.dw_data.ShareDataOff()
```

FIG. 23.2

This is what you see when DataWindow sharing is turned off.

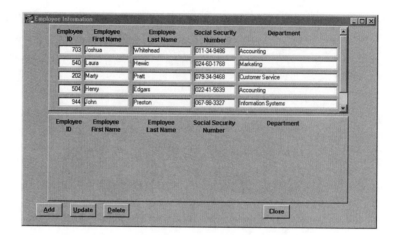

Example #3: Sharing Drop-Down Child DataWindows

As mentioned earlier, the department field does not appear to match in the two shared DataWindows in figure 23.1. This occurs because the department field is defined as a drop-down child DataWindow. When the primary DataWindow is retrieved, the drop-down child DataWindow is automatically retrieved from another table, and the department code is re-placed with the department name. Unfortunately, when the DataWindows are shared, the drop-down child DataWindows are not shared automatically.

The solution to this is to add code to the open event of the w_employee window to share the drop-down child DataWindows (see listing 23.2).

Listing 23.2   Code to Share Data Between Three DataWindows

```
//define 2 temporary variables of type datawindowchild ***New***
datawindowchild dwc_data, dwc_alternate

//Set the transaction object for the primary dw
dw_data.SetTransObject(sqlca)

//Share the primary dw with the secondary dw
dw_data.ShareData(dw_alternate)
```

```
//get the drop down datawindowchild for dw_data ***New***
dw_data.dwGetChild("employee_department",dwc_data)

//get the drop down datawindowchild for dw_alternate ***New***
dw_alternate.dwGetChild("employee_department",dwc_alternate)

//share the child datawindows ***New***
dwc_data.ShareData(dwc_alternate)

//Retrieve the primary dw
dw_data.retrieve()
```

First, two temporary variables of type DataWindowChild must be created, one for the drop-down child DataWindow in each DataWindow. The next two new statements assign the DataWindowChild handles to the temporary variables, using the dwGetChild function. The last new statement is a ShareData function that shares the child DataWindows. Figure 23.3 shows how sharing the drop-down child DataWindows makes the department fields for both DataWindows contain the department name.

FIG. 23.3

The department field on both DataWindows contains the department name.

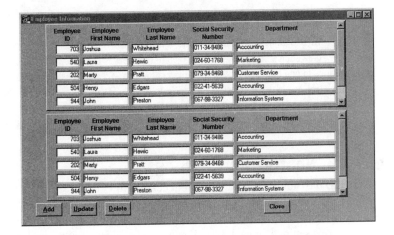

Example #4: Sharing DataWindows with Different Fields

In the next example, the sample application is changed by using different DataWindows in the shared DataWindow control objects. In figure 23.4, dw_alternate now displays a new DataWindow (d_employee_alternate), which has some different fields than the original DataWindow (d_employee_basic). Even though these two DataWindows display different data, they can still share the same data buffers because they use identical data source SQL. All the fields from both DataWindows are added to the data source SQL, and then only the desired fields are displayed.

N O T E To create a DataWindow that uses only part of the fields selected in the data source, simply delete those fields that should not be displayed. In the DataWindow painter, right-click the field to display the pop-up menu and then choose Delete. ■

FIG. 23.4
Shared DataWindows can display like data in different formats.

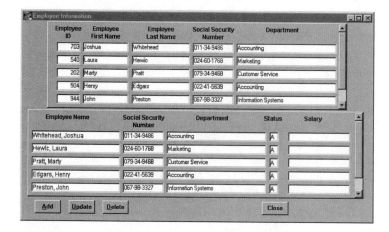

N O T E When sharing many DataWindows, it is often necessary to make the same changes to the data source SQL on several DataWindows. One way to speed up this job is to make the modifications to one data source SQL, and then convert to SQL syntax using the menu option Convert to Syntax. Once converted, it can then be copied to the Clipboard and pasted in the other DataWindows data source SQL painters. The other data source SQL painters must also be converted to SQL syntax before pasting the new SQL. If desired, it can then be converted back to graphic mode. ■

Example #5: Sharing Row Settings

Shared DataWindows can have different current row and selected row settings, and can scroll separately. These independent actions may be desirable in some cases, but there will also be instances when row settings should be shared. One method to accomplish this is to change the current row settings for each DataWindow in the other DataWindow's RowFocusChanged event. This allows either DataWindow to shadow row changes from the other.

> **CAUTION**
>
> Use care when coding RowFocusChanged events that call each other; a looping effect can occur between these events.

One way to code this is to use a window function like wf_share_row, shown in figure 23.5. This function is called from both DataWindows RowFocusChanged events. The current row is passed from the RowFocusChanged event into the parameter variable (passed_row). The current row and selected row (highlighted) from both DataWindows are compared to the value of passed_row, and then changed if they do not match. This causes DataWindow row changes to shadow each other, giving the appearance of sharing row settings.

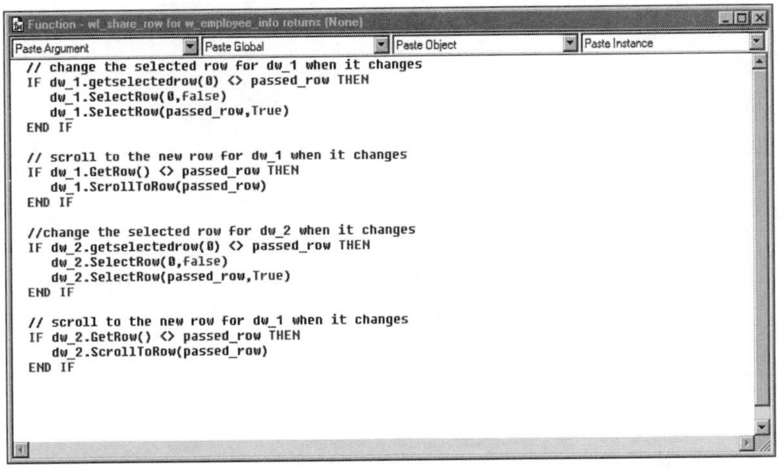
Function - wf_share_row for w_employee_info returns (None)
Paste Argument
Paste Global
Paste Object
Paste Instance
// change the selected row for dw_1 when it changes
IF dw_1.getselectedrow(0) <> passed_row THEN
dw_1.SelectRow(0,False)
dw_1.SelectRow(passed_row,True)
END IF
// scroll to the new row for dw_1 when it changes
IF dw_1.GetRow() <> passed_row THEN
dw_1.ScrollToRow(passed_row)
END IF
//change the selected row for dw_2 when it changes
IF dw_2.getselectedrow(0) <> passed_row THEN
dw_2.SelectRow(0,False)
dw_2.SelectRow(passed_row,True)
END IF
// scroll to the new row for dw_1 when it changes
IF dw_2.GetRow() <> passed_row THEN
dw_2.ScrollToRow(passed_row)
END IF

FIG. 23.5
wf_share_row is a window function that keeps dw_1 and dw_2 on the same row.

From Here...

In this chapter, you learned how to share data between multiple DataWindows. For more on what DataWindows can do, refer to the following chapters:

- Chapter 9, "Creating DataWindows," describes several DataWindow development techniques. You learn how to create three DataWindows and hook your DataWindows to your application.
- Chapter 10, "Enhancing DataWindows," shows you how to modify, enhance, and use your DataWindows.
- Chapter 11, "Manipulating Data Using DataWindows," shows how SQL can be used to define a DataWindow. This chapter covers the SQL toolbox and the SQL syntax behind a DataWindow.

References

CHAPTER 24

Implementing MDI Applications

by Mike Seals

Many applications today use the Multiple Document Interface (MDI). Applications like word processors, spreadsheets, and presentation packages lend themselves to this type of interface because each sheet can represent a different physical file. Applications in which each sheet represents a single file are relatively simple to create, but PowerBuilder is used primarily to create database applications. Creating MDI database applications presents a special set of challenges. Database search windows, maintenance sheets, and report sheets all can interact with one another.

Your challenge is to create an application architecture that presents a consistent interface to the user, makes adding new functionality easy, and is flexible enough to handle unique situations, if necessary.

This chapter will cover ways to achieve these goals with a practical approach to creating database apps with an MDI interface. The first section quickly covers some basics concerning the creation of the fundamental objects in an MDI app, like the frame window, sheet window class, and menus. It then moves on quickly to more advanced and useful real-world techniques that you can use to enhance your PowerBuilder "technique toolbox." ■

PowerBuilder's Application Framework as a Model for How to Create an MDI App

PowerBuilder offers to create an application framework for you when you create a new application object. It contains all of the fundamental MDI objects needed to create a running MDI application. They can then be enhanced to meet your needs. To create the application framework, start with an empty PBL. Go to the Library Painter and select Library|Create.... Give the new library the name PB5MDI.PBL. When you press OK, a new, empty library will be created.

Now create a new application object. When you do, PowerBuilder 5 will offer to create the application framework for you.

Follow these steps to create the application framework in the new PBL:

1. Go to the Application Painter.
2. Select menu item File|New. The dialog box shown in figure 24.1 appears.

FIG. 24.1

This dialog box requests the location and name of the PBL you want to create.

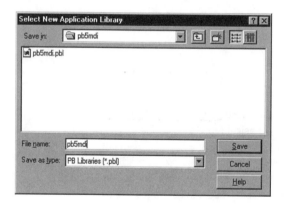

This dialog box asks where you want the new application. I'm sure you are familiar enough with this standard file search dialog box to find the PB5MDI.PBL just created. Select it and click the OK button.

3. Next, give the new application object a name. I like to use the same name as the primary pbl, so I suggest you call this application object ao_pb5mdi. When you click OK, the dialog box shown in figure 24.2 appears.

Click Yes here to allow PowerBuilder to create the Application Template objects along with the application object itself. When it is done, you are returned to the application painter. Close it and return to the library painter. It should now include the objects shown in figure 24.3.

Next, I will briefly describe these objects and how they are related to each other.

FIG. 24.2
Click Yes to allow
PowerBuilder to create
the application
template.

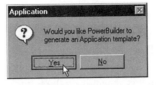

FIG. 24.3
Application Template
objects created by
PowerBuilder.

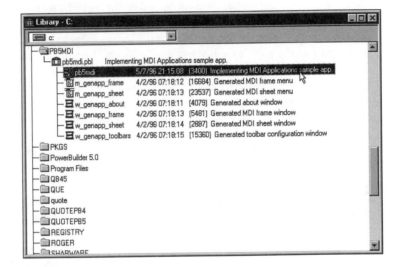

Using the MDI Frame; w_genapp_frame

In an MDI app, the frame is the first window opened, remains open the duration of the app, and is the last window to close. Only one frame is allowed to exist per application. A frame window is simply a window that has the WindowStyle attribute set to MDI! or MDIHelp!. Both create an MDI frame window capable of containing MDI sheets, but MDIHelp! adds the special status bar at the bottom of the frame which is used to display MicroHelp text.

The application template frame is called w_genapp_frame and includes the microhelp area on its frame.

Using the MDI Sheet Window Class; w_genapp_sheet

The MDI Sheet window class is intended to be used as the ancestor of any window that will be opened as a sheet within the MDI frame. This class becomes a convenient place to put code that occurs each time a sheet is opened or closed.

Part
VII

Ch
24

Using the Frame Menu; m_genapp_frame

The frame menu is the menu that is associated with MDI frame. It is only visible when the frame is displayed with no sheets. You will notice that it does not contain an edit menu top level item because edit functionality applies only to an open sheet. No editing can occur if there is no open sheet to receive the edit message, so it is absent from the frame's menu and added at the sheet menu level. Any toolbar bitmaps defined on the frame menu will show up on the frame toolbar and the sheet toolbar. Because the sheet menu is inherited from the frame, it will pick up these toolbar items and display them on the sheet toolbar as well. To make a toolbar bitmap appear only on the frame's toolbar, you must go to the sheet toolbar and make the item invisible at the sheet level. To illustrate this another way, consider the Exit menu item's toolbar bitmap. Open the m_genapp_frame menu and go to the File|Exit menu item. Click the Change… button to display the toolbar dialog for this menu item. Notice that the item is marked as visible. Now open the Sheet menu, m_genapp_sheet, and go to the same File|Exit menu item. Again, click the Change… button and note that the picture property has been reset so that the exit toolbar item does not appear on the sheetbar. You could also have kept the toolbar bitmap name defined, but made it invisible to achieve the same result.

 T I P   A menu item's toolbar button can remain visible even when the visibility of the menu item itself is off. When a menu item is disabled, the button remains visible but is no longer active; pressing it produces only a beep. It is important to give your users the feedback; they need to know which toolbar items are available for use, and which ones are disabled. You can do this by changing the toolbar bitmap to a grayed-out version at the same place in your code where you disable the menu item. This can be done by setting the toolbaritemname property to a string that points to a disabled version of the toolbar bitmap. When you enable the menu item, you can change the toolbaritemname property back to the full color bitmap. The sample application for this chapter includes a global function that you can use that enables or disables a menu item, and toggles its bitmap. The function is called fx_enable_menuitem(menuitem, boolean).

Using the Sheet menu; m_genapp_sheet

While the File|Close command is included on the frame menu generated by PowerBuilder, it is not automatically included on the frame's toolbar. You can include it there by adding the closed folder icon to the Close menu item at the frame level.

> **N O T E**   File | Exit is the menu item used to exit the application. I have seen many MDI implementations where the Close menu item remains available even when there are no sheets open. This can cause confusion for the user as to the exact meaning of the Close menu item. Remember that Close can be selected from a sheet's control menu, or from a sheet's menu. Exit has the function of attempting to close all open sheets and then exiting the application. From the user's perspective, the frame represents the application itself, and so is never actually "closed." The converse is also true of the effect of pressing the Exit button while a sheet is open. Exit should always attempt to close the frame, which in turn attempts to close all open sheets. It should not be used to close only the active sheet. To confirm this, try opening multiple sheets in an MDI word processor or spreadsheet program and see how it responds to the close and exit commands. ■

Using a Menu for Every Sheet

The PowerBuilder manuals describe the set of rules it follows when determining which menu is to be displayed on a frame if a sheet is opened that does not have a menu assigned to it. For example, if an empty frame MDI window is open, and a new sheet with no menu assigned is opened, the frame's menu will be visible and functional. If a sheet with its own menu is open, and a new sheet with no menu is opened, the previous sheet's menu will be visible instead of the frame's.

These rules can be simplified; <u>assign a menu to any and all windows that will be opened as a sheet.</u> This way, you won't need to worry about which menu will be displayed because you will have assigned a menu to all sheets. If a window has no functionality of its own beyond the row maintenance and window close commands added at the sheet level, then assign the sheet menu to it. In fact, the sheet menu is assigned to the sheet window class itself, so if you are inheriting your sheet maintenance windows from this class as you should be, you won't need to assign a menu at all; it will inherit the sheet menu by default.

Selecting Menu Levels for New Menu Items

As you may have noticed, I like to add new control or branching options to a window's menu and toolbar, instead of adding buttons on the sheet. This serves two purposes. First, by adding the item to the menu and toolbar, I have more working space on my window for a larger DataWindow area, or for more controls that can't be placed on a toolbar, like a combo box. Second, placing items at the appropriate inheritance level encourages reuse of code and a modular architecture. The next question becomes, then, "Where do I add new menu items?" New menu items can be added at three levels: maintenance, sheet, or frame level. Use the following chart as a guide:

Menu Level	Criteria	For Example
Frame	Item is always available to the user.	Application Exit.
	(or)	
	Item is available even when there are no sheets open.	Open search window.
Sheet	Not available to the user when there are no sheets open.	DataWindow row maintenance.
	(and)	
	Applies to more than one sheet.	DataWindow row scrolling.

continues

(continued)

Menu Level	Criteria	For Example
	(It can be made invisible on some.)	Close.
Maintenance	Not available to the user when there are no sheets open.	Revert to initial settings.
	Applies only to one maintenance window.	Select all accounts in a list of accounts.

Creating Frame and Sheet Toolbars

In an MDI application, two windows can have the input focus at the same time. These are the MDI frame window and the active sheet. A menu should be assigned to both. The frame toolbar consists of toolbar items that are visible on the frame menu whether the frame menu itself is visible or not. The sheet toolbar is visible when a sheet is active that has toolbar items that are visible on the sheet's own menu. As demonstrated in the application framework, you should inherit the sheet menu from the frame menu. The frame toolbar bitmap for application exit and the minimize/maximize bitmaps are defined and made visible on the frame's menu. This causes them to show up on the frame toolbar. The sheet menu is then opened up and these same toolbar items are made invisible so that they don't show up on the sheet toolbar as well. Then, sheet toolbar bitmaps are assigned to the sheet menu items for which you want toolbar buttons, like the row maintenance and row scrolling items discussed earlier.

- Keep in mind that the frame toolbar remains visible at all times, while a sheet's toolbar remains visible only when that sheet is active.

Enhancing the Application Framework

The application framework that PowerBuilder generates gives you a good starting point when building a new MDI application. There are many things that it does not provide, however. I will cover several of the enhancements that I always make to the application framework to allow it to perform better and provide a greater level of flexibility.

Adding Row Maintenance Entries on the Frame Menu

It is useful to add some database maintenance capabilities to the frame menu so that it's not necessary to add them to each sheet menu you create. I use PowerBuilder's development environment as a model for where to add them. While in the database painter you can open a table definition, select it, and click the Preview icon to open a grid style DataWindow to perform database maintenance against that table. While in this mode, observe the location of row maintenance menu items and place yours in the same location.

First, the Save Changes to Database and Save Rows As... menu items have been added to the File menu item as a section following Close and preceding Print with a separator bar before and after the section. Because these items are to be inserted into the sheet menu instead of appended, it is easiest to simply insert them on the frame menu as invisible items, then make them visible at the sheet level.

Next, a Display top-level menu item has been added after Edit that includes Next Page, Prior Page, and I would add Next Row and Prior Row.

And lastly, another top-level menu item is added after Display called Rows. It includes items for Delete, Described..., Filter..., Import..., Insert, and Sort (see fig. 24.4).

FIG. 24.4
A composite view of the enhancements to the Application Framework's sheet menu.

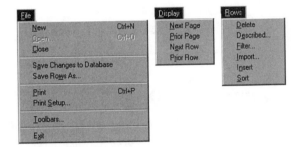

TIP Notice the menu item naming convention that Powersoft uses for these menu items. Items that are "self-contained" and require no further input do not have the ellipsis (3 dots) after the menu item label, while those that display a dialog box of some kind do. You can make your applications more intuitive to your users if you follow this convention also.

All of these will be visible at the sheet level so that they are globally available on any MDI sheet. Later, when you add a database maintenance DataWindow userobject, you will add events that contain code that can provide a default response to these menu commands. For example, you can add code to a ue_rowdelete event that simply deletes the current row in the DataWindow. Because these functions are usually available, you should leave them visible and enabled by default. If any items are invalid on a particular sheet, you can make them invisible on that sheet's menu.

You can add these new menu items to the sheet toolbar, which would now look as shown in figure 24.5.

Generally, you should try to avoid placing application-specific code directly in menu item events. Instead, you should post or trigger events on the current sheet. The sheet can respond in any way appropriate for that particular maintenance type. For example, there are situations where you will want the ue_rowinsert event to simply insert a blank new row in a DataWindow on the current window, and other times where you may need to display a dialog box to the user first. Triggering an event gives you the flexibility to respond to the ue_rowinsert event in whatever way is appropriate for that maintenance sheet.

FIG. 24.5

The sheet menu and sheet toolbar. The sheet toolbar is normally anchored to the left side of the frame.

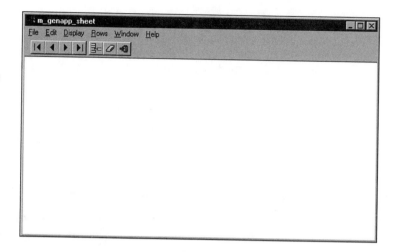

Using File | New and File | Open

In the application template that PowerBuilder builds for you, the File|New and File|Open menu items are patterned after applications with a single maintenance sheet type, such as the document of a word processor. In database applications in particular, you might have dozens of maintenance sheets, not just one. In fact, the entire database application development effort could be seen as simply creating a number of maintainable "views" of your database, with each view becoming a new maintenance sheet of its own. So you need to use a method of opening multiple maintenance views while still adhering to the conventional availability and meaning of the New and Open entries under File. At first, you might be tempted to open a dialog box listing the available maintenance sheets. The problem with this approach is that you cannot launch an MDI sheet while a modal dialog box is displayed on-screen. Windows itself simply doesn't allow it until the dialog box is closed. An effective solution is to add a cascading menu to the New and Open menu items.

 If you convert the application framework to display a cascaded menu when the user selects New, don't forget to remove the code in the New menu item.

Placing a Maintenance Sheet

Assuming you have decided to use the New and Open menu items as cascaded menus, you must decide which maintenance types to place under each menu item. To maintain some consistency with other, non-database applications, you can use New to list all maintenance sheets that are globally available at any time, even when there are no other sheets open.

These can include "top-level" search windows and maintenace windows with no criteria, such as an editable list of all vendors. The Open cascaded menu is reserved for sheets that can be opened only within the context of another sheet. You can take one of two approaches to adding entries to the Open menu. You can add all related maintenance sheets to the Open on the Frame, or you can leave it empty and add only those that apply to a particular maintenance type directly to that sheet's menu. Because one maintenance sheet might be available from several other sheets, you may find it works best to take the first approach and add all related sheets to the Open menu item on the frame.

To illustrate this, a good example is an invoice search sheet that lists a number of criteria objects at the top of the window, a Search button, and a list of invoices at the bottom of the window that match the criteria entered. The Invoice Search window is placed under the New menu item, while the Edit Invoice maintenance window appears under the Open menu item. The user selects File|New|Invoice Search, which opens an invoice search window. The user enters a range of dates in the search fields and clicks the Search button. A list of invoices created between those two dates appears in the DataWindow in the lower portion of the window. The user selects an invoice from the list, then selects File|Open|Edit Invoice to open the maintenance sheet that allows the user to edit the invoice. Nearly all database application maintenance sheets can be broken down into one of these two categories. I will discuss later in the chapter how to create a criteria structure that can be used to pass criteria from one window to another when it is opened from the File|Open menu.

Using a DataWindow userobject

It is good PowerBuilder programming practice to trigger or post events from a menu instead of placing code there. An example of the power and flexibility that this approach provides is in the row maintenance items I suggested you add to the frame menu. You want the Row|Insert menu item to post an event on the current sheet called ue_rowinsert. You don't want to post the message directly to a specific DataWindow, just to whatever window happens to be the active sheet. This is very simple:

```
If isvalid(w_genapp_frame.GetActiveSheet())= true then
    w_genapp_frame.GetActiveSheet().PostEvent ( "ue_rowinsert" )
End If
```

Once the message shows up on the current sheet, you can write code in the ue_rowinsert event to handle it. You can provide some default behavior at the window level, where this ue_rowinsert event arrives, by forwarding it to a DataWindow. By "forward," I mean that you want to trigger the ue_rowinsert event on the current DataWindow within the current sheet (remember, there could be several DataWindows on the window). You can accomplish this by creating an instance variable at the sheet level of type DataWindow to hold a reference to the current DataWindow, since there could be several on the window at any one time. Finally, create a DataWindow userobject that also has the ue_rowinsert event defined on it. When the ue_rowinsert event arrives, the special DataWindow userobject responds by inserting a blank row into the DataWindow. All of this will happen automatically, by default, without the need to write any DataWindow maintenance code except when there are exceptions to the norm. Figure 24.6 summarizes this process in a more graphical way.

FIG. 24.6
This screen shows an event triggered from the menu toolbar that is sent first to the window, and then forwarded to the current DataWindow.

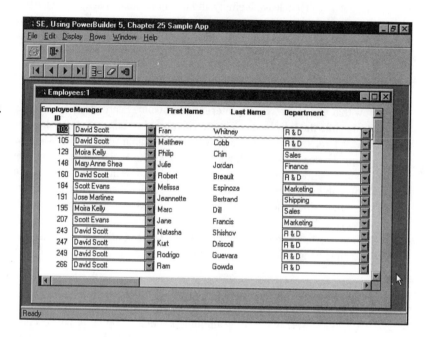

Working with the Criteria Structure

In PowerBuilder, the term criteria is used to describe the parameters passed to the retrieve DataWindow function that can be used as host variables to include in the result set, or to be used for grouping rows or limiting rows via the WHERE clause. In the context of a DataWindow, criteria elements are referred to as retrieval arguments. I expand this concept of criteria elements further than just the DataWindow. You may not realize it, but if you have created a database application in PowerBuilder, you probably have used criteria elements in the form of instance variables or global variables. For example, you may have an invoicing application and a table with a list of all vendors. As mentioned earlier, you might have a sheet that lists search criteria at the top of the sheet, with a list of vendors at the bottom of the sheet. When the user selects one of the vendors in the list, and then chooses to perform some function on it, you must somehow pass the vendor's id to the sheet being opened. You could take one of three common approaches to this.

Setting Global Variables

Set a global variable to the vendor's id, such as gv_vendor_id, and open the sheet. In the open script of the sheet, look at the value in the global variable for the criteria, in this case, the vendor's id.

This approach is a very common one, but it presents some problems. First, if you have multiple criteria, such as vendors that are active within a certain time period, you must create new global criteria elements. These elements take up space the entire time the application is running. Powersoft recommends limiting your use of global variables. A second problem with this approach is that the global variable is only valid for as long as it takes to open a new sheet. The user could open a sheet, go back to the list of vendors and open a maintenance sheet for a different vendor, wiping out the current value of the global variable. You will need to keep the criteria element for as long as the sheet is open, so you must store it in an instance variable on the sheet. Each sheet, then, will have a different set of instance variables to refer to the same criteria elements.

Using the OpenWithParm Function

A better approach is to skip the use of the global variable and use PowerBuilder's OpenWithParm function to pass a structure containing the necessary criteria elements. This call would take whatever criteria elements are needed and package them together in a criteria structure.

Part VII
Ch
24

This approach is on the right track. It eliminates the use of global variables, but creates a few problems of its own. The criteria structure can only be recognized by the window being opened if it is defined as a global structure. You cannot create a criteria structure that is local to two individual sheets, even if they both have the same elements and even the same name. The structure must be defined as a global structure. This repeats our problem of having multiple, global elements defined, but instead of a number of global criteria variables, you have a number of globally defined criteria structures, one for each maintenance sheet you can open. In some ways, you are just trading one problem for another.

Using the OpenWithParm/Criteria Structure

I have found that the best approach to this problem is to create a single criteria structure for your entire application. Essentially, this is a structure that contains all of the key elements in your database, plus any further qualifying elements you may need, like start and end dates used for searches. This solves many of the problems associated with other approaches to handling sheet criteria.

Why Use a Criteria Structure?

First and foremost, it eliminates the need to write code in each maintenance sheet to handle the details of pulling off the criteria structure. Because only one criteria structure is defined that contains all possible criteria elements, code can be placed in the open event of the sheet class to pull the standard criteria off of the message object and store it in an instance variable defined at the sheet class. I usually name the global criteria structure gs_criteria, and the instance variable at the sheet level iv_criteria. You can use your own naming convention, of course.

Further, the criteria structure becomes a convenient place to hold the entire set of criteria that was used to open an instance of a maintenance sheet. For example, if a window needs to be reretrieved, this can be done simply by looking at the appropriate elements of the criteria structure passed to the sheet when it was initially opened. For this reason, it is important to never change the criteria structure that was passed into a sheet.

Another benefit of a single criteria structure is the ability to create drill-down maintenance sheets and reports. An example of a drill-down might be our vendor search list. The application might allow the user to double-click on a vendor in the list to display a maintenance sheet listing all of the SKUs defined for that vendor. From the SKU list, the user could double-click a SKU line to display a sheet listing the locations and quantities available for that SKU. Drill-down reports could be created in the same way, with top-level, summary reports displayed first that allow the user to drill-down into further, more detailed reports by double-clicking a line in the top-level report.

Drill-downs are created by making a local copy of the sheet instance criteria variable, adding additional criteria from the currently selected row in the listbox or DataWindow, and using this new, enhanced criteria variable to open the drill-down sheet or report. The local copy of the criteria variable simply carries along the initial criteria used to open the top-level sheet.

Lastly, using a single criteria structure makes it easy to add criteria elements for new maintenance sheets because no new code needs to be added to handle them. Simply add the new elements to the global criteria structure, and presto! They are automatically passed along to all new sheets and stored in the instance criteria variable.

The Basic Elements of a Criteria Structure

I will discuss in a moment how to obtain the list of criteria elements themselves, but the criteria structure contains some other non-criteria elements as well. In order to promote modular code, set a maintenance_type string element to the type of maintenance window you open, and then call a global function to actually open the sheet. This way, if the sheet is opened from multiple entry points, changes to the open script can be made in a single location. For instance, if you use the maintenance type string of VENDORS, you can change the window that is used from w_vendors to w_vendors_new in just the function, and all of the entry points throughout the application will be up to date.

Another useful element is a flag indication that the sheet is to be opened to a "new" instance of the maintenance type defined in the structure. Let's say your list of vendors is displayed, and one of the options available on the sheet menu is to create a new vendor. If a row is simply inserted in the list, the insert can be handled entirely on the vendor sheet. However, if another sheet window is displayed to the user, you may want to set the new_flg element to True to indicate to the sheet being opened that it needs to generate a new vendor number, and display a blank, freeform record to enter the vendor's demographic information.

Maintenance sheets are not the only windows that can be opened from an application. Often, you must restrict the user from moving to another sheet until a maintenance operation is completed. This is accomplished by opening the maintenance window as a modal window instead of as a sheet. These are essentially dialog boxes. They can still be passed the criteria structure in the same way as a sheet because they benefit from this technique in all the same ways that a sheet does. The criteria structure can also be used to return information gathered while the dialog box is displayed. The new information can be placed in the criteria structure while the dialog is displayed, and the ReturnWithParm function can return the result. When the criteria structure is used in this way, an element to record whether the OK or Cancel button was pressed is useful. I call this element dialog_return, and make it an integer. This way, the same element can support dialogs of various types, such as dialogs with OK and Cancel, as well as Yes, No, and Cancel. Just like PowerBuilder does with its internal MessageBox function, you should assign the value of dialog_return according to the button's ordinal position on the screen with the first button given the value of 1, the second 2, and so forth.

These three elements are included in all applications that use a criteria structure, but the rest of the criteria elements will vary from one application to another.

Defining Key Database Elements

Part
VII

Ch
24

The best place to start when defining criteria elements for the criteria structure is to look at the database model for the tables that appear in your application. Table key values are an obvious candidate for inclusion in the criteria structure. So are elements that you have placed in an index. Of course, including key elements covers all foreign keys by default, so these do not need to be included. Often, a column with the same meaning appears on multiple tables, such as vendor_id. It only needs to be included once in the criteria structure. If you have columns such as start_date on multiple tables, but they have different meanings, such as the start date of a vendor's account and a start date for a client, then they must be represented as two separate elements in the criteria structure. These might be called vendor_start_date, and client_start_date in our example.

Following these simple rules will allow you to create a criteria structure that is as small as required without missing key elements. When in doubt about whether to include a particular database column, include it. As you develop your application, you will find other elements that need to be included. These can be included with minimal concern about their impact on the rest of the application because they are carried along with all other criteria elements.

If storage space is of concern to you, keep in mind that one copy exists for each sheet that is open in your application, and this number will remain small in most applications. Unused elements in the criteria take up space in each sheet, but unused strings occupy only 4 bytes of space; integers, 2 bytes; and long values, 4 bytes. Even in a complex system, a fully loaded criteria structure will occupy a manageable amount of memory, and should not be a concern given the elegance that the criteria structure approach offers you.

Based on the tables in the sample database that ships with PowerBuilder 5, the criteria structure for the sample app for this chapter looks like this:

Data Type	Element Name
string	sheet_type
integer	result
integer	dept_id
integer	customer_id

continues

continued

Data Type	Element Name
integer	contact_id
integer	emp_id
integer	product_id
integer	quarter
integer	ole_id
character	state_id
character	country
integer	sales_order_id
integer	sales_order_item_id

Working with the fx_new_sheet() Function

As mentioned earlier, I like to call a global function to open a new maintenance sheet. In any sheet where I want to open a related sheet, I create a new local instance of the criteria structure, set the maintenance sheet type element, any criteria elements, and call the fx_new_sheet() function passing only the criteria structure. The structure contains all of the information the function needs to open the new sheet with the criteria structure passed as a parameter.

I use a separate function called fx_new_report() to open new reports, but they could be opened from fx_new_report() also.

This function is quite simple. It uses the maint_type element of the criteria structure in a Case statement to jump to the section of code that actually performs the open for that maintenance type.

Other Uses for the Criteria Structure

Graph Drill-Downs

Having a consistent method for passing along criteria to new sheets opens up your application to some potential features that you might not otherwise have the time to implement. I touched on the idea of a drill-down from a report window earlier. Now I'd like to expand on this idea to present a method for using the drill-down to make even graphs, charts, and graphics like maps dynamic.

Powersoft has anticipated that some crazy developers will want to make a graph dynamic because it provides a function to retrieve the data element that is represented by a click on a particular area of a graph. The function is called ObjectAtPointer(). It returns the type of graph object at the mouse pointer, such as TypeLegend!, and TypeTitle!. The type you are interested in for drill-down purposes is TypeData!, because this indicates that the user clicked on a portion of the graph that represents data, such as a bar or pie slice. When the type returned is TypeData!, the seriesnumber and datapoint parameters are populated. These can then be used to determine the additional criteria needed to support a drill-down to another report or graph, providing additional detail. For example, you could provide a high-level graph of sales by region for the year, with each region represented by a separate line on the graph. There may exist a "spike" or dip in the data for one of the regions for one month. You can give your users the ability to double-click the spike or dip to retrieve a detailed sales drill-down report. Of course, further drill-downs would be possible from the detail report, if desired.

The sample app in pb5mdi.pbl contains an example of this type of functionality.

Bar graphs and pie charts work well with this kind of functionality because their surface areas are greater, and so are easier for the user to find. When detecting the double-click on a point on a line, the users must be very careful about the mouse placement, or the ObjectAtPointer() function will report that they are pointing to the background of the graph.

Criteria Summary

The criteria structure can be used to support all of these types of maintenance sheets. You can use them in any combination to make your database application more dynamic and useful. You can drill down from one report to another, or from a report to a graph, and you can drill down from a graphic image to a report or graph. The criteria structure and the code to handle it supports all of these dynamic methods.

The Refresh Structure

PowerBuilder is used primarily to create multi-user database maintenance and reporting applications. For a reporting application, you do not need to be very concerned about the volatility of data. A report can be seen as a view of the data as of an instant in time, or within a time range. In either case, it is assumed that you will request a report that has relatively stable data, such as last month's sales. If you request a sales report for the current month, you would understand that the report would contain dynamic data that would (likely) be different when you requested it later in the same day. So, a view of data like a report can by be ranked along a scale ranging from highly volatile to very stable.

Why Is a Refresh Structure Necessary?

Unlike report windows, table maintenance windows contain highly volatile data by their very nature. Multiple users maintaining data simultaneously can compound problems related to the volatility of data. Data inconsistency can occur at any one of several levels. First, in an MDI application, the user can open two separate maintenance sheets simultaneously. Sometimes, these sheets are totally unrelated to one another. For example, one sheet might be a list of vendors, while the second might be a list of clients. Entering a new client could not make any data on the vendor screen obsolete or out of date, and the vendor list does not influence the client list in any way. These two screens are completely independent of one another. Other windows can present data dependencies. I can think of the example of an invoice sheet with a drop-down DataWindow listing available SKUs. You should be able to go to a vendor's list of SKUs, add one, and have the new SKU automatically appear in the drop-down list on the invoice screen. The same problem could exist in other applications running on the same machine and connected to the same database, and at other users' machines somewhere else on the network. The refresh structure presented here provides a potential solution to many data volatility problems. Using a unified approach such as a refresh structure prevents the proliferation of stop-gap solutions to refreshing, which adds complexity to your code and makes it harder to maintain.

 TIP PowerBuilder provides one helpful way to prevent serious data integrity issues related to data volatility. For DataWindows with update capability, you can force PowerBuilder to specify only key columns, all of the modified columns, or all of the modifiable columns in the where clause when it generates an Update or Delete statement. Specifying one of these options goes a long way toward solving the problems of data volatility. The techniques discussed here present solutions that go beyond the basic data integrity issues solved by PowerBuilder's Update Characteristics settings.

As the architect of your application, only you can decide how critical it is to always have up-to-date data available to all users at all times. If you are developing a simple invoicing system with stable pricing structures, you may not be interested in this at all, or only on a limited basis. If you are creating a real-time stock market trading system, you may be quite interested in this technique's benefits.

Defining the Basic Elements of a Refresh Structure

Just as the criteria structure could be viewed generally as a list of database key columns, the refresh structure can be seen as a list of tables and views that may have changed. As such, its elements are simply booleans indicating whether that table or view has changed. The refresh structure (which includes the criteria structure) is then passed to all open sheets, other applications, and other network users indicating that something has changed in a specific table or tables. It is left to the sheets or applications receiving the refresh structure as to the appropriate way to respond. More often than not, the refresh message is simply ignored because the tables affected could not affect the window or application that received it.

So, a refresh structure is simply a list of elements representing tables and views in the database, with one element of the data type for the criteria structure described earlier. Knowing the tables that have changed, and the current key values used to retrieve the source data, the window or app receiving the refresh message can ignore the message, warn the user of the data volatility, or re-retrieve the data in question.

Utilizing Table Changed Flags

It may help to describe how you might go about creating a refresh structure. You should start with the criteria element. Whenever a change to the database is made on a critical data element, the maintenance sheet generating the refresh message populates this element in a local instance of the refresh structure with its current criteria structure. Next, the refresh structure must contain a boolean element for each individual, updatable table in the database. I call these "table changed" flags. Code tables can be eliminated because their data is highly static. Next, add elements for any distinct view of the underlying tables whether an actual database view is defined or not.

The refresh structure for the sample database that comes with PowerBuilder 5, and on which the sample app for this chapter is based, looks like this:

Data Type	Element Name
s_criteria	criteria
boolean	department
boolean	customer
boolean	contact
boolean	employee
boolean	product
boolean	printer
boolean	ole
boolean	states
boolean	sales_order
boolean	sales_order_items

Part
VII

Ch
24

Broadcasting the Refresh Message to All Open Sheets

Now that the refresh structure is defined, a mechanism must be put in place to broadcast it to all open sheets within an application so they can respond appropriately. Sending a user event message is one option.

5.0

N O T E User-defined events have been available in PowerBuilder since version 2, but their usefulness has been hindered by the fact that you could not pass parameters with the event script or return a value, as you could do with functions. PowerBuilder 5 eliminates that restriction by allowing you to define arguments to be passed along with the event, and even supports the definition of a return value when the event is triggered instead of posted. ▪

Another solution is to create a window level function on the sheet class window, which is the approach I take in the sample app for this chapter. The function as defined on the sheet ancestor does not do anything, it is only a placeholder to assure that the function is defined on all sheets in the application. If a particular maintenance sheet does not need to respond to any refresh, then it can depend on the sheet ancestor's function to simply return. However, if the maintenance sheet does need to respond to a refresh, it can test the elements of the refresh structure to first see if tables it is concerned with have changed. It can also look at the criteria structure to see if the change was for a totally unrelated data element, in which case, it again can ignore it. For example, if a vendor maintenance window is open, and the address changes, a vendor invoice window open to a different vendor will ignore the refresh message because it does not affect it. This is why you should pass along the criteria structure as an element of the refresh structure, to make it easy for a maintenance sheet to decide if it needs to take some action as the result of the refresh.

Re-retrieving a Drop-Down DataWindow

You can re-retrieve a drop-down DataWindow by getting a reference to the child DataWindow with the GetDataWindowChild( ) function, setting its transaction object, and performing a retrieve( ) on the child. This will work even when the child DataWindow has arguments defined.

This DataWindow child technique can be used to re-retrieve a drop-down DataWindow in response to a refresh message.

In the sample app for this chapter, the following code is in the wfx_refresh( ) function for the w_employees sheet:

Listing 24.1 The wfx_refresh() function

```
// This is triggered from other windows as changes are made.
// We are interested in whether the employee list has changed, and
// the list of departments.
DataWindowchild lv_child_dw

If refresh.employee = true then
    // Then the employee list has changed. Re-retrieve the entire list.
    iv_current_dw.GetChild('manager_id', lv_child_dw)
    lv_child_dw.SetTransObject(SQLCA)
    lv_child_dw.Retrieve()
end if

If refresh.department = true then
    // Then the employee list has changed.  Re-retrieve the entire list.
    iv_current_dw.GetChild('dept_id', lv_child_dw)
    lv_child_dw.SetTransObject(SQLCA)
    lv_child_dw.Retrieve()
end if

Return True
```

You can try this in the sample app. Open the employees window by selecting File|New|Employees List. Drop down the department list and not its contents. Now go to the Departments list by selecting File|New|Departments List. Add a department and save it. Now return to the Employees list and drop down the department listbox. The new department was automatically added to the list, by re-retrieving the drop-down DataWindow. You can try the same thing with the manager drop-down. The manager list is actually the employee list, and it can be refreshed just like the department drop-down. Try adding a new employee, saving, then assigning the employee you just added as his/her own manager. This is possible because the refresh function on the frame calls the refresh function on *all* sheets, even the sheet that initiated the refresh. The code above responds by re-retrieving the list of managers whether the new employee was added by the same window or a different one!

I think you will find that using the refreshing techniques described in this section will make your apps more intuitive to your users.

Refreshing Other Applications Within a Windows Session

While this is a less likely scenario than updating other sheets within that same MDI application, you may also find that you have the need to refresh other applications running within the same Windows session. These could take the form of stock price quote feed applications like the service provided by Dow Jones, or an application written in another development tool like Visual Basic or C/C++, or PowerBuilder itself.

Part

VII

Ch

24

Using the RegisterWindowMessage() API Function

You are probably familiar with the ability to create user events that can be triggered from within PowerBuilder on other forms or userobjects. Windows itself provides a facility to register a message number to a particular string dynamically. The number itself is assigned dynamically, so it may not be the same from one Windows session to another, or on different machines. However, if another application calls the RegisterWindowMessage() API call with the exact same string in the same session, Windows will return the same message id (message number), which can then be used to send that message to other Windows applications. The number assigned falls within a range of Windows messages called generically String messages and are assigned message numbers between 0XC000 and 0XFFF (hex). This message number, in conjunction with the API PostMessage() function, becomes a simple way to broadcast refresh messages to all other applications without the overhead and setup time of a DDE link. Two way communication is not needed, just notification. Use the message number returned by the call to RegisterWindowMessage() API function and the null value as the window handle. This broadcasts the message to all windows in the system. Most windows, of course, will ignore it, but others can be programmed to look for the message returned when they called RegisterWindowMessage(). You must pass the address of a string that has been encoded with all of the refresh elements.

Encoding a String with the Entire Refresh Structure

A single string can be encoded to contain the entire refresh structure, including the criteria element. The single string can then be sent to other applications, or across the network, or stored in a database table to be queried periodically by other applications. A technique of encoding a version number into the string will allow you to make changes to the format of the string without causing existing programs to crash.

On the CD

To encode a string, you must write a function that you can pass a refresh structure and have it return a single encoded string. Each element of the criteria structure is separated from the previous one using a vertical pipe (|) character. The pipe is a natural delimiter because it seldom, if ever, appears as part of the data itself, and is available on multiple platforms, including PCs, minicomputers, and mainframes. Simply encode every element of the criteria structure, then every element of the update structure with a propertyvalue1|propertyvalue2… construction. This way, the criteria and refresh elements can be parsed easily. I have included a function on the CD-ROM that makes parsing this string easy, called `fx_break_off_at()`. There is also an example of both an encoder and a decoder on the CD-ROM.

Transferring Information with DDE

DDE is a more common, and probably easier to use method for transferring information between two applications running in the same Windows session. Simply set up a DDE link to other applications that need notification and send and receive the encoded refresh string as described above.

Refreshing Across a Network

If your application warrants it, you may need to refresh other clients running "somewhere else" on the network. You would simply create a refresh string and deliver it across the network to other client machines so that they can be informed of database activity as it happens.

You must decide whether this approach will work for your application given the amount of network traffic this approach can generate. You can anticipate this by calculating the expected size of the refresh string, and multiplying it by the number of expected transactions by all users. For many systems with only a few users, it will still be practical to implement real-time refresh in your application.

There are many methods available to deliver these refresh messages to other client machines. These fall into two general categories. The first is called datagram delivery. This method has low overhead and is fast, but does not guarantee delivery of the string to the destination. The second is called session delivery. In session delivery, a transfer session is first established with the destination client. Then, the string is sent by breaking it down into component parts that are sent down the data pipe, and are reassembled at the other end. Session-oriented network protocols guarantee delivery of the message (in our case, the refresh string). A few example protocols that fall in these two categories follow:

Protocol	Type	Notes
NetBIOS	Datagram	Relatively slow, and cannot be routed over bridges or routers.
NetBUI	Datagram/Session	Routable version of NetBIOS.
IPX	Datagram	PowerBuilder Enterprise comes with a Netware library that includes the IPX/SPX protocols.

Protocol	Type	Notes
IP	Datagram	Available through DLL calls to WINSOCK.DLL. WINSOCK 2.0 will support non-TCP/IP protocols, like native ethernet, as well.
SPX	Session	Session-oriented protocol that works on top of IPX.
TCP	Session	Session-oriented protocol that works on top of the datagram services provided by IP.

Part
VII

Ch
24

From Here...

This chapter moved very quickly on the topics of creating an MDI frame, sheets, menus, and user objects. You can explore these topics in more detail in the following chapters:

- Chapter 4, "Exploring Windows," for a detailed explanation of how to create an MDI frame and sheet windows.

- Chapter 5, "Designing Menus," explains how to modify toolbar bitmaps and inherit new menus from existing ones.

- Chapter 22, "Exploiting the Power of Inheritance," for a discussion of the benefits of using inheritance, and a case study.

In addition, many of the topics covered in this chapter included a discussion of the use of User-Defined Events. You can obtain a more in-depth understanding of these topics in the following chapter:

- Chapter 6, "Using Events, Functions, and the PowerScript Language," contains a discussion of user-defined events.

CHAPTER 25

Function Quick Reference

by Charles A. Wood

PowerBuilder functions make coding your PowerScript easier. If you need to complete some task in your application, chances are that a PowerBuilder function exists that can complete your task for you.

This chapter deals with all the functions used inside PowerBuilder, starting with stand-alone functions that can be used in any PowerScript, and moving on to functions specific to an object or control. ■

N O T E   This reference chapter doesn't provide examples. If you need an example of a function after looking at the description, refer to the online help provided with PowerBuilder. ■

Stand-Alone Functions

Stand-alone functions are callable from any PowerScript. These functions can be separated into nine different categories:

Date Functions	Dates can be difficult to process in many computer languages. PowerBuilder has added many date functions to help out. Date functions are used to set and retrieve dates and date information.
DDE Functions	DDE (Dynamic Data Exchange) is a Windows convention that lets Windows programs "talk" or send data back and forth. DDE Server functions allow your program to be supplied with data from another program. DDE Client functions allow your program to supply another program with data.
Numeric Functions	Numeric functions (also called mathematical functions) perform complex mathematical equations. In addition to using these functions in PowerScript, the DataWindow painter uses the following functions in computed fields, filters, and validation rules.
Print Functions	Many objects and controls provide their own print functions. However, sometimes you may want to send the printer some information developed in PowerScript. Print functions set up print jobs to handle such tasks.
Miscellaneous Functions	The following functions don't fit into a specific grouping, but can be useful nonetheless.
String Functions	PowerBuilder excels in string handling with its string functions. In the DataWindow painter, use the following string functions in computed fields, filters, and validation rules:

File Functions	File functions access any type of file on your system.
Time Functions	Time functions return times and time information.
Conversion Functions	Data type conversion functions convert from one data type to another.

Table 25.1 is a list of all stand-alone functions in PowerBuilder:

Table 25.1   PowerBuilder Functions

Function	Function Type	Description
Abs(number)	Numeric	Obtains the absolute value of a number.
Asc(string)	String	The ASCII value of the first character of a string.
Beep(num)	Miscellaneous	Causes the computer to beep a specified number of times.
Ceiling(num)	Numeric	Obtains the smallest whole number that is greater than or equal to a specified number.
Char(num)	String	The character that corresponds to an ASCII value.
Char(variable)	Conversion	A blob, integer, or string as a char.
Clipboard(string)	Miscellaneous	Obtains the contents of the Microsoft Windows Clipboard.
CloseChannel(handle, windowhandle)	DDE Server	Closes a channel to a DDE server application that was opened by the OpenChannel function.
CommandParm( )	Miscellaneous	Retrieves the parameter string, if any, that was specified when the application was run.
Cos(num)	Numeric	Obtains the cosine of an angle. The angle is measured in radians.
Cpu( )	Miscellaneous	Obtains the number of seconds of CPU time the current application has used.
Date(datetime)**	Conversion	The date portion of a DateTime value retrieved from the database.
Date(string)**	Conversion	A valid date if the string argument is a valid date.
Date(year, month, day)**	Conversion	A date based on the integer values for year, month, and day.
Day(date)	Date	Returns the day of the month.
DayName(date)	Date	Returns the name of the day of the week.
DayNumber(date)	Date	Returns a number representing the day of the week (for example, Sunday is 1 and Wednesday is 4).
DaysAfter(date1, date2)	Date	Returns the number of days one date occurs after another.

Part

VII

Ch

25

continues

Table 25.1 Continued

Function	Function Type	Description
DBHandle(transobj)	Miscellaneous	Returns the DBMS specific interface handle.
Dec(string)	Conversion	The contents of a string as a decimal.
Double(string)	Conversion	The contents of a string as a double.
ExecRemote(command, applname, topicname)	DDE Server	Asks a server application to execute a command. This function has two formats.
ExecRemote(command, handle, windowhandle)	DDE Server	
Exp(num)	Numeric	Obtains e raised to the power of x.
Fact(num)	Numeric	Obtains the factorial of x.
FileClose(filenum)	File	Closes a file.
FileDelete(filename)	File	Deletes a file.
FileExists(filename)	File	Determines whether a file exists.
FileLength(filename)	File	Obtains the length of a file.
FileOpen(filename, file-mode, writemode)	File	Opens a file and returns a file handle.
FileRead(filenum, buffer)	File	Reads a file into buffer.
FileSeek(file#, position, origin)	File	Seeks a position in a file.
FileWrite(filenum, buffer)	File	Writes to a file.
Fill(string, num)	String	A string of a specified length filled with occurrences of a specified string.
GetCommandDDE(string)	DDE Client	Obtains the command the client application has sent.
GetCommandDDEOrigin (appl)	DDE Client	Determines what client application sent the command.
GetDataDDE(string)	DDE Client	Obtains data the client application has sent.
GetDataDDEOrigin (appl,topic, item)	DDE Client	Determines which client application sent the data.
GetDataDDE(string)	DDE Server	Obtains the new data from the hot-linked server application.
GetDataDDEOrigin (appl, topic, item)	DDE Server	Determines the origin of data that has arrived from a hot-linked server application.

Function	Function Type	Description
GetRemote(location, target, applname, topicname)	DDE Server	Asks a server application for data. This function has two formats.
GetRemote(location, target, handle, windowhandle)	DDE Server	
Hour(time)	Time	The hour (an integer between 0 and 23).
Idle(num)	Miscellaneous	Sends an Idle event if no user activity (for example, a keystroke or mouse movement) has occurred for a specified period of time.
Int(num)	Numeric	Obtains the largest whole number that is less than or equal to a specified number.
Integer(string)	Conversion	The contents of a string as an integer.
IsDate(string)	Miscellaneous	Determines whether the specified string contains a valid date.
IsNull(variable)	Miscellaneous	Determines whether the argument is NULL.
IsNumber(string)	Miscellaneous	Determines whether the specified string contains a number.
IsTime(string)	Miscellaneous	Determines whether the specified string contains a valid time.
KeyDown(keycode)	Miscellaneous	Determines whether the specified key is pressed.
Left(string, num)	String	A specified number of characters from a string, starting with the first character.
LeftTrim(string)	String	A copy of a specified string with leading blanks deleted.
Len(string)	String	The length of a string.
Log(num)	Numeric	Obtains the natural logarithm (base e) of a number.
LogTen(num)	Numeric	Obtains the decimal logarithm (base 10) of a number.
Long(string)	Conversion	The contents of a string as a long.
Lower(string)	String	A copy of a specified string with all uppercase letters converted to lowercase.
LowerBound(array,n)	Miscellaneous	Determines the lower bound of a dimension of an array.

Part

VII

Ch

25

continues

Table 25.1   Continued

Function	Function Type	Description
Match(string, pattern)	Miscellaneous	Compares a string to a text pattern and determines whether or not they match.
Max(num1, num2)*	Numeric	Obtains the larger of two numbers.
MessageBox(title, text, icon, button, default)	Miscellaneous	Displays a box containing a message.
Mid(string, start, length)	String	A string containing a specified number of characters copied (starting at a specified position) from a specified string.
Min(num1, num2)*	Numeric	Obtains the smaller of two numbers.
Minute(time)	Time	The minutes (an integer between 0 and 59).
Mod(num)	Numeric	Obtains the modulus of two numbers (the remainder after dividing the first number into the other number).
Month(date)	Date	Returns the month (an integer between 1 and 12).
Now()	Time	The current system time.
OpenChannel(appl, topic,windowhandle)	DDE Server	Opens a channel to a DDE server application.
Pi()	Numeric	Obtains pi (3.14...) times a number.
Pos(string1, string2, start)	String	The starting position of a string within a specified string.
Print(printjobnumber, {beforetab,} string {, aftertab})	Print	Prints a string in the current font. You can specify the tab before and after the string is printed.
PrintBitmap(printjob-number, bitmap, x, y, width, height)	Print	Prints a specified bitmap image at a specified location in the print area.
PrintCancel(jobnum)	Print	Cancels printing.
PrintClose(jobnum)	Print	Closes the print job and sends the page to the printer.
PrintDefineFont (printjobnumber, fontnumber, facename, height, weight, fontpitch, fontfamily, italic, underline)	Print	Defines a font for the print job. PowerBuilder supports eight fonts for each print job.

Function	Function Type	Description
PrintLine(print-jobnumber, x1, y1, x2, y2, thickness)	Print	Prints a line of a specified thickness at a specified location.
PrintOpen(jobname)	Print	Starts the print job and assigns it a print job number.
PrintOval(printjobnumber, x, y, width, height, thickness)	Print	Prints an oval (or circle) with a specified line thickness at a specified location.
PrintPage(jobnum)	Print	Sends the current page to the printer and sets up a new blank page.
PrintRect(printjobnumber, x, y, width, height, thickness)	Print	Prints a rectangle with a specified line thickness at a specified location.
PrintRoundRect(jobnumber, x, y, width, height, xradius, yradius, thickness)	Print	Prints a round rectangle with a specified line thickness at a specified location.
PrintSend(jobnum, string, zerochar)	Print	Sends a specified string directly to the printer.
PrintSetFont(jobnum, fontnumber)	Print	Sets the current print job font to one of the defined fonts.
PrintSetSpacing(jobnum, factor)	Print	Sets the spacing factor that will be used to determine the space between lines.
PrintSetup( )	Print	Calls up the Printer Setup dialog box for the printer driver.
PrintText(job, string, x, y, fontnum)	Print	Prints specified text at a specified location.
PrintWidth(jobnum, string)	Print	Returns the width (in 1/1000 inches) of the specified string in the current font.
PrintX(jobnum)	Print	Returns the X coordinate of the cursor.
PrintY(jobnum)	Print	Returns the Y coordinate of the cursor.
ProfileInt(filename, section, key, default)	Miscellaneous	Obtains an integer from a specified profile file.
ProfileString(filename, section, key, default)	Miscellaneous	Obtains a string from a specified profile file.

Part

VII

Ch

25

continues

Table 25.1 Continued

Function	Function Type	Description
Rand( )	Numeric	Obtains a random whole number (between 1 and a specified number).
Randomize( )	Numeric	Initializes the random number generator.
Real(string)	Conversion	The contents of a string as a real.
RelativeDate(date, n)	Date	Returns the date that occurs a specified number of days after a date.
RelativeTime(time1, numsecs)	Time	The time that occurs a specified number of seconds after a specified time.
Replace(string1, start, len, string2)	String	Replaces part of one string with all or part of another string.
RespondRemote(Boolean)	DDE Client	Indicates to the client whether the command or data was acceptable to the server.
RespondRemote(Boolean)	DDE Server	Indicates to the server whether the command or data was acceptable to the client.
Restart( )	Miscellaneous	Stops the execution of all scripts, closes all windows, commits and disconnects from the database, and restarts the application.
RGB(red, green, blue)	Miscellaneous	Determines the long value that represents a specified color.
Right(string, num)	String	A specified number of characters from the end of a specified string.
RightTrim(string)	String	A copy of a specified string with trailing blanks deleted.
Round(num)	Numeric	Obtains a number rounded to a number of decimal places.
Run(string, windowstate)	Miscellaneous	Executes (runs) a specified program.
Second(time)	Time	The seconds of a specified time (an integer between 0 and 59).
SecondsAfter(time1, time2)	Time	The number of seconds one time is after another.
SetDataDDE(string, appl, topic, item)	DDE Client	Sends data to the client application.
SetNull(variable)	Miscellaneous	Sets a specified variable to NULL.
SetPointer(type)	Miscellaneous	Sets the pointer to a specified type (Arrow, Cross, Beam, HourGlass, SizeNESW, SizeNS, SizeNWSE, SizeWE, or UpArrow).

Function	Function Type	Description
SetProfileString(filename, section, key, value)	Miscellaneous	Writes a value to a specified profile file.
SetRemote(location, value, applname, topicname)	DDE Server	Asks a server application to set an item to a specific value. This function has two formats.
SetRemote(location, value, handle, windowhandle)	DDE Server	
ShowHelp(helpfile, helpcommand, typeid)	Miscellaneous	Provides access to the Microsoft Windows-based system that you created for your PowerBuilder application.
Sign(num)	Numeric	Obtains a number (–1, 0, or 1) indicating the sign of a number.
SignalError()	Miscellaneous	Causes a SystemError event at the application level.
Sin(num)	Numeric	Obtains the sine of an angle. The angle is measured in radians.
Space(num)	String	A string of a specified length filled with spaces.
Sqrt(num)*	Numeric	Obtains the square root of a number.
StartHotLink(location, appl, topic)	DDE Server	Initiates a hot link to a server application so PowerBuilder is notified immediately of specified data changes in the server application.
StartServerDDE (windowname, appl, topic, item)	DDE Client	Causes PowerBuilder to begin acting as a server.
StopHotLink(location, appl, topic)	DDE Server	Ends the hot link with a server application.
StopServerDDE (windowname, appl, topic)	DDE Client	Causes PowerBuilder to stop acting as a server.
String(date, format)	Conversion	A date formatted to a string variable based on the format argument.
String(datetime, format)	Conversion	A datetime formatted to a string variable based on a format argument.
String(number, format)	Conversion	A number formatted to a string variable based on a format argument.
String(string, textpattern)	Conversion	A string reformatted based on a text pattern argument.

Part

VII

Ch

25

continues

Table 25.1 Continued

Function	Function Type	Description
String(time, format)	Conversion	A time formatted to a string variable based on the format argument.
Tan(num)	Numeric	Obtains the tangent of an angle. The angle is measured in radians.
Time(datetime)	Conversion	The time portion of a DateTime value retrieved from the database.
Time(hour, minute, second)	Conversion	Returns a time based on the integer values for hour, minute, and second.
Time(string)	Conversion	Returns a valid time if the string argument is a valid time.
Timer(num, windowname)	Miscellaneous	Sends a timer event to the active window.
Today()	Date	Returns the current system date.
Trim(string)	String	A string with leading and trailing blanks deleted.
Truncate(num)	Numeric	Obtains a number truncated to a specified number of decimal places.
Upper(string)	String	A copy of a specified string with all lowercase letters converted to uppercase.
UpperBound(array, n)	Miscellaneous	Determines the upper bound of a dimension of an array.
Year(date)	Date	Returns the year.

Min, Max, and Sqrt are not valid in the DataWindow painter for computed fields, filters, and validation rules.

**In the DataWindow painter, you can use these date conversion functions in computed fields, filters, and validation rules.*

Object and Control Functions

In addition to global functions that can be accessed by any PowerScript, PowerBuilder also includes object functions. These functions are accessed by listing the object name followed by a period and function name:

```
objectname.function(argument)
Functions are specific to a particular object. For instance, if you wanted to
update your database with the information on dw_my_datawindow, you would
type:dw_my_datawindow.update( )
```

Since update does not require any arguments, none were provided.

Object and Control functions have been separated into ten distinct categories:

Common Functions

Common Functions can be used by any object or control. For instance, the show( ) function can be accessed by a window (i.e., w_mywin.show( )) as well as a command button (i.e., cb_mybutton.show( )).

Common Non-Drawing Functions

Non-drawing functions can be accessed by any object or control except for drawing controls like lines, ovals, rectanges, and round rectangles.

DataWindow Functions

DataWindow Control Functions can be used with DataWindow controls.

Edit Functions

Edit functions can be used with single line edits (SLE), multi-line edits (MLE), drop-down list boxes (DDLB), edit masks (EM), Rich Text Edits (RTE), and DataWindow (DW) controls.

Graph Functions

Graph functions can only be used with graph controls. This includes window graph controls and DataWindows that are graphs.

ListBox Functions

ListBox functions can be used with list boxes, drop-down list boxes (DDLBs), picture list boxes (PLBs), and drop-down picture list boxes (DDPLBs). Some TreeView (TV) functions are included in this category.

ListView Functions

ListView Functions can be used with ListView controls and some TreeView controls.

Menu Functions

Menu functions are available to menus only.

Multi-Line Functions

Multi-Line Functions apply to those controls that can contain multiple lines of information and/or text. Specifically, multi-line edits (MLE), edit masks (EM), Rich Text Edits (RTE), and DataWindow (DW) controls.

OLE 2.0 Functions

OLE 2.0 functions can only be used with OLE objects and DataWindows that are OLE objects.

Picture Functions

Picture Functions can be used with TreeView (TV) controls as well as picture list boxes (PLBs) and drop-down picture list boxes (DDPLBs).

RTE Functions

RTE functions can only be used with rich text edit (RTE) controls. This includes window RTE controls and DataWindows that are RTEs.

Part
VII

Ch
25

Tab Folder Functions	Tab folder functions can only be used with tab folder controls.
TreeView Functions	TreeView functions can only be used with TreeView controls.
User Object Functions	User Object Functions are available to userobjects only.
Window Functions	Window functions are available to windows only.

N O T E   Notice that there is some overlap between function categories. For instance, DataWindows use edit, multi-line, graph, and DataWindow functions. ■

Table 25.2 lists all the functions used in PowerBuilder in alphabetical order, their type, and a short description of their function:

Table 25.2   Object Functions

Function	Function Type	Description
AcceptText( )	DataWindow	Forces all text on the DataWindow to be accepted, especially the text on the current field when Tab or Enter has not been pressed.
AddCategory(string)	Graph	Adds a category (denoted by a string) to a graph. Does not apply to DataWindows.
AddColumn(label, alignment, width)	ListView	Add a column with a specified label, alignment, and width.
AddData(series, xvalue, yvalue)	Graph	Adds data to a scattergraph. Uses series number, and x and y as coordinates. Does not apply to DataWindows.
AddData(series,datavalue, categorylabel)	Graph	Adds data to a series in graphs that aren't scattergraphs. Does not apply to DataWindows.
AddItem(label, pictureindex)	ListView	Adds an item to a listview. Item is the name of the item you are adding.
AddItem(item)	ListView	Adds a picture to a listview. Label is the name of the picture you are adding and pictureindex is the index of the picture you are adding.
AddItem(string)	Listbox	Adds the string to the bottom of a list box or DDLB.

Function	Function Type	Description
AddLargePicture (picturename)	ListView	Add the bitmap, icon, or cursor specified by picturename to the large image list on a listview.
AddPicture (picturename)	Picture	Adds a picture to the image list in a tree list-view or a picture list box.
AddSeries(string)	Graph	Adds a series to the graph. The string parameter is the series name. Does not apply to DataWindows.
AddSmallPicture (picturename)	ListView	Add the bitmap, icon, or cursor specified by picturename to the small image list on a listview.
AddStatePicture (picturename)	ListView	Add the bitmap, icon, or cursor specified by picturename to the state image list on a listview or tree view control.
Arrange ()	ListView	Arranges icons in a listview.
ArrangeSheets (ArrangeType)	Window	Arranges sheets in an MDI application. ArrangeType is an enumerated variable of either Cascade!, Tile!, or Layer!. Icons! is also available for arranging minimized sheets in an MDI application.
CanUndo()	Edit	Returns a boolean TRUE or FALSE if the last edit can be undone. Does not apply to drop-down list boxes.
CategoryCount({control})	Graph	Counts the categories in a graph. If the graph is a datawindow control, the control name also must be passed.
CategoryName({control,} category)	Graph	Returns the category name of a category number. If grCategoryName is used on a DataWindow, the control name also must be passed.
ChangeMenu (menuname, position)	Window	Selects a new menu for a window. If the window is an MDI frame, position can be passed to determine which menu bar item lists the open sheets.
ClassName()	Common	Returns the name of the object or control.
Clear()	Edit	Deletes the selected text.
ClearValues(column)	DataWindow	Deletes all the values of the code table (if one exists) in the specified column.

Part

VII

Ch

25

continues

Table 25.2 Continued

Function	Function Type	Description
Clipboard( )({control})	Graph	Copies the graph control image to the Clipboard. If Clipboard is used on a DataWindow graph, the control name must also be passed.
closetab(dragobject o)	Tab Folder	Removes a tab page from a Tab control that was opened previously with the OpenTab or OpenTabWithParm function. CloseTab executes the scripts for the user object's Destructor event.
Closeuserobject (userobject)	Window	Closes a user object by removing it from view and executing the scripts for its Destructor event.
CollapseItem(handle)	TreeView	Collapses the specified item identified by the handle in a treeview control.
Copy( )	Edit	Puts the selected text in the Clipboard but does not delete (clear) it.
CopyRTF({selected {,band}})	RTE	Copies the selected contents of the RichTextEdit control to a string in rich text format. You can specify TRUE (default) or FALSE to indicate if you want to copy selected text only or the entire RTE. You can also specify which RTE band you want to copy from.
Create(syntax, errorbuffer)	DataWindow	Creates a new DataWindow based on the passed syntax. Any errors are placed in errorbuffer.
CrosstabDialog( )	DataWindow	Displays the CrossTab dialog box that the developer sees when defining a crosstab. This allows dynamic manipulation of crosstabs during execution.
Cut( )	Edit	Deletes the selected text and places the text in the Clipboard.
DataCount(({control,} seriesname)	Graph	Returns the number of data in a series. If grDataCount is used on a DataWindow graph, the control name must also be passed.
DBCancel( )	DataWindow	Cancels a current database retrieval.
DBErrorCode( )	DataWindow	Returns the database specific error number.

Function	Function Type	Description
DBErrorMessage( )	DataWindow	Returns the database specific error message.
DeleteCategory(string)	Graph	Deletes the category name denoted from the string parameter from a graph. Does not apply to DataWindows.
DeleteColumn(index)	ListView	Deletes a column in a listview control.
DeleteColumns( )	ListView	Deletes all columns in a listview control.
DeleteData(seriesnumber, datapointnumber)	Graph	Deletes a datapoint from a series in a graph. Does not apply to DataWindows.
DeletedCount( )	DataWindow	Returns the number of rows that have been deleted from the data window since the last retrieval or update.
DeleteItem(index)	Listbox	Deletes the item referenced by index out of a list box, DDLB, or treeview control.
DeleteItem(index)	ListView	Deletes an item in a listview control.
DeleteItems( )	ListView	Deletes all items in a listview or treeview control.
DeleteLargePicture(index)	ListView	Deletes a large picture from the large picture list in a listview.
DeleteLargePictures( )	ListView	Deletes all large pictures in a listview control.
DeletePicture(index)	Picture	Deletes a picture from the image list in a tree listview or a picture list box.
DeletePictures( )	Picture	Deletes all pictures for the image list in a tree listview or a picture list box.
DeleteRow(rownum)	DataWindow	Deletes a row from the DataWindow. If rownum is 0, the current row is deleted.
DeleteSeries(seriesname)	Graph	Deletes an entire series from a graph denoted by a passed series name. Does not apply to DataWindows.
DeleteSmallPicture(index)	ListView	Deletes a Small picture from the Small picture list in a listview.
DeleteSmallPictures( )	ListView	Deletes all Small pictures in a listview control.
DeleteStatePicture(index)	ListView	Deletes a State picture from the State picture list in a listview or treeview control.

Part

VII

Ch

25

continues

Table 25.2   Continued

Function	Function Type	Description
DeleteStatePictures( )	ListView	Deletes all State pictures in a listview or treeview control.
Describe(string)	DataWindow	Returns the current description of a dynamic DataWindow.
DirList(filespec, filetype, statictext)	Listbox	Populates your list box or DDLB with a directory of files that match the filespec (for example, *.pbl, *.ini, and so on) and filetype.
DirSelect(filename)	Listbox	Retrieves the current selection of a list box or DDLB populated with DirList and places it in filename.
Drag(dragmode)	Common Non-Drawing	Starts or stops the dragging of an object. Dragmode is an enumerated data type of Begin!, End!, or Cancel!.
Draw(x, y)	Picture	Draws a picture control at a specified location in the current window.
EditLabel(handle)	TreeView	Begin editing a specified label in a listview or treeview control.
EventParmDouble (parameter, parmvariable)	User Object	For use with visual basic controls. Returns the double parmvariable denoted by the parameter number in a vbx control.
EventParmString (parameter, parmvariable)	User Object	For use with visual basic controls. Returns the string parmvariable denoted by the parameter number in a vbx control.
ExpandAll(handle)	TreeView	Expands all sub-items in a treeview item identified by handle.
ExpandItem(handle)	TreeView	Expands an item by one level identified by handle.
Filter( )	DataWindow	Displays rows that pass the current filter definition.
FilteredCount( )	DataWindow	Returns the number of rows not displayed because of the filter.

Function	Function Type	Description
find(searchstring, forward, nsensitive, wholeword, cursor)	RTE	Finds a string in an RTE. You can specify the string to search for TRUE or FALSE indicating forward or backward, TRUE or FALSE indicating if the search is case insensitive or not, TRUE or FALSE indicating if a whole word is being searched for or not, and TRUE or FALSE indicating if the search begins at the cursor or if the entire document is to be searched.
Find(condition, rowstart, rowend)	DataWindow	Searches for a row that meets a condition starting at rowstart and ending at rowend.
FindCategory({control,} categoryname)	Graph	Returns the number of the category name. If FindCategory is used on a DataWindow graph, the control name must also be passed.
FindGroupChange (rownum, level)	DataWindow	Searches for the first break in the DataWindow for the group identified by level after rownum.
FindItem(startindex, label, partial, wrap)	ListView	Search for the next item (starting at startindex) that has the same label as the one specified. If partial is TRUE, partial labels will be searched. Wrap indicates whether or not to return to the starting point of the search.
FindItem(string, index)	Listbox	Returns the number of the string item in a list box or treeview control. FindItem starts the search at a given index.
findnext()	RTE	Finds the next occurrence of a string in a rich text edit
FindRequired(dwbuffer, row, colnbr, colname, updateonly)	DataWindow	Reports the next row that is required in a DataWindow, but has a NULL value currently entered.
FindSeries({control,} seriesname)	Graph	Returns the number of the series name. If FindSeries is used on a DataWindow graph, the control name must also be passed.
get_classlongname()	OLE 2.0	
get_classshortname()	OLE 2.0	
GetActiveSheet()	Window	Returns a window data type of the active sheet in an MDI application.

Part
VII

Ch
25

continues

Table 25.2   Continued

Function	Function Type	Description
getalignment( )	RTE	Returns an Alignment enumerated variable describing the alignment of a rich text edit control.
GetBandAtPointer( )	DataWindow	Returns a string containing the band in which the mouse pointer is currently located.
GetBorderStyle(column)	DataWindow	Returns a Border enumerated data type describing the type of border at a column.
GetChild(columnname, dwc)	DataWindow	Sets the DataWindowChild variable (dwc) with the contents of the child DataWindow (the DDDW or nested report). Use this to perform functions on the child DataWindow.
GetClickedColumn( )	DataWindow	Returns the column number that was clicked.
GetClickedRow( )	DataWindow	Returns the row number that was clicked.
GetColumn(startindex, label, partial, wrap)	ListView	Returns the next column index (starting at startindex) that has the same label as the one specified. If partial is TRUE, partial labels will be searched. Wrap indicates whether or not to return to the starting point of the search.
GetColumn( )	DataWindow	Returns the current column number.
GetColumnName( )	DataWindow	Returns the current column name.
getdata(clipboardformat, data)	OLE 2.0	
GetData(datavariable)	Edit	Gets the unformatted text from an EditMask control.
GetData({control,} seriesnumber, datapoint {,datatype})	Graph	Returns the data from the graph referenced by seriesnumber and datapoint. If GetData is used on a DataWindow graph, the control name must also be passed.
GetDataPieExplode ({control} series, datapoint, percentage)	Graph	Reports the percentage that a pie slice is exploded in a pie graph. The value is stored in percentage.

Function	Function Type	Description
GetDataStyle({control,} seriesnumber, datapoint, fillpattern)	Graph	The fill pattern is stored in a fill pattern enumerated data type for a specific datapoint on a series. If DataStyle is used on a DataWindow graph, the control name must also be passed.
GetDataStyle({control,} seriesnumber, grColorType, ColorVariable)	Graph	Stores color information into ColorVariable about a specific series and color type. If DataStyle is used on a DataWindow graph, the control name must also be passed.
GetDataStyle({control,} seriesnumber, datapointnumber, grSymbolType)	Graph	The symbol is stored in an enumerated variable of grSymbolType for a specific datapoint on a series. If DataStyle is used on a DataWindow graph, the control name must also be passed.
GetDataStyle({control,} seriesnumber, datapointnumber, linestyle, linewidth)	Graph	The line style and line width are stored in the appropriate enumerated data types for a specific datapoint on a series. If DataStyle is used on a DataWindow graph, the control name must also be passed.
GetDataValue({control,} seriesnumber, datapoint, datavariable {, xory })	Graph	Obtains the value of a data point in a series of a graph.
GetFirstSheet()	Window	Returns a window variable containing the first window sheet on an MDI frame window.
GetFormat(column)	DataWindow	Returns a string containing the column format.
GetItem(index, column, label)	ListView	Returns the label value of a specified column, index, and label in a listview or treeview control.
GetItemDate(rownum, column)	DataWindow	Returns the date in a date column in the DataWindow.
GetItemDateTime(rownum, column)	DataWindow	Returns the datetime in a datetime column in the DataWindow.
GetItemDecimal(rownum, column)	DataWindow	Returns the decimal number in a decimal column in the DataWindow.
GetItemNumber(rownum, column)	DataWindow	Returns the number in a numeric column in the DataWindow.

Part

VII

Ch

25

continues

Table 25.2 Continued

Function	Function Type	Description
GetItemStatus(rownum, column, dwbuffer)	DataWindow	Returns a dwItemStatus enumerated data type indicating the item status of the item at rownum and column in dwbuffer.
GetItemString(rownum, column)	DataWindow	Returns the string in a string column in the DataWindow.
GetItemTime(rownum, column)	DataWindow	Returns the time in a time column in the DataWindow.
GetMessageText()	DataWindow	Obtains the message text generated by a crosstab DataWindow object in a DataWindow control. (Only crosstab DataWindows generate messages.)
getnativepointer(pobject)	OLE 2.0	
GetNextModified(rownum, dwbuffer)	DataWindow	Returns the next row number that was modified after rownum.
GetNextSheet(window)	Window	Returns a window variable containing the first window sheet on an MDI frame window.
GetObjectAtPointer()	DataWindow	Returns the DataWindow object under the mouse pointer.
GetOrigin(x,y)	ListView	
GetParagraphSetting (paragraphsetting p)	RTE	Returns the paragraph setting (Left!, Indent!, Right!) of selected text in an RTE control.
GetParent()	Common	Returns a PowerObject containing the parent window, user object, or menu of the control, menu, or sheet window.
GetRow()	DataWindow	Returns the current row.
GetSelectedRow(rownum)	DataWindow	Returns the next selected row after the passed rownum.
GetSeriesStyle ({dw_control,} seriesname, fillpatternvariable)	Graph	GetSeriesStyle returns information about the fill pattern of a series. The fill pattern is stored in an enumerated variable.
GetSeriesStyle ({dw_control,} seriesname, grSymbolType)	Graph	GetSeriesStyle returns information about the tickmark symbol. The symbol is stored in an enumerated variable of grSymbolType.

Function	Function Type	Description
GetSeriesStyle ({dw_control,} seriesname, overlay)	Graph	GetSeriesStyle returns information about the tickmark symbol of a series. Overlay is a boolean set to TRUE or FALSE indicating if overlays are allowed.
GetSeriesStyle ({dw_control,} seriesname, Colortype, colorvariable)	Graph	GetSeriesStyle returns information about the color of a series. ColorType is an enumerated data type specifying the color type for which you want to obtain the color. The color is then stored in a long ColorVariable.
GetSeriesStyle ({dw_control}, seriesname, linestyle)	Graph	GetSeriesStyle returns information about the line style of a series. The line style is stored in an enumerated line style variable.
GetSpacing( )	RTE	Returns a Spacing enumerated data type describing the spacing of a rich text edit control at the insertion point.
GetSQLPreview( )	DataWindow	Returns the current SQL statement.
GetSQLSelect( )	DataWindow	Returns a string containing the SQL. Select syntax of the DataWindow.
GetText( )	DataWindow	Returns a string containing the text of the current field on the DataWindow.
gettextcolor( )	RTE	Returns the color of the selected text in a rich text edit.
gettextstyle(textstyle s)	RTE	Stores the font settings for selected text in a textstyle variable in a rich text edit control.
Gettoolbar(integer i, boolean v, alignment, oolbaralignment a, visibility, and string t)	Window	Gets the current values for title of the specified toolbar.
GetToolbarPos (toolbarindex, dockrow, offset)	Window	Gets the row number and offset of a docked toolbar.
GetToolbarPos (toolbarindex, x, y, width, height)	Window	Gets the position and dimensions of a floating toolbar.
GetTrans(transaction)	DataWindow	Returns the transaction of a DataWindow and places it into the passed transaction variable.

Part

VII

Ch

25

continues

Table 25.2 Continued

Function	Function Type	Description
GetUpdateStatus(row, dwbuffer)	DataWindow	Determines what caused the DataWindow to submit SQL to the database server.
GetValidate(column) rule of a column.	DataWindow	Returns a string containing the validation
GetValue(column, index)	DataWindow	Returns the display value of the code table of a column when passed the index.
GroupCalc( )	DataWindow	Recalculates breaks in the grouping levels.
Handle( )	Common	Returns a long integer containing the Windows handle of your object or control.
Hide( )	Common	Hides an object if that object is showing.
ImportClipboard(startrow, endrow, startcolumn, endcolumn, dwstartcolumn)	Graph	Copies the contents of the Clipboard, beginningwith startrow and startcolumn and ending with endrow and endcolumn, to datawindowname (if applicable) starting in column dwstartcolumn. Default is whole clipboard and dwstartcolumn (if applicable) = 1.
ImportClipboard(startrow, endrow, startcolumn, endcolumn, dwcolumn)	DataWindow	Imports tab-delimited Clipboard contents starting at startrow and startcolumn and going to endrow and endcolumn of the file. Places the result in the DataWindow starting at dwcolumn.
ImportFile(filename, startrow, endrow, endcolumn, dwstartcolumn)	Graph	Imports a file in TXT (tab separated) or DBF (dBase II or III) format into a graph. Startrow, endrow, and startcolumn are defaulted to be the entire file.
ImportFile(filename, startrow, endrow, startcolumn, endcolumn, dwcolumn)	DataWindow	Imports a tab-delimited file starting at startrow and startcolumn and going to endrow and endcolumn of the file. Places the result in the DataWindow starting at dwcolumn.
ImportString(filename, startrow, endrow, endcolumn, dwstartcolumn)	Graph	Imports a tab delimited string into a graph.
ImportString(string, startrow, endrow, startcolumn, endcolumn, dwcolumn)	DataWindow	Imports a tab-delimited string starting at startrow and startcolumn and going to endrow and endcolumn of the string. Places the result in the DataWindow starting at dwcolumn.

Function	Function Type	Description
inputfieldchangedata (name, values)	RTE	Modifies the data value for all input fields with a specified field name in a rich text edit control.
inputfieldcurrentname( )	RTE	Returns the name of the selected input field in a rich text edit control.
inputfielddeletecurrent( )	RTE	Deletes the selected input field in a rich text edit control.
inputfieldgetdata (inputfieldname)	RTE	Retrieves data from an input field in a rich text edit control.
inputfieldinsert (inputfieldname)	RTE	Inserts the named input field at the insertion point.
InsertCategory (categoryname, categorynumber)	Graph	Inserts a new category name before the given category number. Does not apply to DataWindows.
InsertColumn(index, label, alignment, width)	ListView	Inserts a column with the specified label, alignment, and width at the specified index in a listview control.
InsertData(seriesnumber, datapoint, datavalue, categorylabel)	Graph	Inserts a new datavalue before the given datapoint in a given series. If a category label is specified, a tickmark is placed on the graph for this new data. Does not apply to DataWindows.
insertdocument(filename, replace {,filetype})	RTE	Inserts the named file in the rich text edit control. Replace is TRUE or FALSE indicating whether or not the current contents are to be replaced or added at the insertion point. Filetype can be set to rich text format (RTF) or ASCII text.
InsertItem({index,} label {,pictureindex})	ListView	Inserts an item to a listview or tree view control.
InsertItem(string, index)	Listbox	Inserts an item string in your list box or tree-view control before a given index.
InsertItemFirst (handleparent, label, pictureindex)	TreeView	Inserts an item as the first child of its parent in a treeview control.
InsertItemLast (handleparent, label, pictureindex)	TreeView	Inserts an item as the last child of its parent in a tree view control.

Part

VII

Ch

25

continues

Table 25.2 Continued

Function	Function Type	Description
InsertItemSort (handleparent, label, pictureindex)	TreeView	Inserts an item in sorted order with its "siblings" in a treeview control.
insertpicture(picturename)	RTE	Inserts the specified picture at the insertion point in a rich text edit control.
InsertRow(rownum)	DataWindow	Inserts a row before the passed row number. If rownum is 0, this inserts a row before the current row.
InsertSeries(seriesname, seriesnumber)	Graph	Inserts a new series name before the given series number. Does not apply to Data-Windows.
ispreview( )	RTE	TRUE or FALSE indicating whether or not the rich text edit control is in preview mode.
IsSelected(rownum)	DataWindow	Returns TRUE or FALSE indicating whether or not the row is selected.
LineCount( )	Multi-line	Returns the number of text lines.
LineLength( )	Multi-line	Returns the length of the cursor line. This function does not apply to DataWindows.
menuitem.Check( )	Menu	Places a check mark next to the menuitem.
menuitem.Disable( )	Menu	Disables the menuitem.
menuitem.Enable( )	Menu	Enables the menuitem.
menuitem.PopMenu(x, y)	Menu	Displays a pop-up menu at coordinates x and y.
menuitem.Uncheck( )	Menu	Removes the check mark from the menuitem.
ModifiedCount( )	DataWindow	Returns the number of changed rows since the last retrieve or update.
Modify(string)	DataWindow	Applies the string to modify the DataWindow.
ModifyData(seriesnumber, datapoint, datavalue_x, categorylabel_y)	Graph	Changes a datavalue at the given datapoint in a given series. If category label (or y value) is specified, then a tickmark is placed on the graph for this new data.

Function	Function Type	Description
Move(x, y)	Common	Moves an object to a new position relative to the parent window.
MoveTab(source, destination)	Tab Folder	Moves a tab page to another position in a Tab control, changing its index number.
ObjectAtPointer({control,} seriesnumber, datapoint)	Graph	If the mouse pointer is pointing at the graph, grObjectAtPointer can tell where by returning the seriesnumber and the datapoint. If ObjectAtPointer is used on a DataWindow graph, the control name must also be passed.
OLEActivate(row, column, OLEverb)	DataWindow	Activates OLE for a given column.
OpenTab(userobjectvar, {userobjecttype, } index)	Tab Folder	Opens a user object as a tab page in a Tab control. If the data type is not known until run time, userobjecttype must be specified.
OpenTabWithParm (userobjectvar, parameter, {userobjecttype, } index)	Tab Folder	Opens a tab after filling the message object with a parameter.
OpenUserObject (uo {,uo_type} {, x, y})	Window	Opens a user object on a window. uo_type specifies the datatype (if not known) and x and y specify location.
OpenUserObjectWithParm (uo, parm {,uo_type} {, x, y})	Window	Opens a user object on a window and passes a parameter. uo_type specifies the datatype (if not known) and x and y specify location.
pagecount( )	RTE	Returns the number of pages in a rich text edit control document.
ParentWindow( )	Window	Returns a window data type of the parent window. Usually, used with a child window.
Paste( )	Edit	Puts the contents of the Clipboard at the cursor location.
pastertf (string s {, band b})	RTE	Inserts a string at the insertion point containing data in RTF format.
PointerX( )	Common Non-Drawing	Moves an object to the left edge of a window in which an object is placed.
PointerY( )	Common Non-Drawing	Returns the number of units from the top edge of a window in which an object is placed.

Part

VII

Ch

25

continues

Table 25.2 Continued

Function	Function Type	Description
Position( )	Edit	Returns the position of the cursor in the edit field.
PostEvent(event, word, long)	Common Non-Drawing	Triggers an event after the current function or event is complete.
preview(previewsetting)	RTE	Preview setting can be TRUE or FALSE indicating whether or not to place a rich text edit control in preview mode (or to take it out of preview mode).
Print({canceldialog})	DataWindow	Prints the contents of the DataWindow. You can optionally specify TRUE or FALSE indicating whether or not you want a response window to display allowing the user to cancel the print job. (Default is TRUE.)
Print(copies, pagerange, collate, canceldialog)	RTE	Prints the contents of a RTE. You can specify the number of copies, the print range (i.e., "1-3"), TRUE or FALSE indicating whether or not to collate printouts, and TRUE or FALSE indicating whether or not you want a response window to display allowing the user to cancel the print job.
Print(jobnum, x, y {, width, height})	Common Non-Drawing	Prints the control with a specified job print number. The printout starts at position x,y of the window and (optionally) continues for a specified length and width or, if omitted, the length and width of the control.
PrintCancel( )	DataWindow	Cancels the current DataWindow print.
releasenativepointer (pobject)	OLE 2.0	
ReplaceText(string)	Edit	Replaces the selected text with a string.
ReselectRow(rownum)	DataWindow	Accesses the database to retrieve all changed columns in a row.
Reset( )	DataWindow	Completely clears the contents of the DataWindow.
Reset( )	Listbox	Deletes all items from a list box or a DDLB.

Function	Function Type	Description
Reset(grResetType)	Graph	Deletes information from your graph with the grResetType enumerated data type specifying whether you want to delete data, categories, series, or the whole graph. Does not apply to DataWindows.
ResetDataColors ({control,} seriesnumber, datapoint)	Graph	Restores the color of a data default color for its series.
ResetTransObject( )	DataWindow	Stops a DataWindow from using programmer-specific transaction objects.
ResetUpdate( )	DataWindow	Clears the update flags in the primary and filter buffers and empties the delete buffer of the DataWindow.
Resize(width, height)	Common	Adjusts an object to a new size and redraws the object.
Retrieve(retrieveargument)	DataWindow	Retrieves data from the database and places it in a DataWindow. If the retrieval argument is passed, retrieve applies that retrieval argument to the DataWindow.
RowCount( )	DataWindow	Returns the number of rows in a Data Window.
RowsCopy(startrow, endrow, copybuffer, targetdw, beforerow, targetbuffer)	DataWindow	Copies rows from one DataWindow control buffer to another DataWindow control buffer.
RowsDiscard(startrow, endrow, buffer)	DataWindow	Discards a range of rows in a DataWindow control.
RowsMove(startrow, endrow, movebuffer, targetdw, beforerow, targetbuffer)	DataWindow	Copies rows from one DataWindow control buffer to another DataWindow control buffer.
SaveAs({control,} filename, saveastype, colheading)	Graph	Saves the contents of a graph. Filename is the name of the file in which you want to save the contents. Saveastype is an enumerated data type specifying the save format. ColHeading is TRUE or FALSE indicating if column headers are to be saved.

continues

Part

VII

Ch

25

Table 25.2   Continued

Function	Function Type	Description
SaveAs(filename, saveas, columnheading)	DataWindow	Saves the contents of the DataWindow in a new format. SaveAs is an enumerated data type describing the new format. Column-heading is a boolean TRUE or FALSE decribing whether or not you want column headings on your output.
savedocument(filename {, filetype})	RTE	Saves a rich text edit control document to a file in RTF format or ASCII format.
Scroll(int)	Multi-line	Scrolls down (or up for negative numbers) a given number of lines.
ScrollNextPage()	RTE	Scrolls forward one page and makes the row one page forward active.
ScrollNextRow()	RTE	Scrolls to the next row in a DataWindow and makes that row active.
ScrollPriorPage()	RTE	Scrolls backward one page and makes the row one page back active.
ScrollPriorRow()	RTE	Scrolls to the previous row in a DataWindow and makes that row active.
ScrollToRow(rownum)	RTE	Scrolls to a row and makes that row active.
SelectedIndex()	Listbox	Returns the number of the selected item of a list box. Not available with drop-down list boxes.
SelectedIndex()	ListView	Returns the number of the selected item in a listview.
SelectedItem()	Listbox	Returns a string containing the selected item of a list box. Not available with drop-down list boxes.
SelectedLength()	Edit	Returns the length of the selected string.
SelectedLine()	Multi-line	Returns the line number where the selection is made.
selectedpage()	RTE	Returns the page number of the insertion point in a rich text edit control.
SelectedStart()	Edit	Returns the starting position of the selection.
SelectedText()	Edit	Returns a string containing the selected text.

Function	Function Type	Description
SelectItem (index)	Listbox	Allows you to select an item in a list box indicated by either an index or a string and a starting search index.
SelectItem (string, index)	Listbox	
SelectRow (rownum, boolean)	DataWindow	Makes a current row selected if boolean is set to TRUE or deselected if boolean is set to FALSE.
SelectTab (tabidentifier)	Tab Folder	Selects the specified tab, displaying its tab page in the Tab control. Tabidentifier can be the tab page index (an integer), the name of the user object (data type DragObject or UserObject), or a string holding the name of the user object.
SelectText (start, length)	Edit	Selects text at a starting point for a given length.
selecttextall( )	RTE	Selects all the text in a rich text edit control.
selecttextline( )	RTE	Selects all the text in the line where the insertion point resides in a rich text edit control.
selecttextword( )	RTE	Selects the word where the insertion point resides in a rich text edit control.
SeriesCount ({control})	Graph	Returns the number of series. If Series-Count is used on a DataWindow graph, the control name must also be passed.
SeriesName ({control,} seriesnumber)	Graph	Returns the name of a series. If SeriesName is used on a DataWindow graph, the control name must also be passed.
SetActionCode (int)	Common Non-Drawing	Sets the action code to control the processing of an event. It should be the last line in the script.
setalignment (alignment a)	RTE	Sets the alignment in a rich text edit control based on a passed alignment enumerated data type.
SetBorderStyle (column, borderstyle)	DataWindow	Changes the column's border to a new border based on a BorderStyle enumerated data type.

Part

VII

Ch

25

continues

Table 25.2   Continued

Function	Function Type	Description
SetColumn(startindex, label, partial, wrap)	ListView	Sets focus on the next column (starting at startindex) that has the same label as the one specified. If partial is TRUE, partial labels will be searched. Wrap indicates whether or not to return to the starting point of the search in a listview control.
SetColumn(column)	DataWindow	Sets a column number or column string to be the current column.
Setdata (clipboardformat, data)	OLE 2.0	
SetDataPieExplode ({control} series, datapoint, percentage)	Graph	Sets the percentage of the exploded pie slice in a pie graph. The value is stored in percentage.
SetDataStyle({control,} seriesnumber, datapoint, fillpattern)	Graph	The fill pattern is set for a specific datapoint on a series. If DataStyle is used on a DataWindow graph, the control name must also be passed.
SetDataStyle({control,} seriesnumber, grColorType, ColorVariable)	Graph	Sets color information based on the Color Variable enumerated data type. If DataStyle is used on a DataWindow graph, the control name must also be passed.
SetDataStyle({control,} seriesnumber, datapointnumber, grSymbolType)	Graph	The tick mark symbol is set for a specific datapoint on a series. If DataStyle is used on a DataWindow graph, the control name must also be passed.
SetDataStyle({control,} seriesnumber, datapointnumber, linestyle, linewidth)	Graph	The line style and line width are set for a specific datapoint on a series. If DataStyle is used on a DataWindow graph, the control name must also be passed.
SetDetailHeight (startrow, endrow, height)	DataWindow	Sets the height of each row from startrow toendrow to the specified height.
SetDropHighlight(handle)	TreeView	Highlight the specified item as the drop target in a tree view.
SetFilter(string)	DataWindow	Sets the filter based on the string.
SetFirstVisible(handle)	TreeView	Set the specified item (identified by handle) as the first visible item in the TreeView control.

Function	Function Type	Description
SetFocus( )	Common Non-Drawing	Sets focus to the object.
SetFormat(column, formatstring)	DataWindow	Sets the display format for a column based on the format string.
SetItem(index, item)	ListView	Sets the state for a particular item in a list-view or treeview.
SetItem(row, column, value)	DataWindow	Sets the item to a new value at the specified row and column. The value's data type must match the column.
SetItemStatus(rownum, column, dwbuffer, status)	DataWindow	Sets the status of an item at rownum, column, in buffer dwbuffer.
SetLevelPictures (level, pictureindex, selectedpictureindex, statepictureindex, overlaypictureindex)	TreeView	Sets the picture indexes for all items at a particular level in a treeview control.
SetMask (maskdatatype, mask)	Edit	Sets the edit mask data type and the edit mask for an EditMask control.
SetMicroHelp(string)	Window	Sets MicroHelp in an MDI application to display a string.
SetOverlayPicture (overlayindex, imageindex)	ListView	Maps an OverlayPicture to a large or small image list index in a listview or treeview.
SetOverlayPicture (Overlayindex, imageindex)	ListView	Maps an OverlayPicture to a large or small image list index in a list view control.
setparagraphsetting (paragraphsetting, long v)	RTE	Sets the alignment of a paragraph.
SetPicture(bitmap)	Picture	Assigns a bitmap stored in a blob to be the image in a Picture control.
SetPosition (position, preceding)	Common Non-Drawing	Sets the position in front to back order of an object in relation to other objects in a window.
SetRedraw(boolean)	Common Non-Drawing	Sets the redraw status of redrawing every attribute change or not. The boolean variable is TRUE or FALSE.
SetRow(rownum)	DataWindow	Sets rownum to be the current row.

continues

Part

VII

Ch

25

Table 25.2 Continued

Function	Function Type	Description
SetRowFocusIndicator (FocusIndicator, X, Y)	DataWindow	Sets the mouse pointer to change to the focus indicator if the row receives focus. X and Y correspond to coordinates offsetting the corner of the row for the new pointer's display to take effect.
SetSeriesStyle ({dw_control,} seriesname, fillpatternvariable)	Graph	SetSeriesStyle sets information about the fill pattern of a series. FillPatternVariable contains the new fill pattern.
SetSeriesStyle ({dw_control,} seriesname, grSymbolType)	Graph	SetSeriesStyle sets information about the tickmark symbol of a series. The new tickmark symbol is stored in grSymbolType.
SetSeriesStyle ({dw_control,} seriesname, overlay)	Graph	SetSeriesStyle sets information about the tickmark symbol of a series. Overlay is a boolean set to TRUE or FALSE indicating if overlays are allowed.
SetSeriesStyle ({dw_control,} seriesname, Colortype, colorvariable)	Graph	SetSeriesStyle sets information about the color of a series. ColorType is an enumerated data type specifying the color type for which you want to set the color. ColorVariable is the new color.
SetSeriesStyle ({dw_control}, seriesname, linestyle)	Graph	SetSeriesStyle sets information about the line style of a series. LineStyle contains the new line style variable.
SetSort(string)	DataWindow	Sets new sort criteria based on the value of the string.
setspacing(spacing)	RTE	Sets the line spacing for the selected paragraphs in a rich text edit control.
SetSQLPreview(string)	DataWindow	Modifies the SQL syntax for the DataWindow.
SetSQLSelect(SQLsyntax)	DataWindow	Replaces the current Select statement with a new Select statement for the DataWindow. (Often, you'll want to use Modify instead.)
SetState(index, boolean)	Listbox	Sets the state of a list box item corresponding to an index. Requires a boolean variable of TRUE (highlighted) or FALSE (unhighlighted). Not available with drop-down list boxes.

Function	Function Type	Description
SetTabOrder (column, tabnumber)	DataWindow	Sets the tab order inside the DataWindow for a given column.
SetText(string)	DataWindow	Sets the text in the current cursor location in the DataWindow.
settextcolor(textcolor)	RTE	Sets the text color in a rich text edit control.
settextstyle(bold, underline, subscript, superscript, italic, strikeout)	RTE	Passes a series of TRUE/FALSE values to set the character style in a rich text edit control.
settoolbar (integer i, boolean v, toolbaralignment a, string t)	Window	
settoolbarpos (integer i, integer r, integer o, boolean b)	Window	
settoolbarpos (integer i, integer x, integer y, integer w, integer h)	Window	
SetTop(index)	Listbox	Places the item corresponding to an index at the top of a list box. Not available with drop-down list boxes.
SetTrans()	DataWindow	Sets the transaction for the DataWindow.
SetTransObject()	DataWindow	Sets the transaction for the entire DataWindow and all child DataWindows.
SetValidate(column, rule)	DataWindow	Sets the validation rule of a column to a new rule contained in a string parameter.
SetValue(column, index, value)	DataWindow	Sets the column number's or name's code table index to a new value.
sharedata(datawindow d)	RTE	Shares data with a DataWindow, creating a document instance for each row in a DataWindow.
ShareData(dw2)	DataWindow	Shares data with DataWindow dw2.
ShareDataOff(dw)	DataWindow	Turns off all sharing on the DataWindow.
Show()	Common	Shows an object if that object is hidden.

Part

VII

Ch

25

continues

Table 25.2 Continued

Function	Function Type	Description
showheadfoot(boolean s)	RTE	Passes TRUE or FALSE indicating if the header and footer can be edited in a rich text edit control.
Sort(grSortType)	ListView	Sorts the items in a ListView or TreeView control.
Sort( )	DataWindow	Sorts the rows of the database based on the sort criteria established in the DataWindow painter or using the SetSort function.
SortAll(handle, grSortType)	TreeView	Sorts the child levels in a TreeView control item.
State(index)	Listbox	Returns a boolean (TRUE or FALSE) indicating the state (highlighted or not highlighted) of the item in a list box that corresponds to the index. Not available with drop-down list boxes.
TabPostEvent(event {, word, long })	Tab Folder	Triggers an event for each tab page in a Tab control after the current function or event is completed. Event is either an enumerated data type or string. Wordparm is a long and longparm is either a string or a long. Both are stored in the Message object.
TabTriggerEvent (event {, word, long })	Tab Folder	Immediately triggers an event for each tab page in a Tab control. Event is either an enumerated data type or string. Wordparm is a long and longparm is either a string or a long. Both are stored in the Message object.
Text(index)	Listbox	Returns the text of an item in a list box or DDLB that corresponds to the index.
TextLine( )	Edit	Returns a string containing the line of text where the cursor currently is placed.
Top( )	Listbox	This returns the index (number) of the item at the top of a list box. This item could be the first item or it could be a later item if the user scrolled down. Not available with drop-down list boxes.
TotalColumns( )	ListView	Returns the number of columns in a listview control.

Function	Function Type	Description
TotalItems( )	ListView	Returns the number of items in a listview control.
TotalItems( )	Listbox	Returns the total number of items in a list box or DDLB.
TotalSelected( )	ListView	Returns the total number of items selected in a listview control.
TotalSelected( )	Listbox	Returns the total number of items selected in a list box. Not available with drop-down list boxes.
TriggerEvent(event, Word, Long)	Common Non-Drawing	Immediately triggers an event. Event is either an enumerated data type or string. Wordparm is a long and Longparm is either a string or a long that is stored in the Wordparm and Longparm variables of the Message object.
TypeOf( )	Common	Returns the type of object or control.
Undo( )	Edit	Reverses the last edit. Does not function with drop-down list boxes.
Update( )	DataWindow	Updates the database with the DataWindow.
WorkSpaceHeight( )	Window	Returns the height of a window.
WorkSpaceWidth( )	Window	Returns the width of a window.
WorkSpaceX( )	Window	Returns the X coordinate of the upper left corner of a window.
WorkSpaceY( )	Window	Returns the Y coordinate of the upper left corner of a window.

Part

VII

Ch

25

DataWindow Computed Functions

In the DataWindow painter, you can use some functions in computed fields, filters, and valida-tion rules that are not allowed in PowerScript. These functions can be separated into two categories:

DW Computed Column Functions DataWindow Computed Functions cannot be used with PowerScript, but can be used within a computed field on a DataWindow.

DW Aggregate Functions — DataWindow Aggregate Functions can be used on DataWindow computed fields to process a series of information. (The Sum( ) function can tally an entire column on a Data Window.)

DW Computed Column Functions

Bitmap(filename)
Bitmap(columnname)
Bitmap(columnnumber) — Places a bitmap in a computed ield. The bitmap can either be a file name, a column name, or a column number. If a column is referenced, that column must contain a bitmap file name.

Describe(string) — Returns the values described in the syntax of the string.

If(condition, TRUE string, FALSE string) — Tests a condition in a computed field, filter, or validation rule and either sets the column to a TRUE string or a FALSE string. (Also available in SetSort or dwModify statements.)

LookUpDisplay(column) — Returns a string value of the corresponding column value in a code table.

Number(string) — Converts the value of a string to a numeric data type.

Page( ) — Returns the current page of a DataWindow or Report.

PageCount( ) — Returns the PageCount of a DataWindow or Report.

WordCap(string) — Capitalizes the first letter in every word of the string.

DataWindow Object Aggregate Functions

In the DataWindow painter, you can use the following aggregate functions in computed fields, filters, and validation rules. You aren't allowed to use these functions inside PowerScript. Most aggregate functions allow the following parameters:

(column, {for range
{ DISTINCT {expression1
{, expression2 for range
{, ...}}}}}) — Column is the column for which you want to apply the function. Column can be the name of the column or the number of the column preceded by a pound sign (#). Values for range are:

All(Default)—Apply the function to all rows in column in the report.
Crosstab(Crosstabs only)—Apply the function to all rows in column in the crosstab.
Graph(Graphs only)—Apply the function to all rows in column for the graph. This value for range has effect only when you specify Page in the Rows option on the Graph.
GroupNbr—Apply the function to all rows in column in the specified group. To specify a group, enter group and then the group number.

For example: for group 1.

Page—Apply the function to the rows in column on a page.
DISTINCT is used like the SQL SELECT DISTINCT. It
eliminates duplicates from the expression.

expression (optional)—One or more expressions that you
want to evaluate. Expression can be the name of a column,
a function, or an expression.

Table 25.3 lists the aggregate DataWindow functions and a brief description of each.

Table 25.3 Aggregate DataWindow Functions

Function	Description
Avg(column {for range { DISTINCT {expression1 {, expression2 {, ...}}}}})	Takes the averages of a column.
Count(column {for range { DISTINCT {expression1 {, expression2 {, ...}}}}})	Returns the number of columns.
CumulativePercent(column {for range { DISTINCT {expression1 {, expression2 {, ...}}}}})	Takes the cumulative percent of the total for a column. Usually, this is in the detail section of the report.
CumulativeSum(column {for range { DISTINCT {expression1 {, expression2 {, ...}}}}})	Returns the cumulative sum of the total for a column. Usually, this is in the detail section of the report.
First(column {for range { DISTINCT {expression1 {, expression2 {, ...}}}}})	Returns the first value in a column.
Last(column {for range { DISTINCT {expression1 {, expression2 {, ...}}}}})	Returns the last value in a column.

Part

VII

Ch

25

continues

Table 25.3   Continued

Function	Description
Max(column {for range { DISTINCT {expression1 {, expression2 {, ...}}}}})	Returns the maximum value of a column.
Min(column {for range { DISTINCT {expression1 {, expression2 {, ...}}}}})	Returns the minimum value of a column.
Percent(column {for range { DISTINCT {expression1 {, expression2 {, ...}}}}})	Converts the number as a percent of total for a column. Usually, this is in the detail section of the report.
StDev(column {for range { DISTINCT {expression1 {, expression2 {, ...}}}}})	Returns the sample standard deviation of a column.
StDevP(column {for range { DISTINCT {expression1 {, expression2 {, ...}}}}})	Returns the standard deviation of a column.
Sum(column {for range { DISTINCT {expression1 {, expression2 {, ...}}}}})	Returns the sum of a column.
Var(column {for range { DISTINCT {expression1 {, expression2 {, ...}}}}})	Returns the sample variance of a column.
VarP(column {for range { DISTINCT {expression1 {, expression2 {, ...}}}}})	Returns the variance of a column.

NOTE Do not confuse the Max and Min aggregate functions with the PowerScript Max and Min functions that compare two numbers and return the maximum or minimum number. Also, you can't nest aggregate functions. (*Nested functions* refer to the fact that you cannot call one aggregate function within another aggregate function.) ■

From Here...

This chapter describes the many functions available to you inside PowerBuilder. For more information, check out the following chapters:

- Chapter 6, "Using Events, Functions, and the PowerScript Language," describes the basic PowerScript programming language, including function calls. Chapter 6 lays a good foundation for understanding PowerScript functions.

- Chapter 14, "Pulling It All Together in an Application," shows much of the PowerScript that is implemented in the Inventory Tracking system.

- Chapter 28, "Enumerated Data Types Quick Reference," lists and describes all the enumerated data types used with PowerBuilder. Many functions use enumerated data types as arguments.

Also, be sure to check out the CD. In the CD, you will find a utility called PBAPI. PBAPI details over 700 functions available to you through the Windows Application Programming Interface (API). These functions can be called from any Windows development langauge, including PowerBuilder.

Part
VII

Ch
25

CHAPTER 26

Event Quick Reference

by Charles A. Wood

Every object and control has attributes. All objects and most controls have events. Attributes determine the state of the object or control, whereas events implement the functionality of the object or control. ■

> **N O T E** Many window controls (like command button and list box) have similar or identical events. (However, group boxes and the drawing objects, like rectangle and line, have no events.) Because of the similarity between window controls, the events for the window controls have been merged into a Window Control Event section. ■

Application Event	Description
Close	Executed upon the close of the application.
Idle	Executed when the specified number of seconds have elapsed during the application with no activity.
Open	Executed upon the opening of the application.
SystemError	Executed during a system error anywhere in the application.
ConnectionBegin	Executed immediately prior to connecting to a database
ConnectionEnd	Executed immediately after connecting to a database

Window Event	Description
Activate	The window has received focus.
Clicked	The user clicked on the window.
Close	The window is closing. This event occurs after the window is closed.
CloseQuery	The window is closing via the control box. This event happens before the close event. A return value of greater than 0 will stop the window from closing.
Deactivate	The window is losing focus.
DoubleClicked	The user double-clicked on the window.
DragDrop	A dragged object was dropped on the window.
DragEnter	A dragged object entered the window.
DragLeave	A dragged object has left the window.
DragWithin	An object is being dragged within the window.
Hide	The window becomes hidden.
HotLinkAlarm	A server application has sent new (changed) data through the DDE.
Key	A key has been pressed (except Alt).
MouseDown	A mouse button is pressed in an empty area on the window.
MouseMove	The mouse is moving.
MouseUp	The mouse button is released in an empty area on the window.

Window Event	Description
Open	The window opens.
Other	A Windows 3.x event has occurred that has not been defined by PowerBuilder.
RButtonDown	The user is holding the right mouse button down on the window.
RemoteExec	A client application has sent a request through the DDE.
RemoteHotLinkStart	A client application wants to start a hotlink through the DDE.
RemoteHotLinkStop	A client application wants to end a hotlink through the DDE.
RemoteRequest	A client application has requested data through the DDE.
RemoteSend	A client application has sent data through the DDE.
Resize	The user is resizing the window.
Show	The window was hidden and is now being shown.
SystemKey	The Alt or Alt+ another key has been pressed.
Timer	The event has been triggered by the Timer function at some timed interval.
ToolBarMoved	Your window's toolbar has been moved (from top to bottom, left to right, top to floating, etc).

MenuItem Event	Description
Clicked	The menu item has been clicked by the mouse.
Selected	The menu item has been selected (but not clicked yet) by the user.

Window Control Event	Description
BeginDrag	A drag has begun using the left mouse button in a listview or treeview control.
BeginLabelEdit	The user has begun to edit the label of a listview or treeview.
BeginRightDrag	A drag has begun using the right mouse button in a listview or treeview control.
ColumnClick	The user has clicked a column in a listview control.
Clicked	The user has clicked the window control.
Constructor	The window has opened and the window control is being constructed.
DataChange	When the server application in an OLE control notifies the control that data has changed.

Part
VII

Ch
26

continues

continued

Window Control Event	Description
DBError	A database error has occurred on the DataWindow control.
DeleteItem	A user has deleted an item off a listview or treeview.
DeleteAllItems	A user has deleted all items in a listview.
Destructor	The parent window is closing and the control is closing (being destroyed) with it.
DoubleClicked	The user has double-clicked the control.
DragDrop	The user has dropped an object on the window control.
DragEnter	A dragged object has entered the window control area.
DragLeave	A dragged object is leaving the window control area.
DragWithin	The user is dragging an object within the window control area.
EditChanged	The user is typing into an edit control.
EndLabelEdit	The user has finished editing the label of a listview or treeview.
Error	The Error event occurs within a DataWindow or DataStore object, or within an OLE object. An Error event is triggered in a DataWindow or DataStore if invalid names of objects are used within the DataWindow. It also occurs when a property isn't valid for the specified OLE object. In most cases, the Error event occurs because of mistyping within a string that cannot be detected during the PowerBuilder compile.
ExternalException	ExternalException occurs when an OLE application has an error, but the error does not directly affect the OLE communication between the Client OLE application and the server OLE application.
FileExists	A document in the RichTextEdit is saved to a file, but a file of the specified name already exists.

 TIP The variable FileName is already passed to the FileExists event.

GetFocus	The window control has received focus.
InputFieldSelected	When the user selects an input field in a richtextedit control by double-clicking it or pressing ENTER after clicking it.

 TIP The variable FieldName is already declared in the InputFieldSelected event. It contains the name of the input field.

Window Control Event	Description
InsertItem	An item has been inserted in a listview.
ItemChanged (DataWindow)	When a field in the DataWindow has been modified and loses focus (for example, the user presses ENTER, the TAB key, or an arrow key, or clicks the mouse on another field).

N O T E The itemchanged event in a DataWindow occurs right before the item actually is accepted. You can reject the change using the SetActionCode(code) function. The following action codes are valid:

Action Code	Description
0 (Default)	Accept the data value
1	Reject the data value and don't allow focus to change. Trigger the ItemError event.
2	Reject the data value but allow the focus to change. Replace the column value just entered with the value originally in the column. ▨

ItemChanged (ListView)	An item has changed value in a listview control.

N O T E Unlike the DataWindow ItemChanged event, the listview itemchanged event happens *after* an item has changed in a listview. The *ItemChanging* event described next happens before an item changes.

The following arguments are sent to the listview ItemChanged event:

- FocusChange is a boolean TRUE/FALSE value indicating the focus state is changing.
- HasFocus is a boolean TRUE/FALSE value indicating the new focus state.
- SelectionChange is a boolean TRUE/FALSE value indicating the selection state is changing.
- Selected is a boolean TRUE/FALSE value indicating the new selected state.
- OtherChange is a boolean TRUE/FALSE value indicating that something other than selection or focus has changed in the item. ▨

ItemChanging	An item is about to change value in a listview control.

T I P The ItemChanging listview event has the same parameters as the ItemChanged listview event.

ItemCollapsed	A treeview item has collapsed.
ItemCollapsing	A treeview item is about to collapse.

Part

VII

Ch

26

continues

continued

Window Control Event	Description
ItemError	An item has not passed its validation test.

TIP In a treeview ItemCollapsing event or ItemExpanding, return 1 to prevent or 0 to allow collapsing/expanding.

ItemExpanded	A treeview item has expanded.
ItemExpanding	A treeview item is about to expand.
ItemFocusChanged	The focus within the DataWindow control has changed.
ItemPopulate	An item is expanding for the first time.

N O T E   If possible, a treeview item's children should be populated in the ItemPopulate event rather than the ItemExpanding event. You should only use the ItemExpanding event to populate the children if they change.

A return value of 1 will prevent action in the ItemCollapsing or ItemExpanding events. ■

N O T E   Handle is a long integer argument passed to every ItemPopulate, ItemExpanding, ItemExpanded, ItemCollapsing, and ItemCollapsed events. Handle identifies the Windows handle of the treeview. ■

Key	A user has pressed a key in a richtextedit, listview, treeview, or tab control.

TIP Keycode (an enumerated data type indicating what key was pressed) and keyflags are passed to the Key event as arguments.

LineLeft	An HScrollBar has just moved one line left.
LineRight	An HScrollBar has just moved one line right.
LineUp	A VScrollBar has just moved one line up.
LineDown	A VScrollBar has just moved one line down.
LoseFocus	The window control is about to lose focus.
Modified	A multi-line edit, single-line edit, list box, or drop-down list box control loses focus and has been changed (modified).
MouseDown	A mouse button is pressed in an empty area on a richtextedit control.
MouseMove	The mouse is moving when a richtextedit control has focus.

Window Control Event	Description
MouseUp	The mouse button is released in an empty area on a richtextedit control.
Moved	When the Horizontal or Vertical scrollbox is moved.
Other	A Windows 3.x event has occurred that is not specific to PowerBuilder.
PageLeft	An HScrollBar has just moved one page left.
PageRight	An HScrollBar has just moved one page right.
PageUp	A VScrollBar has just moved one page up.
PageDown	A VScrollBar has just moved one page down.
PictureSelected	When the user selects bitmap by double-clicking it or pressing ENTER after clicking it in a richtextedit control.
PrintEnd	The DataWindow control has finished printing.
PrintFooter	When the contents of the richtextedit are being printed and a footer is about to be printed for a page.

NOTE The following arguments are generated for the PrintFooter Event:

- currentpage—the number of the current page within the control
- totalpages—the total number of pages being printed
- currentrow—the number of the current row

PrintHeader	When the contents of the richtextedit are being printed and a header is about to be printed for a page.

TIP The arguments for the PrintHeader event are the same as for the PrintFooter event discussed earlier.

PrintPage	A new page is about to start printing.
PrintStart	The DataWindow control is about to print.
RButtonDown	The right mouse button is clicked on the window control.
RButtonUp	The right mouse button is released on the window control.
Rename	When the server application in an OLE control notifies the control that the OLE object has been renamed.
Resize	The DataWindow control is being resized.
RetrieveEnd	A retrieve has just finished.
RetrieveRow	A row has been retrieved.
RetrieveStart	A retrieve is about to start.

Part
VII

Ch
26

continues

continued

Window Control Event	Description
RightClicked	When the user clicks with the right mouse button in the Tab control, treeview, or listview in the display area of the tab page.
RightDoubleClicked	When the user double-clicks with the right mouse button in the Tab control, treeview, or listview in the display area of the tab page.

TIP   When clicking an individual tab page as opposed to a tab, the RButtonDown event for that tab page is triggered instead of the RightClicked event or the RightDoubleClicked event for the tab folder control.

N O T E   In a tab control, index is created as a parameter of the RightClicked and RightDoubleClicked events. Index is an integer whose value is the index of the tab the user clicked, or -1 if a blank area in the tab control was clicked. ■

RowFocusChanged	A new row has received focus.
Save	When the server application in an OLE control notifies the control that data has been saved to file.
ScrollHorizontal	The DataWindow control is being scrolled horizontally.
ScrollVertical	The DataWindow control is being scrolled vertically.
SelectionChanged	The selection has changed in a list box, drop-down list box, treeview, or tab folder.
SelectionChanging	The tab selection or treeview is about to change the tab or item selected.
Sort	Compare the two items passed.

N O T E   The sort listview event seems more like a function than an event. The sort event has two items passed to it: Handle1 and Handle2. The following functionality is supposed to be coded into the sort event:

- Return -1 when Handle1 < Handle2.
- Return 0 when Handle1 = Handle2.
- Return 1 when Handle1 > Handle2.

Handle1 and Handle2 are long integers passed to the event. ■

SQLPreview	A Retrieve, Update, or ReselectRow function call has just been issued, but the function has not yet been executed.
UpdateEnd	An update has just finished.
UpdateStart	An update is about to start.
ViewChange	When the server application in an OLE control notifies the control that the view shown to the user has changed.

From Here...

This chapter describes the events that can be triggered with objects and controls inside PowerBuilder. For more information, check out the following chapters:

- Chapter 6, "Using Events, Functions, and the PowerScript Language," describes the basic PowerScript programming language, including events. Chapter 6 lays a good foundation for understanding PowerScript events.

- Chapter 14, "Pulling It All Together in an Application," shows much of the PowerScript that is implemented in the Inventory Tracking system.

- Chapter 27, "Property Quick Reference," lists and describes all the properties of objects and controls used in PowerBuilder. Many events use or affect the properties of other PowerBuilder controls and objects.

Part VII

Ch

26

Property Quick Reference

by Charles A. Wood

Every object and control has properties. Attributes determine the state of the object or control. ■

NOTE Many window controls (like command button and listbox) have similar or identical properties. Because of the similarity between window controls, the properties for the window controls have been merged into a Window Control Attribute section. ■

Table 27.1 Application Attributes

Attribute	Data Type	Description
AppName	String	A string containing the application name.
DDETimeOut	Integer	An integer specifying the time-out interval in seconds for a DDE conversation.
DisplayName	String	The DisplayName is displayed in user-readable applications (like OLE dialog boxes) that show the application's name. DisplayName defaults to AppName.
dwMessageTitle	String	A string containing the title of the DataWindow message boxes displayed during execution.
MicroHelpDefault	String	A string containing the default text for MicroHelp.
RightToLeft	Boolean	TRUE or FALSE indicating that characters should be displayed in right-to-left order. This is often useful in foreign-language versions of certain operating systems.
ToolbarFrameTitle	String	A string indicating the title of the frame toolbar when it is a floating toolbar. This property has effect only in an MDI frame window.
ToolbarPopMenuText	String	A string that displays on the pop-up menu for toolbars.
ToolbarSheetTitle	String	A string indicating the title of the sheet toolbar when it is a floating toolbar. This property has effect only in an MDI frame window.
ToolbarText	Boolean	A TRUE or FALSE indicating whether or not to display the toolbar text. This property has effect only in an MDI frame window.
ToolbarTips	Boolean	A TRUE or FALSE indicating whether or not to display microtips on your toolbar. The default is TRUE.
ToolbarUserControl	Boolean	A TRUE or FALSE indicating whether or not the end-user is allowed to right-click on your toolbar to customize the toolbar to his or her personal preference. The default is TRUE.

Table 27.2 Window Attributes

Attribute	Data Type	Description
BackColor	Long	An indicator of the background color.
Border	Boolean	A TRUE or FALSE indicating whether or not the window has a border.
BringToTop	Boolean	A TRUE or FALSE indicating if the window is supposed to be on top.
ColumnsPerPage	Integer	An integer indicating the number of units to scroll when the scroll over bar has been clicked on.
Control[ ]	Object array	An array listing the controls. You cannot change the values in this variable.
ControlMenu	Boolean	TRUE or FALSE indicating the presence of the control box and control box menu.
Enabled	Boolean	TRUE allows the window to send and receive messages.
Height	Integer	Indicates the height of the window.
HScrollBar	Boolean	TRUE or FALSE indicating the presence of a horizontal scroll bar.
hWnd	Unsigned Long	The Windows handle of the window.
Icon	String	The icon associated with the window when the window is minimized.
KeyboardIcon	Boolean	TRUE or FALSE indicating whether or not this window supports a keyboard icon.
LinesPerPage	Integer	An integer indicating the number of units to scroll when the scroll down bar has been clicked on.
MaxBox	Boolean	A TRUE or FALSE indicating the presence of a maximize box on the window title bar.
MenuID	Menu	The menu item associated with the window.
MenuName	String	The menu name associated with the menu ID.
MicroHelpHeight	Integer	An integer in the MDI Client (MDI_1) control determining the MicroHelp height.
MinBox	Boolean	A TRUE or FALSE indicating the presence of a minimize box on the window title bar.
Pointer	String	A string containing the name of the file containing the pointer used for the object or control.

Part

VII

Ch

27

continues

Table 27.2 Continued

Attribute	Data Type	Description
Title	String	A string containing the title of the window.
TitleBar	Boolean	TRUE or FALSE indicating the presence of a title bar on your window. Modifying this property in a script will cause an error during execution.
ToolbarAlignment	Enumerated	Controls whether a toolbar is on the top, bottom, left, right, or floating. This property has effect only in MDI frames and sheets.
ToolbarHeight	Integer	Sets the toolbar height. This property has effect only in MDI frames and sheets.
ToolbarVisible	Boolean	This makes the toolbar visible and invisible (TRUE or FALSE).This property has effect only in MDI frames and sheets.
ToolbarWidth	Integer	Specifies the width of a floating toolbar. This property has effect only in MDI frames and sheets.
ToolbarX	Integer	The X coordinate of a floating toolbar. This property has effect only in MDI frames and sheets.
ToolbarY	Integer	The Y coordinate of a floating toolbar. This property has effect only in MDI frames and sheets.
UnitsPerColumn	Integer	Indicates the number of PowerBuilder units a user scrolls when clicking on the scroll left or right.
UnitsPerLine	Integer	Indicates the number of PowerBuilder units a user scrolls when clicking on the scroll up or down.
Visible	Boolean	Makes the window visible or invisible.
VScrollBar	Boolean	TRUE or FALSE indicating the presence of a vertical scroll bar.
Width	Integer	Indicates the width of the window.
WindowState	Enumerated	Indicates what state (maximized, minimized, or normal) in which that window is currently displayed.
WindowType	Enumerated	Indicates the type of window (main, pop-up, MDI Frame, and so on).
X	Integer	Indicates the X coordinate of the upper left corner of the window.
Y	Integer	Indicates the Y coordinate of the upper left corner of the window.

Table 27.3   MenuItem Attributes

Attribute	Data Type	Description
Checked	Boolean	TRUE or FALSE indicating if the menu item is checked.
Enabled	Boolean	TRUE or FALSE indicating if the menu item is able to send and receive messages.
Item[ ]	Menu array	A list of menu items.
MicroHelp	String	The MicroHelp associated with this menu.
Shortcut	Integer	An integer indicating the shortcut key used with this menu item.
ParentWindow	Window	The window containing the menu.
Tag	String	A string containing the tag value of the menu item.
Text	String	The text associated with this menu item.
ToolbarItemDown	Boolean	TRUE or FALSE indicating if the toolbar item defaults to down.
ToolbarItemDownName	String	The name of the picture displayed when a toolbar item is clicked on.
ToolbarItemName	String	The name of the picture displayed on the corresponding toolbar item.
ToolbarItemOrder	Integer	An integer specifying the order of the toolbar items.
ToolbarItemSpace	Integer	The size of the space before a toolbar item when ToolbarText is not displayed.
ToolbarItemText	String	The text displayed with the toolbar item.
ToolbarItemVisible	Boolean	TRUE or FALSE indicating if the toolbar item is visible or not.
Visible	Boolean	TRUE or FALSE indicating if the menu item is visible or not.

Part
VII
Ch
27

Table 27.4   Window Control Attributes

Attribute	Data Type	Control Where Property Is Found	Description
accelerator	integer	Drop Down Listbox	An integer containing the ASCII value indicating the key you want to assign as the accelerator for a control.

continues

Table 27.4 Continued

Attribute	Data Type	Control Where Property Is Found	Description
		Drop Down Picture Listbox Edit Mask Listview Listbox Multi-line edit Picture Listbox Richtextedit Single Line Edit Treeview	
alignment	alignment	Edit Mask	Enumerated data type specifying the alignment of text in a MultiLineEdit, Static Text, or Picture button. Valid values are Center!, Left!, or Right!
		Multi-line edit OLE Static Text Tab	
always-retrieve	boolean	Treeview	Data is always retrieved when an item expands even if the item has been expanded once before.
allowedit	boolean	Drop Down Listbox	TRUE or FALSE allowing the entry of a value not in the code table in a DropDownListBox.
		Drop Down Picture Listbox	
autoarrange	boolean	Listview	TRUE or FALSE indicating whether you want a listview to automatically arrange icons in small icon or large icon listviews.
autohscroll	boolean	Drop Down Listbox	TRUE or FALSE indicating whether you want a field to automatically scroll horizontally.
		Drop Down Picture Listbox Edit Mask Multi-line edit Single Line Edit	

Attribute	Data Type	Control Where Property Is Found	Description
automatic	boolean	CheckBox Radio Button	TRUE or FALSE indicating whether to automatically check or uncheck the Checkbox or RadioButton with a mouse click.
autoskip	boolean	Edit Mask	An Edit mask property indicating whether or not you want to automatically skip this field and go to the next field in the tab order.
autovscroll	boolean	Edit Mask Multi-line edit	TRUE or FALSE indicating whether you want a field to automatically scroll vertically.
backcolor	long	CheckBox Drop Down Listbox Drop Down Picture Listbox Edit Mask Graph Group Box Listview Listbox Multi-line edit OLE Picture Listbox Radio Button Richtextedit Single Line Edit Static Text Tab TabPage Treeview	A feature that uses the RGB function to set to background color of a window control. For example, to set the background color of a multiline edit to purple, you would type **mle_field.backcolor = RGB(255,0,255)**.
beginx	integer	Line	The beginning X point of a line control in a window in relation to the upper left corner.

continues

Part

VII

Ch

27

Table 27.4 Continued

Attribute	Data Type	Control Where Property Is Found	Description
beginy	integer	Line	The beginning Y point of a line control in a window in relation to the upper left corner.
bold-selectedtext	boolean	Tab	TRUE or FALSE indicating whether or not selected tab's text will be bold in a tab control.
border	boolean	DataWindow	TRUE or FALSE indicating whether or not the window control has a border.
		Drop Down Listbox Drop Down Picture Listbox Edit Mask Graph Listview Listbox Multi-line edit OLE Picture Picture Listbox Richtextedit Single Line Edit Static Text TabPage Treeview	
bordercolor	long	Static Text	A feature that uses the RGB function to set to background color of static text. For example, to set the border color of a multi-line edit to purple, you would type **st_text.bordercolor = RGB(255,0,255)**.
borderstyle	border-style	CheckBox	An enumerated variable describing the border style.
		DataWindow Drop Down Listbox Drop Down Picture Listbox Edit Mask Graph Group Box Listview Listbox	

Attribute	Data Type	Control Where Property Is Found	Description
		Multi-line edit OLE Picture Picture Listbox Radio Button Richtextedit Single Line Edit Static Text TabPage Treeview	
bottommargin	long	Richtextedit	A long indicating how long the bottom margin will be in a richtextedit control.
bringtotop	boolean	CheckBox	TRUE or FALSE indicating whether or not to bring the window control to the top of the other controls.
		Command Button DataWindow Drop Down Listbox Drop Down Picture Listbox Edit Mask Graph Group Box HScrollBar Listview Listbox Multi-line edit OLE Picture Picture Button Picture Listbox Radio Button Richtextedit Single Line Edit Static Text Tab TabPage Treeview VScrollBar	

Part
VII

Ch
27

continues

Table 27.4 Continued

Attribute	Data Type	Control Where Property Is Found	Description
buttonheader	boolean	Listview	TRUE or FALSE indicating whether or not a listview's headers appear as text or pushable buttons.
cancel	boolean	Command Button	TRUE or FALSE denoting whether or not to use window control as a cancel button.
		OLE Picture Button	
category	graxis	Graph	Sets the properties of the category axis in a graph control.
categorysort	grsort-type	Graph	Specifies how categories are sorted.
checked	boolean	CheckBox	TRUE or FALSE indicating if a Checkbox or RadioButton is filled in (radio button) or selected with an x (check box).
		Radio Button	
classlong-name	string	OLE	The long name for the server application associated with the OLE object in the OLE window control. This property cannot be changed.
classname	string	TabPage	A string containing the name of the window control.
classshort-name	string	OLE	The short name for the server application associated with the OLE object in the OLE window control. This property cannot be changed.
columns	integer	Listview	The number of columns in a listview.
columnsper-page	integer	TabPage	An integer indicating the number of units to scroll when the scroll over bar has been clicked on.
control[]	window object	Tab	An array listing the window controls. You cannot change the values in this variable.
		TabPage	
controlmenu	boolean	DataWindow	TRUE or FALSE describing whether or not a control box and control box menu are on the DataWindow window control.

Attribute	Data Type	Control Where Property Is Found	Description
cornerheight	integer	Round Rectangle	The height of the rounded corner in a RoundRectangle.
cornerwidth	integer	Round Rectangle	The width of the rounded corner in a RoundRectangle.
createon-demand	boolean	Tab	TRUE or FALSE indicating whether or not a new tab for a tab folder control can be created on demand.
dataobject	string	DataWindow	A string indicating the DataWindow Object associated with the DataWindow control.
default	boolean	Command Button OLE Picture Button	TRUE or FALSE denoting whether or not to use this commandButton or pictureButton as a default button.
deleteitems	boolean	Listview Treeview	TRUE or FALSE indicating whether or not items are allowed to be deleted from a list or treeview with the delete key.
depth	integer	Graph	An integer indicating the percentage the depth is of the width of the graph. For example, if the depth is 75, the depth of the graph is 75 percent of its width.
disabledname	string	Picture Button	The name of the picture to be displayed when a PictureButton is disabled.
disable-dragdrop	boolean	Treeview	TRUE or FALSE indicating whether or not drag and drop will be implemented in a treeview.
disable-noscroll	boolean	Listbox Picture Listbox	TRUE or FALSE indicating if the scroll bar will always be visible (but will be disabled when all the items can be accessed without scrolling) or the scroll bar will be displayed only if it is necessary to view all the items in a listbox.

Part
VII

Ch
27

continues

Table 27.4 Continued

Attribute	Data Type	Control Where Property Is Found	Description
displaydata	string	Edit Mask	A string containing the data that initially appears in an EditMask.
displayname	string	OLE	Read only name for your OLE control. This name is displayed in OLE dialog boxes and windows that show the object's name. Defaults to the name of the OLE control (i.e., ole_1).
displayonly	boolean	Edit Mask	TRUE or FALSE indicating whether or not this field is updatable by the user.
		Multi-line edit Single Line Edit	
document name	string	Richtextedit	The name of the richtextedit document in a richtextedit control.
dragauto	boolean	CheckBox	TRUE or FALSE indicating whether a click puts the window control automatically in Drag mode. (When DragAuto is TRUE, clicking on the control triggers a DragDrop event, not a Clicked event.)
		Command Button DataWindow Drop Down Listbox Drop Down Picture Listbox Edit Mask Graph Group Box HScrollBar Listview Listbox Multi-line edit OLE Picture Picture Button Picture Listbox Radio Button Richtextedit Single Line Edit Static Text Tab TabPage	

Attribute	Data Type	Control Where Property Is Found	Description
		Treeview VScrollBar	
dragicon	string	CheckBox	The icon appears when the user drags the window control.
		Command Button DataWindow Drop Down Listbox Drop Down Picture Listbox Edit Mask Graph Group Box HScrollBar Listview Listbox Multi-line edit OLE Picture Picture Button Picture Listbox Radio Button Richtextedit Single Line Edit Static Text Tab TabPage Treeview VScrollBar	
editlabels	boolean	Listview	TRUE or FALSE indicating whether labels can be edited in a listview or treeview control.
		Treeview	
elevation	integer	Graph	An integer specifying the angle of front-to-back elevation in a graph.
enabled	boolean	CheckBox	TRUE or FALSE indicating whether or not the window control can send and receive messages.
		Command Button DataWindow Drop Down Listbox Drop Down Picture Listbox Edit Mask	

Part

VII

Ch

27

continues

Table 27.4   Continued

Attribute	Data Type	Control Where Property Is Found	Description
		Graph	
		Group Box	
		HScrollBar	
		Line	
		Listview	
		Listbox	
		Multi-line edit	
		OLE	
		Oval	
		Picture	
		Picture Button	
		Picture Listbox	
		Radio Button	
		Rectangle	
		Richtextedit	
		Round Rectangle	
		Single Line Edit	
		Static Text	
		Tab	
		TabPage	
		Treeview	
		VScrollBar	
endx	integer	Line	The ending X point of a line control in a window in relation to the upper left corner.
endy	integer	Line	The ending Y point of a line control in a window in relation to the upper left corner.
extended-select	boolean	Listview	TRUE or FALSE indicating whether or not users can select multiple items by clicking on an item and dragging the mouse up or down to select items; using Click/Shift+Click to select a sequential group of items; or using Control+Click on multiple items.
		Listbox	
		Picture Listbox	

N O T E   The MultiSelect listbox property allows users to select multiple items in a listbox by simply clicking on the items. This differs from ExtendedSelect in that MultiSelect requires a separate click for each item, while ExtendedSelect allows "click and drag," CTRL+click, and SHIFT+click motions with a mouse to select multiple listbox entries. If MultiSelect=TRUE and ExtendedSelect=TRUE, ExtendedSelect takes precedence. ▇

Attribute	Data Type	Control Where Property Is Found	Description
facename	string	CheckBox	A string containing the name of the typeface (for example, Ariel) for the text in a window control.
		Command Button Drop Down Listbox Drop Down Picture Listbox Edit Mask Group Box Listview Listbox Multi-line edit OLE Picture Button Picture Listbox Radio Button Single Line Edit Static Text Tab Treeview	
fillcolor	long	Oval	The color to fill in an oval, rectangle, or roundrectangle control.
		Rectangle Round Rectangle	
fillpattern	fill pattern	Oval	The pattern to fill in a static text, oval, rectangle, or roundrectangle control.
		Rectangle Round Rectangle Static Text	
fixedlocations	boolean	Listview	TRUE or FALSE indicating whether or not users can drag icons to new locations.
fixedwidth	boolean	Tab	TRUE or FALSE indicating whether or not tabs have a fixed width and therefore do not shrink to the length of their text labels.

Part

VII

Ch

27

continues

Table 27.4 Continued

Attribute	Data Type	Control Where Property Is Found	Description
focuson-buttondown	boolean	Tab	TRUE or FALSE indicating whether or not each tab gets focus when the user clicks on it. In either case, the selected tab page comes to the front.
focus-rectangle	boolean	Graph	TRUE or FALSE indicating whether or not to display a rectangle around the control when that control receives focus.
		OLE Picture Static Text	
fontcharset	fontchar set	CheckBox	Specifies the font character set. Valid values are: ANSI!, ChineseBig5!, DefaultCharSet!, HangEul!, Shiftjis!, OEM!, and Symbol!.
		Command Button Drop Down Listbox Drop Down Picture Listbox Edit Mask Group Box Listview Listbox Multi-line edit OLE Picture Button Picture Listbox Radio Button Single Line Edit Static Text Tab Treeview	
fontfamily	font family	CheckBox	Specifies a group of typefaces with similar characteristics for text. Valid values are AnyFont!, Decorative! Modern!, Roman!, Script!, and Swiss!.
		Command Button Drop Down Listbox Drop Down Picture Listbox Edit Mask Group Box	

Attribute	Data Type	Control Where Property Is Found	Description
		Listview Listbox Multi-line edit OLE Picture Button Picture Listbox Radio Button Single Line Edit Static Text Tab Treeview	
fontpitch	fontpitch	CheckBox	Specifies the horizontal spacing (pitch) of text. Valid values are: Default!—use standard pitch for the font (fixed or variable); Fixed!—use fixed pitch; Variable!—use variable pitch.
		Command Button Drop Down Listbox Drop Down Picture Listbox Edit Mask Group Box Listview Listbox Multi-line edit OLE Picture Button Picture Listbox Radio Button Single Line Edit Static Text Tab Treeview	
graphtype	grgraphtype	Graph	An enumerated data type grGraphType specifying the type of a graph.
hasbuttons	boolean	Treeview	TRUE or FALSE indicating whether or not to display '+' and '-' buttons next to parent items in a treeview.

Part

VII

Ch

27

continues

Table 27.4 Continued

Attribute	Data Type	Control Where Property Is Found	Description
haslines	boolean	Treeview	TRUE or FALSE indicating if lines connect objects in a treeview.
headerfooter	boolean	Richtextedit	TRUE or FALSE indicating whether or not a richtextedit control has a header/footer section.
height	integer	CheckBox	A number indicating the height of the window control.
		Command Button	
		DataWindow	
		Drop Down Listbox	
		Drop Down Picture Listbox	
		Edit Mask	
		Graph	
		Group Box	
		HScrollBar	
		Listview	
		Listbox	
		Multi-line edit	
		OLE	
		Oval	
		Picture	
		Picture Button	
		Picture Listbox	
		Radio Button	
		Rectangle	
		Richtextedit	
		Round Rectangle	
		Single Line Edit	
		Static Text	
		Tab	
		TabPage	
		Treeview	
		VScrollBar	
hide-selection	boolean	Edit Mask	TRUE or FALSE indicating whether or not the selection in a control remains highlighted when that control no longer has focus.
		Listview	
		Multi-line edit	
		Single Line Edit	
		Treeview	
hscrollbar	boolean	DataWindow	TRUE or FALSE indicating whether or not the window control has a horizontal scroll bar.
		Drop Down Listbox	
		Drop Down Picture Listbox	

Attribute	Data Type	Control Where Property Is Found	Description
		Edit Mask	
		Listbox	
		Multi-line edit	
		Picture Listbox	
		Richtextedit	
		TabPage	
hsplitscroll	boolean	DataWindow	TRUE or FALSE indicating whether or not the DataWindow control allows split scrolling.
htextalign	alignment	Picture Button	A feature that specifies the alignment of text in a PictureButton control. Valid Values are Center!, Left!, and Right!.
hwnd	unsigned-long	CheckBox	The Windows handle of the window control.
		Command Button	
		DataWindow	
		Drop Down Listbox	
		Drop Down Picture Listbox	
		Edit Mask	
		Graph	
		Group Box	
		HScrollBar	
		Line	
		Listview	
		Listbox	
		Multi-line edit	
		OLE	
		Oval	
		Picture	
		Picture Button	
		Picture Listbox	
		Radio Button	
		Rectangle	
		Richtextedit	
		Round Rectangle	
		Single Line Edit	
		Static Text	
		Tab	
		TabPage	
		Treeview	
		VScrollBar	

Part
VII

Ch
27

continues

Table 27.4   Continued

Attribute	Data Type	Control Where Property Is Found	Description
icon	string	DataWindow	A string indicating the icon (.ICO file) displayed if the window control is minimized.
ignore-default-button	boolean	Edit Mask	TRUE or FALSE indicating whether or not a return causes a carriage return/line feed in the edit mask or multi-line edit, or if it causes the default button control to be pressed when the edit control has focus.
		Multi-line edit	
increment	double	Edit Mask	A feature that specifies the increment used in a numeric Edit mask with spin control.
indent	integer	Treeview	The amount (of PowerBuilder units) to indent a treeview.
inputfield-backcolor	long	Richtextedit	Default background color for input fields. This property uses the RGB function to set the default back ground color in a richtextedit control. For example, to set the default background color of a richtextedit control to purple, you would type **lv_field.inputfield backcolor = RGB(255,0,255)**.
inputfield-namesvisible	boolean	Richtextedit	TRUE or FALSE indicating whether a richtextedit displays the field names (TRUE) or the field values (FALSE).
inputfields-visible	boolean	Richtextedit	TRUE or FALSE indicating whether or not a richtextedit control's input fields are visible.
invert	boolean	Picture	TRUE or FALSE indicating whether or not a picture control is inverted.
isdragtarget	boolean	OLE	TRUE or FALSE indicating whether or not an object can be dropped on an OLE control.
italic	boolean	CheckBox	TRUE or FALSE specifying whether or not the text in a control is in italics.

Attribute	Data Type	Control Where Property Is Found	Description
		Command Button Drop Down Listbox Drop Down Picture Listbox Edit Mask Group Box Listview Listbox Multi-line edit OLE Picture Button Picture Listbox Radio Button Single Line Edit Static Text Tab Treeview	
item[]	string	Drop Down Listbox	An array of display strings in a ListBox or DropDownListBox code table.
		Drop Down Picture Listbox Listview Listbox Picture Listbox	
itempicture-index[]	integer	Drop Down Picture Listbox	An array of picture indexes that corresponds to every item in the item[] array (see previous entry).
		Listview Picture Listbox	
items	integer	Listview	The number of items in a listview.
labelwrap	boolean	Listview	TRUE or FALSE indicating whether or not to word wrap labels or to display them on a single line.
largepicture-height	integer	Listview	The height of large images in a listview.

Part
VII

Ch
27

continues

Table 27.4   Continued

Attribute	Data Type	Control Where Property Is Found	Description
largepicture-mask color	long	Listview	A feature that uses the RGB function to set the masking color of large pictures in a listview for user defined bitmaps. For example, to set the masking color of a listview to purple, you would type **lv_field.largepicture maskcolor = RGB(255,0,255)**.
largepicture-name[]	string	Listview	An array of initial large pictures in a listview added during initialization.
largepicture-width	integer	Listview	The width of large images in a listview.
leftmargin	long	Richtextedit	The length of the left margin in a richtextedit.
lefttext	boolean	CheckBox Radio Button	TRUE or FALSE indicating whether to display the text on the left side (TRUE) or right side (FALSE) of a check box or radio button.
legend	grlegend type	Graph	A number indicating the location of the legend of a graph.
legend-dispattr	grdispattr	Graph	Defines how you want the graph legend to appear.
libraryname	string	TabPage	The name of the dynamic-link library (DLL) that contains a custom user object class.
limit	integer	Drop Down Listbox Drop Down Picture Listbox Edit Mask Multi-line edit Single Line Edit	An integer containing the maximum number of characters (0–32,767) the user can enter in a control. 0 indicates an unlimited number of characters.
linecolor	long	Line Oval Rectangle Round Rectangle	The color to draw lines in a Line, Oval, Rectangle, or RoundRectangle control.

Attribute	Data Type	Control Where Property Is Found	Description
linesatroot	boolean	Treeview	TRUE or FALSE indicating whether or not lines connect all root items.
linesperpage	integer	TabPage	An integer indicating the number of units to scroll when the scroll down bar has been clicked on.
linestyle	linestyle	Line	A Style! enumerated data type specifying the line style in a Line, Oval, Rectangle, or RoundRectangle control.
		Oval Rectangle Round Rectangle	
line-thickness	integer	Line	An integer determining the line thickness in a Line, Oval, Rectangle, or RoundRectangle control.
		Oval Rectangle Round Rectangle	
livescroll	boolean	DataWindow	TRUE or FALSE indicating if the clicking on the scroll bars allows scrolling of the DataWindow.
mask	string	Edit Mask	A string containing the format in an Edit mask control.
maskdatatype	maskdata type	Edit Mask	An enumerated variable assigning a predefined format to an Edit mask control.
maxbox	boolean	DataWindow	TRUE or FALSE indicating the presence of a maximize box on the DataWindow.
maxposition	integer	HScrollBar	An integer containing the value of the position property when a horizontal scroll bar is at the far right or a vertical scroll bar is at the bottom. For use in HScrollBar and VScrollBar controls only.
		VScrollBar	

Part

VII

Ch

27

continues

Table 27.4 Continued

Attribute	Data Type	Control Where Property Is Found	Description
minbox	boolean	DataWindow	TRUE or FALSE indicating the presence of a minimize box on the DataWindow.
minmax	string	Edit Mask	A string containing the minimum and maximum values for a spin control in an Edit mask. The minimum and maximum values are separated with a tab (for example, em_field.minmax = "1000 5000").
minposition	integer	HScrollBar	An integer containing the value of the position property when a horizontal scroll bar is at the far left or a vertical scroll bar is at the top. For use in HScrollBar and VScrollBar controls only.
		VScrollBar	
modified	boolean	Richtextedit	TRUE or FALSE indicating whether or not the richtextedit control's document has been modified since it was opened.
multiline	boolean	Tab	TRUE or FALSE indicating whether or not the tabs in a tab control can appear in more than one row if there's not enough room for all of them on one row.
multiselect	boolean	Listbox	TRUE or FALSE indicating whether or not the user can select multiple values in a ListBox.
		Picture Listbox	

N O T E As explained earlier in this chapter, the MultiSelect listbox property allows users to select multiple items in a listbox by simply clicking on the items. This differs from ExtendedSelect in that MultiSelect requires a separate click for each item, while ExtendedSelect allows "click and drag," CTRL+click, and SHIFT+click motions with a mouse to select multiple listbox entries. If MultiSelect=TRUE and ExtendedSelect=TRUE, ExtendedSelect takes precedence. ■

Attribute	Data Type	Control Where Property Is Found	Description
objecttype	userobjects	TabPage	An enumerated data type specifying the type of user object.

Attribute	Data Type	Control Where Property Is Found	Description
originalsize	boolean	Picture	TRUE or FALSE indicating whether or not to override Height and Width properties in Picture or Picture-Button control and display the picture associated with the control at the original size.
		Picture Button	
overlap-percent	integer	Graph	An integer specifying the percentage of the width of the data markers (for example, bars or columns), if different series overlap in a graph.
password	boolean	Single Line Edit	TRUE or FALSE indicating whether or not to make a Single Line Edit as password field.
perpendic-ulartext	boolean	Tab	TRUE or FALSE indicating whether or not the tab labels are drawn perpendicular to the tab page, thereby making tabs thinner.
perspective	integer	Graph	An integer (1 to 100) indicating the distance the graph is from the front of the window. The larger the number, the greater the distance and the smaller the graph appears.
picture-height	integer	Drop Down Picture Listbox Picture Listbox Treeview	The height of pictures added to a window control.
picturemask-color	long	Drop Down Picture Listbox	A feature that uses the RGB function to set the masking color of a picture in a window control using user defined bitmaps. For example, to set the masking color of a DDPLB to purple, you would type **ddplb_field.picture maskcolor = RGB(255,0,255)**.
		Picture Listbox TabPage Treeview	

Part **VII**

Ch **27**

continues

Table 27.4 Continued

Attribute	Data Type	Control Where Property Is Found	Description
picturename	string	Picture Picture Button TabPage	A string containing the name of the bit map in a window control.
picture-name[]	string	Drop Down Picture Listbox Picture Listbox Treeview	An array of initial pictures in a window control added during initialization.
pictureon-right	boolean	Tab	TRUE or FALSE indicating whether or not a picture that is part of the tab label is to the right of the text. (FALSE tells that the picture is on the left.)
pictures-asframe	boolean	Richtextedit	TRUE or FALSE indicating whether or not a picture in a richtextedit control is displayed as a frame.
picturewidth	integer	Drop Down Picture Listbox Picture Listbox Treeview	The width of a picture.
piedispattr	grdispattr	Graph	Specifies properties of the text in pie graph labels, including the text style, size, color, and rotation.
pointer	string	CheckBox Command Button Drop Down Listbox Drop Down Picture Listbox Edit Mask Graph Group Box HScrollBar Listview Listbox Multi-line edit OLE Picture	A string containing the mouse pointer for this object.

Attribute	Data Type	Control Where Property Is Found	Description
		Picture Button Picture Listbox Radio Button Richtextedit Single Line Edit Static Text Tab TabPage Treeview VScrollBar	
popmenu	boolean	Richtextedit	TRUE or FALSE indicating whether or not the user has access to the richtextedit pop-up menu by clicking the right mouse button on the control.
position	integer	HScrollBar VScrollBar	The current position of a scroll bar. For use in HScrollBar and VScrollBar controls only.
powertips	boolean	Tab	
powertiptext	string	TabPage	TRUE or FALSE indicating whether or not PowerTips are displayed when the mouse pointer pauses over the tab.
raggedright	boolean	Tab	TRUE or FALSE indicating whether or not tabs are stretched so that they fill space along the edge of the control. (TRUE indicates that they are not stretched.)
resizable	boolean	DataWindow Richtextedit	TRUE or FALSE indicating whether or not the DataWindow or richtextedit is resizable.
returns-visible	boolean	Richtextedit	TRUE or FALSE indicating whether or not carriage returns are visible.
rightmargin	long	Richtextedit	The length of the right margin in a richtextedit.

continues

Part
VII

Ch
27

Table 27.4 Continued

Attribute	Data Type	Control Where Property Is Found	Description
righttoleft	boolean	CheckBox	TRUE or FALSE indicating whether typed text goes from right to left (TRUE) or left to right (FALSE). Default is FALSE. (This is useful when programming for other languages whose text goes from right to left.)
		DataWindow Drop Down Listbox Drop Down Picture Listbox Edit Mask Group Box Listbox Multi-line edit Picture Listbox Radio Button Single Line Edit Static Text	
rotation	integer	Graph	An integer indicating how much you want to rotate a graph from left to right.
rulerbar	boolean	Richtextedit	TRUE or FALSE indicating whether or not the ruler bar is visible in a richtextedit control.
scrolling	boolean	Listview	TRUE or FALSE indicating whether or not scrolling is allowed in a listview.
selectedtab	integer	Tab	The index of the selected tab in a tab control.
series	graxis	Graph	Sets the properties of the series axis in a graph control.
seriessort	grsorttype	Graph	Specifies how a series is sorted.
shadecolor	long	Graph	An integer determining the shading color of a graph.
showheader	boolean	Listview	TRUE or FALSE indicating whether or not to show the header in a report view of a listview.

Attribute	Data Type	Control Where Property Is Found	Description
showlist	boolean	Drop Down Listbox	TRUE or FALSE indicating whether or not to always show the list in a DropDownListBox.
		Drop Down Picture Listbox	
showpicture	boolean	Tab	TRUE or FALSE indicating whether or not a picture is shown for each tab in a tab control.
show-selection	boolean	Treeview	TRUE or FALSE indicating if the treeview selection should be shown when the treeview does not have focus.
showtext	boolean	Tab	TRUE or FALSE indicating whether or not text is displayed (as opposed to a picture) in each tab in a tab control.
smallpicture-height	integer	Listview	The height of small pictures added to a listview.
smallpicture-maskcolor	long	Listview	A feature that uses the RGB function to set the masking color of small pictures in a listview for user defined bitmaps. For example, to set the masking color of a listview to purple, you would type **lv_field.smallpicture maskcolor = RGB(255,0,255)**.
smallpicture-name[]	string	Listview	An array of initial small pictures in a listview added during initialization.
smallpicture-width	integer	Listview	The width of small pictures added to a listview.
sorted	boolean	Drop Down Listbox	TRUE or FALSE indicating whether or not to sort the elements in a ListBox or DropDownListBox by their display value.
		Drop Down Picture Listbox Listbox Picture Listbox	

Part

VII

Ch

27

continues

Table 27.4 Continued

Attribute	Data Type	Control Where Property Is Found	Description
sorttype	grsorttype	Listview Treeview	Sets the sorting order in a listview or treeview.
spaces-visible	boolean	Richtextedit	TRUE or FALSE indicating whether or not spaces are visible in a richtextedit control.
spacing	integer	Graph	An integer determining the space between categories in a graph.
spin	boolean	Edit Mask	TRUE or FALSE indicating whether or not an Edit mask has spin control.
statepicture-height	integer	Listview Treeview	The height of state pictures added to a listview or treeview.
statepicture-maskcolor	long	Listview Treeview	A feature that uses the RGB function to set the masking color of state pictures in a listview or treeview for user defined bitmaps. For example, to set the masking color of a listview to purple, you would type **lv_field.statepicture maskcolor = RGB(255,0,255)**.
statepicture-name[]	string	Listview Treeview	An array of initial state pictures in a listview or treeview added during initialization.
statepicture-width	integer	Listview Treeview	The width of state pictures added to a listview or treeview.
stdheight	boolean	HScrollBar	TRUE or FALSE indicating whether to use standard horizontal scroll bar height (TRUE) or system horizontal scroll bar height (FALSE).
stdwidth	boolean	VScrollBar	TRUE or FALSE indicating whether to use standard vertical scroll bar height (TRUE) or system vertical scroll bar height (FALSE).

Attribute	Data Type	Control Where Property Is Found	Description
style	long	TabPage	Controls the appearance of the user object.
tabbackcolor	long	TabPage	A feature that uses the RGB function to set to background color of the selected tab. For example, to set the background color of the selected tab to purple, you would type **mle_field.tabbackcolor = RGB(255,0,255)**.
tabbar	boolean	Richtextedit	TRUE or FALSE indicating whether or not the bar for setting tabs in a richtextedit is visible.
taborder	integer	CheckBox	An integer that describes the tab order of the window control in relation to other controls.
		Command Button	
		DataWindow	
		Drop Down Listbox	
		Drop Down Picture Listbox	
		Edit Mask	
		Graph	
		Group Box	
		HScrollBar	
		Listview	
		Listbox	
		Multi-line edit	
		OLE	
		Picture	
		Picture Button	
		Picture Listbox	
		Radio Button	
		Richtextedit	
		Single Line Edit	
		Static Text	
		Tab	
		TabPage	
		Treeview	
		VScrollBar	
tabposition	tabposition	Tab	Specifies where tabs appear around the tab control.

Part

VII

Ch

27

continues

Table 27.4   Continued

Attribute	Data Type	Control Where Property Is Found	Description
tabstop[]	integer	Edit Mask	A signed integer array containing the position of the tab stops in an Edit mask, Listbox or Multi-Line Edit.
		Listbox Multi-line edit Picture Listbox	
tabsvisible	boolean	Richtextedit	TRUE or FALSE indicating whether or not tabs are visible in a richtextedit.
tabtextcolor	long	TabPage	A feature that uses the RGB function to set the color of the selected tab text. For example, to set the tab text color of the selected tab to purple, you would type **mle_field.tabtextcolor = RGB(255,0,255).**
tag	string	CheckBox	A string containing the tag value of the window control. A tag value is a value assigned to a control by a developer to be used to identify that control or to identify an association of that control.
		Command Button DataWindow Drop Down Listbox Drop Down Picture Listbox Edit Mask Graph Group Box HScrollBar Line Listview Listbox Multi-line edit OLE Oval Picture Picture Button Picture Listbox Radio Button Rectangle Richtextedit	

Attribute	Data Type	Control Where Property Is Found	Description
		Round Rectangle	
		Single Line Edit	
		Static Text	
		Tab	
		TabPage	
		Treeview	
		VScrollBar	
text	string	CheckBox	The text associated with a window control.
		Command Button	
		Drop Down Listbox	
		Drop Down Picture Listbox	
		Edit Mask	
		Group Box	
		Multi-line edit	
		Picture Button	
		Radio Button	
		Single Line Edit	
		Static Text	
		TabPage	
textcase	textcase	Edit Mask	A Case! enumerated variable denoting the case of a text field.
		Multi-line edit	
		Single Line Edit	
textcolor	long	CheckBox	A long indicating the color of text in a field.
		Drop Down Listbox	
		Drop Down Picture Listbox	
		Edit Mask	
		Graph	
		Group Box	
		Listview	
		Listbox	
		Multi-line edit	
		OLE	
		Picture Listbox	
		Radio Button	
		Single Line Edit	
		Static Text	
		Treeview	

Part

VII

Ch

27

continues

Table 27.4	Continued		
Attribute	**Data Type**	**Control Where Property Is Found**	**Description**
textsize	integer	CheckBox	An integer indicating the size of the text in a text field.
		Command Button	
		Drop Down Listbox	
		Drop Down Picture List-box	
		Edit Mask	
		Group Box	
		Listview	
		Listbox	
		Multi-line edit	
		OLE	
		Picture Button	
		Picture Listbox	
		Radio Button	
		Single Line Edit	
		Static Text	
		Tab	
		Treeview	
thirdstate	boolean	CheckBox	TRUE or FALSE indicating whether or not a check box is in its third state.
threestate	boolean	CheckBox	TRUE or FALSE indicating whether or not a check box has three states (TRUE) or only two states (FALSE).
title	string	DataWindow	A string containing the title of the DataWindow or graph.
		Graph	
titlebar	boolean	DataWindow	TRUE or FALSE indicating whether or not the DataWindow has a title bar.
title-dispattr	grdispattr	Graph	A grDispAttr object defining the style of a title in a graph.
toolbar	boolean	Richtextedit	TRUE or FALSE indicating whether or not a toolbar used for formatting text is visible in a richtextedit control.
topmargin	long	Richtextedit	The length of the top margin in a richtextedit.
underline	boolean	CheckBox	TRUE or FALSE specifying whether or not the text in a control is underlined.

Attribute	Data Type	Control Where Property Is Found	Description
		Command Button	
		Drop Down Listbox	
		Drop Down Picture Listbox	
		Edit Mask	
		Group Box	
		Listview	
		Listbox	
		Multi-line edit	
		OLE	
		Picture Button	
		Picture Listbox	
		Radio Button	
		Single Line Edit	
		Static Text	
		Tab	
		Treeview	
undodepth	integer	Richtextedit	The maximum number of activities that an UNDO command will undo.
unitsper-column	integer	TabPage	A feature that indicates the number of PowerBuilder units a user scrolls when clicking on the scroll left or right.
unitsperline	integer	TabPage	A feature that indicates the number of PowerBuilder units a user scrolls when clicking on the scroll up or down.
usecodetable	boolean	Edit Mask	TRUE or FALSE indicating whether or not an Edit mask will use code tables. This is useful for spin controls in non-numeric fields.
values	graxis	Graph	A feature that sets the properties of the values in a graph control.
view	listview view	Listview	A property that changes the display mode in a listview.
visible	boolean	CheckBox	TRUE or FALSE indicating whether or not the window control is visible or not.

Part

VII

Ch

27

continues

Table 27.4   Continued

Attribute	Data Type	Control Where Property Is Found	Description
		Command Button	
		DataWindow	
		Drop Down Listbox	
		Drop Down Picture Listbox	
		Edit Mask	
		Graph	
		Group Box	
		HScrollBar	
		Line	
		Listview	
		Listbox	
		Multi-line edit	
		OLE	
		Oval	
		Picture	
		Picture Button	
		Picture Listbox	
		Radio Button	
		Rectangle	
		Richtextedit	
		Round Rectangle	
		Single Line Edit	
		Static Text	
		Tab	
		TabPage	
		Treeview	
		VScrollBar	
vscrollbar	boolean	DataWindow	TRUE or FALSE indicating whether or not the window control has a vertical scroll bar.
		Drop Down Listbox	
		Drop Down Picture Listbox	
		Edit Mask	
		Listbox	
		Multi-line edit	
		Picture Listbox	
		Richtextedit	
		TabPage	
vtextalign	vtextalign	Picture Button	An enumerated data type specifying the alignment of text in a PictureButton control. Valid values are Bottom!, MultiLine!, Top!, and VCenter!.

Attribute	Data Type	Control Where Property Is Found	Description
weight	integer	CheckBox	An integer containing the weight (line thickness) of the text. Weight is in points. PowerBuilder suggests 400 for normal or 700 for bold.
		Command Button	
		Drop Down Listbox	
		Drop Down Picture Listbox	
		Edit Mask	
		Group Box	
		Listview	
		Listbox	
		Multi-line edit	
		OLE	
		Picture Button	
		Picture Listbox	
		Radio Button	
		Single Line Edit	
		Static Text	
		Tab	
		Treeview	
width	integer	CheckBox	A number indicating the width of the window control.
		Command Button	
		DataWindow	
		Drop Down Listbox	
		Drop Down Picture Listbox	
		Edit Mask	
		Graph	
		Group Box	
		HScrollBar	
		Listview	
		Listbox	
		Multi-line edit	
		OLE	
		Oval	
		Picture	
		Picture Button	
		Picture Listbox	
		Radio Button	
		Rectangle	
		Richtextedit	
		Round Rectangle	

Part

VII

Ch

27

continues

Table 27.4 Continued

Attribute	Data Type	Control Where Property Is Found	Description
		Single Line Edit	
		Static Text	
		Tab	
		TabPage	
		Treeview	
		VScrollBar	
wordwrap	boolean	Richtextedit	TRUE or FALSE indicating whether or not words automatically wrap in a richtextedit.
x	integer	CheckBox	The X coordinate of the window control in relation to the window.
		Command Button	
		DataWindow	
		Drop Down Listbox	
		Drop Down Picture Listbox	
		Edit Mask	
		Graph	
		Group Box	
		HScrollBar	
		Listview	
		Listbox	
		Multi-line edit	
		OLE	
		Oval	
		Picture	
		Picture Button	
		Picture Listbox	
		Radio Button	
		Rectangle	
		Richtextedit	
		Round Rectangle	
		Single Line Edit	
		Static Text	
		Tab	
		TabPage	
		Treeview	
		VScrollBar	
y	integer	CheckBox	The Y coordinate of the window control in relation to the window.

Attribute	Data Type	Control Where Property Is Found	Description
		Command Button	
		DataWindow	
		Drop Down Listbox	
		Drop Down Picture Listbox	
		Edit Mask	
		Graph	
		Group Box	
		HScrollBar	
		Listview	
		Listbox	
		Multi-line edit	
		OLE	
		Oval	
		Picture	
		Picture Button	
		Picture Listbox	
		Radio Button	
		Rectangle	
		Richtextedit	
		Round Rectangle	
		Single Line Edit	
		Static Text	
		Tab	
		TabPage	
		Treeview	
		VScrollBar	

From Here...

This chapter describes the many properties inside PowerBuilder. For more information, check out the following chapters:

- Chapter 6, "Using Events, Functions, and the PowerScript Language," describes the basic PowerScript programming language, including many attribute descriptions. Chapter 6 lays a good foundation for understanding PowerScript functions.

- Chapter 14, "Pulling It All Together in an Application" shows much of the PowerScript that is implemented in the Inventory Tracking system.

- Chapter 25, "Function Quick Reference" lists and describes all the built-in functions used with PowerBuilder. Many functions can affect the properties of an object or control.

Part
VII

Ch
27

CHAPTER 28

Enumerated Data Types Quick Reference

by Charles A. Wood

Enumerated data types are constants defined by PowerBuilder that are used to set the value of many object attributes. Because you are using a descriptive enumerated data type name as opposed to a constant, enumerated data types make developing and future maintenance a little easier. Enumerated data types also ensure data integrity for the PowerBuilder application.

PowerBuilder includes many enumerated data types. Most (but not all) of the enumerated data types can be found through the object browser. To get to the object browser, click on the Object Browser icon on any PowerScript painter PainterBar. The object browser can then be viewed, as seen in figure 28.1.

FIG. 28.1

You can get a list of enumerated data types from the PowerBuilder object browser.

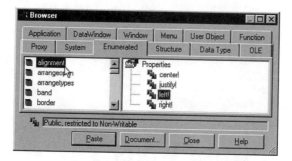

An example of an enumerated data type is as follows:

```
sle_numsold.alignment = Right!
```

Many of the enumerated data types are listed in online help. Table 28.1 lists all of PowerBuilder's enumerated data types.

N O T E   Any time the enumerated name is listed as an attribute of an object or control, you should use the enumerated data type to test and set that attribute. ■

TROUBLESHOOTING

I'm trying to use an enumerated data type, but the script I'm using it in will not compile, and I keep getting errors. When you use enumerated data types, be sure to include a "!" at the end. PowerBuilder will not recognize them without the exclamation point.

Often, PowerBuilder allows you to either use an enumerated data type or a string. If you put an enumerated data type in quotes, PowerBuilder converts it to a string and does not process it as an enumerated data type. This causes a run-time error; therefore, be sure not to put your enumerated data type within quotes.

Table 28.1   Enumerated Data Types

Category	Values	Comments
Alignment	Center! Justify! Left! Right!	The alignment of text in a MultiLineEdit, StaticText, or PictureButton control.
ArrangeOpen	Cascaded! Layered! Original!	How MDI sheets are arranged when opened.

Category	Values	Comments
ArrangeTypes	Cascade! Icons! Layer! Tile! Tile Horizontal!	How open MDI sheets are arranged.
Band	Detail! Footer! Header!	The band where a specific DataWindow column is located.
Border	Box! Lowered! NoBorder! Raised! ResizeBorder! ShadowBox! Underline!	The type of the border.
BorderStyle	StyleBox! StyleLowered! StyleRaised! StyleShadowBox!	The style of the border.
Button	AbortRetryIgnore! OK! OKCancel! RetryCancel! YesNo! YesNoCancel!	Message Box Button.
ClipboardFormat	ClipFormat Bitmap! ClipFormatDib! ClipFormatDif! ClipFormatEnhMetaFile! ClipFormatDrop! ClipFormatLocale! ClipFormatMetaFilePict! ClipFormatOEMText! ClipFormatPalette! ClipFormatPenData! ClipFormatRiff! ClipFormatSylk! ClipFormatText! ClipFormatTiff! ClipFormatUnicodeText! ClipFormatWave!	The format of the data as it resides on the clipboard.

Part

VII

Ch

28

continues

Table 28.1 Continued

Category	Values	Comments
Connect Privilege	connect privilege! connectwith adminprivilege! noconnectprivilege!	The level of access of the connection to the database.
ConvertType	XPixelsToUnits! XUnitsToPixels! YPixelsToUnits! YUnitsToPixels!	How you want to convert units or pixels in the PixelsToUnits and UnitsToPixels functions.
CPUTypes	Alpha! HPPA! I286! I386! I486! m68000! m68020! m68030! m68040! MIPS! Pentium! PowerPC! RS6000! Sparc!	The CPU type the program is currently being executed on.
Direction	DirectionAll! DirectionDown! DirectionLeft! DirectionRight! DirectionUp!	The direction of the mouse.
DragModes	Begin! Cancel! End!	The Drag mode for an object.
dwBuffer	Delete! Filter! Primary!	The DataWindow buffer.
dwItemStatus	DataModified! New! NewModified! NotModified!	The status of a DataWindow item.

Category	Values	Comments
ExceptionAction	ExceptionFail! ExceptionIgnore! ExceptionRetry! ExceptionSubstitute- ReturnValue!	How a user responds to an exception.
FileAccess	Read! Write!	The file access allowed.
FileLock	LockRead! LockReadWrite! LockWrite! Shared!	The file lock for other users.
FileMode	LineMode! StreamMode!	The File mode for reading or writing.
FileType	FileTypeRichText! FileTypeText!	The type of text file.
FillPattern	BDiagonal! Diamond! FDiagonal! Horizontal! Solid! Square! Vertical!	The hatch pattern used to fill a drawing or graph object.
FontCharSet	ANSI! ChineseBig5! DefaultCharSet! HangEul! OEM! Shiftjis! Symbol!	The font character set.
FontFamily	AnyFont! Decorative! Modern! Roman! Script! Swiss!	The font family.
FontPitch	Default! Fixed! Variable!	The font pitch.

Part
VII

Ch
28

continues

Table 28.1   Continued

	Category	Values	Comments
	grAxisDataType	adtDate! adtDateTime! adtDefault! adtDouble! adtText! adtTime!	The type of axis in a graph.
	grColorType	Background! Foreground! LineColor! Shade!	A color type in a graph.
	grDataType	xvalue! yvalue!	The value of a data point in a graph.
	grGraphType	Area3d! AreaGraph! Bar3dGraph! Bar3dObjGraph! BarGraph! BarStack3dObjGraph! BarStackGraph! Col3dGraph! Col3dObjGraph! ColGraph! ColStack3dObjGraph! ColStackGraph! Line3d! LineGraph! Pie3d! PieGraph! ScatterGraph!	The type of graph.
	grLegendType	AtBottom! AtLeft! AtRight! AtTop! NoLegend!	The location of the graph legend.
	grObjectType	TypeCategory! TypeCategoryAxis! TypeCategoryLabel! TypeData! TypeGraph! TypeLegend! TypeSeries! TypeSeriesAxis!	The type of graph object.

Category	Values	Comments
	TypeSeriesLabel! TypeTitle! TypeValueAxis! TypeValueLabel!	
grResetType	All! Category! Data! Series!	The data you want to reset in a graph.
grRoundToType	rndDays! rndDefault! rndHours! rndMicroSeconds! rndMinutes! rndMonths! rndNumber! rndSeconds! rndYears!	
grScaleType	Linear! Log10! LogE!	The type of scale in a graph.
grScaleValue	Actual! Cumulative! CumulativePercent! Percentage!	The value of scale in a graph.
grSortType	Ascending! Descending! Unsorted! UserDefinedSort!	
grSymbolType	NoSymbol! SymbolHollowBox! SymbolHollowCircle! SymbolHollowDiamond! SymbolHollowDownArrow! SymbolHollowUpArrow! SymbolPlus! SymbolSolidBox! SymbolSolidCircle! SymbolSolidDiamond! SymbolSolidDownArrow! SymbolSolidUpArrow! SymbolStar! SymbolX!	The symbol you want to use for a series in a graph.

Part

VII

Ch

28

continues

Table 28.1 Continued

Category	Values	Comments
grTicType	Inside! NoTic! Outside! Straddle!	The type of tick marks in the scale in a graph.
HelpCommand	Index! Keyword! Topic!	The type of command in the ShowHelp function.
Icon	Exclamation! Information! None! Question! StopSign!	The Message Box icon.
KeyCode	key0! key1! key2! key3! key4! key5! key6! key7! key8! key9! keyA! keyAdd! keyAlt! keyB! keyBack! keyBackQuote! keyBackSlash! keyC! keyCapsLock! keyComma! keyControl! keyD! keyDash! keyDecimal! keyDelete! keyDivide! keyDownArrow! keyE! keyEnd!	The keycode argument in the KeyDown function. + on the numeric keypad. Backspace key. ´ and _ keys. \ and I keys. , and < keys. - and _ keys. . on the numeric keypad when NumLock is on. / on the numeric keypad.

Category	Values	Comments
	keyEnter!	
	keyEqual!	= and + keys.
	keyEscape!	
	keyF!	
	keyF1!	
	keyF10!	
	keyF11!	
	keyF12!	
	keyF2!	
	keyF3!	
	keyF4!	
	keyF5!	
	keyF6!	
	keyF7!	
	keyF8!	
	keyF9!	
	keyG!	
	keyH!	
	keyHome!	
	keyI!	
	keyInsert!	
	keyJ!	
	keyK!	
	keyL!	
	keyLeftArrow!	
	keyLeftBracket!	[and { keys.
	keyM!	
	keyMultiply!	* on the numeric keypad.
	keyN!	
	keyNull!	
	keyNumLock!	
	keyNumpad0!	
	keyNumpad1!	
	keyNumpad2!	
	keyNumpad3!	
	keyNumpad4!	
	keyNumpad5!	
	keyNumpad6!	
	keyNumpad7!	
	keyNumpad8!	
	keyNumpad9!	
	keyO!	
	keyP!	
	keyPageDown!	
	keyPageUp!	
	keyPause!	

Part

VII

Ch

28

continues

Table 28.1   Continued

Category	Values	Comments
	keyPeriod! keyPrintScreen! keyQ! keyQuote!	. and > keys. Single-quote and double-quote key.
	keyR! keyRightArrow! keyRightBracket! keyS! keyScrollLock! keySemiColon! keyShift! keySlash! keySpaceBar! KeySubtract! keyT! keyTab! keyU! keyUpArrow! keyV! keyW! keyX! keyY! keyZ!	] and } keys. ; and : keys. / and ? keys. - on the numeric keypad.
LanguageID	languageafrikaans! languagealbanian! languagearabicalgeria! languagearabicbahrain! languagearabicegypt! languagearabiciraq! languagearabicjordan! languagearabickuwait! languagearabiclebanon! languagearabiclibya! languagearabicmorocco! languagearabicoman! languagearabicqatar! languagearabicsaudiarabia! languagearabicsyria! languagearabictunisia! languagearabicuae! languagearabicyemen! languagebasque! languagebulgarian!	Identifies the language in use.

Category	Values	Comments
	languagebyelorussian!	
	languagecatalan!	
	languagechinese!	
	languagechinesehongkong!	
	languagechinesesimplified!	
	languagechinesesingapore!	
	languagechinesetraditional!	
	languagecroatian!	
	languageczech!	
	languagedanish!	
	languagedutch!	
	languagedutchbelgian!	
	languagedutchneutral!	
	languageenglish!	
	languageenglishaustralian!	
	languageenglishcanadian!	
	languageenglishirish!	
	languageenglishnewzealand!	
	languageenglishsouthafrica!	
	languageenglishuk!	
	languageenglishus!	
	languageestonian!	
	languagefaeroese!	
	languagefarsi!	
	languagefinnish!	
	languagefrench!	
	languagefrenchbelgian!	
	languagefrenchcanadian!	
	languagefrenchluxembourg!	
	languagefrenchneutral!	
	languagefrenchswiss!	
	languagegerman!	
	languagegermanaustrian!	
	languagegermanliechtenstein!	
	languagegermanluxembourg!	
	languagegermanneutral!	
	languagegermanswiss!	
	languagegreek!	
	languagehebrew!	
	languagehindi!	
	languagehungarian!	
	languageicelandic!	
	languageindonesian!	
	languageitalian!	
	languageitalianneutral!	

Part
VII

Ch
28

continues

Table 28.1   Continued

Category	Values	Comments
	languageitalianswiss!	
	languagejapanese!	
	languagekorean!	
	languagekoreanjohab!	
	languagelatvian!	
	languagelithuanian!	
	languagemacedonian!	
	languagemaltese!	
	languageneutral!	
	languagenorwegian!	
	languagenorwegianbokmal!	
	languagenorwegiannynorsk!	
	languagepolish!	
	languageportuguese!	
	languageportuguese_brazilian!	
	languageportugueseneutral!	
	languagerhaetoromanic!	
	languageromanian!	
	languageromanianmoldavia!	
	languagerussian!	
	languagerussianmoldavia!	
	languagesami!	
	languageserbian!	
	languageslovak!	
	languageslovenian!	
	languagesorbian!	
	languagespanish!	
	languagespanishcastilian!	
	languagespanishmexican!	
	languagespanishmodern!	
	languagesutu!	
	languageswedish!	
	languagesystemdefault!	
	languagethai!	
	languagetsonga!	
	languagetswana!	
	languageturkish!	
	languageukrainian!	
	languageurdu!	
	languageuserdefault!	
	languagevenda!	
	languagexhosa!	
	languagezulu!	

Category	Values	Comments
LanguageSortID	LanguageSortNative! LanguageSortUnicode!	The sort order of a language.
LibDirType	DirAll! DirApplication! DirDataWindow! DirFunction! DirMenu! DirPipeline! DirProject! DirQuery! DirStructure! DirUserObject! DirWindow!	The type of objects to be included in the directory list.
LibExportType	ExportApplication! ExportDataWindow! ExportFunction! ExportMenu! ExportPipeline! ExportProject! ExportQuery! ExportStructure! ExportUserObject! ExportWindow!	The type of object to be exported.
LibImportType	ImportDataWindow!	The type of object to be imported.
LineStyle	Continuous! Dash! DashDot! DashDotDot! Dot! Transparent!	The style of the line.
ListViewView	ListViewLargeIcon! ListViewList! ListViewReport! ListViewSmallIcon!	How a ListView is viewed.
mailFileType	mailAttach! mailOLE! mailOLEStatic!	Mail file types.
mailLogonOption	mailDownLoad! mailNewSession! mailNewSessionWithDownLoad!	Mail logon options.

continues

Part
VII

Ch
28

Table 28.1 Continued

Category	Values	Comments
mailReadOption	mailBodyAsFile! mailEntireMessage! mailEnvelopeOnly! mailSuppressAttachments!	Mail read options.
mailRecipient Type	mailBCC! mailCC! mailOriginator! mailTo!	Mail recipient types.
mailReturnCode	mailReturnAccessDenied! mailReturnAttachmentNotFound! mailReturnAttachmentOpenFailure! mailReturnAttachmentWriteFailure! mailReturnDiskFull! mailReturnFailure! mailReturnInsufficientMemory! mailReturnInvalidMessage! mailReturnLoginFailure! mailReturnMessageInUse! mailReturnNoMessages! mailReturnSuccess! mailReturnTextTooLarge! mailReturnTooManyFiles! mailReturnUnknownRecipient! mailReturnTooManyRecipients! mailReturnTooManySessions! mailReturnUserAbort!	Mail function return codes.
MaskDataType	DateMask! DateTimeMask! DecimalMask! NumericMask! StringMask! TimeMask!	The EditMask data type.
MenuItemType	MenuItemTypeAbout! MenuItemTypeExit! MenuItemTypeNormal!	The type of menu item.
MenuMergeOption	EditMenu! Exclude! FileMenu! HelpMenu! Merge! WindowMenu!	The type of menu merge.

Category	Values	Comments
Object	application!	The object type.
	checkbox!	
	commandbutton!	
	connection!	
	connectioninfo!	
	connectionobject!	
	cplusplus!	
	datastore!	
	datawindow!	
	datawindowchild!	
	dragobject!	
	drawobject!	
	dropdownlistbox!	
	dropdownpicturelistbox!	
	dwobject!	
	dynamicdescriptionarea!	
	dynamicstagingarea!	
	editmask!	
	environment!	
	error!	
	extobject!	
	functionobject!	
	graph!	
	graphicobject!	
	graxis!	
	grdispattr!	
	groupbox!	
	hscrollbar!	
	line!	
	listbox!	
	listview!	
	listviewitem!	
	mailfiledescription!	
	mailmessage!	
	mailrecipient!	
	mailsession!	
	mdiclient!	
	menu!	
	menucascade!	
	message!	
	multilineedit!	
	nonvisualobject!	
	olecontrol!	
	olecustomcontrol!	
	oleobject!	
	olestorage!	
	olestream!	

continues

Part
VII

Ch
28

Table 28.1 Continued

Category	Values	Comments
	omcontrol!	
	omcustomcontrol!	
	omembeddedcontrol!	
	omobject!	
	omstorage!	
	omstream!	
	oval!	
	picture!	
	picturebutton!	
	picturelistbox!	
	pipeline!	
	powerobject!	
	radiobutton!	
	rectangle!	
	remoteobject!	
	richtextedit!	
	roundrectangle!	
	rteobject!	
	singlelineedit!	
	statictext!	
	structure!	
	subsystem!	
	tab!	
	transaction!	
	transport!	
	treeview!	
	treeviewitem!	
	userobject!	
	vscrollbar!	
	window!	
	windowobject!	
OleFunction CallType	AsStatement!	The type of OLE function call.
OmActivateType	InPlace! OffSite!	
OmActivation	ActiveateManually! ActivateOnDoubleClick! ActivateOnGetFocus!	
OmContent Allowed	ContainsAny!s ContainsEmbeddedOnly! ContainsLinkedOnly!	

	Category	Values	Comments
	OmDisplayType	DisplayAsContent! DisplayAsIcon!	
	OmLinkUpdate Options	LinkUpdateAutomatic! LinkUpdateManual!	
	OSTypes	AIX! HPUX! Macintosh! OSF1! SOL2! Windows! WindowsNT!	The type of operating system.
	ParmType	TypeBoolean! TypeDate! TypeDateTime! TypeDecimal! TypeDouble! TypeInteger! TypeLong! TypeReal! TypeString! TypeTime! TypeUInt! TypeULong! TypeUnknown!	The parameter data type.
	PBTypes	Desktop! Enterprise!	The type of PowerBuilder used in development.
	Pointer	Arrow! Beam! Cross! HourGlass! SizeNESW! SizeNS! SizeNWSE! SizeWE! UpArrow!	The shape of the pointer for the SetPointer function.
	RowFocusInd	FocusRect! Hand! Off!	The method that will be used to indicate that a DataWindow row has focus.
	SaveAsType	Clipboard Csv! dBase2!	The type of file to create when saving the rows of a DataWindow.

Part
VII

Ch
28

continues

Table 28.1   Continued

Category	Values	Comments
	dBase3! Dif! Excel! PSReport! SQLInsert! Sylk! Text! Wk1! Wks! Wfm!	
SeekType	FromBeginning! FromCurrent! FromEnd!	The position at which you want to begin a seek in the FileSeek function.
SetPosType	Behind! NoTopMost! ToBottom! TopMost! ToTop!	Set the order of display in a window control.
Spacing	Spacing1! Spacing2! Spacing15!	
SQLPreview Function	PreviewFunctionReselectRow! PreviewFunctionRetrieve! PreviewFunctionUpdate!	
SQLPreviewType	PreviewDelete! PreviewInsert! PreviewSelect! PreviewUpdate!	The type of function previewed in the SQL Preview Event.
stgReadMode	stgRead! stgReadWrite! stgWrite!	How files are opened.
stgShareMode	stgDenyNone! stgDenyRead! stgDenyWrite! stgExclusive!	How multi-users are handled.
TabPosition	TabsOnBottom! TabsOnBottomAndTop! TabsOnLeft! TabsOnRight!	How tabs are positioned in a tab control.

Category	Values	Comments
TextCase	TabsOnRightAndLeft! TabsOnTop! TabsOnTopAndBottom! AnyCase! Lower! Upper!	The text case.
TextStyle	Bold! Italic! Strikeout! Subscript! SuperScript! Underlined!	The format of text.
Toolbar Alignment	AllignAtBottom! AlignAtLeft! AlignAtRight! AlignAtTop! Floating!	The toolbar alignment.
TreeNavigation	ChildTreeItem! CurrentTreeItem! DropHighlightTreeItem! FirstVisableTreeItem! NextTreeItem! NextVisableTreeItem! ParentTreeItem! PreviousTreeItem! PreviousVisibleTreeItem! RootTreeItem!	
TrigEvent	Activate! BeginDrag! BeginLabelEdit! BeginRightDrag! Clicked! Close! CloseQuery! ColumnClick! Constructor! DataChange! DBError! Deactivate! DeleteAllItems! DeleteItem! Destructor! DoubleClicked! DragDrop!	The type of event to be triggered by the TriggerEvent function.

continues

Table 28.1 Continued

Category	Values	Comments
	DragEnter!	
	DragLeave!	
	DragWithin!	
	EditChanged!	
	EndLabelEdit!	
	FileExists!	
	GetFocus!	
	Hide!	
	HotLinkAlarm!	
	Idle!	
	InputFieldsSelected!	
	InsertItem!	
	ItemChanged!	
	ItemChanging!	
	ItemCollapsed!	
	ItemCollapsing!	
	ItemError!	
	ItemExpanded!	
	ItemExpanding!	
	ItemFocusChanged!	
	ItemPopulate!	
	Key!	
	LineDown!	
	LineLeft!	
	LineRight!	
	LineUp!	
	LoseFocus!	
	Modified!	
	MouseDown!	
	MouseMove!	
	MouseUp!	
	Moved!	
	Open!	
	Other!	
	PageDown!	
	PageLeft!	
	PageRight!	
	PageUp!	
	PictureSelected!	
	PipeEnd!	
	PipeMeter!	
	PipeStart!	
	PrintEnd!	
	PrintFooter!	

Category	Values	Comments
	PrintHeader!	
	PrintPage!	
	PrintStart!	
	RButtonDown!	
	RButtonUp!	
	RemoteExec!	
	RemoteHotLinkStart!	
	RemoteHotLinkStop!	
	RemoteRequest!	
	RemoteSend!	
	Resize!	
	RetrieveEnd!	
	RetrieveRow!	
	RetrieveStart!	
	RightClicked!	
	RightDoubleClicked!	
	RowFocusChanged!	
	Save!	
	ScrollHorizontal!	
	ScrollVertical!	
	Selected!	
	SelectionChanged!	
	SelectionChanging!	
	Show!	
	Sort!	
	SQLPreview!	
	SystemError!	
	Timer!	
	ToolBarMoved!	
	UpdateEnd!	
	UpdateStart!	
	ViewChange!	
UserObjects	CustomVisual!	The type of user object.
	ExternalVisual!	
	vbxVisual!	
VTextAlign	Bottom!	The alignment of text.
	MultiLine!	
	Top!	
	VCenter!	
WindowState	Maximized!	The state in which the window or program will run.
	Minimized!	
	Normal!	

continues

Part

VII

Ch

28

Table 28.1   Continued

Category	Values	Comments
WindowType	Child! Main! MDI! MDIHelp! Popup! Response!	Type of window.
WriteMode	Append! Replace!	The mode for the FileOpen function.

From Here...

Enumerated data types allow the developer to code PowerScript without constantly looking up accepted values. They also aid in the maintenance of a system. For a list of functions that require enumerated data types, refer to the following chapters:

■ Chapter 6, "Using Events, Functions, and the PowerScript Language," describes the basic PowerScript programming language. It's a must for the beginner.

■ Chapter 25, "Function Quick Reference," shows all the functions used inside PowerBuilder, starting with stand-alone functions and moving on to functions specific to an object or control.

■ Chapter 26, "Event Quick Reference," shows all the events used inside PowerBuilder objects and controls.

You could also check out the online help system for help on the enumerated data types or the Function reference provided with PowerBuilder to list how functions use enumerated data types.

CHAPTER 29

Message Quick Reference

by Charles A. Wood

No matter how well you design and implement your system, situations will come up in your application that need to be handled. You already have coded some error handling. This reference discusses ways to handle errors and lists the errors, the corresponding error message, and the meaning of the error. ■

Handling PowerBuilder Messages

PowerBuilder errors are usually handled through the SystemError event in the application object. The exact error that occurred is stored in PowerBuilder's Error object structure.

SystemError Event

You already have coded the SystemError application event. The SystemError event is executed when a serious run-time error occurs. If you don't write a SystemError script, PowerBuilder attempts to handle the error by displaying a message box containing the error number, error message, and Yes and No buttons, so the user can either continue or stop the application.

If the SystemError event has a script, PowerBuilder executes the script instead of displaying the message box. In the script for the SystemError event, you usually access the Error object to determine the error and where the error occurred.

If you want to handle specific errors, usually CHOOSE CASE or IF statements are used. To halt the application, a HALT or HALT CLOSE is used.

Error Object

In the application object's SystemError event, you can access the Error object to determine the error and where the error occurred. To access the error object, statements like the following are executed:

```
int answer
If Error.Number = 1 then
answer = Messagebox("System Error", &
+ "You tried to divide by zero at line " &
+ string(Error.Line) &
+ " in the " &
+ Error.ObjectEvent &
+ " event of the " &
+ Error.Object &
+ "."
End If
```

The Error object structure is defined in table 24.1.

Table 24.1 Error Object Structure

Error Structure Variable	Data Type	Purpose for Variable
Error.Number	Integer	An integer identifying the PowerBuilder error.
Error.Text	String	A string containing the text of the error message.
Error.WindowMenu	String	A string containing the name of the Window or Menu object in which the error occurred.

Error Structure Variable	Data Type	Purpose for Variable
Error.Object	String	A string containing the name of the object in which the error occurred. If the error occurred in a window or menu, Object will be the same as WindowMenu.
Error.ObjectEvent	String	A string containing the event for which the error occurred.
Error.Line	Integer	An integer identifying the line in the script at which the error occurred.

SignalError() Function

Sometimes you'll want to initiate an error in an application. To do this, use the SignalError() function. SignalError() invokes the application SystemError event. To use SignalError(), move values into the Error Object and use the SystemError event.

NOTE The SignalError() function returns 1 if successful and -1 if an error occurs, but usually the return value is not tested. ■

Following is an example of the use of the SignalError function. First assume that a file that should exist on the system has been deleted. The signal error function triggers a custom SystemError event.

```
error.number = 99
error.text = "File not found! Please Restore!"
error.windowmenu = "w_window"
error.object = "cb_openfile"
error.ObjectEvent = "Clicked!"
error.line = 5
SignalError ( )
```

Run-Time Errors

Table 24.2 is a list of PowerBuilder errors, the corresponding message, and the meaning and/or probable cause of the PowerBuilder error.

Table 24.2 PowerBuilder Error Messages

Number	Message	Meaning
1	Divide by zero	You tried to divide by zero. Probably one of your variables was inadvertently set to zero.
2	Null object	You tried to access a variable reference or object that has not been declared or opened yet.

continues

Table 24.2 Continued

Number	Message	Meaning
3	Array boundary	You have declared an array but exceeded the upper limit. This happens often with variable length arrays that are set with the first access.
4	Enumerated value	The function you have called requires an enumerated data type. The value you passed the function is out of range for the enumerated data type.
5	Negative value	This is a low level error that occurs when a function tries to reference a negative memory address.
6	Invalid DataWindow	You tried a DataWindow row row/column specified function on a row that doesn't exist in your DataWindow, or you tried to access a column (probably with a string) that does not exist. This happens often when you misspell a column name.
7	Unresolvable	Some DLLs can have multiple external functions that use the same name. If this happens, PowerBuilder will not be able to resolve which function to call.
8	Reference of array	The offset integer you used with NULL subscript with your array has been set to NULL. This happens often if an SQL call to fill your offset integer has failed.
9	DLL function not found in current application	You made a function call to a DLL but deleted the reference to it in the external references.
10	Unsupported argument type in DLL	A function in your DLL requires an argument whose data type is not supported in PowerBuilder.
12	DataWindow column does not match GetItem type	You issued a GetItem function, but the type of variable listed in the GetItem function is not the type of variable declared on the DataWindow.
13	Unresolved attribute reference	The attribute you are trying to set does not exist for this object. This happens when you use a PowerObject variable type to store an object, and then try to reference an attribute of that variable type.
14	Error opening DLL library for external function	The DLL you specified in your external definition does not exist or cannot be opened for some reason. A corrupted DLL will also cause this message.

Number	Message	Meaning
15	Error calling external function	You tried to link your program with a function inside an external DLL, but PowerBuilder could not find the function. This happens often when you misspell the function name. Also, some C and especially some C++ programs perform "name maligning" to support polymorphism. Name Maligning must be turned off for PowerBuilder to access your DLL.
16	Maximum string size exceeded	Strings can only be 32K in PowerBuilder. Somehow you have exceeded this. Look for a runaway loop.
17	DataWindow referenced in does not exist	You tried to define a DDDW (Drop Down DataWindow) in your DataWindow that does not exist.
50	Application Reference could not be resolved	You have made a reference in your application that has one or more possible reference targets.
51	Failure loading dynamic library	You declared a dynamic library resource that does not exist.

Handling Sybase SQL Anywhere Messages

Sybase SQL Anywhere also has error messages. These messages are listed alphabetically in a quick reference format, as well as in a descriptive format, in your Sybase SQL Anywhere book that comes with PowerBuilder. Table 24.3 gives you quick access to all your SQL Anywhere SQLDBCODE messages, and lets you limit the number of books you have to carry around with you.

N O T E An '%s' in table 24.3 refers to a string in the message that SQL Anywhere passes back to the application. ▪

Table 24.3 Sybase SQL Anywhere Messages

SQLDBCODE	Description of Message
0	(No error and no message)
100	Row not found
101	Value truncated
102	Using temporary table
103	Invalid data conversion
104	Row has been updated since last time read

continues

Table 24.3 Continued

SQLDBCODE	Description of Message
105	Open or Resume has caused a stored procedure to execute to completion or a cursor to restart
200	Warning
400	The supplied buffer was too small to hold all requested query results
-073	Communication buffer underflow
-074	Database is in an inactive state
-075	Access was denied
-076	No loaded databases
-077	Database name is conflicting with the name of another loaded database
-078	Could not allocate dynamic memory
-079	Bad switch has passed
-080	Unable to start database engine
-081	Invalid database engine command line
-082	Unable to start specified database
-083	Specified database not found
-084	Specified database is invalid
-085	Communication error
-086	Not enough memory to start
-087	Database name required to start engine
-088	Client/server communications protocol mismatch
-089	Database engine not running in multi-user mode
-095	Could not parse string parameter in a START command
-096	Database engine is already running
-097	The database page size is too big
-098	Authentication violation
-099	Connections to database have been disabled
-100	Database engine not running
-101	Not connected to SQL database
-102	Too many connections to database
-103	Invalid UserID or password

SQLDBCODE	Description of Message
-104	Invalid UserID and password on preprocessed module
-105	Cannot be started — '%s'
-106	Cannot open log file '%s'
-107	Error writing to log file
-108	Connection not found
-109	There are still active database connections
-110	'%s' already exists
-111	Index name '%s' not unique
-112	Table already has a primary key
-113	Column '%s' in foreign key has a different definition than primary key
-114	Number of columns does not match SELECT
-116	Table must be empty
-118	Table '%s' has no primary key
-119	Primary key column '%s' already defined
-120	'%s' already has grant permission
-121	Do not have permission to '%s'
-122	Operation would cause a group cycle
-123	'%s' is not a user group
-125	ALTER clause conflict
-126	Table cannot have two primary keys
-127	Cannot alter a column in an index
-128	Cannot drop a user that owns tables in run-time engine
-130	Invalid statement
-131	Syntax error near '%s'
-132	SQL statement error
-133	Invalid prepared statement type
-134	'%s' not implemented
-135	Language extension
-136	A table is in an outer join cycle
-137	A table requires a unique correlation name

continues

Table 24.3 Continued

SQLDBCODE	Description of Message
-138	Tablespace could not be found
-139	More than one table is identified as '%s'
-140	UserID could not be found
-141	Table '%s' not found
-142	Correlation name '%s' not found
-143	Column '%s' not found
-144	Column '%s' found in more than one table—need a correlation name
-145	Foreign key name '%s' not found
-146	No way to join '%s' to '%s'
-147	More than one way to join '%s' to '%s'
-148	Unknown function '%s'
-149	Column '%s' cannot be used unless it is in a GROUP BY
-150	Aggregate functions not allowed on this statement
-151	Subquery allowed only one select list item
-152	Number in ORDER BY is too large
-153	SELECT lists in UNION do not match in length
-154	Wrong number of parameters to function '%s'
-155	Invalid host variable
-156	Invalid expression near '%s'
-157	Cannot convert '%s' to a '%s'
-158	Value '%s' too large for destination
-159	Invalid column number
-160	Can only describe a SELECT statement
-161	Invalid type on DESCRIBE statement
-170	Cursor has not been declared
-172	Cursor already open
-180	Cursor not open
-181	No indicator variable provided for NULL result
-182	Not enough fields allocated in SQLDA
-183	Cannot find index named '%s'

SQLDBCODE	Description of Message
-184	Error inserting into cursor
-185	SELECT returns more than one row
-186	Subquery cannot return more than one result
-187	Invalid operation for this cursor
-188	Not enough values for host variables
-189	Unable to find in index '%s' for table '%s'
-190	Cannot update an expression
-191	Cannot modify column '%s' in table '%s'
-192	Invalid operation on joined tables
-193	Primary key for table '%s' is not unique
-194	No primary key value for foreign key '%s' in table '%s'
-195	Column '%s' in table '%s' cannot be NULL
-196	Index '%s' for table '%s' would not be unique
-197	No current row of cursor
-198	Primary key for row in table '%s' is referenced in another table
-199	INSERT/DELETE on cursor can modify only one table
-200	Invalid option '%s'—no PUBLIC setting exists
-201	Invalid setting for option '%s'
-207	Wrong number of values for INSERT
-208	Row has changed since last read—operation canceled
-209	Invalid value for column '%s' in table '%s'
-210	'%s' has the row in '%s' locked
-211	Not allowed while '%s' is using the database
-212	CHECKPOINT command requires a rollback log
-213	SAVEPOINT was attempted without a rollback log
-214	Table in use
-215	Procedure in use
-220	Subtransaction '%s' not found
-221	Tried to rollback within an atomic compound statement

continues

Table 24.3   Continued

SQLDBCODE	Description of Message
-222	SELECT without INTO or a RESULT CURSOR was attempted within an atomic compound statement
-230	Sqlpp/dblib version mismatch
-231	Dblib/database engine version mismatch
-232	Server/database engine version mismatch
-240	Unknown backup operation
-241	Database backup not started
-242	Incomplete transactions prevent transaction log renaming
-243	Unable to delete database file
-250	Identifier '%s' too long
-251	Foreign key '%s' for table '%s' duplicates an existing foreign key
-260	Variable '%s' not found
-261	Already a variable named '%s'
-262	Label '%s' not found
-263	Invalid absolute or relative offset in FETCH
-264	Wrong number of variables in FETCH
-265	Procedure '%s' not found
-266	Database was initialized with an older version of the software
-267	COMMIT/ROLLBACK not allowed within ATOMIC compound statement
-268	Trigger '%s' not found
-269	Cannot delete a column referenced in a trigger definition
-270	Cannot drop a user that owns procedures in run-time engine
-271	Trigger could not be created because of conflicts with an existing trigger
-272	Invalid REFERENCES clause in trigger definition
-273	COMMIT/ROLLBACK not allowed within trigger actions
-274	Infinite loop caused by a procedure or trigger
-275	Triggers and procedures are not supported in run-time engine
-280	Publication is not found
-297	Stored procedure or trigger signaled a user-defined exception

SQLDBCODE	Description of Message
-298	Attempted two active database requests
-299	Statement interrupted by user
-300	Run-time SQL error—'%s'
-301	Internal database error '%s' transaction rolled back
-302	Terminated by user transaction rolled back
-304	Disk full transaction rolled back
-305	I/O error '%s' transaction rolled back
-306	Deadlock detected
-307	All threads are blocked

From Here...

Messages are important to check during any system error or DBError event, and return codes should *always* be checked after using embedded SQL.

For more information about checking messages, check out the following chapters:

- Chapter 7, "Programming in PowerScript," shows you basic coding practices in PowerScript.
- Chapter 8, "Using SQL in PowerBuilder," details how to code embedded SQL in your PowerBuilder application.
- Appendix B, "Using SQL Anywhere Database and SQL Anywhere," goes into detail on how to use SQL Anywhere.

Appendixes

Using Naming Conventions

by Charles A. Wood

The naming conventions in this appendix are suggestions. Use the ones that best suit your needs—the important thing is to use naming conventions while developing. They make maintenance and debugging much easier.

These naming conventions rely on a prefix that indicates exactly what kind of variable or data you are dealing with. ■

Naming Objects

PowerBuilder uses seven object types within an application to build its systems. Table A.1 shows the naming conventions for object types.

Table A.1   Naming Object Types

Object Name	Convention	Example
DataWindow Object	d_	d_client
Function (global)	f_	f_display_error
Menu	m_	m_client
Project	p_	p_inventory_tracking
Structure	s_	s_employee
Query	q_	q_clients_for_agent
User Object	u_	u_request
Window	w_	w_ancestor

Naming Window Controls

Every window can have several controls. These controls have default names, but should be renamed to be more descriptive and to make your application more manageable. Table A.2 shows the suggested window control prefixes.

Table A.2   Naming Window Controls

Control Name	Convention	Example
CheckBox	cbx_	cbx_draft
CommandButton	cb_	cb_OK
DataWindow Control	dw_	dw_data
DropDownListBox	ddlb_	ddlb_agents
Edit Mask	em_	em_phone
Window Function	wf_	wf_sqlerr
Graph	gr_	gr_income_per_agent
GroupBox	gb_	gb_output_choice

Control Name	Convention	Example
HScrollBar	hsb_	hsb_red
Line	ln_	ln_shortline
ListBox	lb_	lb_agents
ListView	lv_	lv_files
MultiLineEdit	mle_	mle_comments
Oval	oval_	oval_team
Picture	p_	p_employee
PictureButton	pb_	pb_update
RadioButton	rb_	rb_construction
Rectangle	r_	r_rect
RichTextEdit	rte_	rte_document
RoundRectangle	rr_	rr_screen
SingleLineEdit	sle_	sle_customer_name
StaticText	st_	st_customer_prompt
TabControl	t_	t_entry_screens
TreeView	tv_	tv_directories
UserObject	uo_	uo_request
VScrollBar	vsb_	vsb_percent_done

App

A

Naming Variables

Every variable has a scope (when it can be accessed) and a data type. The scope should always be as limited as possible. For example, don't use an instance variable when a local variable will suffice. Limiting scope will aid in encapsulation, release memory sooner and make the application easier to maintain.

In the variable scope, x indicates the data-type convention that follows the variable-scope conventions.

Naming by Scope

Table A.3 describes the conventions for naming by scope.

Table A.3   Naming by Scope

Variable Scope	Convention
Local	lx_ or nothing (a prefix on local variables is optional)
Global	gx_
Instance	ix_
Shared	sx_
Argument	ax_

Naming by Data Type

Table A.4 describes the conventions for naming by data type.

Table A.4   Naming by Data Type

Data Type	Convention
Window	w
MenuItem	m
DataWindow Control	dw
Structure	str
User Object	uo
Integer	i
Unsigned Integer	ui
Long	l
Unsigned Long	ul
Boolean	b
String	s
Double	db
Real	r
Decimal	dc
Date	d
Time	t
DateTime	dt or ts (TimeStamp)

Naming Variable Examples

Table A.5 lists naming variable examples.

Table A.5   Naming Variable Examples

Variable Name	Data Type Description
sstr_data_points[ ]	Shared structure array
iul_client_id	Instance of an unsigned long
ss_name	Shared string
ii_count	Instance of an integer
loop_count	Local variable (prefix not required)
li_loop_count	Local integer (optional prefix added)
lw_window_instance	Local instance of a window variable
as_error	Argument string (passed)

Object Functions

Along with global functions, functions can be attached to individual objects. The object prefix should precede the function prefix to indicate a function that is tied to a specific object.

Table A.6 describes naming object functions.

Table A.6   Naming Object Functions

Function Object Type	Convention	Example
Global function	f_	f_sql_error
Menu function	mf_	mf_exit
User Object function	uf_	uf_request
Window function	wf_	wf_update

Using SQL Anywhere Database and SQL Anywhere

by Scott L. Warner

Sybase SQLAnywhere is one of the many databases supported by PowerBuilder. A development copy of SQLAnywhere is included in every version of PowerBuilder as well as other Powersoft products like InfoMaker.

If you've used Watcom SQL in the past but felt the product wasn't meeting your needs, you may be in for a surprise! Sybase SQLAnywhere has increased performance and enhanced high-level features such as stored procedures, triggers, cascading updates and deletes, multiple database-single server support, and temporary tables. These features were in the latest version of Watcom SQL but this Sybase version has definitely improved them.

If money is a factor or if you have a limited support staff coupled with a department-wide or peer-to-peer database, or want to distribute a stand-alone copy of your work, SQLAnywhere should be your database of choice. ■

Understanding SQL Anywhere Files

SQLAnywhere uses DOS files to store data. These files include the .DB file, .LOG file, and several temporary files used for processing. The .LOG and .DB files are defined in this section.

Understanding the SQL Anywhere DB (Database) File

All your tables go into a single database (DB) file on your hard drive. All the tables that are created in the database painter in chapter 2 are stored in the INVENTRY.DB file. Your database file (INVENTRY.DB) should be backed up on a regular basis using backup software or the backup utility that comes with Windows 95.

Understanding the SQL Anywhere LOG (Transaction Log) File

Your PowerBuilder SQLAnywhere application also generates a log, which is a file with a LOG extension. (The Inventory Tracking system described in this book uses INVENTRY.LOG.) This log file is called the transaction log or the forward log file. The transaction log is optional when the database is created, but if created inside PowerBuilder, the transaction log always exists.

The log is used to record transactions to the database. Without a log, SQLAnywhere is forced to perform a checkpoint every time you write to disk. (A checkpoint writes a copy of any updates you make to the hard disk into a temporary file.) Often, this can slow down database updates.

A transaction log is also used to make SQLAnywhere more stable. If the SQLAnywhere database file was corrupted, the transaction log and the previous backup could be used to restore your database up to the moment of failure! This is because all database transactions are recorded in the transaction log.

If you have a machine with two physical hard drives, it's good to write the log to a separate hard drive from the database. If the disk with the database file crashes, the transaction log will remain intact on the other hard drive. The transaction log can then be used to restore the database.

SQLAnywhere defaults to using a transaction log with the same file name as your .DB file but with a .LOG extension (for example, INVENTRY.LOG). You can change the default status of your log with the DBINIT program when you create your database. You can also change the log settings of a database with the DBLOG program if your database is in existence, or convert your log to SQL using the DBTRAN program. These SQLAnywhere programs are included with PowerBuilder, and are discussed in the next section.

Using SQL Anywhere

The PowerBuilder version of SQLAnywhere includes several programs that can help you manage your SQLAnywhere database—especially upon distribution. These programs are on your disk and are probably in either your PowerBuilder directory or your SQLAny(where) directory (depending on which directory you chose). Examples are given later in this chapter.

SQLAnywhere programs will not run within the PowerBuilder environment. It is necessary to run the SQLAnywhere programs by opening the Start menu and choosing Run in Windows 95. Several of the programs take command line options, but you also can run them through an icon if you want to set one up.

This documentation will discuss the purpose of each program. If the syntax documentation provided by PowerBuilder is incomplete, a fuller syntax definition will follow. All of the programs are included with PowerBuilder, but are run outside of the PowerBuilder environment. However, many can be duplicated with the database painter from within the PowerBuilder environment.

App

B

Understanding Connection Parameters

SQLAnywhere commands establish connections to databases. These commands can be cryptic and hard to use. In SQLAnywhere, connection parameters are clearly marked.

Connection parameters are used when you want to connect to a database. Commands that use connection parameters are DBBACKUP, DBUNLOAD, DBVALID, DBWATCH, and ISQL. (These commands are reviewed later in this section.) Table B.1 lists the verbose keyword, the short form of the keyword, an example of how to use the connection parameter, and a description of each.

Table B.1 Command Parameters

Verbose Keyword	Short Form	Example	Description
Userid	UID	UID=dba	The user id defined in the Grant SQL statement.
Password	PWD	PWD=SQL	The password of the user id.
Connection	CON	CON=conn1	The name of the connection used to connect to the database (for multiple database connections).
EngineName	ENG	ENG=Sample	The name of the ODBC engine to start.
Database Name	DBN	DBN=Powersoft	The name of the Demo DB database assigned by the database configuration in the database painter.
Datasource Name	DSN	DSN=Sybase	The name that identifies the location of information about a database in the odbc.ini file.
Database File	DBF	DBF=\wsql\	The file of the sample.db database.
DatabaseSwitches	DBS	DBS=-d	Switches used in the database.

continues

Table B.1   Continued

Verbose Keyword	Short Form	Example	Description
AutoStop	AutoStop	AutoStop	(In PB.INI, use AUTOSTOP=TRUE) Disconnects from the database after the command that's using the connection parameters is finished if there are no other connections to the database.
Start	Start	Start=DB32W	The name of the SQLAnywhere program used to start the database Engine.

The following is an example of how to use a connection parameter:

```
UID=dba;PWD=sql;ENG=sample
```

You'll notice this line is similar to the CONNECTSTRING parameter found in the PB.INI file. You can also connect using positional parameters without qualifiers as was necessary in PowerBuilder 3 as follows:

```
dba,sql,sample
```

Using the old positional connection parameters will connect to a database engine, but using positional connection parameters will disable the use of multiple databases running on one server.

Using Dbeng50.EXE, DBSTART.EXE

SQLAnywhere programs Dbeng50.EXE and DBSTART.EXE are the SQLAnywhere database engines. You choose one of the database engines when starting your database to describe the access your program will have when your database is running.

The database engines are the only SQLAnywhere program that you can run within PowerBuilder. To define your database engine, get into the database painter by clicking the Database icon. Then click File and choose Configure ODBC. The Configure ODBC dialog box appears. Click the database driver for your database and choose your database (data source).

This pulls up the SQLAnywhere ODBC Configuration dialog box. In the Execute text box, type in the database engine with flags that you want to use.

The syntax for the SQLAnywhere start program is as follows:

```
program_name [flags] database_file
```

program_name can be Dbeng50 or DBSTART.

database_file is the name of the database file on your hard drive. (For the Inventory Tracking database, it is INVENTRY.DB.)

Flags   The flags in use are as follows:

- @environment-variable. Command-line switches can be supplied using an environment variable. The environment variable may contain any combination of command line switches. Below, several switches are set and passed as parameters using an environment variable:

```
set envvar=-c 4096 c:\sqlany50\sademo.db

DBENG50 @envvar
```

- -b   Use Bulk mode. Although this is handy for large quantities of data at a time, it is not recommended for everyday use because it forces autocommit (which commits automatically after every SQL instruction) and only allows one user.

- -c   Set cache size. This is a number that sets the size of the cache. Any cache size less than 10,000 is assumed to be kilobytes (K). If an M is placed at the end of the number, megabytes is assumed. By default, the database uses 2M cache.

- -n   Set the name of the database engine. By default, the name is the name of the database file. (For the Inventory Tracking system, the default is INVENTRY.)

- -q   Quiet mode. Don't print any messages.

- -v   Log old values of columns on SQL Updates as opposed to only enough information to uniquely identify the key. This is useful if you are working on a copy of the database.

- -a translog   Apply the transaction log named by translog. This option applies the log and then terminates.

- -f   Force-start the database. This starts the database without a log, and immediately terminates. This is handy for clearing the database once the log has been lost.

- -d   Use synchronous I/O rather than asynchronous I/O. Asynchronous I/O is generally the preferred option.

- -di   For DOS and Windows 3.x database engines and servers only. If you supply the -di switch, the database engine uses low-level direct calls rather than normal DOS calls where possible.

- -ga   Applications can cause databases to be started and stopped. This switch causes the engine to shut down when the last database is stopped.

- -gb level   OS/2 and Windows NT only. This switch sets the database process priority class to level. Level must be one of idle, normal (the default), high, or maximum. Low and high are the commonly used settings.

- -gc num   This switch sets the maximum desired length of time (in minutes) that the database engine will run without doing a checkpoint. When multiple databases are running, the checkpoint time specified by the first database started will be used unless overridden by this switch.

- -gd level   Set the database starting permission to level. The level can be one of the following (default setting is all):

    dba, all, none

- -ge size   Sets the stack size for threads running external functions. The default is 16384 bytes (16K). Used only for OS/2, Windows NT, and NetWare.

- -gf   Disable firing of triggers by the engine.

- -gn num   Sets the number of execution threads used in the database engine while running with multiple users. When multiple databases are opened, the thread count specified by the first database started will be used unless overridden by this switch.

- -gp size   Sets the maximum page size allowed, in bytes. The size specified must be one of: 512, 1024, 2048, or 4096.

- -gr num   Set the maximum desired length of time (in minutes) that the database engine will take to recover from system failure. When multiple databases are opened, the recovery time specified by the first database started will be used unless overridden by this switch.

- -gs size   Sets the stack size of every thread in the engine. The value entered is multiplied by four to produce the stack size in bytes.

- -gx   Disable dual threading. This option is available for the Windows 95, Windows NT, OS/2, and NetWare versions.

TROUBLESHOOTING

My SQLAnywhere program works fine on my computer and on all computers with PowerBuilder or SQLAnywhere installed, but when I try to make a stand-alone version, I can't access the database. What should I do? SQLAnywhere requires support files to be distributed stand-alone databases in order for them to work properly. Without these files, run-time errors will occur.

Using DBBACKUP.EXE

DBBACKUP makes a backup copy of all the files that make up a single database, which include all tablespaces and log files. From here, you also can erase and restart your transaction file. An example of the function call is as follows:

```
DBBACKUP -c UID=dba,PWD=sql,ENG=inventry \book\inventry
```

In the DBBACKUP command, you can specify the database and where it's located. For a complete description on uses of the DBBACKUP command, see your Watcom SQL reference manual.

Using DBCOLLAT.EXE

This extracts a *collation* (sorting sequence) from your database, suitable for use with DBINIT, to create a database using a custom collation. This is for the really advanced database power user. A *custom collation* is a sort order that is not ascending or descending. For instance, if you want city names to appear in ZIP code order when indexing your file, you can use a custom collation. DBCOLLAT extracts that collation, if one exists.

The syntax for DBCOLLAT is as follows:

```
DBCOLLAT [flags] output_file
```

The flags are as follows:

- -c [connection parameters]   Supply the database-connection parameters.
- -e   Include empty mappings. Normally, collations don't specify the actual value that a character is to sort to. Instead, each line of the collation sequence sorts to one higher than the last one. However, older collations have gaps between some sort positions. DBCOLLAT skips these gaps unless the -e flag is specified.
- -o filename   Output log messages to file.
- -q   Quiet mode. Don't print any messages.
- -x   Use hex for extended characters. Some sites support extended characters, especially for foreign languages. If an extended character goes above hex 7F, this flag converts the character to a two-digit hexadecimal number.
- -y   Replace the existing output file without asking for permission.
- -z col-seq   Specify the collating sequence label. Use this if the label is different than the one being used by the database.

output_file is the name of the file you want to place your collating sequence in.

Using DBERASE.EXE

DBERASE erases a database, log file, or write file. This is useful because SQLAnywhere database and log files are marked read-only. The format for DBERASE is as follows:

```
DBERASE [flags] filename
```

The flags are as follows:

- -o   Output log messages to file.
- -q   Do not print any messages.
- -y   Erase database without confirmation.

filename is the name of the log file, database file, or write file you wish to delete.

Using DBEXPAND.EXE

DBEXPAND expands a compressed database created by DBSHRINW, which is a good method for distribution. The format for DBEXPAND is:

```
DBEXPANd [flags] compressed_file database
```

The flags are as follows:

- -q   Do not print any messages.
- -y   Operate without confirming actions.

compressed_file is the name of the compressed file created by DBSHRINW. If no extension is listed, a .CDB extension is used.

database is the name of the database you want to create. If no extension is listed, a .DB extension is used.

Using DBINFO.EXE

DBINFO displays information about a database file or write file, including the options that were used to create the database, the name of the transaction log file, and other information. The database engine shouldn't be running when you run DBINFO. The format for DBINFO is:

```
DBINFO [flags] filename
```

The flags are as follows:

- ■ -c[connection parameters]   Supply the database-connection parameters.
- ■ -o   Output messages to a file.
- ■ -q   Do not print any messages.
- ■ -u   Output page-usage statistics.

filename is the name of the database or write file that you want information about.

Using DBINIT.EXE

This creates a new database. An example of its use is as follows:

```
DBINIT INVENTRY.DB
```

The SQLAnywhere manual provided with PowerBuilder does a fine job describing DBINIT, except that you can also use the -l flag to list available collating sequences.

Using DBLOG.EXE

DBLOG is used to display or change the name of the transaction log. Its format is as follows:

```
DBLOG [flags] database
```

The flags are as follows:

- ■ -m mirror-name   Set transaction log mirror name.
- ■ -n   Do not use a transaction log.
- ■ -o   Output messages to file.
- ■ -q   Do not print any messages.
- ■ -r   No longer use a transaction log mirror.
- ■ -t log_name   Change the name of the transaction log file to log_name.

database is the name of the database you want to access.

Using **DBSHRINK.EXE**

DBSHRINK compresses a database that can later be expanded using DBEXPAND. This is a good method for distribution. The format for DBSHRINK is:

```
DBSHRINK [flags] database compressed_file
```

The flags are as follows:

- -q Do not print any messages.
- -y Erase existing output file without confirmation.

database is the name of the database you want to compress. If no extension is listed, a .DB extension is used.

compressed_file is the name of the compressed file to be created. If no extension is listed, a .CDB extension is used.

Using **DBTRAN.EXE**

DBTRAN translates the log file into an ASCII SQL command file. An example of DBTRAN is as follows:

```
DBTRAN INVENTRY.LOG INVENTRY.SQL
```

This command translates the inventory transaction log file to INVENTRY.SQL.

Using **DBUNLOAD.EXE**

DBUNLOAD is used to unload a database into an ASCII file containing SQL statements called RELOAD.SQL (unless you use the flags described in the Sybase SQLAnywhere manual to change the name of your output file). An example of DBUNLOAD is as follows:

```
DBUNLOAD -c UID=dba,PWD=sql,ENG=inventry \book\inventry
```

This command creates RELOAD.SQL in the \book\inventry directory, which will contain SQL calls to duplicate the inventory database.

Using **DBVALID.EXE**

DBVALID validates all indexes on a table in the database. It is good to use in conjunction with DBBACKUP. An example of DBVALID is as follows:

```
DBVALID -c UID=dba,PWD=sql,ENG=inventry
```

The above statement validates the item table in the inventory database.

 TIP Write files are good to use for testing because they don't allow corruption or data manipulation of the database.

Using DBWRITE.EXE

DBWRITE is used to manage database *write files*, which are files that contain all the changes to a particular database, leaving the original database unchanged. An example of starting up a write file using DBWRITE is as follows:

```
DBWRITE \book\inventry\inventry.db \book\inventry\inventry.wrt
```

This statement creates a write file for the inventory database.

Using ISQL.EXE and RTSQL.EXE

ISQL (and RTSQL in the run-time version) allows you to run ASCII files containing interactive SQL statements. Interactive SQL (or ISQL) is a broader set of SQL statements. The format for ISQL and RTSQL is as follows:

```
command [flags] sqlfile/sqlcommand
```

The *command* can be ISQL or RTSQL.

The flags are as follows:

- ■ -b   Do not print banner.
- ■ -c [connection_parameters]   Supply the database-connection parameters.
- ■ -q   Do not print any messages.
- ■ -s "cmd"   The command to start the database. Defaults to DBSTARTW.
- ■ -v   Verbose mode; output information on commands.
- ■ -x   Syntax check only; no commands are executed.

sqlfile/sqlcommand can either be a single command or an SQL file containing many SQL commands.

RTSQL is really useful for installation programs—you can issue ISQL commands that aren't available to you in PowerScript.

Exploring Embedded SQL and ISQL

Embedded SQL is the SQL you can use within a programming language such as PowerScript. ISQL or interactive SQL is SQL that can be used from the ISQL and RTSQL programs.

There are several ISQL commands that are useful, especially in installation programs (they aren't available in PowerScript). A listing of available commands can be reviewed in the Listing ISQL Commands section later in this chapter.

Comparing the Run-Time Version and the Developer's Version

There are certain commands you can run in PowerScript or in ISQL that aren't available when using RTSQL. Inconsistencies between the developer's version of SQLAnywhere and the run-time version of SQLAnywhere can cause many problems if you're running under one environment but distributing under another.

Using the run-time version, you can't issue any CREATE, ALTER, or DROP SQL statements. Although they work in your test environment, they no longer work when you distribute with the run-time environment.

Using RTSQL or ISQL, you can execute your own SQL. In a DOS editor, create your SQL statements in an ASCII file. The following command runs the SQL commands in sqlfil.sql against the Inventory Tracking database:

```
\pb3\RTSQL.EXE -v -c dba,sql,\book\inventry\inventry
Â\book\inventry\sqlfil
```

In the above example, inventry is the database and sqlfil is the file with the SQL statements.

 TIP When using the RTSQL program, if you leave off the extension on your database or your SQL file, .DB or .SQL are assumed.

App B

Listing ISQL Commands

No ISQL commands appear in the SQLAnywhere. This section lists ISQL commands available to you through RTSQL and ISQL.

Using CONFIGURE

CONFIGURE allows you to design your database environment. The syntax for the CONFIGURE command is simply:

```
CONFIGURE;
```

The CONFIGURE command pulls up the ISQL Configuration dialog box which allows you to configure your ISQL commands.

 TIP The -v flag on the RTSQL command forces verbose messages. By typing CONFIGURE at the end of your SQL file, you force the RTSQL program to stop at the end until you're ready to go on.

Using Variables

Variables can be used inside an SQL script. Where typically you need a programming language to use variables, Sybase gives the developer the capability to declare variables without resorting to programming in a conventional language like PowerScript. You can manipulate variables with the following SQLAnywhere commands:

```
CREATE VARIABLE identifier data_type
SET identifier = constant or identifier;
DROP VARIABLE identifier;
```

The CREATE VARIABLE statement creates a variable in SQL and specifies a data_type. The variable created contains a NULL until it is set by the SET command. The DROP VARIABLE command releases the variable. The variable is dropped at disconnect if no drop statement is made.

Assume the following rows exist on the Customer table:

customer number	customer name	customer contact	customer address1
1	Zeppelins and Blimps	Robert Plant	123 4th St.
2	Silver Bullets and More	Bob Seger	231 123rd St.
3	Queen Headgear	Freddie Mercury	33 Bohemian Avenue
4	Grapes, Nuts, and Health Foods	Euell Gibbons	8 Pine Tree
5	Doors, Inc.	Jim Morrison	23 Stormriders Court

The following ISQL runs through RTSQL:

```
Create Variable avg_cust int;
Set avg_cust = 3;
select customer_name
from customer
where customer_number > avg_cust;
output to \book\inventry\highcust.dat format ASCII;
configure;
The resulting output in \book\inventry\highcust.dat is:
 'Grapes, Nuts, and Health Foods'
 'Doors, Inc.'
```

All customer_names were selected whose corresponding customer number was greater than 3.

TIP If possible, test your SQL function calls through RTSQL using the verbose flag.

Using INPUT

The INPUT command uses a file or the keyboard to place data into a table in the database:

```
INPUT INTO {creator}.table
FROM filename or PROMPT
{ FORMAT filetype }
{ BY NAME }
{ DELIMITED BY string }
{ COLUMN WIDTHS (integer, ....)};
{ NOSTRIP }
{ (column_name,...) };
```

filename. The name of the input file. You can see the PROMPT clause instead of the FROM clause, and the user will be prompted for the file name.

filetype. The type of file format. Allowable formats are ASCII, DBASEII, DBASEIII, DIF, FIXED, LOTUS, SQL, TEXT, and WATFILE. If this clause is left out, INPUT tries to determine the file type on its own.

BY NAME. Allows you to input into a table, based on the name of the field, if your input file format is one that contains column names. If this is left out, INPUT will try to read the input file BY ORDER.

NOSTRIP and DELIMITED BY. For ASCII file formats only. Normally, space padding is stripped out by the INPUT command. The NOSTRIP clause leaves any space padding in. DELIMITED BY string will put a specified delimiter between columns. (The default is commas.)

COLUMN WIDTHS. Valid only for FIXED format. This specifies the width of each column. The default is computed for the data type for that column, and is large enough to hold any value of that data type.

column_names. Allows you to specify which columns will be input and in what order.

Using OUTPUT

```
OUTPUT TO filename
FORMAT filetype
{ DELIMITED BY string }
{ QUOTE quote_string {ALL}}
{ COLUMN WIDTHS (integer, ....)};
```

filename. The name of the output file.

filetype. The type of file format. Allowable formats are ASCII, DBASEII, DBASEIII, DIF, FIXED, LOTUS, SQL, TEXT, and WATFILE.

The DELIMITED BY and QUOTE clauses are for ASCII file formats only. The DELIMITED BY string will put a specified delimiter between columns. (The default is commas.) The quote_string specifies what quote symbol will be placed around string variables (default ' — single quote). It specifies all placed quotes around all columns, not just string columns.

App
B

COLUMN WIDTHS. Valid only for FIXED format. This specifies the width of each column. The default is computed for the data type for that column, and is large enough to hold any value of that data type.

See the CREATE VARIABLE example to view the OUTPUT command.

Using PARAMETERS

```
PARAMETERS parameter1, parameter2, ...
```

PARAMETERS. Allows you to specify input parameters coming in from the command line. If this command is invoked, and those parameters are missing, you are prompted for them.

```
READ filename { parameters}
```

The READ command causes RTSQL to execute a series of SQL commands *filename*. Parameters are needed if a PARAMETER clause is specified; otherwise, they are ignored.

RTSQL issues its own read when you pass it a file name.

```
SET { TEMPORARY } OPTION { UserId. or PUBLIC.}option_name = value;
```

SET OPTION. Allows you to set an option that the end user can set with the CONFIGURE command or during the Watcom installation.

TEMPORARY. Specifies that this option change is valid for the current database connection only.

UserId. Allows you to specify someone else's options. You must have DBA authority to use this.

PUBLIC. Allows you to specify a default option for any user who hasn't set their own options.

Tables B.2 and B.3 show the different options you can specify.

Table B.2   Watcom Database Options

Option	Values	Default
BLOCKING	ON, OFF	ON
CHECKPOINT_TIME	number of minutes	60
CONVERSION_ERROR	ON, OFF	ON
DATE_FORMAT	string	'MM/DD/YYYY'
DATE_ORDER	'YMD,' 'DMY,' 'MDY'	'MDY'
ISOLATION_LEVEL	0, 1, 2, 3	0
PRECISION	number of digits	30
RECOVERY_TIME	number of minutes	2
ROW_COUNTS	ON, OFF	OFF

Option	Values	Default
SCALE	number of digits	6
THREAD_COUNT	number of threads	0
TIME_FORMAT	string	'HH:NN:SS.SSS'
TIMESTAMP_FORMAT	string	'YYYY-MM-DD HH:NN:SS.SSS'
WAIT_FOR_COMMIT	ON, OFF	OFF

Table B.3   ISQL options

Option	Values	Default
AUTO_COMMIT	ON, OFF	OFF
AUTO_REFETCH	ON, OFF	ON
BELL	ON, OFF	ON
COMMIT_ON_EXIT	ON, OFF	ON
ECHO	ON, OFF	ON
HEADINGS	ON, OFF	ON
INPUT_FORMAT	ASCII, FIXED, DIF, DBASE, DBASEII, DBASEIII, LOTUS, WATFILE	ASCII
ISQL_LOG	file_name	'' (empty string)
NULLS	string	'(NULL)'
ON_ERROR	STOP, CONTINUE, PROMPT, EXIT	PROMPT
OUTPUT_FORMAT	ASCII, FIXED, DIF, DBASEII, DBASEIII, LOTUS, SQL, WATFILE	ASCII
OUTPUT_LENGTH	integer	0
STATISTICS	0, 3, 4, 5, 6	3
TRUNCATION_LENGTH	integer	30

Defining the best way to set each of the options listed in the tables is another book in itself. If you have a question about ways to configure your options, contact Powersoft or Sybase technical support. You should also consider buying a full version of SQLAnywhere for your Database Analyst (DBA).

From Here...

Hopefully, there's enough Sybase information here to help you better manage the SQLAnywhere database that came with PowerBuilder. If not, here are some other places you can go for help:

- You can find some information in the SQLAnywhere manual that comes with PowerBuilder.

- If you need more DBA type assistance, don't be shy about calling for technical support. Sybase's technical support is pretty good, and they have a knowledgeable staff.

- Finally, at least one person in your organization should buy a stand-alone copy of SQLAnywhere, if that is the database you're using. The user's guide that accompanies SQLAnywhere is a good reference book.

Implementing Advanced Procedures

by Raghuram Bala

There are some PowerBuilder features not covered in this book that you may want to be aware of. This appendix is designed to inform you of the existence of these features and to perhaps lead you in the right direction if you decide to use them. ■

Using Queries

Queries are used in place of SQL Selects when creating a DataWindow. You can even save your SQL select as a query in the SQL select painter that you get to from the DataWindow painter. Think of a query as a permanent SQL select that can be used with many DataWindows.

To declare a query, click the Query icon. The Select Query dialog box appears, as seen in figure C.1. To start building your query, click New.

FIG. C.1

The Select Query dialog box lets you modify or create a query.

Now you will be allowed to choose which tables go into the query through the familiar Select Tables dialog box, as seen in figure C.2. Choose the tables you want and click Open.

FIG. C.2

The Select Tables dialog box lets you select tables for your query.

Now you are in the query painter, shown in figure C.3. (Look familiar? It should! This painter is identical to the SQL select painter.)

FIG. C.3

Choose the columns you would if you were creating an SQL Select DataWindow, and then save. You can use the finished query as a data source for a DataWindow.

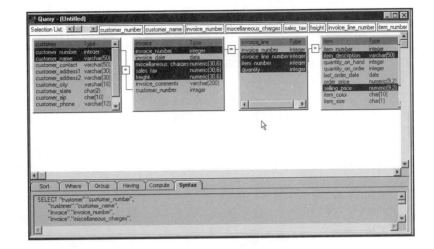

NOTE When a query is used as a data source, it is immediately converted to an SQL select. Later modifications to the query *do not* affect the DataWindow that used that query for a data source.

Because most DataWindows don't share the exact same SELECT (with the exception of DataWindows employing the dwShareData() function), usually a query is not needed, and an SQL Select is used as the data source instead. In fact, most PowerBuilder developers don't use them at all. ■

Using Views

Often, database administrators (DBAs) like to limit the access one has to both data and updatability. To accomplish this, they use views. Views are a cross section of the databases that are used primarily for display.

You need to be in the database painter to create a view. Once in the database painter, you can click the View icon. The Select Tables dialog box opens and lets you select which tables you want for your view (see fig. C.4).

App

C

FIG. C.4

The Select Tables dialog box lets you select tables for your view.

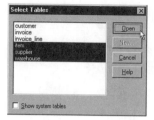

When you're done selecting tables, you are returned to the view painter, as seen in figure C.5. Here you pick the columns you want for your view, and save your view using the Save View Definition dialog box, shown in figure C.6.

FIG. C.5

The view painter allows you to pick the columns for your view.

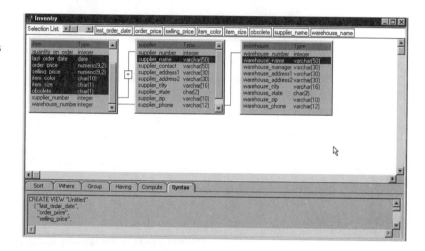

FIG. C.6

The Save View Definition dialog box allows you to name and save your view.

The view is immediately displayed in the database painter, as seen in figure C.7.

FIG. C.7

The view you created is now displayed in the database painter.

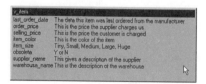

When you double-click your view, instead of getting an Alter Table dialog box as you would with a table in the database painter, you get a Select statement (see fig. C.8), which describes the view you have just created.

FIG. C.8

Instead of an Alter Table dialog box, you get a Select SQL statement when you try to modify the definition of a view.

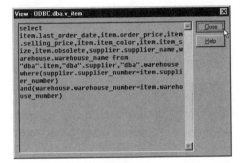

N O T E   The view was dropped after creation from the Inventory Tracking system, because the view was not used by the system. ■

App

C

Using INI Files

In the Inventory Tracking system, all access to the database was hard coded in the application open event. Many PowerBuilder programs instead use an INI file to give the power users greater flexibility. An INI file is an application initialization file that contains variables used by the applications and allows customization of an application by the user.

If an INVENTRY.INI file existed with the following lines:

Listing C.1   The Layout of a Windows Initialization File (INVENTRY.INI)

```
[sqlca]
dbms=ODBC
database=inventry.db
userid=dba
dbpass=sql
logid=
logpass=
servername=
DbParm=ConnectString='DSN=Inventory Tracking;UID=dba;PWD=sql'
```

you could then access that INI file using the ProfileString() PowerBuilder function as follows:

```
sqlca.DBMS     = ProfileString("inventry.ini","sqlca","dbms","")
sqlca.database = ProfileString("inventry.ini","sqlca",
                   Â"database","")
sqlca.userid   = ProfileString("inventry.ini","sqlca",
                   Â"userid","")
```

```
sqlca.dbpass    = ProfileString("inventry.ini","sqlca",
     Â"dbpass","")
sqlca.logid    = ProfileString("inventry.ini","sqlca","logid","")
sqlca.logpass  = ProfileString("inventry.ini","sqlca",
     Â"logpass","")
sqlca.servername = ProfileString("inventry.ini","sqlca",
     Â"servername","")
sqlca.dbparm    = ProfileString("inventry.ini","sqlca",
     Â"dbparm","")
```

In ProfileString (filename, section, key, default), ProfileString allows a PowerBuilder program to access a DOS file. Filename is the name of the file being searched; section is the name of a bracketed entry (for instance, [sqlca]). The key is the specific parameter under the section for which the program is looking, and the default is a string containing the value if no value is found.

In the Inventory Tracking system, you substituted flexibility for security and did not allow the use of an INI file. Many systems, however, include an INI file to allow the user to pass a large set of parameters to the application.

Using the Registry

The Registry is a database that contains information about hardware, software, and users of a machine. Although the Registry is available in Windows 3.1, it plays a more prominent role in Windows 95 and NT and its capabilities have been beefed up significantly. The Registry has in many cases replaced INI files for newer software coming on the market by storing configuration and state information.

Furthermore, the Registry contains entries for OLE-enabled software components. Every OLE component needs to register itself in the registry and publish its interface, that is, the means by which methods can be invoked upon it by external software. For instance, Microsoft Word's external interface is known as "Word.Basic." With this interface, any external program, e.g., your PowerBuilder application, can invoke functions on the Word.Basic object as though it was invoked from within Word.

Advanced users can view and modify the Registry by using REGEDIT.EXE on Windows 95 and REGEDT32.EXE on NT. However, any changes made in the registry can affect your system's performance and must be undertaken carefully if at all. PowerBuilder 5 offers the following new functions to enable your PowerBuilder applications to maintain Registry entries.

Table C.1 Registry Functions

Function	Description
RegistryDelete	Delete a key or value for an entry in the Registry.
RegistryGet	Retrieve value for a particular key from the Registry.
RegistryKeys	Retrieve the subkeys available for a particular key.

Function	Description
RegistrySet	Set or Create a value for a particular key in the Registry.
RegistryValues	Get the set of named values for a particular key.

Designing Dynamic Menus

A frequently asked question on coding techniques is, "How would you provide menu customization at run time?" This question is not easily answered. As discussed in Chapter 5, "Designing Menus," PowerBuilder provides an easy-to-use menu painter for fast development of application menus, but provides only limited functionality to change a menu dynamically.

PowerBuilder menus are not true objects. Rather, they are properties of the parent window to which they are attached. Unlike other PowerBuilder objects, menus do not allow you to define user events. They are lacking the standard methods and attributes, and expose quirks in behavior when you try to modify them dynamically.

You can use a few well-described techniques to customize menus at run time:

- Switch the current menu to a completely different one, using the ChangeMenu() function. This method is useful when two menus have very little in common.
- Define (if applicable) invisible menu items in the original menu and switch the menu items' visibility, using the hide() and share() functions, or by setting the menuitem.visible attribute to either TRUE or FALSE. This method is useful when two windows share the same major set of menu items.

Please note that in both cases, you have to know all menu items and their locations at design time. This may be acceptable when you have just a few menu options you want to enable or disable during run time, but these methods will not be sufficient for the menuing needs of some applications.

Consider these other desired behaviors that cannot be effectively handled using static menus:

- An object or control that is activated on a window dynamically could attach a submenu to the Window's main menu.
- A security system can allow access to application menu options based on the user's profile.

The ultimate solution is to create and attach menu items dynamically. The following techniques demonstrate a proven method of designing menu objects dynamically.

Attaching Menu Item to an Existing Menu

For this example, assume that the menu you are designing is called m_main, and it contains a top-level menu item, m_option. Now add a menu item with the text "A dynamic item" to the end of m_option's submenu list.

Step 1: Create a Menu Object, m_dynamic   This menu should contain only one menu item: m_Item.

Within m_dynamic, declare two instance variables:

```
window iwCreator
string  isNotificationEvent
```

In the PowerScript for the Clicked! event for m_Item item, place the following code:

```
IF IsValid(iwCreator) THEN
iwCreator.TriggerEvent(isNotificationEvent)
 END IF
```

You'll change the value of isNotificationEvent to the name of the event that has to be triggered when the item gets clicked. You'll change the value of iwCreator to the window that has to be notified of that click.

Step 2: Add Your Item   In the window that will eventually process the dynamic menu item's function, declare a user event ue_dynamic_item_clicked. Then, in the clicked event of the "A dynamic item menuitem," place the following code:

Listing C.2   Clicked Event Code for a Dynamic Menu Item

```
 m_main    mCurrentMenu
m_dynamic  mAdditional
int     ii
mCurrentMenu = MenuId
mAdditional = create m_dynamic
mAdditional.m_item.Text = "A dynamic &item"
mAdditional.iwCreator = this
mAdditional.isNotificationEvent = "ue_dynamic_item_clicked"
ii = UpperBound(mCurrentMenu.m_option.Item) + 1
mCurrentMenu.m_option.Item[ii] = mAdditional.m_item
```

Step 3: Force Menu to Redraw   A dynamic menu now is attached! However, the menu is not redrawn, and you can't see any changes yet. To force redrawing of the menu, add two more lines of code:

```
mCurrentMenu.m_option.Item[1].Visible = NOTmCurrentMenu.m_option.Item[1].Visible
mCurrentMenu.m_option.Item[1].Visible = NOTmCurrentMenu.m_option.Item[1].Visible
```

Removing Menu Items

Menu items are collected in arrays. Unfortunately, PowerBuilder does not allow you to reduce the bounds of arrays. If you need to delete an item(s) from an array, create an empty array of the same type, copy the entries you want to keep there, replace the new array in control sequence, and destroy the original one.

Designing a Menu Configuration System

This section will show you how to create menus at execution time based on user profile. It can be used as a part of a security system to allow control of the options available to each user. A complete set of functions and objects for creating and maintaining dynamic menus is included on the *Using PowerBuilder 5 Companion CD* in the DynaMenu Toolkit. The complete system allows you to do the following:

- Import existing (PBL-based) menus and store them in a database
- Create new menus in the special menu painter
- Edit database-kept menus, providing user-specific profiles for each menuitem

Here you'll examine the structure and more important functions used in that system. First of all, you need to establish tables to keep information about nodes and users who are granted permission to particular nodes.

The first table (t_menu_node_info) keeps all the information about all the nodes for all the menus (or applications) being used. The second table keeps IDs for those users who are authorized to use that system. The following example creates menu information for a particular user. Please note that users get access to nodes that are authorized for a group they belong to.

App

C

Listing C.3 This Code Provides Security on Menus Based on User Ids(INVENTRY.INI)

```
string sSQLStatement, sUserGroupName
int iiGroupUId
SELECT a.gid INTO :iiGroupUId FROM sysusers a WHERE name = :sqlca.userid;
select name into :sUserGroupName from sysusers where uid = :iiGroupUId;
s_SQL_Statement = "SELECT a.* FROM t_menu_node_info a, t_menu_users b "+ &
"WHERE a.generated_id = b.generated_id AND a.appname_s = b.appname " +&
" AND a.appname_s = '"+gsMenuName+"' " + &
" AND ( b.user_id = '"+gsUserName+"' " or b.user_id ='" &
+s_UserGroupName+"')"
 f_array_from_database(sSQLStatement)
f_array_to_menu(w_test_menu_sheet)


global subroutine f_array_from_database (string is_sql_statement)
// Clean Out whatever they had before
s_MenuNode istr_EmptyConstructor[]
s_MenuNode istr_Node
gstr_MenuNode = istr_EmptyConstructor
DECLARE my_cursor DYNAMIC CURSOR FOR SQLSA ;
PREPARE SQLSA FROM :is_SQL_Statement;
OPEN DYNAMIC my_cursor ;
int i = 1
DO
FETCH my_cursor INTO :istrMenuNode;
IF (sqlca.sqlcode = 0) THEN gstr_menunode[i] = istr_node
i += 1
```

(continues)

Listing C.3   Continued

```
LOOP WHILE SQLCA.SQLCODE = 0
CLOSE my_cursor ;
end subroutine


global subroutine f_Array_to_Menu ( window pwParentWindow)
menu m_out_menu
 int j, i = 1
if IsValid(UserWindow.MenuId ) then Destroy( UserWindow.MenuId )
UserWindow.ChangeMenu(m_empty)
m_out_menu = UserWindow.MenuId
 FOR j = 1 to UpperBound(gstr_MenuNode)
IF gstr_MenuNode[j].gen_Parent_Id =0 THEN
m_out_menu.Item[i+1] = f_Create_Menu_Node_From_Array( UserWindow,&
gstr_MenuNode[j].itemorder )
i = i + 1
END IF
NEXT
m_out_menu.Item[1].Visible = NOT m_out_menu.Item[1].Visible
m_out_menu.Item[1].Visible = NOT m_out_menu.Item[1].Visible
m_out_menu.Item[1].ToolBarItemVisible = &
NOT m_out_menu.Item[1].ToolBarItemVisible
m_out_menu.Item[1].ToolBarItemVisible = &
NOT m_out_menu.Item[1].ToolBarItemVisible
end subroutine


global function menu f_Create_Menu_Node_From_Array ( &
ref window pwParentwindow, int nodeid)
menu im_menu
int i, j = 0
im_menu = create m_dynamic_item
FOR i = 1 to UpperBound(gstr_MenuNode)
IF gstr_MenuNode[i].gen_Parent_Id = NodeId THEN
j = j + 1
im_menu.Item[j] =f_Create_Menu_Node_From_Array(iw_ParentWindow, &
gstr_MenuNode[i].itemorder)
END IF
NEXT
f_structure_to_menunode(gstr_MenuNode[f_Index_from_Id(NodeId)], im_menu)
im_Menu.ParentWindow = pwParentWindow
return im_Menu
end function
```

Implementing OLE 2.0

PowerBuilder 5 supports the Object Linking and Embedding (OLE) 2.0 standard in four ways:

■ OLE 2.0 controls

- OCX controls
- Outbound OLE Automation
- Inbound OLE Automation

OLE 2.0 Controls

In the window painter, select the OLE 2.0 control icon from the toolbar and place the control on your window. The Insert Object dialog box appears, as seen in figure C.9.

FIG. C.9
The Insert Object dialog box allows you to insert an OLE 2.0 object into a window.

App

C

Here you choose which program you want to insert in your Window. In figure C.9, Paintbrush is selected. When you place the control on your window by clicking the Insert button, Power-Builder immediately takes you to the target application and allows you to edit the control before it is placed on your window (see fig. C.10).

FIG. C.10
The bitmap being edited in its native application.

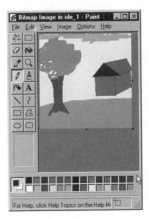

After the bitmap is edited, you exit Paintbrush and the bitmap appears within your PowerBuilder window, as seen in figure C.11.

FIG. C.11

Through OLE, the bitmap now appears with your window.

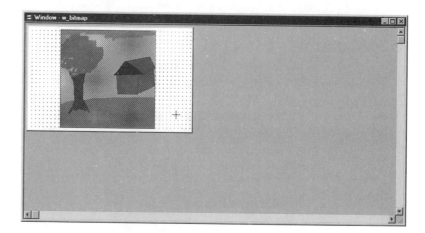

To edit the bitmap, you can click the right mouse button on your PowerBuilder window and select the Open menu option.

FIG. C.12

Editing the OLE 2.0 control.

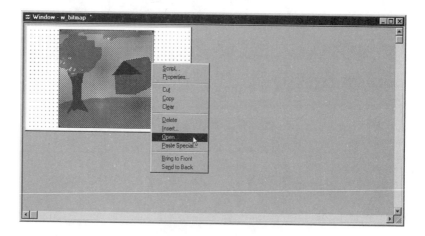

During run time, the user can edit the bitmap by double-clicking the bitmap. This would cause the Inplace OLE activation to take place. This means that the target application, in this case Paintbrush, will "take over" the menu and toolbar of your application temporarily while you edit the bitmap. Once you finish editing the bitmap, your original menu will return. See figures C.13 and C.14.

FIG. C.13

Your window with an OLE 2.0 bitmap.

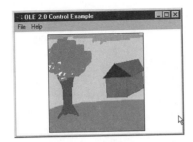

CAUTION

Using OLE 2.0 can really slow down an application and consume significant amounts of system resources. OLE 2.0 is a really neat feature of Windows and PowerBuilder, but don't use it frivolously or you will sacrifice execution speed.

FIG. C.14

Inplace activation of OLE 2.0 bitmap.

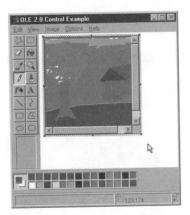

N O T E The embedded Paintbrush bitmap was not saved into the final system. ■

OCX Controls 32-bit OCX controls are descendants of 16-bit VBX controls. OCX controls embody the spirit of component-ware and are prefabricated components that can be easily plugged into your application. They have properties that can be modified for customization within your application.

In order to place an OCX control in your application, first click the OLE 2.0 icon in your Window Painter. Then click the window. This brings up the Insert Object dialog box. Now select the *Insert Control* tab. Here, you will find all the OCX controls that have been registered on your machine. If you need to register a new control, click the *Register New* button. See figure C.15.

FIG. C.15

Selecting an OCX control.

After selecting the OCX control, click the Insert button and position the OCX control in your window. OCX controls have attributes just as any other control. These properties can be viewed by clicking the right mouse button. This brings up a pop-up menu with all the different attributes. Among them, you will notice the *OCX Properties* menu item that is unique to OCX controls. See figure C.16.

FIG. C.16

Placing an OCX control on your window.

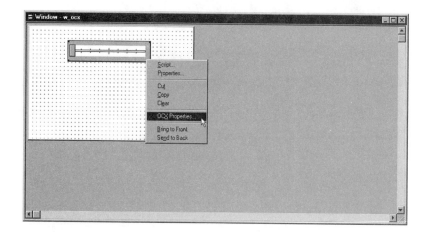

The OCX Properties menu item displays properties specific to that OCX control. See figure C.17.

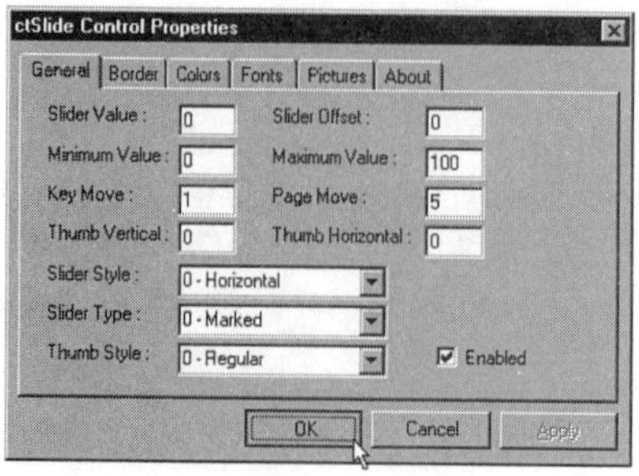

FIG. C.17

Properties specific to an OCX control.

The OCX properties can be modified programmatically by accessing the *object* attribute of the OCX control and modifying attributes thereof. In figure C.18, we have a slider OCX control that comes with PowerBuilder 5 and two command buttons used to move it five units in either direction.

FIG. C.18

Placing an OCX control in a window.

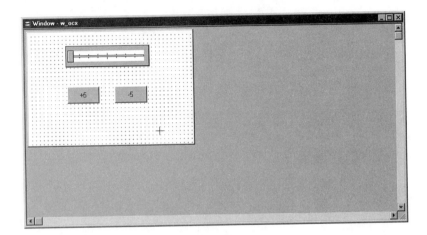

The code behind the *+5* button is shown in figure C.19. You can move the slider to the right or left by adding or subtracting to the *value* field of the *object* attribute of the OCX control.

FIG. C.19

Manipulating properties of an OCX control programmatically.

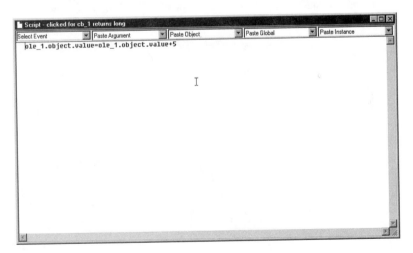

Outbound OLE Automation

Outbound OLE Automation refers to the scenario when your PowerBuilder application acts as a client and invokes another application, e.g., Microsoft Word, via OLE.

You can create a form letter in Word using bookmarks as placeholders, and fill in the values using data from your PowerBuilder application.

Figure C.20 shows a simple form letter where the Name of the person to whom it is addressed is marked using a bookmark called *Name*.

FIG. C.20

Form letter written in Microsoft Word.

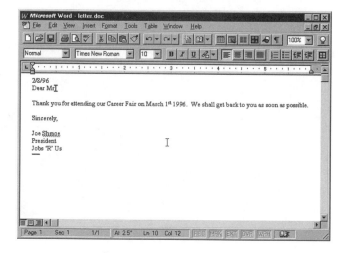

You can create a simple window, as in figure C.21, to invoke, fill in the Name, and print the form letter. The window has a singlelineedit and a commandbutton. The singlelineedit captures the name of the person to whom the letter is addressed. The commandbutton takes the value from the singlelineedit and passes it to Word via OLE Automation.

FIG. C.21

OLE Automation client application.

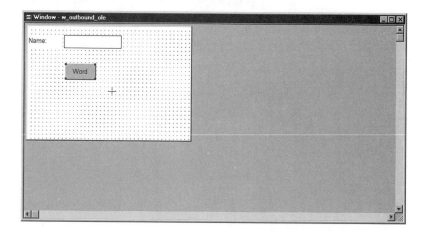

The code behind the commandbutton is as follows:

Listing C.4   Word OLE Automation Object Invoked from PowerBuilder

```
integer result

OLEObject myoleobject

myoleobject = CREATE OLEObject
result = myoleobject.ConnectToNewObject("word.basic")

IF result = 0 THEN
     myoleobject.fileopen("c:\book\letter.doc")
     myoleobject.editgoto("Name")
     myoleobject.insert(sle_name.text)
     myoleobject.fileprint()
END IF
DESTROY myoleobject
```

Figure C.22 shows the end-product of this exercise.

FIG. C.22

PowerBuilder to Word OLE Automation.

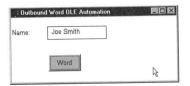

Inbound OLE Automation

Inbound OLE Automation allows PowerBuilder to act as an OLE Server. For example, you could write a PowerBuilder user object that is called from Excel.

PowerBuilder allows for two flavors of inbound OLE Automation. The first type requires an application to register itself in the Registry and then "advertise" the different methods that can be invoked on it. The second method is to have a PowerBuilder user object piggyback on the PowerBuilder application entry in the registry and be invoked through PowerBuilder itself.

The first method does not require the PowerBuilder environment to be present on a machine in order to use it, whereas the second one does. The second method is easier to test and implement.

You can create a simple PowerBuilder user object that is called from an Excel macro written in Visual Basic for Applications. Create a PowerBuilder custom user object called u_msg. This user object has two methods: uf_msgbox and uf_add. The uf_msgbox function displays a message box when invoked, while the uf_add function increments the argument passed to it by 1 and returns that value. See figure C.23.

FIG. C.23

User object functions.

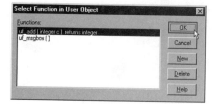

The code for the two functions is shown in figures C.24 and C.25.

FIG. C.24

Code for uf_msgbox function.

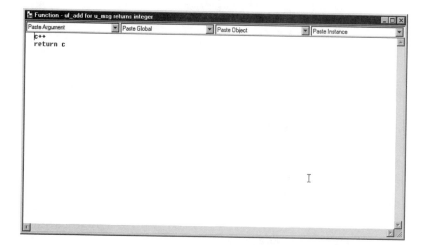

FIG. C.25

Code for uf_add function.

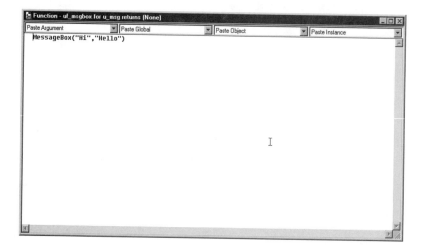

Next, compile the PBL where the user object is stored into a dynamic link library (DLL) in the Library Painter. See figure C.26.

FIG. C.26
Building a DLL.

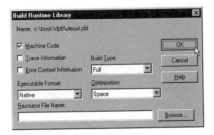

After having written and compiled the PowerBuilder user object, you need to write your Visual Basic for Applications macro in Excel. The macro will create two OLE objects in memory. The first OLE object hooks into PowerBuilder. Using the handle from the first OLE object, the *LibraryList* attribute is set to our DLL compiled earlier. Having done this, you can instantiate a handle to the u_msg user object. After this, you can invoke the uf_msgbox and uf_add functions, as shown in figure C.27.

App C

FIG. C.27
Visual Basic for Applications code in Excel accessing a PowerBuilder user object.

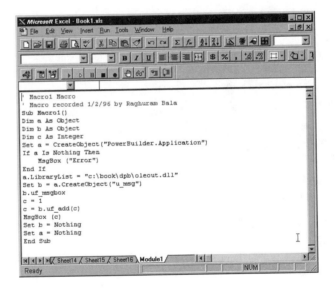

```
' Macro1 Macro
' Macro recorded 1/2/96 by Raghuram Bala
Sub Macro1()
Dim a As Object
Dim b As Object
Dim c As Integer
Set a = CreateObject("PowerBuilder.Application")
If a Is Nothing Then
    MsgBox ("Error")
End If
a.LibraryList = "c:\book\dpb\oleout.dll"
Set b = a.CreateObject("u_msg")
b.uf_msgbox
c = 1
c = b.uf_add(c)
MsgBox (c)
Set b = Nothing
Set a = Nothing
End Sub
```

When the uf_msgbox method is invoked from Excel, a MessageBox appears on the screen, as if it were invoked from any other PowerBuilder application. See figure C.28.

FIG. C.28

Calling the uf_msgbox
user object function
from Excel.

When the uf_add method is invoked with an argument of 1, it returns 2 and this is stored in the local variable c. The MsgBox function is then called and it displays the value of c, as shown in figure C.29.

FIG. C.29

Calling the uf_add user
object function from
Excel.

Introducing DDE

DDE is the predecessor of OLE and primarily used on Windows 3.x platforms. Although DDE is still available as a method of interprocess communication, OLE is preferable especially on Windows 95 and NT platforms.

To use the DDE in your application, you need to perform the following steps:

1. Open a PowerBuilder window if one is not already opened.
2. Start communication with the client application using the OpenChannel( ) PowerBuilder function. (The client application is the application you want to access.)
3. Identify your application as a DDE server using the StartServerDDE( ) PowerBuilder function. (The server application is the application that invokes the client application.)
4. Execute the client functions by using the ExecRemote( ) PowerBuilder function for each client function you want to access.
5. When you're finished executing client functions, close the DDE channel with the CloseChannel( ) PowerBuilder function.
6. Close the PowerBuilder window opened in step 1 unless you want to keep it open for other processing.

The following list gives a detailed description of the functions used to implement DDE in your application:

■ Handle = OpenChannel (applname, topicname, {windowhandle}): OpenChannel opens a DDE channel to another application. *Handle* is an integer identifying the DDE connection. *Applname* is a string containing the DDE name of the DDE. *Topicname* is a string identifying either the data or instance of the program you want to use. If only one instance of the program is available, *topicname* is often the same as *applname*. *Windowhandle* is the handle of the window acting as a DDE client. Use this if you have more than one open window.

- StartServerDDE ({windowname}, applname, topic{, items}): *StartServerDDE* causes the application denoted by *applname* to begin acting as a DDE server. *Windowname* is the name of the server window. The default is the current window. *Applname* is the DDE name for your PowerBuilder application. *Topic* is a string containing the basic data grouping of the server application to be accessed by the client application. *Items* is a comma-delimited string list of what the DDE server will support.

- StartServerDDE ({windowname}, applname, topic{, items}): *StartServerDDE* causes the application denoted by *applname* to begin acting as a DDE server. *Windowname* is the name of the server window. The default is the current window. *Applname* is the DDE name for your PowerBuilder application. *Topic* is a string containing the basic data grouping of the server application to be accessed by the client application. *Items* is a comma-delimited string list of what the DDE server will support.

- ExecRemote (command, handle{,windowhandle}): ExecRemote executes a remote function from the server application. *Command* is a string containing the name of the command you want to execute. Although the format of the command depends on the DDE application you want to access, usually the command is surrounded in brackets. *Handle* is the handle returned by the OpenChannel function. *Windowhandle* is the handle of the window acting as a DDE client. Use this if you have more than one open window.

- CloseChannel (handle{, windowhandle}): CloseChannel closes the DDE channel opened by OpenChannel and identified by handle. *Handle* is the handle returned by the OpenChannel function. *Windowhandle* is the handle of the window acting as a DDE client. Use this if you have more than one open window.

One good use of DDE is to create a Windows 3.x group and insert a Windows icon for your application during the install process. If you are making a stand-alone application for distribution, you'll also need to write an install program to make your application accessible from Windows 3.x without burdening the end user. In your install program, you can manipulate Windows 3.x groups and icons with the following PowerScript:

App

C

Listing C.5   Manipulating Windows 3.x Groups via DDE from PowerBuilder

```
int handle     // Define the handle for identifying the remote application
Open (w_dde)      // Open a PowerBuilder Window
// Now open a remote DDE channel to PROGMAN
handle = OpenChannel ("PROGMAN","PROGMAN")
// Define your app as a DDE server
StartServerDDE(w_dde, "dde", "System")
// Execute PROGMAN functions
//      Add a group
ExecRemote("[CreateGroup(MyGroup)]", handle)
//      Add an item to the group with a path and description
ExecRemote("[AddItem(C:\PROGPATH\PROGNAME.EXE, Description]", handle)
CloseChannel(handle) // Close the remote DDE channel to PROGMAN
Close(w_dde)      // Close the PowerBuilder window
```

To learn more about DDE, look up DDE in the online help that comes with PowerBuilder or read the User's Guide on Dynamic Data Exchange.

Using External DLLs

Before Windows, developers were expected to develop in only one language. If multiple languages were used in an application, calling modules and called modules usually required special processing to pass data back and forth between modules.

When Microsoft developed Windows, the company added a common interface for "sections" of code called *DLLs*, or *Dynamic Link Libraries*. DLLs can be generated by most compilers and called by most Windows programs without additional research and coding required to handle parameters. DLLs—or Microsoft SDK (Software Developers Kit) EXEs—are much like PBDs (PowerBuilder Dynamic Libraries) in that they are not linked into a program until run time.

PowerBuilder can interface with DLLs written in other languages like C++ or Visual Basic and EXEs used in the SDK.

To declare an external function inside a DLL to be accessible to PowerBuilder, Declare, Global External Functions. (The Declare option is available in most painters.) This opens the Declare Global External Functions editor. Here you can declare a function using the Function data type.

As you can see in figure C.30, you wrote a function to attach to another drive and directory. This function is one of many inside a DLL called CFUNCS.DLL. By this declaration, you are allowing PowerBuilder to access your function.

FIG. C.30

PowerBuilder is allowed to access CHANGEDIR inside CFUNCS.DLL.

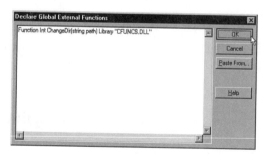

Implementing Drag and Drop

The drag-and-drop metaphor provides applications with an intuitive user interface. PowerBuilder supports drag and drop by providing the following attributes, events and functions:

Table C.2 Drag-and-Drop Attributes

Attribute	Data Type	Description
DragIcon	String	The name of the icon when in drag mode
DragAuto	Boolean	Indicates if control is automatically in dragdrop mode

Table C.3 Drag-and-Drop Events

Events	Description
DragDrop	Indicates if a dragged control has been dropped on the control
DragEnter	Indicates if a dragged control is entering the control
DragLeave	Indicates if a dragged control is leaving the control
DragWithin	Indicates if a dragged control is being moved within the control

Table C.4 Drag-and-Drop Functions

Function	Description
Drag(DragMode)	Starts or ends dragging of a control
DraggedObject()	Returns a reference to the object being dragged

The most important event is the DragDrop event that is available to all PowerBuilder controls in a window. It indicates whether another control has been dropped on it. The Drag function is equally important as it enables one to programmatically put a control in drag mode. Whenever a dragged control is dropped on another control, it automatically snaps out of the drag mode.

Figure C.31 shows a simple window with two listboxes and with the goal of dragging items from the left listbox to the right listbox.

App

C

FIG. C.31

Simple window for Dragdrop exercise.

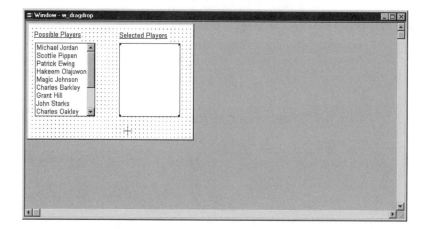

You can modify the Properties of the left listbox by right-clicking and selecting Properties from the pop-up menu. Select the Drag and Drop tab on the Properties sheet and modify the Drag Icon as shown in figure C.32.

Whenever the user selects an item in the left listbox, you need it to go into dragdrop mode. In order to achieve this, you need to place the code shown in figure C.33 in the *selectionchanged* event of the left listbox.

FIG. C.32

Modifying drag-and-drop properties.

FIG. C.33

Forcing a control into dragdrop mode programmatically.

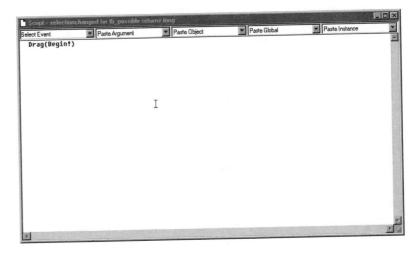

When the user drags an item from the left listbox and drops it in the right listbox, the right listbox needs to be receptive to this fact. In order to achieve this, the *dragdrop* event of the right listbox needs to have the code shown in figure C.34.

FIG. C.34

Code for dragdrop event.

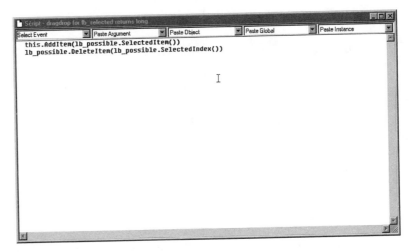

The end-product of this exercise is shown in figure C.35 where an item is dragged from the left listbox to the right listbox. Notice that the left listbox item is represented by the Drag Icon selected earlier.

FIG. C.35

Dragdrop application in action.

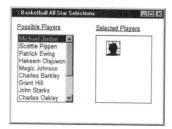

Writing PowerBuilder Applications for Multiple Platforms

This book concentrates primarily on developing PowerBuilder applications for the Windows 95 environment. However, PowerBuilder is available on Windows NT, Windows 3.x, the Apple Macintosh, and Sun Solaris 2.4.

Although applications are transportable, certain system specific functions like OLE and DDE will not work in a non-Windows environment. PowerBuilder lets you test for this with the new global parameter *g_platform*. You can use *g_platform* in a CHOOSE CASE statement to code for operating-system-specific script as follows:

Listing C.6   Code for *g_platform* in a CHOOSE CASE Statement for Operating-System-Specific Script

```
CHOOSE CASE g_platform
     CASE Windows!
          .
          .
          .
     CASE Macintosh!
          .
          .
          .
END CASE
```

Coding in this manner will let you take your complete PowerBuilder application and port it *without changes* to another platform! For the software developer, this could mean easy access to other markets with a minimal amount of effort. ●

Getting Help with Your PowerBuilder Applications

by David J. O'Hearn

PowerBuilder is relatively easy to learn and use, once you understand "event driven," as opposed to "procedural" programming. However, every developer needs help and advice at one time or another. This appendix is designed to help you find the advice you need.

You can get many Powersoft products and third-party PowerBuilder support products through most retail software outlets. If you need more than just software—like support and training—help is not far away. In addition to a robust online help system, Powersoft has designated PowerBuilder Development Consultants and Powersoft Authorized Training Partners. ■

N O T E Are you having trouble finding information to help you when developing your PowerBuilder application? Before you seek assistance from other sources, try the online help system built into PowerBuilder. Just click the Help icon and then search for your topic. PowerBuilder has very extensive online help. Such comprehensive help systems are rare in Windows 3.x development products. ■

Getting Help from Powersoft

If you still can't find what you need, you can contact Powersoft by calling 1-800-395-3525. You usually don't have to wait that long, and the call is toll free. Although this number can't give you technical support beyond installation assistance, the service representatives can often steer you toward a support plan that fits your needs and resources. If you have a bug you want fixed or an enhancement you want added, you can report it here.

Getting Free PowerBuilder Support

Many of your questions can be answered by PowerBuilder's FaxLine™ service (also known as the FaxBack system). If you have access to a fax, the service is free. Call PowerBuilder's FaxLine™ service at 1-508-287-1600. (At the risk of insulting your intelligence, don't dial this number with your fax. That would just confuse both machines. Use a regular voice telephone.) PowerBuilder's FaxLine™ automated voice mail will guide you first through ordering a catalog of available faxes, and then (on a second call) ordering the fax help you need. You'll be surprised how helpful this is.

If you have access to CompuServe, you can access the Powersoft forum by typing GO POWERSOFT. This free service (other than the normal CompuServe usage fees) is probably one of the better ways to eventually communicate with a live technical support person from Team Powersoft (TEAMPS). Team Powersoft is a worldwide web of independent developers who help those in need with their Powersoft problems. It was organized by Powersoft to answer the growing need for PowerBuilder technical support. Alternatively, Powersoft also has its own Bulletin Board System (BBS) where you can leave questions and download patches and bug fixes. The BBS number is 1-508-287-1850, and the connection is 8-N-1 (8 data bits, No Parity, one stop bit).

If you don't have a CompuServe account, but have access to the Internet, Powersoft maintains a site on the World Wide Web. Although not as well developed as the CompuServe forum, there is still a wealth of information available here. It can be accessed by pointing your web browser to the Uniform Resource Locator (URL) http://www.Powersoft.com/. Powersoft also maintains an FTP site (ftp.Powersoft.com) which contains all the maintenance and sample files currently available on the Powersoft BBS.

Buying PowerBuilder Support

As easy as PowerBuilder is to use, sometimes you may find yourself needing a little extra support. Powersoft has many programs available to meet your budget and needs. You find a price comparison listed at the end of this section in table D.1.

- If you need to purchase support but either have limited resources or have a small development shop with experienced PowerBuilder developers, the Quantity Pack Support Program is for you. This plan comes in packages of five issues (or problems) and can be purchased for the desktop or the enterprise editions.

- If you need a little extra support, Powersoft provides annual support programs for PowerBuilder Desktop. The desktop annual support is limited to 15 issues, but you get support for PowerBuilder Desktop, InfoMaker, Watcom VX-REXX (for OS/2), Watcom SQL Single User Editions, Watcom C/C++, and Watcom FORTRAN 77. You also get the single user Infobase CD-ROM annual subscription and any bug fixes.

- If you have the PowerBuilder Enterprise edition, there's a Powersoft Enterprise annual support program. The Enterprise annual support includes either unlimited issues or two contacts with 55 issues, and you support all products carried by the desktop annual support as well as support for PowerBuilder Enterprise and the Watcom SQL Network Server Editions. You also get the multi-user Infobase CD-ROM Server subscription, all the bug fixes, and two printed copies of the documentation.

- If you've bought the Enterprise annual support program but have used up your support, you can purchase the Add-on Enterprise Support, which allows you one additional contact or 25 additional issues.

- For the big corporations with large numbers of PowerBuilder developers, there's the PowerBuilder's Custom Annual Support program. This program allows you two contacts or 100 issues, guaranteed 15 minute response, monthly report of calls, Infobase Server Subscription, scheduled conference calls to cover the status of any open problem, two copies of documentation, and an annual technology briefing.

- Powersoft also provides a Credit Card Support Program. You can use your American Express, VISA, or Master Card to purchase support on a per-issue basis. The credit card phone number is 508-287-1950.

App

D

Table D.1   PowerBuilder Support Pricing

Product	U.S. Dollars	Canadian Dollars
Infobase annual subscription	$90.00	
Credit Card Pay-Per-Issue Desktop Products (1 issue)	$75.00	$105.00
Credit Card Pay-Per-Issue Enterprise Products (1 issue)	$100.00	$140.00
Pay-Per-Issue Desktop Products (5 issues)	$375.00	$525.00
Pay-Per-Issue Enterprise Products (5 issues)	$500.00	$700.00

continues

Table D.1   Continued

Product	U.S. Dollars	Canadian Dollars
Annual Support Desktop Products (15 issues)	$950.00	$1,300.00
Annual Support Enterprise Products	$5,000.00	$7,000.00
Add-on Annual Enterprise Support	$2,500.00	$3,500.00
Custom Annual Support	$25,000.00	$35,000.00

 TIP Powersoft Training Partners can teach you PowerBuilder, and most of them also provide consulting services.

Getting Help from Third-Party Sources

Finally, you could always take a class to increase your PowerBuilder skills. Powersoft Training Partner instructors go through a thorough, rigorous training process before they become qualified PowerBuilder instructors. Table D.2 is a list of the Powersoft Training Partners ordered by state (or province) and name. (Canadian training partners follow the United States training partners.)

Table D.2   Powersoft Authorized Training Partners

UNITED STATES

ARIZONA

MIDAK Contact: Lawana Diffie	2800 North Central Avenue, Suite 100	Phoenix, AZ 85004	(800) 264-9029

CALIFORNIA

American Digital Technologies Contact: Scott Shulga	3100 Bristol St., Suite 380	Costa Mesa, CA 92626	(714) 433-1300
IG Systems, Inc. Contact: Ron York	2800 28th St., Suite 250	Santa Monica, CA 90405	(310) 396-0042
Inventa Corporation Contact: Ashok Santhanum	2620 Augustine Dr., Suite 225	Santa Clara, CA 95054	(408) 987-0220

UNITED STATES

CALIFORNIA

NetBase Computing, Inc. Contact: Donna Reed	1065 East Hillsdale Blvd., Suite 413	Foster City, CA 94404	(800) 795-6224
Panttaja Consulting Group Contact: Paul Hamberis	55 Francisco St., Suite 300	San Francisco, CA 94133	(415) 705-6868

COLORADO

Greenbrier & Russel Contact: Mary Delutri	999 18th St., Denver Plaza South Tower, Suite 1590	Denver, CO 80202	(800) 453-0347
Semiotix, Inc. Contact: Julie Wilson	10620 East Bethany Drive	Aurora, CO 80014	(303) 743-1400

CONNECTICUT

Linc Systems Contact: Kerry Leslie	310 West Newberry Road	Bloomfield, CT 06002	(203) 286-9060
MetaCorp Strategies International Contact: Russell Nugent	325 Riverside Avenue	Westport, CT 06880	(203) 222-6685
Computer Science Management, Inc. Contact: Dave Sagers	111 Charter Oak Ave.	Hartford, CT 06106	(203) 278-0244

FLORIDA

PowerCerv Contact: Marc Fratello	400 North Ashley Dr., Suite 1910	Tampa, FL 33602	(813) 226-2378
Computer Task Group Contact: Mike Niemann	7650 Courtney Campbell Causeway, Suite 605	Tampa, FL 33607	(813) 289-4471

App
D

continues

Table D.2   Continued

UNITED STATES

FLORIDA

Systems Group Consulting Contact: Jeff Manchester	760 NW 107th Ave., Suite 310	Miami, FL 33172	(305) 225-3325

GEORGIA

Greenbrier & Russel Contact: Mary Delutri	300 Galleria Pkwy. Suite 290	Atlanta, GA 30339	(800) 453-0347
Omni Training Center Contact: Rhonda Sides	1150 Hammond Drive Building A, Suite 1190	Atlanta, GA 30326	(404) 395-0055
OSoft Development Corp. Contact: Mike Kelleher	6 Piedmont Center, Suite 303	Atlanta, GA 30305	(404) 814-6030

ILLINOIS

Greenbrier & Russel, Inc. Contact: Mary Delutri	1450 E. American Lane, Suite 1640	Schaumburg, IL 60173	(800) 453-0347
Client/Server, Inc. Contact: Harvey Mayerowicz	5701 N. Sheridan Rd., Suite 160	Chicago, IL 60660	(312) 275-2513
DC Systems Contact: Leslie Kuster	533 S. York Road, Suite B	Elmhurst, IL 60126	(708) 834-2095

INDIANA

Analytical Technologies, Inc. Contact: Debbie Yasenka	6060 Castleway West Drive, Suite 233	Indianapolis, IN 46250	(800)ANATEC -3

KANSAS

Analytical Technologies, Inc. Contact: Debbie Yasenka	9401 Nall Ave., Suite 100	Shawnee Mission, KS 66207	(800)ANATEC -3

UNITED STATES

MARYLAND

The Orkand Corporation Contact: Cori Asaka	8484 Georgia Ave., Suite 1000	Silver Spring, MD 20910	(301) 585-8480

MASSACHUSETTS

CSC Partners Contact: Bill Heys	One Newton Exec. Park	Newton, MA 02162	(617) 332-3900

MICHIGAN

Analytical Technologies, Inc. Contact: Debbie Yasenka	30300 Telegraph Rd., Suite 200	Bingham Farms, MI 48025	(800)ANATEC -3

MINNESOTA

Connect Education Services Contact: Kathy Carroll	9855 West 78th Street	Eden Prairie, MN 55344	(612) 946-0210
Fourth Generation Contact: Chiam Titlebaum	Galtier Plaza, Suite 763 175 East Fifth Street	St. Paul, MN 55101	(612) 224-9919

MISSOURI

Grant Thornton Contact: John Hart	500 Washington St. #1200	St. Louis, MO 63101	(314) 241-3232
SoluTech Contact: Randy Schilling	117 S. Main Street, Suite 111	St. Charles, MO 63301	(314) 947-9393

NEW JERSEY

Indus Consultancy Services Contact: Angelique Ramsey	140 East Ridgewood Avenue	Paramus, NJ 07652	(201) 261-3100
Trecom Business Systems Contact: Allison O'Neill	333 Thornall Street	Edison, NJ 08837	(908) 549-4100
PC Strategies & Solutions Contact: Carol Lee	6 Century Drive	Parsippany, NJ 07054	(201) 984-1000

App

D

continues

Table D.2   Continued

UNITED STATES

NEW YORK

Advanced Communication Resources Contact: Maria Colavito	350 Fifth Ave., Suite 7803	New York, NY 10118	(212) 629-3370
Systar Technologies Contact: Jeff Bernstein	1890 Palmer Avenue	Larchmont, NY 10538	(914) 833-0300

NORTH CAROLINA

Cedalion Systems Contact: Debbie Martin	1300 Charlotte Plaza	Charlotte, NC 28244	(800) 277-4526
Cedalion Systems Contact: Walt Wintermute	79-4401 Alexander Dr., P.O. Box 13239	Raleigh, NC 27709-3239	(800) 277-4526
Financial Dynamics Contact: Carolyn Caldwell	3600 Glenwood Avenue Suite 100	Raleigh, NC 27612	(800) 486-5201 ext. 122

OHIO

ComputerPeople Contact: Ellen Saunders	50 Northwoods Boulevard	Worthington, OH 43235	(614) 433-0133
McHale USConnect Contact: Kathleen Binder	31200 Bainbridge Road	Solon, OH 44139	(216) 498-3550
New Media Contact: Joe Bains	503 East 200th St., Suite 202	Cleveland, OH 44119	(216) 481-7900

OKLAHOMA

Business Consulting Group Contact: Alan Lipe	4500 South Garnett, Ste. 620	Tulsa, OK 74146	(918) 665-0883

PENNSYLVANIA

Cutting Edge Computer Solutions Contact: Tom Olenzak	5 Great Valley Parkway	Malvern, PA 19355	(610) 648-3881

UNITED STATES

PENNSYLVANIA

Information Technologists, Inc. Contact: Kristine Waters	555 North Lane, Suite 5040	Conshohocken, PA 19428	(215) 832-1000
Information Technologists, Inc. Contact: Tim O'Shea	101 North Meadow Dr., Suite 113	Wexford, PA 15090	(412) 934-5885

SOUTH CAROLINA

The Database Group Contact: Susan Moffit	11 Technology Circle	Columbia, SC 29203	(803) 935-1100

TEXAS

Analytical Technologies, Inc. Contact: Steven McDermott	21515 SH 249 Trombell Pkwy., Suite 330	Houston, TX 77070	(713) 379-1006
B. R. Blackmarr & Associates Contact: Tanna Bailey	1950 Stemmons Freeway, Suite 3031	Dallas, TX 75237	(214) 756-4779
BSG Educational Services Contact: Toni Trivelli	11 Greenway Plaza, Suite 900	Houston, TX 77046	(800) 937-2001
Coopers & Lybrand Contact: Michelle Bode	2711 LBJ Freeway, Suite 312	Dallas, TX 75234	(214) 243-1256
Powersoft Latin America Contact: Yolanda Berea	2929 Briar Park, Suite 529	Houston, TX 77042	(713) 977-0752
ScottSoftware Contact: Richard Scott	90 South Trace Creek Drive	The Woodlands, TX 77381	(713) 367-2734
Software Integration Consulting Group	10000 Richmond, Suite 660	Houston, TX 77042	(713) 977-6421

App

D

continues

Table D.2   Continued

UNITED STATES

TEXAS

Contact: Dwight Williams

Systems Evolution, Inc. Contact: Karen Stephenson	3023 Pecan Point Drive	Sugar Land, TX 77478-4224	(713) 265-7075
Techsys Computer Associates Contact: Robert Chadwell	1420 W. Mockingbird Lane, Suite 270	Dallas, TX 75247	(214) 638-8324
The Austin Software Foundry Contact: Don Hudecek	P.O. Box 1522	Austin, TX 78767	(512) 292-0984

UTAH

Erudite Software & Consulting Contact: Gene Loveridge	2474 N. University Avenue Suite 100	Provo, UT 84604	(801) 373-6100

VIRGINIA

Financial Dynamics Contact: Carolyn Caldwell	5201 Leesburg Pike, Ste. 701	Falls Church, VA 22041	(703) 671-3003
IPC Technologies Contact: Jeffrey Brownstein	7200 Glen Forest Drive	Richmond, VA 23226	(804) 285-9300
Noblestar Systems Corp. Contact: Stuart Hill	3141 Fairview Park Drive Suite 400	Falls Church, VA 22042	(703) 641-8511

WASHINGTON

ServerLogic Corp. Contact: Terry LeLievre	2800 Northup Way, Suite 205	Bellevue, WA 98004	206-803-0378

WISCONSIN

Greenbrier & Russel, Inc. Contact: Mary Delutri	13555 Bishops Court Suite 201	Brookfield, WI 53005	(800) 453-0347

CANADA

ALBERTA

DCS Systems, Ltd. Contact: Kirsten Harty	Bay #1, 4001A-19 St., NE	Calgary, AB T2E-6X8	(403) 291-5343
Computronix Holdings, Ltd. Contact: Jeff Pfahl	One Thornton Court, Ste. 700	Edmonton, AB T5J-2E7	(403) 424-1617

BRITISH COLUMBIA

BPR Consulting Contact: Derek Ball	1205 Deeks Place	Victoria, BC V8P-5S7	(604) 472-0688
DCS Systems, Ltd. Contact: Roxanne Lemire	#120, 4170 Still Creek Drive	Burnaby, BC V5C-6C8	(604) 291-0015

MANITOBA

Online Business Systems Contact: Tim Siemens	130 Scott Street	Winnipeg, MB R3L-0K8	(204) 452-0614

ONTARIO

Ajja Educational Services Contact: E. F. Lloyd Hiscock	457 Catherine Street	Ottawa, ON K1R-5T7	(613) 563-2552
Visual Systems Development Corporation Contact: Suzanne Starr	One University Ave., Ste. 303	Toronto, ON M5J-2P1	(416) 368-5464

App

D

Joining PowerBuilder User Groups

One of the best places to meet other PowerBuilder developers and figure out those hard-to-solve PowerBuilder problems is to attend a user group meeting. You'll usually get a good speech on some interesting technique and/or third-party software, and you can always discuss what PowerBuilder problems you have with the other members.

Table D.3 shows a list of all PowerBuilder user groups at the time of publication. If you can't find a user group near you, call Powersoft. New user groups are opening all the time, and Powersoft keeps an up-to-date list of user groups and how to join them. Also, kudos to Powersoft for keeping the user groups relatively independent. Powersoft truly acts as a resource—as opposed to a controller—for the PowerBuilder user groups.

Table D.3 PowerBuilder User Groups

GROUP LOCATION	CONTACT PERSON	TELEPHONE #	MEETING SCHEDULE
Eastern Region			
Alabama - Birmingham	Dave Seaman Vulcan Materials	205-877-3045	
Connecticut	Muffie Fox-Dyer Pitney Bowes, Inc.	203-351-7316	
Florida - South	Ruth Howard	508-287-1859	6/29/94
Florida-Tampa Bay	Mike Nieman	813-289-4471	2nd Thursday of every other month
Georgia - Atlanta	Steve Benfield	404-813-1201	3rd Thursday, every month
Massachusetts - Boston	John Dacy Waterfield Technology	617-863-8400	
New Jersey	Bob Champolian Johnson & Johnson	908-524-3930	
New York City	Mike Ryan	212-236-9359	
New York - Buffalo	Ruth Howard	508-287-1859	6/30/94
New York State	Mark Balley	315-428-6504	Bi-monthly
North Carolina - Charlotte	Tanya Watkins	704-335-1200 x2213	
North Carolina - Central	Phyllis Weldon Burroughs Welcome Company	919-315-4984	Quarterly, 3rd Thursday of the month
Pennsylvania - Philadelphia	Bill Turocy National Liberty	215-648-5473	Bi-monthly
Pennsylvania - Pittsburgh	Ruth Howard	508-287-1859	
South Carolina	Joseph Grant Graniteville Company	803-663-2235	3rd Tuesday, every 3 months, 3:00-6:00pm
Tennessee - Nashville	Greg Coe DRT International	615-366-4074	2nd Tuesday of every month
Washington, DC	Stuart Hill Noblestar	703-641-8511	Quarterly (1/2 day)

GROUP LOCATION	CONTACT PERSON	TELEPHONE #	MEETING SCHEDULE
Eastern Region			
Baltimore, Maryland	Ruth Howard	508-287-1859	7/6/94
Virginia/Maryland - Federal	Robert Williams Mindbank	703-893-4700	
Virginia - Richmond	Dan Black Blue Cross	804-354-3316	
Central Region			
Colorado - Denver	Scott Levin	303-783-0607	
Illinois-Decatur	Ruth Howard	508-287-1859	7/13/94
Illinois - Chicago	Jeff Barnes	312-727-4422	First Tuesday of every month
Indiana-Indianapolis	Ruth Howard	508-287-1859	6/29/94
Iowa - Des Moines	Mark Herbsleb Principal Financial Group	515-248-3349	3rd Thursday of every month 6:30-9:30
Kansas	Ruth Howard	508-287-1859	
Michigan - Detroit	Debbie Yasanka Anatech	313-540-4440	
Minnesota - Minneapolis	Steve Anastasi Insight Software, Inc.	612-227-8682	3rd Wednesday every odd # month, 1:00-4:00pm
Missouri - St. Louis	Randy Schilling SoluTech	314-947-9393	3rd Thursday of every month, 6:00-8:00
Nebraska - Omaha	Jerry Pape Applications Design & Development	402-691-8774	
Ohio - Cincinnati	Molly Quinn	708-706-9600	
Ohio - Cleveland	Marleane Troxel	216-344-4760	
Ohio - Columbus	Don Long White Castle	614-228-5781x709	
Oklahoma - Tulsa	Ruth Howard	508-287-1859	7/6/94
Oklahoma - Oklahoma City	Ruth Howard	508-287-1859	

App

D

continues

Table D.3 Continued

GROUP LOCATION	CONTACT PERSON	TELEPHONE #	MEETING SCHEDULE
Central Region			
Texas - San Antonio	Ruth Howard	508-287-1859	7/19/94
Texas - Austin	Bill Reynolds	512-343-7964	Quarterly on U.T. campus
Texas - Dallas	James Pujals Client/Server Campaign	214-393-3586	2nd Tuesday, every month
Texas - Houston	Scott Heath BSG	713-965-1330	4th Friday, every month,
Utah	Doug Austin	801-373-6100	Quarterly
Western Region			
Arizona - Phoenix	Jeff Colyar	602-554-4372	
California - San Francisco	Edie Harris Harris & Associates	510-865-7417	Next meeting March 16th
California - San Diego	Marie Gajo San Diego City Schools	619-293-4489	
California - Orange County	Jon Bruce	714-436-4390	
California - Northern LA	Tony Tortorice DRT Systems	310-590-8805	
Oregon - Portland	Doug Atterbury City of Portland	503-823-7090	
Washington - Seattle	Mike Carney Washington Natural Gas	206-521-5667	
Canada			
Calgary	Glen Murphy	403-290-6515	
Ottawa	Kevin Light Department of Government Services	613-736-2906	
Regina	Ruth Howard	508-287-1859	
Toronto	Stephen Kwiecien LGS	416-492-3003	
Vancouver	Michael Li Infocam Management	604-432-1709	
Winnipeg	Susan Hogan Online	204-452-0614	

Getting Your CPD

by Chuck Boudreau

As you continue to develop in PowerBuilder, you might want to apply for CPD certification at some point. This appendix shows you how. ■

Why Does the CPD Program Exist?

When PowerBuilder first arrived on the scene in 1991, Powersoft marketed it exclusively to corporate information systems organizations. For the first two releases of the product, PowerBuilder was priced way out of the range of the average xBase developer. Besides, it didn't even come with a local database. The typical PowerBuilder developer was an information systems professional for a large corporation.

In early 1994, PowerBuilder Desktop changed all that. It came with a local database, ODBC connectivity, and exceptional functionality at a retail price that any xBase developer could swallow. Soon thereafter, it seemed that everyone and their cousins were creating applications with PowerBuilder.

Consequently, the market was flooded with people claiming to be expert PowerBuilder developers. Companies wanting to hire client-server gurus were too new to the technology to discern an experienced developer from an inexperienced developer. With these fledgling PowerBuilder developers commanding salaries comparable to their COBOL and xBase comrades with 10 years of experience, it became necessary for Powersoft to take action. They had to provide a reality check on what constituted an "expert."

Powersoft's response to this situation was to introduce the Certified PowerBuilder Developer (CPD) program. It is a formal certification process that requires a PowerBuilder developer to pass a rigorous set of examinations. At the onset of the program, a developer was required to be recertified on an annual basis.

The program has now evolved to two levels of CPD certification: Associate and Professional. A candidate attains CPD Associate level upon completing and passing a pair of computer-based exams in a controlled environment. To attain CPD Professional level, a candidate must write an actual application in a controlled exam environment. Powersoft does not allow a candidate to use books, manuals, or any other resources during an exam.

Also, CPD certification is now associated with a particular version of PowerBuilder. Developers maintain their certification for that version for as long as Powersoft officially supports the version. CPD certification for a version expires after two subsequent versions of PowerBuilder are released. This means that when PowerBuilder 5.0 is released, CPD certification for PowerBuilder 3.0 is no longer valid. At that time, only certifications for versions 4.0 and 5.0 are recognized.

CPD certification requirements are subject to change at Powersoft's discretion. For more specific information, contact their FaxLine at 508-287-1600 and request document #1616. For information on where to take the Associate exams, contact Sylvan Prometric at 800-407-3926. For information on where to take the Professional exams, contact Powersoft for one of their authorized training partners.

Exams must be scheduled ahead of time so that the testing center can acquire the appropriate exam. The testing center charges a fee to administer each of the various exams. You can pay by credit card at the time of the exam. Also, before you conclude that the entire CPD program is a racket, you should know that the CPD certification department at Powersoft is not a profit center.

What to Expect at the Exam Center

CPD Associate exams are administered in a wide variety of cities by Drake Exams. The testing centers have dedicated computers for you to use during your exam. Personnel at the exam center generally administer a variety of professional certification exams. Don't expect them to know anything about PowerBuilder or the questions on the exams.

CPD Associate exams are multiple choice, true/false, and matching. They are presented one panel at a time. If you're unsure of your answer to a particular question, you can mark that question and review it before submitting your final answers. Your exam is scored automatically by the software upon completion or after time expires.

CPD Professional exams are administered in selected cities by authorized Powersoft training partners. The testing centers have dedicated computers for you to use during your exam. Experienced PowerBuilder personnel review your exam upon completion and results are available in six to eight weeks.

How to Prepare for the CPD Exams

Preparing for the CPD Associate exam requires that you attain a reasonable level of PowerBuilder proficiency. Powersoft doesn't necessarily expect you to master the most in-depth, esoteric aspects of their product. However, they expect you to have a good understanding about the individual painters, datawindow objects, datawindow controls, PowerScript, functions, event-driven programming, the Microsoft Windows environment, object instantiation, variable scope, inheritance, encapsulation, and polymorphism.

App

E

You can prepare for your CPD exam using several approaches depending upon your particular situation. Powersoft rightfully suggests that the best way to prepare for the CPD exam is to use the product. However, if after using the product for several months you're still feeling squeamish at the prospect of taking the exam, you may want to consider some of the following approaches.

The first method for preparing for the exam involves finding a study partner or group. Many PowerBuilder User Groups have CPD study groups that meet regularly to prepare for the exams. These groups often have CPDs involved in them.

If you are unable to locate such a group, you may want to arrange a meeting with another PowerBuilder developer to form a study partnership. Quiz each other using flash cards you develop. Create your questions from sections in the PowerBuilder documentation. This is an excellent method for reviewing during business commutes and on the way to the CPD exam.

If no developers are in your area, consider networking with other developers in the Powersoft CompuServe forum, or on one of the many Internet USENET forums. These forums provide a rich source of PowerBuilder material for you to acquaint yourself with.

Another popular but slightly costly approach is to use CPD exam preparation software. This type of software provides a set of tests that approximate the actual exam experience. If you suffer from pre-test anxiety, this is a great way to go through a few actual exams. This type of software costs around $40–50 and is advertised regularly in various PowerBuilder trade magazines under the names of PowerQuiz and PowerPrep.

A third, even more expensive approach is to attend training, in person, via video tape, or via computer. A variety of training options are available from Powersoft and their partners. This is costly, but they provide you with an effortless way of reviewing key concepts of mastery.

Going for CPD Associate

If you just bought PowerBuilder last week, don't even think about taking the first CPD Associate exam for several months. You may find it helpful to know the types of things you'll be asked about. This is difficult to predict because Powersoft has several exams that they administer and they change them from time to time.

The following list highlights some of the topics you should be familiar with in order to achieve CPD Associate certification. Use it to create your own mastery plan. A study guide is also available on Powersoft's FaxLine service (508-287-1600, document #1627).

> Know the various window Open() functions calls and their usage, especially using window variables, window types, and parameters.
>
> Understand the use of tildes and tilde quotes and tildes in literal strings.
>
> Know valid datatypes you can pass to and from a user-defined function and the difference between passing by value vs. reference.
>
> Know how ChildDatawindows work (when they retrieve, sort, filter, and so on).
>
> Know about the PowerBuilder system object hierarchy. Know which controls are drag objects and which are not.
>
> Understand the basics of window performance (don't use over 20 controls in a window, don't write long open event scripts, and so on).
>
> Know how to instantiate user objects using CREATE and DESTROY.
>
> Know how to test for database connectivity without checking SQLCA.SQLCode.
>
> Know how to read PowerScript (lots of code in the exam), especially reference variables, variable declarations, and the ++ operator.
>
> Understand the implications of assigning a PSR file to the dataobject attribute of a datawindow control.
>
> Know about shared datawindow functionality.

Understand the addressability of user-defined windows functions in PowerScript (especially using inheritance).

Know the MDI frame functions GetFirstSheet() and GetNextSheet().

Understand object instantiation, reference variables, and the IsValid() function.

Understand that the result of using a null in an arithmetic expression is null.

Know the attributes of the Environment structure.

Learn about the GetEnvironment( ) function call.

Know which events are triggered when a HALT CLOSE is called from PowerScript.

Understand SQL SELECT syntax and joins.

Understand how to trigger custom events using PostEvent(), TriggerEvent(), Send() function calls and using the enumerated datatype pbm_custom01!, and so on.

Know transaction management in a multi-user database environment (especially COMMIT, ROLLBACK, using datawindows to derive the WHERE clause, and so on).

Understand the syntax for user object external function declarations to stored procedures.

Understand MDI sheet menu and sheet toolbar behavior.

Know how EXEs are created. Know where the object code is put when you use PBDs and EXEs together.

Understand composite reports and retrieval arguments for multiple reports.

Understand how to use datawindow expressions to dynamically set a column's Protect attribute based on another column's value (for example, IF(<colname>="Y",0,1)).

Know when COMMITs occur implicitly.

Know about the default error message in the datawindow DBError event.

Know about the effect that Sort and Filter criteria have on a datawindow object that has the RetrieveAsNeeded attribute set on.

Know the visibility of private, protected, and public functions, and variables in objects such as windows, menus, and user objects. In other words, understand how inheritance works.

Going for CPD Professional

Attaining Professional certification requires a proficiency that is normally acquired over years as opposed to months. Of course, there are exceptions to this rule.

To prepare for this exam, you should have experience with all of the PowerBuilder core competencies:

App

E

SQL and relational database concepts

Object-oriented programming

Graphical user interface design

This certification is awarded to those developers who display an understanding of the efficiencies that PowerBuilder affords them. Keep in mind that Powersoft is looking for candidates to display an understanding of the following:

How well the solution meets the specified requirements

How to implement ancestor objects and effectively use inheritance with reuse in mind

How to design an optimum system implementation

How to design a GUI effectively with attention to standards

How to code according to consistent in-line standards

How to handle errors in processing effectively ●

The Windows API and Third-Party Products (What's on the CD?)

by Charles A. Wood

In this appendix, you learn about the software included on the *Special Edition Using PowerBuilder 5 Companion CD*. These products may be useful when developing and managing PowerBuilder development projects. ■

The CD-ROM that accompanies this book contains applications, tools, and demonstration products. There are four major sections:

■ Two PowerBuilder programs written by author Chuck Wood. One is the Inventory Tracking system developed throughout this book. The other is a new utility, PBAPI, that lists over 700 calls made from PowerBuilder to the Windows API.

NOTE   When you run your Inventory Tracking system through PowerBuilder, you may get a message that the Inventory Tracking system is not version 5, and must be migrated. If this happens to you, read the README.TXT that comes with the Inventory Tracking system if you need help migrating from the beta version to the production version of PowerBuilder 5. ■

■ A collection of demonstration applications, scaled-down software, and shareware that all work with (or around) PowerBuilder.

■ All of the sample code from the book.

■ The entire contents of this book formatted electronically as HTML documents that can be read on your computer using any Web Browser.

PBAPI

The CD contains two utilities written by author Chuck Wood. The first is the Inventory Tracking System (discussed throughout this book). The second is a utility (complete with source code) for looking up Windows API calls called PBAPI. You can find these utilities under the \samples subdirectory of the CD.

Understanding the Windows API

PowerScript is a very robust language, containing several hundred functions. Many PowerBuilder developers never have needed to call any external functions. However, there are some functions that are not included in PowerBuilder but *are* listed in the Windows API (Application Programming Interface). The Windows API contains several hundred functions, some of which are not available within PowerScript. These functions are contained *within* windows. No additional software needs to be purchased.

Using External Functions with PowerScript

PowerBuilder allows you to call external functions. External functions are functions that are defined in a DLL (Dynamic Link Library) outside your PowerBuilder environment. Some of the most popular external functions are contained in the Windows API.

To define an external function, get into any PowerScript painter. Then click Declare, Global External Functions as seen in figure F.1.

FIG. F.1

Defining an external function occurs through the PowerScript painter menu.

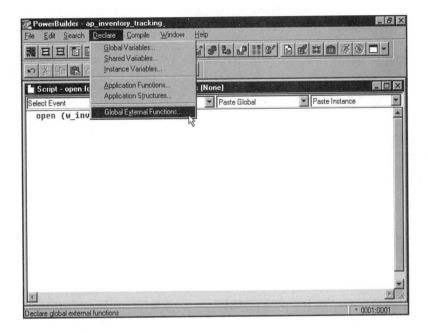

Then, the Declare Global External Functions dialog box appears. Here, you type in your *function prototype*, as shown in figure F.2. A function prototype indicates to PowerBuilder that you are going to call an external function. Futhermore, a function prototype sets up the proper syntax for the external function so you can reference it within PowerScript without a compiler error.

FIG. F.2

The Declare Global External Functions dialog box allows you to define your external function to PowerBuilder by typing in a function prototype.

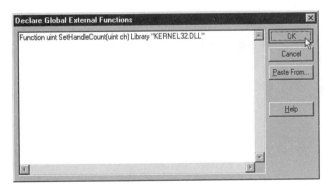

App

F

A function prototype is shown below:

```
Function uint SetHandleCount(uint num) Library "KERNEL32.DLL"
```

Any function prototype can be separated into 4 segments:

Segment	Example	Description
return value	Function uint	The return value defines the return value of the function. In the example, uint means that the functions will return an unsigned integer to the calling PowerScript which may or may not be captured by the developer.
function name	SetHandleCount	The function name is the name of the function in the external DLL that will be called by an external PowerScript function call.
parameters	(uint num)	Most functions require some parameter to be passed from the calling module to the called function. This parameter also may be passed by reference to allow the calling program to change the function.
external library	Library "KERNEL32.DLL"	Finally, you must tell PowerBuilder where the external function is located. In Windows 95, KERNEL32.DLL is where roughly half of all Windows API functions are located.

After you're done defining your external function in the Declare Global Functions dialog box, you can use it in your PowerBuilder events and functions, as seen in figure F.3.

FIG. F.3
You can use external functions in your PowerScript after they've been defined in the Global Functions dialog box.

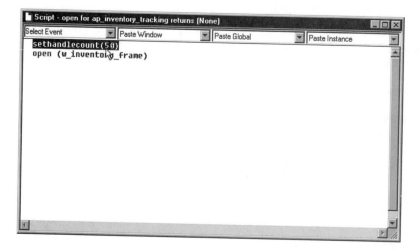

Third-Party Products

Following is a brief description of the products and demos you'll find on the disc from third-party vendors.

> **N O T E** The products on the CD are Demos and Shareware. You may have some difficulty running them on your particular machine. If you do, feel free to contact the vendor. (They'd rather have you evaluate their product than ignore it.) ■

EasyCASE

Evergreen CASE Tools, Inc.
8522 154th Ave. NE
Redmond, WA 98052
Phone Number: 206-881-5149
Fax Number: 206-883-7676

Product Description   EasyCASE is an easy-to-use, low cost, highly-functional Computer Aided Software Engineering (CASE) tool that supports a wide range of methods for process event and data modeling. It is used primarily during the analysis and design phases of system development. It can be used for logical and physical data modeling, which results in the generation of SQL database creation scripts and supports forward and reverse engineering of xBASE databases.

EasyCASE allows you to data model using several different design methods, such as IDE1FX, Bachman, Martin, and so on. Although EasyCASE is not for the beginner, you can use this tool for some great documentation of your database.

To install the application, run **setup.exe** from the \3RDPRTY\EVERGRN\EASYCASE directory on your CD.

> **N O T E** Be sure you run your projects from your C drive. EasyCASE needs to be able to write to your project, and you can't write to a CD. ■

Price $1,295

Chen DB Designer

Chen & Associates
4884 Constitution Ave., Suite 1-E
Baton Rouge, LA 70808
Phone Number: 800-448-2436
Fax Number: 504-928-9371

Product Description   The enclosed demo is a self-guided tour. Type **SGT** to run the program.

App

F

The Chen PowerBuilder Companion is a Case tool for optimal database design. The user can launch a PowerBuilder script to implement the design on the host DBMS. Schema changes are supported, as are links to the CHEN ER-Modeler Workbench, which includes data and process modeling and reverse engineering for more than 30 DBMSes. Migration/conversion is supported. Dictionary reports are produced. The sophisticated Chen Normalizer can decompose records and relations into more desirable formats, including 3NF. Links to major data dictionaries and CASE tools are provided. Stand-alone and network operations are supported.

To install the application, run **setup.exe** from the \3RDPRTY\CHENDB directory on your CD.

PowerClass

ServerLogic Corp
2800 Northup Way, Suite 205
Bellevue, WA 98004

Description   PowerClass is a PowerBuilder class library that can reduce the amount of code and time needed to create PowerBuilder applications by 40-60%. It provides a foundation for application standards, a consistent look and feel to an application, reduces application maintenance, and includes a 700-page user manual, tutorial, and sample applications.

- PowerLock is a PowerBuilder security library and administration tool that provides access control down to the DataWindow field level.
- PowerObjects is a collection of stand-alone PowerBuilder objects that includes a tabbed folder, configurable toolbar, calendar, and several multi-media objects.

Price   Several pricing packages are available.

Key Features   Code reusability; fully integrated object functionality.

To install the demo, run **pc414dem.exe** from the \3RDPRTY\SERVER\PWRCLASS directory on your CD.

PowerFrame Application Security Library Version 2.0

MetaSolv Software, Inc.
14900 Landmark, Suite 240
Dallas, TX 75240

Description PowerFrames' Application Security class library provides a comprehensive application security system that can secure PowerBuilder applications at run time. Applications can be secured at a window, window control (menu items, command buttons, data window, etc.), and database column level. Security authorizations may be granted at a user and/or group level.

Price $1,495 per production server.

PowerTOOL

PowerCerv
400 N. Ashley Dr. #1910
Tampa, FL 33602

Description PowerTOOL is a library of reusable PowerBuilder objects. These objects embody a powerful, standardized methodology for the development of PowerBuilder applications. This methodology provides developers an accelerated foundation for large scale, client-server application development. PowerTOOL promotes a standard use of inheritance and provides a proven method for navigational control and application security. PowerTOOL saves the PowerBuilder developer time usually measured in months.

Price $8,995 unlimited developers; $4,995 for 5 developers; $1,200 single developer. For PowerBuilder Desktop: $249 list price, with an introductory promotion in place with some resellers.

Key Features Complete support for MDI Applications, Object-Oriented Class Library, Application Template, Window Ancestor Hierarchy, DataWindow Ancestor Hierarchy, Naming Conventions, Database-driven Navigation/Security Methodology, Intersheet Communication, Comprehensive Tutorial.

Finding Powersoft CODE Partners

The Powersoft CODE (Client/server Open Development Environment) partners all have products designed to work with PowerBuilder. Current CODE partners are listed in table F.1, along with their product, the product's category, and a telephone number and fax number where they can be reached. Table F.1 lists CODE partners by name.

N O T E For a more updated list, contact Powersoft. ▪

App
F

Table F.1   CODE Partners Sorted by Name

Company	Product Name	Category
Arbor Software	Essbase Analysis Server	Executive Info System
Arcland	DesignPad	Diagramming Productivity Tools
Asymetrix Corporation	Info Modeler	CASE/Methodology
Attachmate Corporation	Extra!	Host Connectivity
AutoTester, Inc	AutoTester	Automated Testing
Bachman Information Systems, Inc.	Generator for PowerBuilder	CASE/Methodology
Banyan Systems, Inc.	ENS	Connectivity
Blue Sky Software	RoboHelp	System Development Tool
Born Software Development Group	ODBC for the As/400	Database/ODBC
BrownStone Solutions	DataDictionary/ Solution	Repository
CASE/MATE	Power-Aid	CASE/Methodology
Chen & Associates	ER-Modeler	CASE/Methodology
Cincom	Supra	Database/ODBC
Computer Associates	CA-QbyX	Database/ODBC
Control Data A/S	The NIAM Suite	Data Modeling Tool
Corporate Computing	GUI Guildelines	Class Libraries & Custom Controls
Datawatch Corporation	DataSync	Database Services
DCA	Irma	Host Connectivity
Dharma Systems, Inc.	SQL Access	Database/ODBC
Digital Equipment Corporation	Rdb	Database/ODBC

Contact	Phone	Fax #	Start Date
Matt Slavik	(408) 727-5800	(408) 727-7140	11/93
Alex Ramsay	(215) 993-9904	(215) 993-9908	12/93
Bruce Linn	(206) 637-2488	(206) 637-2435	4/94
Mark Leff	(203) 325-0066	(203) 325-1216	4/93
Larry Goldsticker	(214) 368-1196	(214) 750-9668	4/94
Kelly O'Rourke	(617) 273-9003	(617) 229-9904	9/92
John Fratus	(508) 898-1713	(508) 836-2880	4/94
Roger Zucchett	(619) 459-6365	(619) 459-6366	2/94
Rob Velasco	(507) 280-8083	(507) 280-6555	9/93
Flint Lane	(212) 370-7160	(212) 867-7820	6/94
Garland Favorito	(404) 448-0404	(601) 437-2146	3/94
Dave Hewins	(504) 928-5765	(504) 928-9371	3/94
Ed Lennon	(513) 573-3434	(513) 459-0612	12/93
Bill Pollack	(201) 592-0009	(201) 585-6745	
Bjorn-Harold Sjogren	(472) 289-2389	(472) 215-9821	7/93
Christine Comaford	(708) 374-1995	(708) 374-1124	10/93
Peter Kusterer	(919) 549-0711	(919) 549-0065	4/94
Bob McGowan	(404) 442-4556	(404) 442-4397	8/93
Swaroop Conjeevaram	(603) 886-1400	(603) 883-6904	9/93
Mike O'Connell	(603) 881-1627	(603) 881-0120	7/93

App
F

continues

Table F.1   Continued

Company	Product Name	Category
Ernst & Young	Navigator	CASE/Methodology
Evergreen CASE Tools, Inc.	EasyCASE System Designer	CASE/Methodology
FileNet	WorkFLO	Imaging & Document Mgmt
FileT Software Corp	FileT/PC	Data Access Library
Folio Corporation	Folio VIEWS	Text Processing
Frustram Group	TransPortal PRO	Host Connectivity
Fulcrum Technologies, Inc.	Ful/Tex	Text Processing
Greystone Technology	GTM	Database
Gradient Technologies, Inc.	Visual-DCE	Distributed Computing
Greenbrier & Russell	ObjectStart	Class Libraries & Custom Controls
Information Engineering	IE: Advantage, IE: Advisor	CASE/Methodology
Hewlett Packard Company	ALLBASE/SQL, IMAGE/SQL	Database
IBM Corporation	DB2/2, DB2/6000	Database
IBM Corporation	DDCS/2 to DB2, SQL/DS	Database/ Connectivity
Information Builders	EDA/SQL	Database/ Connectivity
Informix Software	Online Dynamic	Database Server
Integre France	Powertalk	Prototype Generator
Intersolv	Excelerator	CASE/Methodology
Intersolv	PVCS	Version Control
IRI Software	EXPRESS	Imaging & Document Mgmt
Lante Corporation	Lotus Notes	Groupware

Contact	Phone	Fax #	Start Date
David Bonner	(214) 444-2100	(214) 444-2102	
Rob Pritt	(206) 881-5149	(206) 883-7676	9/93
Michael Piti	(714) 966-3400	(714) 966-3490	3/94
Glenn Englund	(719) 661-8371	(719) 576-0832	1/94
Mike Judson	(801) 344-3671	(801) 344-3787	
Chris Davis	(212) 338-0721	(914) 428-0795	5/93
Colin McAlpin	(613) 238-1761	(613) 238-7695	11/93
Robert Shear	(617) 937-9000	(617) 937-9022	3/94
Dave Zwicker	(508) 624-9600	(508) 229-0338	
Deb Turkot	(708) 706-4000	(708) 706-4020	1/94
Cathy Begley	(703) 739-2242	(703) 739-0074	4/94
Todd Hirozawa	(408) 447-5705	(408) 447-4597	
Larry Chan	(416) 448-4291	(512) 823-2110	
Larry Chan	(416) 448-4291	(416) 448-4439	
Gary Goldberg	(212) 736-4433	(212) 564-1726	4/93
Susan Nurse	(415) 926-6688	(415) 322-2805	
France Thebault	33-1-40911060	33-1-4011032	5/94
Kelle McConnell	(301) 230-3349	(301) 230-2883	
Kelle McConnell	(301) 230-3349	(301) 230-2883	
Dave Meninger	(617) 672-4689	(617) 672-4660	4/94
Jeff Weinberg	(312) 236-5100	(312) 236-0664	

App
F

continues

Table F.1   Continued

Company	Product Name	Category
LaserData	DocuData	Imaging & Document Management
LBMS - System Engineer	System Engineer	CASE/Methodology
Legent Corporation	Endevor	Version Control
LexiBridge Corporation	LexiBridge Transformer	CASE/Methodology
Logic Works, Inc.	ERwin/ERX	CASE/C72 Methodology
Lotus Development Corporation	Notes	Groupware
Magna Software	MAGNA.X	DCE
MapInfo Corporation	MapInfo	Mapping
MediaWay, Inc.	MediaDB	Database
MetaSolv Software, Inc.	PowerFrame	Class Libraries
Mercury Interactive	Win Runner	Automated Testing
MicrodecisionWare	Database Gateway	Database/ Connectivity
Microsoft Corporation	SQL Server	Database
Microsoft Corporation	Microsoft Test	Automated Testing
Millennium Corporation	PowerBase	Reporting
Mortice Kern Systems, Inc.	RCS	Version Control
Netwise, Inc.	TransAccess DB2/ Integrator	Database/ Connectivity
NobleNet	WinRPC	Distributed Computing
Open Environment Corporation	POWERextender	Distributed Computing
Open Horizon, Inc.	Connection/DCE	Connectivity/DCE
Oracle Corporation	Oracle Server	Database

Contact	Phone	Fax #	Start Date
Rich Grady	(508) 649-4600	(508) 649-4436	8/93
Jim Fatiuk	(800) 231-7515	(713) 623-4955	12/92
Bruce Hall	(508) 870-1900	(508) 836-5992	3/93
Fred Holahan	(203) 459-8228	(203) 459-8220	
Barbara Bogart	(609) 243-0088	(609) 243-9192	3/93
Jeff Brown	(617) 693-4875	(617) 229-8678	
Ross Altman	(212) 727-6719	(212) 691-1968	2/94
Geoff LeBloud	(518) 266-7289	(518) 272-0014	6/94
Debbie Gronski	(408) 748-7402	(408) 748-7405	7/94
Dana Brown	(214) 239-0692	(214) 239-0653	1/94
Inbar Lasser-Raab	(408) 987-0100	(405) 982-0149	9/93
Chris Matney	(303) 546-1228	(303) 546-1110	4/93
Brian Lania	(617) 487-6450	(617) 487-7925	
Bob Saile	(206) 936-3468	(206) 936-7329	6/94
Kent Marsh	(206) 868-3029	(206) 868-5093	6/94
Chuck Lownie	(519) 884-2251	(519) 884-8861	12/93
Bill Jacobs	(303) 442-8280	(303) 442-3798	4/93
Bill Bogasky	(508) 460-8222	(508) 460-3456	1/94
Peter Foster	(617) 562-5852	(617) 562-0038	8/93
Kurt Dahm	(415) 593-1509	(415) 593-1669	6/94
Gini Bell	(415) 506-6337	(415) 506-7225	

App
F

continues

Table F.1   Continued

Company	Product Name	Category
OSoft Development Corp.	Spinlist	Class Libraries & Custom Controls
PARADIGM Computer Solutions	PowerPlate	Class Libraries
Pegasus Imaging Corp.	PIC View	Imaging/Graphics
Popkin Software Systems, Inc.	System Architect	CASE/Methodology
PowerCerv	PowerTool	Class Libraries & Custom Controls
Praxis International	Connect*	Database/ODBC
Promark, Inc.	Rhobot/Client-Server	Automated Testing
Quadbase Systems, Inc.	Quadbase SQL	Database/ODBC
Red Brick Systems	Red Brick Warehouse	Database/ODBC
SDP	S-Designor	Database Design
Sietec Open Systems	ViSietec	Imaging & Document Mgmt
Select Software Tools	Select OMT	CASE/Methodology
Segue	QA Partner	Automated Testing
Server Logic Corp	PowerClass	Class Libraries & Custom Controls
ShowCase Corporation	ShowCase ODBC	Database/ODBC
Softbridge, Inc.	Automated Test Facility	Automated Testing
Soft-tek International	GRAFSMAN	Graphics
Software Quality Automation	Team Test	Automated Testing
Sterling Software	Answer Testpro	Automated Testing
Strategic Mapping, Inc./TerraLogics	TerraView	Mapping
Stylus Innovation, Inc.	Visual Voice	Voice Processing

Contact	Phone	Fax #	Start Date
Michael J. Gora	(404) 814-6030	(404) 814-8401	9/93
Gary Cook	(800) 593-5106	(403) 256-8398	3/94
Chris Lubeck	(813) 875-7575	(813) 875-7705	3/94
Ron Sherma	(212) 571-3434	(212) 571-3436	
Bernie Borges	(813) 226-2378	(813) 222-0886	12/93
Joan Kaminski	(617) 492-8860	(617) 497-1072	2/94
Daniel Rosen	(201) 540-1980	(201) 540-8377	6/94
Frederick C. Luk	(408) 738-6989	(408) 738-6980	
Sylvia Waelter	(408) 354-7214	(408) 399-3277	10/93
Serve Levy	(708) 947-4250	(708) 947-4251	11/93
David Macklem	(416) 496-8510	(416) 496-8524	4/94
Terri Rodriguez	(714) 957-6633	(714) 957-6219	2/94
Christina Kasica	(617) 969-3771	(617) 969-4326	3/94
Terry LeLievre	(206) 803-0378	(206) 803-0349	1/94
Amy Johnson	(507) 288-5922	(507) 287-2803	4/93
David Stookey	(617) 576-2257	(617) 864-7747	1/93
Michael Christensen	(316) 838-7200	(316) 838-3789	4/94
Eric Schurr	(617) 932-0110	(617) 932-3280	3/93
Douglas Turner	(818) 716-1616	(818) 998-2171	2/94
David C. Snow	(508) 656-9900 x909	(508) 656-9999	7/93
Michael Casidy	(617) 621-9545	(617) 621-7862	2/94

App
F

continues

Table F.1   Continued

Company	Product Name	Category
Sybase	SQL Server	Database
Tandem Computers	NonStop SQL	Database/ODBC
Tangent International	Distributed Computing Integrator	Distributed Computing
Techna International	SEMREC	Reengineering
TechGnosis, Inc.	SequeLink	Database/ Connectivity
Text Systems International	SYSQL, ADAQL	Connectivity
The Ask Group	Ingres	Database/ODBC
Thinking Machines	Decision SQL	Database
Transarc Corporation	Encina	Distributed Computing
Trinzic Corporation	Infohub, Infopump	Database/ Connectivity
UniSQL, Inc.	UniSQL/M	Connectivity
UniSQL, Inc.	UniSQL/X	Database/ODBC
Visible Systems Corporation	Visable Analyst Workbench	CASE/Methodology
Visual Tools	First Impression, Formula One	Class Libraries & Custom Controls
Vmark/Constellation	HyperSTAR	Database/ Connectivity
Walker Richer & Quinn	Reflection	Connectivity
Wall Data, Inc.	Rumba	Host Connectivity
Wang Laboratories, Inc.	Open Image	Imaging & Document Mgmt
WATCOM	WATCOM SQL	Database

Contact	Phone	Fax #	Start Date
Tom Barrett	(510) 922-8534	(510) 922-4747	
Allyn Beekman	(408) 285-8550	(408) 285-6004	12/93
Enzo Greco	(212) 809-8200	(212) 968-1398	5/94
Dave Ghosh	(408) 982-9131	(408) 982-9132	9/93
Don Plummer	(617) 229-6100	(617) 229-0557	6/94
Itzhak Margolis	(203) 637-4549	(203) 698-2409	12/93
Barbara Skrbino	(510) 769-1400	(510) 748-2546	
Franklin Davis	(617) 234-2060	(617) 234-4444	3/94
Peter Oleinick	(412) 338-4368	(412) 338-4404	
Eric Egertson	(617) 891-6500 x2963	(617) 622-1544	4/94
Robert Albach	(512) 343-7297 x137	(512) 343-7383	6/94
Robert Albach	(512) 343-7297 x137	(512) 343-7383	6/94
Stewart Nash	(617) 890-2273	(617) 890-8909	10/93
Tom Debaaco	(913) 599-6500 x102	(913) 599-6597	
Barry Cushing	(508) 620-0200	(508) 620-7443	2/94
Leonard Bargellini	(206) 217-7100	(206) 217-0292	4/94
Rob Spence	(206) 883-4777	(206) 861-3175	4/93
Wang Telesales	(800) 639-WANG	(508) 967-0828	6/93
Chris Kleisath	(519) 886-3700	(519) 747-4971	

App
F

continues

Table F.1   Continued

Company	Product Name	Category
Watermark Software	Watermark Discovery Edition	Imaging & Document Mgmt
XDB	XDB	Database

Contact	Phone	Fax #	Start Date
Kevin Lach	(617) 229-2600	(617) 229-2989	6/93
Kathy Magenheim	(301) 317-6800	(301) 317-7701	4/93

Using the Electronic Book

Special Edition, Using PowerBuilder 5 is available to you as an HTML document that can be read from any World Wide Web browser you may have currently installed on your machine, such as NetScape or Mosaic.

If you do not have a Web Browser, we have included Microsoft's Internet Explorer 2.0 for you.

Reading the Electronic Book

To read the electronic book, you will need to start your Web Browser, then open the document file TOC.HTML located on the \EBOOK subdirectory of the CD. Alternatively, you can browse the CD directory using your file manager and can double-click the TOC.HTML.

Once you have opened the TOC.HTML page, you can access all of the book's contents by clicking the highlighted chapter number or topic name. The electronic book works like any other web page; when you click a hot link, a new page is opened or the Browser will take you to the new location in the document. As you read through the electronic book, you will notice other highlighted words or phrases. Clicking these cross-references will also take you to a new location within the electronic book. You can always use your Browser's forward or backward buttons to return to your original location.

Installing the Internet Explorer

If you do not have a Web Browser installed on your machine, Microsoft's Internet Explorer 2.0 is included on this CD-ROM.

The Microsoft Internet Explorer 2.0 can be installed from the self-extracting file in the \EXPLORER directory. Double-click the MSIE20.exe or use the Control Panel's Add/Remove Programs option and follow the instructions in the install routine. Please be aware you MUST have Windows 95 installed on your machine to use Internet Explorer 2.0. ●

Index

T

Complete and Return this Card
for a *FREE* Computer Book Catalog

Thank you for purchasing this book! You have purchased a superior computer book written expressly for your needs. To continue to provide the kind of up-to-date, pertinent coverage you've come to expect from us, we need to hear from you. Please take a minute to complete and return this self-addressed, postage-paid form. In return, we'll send you a free catalog of all our computer books on topics ranging from word processing to programming and the internet.

r. ☐   Mrs. ☐   Ms. ☐   Dr. ☐

Name (first) ☐☐☐☐☐☐☐☐☐☐☐ (M.I.) ☐ (last) ☐☐☐☐☐☐☐☐☐☐☐☐☐☐☐

Address ☐☐☐☐☐☐☐☐☐☐☐☐☐☐☐☐☐☐☐☐☐☐☐☐☐☐

☐☐☐☐☐☐☐☐☐☐☐☐☐☐☐☐☐☐☐☐☐☐☐☐☐☐

City ☐☐☐☐☐☐☐☐☐☐☐☐☐ State ☐☐ Zip ☐☐☐☐☐ ☐☐☐☐

Phone ☐☐☐ ☐☐☐ ☐☐☐☐ Fax ☐☐☐ ☐☐☐ ☐☐☐☐

Company Name ☐☐☐☐☐☐☐☐☐☐☐☐☐☐☐☐☐☐☐☐☐☐☐☐

E-mail address ☐☐☐☐☐☐☐☐☐☐☐☐☐☐☐☐☐☐☐☐☐☐☐☐

1. Please check at least (3) influencing factors for purchasing this book.

Front or back cover information on book .... ☐
Special approach to the content .... ☐
Completeness of content .... ☐
Author's reputation .... ☐
Publisher's reputation .... ☐
Book cover design or layout .... ☐
Index or table of contents of book .... ☐
Price of book .... ☐
Special effects, graphics, illustrations .... ☐
Other (Please specify): _____

2. How did you first learn about this book?

Saw in Macmillan Computer Publishing catalog .... ☐
Recommended by store personnel .... ☐
Saw the book on bookshelf at store .... ☐
Recommended by a friend .... ☐
Received advertisement in the mail .... ☐
Saw an advertisement in: _____ ☐
Read book review in: _____ ☐
Other (Please specify): _____ ☐

3. How many computer books have you purchased in the last six months?

This book only .... ☐   3 to 5 books .... ☐
2 books .... ☐   More than 5 .... ☐

4. Where did you purchase this book?

Bookstore .... ☐
Computer Store .... ☐
Consumer Electronics Store .... ☐
Department Store .... ☐
Office Club .... ☐
Warehouse Club .... ☐
Mail Order .... ☐
Direct from Publisher .... ☐
Internet site .... ☐
Other (Please specify): _____ ☐

5. How long have you been using a computer?

☐ Less than 6 months   ☐ 6 months to a year
☐ 1 to 3 years   ☐ More than 3 years

6. What is your level of experience with personal computers and with the subject of this book?

	With PCs	With subject of book
New	☐	☐
Casual	☐	☐
Accomplished	☐	☐
Expert	☐	☐

Source Code ISBN: 0-0000-0000-0

7. Which of the following best describes your job title?

- Administrative Assistant ☐
- Coordinator ☐
- Manager/Supervisor ☐
- Director ☐
- Vice President ☐
- President/CEO/COO ☐
- Lawyer/Doctor/Medical Professional ☐
- Teacher/Educator/Trainer ☐
- Engineer/Technician ☐
- Consultant ☐
- Not employed/Student/Retired ☐
- Other (Please specify): _____ ☐

8. Which of the following best describes the area of the company your job title falls under?

- Accounting ☐
- Engineering ☐
- Manufacturing ☐
- Operations ☐
- Marketing ☐
- Sales ☐
- Other (Please specify): _____ ☐

9. What is your age?

- Under 20 ....
- 21-29 ....
- 30-39 ....
- 40-49 ....
- 50-59 ....
- 60-over ....

10. Are you:

- Male
- Female ....

11. Which computer publications do you read regularly? (Please list)

_____
_____
_____
_____
_____
_____
_____
_____
_____
_____
_____

Comments: _____
_____
_____

Fold here and scotch-tape to ma

Go for the end zone *with full-contact* PowerBuilder 5.0 training.

Interactive courses let you train right at your desktop!

Score quickly with PowerBuilder® 5.0 by taking advantage of clear, hands-on, play-by-play instruction. Computer-based training (CBT) and the new multimedia courses are like having a PowerBuilder coach right by your side while you learn.

Each CBT lesson includes interactive, graphical exercises that walk you through the application development process. Multimedia courses combine sight and sound in "video" demos and instruction for a highly effective training program.

Best of all, you learn at your own pace — anytime, anywhere.

So before you tackle your next development project, order these self-paced training courses and take 15% off with this ad! See reverse for course topics and order form or call **800-395-3525** today.

Discount is valid only on purchases made through Powersoft from Jan. 1 - Dec. 31, 1996.

Save 15% on any PowerBuilder 5.0 self-paced training course.

Save 15% on PowerBuilder 5.0 Self-Paced Training (with this ad.)

Get up to speed quickly on the latest PowerBuilder® release with any of these highly effective, self-paced training courses. And be sure to check out the Powersoft® home page on the World Wide Web for full course descriptions, plus new video, multimedia, and CBT course offerings. Visit us at *www.powersoft.com* today.

Name

Title

Company

Address

City

State/Province   Zip/Postal Code

Phone   FAX

Qty	Course	Item #	Price Save 15%!	Total
	Making the Most of PowerBuilder 5.0 CBT	50300	$249~ $212	
	Introduction to PowerBuilder CBT Series			
	• PowerBuilder: The Basics	50303	$249~ $212	
	• DataWindow Concepts	50306	$249~ $212	
	• Implementing a User Interface	50309	$249~ $212	
	• Object-Oriented Essentials in PowerBuilder	50312	$249~ $212	
	• All four Introduction to PowerBuilder CBT modules	50320	$695~ $591	
	Fast Track to PowerBuilder 5.0 Multimedia CD	50323	$649~ $552	
	This series includes the following course topics:	*Available May, 1996*		
	• Preparing for Distributed Computing			
	• Developing PowerBuilder Applications in Windows 95™			
	• Extending PowerBuilder: Exploiting OLE and OCX			
	• Leveraging PowerBuilder 5.0 Object-Oriented Language Features			
	• Accelerating Development Using PowerBuilder Foundation Classes			

Note: All pricing is in U.S. dollars. *To receive pricing and ordering information for countries within Europe, the Middle East, and Africa, please contact PW direct at tel: + 494 55 5599 or email: pwdsales@powersoft.com.*
For all other countries, please contact your local Powersoft office or representative.

Subtotal

Applicable Sales Tax

Shipping ($8.50 per product)

TOTAL

TU AYRTUB6MO

Method of Payment:

Make checks payable in U.S. dollars to **Powersoft** and include payment with order. Please do not send cash.

❑ Check   ❑ Purchase Order   ❑ MasterCard   ❑ Visa   ❑ American Express

Credit Card number, Purchase Order number, or Check number   *Expiration date*

Name on Credit Card

Cardholder's Signature

THREE EASY WAYS TO ORDER!

#1 CALL Powersoft at **800-395-3525**.

#2 FAX this order form to **617-389-1080**.

#3 Or **MAIL** this order form along with payment to Powersoft, P.O. Box 9116, Everett, MA 02149.

 **Powersoft.**

QUE® has the right choice for every computer user

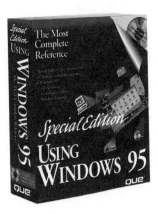

From the new computer user to the advanced programmer, we've got the right computer book for you. Our user-friendly *Using* series offers just the information you need to perform specific tasks quickly and move onto other things. And, for computer users ready to advance to new levels, QUE *Special Edition Using* books, the perfect all-in-one resource—and recognized authority on detailed reference information.

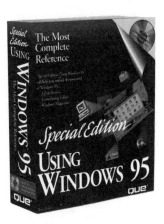

The *Using* series for casual users

Who should use this book?

Everyday users who:

- Work with computers in the office or at home
- Are familiar with computers but not in love with technology
- Just want to "get the job done"
- Don't want to read a lot of material

The user-friendly reference

- The fastest access to the one best way to get things done
- Bite-sized information for quick and easy reference
- Nontechnical approach in plain English
- Real-world analogies to explain new concepts
- Troubleshooting tips to help solve problems
- Visual elements and screen pictures that reinforce topics
- Expert authors who are experienced in training and instruction

Special Edition Using for accomplished users

Who should use this book?

Proficient computer users who:

- Have a more technical understanding of computers
- Are interested in technological trends
- Want in-depth reference information
- Prefer more detailed explanations and examples

The most complete reference

- Thorough explanations of various ways to perform tasks
- In-depth coverage of all topics
- Technical information cross-referenced for easy access
- Professional tips, tricks, and shortcuts for experienced users
- Advanced troubleshooting information with alternative approaches
- Visual elements and screen pictures that reinforce topics
- Technically qualified authors who are experts in their fields
- "Techniques form the Pros" sections with advice from well-known computer professionals

Check out Que® Books on the World Wide Web
http://www.mcp.com/que

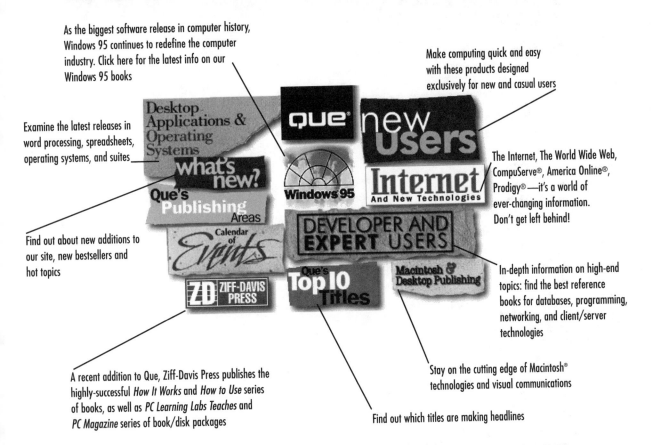

As the biggest software release in computer history, Windows 95 continues to redefine the computer industry. Click here for the latest info on our Windows 95 books

Make computing quick and easy with these products designed exclusively for new and casual users

Examine the latest releases in word processing, spreadsheets, operating systems, and suites

The Internet, The World Wide Web, CompuServe®, America Online®, Prodigy® —it's a world of ever-changing information. Don't get left behind!

Find out about new additions to our site, new bestsellers and hot topics

In-depth information on high-end topics: find the best reference books for databases, programming, networking, and client/server technologies

A recent addition to Que, Ziff-Davis Press publishes the highly-successful *How It Works* and *How to Use* series of books, as well as *PC Learning Labs Teaches* and *PC Magazine* series of book/disk packages

Stay on the cutting edge of Macintosh® technologies and visual communications

Find out which titles are making headlines

With 6 separate publishing groups, Que develops products for many specific market segments and areas of computer technology. Explore our Web Site and you'll find information on best-selling titles, newly published titles, upcoming products, authors, and much more.

- Stay informed on the latest industry trends and products available
- Visit our online bookstore for the latest information and editions
- Download software from Que's library of the best shareware and freeware

Licensing Agreement

By opening this package, you are agreeing to be bound by the following:

The software contained on this CD is in many cases copyrighted and all rights are reserved by the individual software developer and or publisher. You are bound by the individual licensing agreements associated with each piece of software contained on the CD. THIS SOFTWARE IS PROVIDED FREE OF CHARGE, AS IS, AND WITHOUT WARRANTY OF ANY KIND, EITHER EXPRESSED OR IMPLIED, INCLUDING BUT NOT LIMITED TO THE IMPLIED WARRANTIES OF MERCHANTABILITY AND FITNESS FOR A PARTICULAR PURPOSE. Neither the book publisher nor its dealers and distributors assumes any liability for any alleged or actual damages arising from the use of this software. (Some states do not allow exclusion of implied warranties, so the exclusion may not apply to you.)